T0230330

Lecture Notes in Computer Science 692

Edited by G. Goos and J. Hartmanis

Advisory Board: W. Brauer   D. Gries   J. Stoer

David Abel Beng Chin Ooi (Eds.)

Advances in
Spatial Databases

Third International Symposium, SSD '93
Singapore, June 23-25, 1993
Proceedings

Springer-Verlag
Berlin Heidelberg New York
London Paris Tokyo
Hong Kong Barcelona
Budapest

David Abel   Beng Chin Ooi (Eds.)

Advances in Spatial Databases

Third International Symposium, SSD '93
Singapore, June 23-25, 1993
Proceedings

Springer-Verlag
Berlin Heidelberg New York
London Paris Tokyo
Hong Kong Barcelona
Budapest

Series Editors

Gerhard Goos
Universität Karlsruhe
Postfach 69 80
Vincenz-Priessnitz-Straße 1
W-7500 Karlsruhe, FRG

Juris Hartmanis
Cornell University
Department of Computer Science
4130 Upson Hall
Ithaca, NY 14853, USA

Volume Editor

David Abel
Centre for Spatial Information Systems
CSIRO Division of Information Technology
GPO Box 664, Canberra, ACT 2601, Australia

Beng Chin Ooi
Dept. of Information Systems and Computer Science
National University of Singapore, Kent Ridge, Singapore 0511

CR Subject Classification (1991): H.2, H.3, H.5, J.6, I.4, I.5

ISBN 3-540-56869-7 Springer-Verlag Berlin Heidelberg New York
ISBN 0-387-56869-7 Springer-Verlag New York Berlin Heidelberg

This work is subject to copyright. All rights are reserved, whether the whole or part
of the material is concerned, specifically the rights of translation, reprinting, re-use
of illustrations, recitation, broadcasting, reproduction on microfilms or in any other
way, and storage in data banks. Duplication of this publication or parts thereof is
permitted only under the provisions of the German Copyright Law of September 9,
1965, in its current version, and permission for use must always be obtained from
Springer-Verlag. Violations are liable for prosecution under the German Copyright
Law.

© Springer-Verlag Berlin Heidelberg 1993
Printed in Germany

Typesetting: Camera ready by author/editor
Printing and binding: Druckhaus Beltz, Hemsbach/Bergstr.
45/3140-543210 - Printed on acid-free paper

Preface

The 3rd International Symposium on Large Spatial Databases (SSD'93) was held at the National University of Singapore, June 23–25, 1993. The previous meetings of the series were at Santa Barbara (1989) and Zurich (1991). SSD'93 again was planned as a forum for researchers and practitioners specialising in database theory and for advanced applications of Spatial Information Systems.

Seventy submitted papers were each reviewed by three referees. Twenty-six papers were accepted for presentation. The technical program also included three keynote papers (Kim, Schek, and Stonebraker), one invited paper (Tang-Kwong), two panels and four tutorials (Egenhofer, Freeston, Han, and Samet). The growth in the number of submissions over the SSD series to date is evidence of the increasing interest in Spatial Information Systems in general and spatial database in particular. This interest undoubtedly stems from both the research challenges for computer scientists in spatial data management and the potential real-world significance of advances in the state of the art.

Comparison of the papers presented at SSD'93 and SSD'91 shows further progress in the core areas of spatial database and registration of new problems arising from new types of applications. The core topics of data modelling, spatial indexing, storage management and query processing continued to be strongly represented although the influence of changing styles of use of Spatial Information Systems can be seen in new problems within these traditional areas. Ng and Kameda, for example, considered concurrent access to R-trees and Becker and his colleagues indexing for multiple versions of objects. New topics included interoperability of spatial databases, where the paper of Schek and Wolf was complemented by the case study by Kolovson, Neimat and Potamianos, deductive database (Abdelmoty, Williams and Paton) and parallel processing (Franklin and Kankanhalli).

Specialisations such as spatial databases rely on fresh problems to retain their vigour. Stonebraker, Frew and Dozier considered the challenges to the existing technology posed by very large environmental databases and noted some solutions under investigation in the SEQUIOA 2000 Project. Williams and Woods posed another new form of problem in representing and manipulating expectations and conclusions.

Results of research into spatial databases have found their way into commercial implementations of geographical information systems. Kim, Garza and Keskin identified a number of key issues in spatial databases that need to be addressed from an object-oriented system point of view before we can expect to see a rich support of spatial data management in commercial database systems.

As Co-Chairs of the Program Committee, we wish to place on record our appreciation of the contributions of many people. Clearly any conference relies on the number and quality of the submitted papers and we acknowledge the support of the 70 individuals or groups making submissions. The peer review process itself required 210 individual reviews by the members of the Program Committee and other colleagues who were co-opted. The short period between the closing date for submissions and the Program Committee meeting placed particular demands on the referees and we thank them for their diligence and cooperation. We also thank Hans Schek and ETH for providing facilities for the PC meeting at Zuerich, and Max Egenhofer, Tok Wang Ling, Hongjun Lu, Ron Sacks-Davis, Hans Schek, Soon Kiang Wee, Yuk-Wah Tang-Kwong and Chung Kwong Yuen for their support. Finally, we thank Siew Foong Ho, Line Fong Loo and Ronghui Luo for their assistance in preparation of Calls for Papers and Participations, and Cuie Zhao for her assistance in preparation of this proceedings.

Singapore, June 1993   David J. Abel and Beng Chin Ooi

Message from the General Chair

The Department of Information Systems and Computer Science, National University of Singapore, is honoured to have headed the organizational effort for the 1993 International Symposium on Large Spatial Databases, SSD'93. Like research into database techniques in the storage and representation of knowledge during the eighties, databases for geometric, pictorial and multimedia information are at the current forefront of research. Being the international conference specializing in this exciting field of endeavour, SSD'93 will do much to heighten regional awareness and promote international cooperation in research. As the reader can see from the table of contents the conference has attracted eminent keynote speakers and an active group of researchers to present their research, producing altogether an excellent programme.

I wish to acknowledge the assistance and cooperation we received from the sponsoring organizations, the programme committee, the referees, and numerous other individuals who put in many hours of work to make the event a success. They have been listed in the appropriate places in this volume. Last but not least, I thank the publisher for the smooth production of the proceedings in time for distribution at the conference.

C. K. Yuen
SSD'93 General Chair

Acknowledgements

Opening Speaker:
Mr. Tan, Chin Nam, Chairman of National Computer Board
and Managing Director, Economic Development Board, Singapore

Sponsor:
IEEE Computer Chapter Singapore Section

Organisations In Cooperation:
ACM SIGMOD
IEEE Computer Society
Information Processing Society of Japan

Corporate Sponsors:
Automated Systems Pte. Ltd.
Control Data Indo-Asia Pte. Ltd.
Digital Equipment Singapore Pte. Ltd.
ESRI South Asia Pte. Ltd.
Intergraph Systems S.E.A. Pte. Ltd.
IT Asia
Mapindo Parama
Siemens Nixdorf Information System Pte. Ltd.
Spot Asia Pte. Ltd.
SysScan Asia Pte. Ltd.
Tang Dynasty City

Conference Organisation

General Chair:
Yuen, Chung Kwong, National university of Singapore, Singapore

Organizing Co-Chairs and Coordination:
Egenhofer, Max, University of Maine, USA
Ling, Tok Wang, National University of Singapore, Singapore
Sacks-Davis, Ron, CITRI, Australia
Schek, Hans-Jörg, ETH-Zentrum, Switzerland

Programme Committee Co-Chairs:
Abel, David, CSIRO, Australia
Ooi, Beng Chin, National University of Singapore, Singapore

Industrial Chair:
Tang-Kwong, Yuk Wah, Land Systems Support Unit, Singapore

Tutorial Chair:
Lu, Hongjun, National University of Singapore, Singapore

Panel Chair:
Waugh, Tom, University of Edinburgh, U. K.

Local Arrangement Co-Chairs:
Lian, Benjamin, National University of Singapore, Singapore
Tan, Gary, National University of Singapore, Singapore

Publicity Chair:
Wee, Soon Kiang, Ministry of Law, Singapore

Secretariat:
Ho, Siew-Foong, National University of Singapore, Singapore

Programme Committee:
Ang, Chuan Heng, National University of Singapore, Singapore
Casanova, Marco, IBM, Brazil
Chang, Chin-Chen, National Chung Cheng University, Taiwan
Chang, Shi-Kuo, University of Pittsburgh, USA
Egenhofer, Max, University of Maine, USA
Frank, Andrew, University of Vienna, Austria
Freeston, Mike, ECRC, Germany
Guenther, Oliver, FAW, Germany
Gueting, Ralf, University of Hagen, Germany
Han, Jiawei, Simon Fraser University, Canada
Herring, John, Intergraph, USA
Jain, Ramesh, U.C. San Diego, USA
Kambayashi, Yahiko, Kyoto University, Japan
Kriegel, Hans, University of Munich, Germany
Kunii, Tosiyasu, University of Tokyo, Japan
Lu, Hongjun, National University of Singapore, Singapore
Lum, Vincent, Chinese University of Hong Kong, Hong Kong
Masunaga, Yoshifumi, University of Library and Inf. Sc., Japan
Nievergelt, Jurg, ETH Zurich, Switzerland
Sacks-Davis, Ron, CITRI, Australia
Samet, Hanan, University of Maryland, USA
Schek, Hans, ETH Zurich, Switzerland
Scholl, Michel, CNAM, France
Shi, Zhongzhi, Academia Sinica, China
Smith, John, CSIRO, Australia
Smith, Terry, UC Santa Barbara, USA
Svensson, Per, Swedish Defence Research Establishment, Sweeden
Waugh, Tom, University of Edinburgh, U.K.
Whang, Kyu-Young, KAIST, Korea

Contents

Knowledge Engineering in SDS

3-Dimensional Data Handling

Spatial Data Management in Database Systems: Research Directions

Won Kim, Jorge Garza, Ali Kesim
UniSQL, Inc.
9390 Research Blvd.
Austin, Texas 78759

Abstract

Spatial data management has been an active area of research during the past two decades, and results of research into spatial data structures and research into mapping spatial data into records of relational databases have found their way into commercial implementations of geographical information systems. However, no commercial database system today directly supports spatial data management. In particular, data definition and query facilities for spatial data. The objective of this report is to detail a number of key issues that need to be addressed in the near term before we can expect to see a rich support of spatial data management in commercial database systems.

1. Introduction

During the past two decades, management of spatial data has been an active area of research. A major focus of research has been on data structures for storing and retrieving spatial data. The data structures which have been proposed include multidimensional hash structures, such as the Grid File (NIEVSA) (and Gamma File (FFREE87), which is a variation of the Grid File); tree structures extended for multidimensional point data, such as quad trees (FINK74, BENT75, SAMET90), K-D trees (BENT75) (also K-D-B trees (ROBI81), which extends the K-D tree with secondary storage considerations; and spatial K-D trees (OOI90), and tree structures extended for rectangular objects, such as R-trees (GUTT84) (also R+ trees (STON88, SELL87, GREE89), R* trees (BECK90), and Parallel R-trees (KAME92), which are optimized/extended versions of the R-trees), among others. The results of this line of research have found their way into various commercial geographical information systems (G93).

Another direction of research and development adopted during the past decade has been the integration of spatial data management into relational database systems. A number of this research have been, based, on top of relational database systems to retrieve spatial data, as shown in tables. PSQL, TOPS, at SIRO-DBMS (ABEL89), GEO-VIEW (WAGG90) and Generation 5 (GEM90) are relatively recent systems that have been built on top of relational systems.

In view of the fact that spatial data management has been an active area of research in the database field for two decades, it is surprising that today there is no commercial database system that directly supports spatial data management. In particular, no commercial database system provides facilities for directly defining spatial data and formulating queries based on research conditions on spatial data. As a consequence, no commercial database system provides a data structure for spatial data. This has turned the recent research trend in spatial data management in extending the architecture of

Spatial Data Management In Database Systems: Research Directions

Won Kim, Jorge Garza, Ali Keskin
UniSQL, Inc.
9390 Research Blvd.
Austin, Texas 78759

Abstract

Spatial data management has been an active area of research during the past two decades, and results of research into spatial data structures and research into mapping spatial data into records in relational databases have found their way into commercial implementations of geographical information systems. However, no commercial database system today directly supports spatial data management, in particular, data definition and query facilities for spatial data. The objective of this paper is to identify a number of key issues that need to be addressed in the near term before we can expect to see a rich support of spatial data management in commercial database systems.

1. Introduction

During the past two decades management of spatial data has been an active area of research. A major focus of research has been on data structures for storing and retrieving spatial data. The data structures which have been proposed include multidimensional hash structures, such as the Grid File [NIEV84] (and Bang File [FREE87], which is a variation of the Grid File); tree structures extended for multidimensional point data, such as quad trees [FINK74, BENT75, SAME84], K–D trees [BENT75] (also K–D B trees [ROBI81], which extends the K–D trees with secondary storage considerations; and spatial K–D trees [OOI90]); and tree structures extended for rectangular objects, such as R–trees [GUTT84] (also R+ trees [STON83, FALO87, SELL87, GREE89], R* trees [BECK90], and Parallel R–trees [KAME92], which are optimized/extended versions of the R–trees), among others. The results of this line of research have found their way into various commercial geographical information systems (GIS).

Another direction of research and development adopted during the past decade has been the integration of spatial data management into relational database systems. A number of GIS systems have been built on top of relational database systems to take advantage of the query facilities of relational systems to retrieve spatial data that is mapped to tuples in tables. PSQL [ROUS88], SIRO–DBMS [ABEL89], GEO–VIEW [WAUG89] and Generation 5 [GEN90] are relatively recent systems that have been built on top of relational systems.

In view of the fact that spatial data management has been an active area of research in the database field for two decades, it is surprising that today there is no commercial database system that directly supports spatial data management. In particular, no commercial database system provides facilities for directly defining spatial data and formulating queries based on search conditions on spatial data. As a consequence, no commercial database system provides a data structure for spatial data. This has fueled the recent research trend in spatial data management in extending the architecture of current database systems to accommodate management of both spatial and aspatial data [ORE86, OOI90, AREF91].

The objective of this paper is to provide directions for further research in spatial data management with the view to promoting direct support of spatial data management facilities in future database systems. Broadly, we believe the following are the relevant issues on which near–term research should be focused.

First, although numerous data structures have been proposed for spatial data storage, and some performance analysis work on some of the data structures has been done, a lot more work needs to be done on experimental validation of their relative performance, with consideration of a much broader set of operations than just a few typical operations.

Second, relational query optimization techniques need to be extended to deal with spatial queries, that is, queries that contain search conditions on spatial data. In particular, a reasonable cost model for computing the selectivity of spatial predicates needs to be developed.

Third, it is difficult to build into a single database system multiple data structures for spatial indexing, and all spatial operators that are useful for a wide variety of spatial applications; as such, it is desirable to build a database system so that it will be as easy as possible to extend the system with additional data structures and spatial operators.

Fourth, some aspects of the object–oriented paradigm need to be applied to extend the current capabilities of relational database systems. These include support for arbitrary data types in a data definition language, and management (by the database system) of objects in the application workspace (virtual memory) loaded from the database. Performance consequences of these for spatial data management need to be understood better.

In the remainder of this paper, we will explore each of these issues in turn in some detail.

2. Spatial Indexing

Of the known data structures, R–trees seem to be the most popular for storing non–point objects (in particular, rectangular regions). Quad trees and K–D trees necessitate conversion of spatial data into point data in a multidimensional space. R–trees are an extension of B–trees for multidimensional objects. As such, they have the logarithm performance behavior for secondary–storage–resident indexes. R–trees, although developed for a database of 2–dimensional rectangular objects, can be generalized/specialized to accommodate point objects and k–dimensional (k > 2) objects. One serious problem with R–trees is that it allows bounding rectangles to overlap. Since objects within an overlapped area belong to only one of the bounding rectangles, in general multiple branches of the index tree need to be traversed. Some optimization techniques have been suggested in the literature for R–trees [ROUS85, SELL87, BECK90].

concurrency and recovery

Current proposals for R–tree variants do not take into account concurrency control and recovery. In particular, the splitting and merging of index pages will need to be designed with the view to maximizing concurrency (i.e. number of concurrent users) and minimizing the overhead for recovery even while guaranteeing recoverability.

performance studies

Although some work has been done on the relative performance of the R–tree variants and some other data structures [ROUS85, SELI87, FALO87, GREE89, BECK90, HOEL92], it is not clear if the results are conclusive. There are a few problems with the current results. First, most of the current performance studies are not based on actual implementations of the data structures within a full–blown database system; [GREE89] is more realistic than others. It is not clear to what extent the simplifying assumptions made in analytic studies invalidate the results. For example, the effects of concurrency control and recovery protocols incorporated into spatial index structures have not been considered.

Second, most performance studies consider only a few types of spatial operators (e.g., find all objects that contain a given point, find all regions that intersect a given region); the set of spatial operators needs to be expanded. For example, for applications that deal with only points, lines, and regions, there are six classes of spatial operators: region vs. region, line vs. region, point vs. region, line vs. line, point vs. line, and point vs. point. Of course, within each class, there are several meaningful operators. For example, within the region vs. region class, useful operators include, besides the obvious "exact match", intersect, containment, one–side–of (left of, right of, above, below), within–distance–of, nearest (farthest), etc. A data structure that performs well for the region vs. region class of spatial operators may not be suitable at all for, say the line vs. line class of spatial operators.

3. Query Optimization and Processing

Spatial operators manifest themselves as comparison operators in search predicates in queries, or as postprocessing functions against the results of queries. For example, the following comparison operators, corresponding to the spatial operators of the region vs. region class, may be used in a search predicate. Each of these operators allows comparison of a user–supplied spatial object with the value of a spatial attribute (i.e. the attribute whose domain is a spatial data type) in each record in a database:

    MATCHES
    INTERSECTS
    IS–CONTAINED–IN, CONTAINS
    LEFT–OF, RIGHT–OF, ABOVE, BELOW
    WITHIN–DISTANCE–OF
    NEAREST, FARTHEST

Further, a spatial aggregate function, NEAREST (FARTHEST), may be used in the SELECT clause. This is the spatial equivalent of the MIN (MAX) aggregate function.

extensions to query processor and query optimizer

To support spatial operators, the following changes/extensions need to be made to the query processor and query optimizer.

– The query processor should be able to evaluate spatial predicates. A spatial predicate is a predicate which includes any spatial comparison operator.

– The cost model for computing the selectivity of a predicate needs to be extended to take spatial predicates into account.

The first point above is important, regardless of whether spatial indexes are used for query processing. Since minimum bounding rectangles are used to approximate arbitrary shapes of interest to applications, the objects identified through a spatial index on rectangular regions need in general to go through a postprocessing phase.

In relational database systems, the query optimizer does not always generate a query–execution plan using an index, even if one is available. This is because, for predicates whose selectivity is low (e.g., Employee.Age < 80, Employee.Salary > $10,000), it is often better to do a sequential search of all target records. Similarly, the query optimizer should determine when a spatial index can profitably be used in place of a sequential search. To the best of my knowledge, the current literature does not show the cost model for spatial predicates.

query execution cost model

It is not desirable or even necessary to define a very detailed and precise cost model. The cost model used in relational query optimizers is based on a few not–exactly–realistic assumptions (e.g., uniform distribution of indexed–key values, independence of values in different columns) and existence of statistics about the database (e.g. cardinality of a table, minimum and maximum value of an indexed key, etc.) where the statistics are not in general up to date [SELI79]. An approximate cost model comparable in precision to that used in relational query optimization is essentially what is needed for optimizing spatial queries.

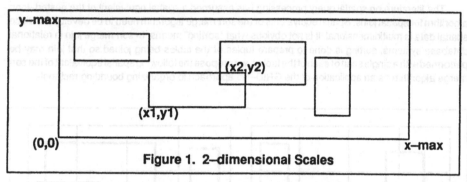

Figure 1. 2–dimensional Scales

We propose the following as the basis of the cost model for computing the selectivity of spatial predicates. To support it, the database system needs to maintain the following information (assuming rectangular regions only, for expository simplicity — extensions for k–dimensional data are straightforward).

N: cardinality – total number of spatial objects
scale for each dimension (i.e. the maximum value and minimum value for each dimension)

The selectivity for the exact match operator is 1/N; this is equivalent to the selectivity of the standard equality predicate. The lowest selectivity is 1, when all records satisfy the predicate.

The selectivity of left–of, right–of, above, or below, a given coordinate value is computed as that for standard predicates involving < or >:
1 / (maximum value of the scale of the i–th dimension – the given coordinate)
For example, for the predicate "left of a region {(x1,y1), (x2,y2)}, where x2 > x1, and the maximum value of the x coordinate is x–max and the minimum value is 0, the selectivity of the predicate would be
1 / (x–max – x1).
Note that this selectivity can be easily fine–tuned by maintaining more precise information about each scale. For example, if each scale is partitioned into a number of unequal–length partitions, the precise scale information may be maintained and used in selectivity computation.

The selectivity computation for the contained–in, contains, within–distance–of, nearest and farthest may straightforwardly be reduced to a union and/or intersection of selectivities along each dimension. For example, the selectivity for the predicate "intersects a region {(x1,y1), (x2,y2)}", shown in Figure 1, where x2 > x1, and the maximum values of the x–dimension is x–max, and the maximum value of the y–dimension is y–max, with their respective minimum values being 0, would be computed by first computing the selectivities for the predicates "above y2", "below y1", "left of x1", and "right of x2"; and then computing the union of the four selectivities.

processing spatial "join"s

In relational database systems, join is used to correlate tuples of two or more tables on the basis of the values of user–specified columns of the tables. Relational database systems typically support two algorithms to evaluate join queries: nested–loop algorithm, and sort merge algorithm. The spatial intersect operator involving two or more sets of spatial objects requires spatial joins. A spatial join correlates spatial tuples (i.e. tuples containing spatial data) belonging to two or more tables on the basis of user–specified spatial attributes of the tables.

The literature on spatial query processing has assumed a spatial equivalent of the nested–loop algorithm for spatial joins. Spatial equivalents of the sort merge algorithm need to be developed. Since spatial data is multidimensional, it is not obvious what "sorting" means. In sort merge join in relational database systems, sorting is done to prepare tuples of the tables being joined so that join may be performed with a single scan of each of the tables. we propose the following spatial equivalent of the sort merge algorithm as an application of the GRID–file approach to organizing bounding rectangles.

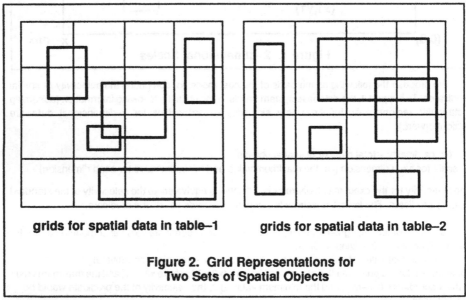

grids for spatial data in table–1   grids for spatial data in table–2

**Figure 2. Grid Representations for
Two Sets of Spatial Objects**

The idea is to partition a region of interest into uniform–sized grids, and assign a storage bucket for each grid. In the "sorting" phase, bounding rectangles are defined for spatial data, and records with bounding rectangles falling in the same grid are stored in the same storage buckets. Figure 2 shows two uniform–sized grids, and bounding rectangles for spatial data on each grid. A bounding rectangle may span more than one grid, and need to be stored in all corresponding storage buckets.

In the "merge" phase, for each corresponding pair of grids for the tables being joined, the corresponding storage buckets are fetched, and spatial join is performed. Since some rectangles are stored in more than one storage bucket, duplicate results must of course be removed from the final result of the join.

4. Object–Oriented Model

The object–oriented data model differs from the relational model in a few fundamental ways [KIM90]. In particular, it provides a framework for a uniform treatment of arbitrary data types, including spatial data types such as points, lines, rectangles, etc. It makes it possible for the attribute definitions to be systematically reused. It also makes it possible for application code to be stored in the database and systematically reused. Further, it provides a basis for supporting navigational access through interrelated objects that are memory–resident. Let us examine these.

arbitrary data types

The object–oriented data model allows the domain of an attribute of a class (roughly corresponding to a table in a relational database) to be an arbitrary user–defined class or a system–defined type (e.g. integer, string, etc.). The value of an attribute is the identifier of the object(s) that belong to the domain of the attribute. The fact that the domain of an attribute may be an arbitrary user–defined class means that the class may be shared easily by many other classes.

For example, suppose that we have defined classes State_Map, Cities_Map, and Highways_Map as follows, and assume that Rectangle and Curve are system–provided classes. The classes Cities_Map and Highways_Map are used as the domains of the two attributes of the class State_Map. They may be used as the domains of attributes of any other classes that may be defined.

```
CREATE CLASS  State_Map (
    Cities  set_of Cities_Map,
    Highways set_of Highways_Map);

CREATE CLASS  Cities_Map (
    City_Name  string,
    City Rectangle);

CREATE CLASS  Highways_Map (
    Highway_Name  string,
    Highway Curve);
```

The values stored in the Cities and Highways attributes of the class State_Map are sets of identifiers of the Cities_Map and Highways_Map objects, respectively. The values stored in the City attribute of the class Cities_Map, and the Highway attribute of the class Highways_Map, are the object identifiers of Rectangle and Curve objects, respectively. Figure 3 illustrates the storage representation of instances of these classes.

navigational access in workspace

The fact that object identifiers of the domain classes are stored for the values of an attribute means that the object identifiers may be used as the search key in fetching the corresponding objects. For example, once an instance of the State_Map class has been fetched, all Cities_Map objects and/or Highways_Map objects that describe it may be fetched using the object identifiers stored in the State_Map object as the search key.

This is the basis for a potentially dramatic advantage in performance that object–oriented database systems can deliver, over relational database systems. The performance advantage of the object–oriented approach becomes dramatic when the ability to store object identifiers as values of attributes is combined with the facility for managing memory–resident objects. The idea is to load objects into the workspace in virtual memory, and transform the object identifiers stored in the objects

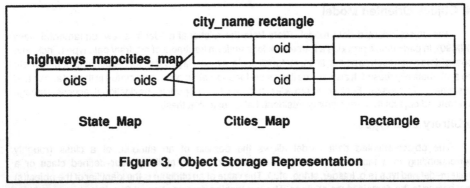

Figure 3. Object Storage Representation

into memory pointers. This is illustrated in Figure 4 for the example State_Map and its constituent Cities_Map objects. The memory pointers to objects are made available to application programs. The application programs may navigate, possibly repeatedly, from one object recursively to all objects references via memory pointers. The database system manages not only the buffer pool of disk pages brought in from the disk, but also the workspace, which is essentially a buffer pool for objects whose representation has been transformed from the disk representation used for the database into memory representation for manipulation by the application programs.

The workspace management technique has been implemented in UniSQL/X unified relational and object–oriented database system from UniSQL, Inc. It is essentially the technique developed in early 1980s to provide persistence to programming languages, for example, LOOM [KAEH81] and PS–ALGOL [ATKI83]. It has also been implemented in the first wave of commercial object–oriented database systems such as ObjectStore, Ontos, and ORION/ITASCA to provide persistence to objects generated by C++ programs [KIM88].

Relational database systems do not provide a workspace management facility. That is, they do not store tuple identifiers as values of attributes, and they do not have a workspace. As such, they do not convert tuples to memory pointers once tuples are brought into memory. If an application program is to fetch tuples related to a tuple already fetched, it must issue explicit "fetch next" command on a cursor, or issue a query with search conditions that will select the desired tuples. This is a far cry from being able to fetch desired objects in memory via memory lookups.

extensions needed

Although the object–oriented data model provides a good framework for supporting spatial data management, the database system needs to provide a number of spatial data types as primitive data types. These data types include *point, line, rectangle, curve, polygon*, etc. For example, if *point* is provided as a primitive data type, it may be used as the domain of an attribute in a class.

> *CREATE CLASS City (*
> *City_Name string,*
> *City_Center point (x: float, y:float));*

These additional spatial data types may be defined as follows.

> *point (x: float, y: float)*
> *line (x1: float, y1: float, x2: float, y2: float)*
> *rectangle (x1: float, y1: float, x2: float, y2: float)*
> *curve (num_segments integer, set_of point)*
> *polygon (num_segments integer, set_of point)*

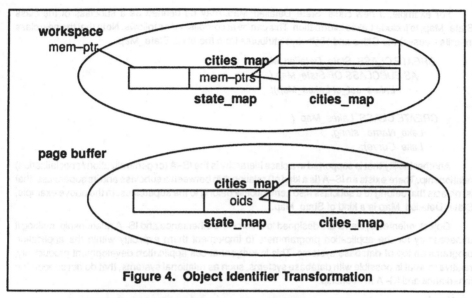

Figure 4. Object Identifier Transformation

We emphasize that these additional data types should ideally be primitive data types, rather than merely system-provided classes. For example, if the point data type is a system-provided class, the above definition of the class City would be as follows.

```
CREATE CLASS City (
    City_Name  string,
    City_Center point);

CREATE CLASS Point (
    X: float,
    Y: float )
```

The use of spatial primitive data types offers two advantages. First, the specification of the domain of a spatial attribute of a class does not require the use of a class (whose definition is given outside the current class). That is, it can make the definition of a class containing spatial attributes more self-contained. Second, a spatial primitive data type consists of two or more elements, and storing the values of all elements of a primitive data type, rather than object identifiers for instances of system-provided classes, will eliminate the need to fetch objects using the object identifiers as the search key (i.e., eliminate the indirection).

Inheritance

Another key feature of the object-oriented data model is the inheritance hierarchy, which makes it possible for spatial attributes defined in one class and methods that operate on them to be automatically reused by other classes. In object-oriented systems, classes are organized in a hierarchy (actually, a directed acyclic graph). The class hierarchy is used as the framework for supporting two different facilities. One is inheritance. A class C (subclass) inherits (reuses) all the attributes and methods defined in a class S (superclass) which is an ancestor of the class C. This makes it unnecessary for the designer (creator) of a class to manually duplicate all the attribute and method specifications in a class that already exists in the database.

For example, a new class, State_Detailed_Map, may be defined as a subclass of the class State_Map, to include Lakes information. This can be accomplished as follows. Note that the new class inherits (reuses) the Cities and Highways attributes from the class State_Map.

```
CREATE CLASS State_Detailed_Map
    AS SUBCLASS OF State_Map (
        Lakes set_of Lakes_Map);

CREATE CLASS Lakes_Map (
    Lake_Name  string,
    Lake Curve);
```

Another facility that is supported in a class hierarchy is the IS–A (or generalization / specialization) relationship. There exists an IS–A (is a kind of) relationship between a subclass and its superclass; that is, objects that belong to a subclass also semantically belong to the superclass. In the above example, State_Detailed_Map is a kind of State_Map.

Object–oriented systems are designed to enforce the inheritance and IS–A relationship, making it unnecessary for the application programmers to implement them explicitly within the application programs on top of database systems. This in turn enhances application development productivity, relative to what is possible with database systems, such as relational systems, that do not support the inheritance and IS–A relationship.

methods

Spatial database applications can clearly benefit from the use of methods. A method is an arbitrary user–written program that is stored in the database, and is loaded and executed either dynamically or statically. Methods are defined, along with the attributes, as a property of a class (table), and are often designed to perform some computations on the data of the objects of the class. They are an arbitrarily powerful and useful facility for any application, rather than just spatial applications. For example, we may write a method for drawing each rectangle and curve representing a city and a highway, and attach them to the classes Cities_Map and Highways_Map, respectively, as follows.

```
CREATE CLASS Cities_Map (
    City_Name  string,
    City Rectangle)
    Method Draw_City;

CREATE CLASS Highways_Map (
    Highway_Name  string,
    Highway Curve)
    Method Draw Highway;
```

In the context of spatial data management, methods may be used to implement various commonly useful spatial data analysis functions. This makes it possible to offload these application functions into a single integrated database. Further, when brought into the inheritance framework, the methods may be reused in a systematic way in various related entities.

5. Extensible Architecture

There have been a few proposals for "extensible" database systems, ranging from proposals for designing an elaborate extensible query optimizer [FREY87], even an optimizer generator to accommodate different data models [GRAE87], and even a database system configurator that constructs a database system from a set of database system building–block modules [BATO88].

objectives of extensible systems

In my view, the overall objectives of an extensible database system have not been clearly defined. In fact, it is not clear when a database system may be regarded as "extensible"; that is, there is not even a qualitative metric for extensibility. Simply put, any database system can be extended to provide additional functions, given enough time and resources. It is also often unclear just for whom extensibility is to be provided. we believe that a much simpler approach can be used than the proposals in the literature for an acceptably extensible query optimizer, at least to satisfy a limited set of objectives for extensibility as we outline below.

First, it is reasonable to assume that the "users" who will extend a database system with new index structures and spatial operators are really the implementors of the database system. It is difficult to imagine that database application programmers or end–users should be allowed to add their own spatial index structures or spatial operators. In the context of a query optimizer, perhaps the cost model may be parameterized and the application programmers may be allowed to provide some of the parameters.

Second, it is reasonable to assume that at least the infrastructure for supporting a class of functions is already available in a database system. For example, if spatial data management is to be supported, at least the infrastructure for it should be built into a database system, so that it will serve as the basis for future extensions. In other words, it is not reasonable to assume that a database system designed without any consideration for spatial data management can be extended painlessly to accommodate spatial indexing and spatial query processing at a later date.

Third, it is also unrealistically ambitious to try to architect a query optimizer and query processor so that they may be easily extended to accommodate fundamental changes in the data model supported by the database system. That is, a query optimizer and processor should only be designed with the view to accommodating only new index structures and new spatial operators. For example, when a query optimizer is being designed to support the relational model, it is unreasonable to expect that the designer of the query optimizer will allow for future extensions to accommodate some data modeling concepts that are not a part of the relational model, such as the concept of a set–valued attribute and methods.

extensibility for spatial data management

There is a reasonable case for an extensible architecture to support spatial objects. First, the index data structure supported in a database system is likely to be unsuitable for some of the applications. Second, it may not be practical to support all possible spatial operators; that is, some applications may require spatial operators beyond those that are built into a database system for a wide variety of applications.

If a database system is to allow installations to add their own index data structures and/or spatial operators, it must be designed for extensibility in the first place. The following discussion outlines how the design–for–extensibility affects the database system architecture.

First, let us see what it will take to allow a new index data structure to be added to a database system. The new data structure will co–exist with other index data structures. For each data structure, there needs to be a separate index manager that supports index primitives. Index primitives include minimally the following operations on an index data structure.

– search for an index entry

– search for a set of index entries within a specified range of indexed key values

– insertion/deletion/update of an index entry

– deletion/update of a set of index entries within a specified range of indexed key values

– index–create

– index–drop

– index–load

– index–statistics update

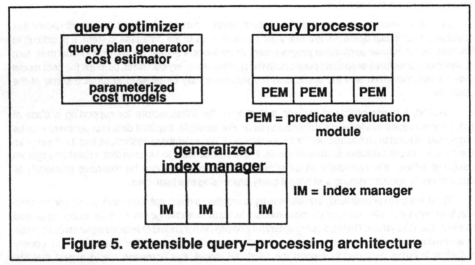

Figure 5. extensible query–processing architecture

Between the index managers and the query processor, there needs to be a software module, called a generalized index manager (GIM). The GIM is a thin layer on top of the individual index managers. It is a collection of modules that implement higher–level index operations than are supported directly within each individual index managers; for example, the closed–area search operation, if not supported directly as an index primitive, may be implemented in the GIM in terms of a set of primitive index search operations; or insertion of a set of index entries may be implemented on top of an index manager by repeatedly inserting one index entry at a time. Each of such index operations may be implemented as a module in terms of the primitives of the underlying index managers.

The query optimizer needs to be designed so that the cost models for any spatial operators that the installations may choose to include may be added without requiring changes to the existing query optimizer code. The part of the query optimizer that computes the selectivities of predicates should be structured so that new types of predicates and their selectivities may be added as query optimizer parameters. For example, a data structure may be designed to maintain the selectivity model for each type of the predicates supported, and a set of commands may be defined to add/delete/update the cost model of any predicate.

The query processor also needs to be designed to invoke installation–supplied algorithms, i.e., modules, that evaluate predicates that involve installation–defined spatial operators.

Figure 5 summarizes the essence of the architectural changes to the query processor, query optimizer, and index manager.

6. Summary

Spatial data management has been an active area of research and development for two decades, and much of the results of research has been incorporated in commercial geographical information systems. However, today no commercial database system directly supports such spatial data management features as spatial index structures and spatial query optimization and processing. In this paper, we identified directions for near–term research and development with the view to encouraging development of commercial database systems that will directly support key features of spatial data management. In particular, we discussed the need for better understanding of the relative performance of various promising spatial data structures; the need for a reasonable cost model for use in a database query optimizer; and the need for an extensible infrastructure for allowing easy addition of new spatial data structures and spatial operators.

References

[ABEL89]   Abel, D. "SIRO–DBMS: A Database Tool–Kit for Geographical Information Systems," Intl. Journal of Geographical Information Systems, vol. 3, no. 2, April–June, 1989, pp. 103–116.

[AREF91]   Aref, W., and H. Samet. "Extending a DBMS with Spatial Operations," technical report, Computer Science Department, University of Maryland, College Park, Maryland, Feb. 1991.

[ATKI83]   Atkinson, M., et al. "An Approach to Persistent Programming," Computer Journal, vol. 26, no. 4, November 1983, pp. 360–365.

[BATO88]   Batory, D., et al. "GENESIS: An Extensible Database Management System," IEEE Trans. on Software Engineering, vol. 14, no. 11, Nov. 1988.

[BECK90]   Beckman, N., H–P Kriegel, R. Schneider, and B. Seeger. "The R*–Tree: An Efficient and Robust Access Method for Points and Rectangles," in Proc. ACM SIGMOD Intl. Conf. on Management of Data, Atlantic City, New Jersey, May 1990, pp. 322–331.

[BENT75]   Bentley, J. "Multidimensional Binary Search Trees Used for Associative Searching," Comm. of ACM, vol. 18, no. 9, 1975.

[FALO87]   Faloutsos, C., T. Sellis, and N. Roussopoulos. "Analysis of Object–Oriented Spatial Access Methods," in Proc. ACM SIGMOD Intl. Conf. on Management of Data, San Francisco, Calif., May 1987, pp. 426–439.

[FINK74]   Finkel, R., and J. Bentley. "Quadtrees: A Data Structure for Retrieval on Composite Keys," Acta Informatica, vol. 4, no. 1, 1974.

[FREE87]   Freeston, M. "The BANG File: A New Kind of Grid File," in Proc. ACM SIGMOD Intl. Conf. on Management of Data, San Francisco, Calif., May 1987, pp. 260–269.

[FREY87]   Freytag, J. "A Rule–Based View of Query Optimization," in Proc. ACM SIGMOD Intl. Conf. on Management of Data, pp. 173–180, San Francisco, Calif., 1987.

[GEN90]   G5.New, vol. 2, no. 1, The Generation 5 Technology, 1990.

[GRAE87]   Graefe, G., and D. DeWitt. "The EXODUS Optimizer Generator," in Proc. ACM SIGMOD Intl. Conf. on Managment of Data, pp. 160–172, San Francisco, Calif., 1987.

[GREE89]   Greene, D. "An Implementation and Performance Analysis of Spatial Data Access Methods," in Proc. IEEE Intl. Conf. on Data Engineering, Feb. 1989, Los Angeles, Calif., pp. 606–615.

[GUTT84]   Guttman, A. "R–Trees: A Dynamic Index Structure for Spatial Searching," in Proc. ACM SIGMOD Intl. Conf. on Management of Data, Boston, Mass., June 1984, pp. 47–57.

[HOEL92]   Hoel, E., and H. Samet. "A Qualitative Comparison of Data Structures for Large Line Segment Databases" in Proc. ACM SIGMOD Intl. Conf. on Management of Data, San Diego, Calif. June 1992.

[JAGA90a] Jagadish, H. "Linear Clustering of Objects with Multiple Attributes," in *Proc. ACM SIGMOD Intl. Conf. on Management of Data*, Atlantic City, New Jersey, May 1990, pp. 332–342.

[JAGA90b] Jagadish, H. "On Indexing Line Segments,"in *Proc. Intl Conf. on Very Large Data Bases*, Brisbane, Australia, August 1990, pp. 614–625.

[KAEH81] Kaehler, T. "Virtual Memory for an Object–Oriented Language," *BYTE*, pp. 378–387, August 1981.

[KAME92] Kamel, I., and C. Faloutsos. "Parallel R–Trees," in *Proc. ACM SIGMOD Intl. Conf. on Management of Data*, San Diego, California, June 1992.

[KIM88] Kim, W. et al. "Integrating an Object–Oriented Programming System with a Database System," in *Proc. 3rd. Intl. Conf. on Object–Oriented Programming Systems, Languages, and Applications*, San Diego, Calif. Sept. 1988.

[KIM90] Kim, W. *Introduction to Object–Oriented Databases*, MIT Press, November 1990.

[MAIE89] Maier, D. "Making Database Systems Fast Enough for CAD Applications," *Object–Oriented Concepts, Applications, and Databases*, (ed. W. Kim, and F. Lochovsky), Addison–Wesley, 1989.

[NIEV84] Nievergelt, J., H. Hinterberger, and K. Sevcik. "The Grid File: An Adaptable, Symmetric Multikey File Structure," *ACM Trans. on Database Systems*, vol. 9, no. 1, March 1984.

[OOI90] Ooi, B–C. *Efficient Query Processing in Geographic Information Systems*, Lecture Notes in Computer Science, Springer–Verlag, 1990.

[OREN86] Orenstein, J. "Spatial Query Processing in an Object–Oriented Database System," in *Proc. ACM SIGMOD Intl. Conf. on Management of Data*, Washington, D.C., May 1986, pp. 326–336.

[ROBI81] Robinson, J. "The K–D–B Tree: A Search Structure for Large Multidimensional Dynamic Indexes," in *Proc. ACM SIGMOD Intl. Conf. on Management of Data*, Ann Arbor, Michigan, April 1981.

[ROUS85] Roussopoulos, N., and D. Leifker. "Direct Spatial Search on Pictoral Databases Using Packed R–Trees," in *Proc. ACM SIGMOD Intl. Conf. on Management of Data*, Austin, Texas, May 1985.

[ROUS88] Roussopoulos, N., C. Faloutsos, T. Sellis. "An Efficient Pictorial Database System for PSQL," IEEE Trans. on Software Engineering, vol. 14, no. 5, pp. 639–650, 1988.

[SAME84] Samet, H. The Quadtree and Related Hierarchical Data Structures, *ACM Computing Surveys*, vol. 16, no. 2, June 1984.

[SEEG90] Seeger, B., H–P Kriegel. "The Buddy–Tree: An Efficient and Robust Access Method for Spatial Data Base Systems,"in *Proc. Intl Conf. on Very Large Data Bases*, Brisbane, Australia, August 1990, pp. 590–601.

[SELI79] Selinger, P., et. al. "Access Path Selection in a Relational Database Management System," in *Proc. ACM SIGMOD Intl. Conf. on Management of Data*, Boston, Mass., May 1979, pp. 23–34.

[SELL87] Sellis, T., N. Roussopoulos, and C. Faloutsos. "The R+–Tree: A Dynamic Index for Multi–Dimensional Objects," in *Proc. Intl Conf. on Very Large Data Bases*, Brighton, England, 1987, pp. 507–518.

[STON83] Stonebraker, M., B. Rubenstein, and A. Guttman. "Application of Abstract Data Types and Abstract Indices to CAD Data Bases,"

[WAUG87] Waugh, T., and R. Healey. "The GEOVIEW Design: A Relational Data Base Approach to Geographical Data Handling," Intl. Journal of Geographical Information Systems, vol. 1, no. 2, April–June, 1987, pp. 101–118.

Realms: A Foundation for Spatial Data Types in Database Systems[1]

Ralf Hartmut Güting and Markus Schneider

Praktische Informatik IV, FernUniversität Hagen
Postfach 940, D-5800 Hagen, Germany
gueting@fernuni-hagen.de, schneide@fernuni-hagen.de

Abstract. Spatial data types or algebras for database systems should (i) be fully general (which means, closed under set operations, hence e.g. a region value can be a set of polygons with holes), (ii) have formally defined semantics, (iii) be defined in terms of finite representations available in computers, (iv) offer facilities to enforce geometric consistency of related spatial objects, and (v) be independent of a particular DBMS data model, but cooperate with any. We offer such a definition in two papers. The central idea, introduced in this (first) paper, is to use *realms* as geometric domains underlying spatial data types. A realm as a general database concept is a finite, dynamic, user-defined structure underlying one or more system data types. A geometric realm defined here is a planar graph over a finite resolution grid. Problems of numerical robustness and topological correctness are solved below and within the realm layer so that spatial algebras defined above a realm enjoy very nice algebraic properties. Realms also interact with a DBMS to enforce geometric consistency on object creation or update.

Keywords. Spatial data types, algebra, realm, finite resolution, numerical robustness, topological correctness, geometric consistency.

1 Introduction

We consider a *spatial database system* to be a full-fledged DBMS with additional capabilities for the representation and manipulation of geometric data. As such, it provides the database technology needed to support applications such as *geographic information systems*. The standard DBMS view for the organization of spatial information is the following: A database consists of several classes of objects. A *spatial object* is just an object with an associated value ("attribute") of a *spatial data type*, such as, for example, *point*, *line*, or *region*. This is true regardless of whether the DBMS uses a relational, complex object, object-oriented or some other data model. Hence the definition and implementation of spatial data types is probably the most fundamental issue in the development of spatial database systems.

Although spatial data types (SDTs) are used routinely in the description of spatial query languages (e.g. [LiN87, JoC88, SvH91]), have been implemented in some prototype systems (e.g. [RoFS88, OrM88, Gü89]), and some formal definitions have been given [Gü88a, ScV89, GaNT91], there is still no completely satisfactory solution available according to the following criteria:

- *Generality.* The geometric objects used as SDT values should be as general as possible. For example, a region value should be able to represent a collection of disjoint areas each of which may have holes. More precisely, this means that the domains of data types *point*, *line*, and *region* must be closed under union, intersection, and difference of their underlying point sets. This allows for the definition of powerful data type operations with nice closure properties.

[1] This work was supported by the DFG (Deutsche Forschungsgemeinschaft) under grant Gu 293/1-1.

- *Rigorous definition.* The semantics of SDTs, that is, the possible values for the types and the functions associated with the operations, must be defined formally to avoid ambiguities for the user and the implementor.
- *Finite resolution.* The formal definitions *must take into account the finite representations available in computers.* This has so far been neglected in definitions of SDTs. It is left to the programmer to close this gap between theory and practice which leads rather inevitably not only to numerical but also topological errors.
- *Treatment of geometric consistency.* Distinct spatial objects may be related through geometric consistency constraints (e.g. adjacent regions have a common boundary). The definition of SDTs must offer facilities to enforce such consistency.
- *General object model interface.* Spatial data types as such are rather useless; they need to be integrated into a DBMS data model and query language. However, a definition of SDTs should be valid regardless of a particular DBMS data model and therefore not depend on it.[2] Instead, the SDT definition should be based on an abstract interface to the DBMS data model which we call the *object model interface.*

The purpose of this paper (together with a companion paper) is to develop a formal definition of spatial data types, called the *ROSE algebra,* fulfilling these criteria. The central idea is to introduce into the DBMS the concept of a *realm.* A realm is in general a finite, user defined structure that is used as a basis for one or more system data types. Realms are somewhat similar to enumeration types in programming languages. A realm used as a basis for spatial data types is essentially a finite set of points and *non-intersecting* line segments. Intuitively, it describes the complete underlying geometry of an application. All points, lines and regions associated with objects (from now on called *spatial attribute values*) can be defined in terms of points and line segments present in the realm. In fact, in a database spatial attribute values are then never created directly but only by selecting some realm objects. They are never updated directly. Instead, updates are performed on the realm and from there propagated to the dependent attribute values.

Hence, all attribute values occurring in a database are *realm-based.* Furthermore, the algebraic operations for the spatial data types are defined to construct only geometric objects that are realm-based as well. So the spatial algebra is closed with respect to a given realm. This means in particular that no two values of spatial data types occurring in geometric computation have "proper" intersections of line segments. Instead, two initially intersecting segments have already been split at the intersection point when they were entered into the realm. One could say that any two intersecting SDT values (say, lines or regions) "have become acquainted" already when they were entered into the realm. This is a crucial property for the correct and efficient implementation of geometric operations.

Realm objects - points and segments - are defined not in abstract Euclidean space but in terms of finite representations. All geometric primitives and realm operations (e.g. updates) are defined in error-free integer arithmetic. For mapping an application's set of intersecting line segments into a realm's set of non-intersecting segments the concept of redrawing and finite resolution geometry from [GrY86] is used. Although intersection points computed with finite resolution in general move away from their exact Euclidean position, this concept ensures that the unavoidable distortion of geometry (that is, the numerical error) remains bounded and very small and that essentially[3] no topological errors occur. This means that a programmer has a precise specification that directly lends itself to a correct implementation. It also means that the spatial algebra obeys algebraic

---

[2] This also holds for the implementation level: A spatial type extension package (STEP) should be able to cooperate with any extensible DBMS offering a suitable interface regardless of its data model.

[3] See the discussion in Sections 2 and 8.

laws precisely in theory as well as in practice. Furthermore, it is rather obvious that realms also solve the geometric consistency problem.

Most closely related to this work are the formal definitions of spatial data types (or algebras) given by Güting [Gü88a, Gü88b], Scholl and Voisard [ScV89, Vo92], and Gargano et al. [GaNT91]. All of these proposals do not fulfill most of the criteria given above. In [Gü88a, Gü88b] data types for points, lines, and regions are available but too restricted, e.g. a region is a single simple polygon (without holes). In [ScV89] general regions are defined; in Voisard's thesis [Vo92] this has been extended to general types for points and lines. However, the definitions are unnecessarily complex. In [GaNT91] there is only a single type for all kinds of geometric objects; a value is essentially a set of sets of pixels. We feel this is not sufficient, since many interesting spatial operations cannot be expressed. As mentioned, all of these proposals give formal definitions. However, those of Güting and of Scholl and Voisard are not based on finite resolution; hence the numeric correctness problems are not addressed. Gargano et al. base their definitions in principle on a finite underlying set (of pixels). But this is not practical since these finite representations are far too large to be efficiently manageable. The geometric consistency problem is not solved in any of these proposals; there is some weak support in [Gü88a] through an AREA data type, but it is not sufficient. Finally, all three proposals have connected their spatial types to a fixed data model – Güting and Gargano et al. to the relational model and Scholl and Voisard to a complex object algebra [AbB88]. Only Scholl and Voisard emphasize a clean interface between the spatial algebra and the general object model. We shall extend their work by offering an abstract interface not dependent on any particular data model.

The topological data model based on simplicial complexes suggested by Egenhofer et al. [EgFJ89] has a similar purpose as our concept of realms. Essentially they offer an irregular triangular network partition of the plane as a geometric domain over which spatial objects could be defined. However, the connections are missing to the underlying finite arithmetic as well as to spatial data types based on this model. Also, in our view a triangular partition contains too much information; it is sufficient to keep those points and segments in a geometric domain that are needed for spatial attribute values. Finally, their model is an abstract one whereas we show realms within a database context.

Our description and formal development of *realm-based spatial data types* is given in two papers. In this paper the lower layers, namely numerically robust geometric primitives, realms and their operations and the structure of values of the spatial data types are defined. In [GüS93] the object model interface and the spatial data types and operations, that is, the spatial algebra, are described. In the following section we first provide an informal overview of the complete concept.

2 Overview: Realm-Based Spatial Data Types

A *realm* is a set of points and non-intersecting line segments over a discrete domain, that is, a grid, as shown in Figure 1.

Values of spatial data types can be composed from the objects present in a realm. Figure 2 shows some values definable over the realm of Figure 1. Our realm-based spatial data types are called *points*, *lines*, and *regions*, hence A and B represent *regions* values, C is a *lines* value, and D a *points* value. The precise structure of these values is not yet relevant here. One can imagine A and B to belong to two adjacent countries, C to represent a river, and D a city.

The underlying grid of a realm arises simply from the fact that numbers have a finite representation in computer memory. In practice, these representations will be of fixed length and correspond to INTEGER or REAL data types available in programming languages. Of course, the resolution will be much finer than could be shown in Figure 1.

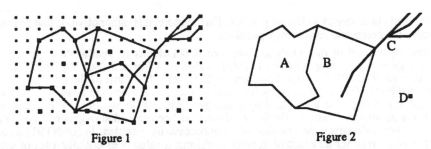

Figure 1   Figure 2

The concept of realm as a basis of spatial data types serves the following purposes:

- It enforces *geometric consistency* of related spatial objects. For example, the common part of the borders of countries A and B is exactly the same for both objects.
- It guarantees nice *closure properties* for the computation with spatial data types above the realm. For example, the intersection of region B with line C (the part of river C lying within country B) is also a realm-based *lines* value.
- It shields geometric computation in query processing from numeric correctness and robustness problems. This is because such problems arise essentially from the computation of intersection points of line segments which normally do not lie on the grid. With realm-based SDTs, there are *never any new intersection points computed* in query processing. Instead, the numeric problems are treated *below* the realm level, namely, whenever updates are made to a realm.
- Additionally, a data structure representing a realm can be used as an index into the database. Our implementation concept assumes that each point and segment in a realm has an associated list of logical pointers to the spatial attribute values defined over it in the database.

Let us now focus on the treatment of numeric correctness problems below and within the realm level. This is necessary because geometric data coming from the application are not intersection-free, as required for a realm. Application data can at the lowest level of abstraction be viewed as a set of points and *intersecting* line segments. These need to be transformed into a realm. As mentioned before, the fundamental problem is that intersection points usually do not lie on the grid.

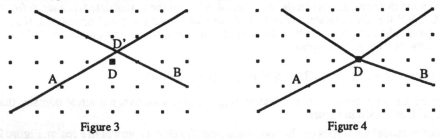

Figure 3   Figure 4

In Figure 3, the intersection point D' of line segments A and B will be moved to the closest grid point D. This leads, for example, to the following topological errors: (1) A test whether D lies *on* A or B fails. (2) A test whether D lies properly within some area defined below A and B will incorrectly yield *true*. (3) If there is another segment C between the true intersection point and D, D will be reported to lie on the wrong side of C. The basic idea to avoid these errors is to slightly change segments A and B by transforming them into chains of segments going through D, as shown in Figure 4. However, this does not suffice, since it allows a segment to drift (through a series of intersections) by an arbitrary distance from its original position. For example, a further intersection of A with some segment C (Figure 5) is resolved as shown in Figure 6, where intersection point E has already a considerable distance from the true intersection point of A and C. Note in particular, that segment A has in Figure 6 been moved to the other side of a grid point (indicated by the arrow) which may later be reported to lie on the wrong side of A.

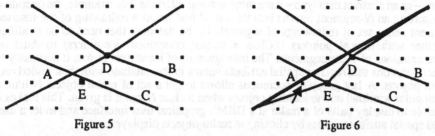

Figure 5   Figure 6

A refined solution was proposed by Greene and Yao [GrY86]. The idea is to define for a segment *s* an *envelope E(s)* roughly as the collection of grid points that are immediately above, below, or on *s*. An intersection of *s* with some other segment may lead to a requirement that *s* should pass through some point *P* on its envelope (the grid point closest to the true intersection point). This requirement is then fulfilled by *redrawing s* by some polygonal line *within the envelope* rather than by simply connecting *P* with the start and end points of *s*. Figure 7 shows a segment *s* (drawn fat) together with the grid points of its envelope. Slightly above *s* a *redrawing* of *s* through *P* is shown.

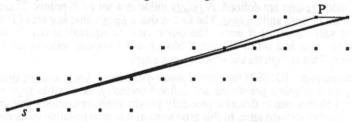

Figure 7

Intuitively, the process of redrawing can be understood as follows: Think of segment *s* as a rubber band and the points of the envelope as nails on a board. Now grip *s* at the true intersection point and pull it around *P*. The resulting polygonal path is the redrawing. The number of segments of this path is in the worst case logarithmic in the size of the grid, but it seems that in most cases only very few segments are created.

This approach guarantees that the polygonal line describing a segment always remains within the envelope of the original segment. We adopt the technique for realms. It then means that by redrawing a segment can never drift to the other side of a realm point. It might still happen, though, that after a redrawing a realm point is found to lie *on* a segment which it did not originally.

The formal definition of realm-based SDTs is organized as a series of layers. Each layer defines its own structures and primitives, using the notions of the layers below. We describe these layers bottom-up in the rest of this paper and the companion paper [GüS93]. Let us briefly provide an overview of this development.

Robust geometric primitives are introduced in Section 3 (and an appendix). This lowest layer defines a discrete space $N \times N$ where $N = \{0, ..., n - 1\}$ is a subset of the natural numbers. The objects in this space are points and line segments with coordinates in N, called *N-points* and *N-segments*. A number of operations (predicates) such as whether an *N*-point lies *on* an *N*-segment or whether two *N*-segments *intersect*, and which *N*-point is the result of intersecting two *N*-segments, are defined. The crucial point is that these definitions are given in terms of error-free integer arithmetic, hence they are directly implementable.

In Section 4 geometric *realms* are defined as described above; elements are called *R-points* and *R-segments*. Basic operations on realms (given in Section 5) are insertion and deletion of *N*-points and *N*-segments. However, to cooperate with a database system, a realm – as an abstract data type – has a more general interface. For example, the operation of inserting an *N*-segment returns besides a modified realm a redrawing of the inserted segment and a set of redrawings of segments in the database that need to be modified together with logical pointers (SCIDs = spatial component identifiers) to database representations of these segments. The management of identifiers makes it necessary to offer operations that *register* spatial attribute values in the database with their underlying realm objects. A last group of operations allows to get a set of realm objects (within a rectangular window) and to identify objects when a close *N*-point is given. This makes it possible to display parts of a realm at a DBMS graphical user interface and to let a user build spatial attribute values by clicking at realm objects displayed.

The next layer (Section 6) defines certain structures present in a realm that serve as a basis for the definition of SDTs. A realm can be viewed as a planar graph; an *R-cycle* is a cycle of this graph. An *R-face* is an *R*-cycle possibly enclosing some other disjoint *R*-cycles corresponding to a region with holes. An *R-unit* is a minimal *R*-face. These three notions support the definition of a *regions* data type. An *R-block* is a connected component of the realm graph; it supports the definition of a *lines* data type. For all of these structures there are also predicates defined to describe their possible relationships.

After these preparations in the next layer (Section 7) the domains of spatial data types *points*, *lines*, and *regions* are defined. A *points* value is a set of *R*-points. There are two alternative views of *lines* and *regions*. The first is that a *lines* value is a set of *R*-segments and a regions value a set of *R*-units. The other view is equivalent but "semantically richer": A lines value is a set of disjoint *R*-blocks and a regions value a set of (edge-) disjoint *R*-faces. This completes the scope of this paper.

In the companion paper [GüS93] the *spatial data types points, lines*, and *regions* together with some *spatial algebra primitives* are defined formally. A flexible type system is introduced that allows one to describe precisely polymorphic operations that are central to the ROSE algebra defined later. In this type system it is also possible to model cleanly partitions of the plane (maps) so that operations can be constrained to be applicable to maps or map regions. A *map* is essentially a set of objects whose *regions* attribute values are disjoint. Next, the *object model interface (OMI)* is defined. The OMI has two parts. The first part is needed to define the semantics of operations of the ROSE algebra. The second part is needed to embed the ROSE algebra into a query language. Then as a top layer of the formal development the *ROSE algebra* is described; the semantics of all operations are formally defined. There are four classes of operations: (i) spatial predicates (e.g. inside, adjacent), (ii) operations returning spatial values (e.g. intersection, contour), (iii) operations returning numbers (e.g. length, dist), and (iv) operations on sets of objects (e.g. overlay, fusion). Finally the ROSE algebra is integrated with a DBMS data model and query language, choosing O_2 as an example. Example queries in O_2Query/ROSE are also shown to demonstrate the "expressive power" of this spatial algebra.

3 Robust Geometric Primitives

The bottom layer of the formal development introduces a finite discrete space, points and line segments over this space, and some simple predicates and operations on them. Let $N = \{0, ..., n - 1\} \subseteq \mathbb{N}$. An *N-point* is a pair $(x, y) \in N \times N$. An *N-segment* is a pair of distinct *N*-points (p, q). P_N denotes the set of all *N*-points and S_N the set of all *N*-segments. We introduce the primitives shown in Figure 8 on *N*-points and *N*-segments. In this graph representation, undirected edges denote predicates and directed edges other operations (here *intersection* takes two *N*-segments and returns an *N*-point).

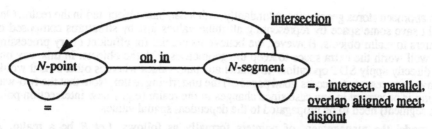

Figure 8

In the appendix these operations are defined in terms of integer arithmetic. Therefore they have a straightforward implementation free of numerical errors. We briefly explain them informally here: Two N-segments *meet* if they have exactly one end point in common. They *overlap* if they are collinear and share a (partial) N-segment. If they are collinear and do not share a (partial) N-segment, we call them *aligned*. If they have exactly one common point but do not meet, they *intersect*. If they have the same slope, they are *parallel*. They are *disjoint* if they are neither equal nor meet nor intersect. The *on* primitive tests if an N-point lies on an N-segment; the *in* primitive does nearly the same but the N-point must not coincide with one of the end points of the N-segment. The *intersection* primitive calculates the intersection point of two N-segments and rounds it to the nearest N-point.

4 Realms

Given N, a *realm over N*, or N-realm for short, is a set $R = P \cup S$ such that

(i) $P \subseteq P_N, S \subseteq S_N$

(ii) $\forall s \in S : s = (p, q) \Rightarrow p \in P \wedge q \in P$

(iii) $\forall p \in P \ \forall s \in S : \neg (p \underline{\text{ in }} s)$

(iv) $\forall s, t \in S : \neg (s = t) \wedge \neg (s \text{ and } t \underline{\text{ intersect}}) \wedge \neg (s \text{ and } t \underline{\text{ overlap}})$

The elements of P and S are called *R-points* and *R-segments*. There is an obvious interpretation of a realm as a spatially embedded planar graph with set of nodes P and set of edges S.

5 Operations on Realms / The Realm Interface

Obviously the fundamental operations on realms are the insertion of an N-point or N-segment and the deletion of an R-point or R-segment. However, the interface is a bit more complex since we study realms not just as abstract entities but in connection with spatial databases. That means that there are spatial attribute values in the database depending on realm objects. This dependency needs to be modeled and treated by the operations.

Our approach to implement the dependency is the following: We assume that (the geometry of) a spatial attribute value of some object is stored together with the object in the database and there is a logical pointer from each segment or point describing the spatial value to the underlying realm object. Furthermore, associated with each realm object (point or segment) is a set of logical pointers; one pointer to each corresponding component of a spatial value in the database. In other words, points and segments in the database are doubly linked with the corresponding points and segments in the realm. Pointers from the database into the realm are realized by *realm object identifiers* from a set *ROID*, pointers from the realm into the database by *spatial component identifiers* from a set *SCID*. It is assumed that each *roid* or *scid* uniquely identifies the corresponding entity and that the implementation guarantees fast access to these components. Additionally, a *scid* also identifies the spatial value as a whole.

This approach stores geometries redundantly with a database object and in the realm. One might save some space by representing attribute values just by structures composed of pointers to realm objects. However, we believe its crucial for efficient query processing and well worth the extra space to keep the geometries with the objects. In this way one can directly apply SDT operations to spatial attribute values whereas otherwise it would always be necessary to access (load pages of) the underlying realm. Note that the two-way linking is necessary in any case since changes in the realm (e.g. a new intersection point on a segment) need to be propagated to the dependent spatial values.

We model the management of pointers formally as follows: Let R be a realm. A *representation of R* is a set of triples $\{(r, roid(r), scids(r)) \mid r \in R\}$ where *roid* is a function giving for a realm object its unique identifier in *ROID* and *scids* is a function returning the set of *SCIDs* of dependent components of spatial attribute values. We also allow the notation $roid(v)$ to assign a new *ROID* to a newly created realm object v.

The realm interface is described by the following signature. Slightly extending standard notations we allow operators to return tuples of values and sets of values – the type of a set of X values is denoted by X*. The first group of operations are those mentioned above:

sorts   *Realm, Point, Segment, RealmObject, ROID, SCID, Rectangle, Bool, Integer*

ops   *InsertNPoint*:   *Realm* × *Point*   → *Realm* × *ROID* × (*SCID* × (*Segment* × *ROID*)*)*

   InsertNSegment: *Realm* × *Segment*   → *Realm* × (*Segment* × *ROID*)* × (*SCID* × (*Segment* × *ROID*)*)* × *Bool*

   Delete: *Realm* × *ROID*   → *Realm* × *Bool*

The sort (type) *Realm* refers to a realm representation, *Point* to the set P_N, *Segment* to the set S_N. *RealmObject* is a union type of *Point* and *Segment*; we assume one can recognize whether a given instance is a point or a segment. *ROID* and *SCID* have been discussed above. *Rectangle* denotes the set of axis-parallel rectangles definable over space $N \times N$, that is, *N-rectangles*.

The update operations implement the approach of Greene and Yao [GrY86] described in Section 2 to preserve the topology for a set of intersecting line segments when they are represented over a finite grid. Greene and Yao do not deal with collections of points that are part of our realms. We extend their approach by an additional integrity rule for points and line segments that are very close to each other. In Section 2 the concept of an *envelope* was already introduced as a set of grid points "adjacent" to a segment (formally defined in [GrY86]). Let us call the "proper envelope" the subset of envelope points that are not end points of the segment (denoted $E(s)$ for segment s). Then the rule is:

   No R-point lies on the proper envelope of any R-segment.

The intuition behind this is that points that are so close are meant to lie on the segment. Update operations maintain this constraint by redrawing the segment whenever a point is discovered to lie on its proper envelope (which can happen on point insertion or on segment insertion).

The operation *InsertNPoint* takes a realm and an *N*-point. It returns (i) the modified realm, (ii) an identifier for the inserted point, which could be an old one if the point was in the realm already, and (iii) a set of segments in the database that need to be redrawn, which may be empty. A segment may need redrawing because the point lies on its proper envelope. For each such segment its "address" in the database (SCID) together with a list of pairs $(s, roid(s))$ (where s is a segment of the redrawing) is returned. It is then the task of the DBMS to replace segments by their redrawings.

The operation *InsertNSegment* takes a realm and an *N*-segment. It returns (i) the modified realm, (ii) a list of segments with their *roids* which may contain either the original segment as the only element or a redrawing of this segment, (iii) a possibly empty set of segments that need to be redrawn (as for *InsertNPoint*). Here the inserted segment may need redrawing because it or its proper envelope touches *R*-points or because it intersects *R*-segments. The other segments need redrawing because they are intersected by this segment. The last parameter (iv) indicates whether insertion was performed; it was rejected, if not both end points of the segment were present in the realm.

The operation *Delete* takes a realm and the identifier of a realm object (point or segment) and removes the object from the realm if this doesn't violate certain integrity constraints. It returns (i) the modified realm and (ii) an indication whether the object was removed. The following conditions are checked: A point is only removed if there is no segment ending in the point. Any realm object is only removed if its set of *scids* (dependent objects) is empty.

The second group of operations supports the management of the two-way linking between realm objects and components of spatial values in the database:

Register:	*Realm × ROID × SCID*	→ *Realm*
Unregister:	*Realm × ROID × SCID*	→ *Realm*
GetSCIDs:	*Realm × ROID*	→ *SCID**
GetRealmObject:	*Realm × ROID*	→ *RealmObject*

Here *Register* informs a realm object *roid* about a spatial component *scid* depending on it. *Unregister* removes such an information. *GetSCIDs* returns the *scids* of spatial components depending on the given *roid*, *GetRealmObject* returns the geometry. These operations are to be used, for example, as follows: A spatial attribute value is constructed by selecting a number of realm objects in a certain order (this is supported by the last group of operations, see below). After all components have been selected, the representation of this value is built and stored in the database. Then all components are registered with their underlying realm objects. When a spatial attribute value is deleted, the registration is removed for all objects. *GetSCIDs* and *GetRealmObject* are general purpose operations to support query processing.

The last group of operations supports the selection of realm objects for the construction of spatial values:

Window:	*Realm × Rectangle*	→ (*RealmObject × ROID*)*
Identify:	*Realm × Point × Integer*	→ *ROID × Bool*

Window returns all realm objects together with their *roid* that are inside or intersect a given rectangular window. *Identify* tries to identify a realm object close to the *N*-point given as a parameter. The number given as a third parameter controls the "pick distance". A *roid* (possibly undefined) is returned together with an indication whether identification was successful. These two operations can be used to retrieve a portion of a realm in order to define spatial attribute values over it. For example, this portion may be displayed at a graphical user interface. With a pointing device one can select *N*-points which through *Identify* determine realm objects from which the spatial values can be built.

We now define the semantics of the realm operations *InsertNPoint* and *InsertNSegment*. All the other operations are rather simple so that their meaning should be clear from the explanations above. *InsertNPoint* and *InsertNSegment* are described by giving algorithms for them. As mentioned before, the concepts of Greene and Yao [GrY86] are applied and extended, some of which need now to be explained in more detail. In [GrY86], for a set of line segments redrawings are computed in two phases. First, for each segment that needs to be redrawn, the set of points on its envelope, that need to be passed by the redrawing, is computed. These points are attached to the segment in the form of "hooks". A hook is a short directed line segment (an "arrow") from a point on the segment to the envelope point that needs to be passed.

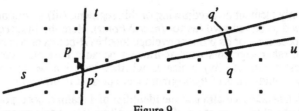

Figure 9

Figure 9 shows a segment *s* with two hooks <*p'*, *p*>and <*q'*, *q*>. Such a "hooked segment" is represented as a list (*s*; <*p'*, *p*>, <*q'*, *q*>). The first hook arises from the intersection of segments *s* and *t* in *p'*; when this intersection is discovered, the hook <*p'*, *p*> is added to *both* segments *s* and *t*. Let us assume that the other hook in Figure 9 arises from the fact that point *q* was inserted into the realm; since it lies on the envelope of *s*, *s* should go through *q*. In such a case we take the point on the segment closest to the target point (in this case *q'*) as the start point of the hook and denote it as *base*(<target>,), in this case *q'* = *base*(*q*, *s*).[4]

Figure 9 also illustrates that for each hook created one generally needs to check whether any segments are intersected by it. In the example an intersection with segment *u* would be discovered and a corresponding hook <*q"*, *q*> be added to segment *u* (where *q"* is the intersection point of the hook and *u*). Only after all hooks have been determined, redrawings (polygonal lines within the envelope) are computed. This can now be done for each hooked segment independently from all other segments. See [GrY86] for a description of how redrawings are computed.

The algorithm *InsertNPoint* has to treat the following cases: (i) the point is already present in the realm, (ii) the point is new and does not lie on any envelope, and (iii) the point falls on one or more proper envelopes. Only the last case is a bit more complex: All segments whose envelopes are touched get a hook. Later, all those segments are redrawn. The description uses predicates *ExistsRPoint* and *ExistsRSegment* with the obvious meaning to check whether a realm object to be created is present already.

algorithm *InsertNPoint* (R, p, R', r, SP)
{Inputs are a realm $R = P \cup S$ and an N-point p. Outputs are the modified realm R', a realm object identifier r for p, and a set SP of spatial component identifiers and redrawings for the spatial objects which have to be updated.}

Step 1
$SP := \emptyset$;
if $\exists\, q \in P : p = q$ (at most one such R-point can exist)
then $r := roid(q); R' := R$
else if $\forall\, s \in S: p \notin \bar{E}(s)$
       then $r := roid(p); R' := R \cup \{(p, r, \emptyset)\}$
       else (R-segments exist whose proper envelopes contain p)
          $S_{rd} := \emptyset$; (a set of R-segments which have to be redrawn)
          $r := roid(p)$;
          $S_{env} := \{s \in S \mid p \in \bar{E}(s)\}$;
          for each s **in** S_{env} **do**
              Insert a hook $h = \;<base\,(p, s), p>$ on s; $S_{rd} := S_{rd} \cup \{s\}$
              (one does not need to check for segments in S intersecting
              h because they are already in S_{env})

---

[4] In [GrY86] all hooks arise from segment intersections.

Step 2 (redraw hooked lines)

Let $S_{rd} := \{t_1, ..., t_n\}$. Let $\{t_{i,1}, ..., t_{i,k_i}\}$ be the set of k_i R-segments of the redrawing of t_i through p. Let $t_{i,j} = (p_{i,j}, q_{i,j}), i \in \{1, ..., n\}, j \in \{1, ..., k_i\}$

Step 3 (update realm)

$R' := R \setminus \{(t_i, roid(t_i), scids(t_i)) \mid i \in \{1, ..., n\}\}$

(Insert the end points of the R-segments of the redrawings and the R-segments themselves if they do not already exist in the realm)

for each i **in** $1..n$ **do**

    for each j **in** $1..k_i$ **do**

        if not *ExistsRPoint*$(p_{i,j})$ **then** $R' := R' \cup \{(p_{i,j}, roid(p_{i,j}), \varnothing)\}$;

        if not *ExistsRPoint*$(q_{i,j})$ **then** $R' := R' \cup \{(q_{i,j}, roid(q_{i,j}), \varnothing)\}$;

        if not *ExistsRSegment*$(t_{i,j})$ **then** $R' := R' \cup \{(t_{i,j}, roid(t_{i,j}), \varnothing)\}$;

$$SP := \bigcup_{i=1}^{n} \{(sc, \{(t_{i,j}, roid(t_{i,j})) \mid j \in \{1, ..., k_i\}\}) \mid sc \in scids(t_i)\}$$

end *InsertNPoint*.

The algorithm *InsertNSegment* first checks whether the end points of the segment are present in the realm; otherwise it rejects insertion. This agrees with the graph-theoretic view of a realm: An edge can only exist if its nodes are there. It implies that the user of the realm layer has to make sure that the points are present (in case of doubt just insert them first; this doesn't hurt). Hence, when a segment is inserted, it is known that the end points have already interacted properly with envelopes of other segments. The following cases are now distinguished: (i) the segment is in the realm already, (ii) the segment is new and doesn't touch anything, and (iii) the segment may intersect some other segments and / or its envelope touches some realm points.

algorithm *InsertNSegment* (R, s, R', RD, SP, ok)

{Inputs are a realm $R = P \cup S$ and an N-segment s. Outputs are the modified realm R', a set RD of pairs of R-segments and realm object identifiers either for s or a redrawing of s, a set SP of spatial component identifiers and redrawings for the spatial objects which have to be updated, and a parameter ok which indicates whether the insertion was performed. Insertion was rejected if the end points of s were not present in the realm.}

Step 1 (initializations)

    $SP := \varnothing$;

Step 2 (check, whether end points of s have already been inserted)

    Let $s = (q_1, q_2)$. $ok := ExistsRPoint(q_1)$ **and** $ExistsRPoint(q_2)$;

if ok **then** (execute steps 3-5)

    Step 3 (insert hooks)

        if $\exists t \in S : s = t$ (at most one such R-segment can exist)

        then $R' := R; RD := \{(s, roid(t))\}$

        else if $\forall t \in S : s$ and t are <u>disjoint</u> $\wedge \forall p \in P : p \notin \bar{E}(s)$

            then $R' := R \cup \{(s, roid(s), \varnothing)\}; RD := \{(s, roid(s))\}$

            else (*s* intersects R-segments and/or there are R-points in the

                    proper envelope of *s*)

                $S_{rd} := \varnothing$ (the set of R-segments which have to be redrawn)

(Get all R-points lying in the proper envelope of s except for the end points. Get all R-segments intersecting S.)

$P_{env}(s) := \{p \in P \mid p \in \bar{E}(s)\}$

$S_{intersect}(s) := \{t \in S \mid s$ and t <u>intersect</u>$\}$

for each p **in** $P_{env}(s)$ **do**

    Insert a hook $h = <base(p, s), p>$ on s

    for each t **in** S **do**

        if h and t intersect at p'

        then

            Insert a hook $h = <p', p>$ on t; $S_{rd} := S_{rd} \cup \{t\}$

for each t **in** $S_{intersect}(s)$ **do**

    Insert a hook $h = <q, p>$ both on s and on t from the intersection point q of s and t to the closest grid point p

    (Note that $p = q$ is possible if q is a grid point)

    $S_{rd} := S_{rd} \cup \{t\}$

    for each v **in** S **do**

        if h and v intersect at p'

        then

            Insert a hook $h' = <p', p>$ on v; $S_{rd} := S_{rd} \cup \{v\}$

Step 4 (redraw hooked lines)

Redraw s. Let $\{s_1, ..., s_m\}$ be the R-segments of the redrawing of s. Let $s_i = (p_i, q_i)$, $i \in \{1, ..., m\}$. Redraw all R-segments of $S_{rd} := \{t_1, ..., t_n\}$. Let $\{t_{i,1}, ..., t_{i,k}\}$ be the set of k_i R-segments of the redrawing of t_i. Let $t_{i,j} = (p_{i,j}, q_{i,j})$, $i \in \{1, ..., n\}$, $j \in \{1, ..., k_i\}$

Step 5 (update realm)

$R' := R \setminus \{(t_i, roid(t_i), scids(t_i)) \mid i \in \{1, ..., n\}\}$

(Insert the end points of the R-segments of the redrawings and the R-segments themselves if they do not already exist in the realm.)

for each i **in** $1..m$ **do**

    if not $ExistsRPoint(p_i)$ **then** $R' := R' \cup \{(p_i, roid(p_i), \varnothing)\}$

    if not $ExistsRPoint(q_i)$ **then** $R' := R' \cup \{(q_i, roid(q_i), \varnothing)\}$

    if not $ExistsRSegment(s_i)$ **then** $R' := R' \cup \{(s_i, roid(s_i), \varnothing)\}$

for each i **in** $1..n$ **do**

    for each j **in** $1..k_i$ **do**

        if not $ExistsRPoint(p_{i,j})$ **then** $R' := R' \cup \{(p_{i,j}, roid(p_{i,j}), \varnothing)\}$

        if not $ExistsRPoint(q_{i,j})$ **then** $R' := R' \cup \{(q_{i,j}, roid(q_{i,j}), \varnothing)\}$

        if not $ExistsRSegment(t_{i,j})$ **then** $R' := R' \cup \{(t_{i,j}, roid(t_{i,j}), \varnothing)\}$

$RD := \{(s_i, roid(s_i)) \mid i \in \{1, ..., m\}\}$

$$SP := \bigcup_{i=1}^{n} \{(sc, \{(t_{i,j}, roid(t_{i,j})) \mid j \in \{1, ..., k_i\}\}) \mid sc \in scids(t_i)\}$$

end *InsertNSegment*.

6 Realm-Based Structures and Primitives

We can now assume that the problems of numerical robustness and topological correctness are solved by the lower layers. Given is a realm which can be viewed as a planar graph over the grid $N \times N$. Within a realm one can discover certain structures and relationships between these structures useful for the definition of spatial data types. These structures are called *R-cycle*, *R-face*, *R-unit*, and *R-block*. For the relationships we will define a number of predicates (primitives).

An *R-cycle* c is just a cycle in the graph interpretation of a realm, defined by a set of R-segments $S(c) = \{s_1, ..., s_m\}$, such that

(i) $\forall i \in \{1, ..., m\} : s_i$ meets $s_{(i+1) \bmod m}$
(ii)   No other pairs of segments in $S(c)$ meet.

Obviously the following relationships may exist between an N-point p and an R-cycle c:

(i) p on c $:\Leftrightarrow$ $\exists s \in S(c) : p$ on s

For $p = (x, y)$ let $s_p = ((x, y), (x, n - 1))$ (that is, a vertical segment extending from p upwards to the edge of the grid). Let $S_r(c)$ be the segments in $S(c)$ whose right end point, but not the left one, is on s_p. Let $S_i(c)$ be the segments in $S(c)$ that intersect s_p. Then

(ii) p in c $:\Leftrightarrow$ $\neg p$ on $c \wedge |S_r(c)| + |S_i(c)|$ is odd[5]

(iii) p out c $:\Leftrightarrow$ $\neg (p$ on $c \vee p$ in $c)$

Hence c partitions the set P_N into three subsets $P_{in}(c)$, $P_{on}(c)$, and $P_{out}(c)$. Let $P(c) := P_{on}(c) \cup P_{in}(c)$.

Cycles are interesting because they are the basic entities for the definition of regions over realms. The relationships shown in Figure 10 may be distinguished between two R-cycles c_1 and c_2 :

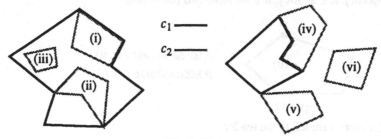

Figure 10

We introduce the following terminology for these configurations:

c_2 is
- *(area-)inside* (i, ii, iii)
- *edge-inside* (ii, iii)
- *vertex-inside* (iii)

c_1.

c_1 and c_2 are
- *area-disjoint* (iv, v, vi)
- *edge-disjoint* (v, vi)
- *(vertex-)disjoint* (vi)

The meaning is that (i) c_2 is (w.r.t *area*) *inside* c_1, (ii) additionally has no common edges with c_1, (iii) has not even common vertices with c_1. Similarly (iv) c_2 is *disjoint* w.r.t. *area* with c_1, (v) additionally has no common edges with c_1, (vi) additionally has not even common vertices with c_1. *area-inside* is the standard interpretation of the term *inside*, *vertex-disjoint* the standard interpretation of the term *disjoint*.

---

[5]   This is a precise grid-based formulation of the well-known "plumbline" algorithm.

Furthermore there are two positive notions: c_1 and c_2 are *adjacent* if they are area-disjoint and have common edges, they *meet* if they are area-disjoint and have common vertices. These predicates are formally defined as follows:

c_1 *(area-)inside* c_2 $:\Leftrightarrow$ $P(c_1) \subseteq P(c_2)$

c_1 *edge-inside* c_2 $:\Leftrightarrow$ c_1 *area-inside* $c_2 \wedge S(c_1) \cap S(c_2) = \emptyset$

c_1 *vertex-inside* c_2 $:\Leftrightarrow$ c_1 *edge-inside* $c_2 \wedge P_{on}(c_1) \cap P_{on}(c_2) = \emptyset$

c_1 and c_2 are *area-disjoint* $:\Leftrightarrow$ $P_{in}(c_1) \cap P(c_2) = \emptyset \wedge P_{in}(c_2) \cap P(c_1) = \emptyset$

c_1 and c_2 are *edge-disjoint* $:\Leftrightarrow$ c_1 and c_2 are *area-disjoint* $\wedge S(c_1) \cap S(c_2) = \emptyset$

c_1 and c_2 are *(vertex-)disjoint* $:\Leftrightarrow$ c_1 and c_2 are *edge-disjoint* $\wedge$
$P_{on}(c_1) \cap P_{on}(c_2) = \emptyset$
(which is equivalent to saying that
$P(c_1) \cap P(c_2) = \emptyset$)

c_1 and c_2 are *adjacent* $:\Leftrightarrow$ c_1 and c_2 are *area-disjoint* $\wedge S(c_1) \cap S(c_2) \neq \emptyset$

c_1 and c_2 *meet* $:\Leftrightarrow$ c_1 and c_2 are *edge-disjoint* $\wedge$
$P_{on}(c_1) \cap P_{on}(c_2) \neq \emptyset$

One can observe similar ways how an R-segment s can lie within an R-cycle c:

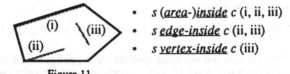

- s *(area-)inside* c (i, ii, iii)
- s *edge-inside* c (ii, iii)
- s *vertex-inside* c (iii)

Figure 11

For an R-point p and an R-cycle c we have two possibilities:

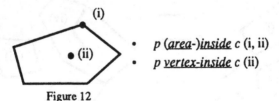

- p *(area-)inside* c (i, ii)
- p *vertex-inside* c (ii)

Figure 12

Formal definitions are left to the reader.

Based on the concept of R-cycles, for the definition of a spatial data type for regions the notions R-*face* and R-*unit* are introduced which describe regions from two different perspectives and which are used equivalently. Both of them essentially define polygonal regions with holes. An R-unit is a "minimal" R-face in the sense that any R-face within the R-unit is equal to the R-unit. Hence R-units are the smallest region entities that exist over a realm. We will see that any two R-units are area-disjoint and that any R-face can be described as a set of R-units. In the next section a region (data type) will be defined that can either be viewed as a set of R-faces or, equivalently, as a set of R-units. The first view emphasizes a minimal representation of the boundary of a region whereas the latter view supports the definition of set operations for regions. We will define operations to convert between the two (formal) representations.

Let $C(R)$ denote the set of all R-cycles. An R-*face* f is a pair (c, H) where c is an R-cycle and $H = \{h_1, ..., h_m\}$ is a (possibly empty) set of R-cycles such that the following conditions hold (let $S(f)$ denote the set of all segments of all cycles of f):

(i) $\forall i \in \{1, ..., m\} : h_i$ *edge-inside* c

(ii) $\forall\, i, j \in \{1, ..., m\}, i \neq j : h_i$ and h_j are _edge-disjoint_
(iii)   Each cycle in $S(f)$ is either equal to c or to one of the cycles in H (no other cycle can be formed from the segments of f)

The last condition ensures uniqueness of representation, that is, there are no two different interpretations of a set of segments as sets of faces. For example, it guarantees that the configuration shown in Figure 13 must be interpreted as two faces, and not as a single face with 5 holes (since under the latter interpretation the cycle drawn fat would violate condition (iii)).

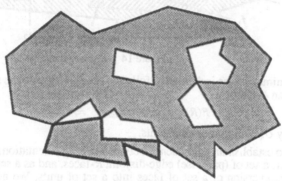

Figure 13

With terms defined below condition (iii) can be rephrased as "an R-face cannot be decomposed into two or more edge-disjoint R-faces".

The grid points belonging to an R-face f are defined as:

$$P(f) := P(c) \setminus \bigcup_{i=1}^{m} P_{in}(h_i)$$

Let $S(F)$ denote the set of all R-segments of a set of R-faces F.

The possible relationships between an R-point p or an R-segment s and an R-face $f = (c, H)$ are:

(i) p _(area-)inside_ f $:\Leftrightarrow$ p _area-inside_ $c \wedge \forall\, h \in H : \neg\, p$ _vertex-inside_ h
(ii) s _(area-)inside_ f $:\Leftrightarrow$ s _area-inside_ $c \wedge \forall\, h \in H : \neg\, s$ _edge-inside_ h

The various notions of _inside_ and _disjoint_ can be extended for the comparison of two R-faces $f = (f_0, \bar{F})$ and $g = (g_0, \bar{G})$, for example:

f _(area-)inside_ g $:\Leftrightarrow$ f_0 _area-inside_ $g_0 \wedge \forall\, \bar{g} \in \bar{G} : \bar{g}$ _area-disjoint_ $f_0\ \vee$
$\hspace{4.5cm} \exists\, \hat{f} \in \bar{F} : \bar{g}$ _area-inside_ $\hat{f}$

This definition is illustrated in Figure 14.

f _area-disjoint_ g $:\Leftrightarrow$ f_0 _area-disjoint_ $g_0 \vee \exists\, \bar{g} \in \bar{G} : f_0$ _area-inside_ $\bar{g}\ \vee$
$\hspace{4.5cm} \exists\, \hat{f} \in \bar{F} : g_0$ _area-inside_ $\hat{f}$

f _edge-disjoint_ g $:\Leftrightarrow$ f_0 _edge-disjoint_ $g_0 \vee \exists\, \bar{g} \in \bar{G} : f_0$ _edge-inside_ $\bar{g}\ \vee$
$\hspace{4.5cm} \exists\, \hat{f} \in \bar{F} : g_0$ _edge-inside_ $\hat{f}$

The meaning of the remaining predicates _edge-inside_, _vertex-inside_, _vertex-disjoint_, _adjacent_, _meet_ should be clear; definitions are omitted for brevity.

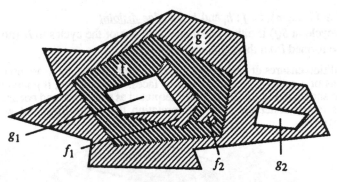

Figure 14

An R-unit as a minimal R·face is defined as follows. Let $F(R)$ denote the set of all possible R-faces. Let f be an R-face.

f is an R-*unit* $:\Leftrightarrow \forall g \in F(R) : g$ *area-inside* $f \Rightarrow g = f$

We also denote by $U(R)$ the set of all R-units.

Our goal is now to establish an equivalence between two representations of a region over a realm, namely, as a set of (pairwise) edge-disjoint R-faces, and as a set of R-units. First we consider the conversion of a set of faces into a set of units. We need two lemmas, whose proofs are technical and are only sketched:

Lemma 6-1 Let f be an R-face and u an R-unit. Then either u *area-inside* f or u *area-disjoint* f.

The idea of the proof is that if this is not the case, then one of the cycles of f, say f', must properly intersect one of the cycles of u, say u'.

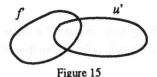

Figure 15

But then a part of f' lies within u and forms a cycle there with a part of u'. Hence there would be a face contained in u different from u which contradicts the definition of an R-unit.

Lemma 6-2 Let f be an R-face and u an R-unit such that u *area-inside* f. Then "subtracting" u from f results in a set of R-faces.

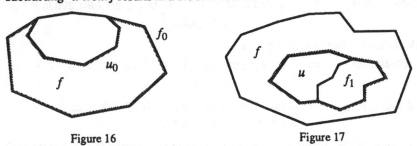

Figure 16   Figure 17

The idea of the proof is the following: If u is even *edge-inside* f then removing the area of

u from f just adds another hole to f. If u's outer cycle u_0 has some adjacent parts with f's outer cycle f_0, then a "bay" is formed in f_0 (Figure 16). If it is adjacent with a hole f_1 in f, then f_1 will grow (Figure 17). If several adjacencies are present, then f may be decomposed into several faces.

The second lemma implies that the units inside a face f cover the area of f completely. For, if some area were left, it would form its own face which could again be decomposed into units.

Therefore the following definition correctly decomposes faces into units. Let F be a set of edge-disjoint R-faces.

$$units(F) := \{u \in U(R) \mid \exists f \in F: u \; \underline{area\text{-}inside} \; f\}$$

We now consider the conversion of a set of units into a set of faces. Given a set of R-segments S, we say, S *describes a set of pairwise edge-disjoint R-faces* :$\Leftrightarrow$ there exists a set of edge-disjoint R-faces F such that $S = S(F)$. Furthermore, let Δ denote the operator for symmetrical set difference, that is, $V \Delta W = (V \setminus W) \cup (W \setminus V)$. Δ forms the union of two sets removing their intersection. The operator is associative and commutative. The basis for the conversion is the following lemma:

Lemma 6-3 Let f and g be two area-disjoint R-faces. Then $S(f) \Delta S(g)$ describes a set of edge-disjoint R-faces.

The basic idea is that the Δ operator just removes segments that are common to both faces. The area-disjointness condition makes sure that only boundaries between adjacent areas are removed (and not boundaries between a covered region in one face and a hole in the other face).

The lemma can be extended to two sets of faces: Let F, G be two sets of edge-disjoint R-faces such that the faces in $F \cup G$ are pairwise area-disjoint. Then $S(F) \Delta S(G)$ describes a set of edge-disjoint R-faces. Let the resulting set of R-faces be denoted as $F + G$. Now the conversion from units to faces can be defined as follows. Let U be a set of R-units.

$$faces(U) = \sum_{u \in U} \{u\}$$

We summarise the equivalence in

Theorem 6-4 $\forall F \subseteq F(R): faces(units(F)) = F$

For the definition of a spatial data type for lines the notion of an R-*block* is introduced. A set S of R-segments is called *connected* :$\Leftrightarrow$ $\forall r, t \in S \; \exists s_1, ..., s_m, s_i \in S : r = s_1, t = s_m$, and $\forall i \in \{1, ..., m-1\} : s_i$ and s_{i+1} meet. An R-*block* is a connected set of R-segments. Two R-blocks b_1 and b_2 are *disjoint* :$\Leftrightarrow$ $\forall s_1 \in S(b_1) \; \forall s_2 \in S(b_2) : s_1$ and s_2 are disjoint. For an R-point p we consider the angularly sorted cyclic list L_p of R-segments $s \in S(b_1) \cup S(b_2)$ that meet in p. p is called a *meeting point* if L_p can be subdivided into two sublists $L_{p,1}$ and $L_{p,2}$ (whose concatenation leads to L_p) so that all R-segments of $L_{p,1}$ are elements of $S(b_1)$ and all R-segments of $L_{p,2}$ are elements of $S(b_2)$, or vice versa (see Figure 18).

Two R-blocks b_1 and b_2 *meet* :$\Leftrightarrow$

(i) $\forall s \in S(b_1) \; \forall t \in S(b_2) : s \neq t$

(ii) $\forall s \in S(b_1) \; \forall t \in S(b_2) : s$ and t meet $\Rightarrow s$ and t meet in a meeting point.

Figure 18: p is a meeting point, p' is not a meeting point.

Again, we have two equivalent representations of a lines value, namely, as a set of segments, or as a set of disjoint R-blocks. For a set of segments $S' \subseteq S$ let $blocks(S')$ denote its partition into maximal connected components. Then $S(blocks(S')) = S'$.

7 Realm-Based Spatial Data Types

A formal definition of realm-based spatial data types (including operations) is given in the companion paper [GüS93]. However, to conclude this paper we show the connection between the realm-based structures of the previous section and the domains of the spatial data types. The basic types introduced are called *points*, *lines*, and *regions*. There is a "flat" and a "structured" view of values of these types. The "flat" view is the following:

> *For a given realm R, a value of type points is a set of R-points, a value of type lines is a set of R-segments, and a value of type regions is a set of R-units.*

The structured view, that we shall assume as the formal definition, is as follows:

> *For a given realm R, a value of type points is a set of R-points, a value of type lines is a set of pairwise disjoint R-blocks, and a regions value is a set of pairwise edge-disjoint R-faces.*

We have shown in the previous section that the two views are equivalent. The first view is conceptually very simple and supports a direct understanding of set operations. The second view shows *lines* and *regions* values as consisting of a number of *components* (blocks or faces), allows one to express relationships between these components and also emphasizes the representation of the boundary in case of regions. Figure 19 illustrates the data types.

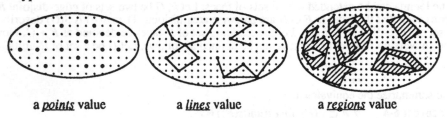

a *points* value   a *lines* value   a *regions* value

Figure 19

It should be obvious now that these data types have very nice closure properties. For example, the set operations are defined as follows. Let P_1 and P_2 be two *points* values, L_1 and L_2 two *lines* values, and R_1, R_2 two *regions* values. Then

$union\ (P_1, P_2) := P_1 \cup P_2$

$union\ (L_1, L_2) := blocks(S(L_1) \cup S(L_2))$

$union\ (R_1, R_2) := faces(units(R_1) \cup units(R_2))$

For *intersection* and *difference* the definitions are analogous. The primitives introduced in the previous sections offer a formal basis for the definition of operations of a spatial algebra. For example, one can define what it means for two regions to be adjacent:

F and G are *adjacent* $:\Leftrightarrow$ F and G are *area-disjoint* $\wedge$

$\exists f \in F \ \exists g \in G : f$ and g are *adjacent*

(assuming *area-disjoint* to be defined already for regions).

8 Conclusions

In this paper we have offered geometric realms as a concept to solve several problems related to spatial data types for database systems. In particular, realms solve the geometric consistency problem as well as problems of numeric robustness and topological correctness. Realm-based structures can be used for the definition of quite general spatial data types and guarantee all the desired closure properties in theory as well as in computational practice. Starting from integer arithmetics, we have developed bottom-up a precise formal framework that makes it easy to define spatial algebras and to implement them correctly. Indeed, such a realm-based algebra is defined in [GüS93].

In closing, let us briefly discuss some open problems and questions that arise with this approach.

Topological correctness. Although it goes a long way, the approach of Greene and Yao does not completely guarantee topological correctness. As is also stated in [GrY86], through the finite representation "... disjoint points and lines may collapse. However, aside from such degeneracies, we do guarantee that topology does not change." There has been a lot of work on numeric robustness and topological correctness for geometric computation (e.g. [OtTU87, GuiSS89, EdM88, NaME90]). We have selected [GrY86] because it fits well with our idea of realms as grid-based planar graphs underlying spatial data types. However, one might try to extend this by adding further integrity constraints (such as our rule that R-points must not lie on envelopes) or by techniques from the other approaches (e.g. symbolic reasoning) to avoid the remaining anomalies.

Efficiency. The realm update algorithms of Section 5 have been given in rather abstract terms, one might be concerned, whether they are efficiently implementable. We suggest to represent a realm in a spatial index structure (e.g. [Gut84]) and are currently implementing realms on the basis of LSD-Trees [HeSW89]. The lookup operations needed in the algorithms can then be performed efficiently. Such a realm representation can at the same time be used as an index into the database. A separate issue is the efficiency of spatial algebra operations (such as intersecting two regions). This can be done by variations of plane-sweep algorithms such as [NiP82, BeO79]. Indeed, these algorithms are now much simpler and more efficient since they do not need to discover new intersections and do not have to treat special cases. The study of algorithms for realm-based data types might become an interesting field of its own.

Space overhead. By redrawing, many more segments may be created than were present in the original set of intersecting line segments. How many more, is an interesting question that should be studied theoretically as well as in experiments with "real life" data. In any case, we feel one cannot trade correctness for space.

Multiple realms. In this paper we have only discussed the case of a single realm underlying all spatial data (of a certain application area). There are several reasons why one might be interested in several realms over the same area. One is to reduce space overhead (by not intersecting spatial values of different realms). Another reason is that there exist interesting SDT operations that are not closed with respect to a realm. An example is the creation of a "buffer area" around a polyline. To accommodate such operations one might dynamically create a realm containing just the "new" spatial values, select a set of SDT values that might interact with these new geometries and create a "small" realm for them, and then use a "merge" operation on realms to compute all intersections correctly.

Appendix: Definition of Geometric Primitives

As a basis for definition and implementation we only assume that the following arithmetic primitives are available and are error-free with respect to overflow.

$$\text{INT} \times \text{INT} \rightarrow \text{INT} \qquad +, -, *, \textbf{div}, \textbf{mod}$$
$$\text{INT} \times \text{INT} \rightarrow \text{BOOL} \qquad =, \neq, <, \leq, \geq, >$$

To fulfill this requirement in an implementation it is sufficient that the INT data type can represent numbers in the range $[-2n^3, 2n^3]$ where $n = |N|$ (see below). Either this relationship holds between N needed by the application and a programming language integer type, or one needs to implement a special integer type with these operations.

For an N-point p we denote by $p.x$ and $p.y$ its first and second component, respectively. Two N-points p and q are equal,

$$p = q \quad :\Leftrightarrow \quad p.x = q.x \wedge p.y = q.y \, .$$

Two N-segments $s_1 = (p_1, p_2)$ and $s_2 = (q_1, q_2)$ are equal,

$$s_1 = s_2 \quad :\Leftrightarrow \quad (p_1 = q_1 \wedge p_2 = q_2) \vee (p_1 = q_2 \wedge p_2 = q_1)$$

Let $s_1 = (p_1, p_2) = ((x_{11}, y_{11}), (x_{12}, y_{12}))$ and $s_2 = (q_1, q_2) = ((x_{21}, y_{21}), (x_{22}, y_{22}))$ be two N-segments. For the calculation of a possible intersection point of the two N-segments we use the following matrix representation where λ, μ are rational numbers (to be represented by pairs of INT values).

$$\begin{bmatrix} x_{11} \\ y_{11} \end{bmatrix} + \lambda \left(\begin{bmatrix} x_{12} \\ y_{12} \end{bmatrix} - \begin{bmatrix} x_{11} \\ y_{11} \end{bmatrix} \right) = \begin{bmatrix} x_{21} \\ y_{21} \end{bmatrix} + \mu \left(\begin{bmatrix} x_{22} \\ y_{22} \end{bmatrix} - \begin{bmatrix} x_{21} \\ y_{21} \end{bmatrix} \right)$$

This leads to the following inhomogeneous linear equation system in two variables:

$$x_{11} - x_{21} = -\lambda (x_{12} - x_{11}) + \mu (x_{22} - x_{21})$$
$$y_{11} - y_{21} = -\lambda (y_{12} - y_{11}) + \mu (y_{22} - y_{21})$$

Let $a_{11} := x_{11} - x_{12}, a_{12} := x_{22} - x_{21}, b_1 := x_{11} - x_{21}, a_{21} := y_{11} - y_{12}, a_{22} := y_{22} - y_{21}$, and $b_2 := y_{11} - y_{21}$. Then

$$a_{11} \lambda + a_{12} \mu = b_1 \qquad \qquad \lambda (a_{11} a_{22} - a_{12} a_{21}) = b_1 a_{22} - b_2 a_{12}$$
$$a_{21} \lambda + a_{22} \mu = b_2 \qquad \Rightarrow \qquad \mu (a_{11} a_{22} - a_{12} a_{21}) = b_2 a_{11} - b_1 a_{21}$$

With $D := a_{11} a_{22} - a_{12} a_{21}, D_1 := b_1 a_{22} - b_2 a_{12}, D_2 := b_2 a_{11} - b_1 a_{21}$, and $D \neq 0$ we get

$$\lambda = \frac{D_1}{D}, \mu = \frac{D_2}{D}. \tag{EQ1}$$

Two N-segments intersect if $D \neq 0$ and $0 < \lambda < 1$ and $0 < \mu < 1$. Note that the situation where an end point of one segment lies on the other segment is excluded. In particular no two end points are equal. Two N-segments are parallel if $D = 0$.

For an N-segment $s = ((x_1, y_1), (x_2, y_2))$, $x\text{-}ext(s) := \{min(x_1, x_2), ..., max(x_1, x_2)\} \subseteq N$ and $y\text{-}ext(s) := \{min(y_1, y_2), ..., max(y_1, y_2)\} \subseteq N$ denote the x- and y-intervals of its bounding box. The resulting intervals are called N-intervals. Two N-intervals I_1 and I_2 overlap if $card(I_1 \cap I_2) > 1$. They are disjoint if $I_1 \cap I_2 = \emptyset$. Two N-segments s_1, s_2 overlap if

(i) $\quad D = 0$

(ii) $\quad D_1 = D_2 = 0$

(iii) $\quad x\text{-}ext(s_1)$ and $x\text{-}ext(s_2)$ overlap $\vee$ $y\text{-}ext(s_1)$ and $y\text{-}ext(s_2)$ overlap.

If condition (iii) does not hold and the x- and y-intervals of s_1 and s_2 are disjoint, the two N-segments are called aligned. Two N-segments $s_1 = (p_1, p_2)$ and $s_2 = (q_1, q_2)$ meet if they have exactly one end point in common. Two N-segments are disjoint if they are neither equal nor meet nor intersect. If two N-segments $s_1 = (p_1, p_2) = ((x_{11}, y_{11}), (x_{12}, y_{12}))$ and $s_2 = (q_1, q_2)$ intersect, then intersection(s_1, s_2) is the N-point $(x, y) := (round\_to\_N(x_0), round\_to\_N(y_0))$ where

(i) $\quad x_0 = x_{11} + \lambda (x_{12} - x_{11})$

$$\tag{EQ2}$$

$$y_0 = y_{11} + \lambda \, (y_{12} - y_{11})$$

x_0 and y_0 are two rational numbers resulting from solving the two equations in exact rational arithmetic (to be implemented through the INT primitives alone). λ is chosen as mentioned in (EQ 1).

(ii)   the function *round_to_N* rounds a rational number to the "nearest" number in *N*.

For the function *round_to_N* we give a simple algorithm to show that integer arithmetic is sufficient to calculate the "nearest" number in N from a rational number $c = \dfrac{a}{b}$:

function *round_to_N* $(a, b : integer) : integer$;
var z : *integer*;
begin
    if $a \geq b$ **then** $z := a$ **div** b; $a := a$ **mod** b **else** $z := 0$ **end**; (* now $a < b$ so that
                                                            $0 < a/b < 1$ hold *)
    if $a = 0$ **then return** z **end**;
    if $2 * a \leq b$ **then return** z **else return** $z + 1$ **end**
end *round_to_N*;

Let $s = (p_1, p_2) = ((x_1, y_1), (x_2, y_2))$ be an N-segment and let $p = (x, y)$ be an N-point. p lies on s, for short: p <u>on</u> s, if

(i) $(x_2 - x_1)(y - y_1) + (x - x_1)(y_1 - y_2) = 0$
(ii) $x \in x\text{-}ext(s) \vee y \in y\text{-}ext(s)$

An N-point p lies within an N-segment s, for short: p <u>in</u> s, if additionally to (i) and (ii) holds

(iii) $x \notin \{x_1, x_2\} \vee y \notin \{y_1, y_2\}$.

One can observe that the largest numbers occur in the equations (EQ 2)

$$x_0 = \frac{x_{11}D + D_1(x_{12} - x_{11})}{D}, \, y_0 = \frac{y_{11}D + D_1(y_{12} - y_{11})}{D}$$

which leads to the requirement that numbers up to $|2n^3|$ should be representable.

References

[AbB88]   Abiteboul, S., and C. Beeri, On the Power of Languages for the Manipulation of Complex Objects. Technical Report 846, INRIA (Paris), 1988.

[BeO79]   Bentley, J.L., and T. Ottmann, Algorithms for Reporting and Counting Geometric Intersections. *IEEE Trans. on Computers C-28 (1979)*, 643-647.

[EdM88]   Edelsbrunner, H., and E.P. Mücke, Simulation of Simplicity. Proc. ACM Symposium on Computational Geometry (Urbana-Champaign, Illinois), 1988.

[EgFJ89]   Egenhofer, M.J., A. Frank, and J.P. Jackson, A Topological Data Model for Spatial Databases. Proc. SSD 89 (Santa Barbara, California), 1989, 271-286.

[GaNT91]   Gargano, M., E. Nardelli, and M. Talamo, Abstract Data Types for the Logical Modeling of Complex Data. *Information Systems 16, 5 (1991)*.

[GrY86]   Greene, D., and F. Yao, Finite-Resolution Computational Geometry. Proc. 27th IEEE Symp. on Foundations of Computer Science, 1986, 143-152.

[GuiSS89]   Guibas, L., D. Salesin, and J. Stolfi, Epsilon-geometry: Building Robust Algorithms from Imprecise Computations. Proc. SIAM Conf. on Geometric Design (Tempe, Arizona), 1989.

[Gut84]   Guttman, A., R-Trees: A Dynamic Index Structure for Spatial Searching. Proc. ACM SIGMOD Conf. 1984, 47-57.

[Gü88a]   Güting, R.H., Geo-Relational Algebra: A Model and Query Language for Geometric Database Systems. Proc. of the Intl. Conf. on Extending Database Technology (Venice, Italy), 1988, 506-527.

[Gü88b]   Güting, R.H., Modeling Non-Standard Database Systems by Many-Sorted Algebras. Fachbereich Informatik, Universität Dortmund, Report 255, 1988.

[Gü89]   Güting, R.H., Gral: An Extensible Relational Database System for Geometric Applications. Proc. of the 15th Intl. Conf. on Very Large Databases (Amsterdam, The Netherlands), 1989, 33-44.

[GüS93]   Güting, R.H., and M. Schneider, Realm-Based Spatial Data Types: The ROSE Algebra. Fachbereich Informatik, FernUniversität Hagen, Report 141, 1993.

[HeSW89]   Henrich, A., H.-W. Six, and P. Widmayer, The LSD Tree: Spatial Access to Multidimensional Point- and Non-Point-Objects. Proc. of the 15th Intl. Conf. on Very Large Data Bases (Amsterdam, The Netherlands), 45-53.

[JoC88]   Joseph, T., and A. Cardenas, PICQUERY: A High Level Query Language for Pictorial Database Management. IEEE Trans. on Software Engineering 14 (1988), 630-638.

[LiN87]   Lipeck, U., and K. Neumann, Modelling and Manipulating Objects in Geoscientific Databases. Proc. 5th Intl. Conf on the Entity-Relationship Approach (Dijon, France, 1986), 1987, 67-86.

[NaME90]   Nagy, G., M. Mukherjee, and D.W. Embley, Making Do with Finite Numerical Precision in Spatial Data Structures. Proc. 4th Intl. Symp. on Spatial Data Handling (Zürich, Switzerland), 1990, 55-65.

[NiP82]   Nievergelt, J., and F.P. Preparata, Plane-Sweep Algorithms for Intersecting Geometric Figures. Communications of the ACM 25 (1982), 739-747.

[OrM88]   Orenstein, J., and F. Manola, PROBE Spatial Data Modeling and Query Processing in an Image Database Application. IEEE Trans. on Software Engineering 14 (1988), 611-629.

[OtTU87]   Ottmann, T., G. Thiemt, and C. Ullrich, Numerical Stability of Geometric Algorithms. Proc. 3rd ACM Symp. on Computational Geometry, 1987, 119-125.

[RoFS88]   Rossopoulos, N., C. Faloutsos, and T. Sellis, An Efficient Pictorial Database System for PSQL. IEEE Trans. on Software Engineering 14 (1988), 639-650.

[ScV89]   Scholl, M., and A. Voisard, Thematic Map Modeling. Proc. SSD 89, (Santa Barbara, California), 1989, 167-190.

[SvH91]   Svensson, P., and Z. Huang, Geo-SAL: A Query Language for Spatial Data Analysis. Proc. SSD 91 (Zürich, Switzerland), 1991, 119-140.

[Vo92]   Voisard, A., Bases de données géographiques: du modèle de données à l'interface utilisateur. Ph.D. Thesis, University of Paris-Sud (Centre d'Orsay), 1992.

A Canonical Model for a Class of Areal Spatial Objects

Michael F. Worboys and Petros Bofakos

Department of Computer Science
Keele University, Keele ST5 5BG UK
michael@cs.keele.ac.uk
petros@cs.keele.ac.uk

Abstract. This study aims to model an appropriate set of 2–dimensional spatial objects (i.e. areas) embedded in R^2 with the usual metric and topology. The set of objects to be modelled is an extension of the set of 2–dimensional objects which can be represented within the vector–based data model. The model aims to capture explicitly some important topological properties of the spatial objects, e.g. connectedness and region inclusion. The construction discussed in this paper is capable of representing a large class of areal objects, including objects with holes which have islands (to any finite level). It has the virtue of being canonical, in the sense that any appropriate areal object has a unique representation in this model. The paper describes the model by specifying the areal objects under consideration and providing their representation. It also defines a set of operations and discusses algorithms for their implementation.

1 Introduction

The construction of an appropriate data model for areal spatial objects provides a central foundation for the analysis and design of spatial databases. Traditionally, vector–based data models represent spatial objects as points, chains and polygons. Thus, they have a limited power to model the complex patterns of spatial phenomena. Several vector–based GIS allow ad–hoc extensions of their underlying data model in order to cope with spatial objects having complex embedding. However, such extensions fail to capture explicitly important topological properties of the objects. For example, varieties of connectivity are not explicitly distinguished, neither are all types of holes explicitly recognized. Moreover, the lack of a substantial model of topological structure makes some spatial operations expensive and difficult to perform.

There are many applications where the underlying spatial structure is complex and it is important to have explicitly as full as possible a structural description. To mention just one example, patterns of wildlife distribution are typically highly complex structures, incorporating complicated connectivity and systems of holes (see [2]).

We assume as given a spatial data model which is able to represent areal objects (termed *atoms*) topologically equivalent to the closed disk. This model is extended to incorporate regular closed areal objects (i.e. areas containing their boundaries and without cuts or missing points). Areal objects with complex embedding in the plane are expressed as constrained and structured aggregations of atoms. The objects are structured according to certain topological concepts, namely types of connectivity and area inclusion. A critical advantage of this model is that every regular closed areal object is *uniquely* represented within it. The only constraint is the requirement that spatial objects should be finitely expressible, in the sense that they are combinations of a finite number of atoms, so that they are computationally tractable.

2   Background

This section discusses some of the background to the development of semantically rich models of areal objects. The main components of this work rests in the fields of databases, graphics and computational geometry. The underlying approach to the work described in this paper stems from the object modelling tradition of systems analysis and design. There is beginning to emerge a consensus amongst the community on what constitutes an object-oriented approach to data modelling. The Object-Oriented Database Task Group (OODBTG), organised by the ASC X3/SPARC Database Systems Study Group operating under the procedures of the American National Standards Institute (ANSI), have published the report [18] setting out possible definitions. The model is populated with objects, each with an attribute-independent identity and supporting sets of operations (*protocols*). Object with like protocols are grouped into classes. Object classes form an *inheritance hierarchy*, where subclasses inherit operations from super-classes. Objects may be aggregated into composites, where composites depend for their existence upon their components. Thus, applying the object modelling approach to areal entities, the problem is to give precise descriptions of the areal objects including the operations they support, classify the objects and construct an inheritance hierarchy. The object-oriented approach to spatial data handling has been propounded in many papers to be found in the literature. We mention work of Egenhofer and Frank [4, 3], which provides a catalogue of requirements for such systems and explores the modelling of spatial objects. Later work, which applies the object-oriented approach to spatial database design and to a general analysis of spatial object classes is reported in [17, 15].

Güting [6] constructs a many-sorted algebra based upon relational algebra which contains spatial sorts and presents a typology of spatial objects and operations. This work is extended in [7] to handle spatial networks and generalisation queries. Such work is a contribution to the 'extensible relational database' concept, whose aim is to enhance relational technology so that it supports non-standard as well as standard corporate applications. Other work in this direction includes [11].

Methods supported by objects do not, of course, act upon the objects themselves, but upon the representations of the objects in data structures. Algorithms and data structures for spatial objects have been the subject of research for many years (see, for example, [12], for an excellent survey of earlier work). Such geometric algorithms have been studied by those engaged in research in the fields of computational geometry, CAD and graphics. An excellent introductory survey of work related to that contained in this paper is contained in [5] (especially Chapter 11), which contains descriptions of techniques from solid modelling. Many concepts here, for example regularized set operations, may be usefully applied in the context of GIS. Further material, some of it directly applied to GIS and containing treatments of access methods, may be found in [9, 10, 14, 8].

This paper describes in an intermediate level of detail the model which we have constructed. This model may be viewed as standing next in the sequence which contains the spaghetti and topological spatial data models as first and second members. The so-called 'spaghetti' model handles each spatial configuration of points, lines and areas, embedded in the Euclidean plane, as a set of point-sequences. Each point-sequence models an approximation to a strand or loop of finite length. Areas are defined by their boundary loops. Thus, topological properties of the configuration, such as adjacency, connectivity and simple-connectedness are not given explicitly by the model but must be calculated when required. The 'topological' model allows a richer class of topological properties to be explicitly handled. The node-arc-polygon structure, with its winged-edge representation, allows the explicit declaration of adjacency relationships. However, connectivity properties are still implicit. The model proposed in this paper allows connectivity properties, including the structure of holes, islands within holes, to any level, to be explicitly declared. Space precludes a complete discussion of the model, which would include formal proofs. Further details may be found in [16].

3 Basic Concepts from Topology

The spatial objects of interest are embedded in the Euclidean plane $\mathcal{R}^2$. If X is a subset of $\mathcal{R}^2$, then $\overline{X}$, X° and ∂X denote the closure, interior and boundary of X respectively. A topological concept often used in this paper is that of regular closed sets [13].

Definition: A subset X of $\mathcal{R}^2$ is called *regular closed* (or an *rc–set*) if, and only if, $\overline{X^\circ} = X$.

Intuitively, an rc–set does not have separate line or point features, neither does it have missing lines and points in the form of cuts and punctures. Thus, it is 'entirely areal' in nature. Obviously, all closed sets do not have the above properties. However, if we eliminate these features, the resulting set is an rc–set. The following proposition is clear.

Proposition: Let X be subset of $\mathcal{R}^2$. The set $\overline{X^\circ}$ is an rc–set.

The above proposition indicates that we can define a function *reg* which associates every subset X of $\mathcal{R}^2$ with a regular closed set, as follows:

$$\text{reg}(X) = \overline{X^\circ}$$

An example of *regularization* is shown in Fig. 1, where the configuration is made up of areal, line and point objects. The areal objects contain only parts of their

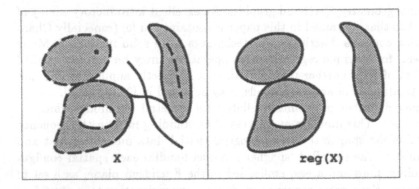

Fig. 1. Regularization

boundaries (shown with broken lines), and have cuts (shown with broken lines) and punctures. The regularization results in the elimination of points, line objects, cuts and punctures, and the inclusion of the full boundaries of the areal objects.

The union of a finite number of regular closed sets is regular closed. The intersection and set–difference of regular closed sets are not necessarily rc–sets. We define the *regularized* union, intersection and set–difference as below. The domain of rc–sets is closed under these operations.

$$A \cup_r B = (A \cup B)$$
$$A \cap_r B = \text{reg}(A \cap B)$$
$$A \setminus_r B = \text{reg}(A \setminus B)$$

The subclass of general objects studied in this work is the class of areal objects. It is possible to define such a subclass quite generally using the concept of *dimensionality*. A full general treatment of dimension theory and an exposition of combinatorial topology may be found in [1].

The ideas in this paper are associated with various forms of connectedness. A bounded rc–set of dimension n is *strongly connected* if, and only if, it is not possible to separate it by a closed set of dimension $n - 2$ or less. For example, an atom is strongly connected. A point-set is *weakly connected* if, and only if, it is not strongly connected. Finally, a connected areal object is *simply connected* if it has no holes.

4 Areal Object Classes

4.1 Basic Definitions

We start the description of the model by defining its basic objects:

Definition: An *atom* is a subset of R^2 which is topologically equivalent to the closed disc.

The boundary of an atom is a *Jordan curve* and, thus, the following theorem (not proved here) holds:

Theorem (Jordan curve theorem for atoms): The boundary of an atom separates the Euclidean plane into two open connected sets: The *interior* of the atom which is bounded and the *exterior* of the atom which is unbounded. The boundary of the atom is also the boundary of both its interior and exterior. Clearly, an atom is equal to the union of its interior and boundary.

The next step in the construction is to build up aggregations of atoms under the following constraints upon the resulting composite object:

- Any two distinct constituent atoms have finite intersection (in particular, the atoms have non-overlapping interiors);
- The composite object has no holes.

The resulting class of aggregated atoms will be called the class of *base areas*. To make this construction more precise, the following definitions are made:

Definition: Let A be a finite set of atoms. The *skeleton* of A, denoted Σ_A, is a graph whose vertices are labelled by the atoms of A. If a, a' are two distinct atoms of A, an edge exists between vertices v_a and $v_{a'}$ if, and only if, $a \cap a' \neq \emptyset$. In addition, a subset A' of A is a *component* of A if, and only if, the set of vertices $\{v_x : x \in A'\}$ is a component (in the graph-theoretical sense) of Σ_a.

Definition: Let $A = \{a_1, a_2, \ldots, a_n\}$ be a finite set of atoms. A is called a *base area* if, and only if, it has the following properties:

1. For every pair of distinct atoms a_i, a_j in A, their intersection is either empty or a singleton set.
2. Σ_A is acyclic.

The embedding of A is defined as

$$emb(A) = \bigcup_{i=1}^{n} a_i \qquad (1)$$

Note that the embedding of a base area is an rc–set since it is the finite union of rc–sets. Note also that we allow the possibility of a base area which is an empty set of atoms. We call this the *null base area*.

Define a base area to be *connected* if it has a connected embedding. It is immediate that a base area is connected if, and only if, its skeleton is connected. Thus, a base area is an aggregation of atoms which are placed according to certain topological rules. Figure 2 shows valid and invalid configurations of atoms, which in the case of (1) constitutes a base area but in the other cases do not constitute base areas. Figure 3 shows the underlying skeleton of sets of atoms in Figure 2. Rule (1) in the above definition, ensures that A does not have two atoms, the union of which is also an atom. In addition, it does not allow two atoms to create a hole between them (Fig. 2(III)). Rule (2) ensures that the embedding of A does not contain holes formed from more than two of its atoms

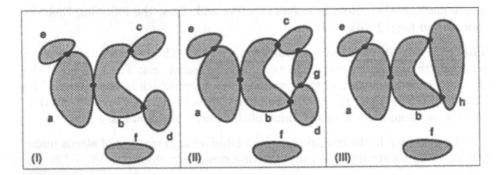

Fig. 2. Valid (I) and invalid (II,III) base areas

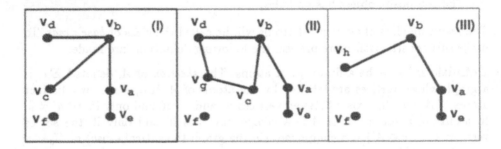

Fig. 3. Skeleton of sets of atoms in Fig. 2

(Fig. 2(II)). The definition also disallows a relationship between atoms which is not finitely representable.

An important property of this base area definition is that it provides a unique description. That is, two areas which have the same embedding must have essentially the same representation in terms of atoms and skeleton. Thus, the function *emb* is one-one and has an inverse.

The representation of a base area is minimal in terms of number of atoms. This is seen by considering the fact that no two atoms can be substituted for one atom without changing the embedding of the base area. In addition, the connectedness of the embedding of a base area is completely expressed by the connectivity properties of its skeleton.

4.2 Generic Areas

Up to this stage the model enables us to express appropriate areas, but without holes. We now proceed to construct a representation of areal objects with holes and islands recursively, up to any finite level. The data structure which we use to hold this representation is the tree, which will be labelled with atoms.

Let $T = <V_T, E_T>$ be a tree with vertex set V_T and edge set E_T. For each $x \in V_T$, define $s(x)$ to be the set of immediate successors of x. In what follows, when no confusion arises, we use the same symbol to denote a vertex and the atom (point–set) which it labels.

Definition: A *generic area* G is a tree, where all non-root nodes are labelled by names of atoms, such that:

1. For each vertex $v \in V_G$, $\{w : w \in s(v)\}$ is a base area.
2. For each non-root vertex $v \in V_G$ and each $w \in s(v)$
   (a) $w \subset v$
   (b) The set $w \cap \partial v$ has finite cardinality.

We allow the possibility that, apart from the root, the tree is empty. Such a generic area is called the *null generic area* or *null area* if no confusion arises. A further useful concept is that of depth. The *depth* of a generic area is defined to be the depth of its tree, that is, the maximum number of edges on direct paths between root and leaves. Associated with this idea is the notion of level. The *nth level* of a generic area refers to the set of atoms which are at distance n (in terms of number of edges on direct paths) from the root. It is clear from the definition of base area that the set of atoms at a particular level constitute a base area.

The connection between the generic area tree structure and the appropriate set of areas in the plane is made using the embedding function defined below. We begin by defining, for each non-root vertex $v \in V_G$, G_v to be the tree constructed by taking the subtree of G rooted at v and attaching above v a new root. It is clear from the definition that G_v is a generic area. The function *emb* which gives the embedding of generic areas in the plane is defined as follows.

$$emb(G) = \bigcup_{w \in s(r)} emb(G_w) \text{ where } r \text{ is the root of } G$$

$$emb(G_v) = \begin{cases} v & \text{if } v \text{ is a leaf vertex of } G \\ v \setminus \bigcup_{w \in s(v)} emb(G_w)^\circ & \text{otherwise} \end{cases}$$

The embedding of a generic area is an rc–set. An example of the embedding of a generic area is shown in Fig. 4. This area is of depth 3, having islands within holes. Figure 5 shows the area in levels, with atoms a and b, constituting a base area at level 1, shown on the left and the combination of levels 1 and 2 shown on the right. Figure 6 shows the full generic area represented as a labelled tree.

4.3 Uniqueness of Representation

The representation of generic areas given in this paper is canonical. More specifically, equal generic areas have the same embedding in the plane and, vice versa, generic areas having the same embedding in the plane are equal. Equality between generic areas is defined as follows.

Definition: Two generic areas G_1 and G_2 are *equal* if, and only if, there exists a graph isomorphism from G_1 to G_2 which preserves the labelling.

It can be shown that two generic areas are equal if, and only if, they have the same depths and at each level have the same base areas.

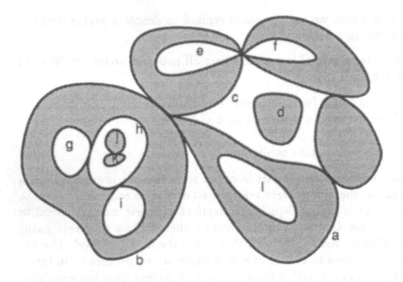

Fig. 4. Example of a generic area embedding

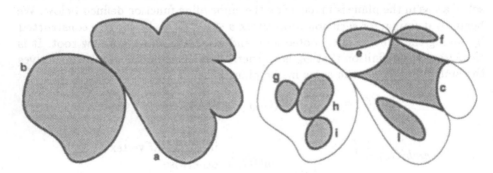

Fig. 5. Base areas at levels 1 and 2

The following theorem is the main theoretical result presented in this paper and indicates that our model is well–defined and provides a unique representation of the spatial objects of interest. The proof is not given here. Full details can be found in [16]. A key fact which is used in the proof of this result, and other results on generic area, is that at each level of the tree (except the root) the set of atoms together constitute a base area. Furthermore, except for the root, all the successors of a particular node are labelled by atoms which are contained in the extent of that node.

Theorem: Let G_1, G_2 be generic areas. Then,

$$G_1 = G_2 \iff emb(G_1) = emb(G_2)$$

This result has amongst its corollaries the conclusion that the function emb,

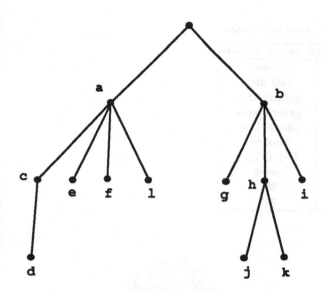

Fig. 6. Labelled tree representation of generic area

extended to the domain of generic areas, is essentially (up to equality of generic areas) one-one and so has an inverse. The inverse is used later.

5   Operations upon Areal Objects

This section presents work on the operations upon areal objects represented in our model. The operations discussed are mainly set-theoretic and topological. Certain operations upon atoms are taken to be primitive. The primitive operations are discussed in the next subsection. The general approach is to construct operations on base areas from primitive operations on atoms and then to construct operations on generic areas from operations on base areas. The full details of the representations and algorithms are long, so in this paper the constructions are presented in a level of detail which it is hoped will provide the essence.

5.1   Primitive Operations on Atoms

A set of primitive spatial operations defined on atoms is provided in Table 1. These operations are to be used as the foundation for defining operations on base and generic areas.

It can be shown that the regularized intersection of two atoms has no holes and thus is equal to the embedding of a base area. We do not prove this here, but an example is illustrated in Fig. 7. The spatial intersection between the atoms a, b is defined as follows:

$$a \cap_s b = emb^{-1}(a \cap_r b)$$

Table 1. Primitive spatial operations on atoms

Operator	Arity	Resultant domain
equals (=)	2	boolean
spatial intersection ($\cap_s$)	2	base area
spatial difference ($\backslash_s$)	2	generic area
spatial union ($\cup_s$)	2	generic area
boundary (∂)	1	simple loop
subset ($\subseteq$)	2	boolean
adjacent	2	$\{-1, 0, 1, 2\}$
centroid	1	point
area	1	$\mathcal{R}^+$
perimeter	1	$\mathcal{R}^+$

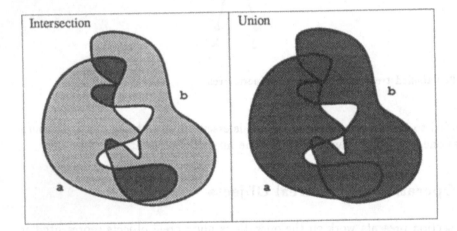

Fig. 7. Regularized intersection and union of atoms

where emb^{-1} is the inverse of the base areas embedding function. Thus, the spatial intersection of two atoms is given as a base area.

The regularized difference of two atoms has a hole when b is a subset of a and the boundary of b intersects with the boundary of a at a finite number of points (see Fig. 8). More specifically, the type of the regularized difference between a and b is determined by their spatial relationship according to Table 2.

Table 2. Regularized difference of atoms

Relationship	Description	$a \backslash_s b$
R_{d_1}	$a \cap_r b = \emptyset$	$\{a\}$
R_{d_2}	$a \subseteq b$	null area
R_{d_3}	$b \subset a$, $b \cap \partial a$ is finite	generic area
R_{d_4}	other	base area

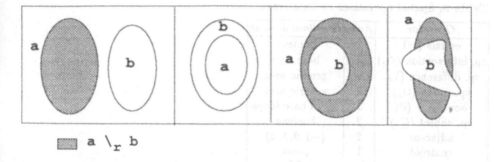

$$\boxed{} \quad a \setminus_r b$$

Fig. 8. Regularized difference of atoms

The spatial difference between two atoms is a generic area, defined as follows:.

$$a \setminus_s b \;=\; emb^{-1}(a \setminus_r b)$$

where emb^{-1} is the inverse of the generic areas embedding function.

The union of two atoms might form holes (Fig. 7) and so not be a base area. The spatial union of two atoms is defined as follows:

$$a \cup_s b \;=\; emb^{-1}(a \cup b)$$

It can be shown that the spatial union of two atoms is a generic area having depth at most two (i.e. it does not contain islands within lakes). It can also be shown that, if the intersection of two atoms consists of n components ($n > 0$), then their union has $n - 1$ holes.

The other operations given in Table 1 are straightforward. The result of the operation *adjacent* is the dimension of the point–set $a \cap b$. If the atoms a, b are disjoint, the result of the operation is -1.

5.2 Operations on Base Areas

The list of operations defined on atoms is extended to the domain of base areas as shown in Table 3. We discuss in detail set–oriented spatial operations, namely spatial intersection, difference and union. These operations are defined as follows:

$$A \cap_s B \;=\; emb^{-1}(emb(A) \cap_r emb(B))$$
$$A \setminus_s B \;=\; emb^{-1}(emb(A) \setminus_r emb(B))$$
$$A \cup_s B \;=\; emb^{-1}(emb(A) \cup emb(B))$$

Spatial Intersection. The spatial intersection of two base areas is a base area. We sketch out below a construction for this spatial intersection. Our claim is that:

$$A \cap_s B = \bigcup \{a \cap_s b : a \in A, b \in B\}$$

To show that this set of atoms forms a base area, we must check two conditions. We note, firstly, that if $x, y \in A \cap_s B$ and $x \neq y$, then the intersection of

Table 3. Spatial operations on base areas

Operator	Arity	Resultant domain
equals ($=$)	2	boolean
sp. intersection ($\cap_s$)	2	base area
sp. difference ($\backslash_s$)	2	generic area
sp. union ($\cup_s$)	2	generic area
boundary (∂)	1	set of base loops
sp. subset ($\subseteq_s$)	2	boolean
adjacent	2	$\{-1, 0, 1, 2\}$
centroid	1	point
area	1	$\mathcal{R}^+$
perimeter	1	$\mathcal{R}^+$
cardinality	1	$\{0, 1, 2, \ldots\}$
components	1	set of base areas
connected	1	boolean
strongly_connected	1	boolean

the embeddings of x and y is either empty or a singleton point. Secondly, the acyclicity of $\Sigma_{A\cap_s B}$ follows from the acyclicity of Σ_A and Σ_B.

Finally, it is not hard to check that $A\cap_s B$, as defined above, represents precisely the area required.

Spatial Difference. The spatial difference $A \backslash_s B$ of base areas A and B is a generic area, having depth at most two. The construction is outlined below:

1. Create a null generic area G.
2. For each $a \in A$, do steps (3) - (8) below.
3. Form the sets

$$B_2(a) = \{b \in B : aR_{d_2}b\},$$
$$B_3(a) = \{b \in B : aR_{d_3}b\},$$
$$B_4(a) = \{b \in B : aR_{d_4}b\}.$$

where relationships R_{d_2}, R_{d_3} and R_{d_4} are as in Table 2.

4. If $B_2(a) \neq \emptyset$, skip steps (5) to (8) below and proceed with next atom from A (if any).
5. Form the set $A^*(a) = \{a\}$.
6. For each $b \in B_4(a)$, form the base area $A^*(a) \backslash_s \{b\}$ and reassign this to $A^*(a)$.
7. Insert the atoms of $A^*(a)$ into the first level of the tree G.
8. Every $b \in B_3(a)$ is a hole of some atom of $A^*(a)$, because $b \subset a$ and the atoms of B subtracted from the atom a during step (6) are non-overlapping with b. Determine which atom contains b and insert b in G as a successor of this atom.

The resulting tree G is a generic area because:

- Atoms at the first level of G are subsets of atoms of A and, thus, their intersection is either void or a singleton set. Moreover, it may be checked that their skeleton graph is acyclic.
- Atoms at the second level of the tree are subsets of their ancestors. Furthermore, the set of atoms at level two is a subset of B and thus is a (possibly null) base area.

Finally, we note that the embedding of G is equal to the regularized difference of $emb(A)$ and $emb(B)$.

Spatial Union. The spatial union of two atoms is a generic area of depth at most two. However, the spatial union of base areas might be a generic area of greater depth. For an example, see Fig. 9. The problem of forming the spatial

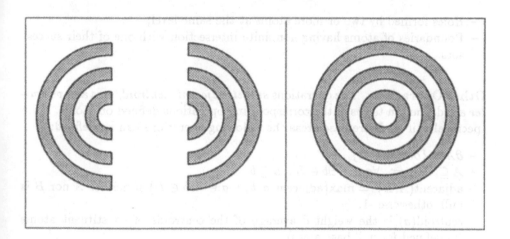

Fig. 9. Spatial union of two base areas resulting in a generic area of depth 6

union of two base areas can be reduced to a series of union operations between a generic area and an atom. The union operations are performed using the identities:

1. $(x \setminus_r y) \cup_r z = (x \cup_r z) \setminus_r (y \setminus_r z)$
2. $(x \setminus_r y) \setminus_r z = (x \setminus_r z) \setminus_r (y \setminus_r z)$

Note in (1) that if $y \subseteq x$ then $y \setminus_r z \subseteq x \cup_r z$. Moreover in (2), if $y \subseteq x$ then $y \setminus_r z \subseteq x \setminus_r z$. Thus, in order to calculate the union of an atom a and a generic area G:

- Consider the base area B at the first level of the generic area G. Construct the union of B with a as follows:
  - Let B_1 be the base area $\{b \in B : dim(a \cap b) > 0\}$. Form the spatial union $(\bigcup_s B_1) \cup_s a$. The resulting structure is a generic area having depth at most two.

- Attach to this tree structure the atoms of B that do not belong to B_1 (if any) at the correct level of the tree (note that some of them might be spatially contained in siblings).

The resulting tree is a generic area G_1 because each atom of B does not overlap with atoms spatially contained in any other atom of B.

- Attach to each atom of G_1, which has been formed from a union operation with an atom of B, the subtree of G rooted at this atom.
- Identities (1) and (2) above indicate that identity (2) should be recursively applied to the atoms of the attached subtrees until the leaves of the tree have been reached.

In the resulting tree, atoms at the same level have disjoint interiors and successors of an atom are subsets of the atom. However, the tree may not be a generic area. We must identify the following illegal cases and restore the violated properties:

- Holes formed by two or more atoms at the same level;
- Boundaries of atoms having non finite intersection with one of their successors.

Other Operations. The operations *subset, adjacent, centroid, area* and *perimeter* are defined in terms of the corresponding operations defined on atoms. More specifically, if A, B are base areas the following operations can be defined:

- $\partial A = \{\partial a : a \in A\}$
- $A \subseteq_* B \iff \forall a \in A \, \exists b \in B : a \subseteq b$
- $\mathrm{adjacent}(A, B) = \max\{\mathrm{adjacent}(a, b) : a \in A, b \in B\}$ if neither A nor B is null, otherwise -1.
- $\mathrm{centroid}(a)$ is the weighted average of the centroids of constituent atoms (undefined for null base areas).
- $\mathrm{area}(A) = \sum_{a \in A} \mathrm{area}(a)$
- $\mathrm{perimeter}(A) = \sum_{a \in A} \mathrm{perimeter}(a)$

It should be noted that the calculations of the area and perimeter of A are simplified by the fact that the interiors of the atoms of A are disjoint and boundaries intersect only at isolated points.

The operation *cardinality* returns the number of atoms (that is, strongly connected components) in the base area. The operations *components* and *connected* can be performed by performing the equivalent operations on the skeleton graph of the base area. Finally, a base area is strongly connected if and only if it is a singleton set.

6 Operations on Generic Areas

Let G be a non–null generic area. The base area at level one of G is called the *frame* of G. The *complementary area* of G is either the null generic area (if G has depth one) or the generic area formed by all the subtrees rooted at level one.

Table 4. Spatial operations on generic areas

Operator	Arity	Resultant domain
equals (=)	2	boolean
sp. intersection ($\cap_s$)	2	generic area
sp. difference ($\backslash_s$)	2	generic area
sp. union ($\cup_s$)	2	generic area
boundary (∂)	1	set of base loops
sp. subset ($\subseteq_s$)	2	boolean
adjacent	2	$\{-1, 0, 1, 2\}$
centroid	1	point
area	1	$\mathcal{R}^+$
perimeter	1	$\mathcal{R}^+$
cardinality	1	$\{0, 1, 2, \dots\}$
components	1	set of generic areas
connected	1	boolean
strongly_connected	1	boolean
simply_connected	1	boolean
depth	1	$\{0, 1, 2, \dots\}$
frame	1	base area
complementary_area	1	generic area

The frame and the complementary area of the null generic area are defined to be the null base area and the null generic area respectively.

The spatial intersection, difference and union of generic areas are defined similarly to the corresponding operations upon base areas. These operations can be complicated. For example consider the spatial intersection of two generic areas G_1, G_2 which have adequate depth. The identity

$$(A_1 \backslash_r B_1) \cap_r (A_2 \backslash_r B_2) = (A_1 \cap_r A_2) \backslash_r (B_1 \cup_r B_2)$$

suggests that the regularized intersection of G_1 and G_2 might be accommodated in a tree structure T as follows:

1. Form the spatial intersection of the frames of G_1, G_2 and insert its atoms at the first level of T.
2. Each atom x created at step (1) is a subset of just one atom a_1 from A_1 and just one atom b_1 from B_1. Attach under x the two trees rooted at a_1 and a_2, which are subtrees of G_1 and G_2 respectively.

Although the resulting tree T has precisely the same embedding as the generic area $G_1 \cap_s G_2$, it does not satisfy two fundamental properties of generic areas. Atoms at the second level of T are not necessarily subsets of their ancestors; also they might overlap each other, since they originate from different base areas.

Restoration of the above constraints is computationally expensive because of interactions recursively propagated down the tree. Construction of efficient algorithms for restoring the properties of a generic area is the subject of ongoing research.

Additional operations have been defined upon generic areas as shown in Table 4. Details of algorithms for constructing the results of such operations can be found in [16].

7 Conclusion

This paper describes the development of a formal model of a well-behaved subset of areal objects embedded in the Euclidean plane. The model is constructed in three stages. Firstly, atoms are constructed as objects topologically equivalent to discs. In the second stage, base areas are introduced which contain atoms as strongly connected components. The most general objects are generic areas, allowed to have holes and represented as trees. The contribution made here is to find a model which provides a unique representation of such a class of objects. Loosely speaking, the object classes 'atom', 'base area' and 'generic area' form part of an inheritance hierarchy, where 'atom' is a subclass of 'base area' which itself is a subclass of 'generic area'. More precisely, each embedding of an atom is the embedding of a base area and each embedding of a base area is the embedding of a generic area. The paper also outlines the representation of some of the operations upon such object classes.

The underlying motivation for the construction of such a model and representation is the perceived need for an approach to spatial data modelling which captures explicitly as much as possible of the topological structuring of the data objects. Thus, this work is a contribution to the line of development from spaghetti to topological data structures.

The model is being implemented using the object-based system, Smallworld GIS. Some of the detailed algorithms for operations upon generic areas still need to be constructed and proved in implementation. The authors are also exploring the tree structure of a generic area as a possibly useful access structure based upon the topological organization of the objects, in contrast to metric organization in traditional spatial indexes.

Acknowledgements

The authors are grateful to Richard Newell of Smallworld Systems for the use of Smallworld GIS as a testbed for many of the ideas contained in this paper. They also acknowledge with thanks one of the anonymous refereees, whose detailed comments allowed them to make several improvements to the paper.

References

1. P.S. Aleksandrov. *Combinatorial Topology*, volume 1. Graylock Press, Rochester, NY, USA, 1956.
2. R. Aspinall. Spatial analysis of wildlife distribution and habitat in GIS. In *Proc. 5th International Symposium on Spatial Data Handling*, volume 2, pages 444–453, Charleston, SC, USA, 1992.
3. M Egenhofer. *Spatial Query Languages*. PhD thesis, Univ. Maine, Orono, US, April 1989.

4. M.J. Egenhofer and A. Frank. Object-oriented databases: Database requirements for GIS. In *Proc. Int. GIS Symposium: The Research Agenda, Vol.2*, pages 189–211, Washington DC, 1987. US Govt. Printing Office.
5. J.D. Foley, A. van Dam, S.K. Feiner, and J.F. Hughes. *Computer Graphics: Principles and Practice*. System Programming Series. Addison-Wesley, 2nd edition, 1990.
6. R.H. Güting. Geo-relational algebra: A model and query language for geometric database systems. In *Proc. Conf. Extending Database Technology (Lecture Notes in Computer Science 303)*, pages 506–527, 1988.
7. R.H. Güting. Extending a spatial database system by graphs and object class hierarchies. In G. Gambosi and H. Six, editors, *Proceedings of the Int. Workshop on Database Management Systems for Geographical Applications*, Capri, May 1991.
8. G.H. Kirby, M. Visvalingam, and P. Wade. Recognition and representation of a hierarchy of polygons with holes. *Computer Journal*, 32(6):554–562, 1989.
9. H-P. Kriegel, T. Brinkhoff, and R. Schneider. The combination of spatial access methods and computational geometry in geographic database systems. In O. Günther and H-K. Schek, editors, *Advances in Spatial Databases, 2nd Symposium, SSD'91, Zurich, Switzerland*, Lecture Notes in Computer Science, pages 5–21. Springer, 1991.
10. H-P. Kriegel, H. Horn, and M. Schiwietz. The performance of object decomposition techniques for spatial query processing. In O. Günther and H-K. Schek, editors, *Advances in Spatial Databases, 2nd Symposium, SSD'91, Zurich, Switzerland*, Lecture Notes in Computer Science, pages 257–276. Springer, 1991.
11. B.C. Ooi, R. Sacks-Davis, and K.J. McDonell. Extending a DBMS for geographic applications. In *Proc. IEEE Int. Conf. on Data Engineering*, L.A., California, US, 1989.
12. F.P. Preparata and M.I. Shamos. *Computational Geometry: An Introduction*. Texts and Monographs in Computer Science. Springer, 1985.
13. A.A.G. Requicha. Mathematical models of rigid solids. Tech. memo 28, Univ. Rochester, Rochester, New York, USA, November 1977.
14. A.A.G. Requicha and H.B. Voelcker. Representation for rigid solids: Theory, methods and systems. *ACM Computing Surveys*, 12(4):437–464, 1980.
15. M. F. Worboys. A generic model for planar geographical objects. *International Journal of Geographic Information Systems*, 6(5):353–372, 1992.
16. M. F. Worboys and P. B. Bofakos. A canonical model for a class of areal spatial objects. Technical Report TR92-15, Department of Computer Science, Keele University, Keele, Staffordshire, UK., 1992.
17. M.F. Worboys, H.M. Hearnshaw, and D.J. Maguire. Object-oriented data modelling for spatial databases. *Int. J. Geographical Information Systems*, 4(4):369–383, 1990.
18. X3/SPARC/DBSSG/OODBTG. Final technical report. Technical report, American National Standards Institute, National Institute of Standards and Technology, Gaithersburg, MD 20899, USA, September 1991.

Strong Integration of Spatial Domains and Operators in a Relational Database System

Thierry Larue *, Dominique Pastre *, Yann Viémont **

* EDS/GFI/INFOSYS
Research and Development Department
Le Guillaumet
60, avenue du Président Wilson
Cedex 70
92046 Paris-la-Défense France

** Laboratoire MASI, Université de Versailles-Saint Quentin
45 av. des Etats-Unis, 78000 Versailles France

Abstract. Managing and manipulating spatial data requires selective access to these data, performance at access level, and data protection. The need for a single spatial database system, integrating in a single model both alphanumeric and geometric data, is discussed. Such a database system, GéoSabrina, has been developed as an extension of an already existing relational database system. The system supports spatial data with corresponding spatial operators. Data manipulation is easily made through a spatial extension of SQL. Optimization techniques are used, providing for a strong integration of spatial operators based on spatial indexing and join-indices techniques. Built-in spatial functionalities may be further extended by application programmers through object oriented features.

1. Introduction: Spatial Data Management

The main difference between geographical data and traditional data is their complexity. This complexity arises from the mix of alphanumeric and geometric information necessary to describe a geographical object, as much as from the complexity of the geometric information itself. Through the remainder of this paper, we will name the alphanumeric and the geometric parts of an object description respectively the *non-spatial* part and the *spatial* part (or geometries).

Typical data manipulations on these objects affect either the non-spatial part, on the spatial part, and often both. To support extensive data retrieval, predicates need to be symmetrically defined on both parts. To support data-intensive computations, functions need to be provided on both parts. In addition, data access based on spatial expressions should be as efficient as any other access and described through a unified assertional data language.

More generally, data management comprises: (1) data modeling, with a conceptual model providing data independence, (2) data storing, using efficiently the available storage, (3) data access, specified with multiple predicates, and (4) data protection, to guarantee security, integrity, proper concurrent access, and fault tolerance [Frank88]. Any feature of the system should apply to both the non-spatial and the spatial properties of an object through a unique model and with the same language constructs.

Numerous Geographical Information Systems (GIS) exist. They may be classified in four generations. This classification is provided to highlight the natural evolution of these systems towards a greater integration of non-spatial and spatial data and of the corresponding processing.

The first generation was based on systems built directly over a set of files. The functionality provided by these systems was very limited with respect to the aforementioned definition of data management. Moreover, the system was mostly handcoded, with a few data definition possibilities and evolution capabilities.

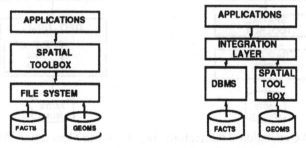

fig. 1. First Generation Architecture   **fig. 2.** Second Generation Architecture

The second generation architecture uses a traditional database system, usually relational, for the non-spatial part management of objects, and a set of separate data structures (in files) for the spatial part. Arc-Info [Morehouse85] [Morehouse89] [Chambers89] belongs to this category; Sand [Aref91] and GeoQL [Ooi90], though providing an interesting extended-SQL interface at the integration layer interface should also be considered as belonging to the second generation from this point of view.

Data non-integration results in two foreign models, two languages, and two data integrity mechanisms. Consequently, an integration layer in the architecture is necessary to process a request linking spatial and non-spatial properties of some objects. Although the performance of each subsystem might be satisfactory, overall performance is significantly affected by the integration layer. Moreover data integrity is only ensured at the integration level.

The third generation tries to manage both non-spatial and spatial data in the same database system. The corresponding architectures are made of a layer built on top of a conventional, usually relational, database system. Geometries are implemented as unstructured data, in the form of some long (binary) attribute. Rough spatial indexing is achieved by re-using a traditional index and playing with the access key, e.g., some bit interleaving scheme such as Z-order. GeoView [Waugh87] and SIRO DBMS [Abel89] are examples of such systems.

This generation offers, to the users, a unique conceptual model, usually derived from the relational model. Data protection is only partly ensured and spatial integrity is missing. However, spatial semantics of geometric attributes is unknown by the system which sees these attributes as binary strings. The database system stores these data but does not provide much help to process complex spatial retrievals based on spatial relationships. The corresponding operators expressing these relationships must be implemented in the top-layer, far from the database accelerators. As a result, the spatial data access language is more a primitive-call interface than a true language. With the lack of knowledge about spatial operator semantics, the database system is unable to perform the desired optimization. System performance is badly compromised.

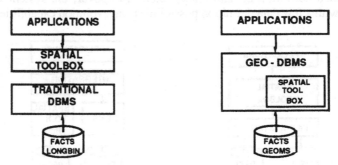

fig. 3. Third Generation Architecture **fig. 4.** Fourth Generation Architecture

The fourth generation, recently appeared, consists of systems which are based on extended database system, fully supporting spatial information as traditional information. These systems rely on spatial basic data types and operators to achieve a much higher level of integration.

Full data integration, if achieved, promises to offer following advantages:

- efficient data access with ad-hoc spatial indexing, clustering techniques and other database oriented technologies
- powerful selective criteria for spatial queries, with a generic predicate mechanism
- extended integrity constraint definition possibilities, as well as view definition possibilities, through the same operators

- query results fit in with the model, hence ready to be reused for further data manipulation in the same data language

A first step towards this goal can be made by using the abstract data type (ADT) [Osborn86] capabilities of some extended-relational systems such as POSTGRES [Stonebraker86]. A good example is given by the Geo System [Oosterom91] built on POSTGRES. A spatial package is provided by the system developer which comprises spatial types, operators, and indexes. This remains a weak integration however, since the system still does not know spatial data semantics outside this package, restricting full optimization. The lack of a well-accepted conceptual model for spatial data is especially a problem when defining a spatial-extended relational language.

To fully benefit from the promises of the fourth generation, a strong integration of spatial and non-spatial data support and processing is mandatory. To achieve it, the database system kernel itself must be extended to recognize spatial information as such and to optimize the corresponding operators. This requires an extension of the relational algebra itself to support spatial versions of the traditional select, project, join and aggregate operators [Güting88] [Güting89] [Scholl89] [Svensson91]. This way, a real spatial database system is obtained. This approach guided the design of the GéoSabrina system.

GéoSabrina is an integrated spatial database system designed and developed as an extension of the commercial Sabrina® relational database system (Sabrina is a trademark of Infosys) [Gardarin87]. This development is the result of a tight co-operation between the MASI laboratory and the Infosys company.

GéoSabrina offers a built-in spatial domain and dedicated operators, as described in the following section. The third section shows how data definition and data manipulation for both the non-spatial and the spatial part of geographic objects (tuples) is uniformly provided through an extended SQL. To encompass the difficulty created by the lack of a well-accepted spatial data model, the fourth section describes object-oriented extensions allowing users to define their own types and operators to better suit their needs, while keeping the benefits of the built-in mechanisms. Future enhancements and conclusions are presented in the last section.

2. An Integrated Spatial Database System

GéoSabrina integrates the management of both non-spatial and spatial data in a unique conceptual model: a relational model extended with basic spatial domains [David91]. In this model, geographical objects are described as tuples in tables taking both non-spatial attributes, that is alphanumeric, and spatial attributes, geometries describing object shapes and positions.

Integrating within the database system kernel (1) a general spatial domain capable of representing spatial attribute values for geographic objects, (2) operators defined on the values of this domain, and (3) indexing techniques supporting this domain and guaranteeing efficient access, makes GéoSabrina a true spatial database system.

2.1. A General Spatial Domain

In addition to the traditional domains of DBMSs, integer, real, character, string, date, long-text, long-unstructured, ..., GéoSabrina offers a general spatial domain called GEOMETRY. Values of this domain represent geometries, they are structured and have a well-defined semantics recognizable by the system.

As for other relationships in the relational model, spatial relations that may link specific objects, such as topological relations, intersection, inclusion, or adjacency, are not described in any specific data structure but are established through querying. The cost of the corresponding geometric computations can be kept low by using specific algorithms taking advantage of database-like techniques such as spatial indexing and join indices [Valduriez87].

Thus, the GEOMETRY domain is defined as a collection of independent geometric values, according to spaghetti model [Peuquet84]. The choice of a spaghetti model rather than a topological one [Spooner89] [Egenhofer90] [Egenhofer91] has been directed by three major considerations:

- first, the geometric representation model can be tuned to specifically fit to the description need of each object:

(1) The dimension of the space used in the representation of two objects may be different. Data represented in modeling spaces of various dimensions may be mixed and processed in an unified way.

(2) applications need to mix objects stemming from heterogeneous sources and described using various scales.

Such different modeling needs aren't provided by topology which represents all geometric data of the database in a single structure and impose all of them the same modeling capability and the same behaviour.

- second, a geometric constant or a geometric function result which are external geometries, not already known by the system, may be represented in the same model as already known internal objects are. This implies that queries may deal with internal and external objects in the same way. Moreover, geometric constant may be complex values, thus, spatial selection is not limited to 'point' and 'window' queries.

- finally, topology is traditionally chosen as an internal geometry model for performance considerations: actually, topology allows to increase performance of a subset of spatial predicates, the topological predicates, like intersection or adjacency. Yet, topology increases the cost of most other manipulations as (1) non-topological predicates, (2) objects reconstruction by geometric union of topological primitives from the topological graph, (3) updates of objects which infer complex and expensive updates of the topology structure and (4) the merge of several map layers needed to catch topological relationships between data from different layers. Topology is consequently ill-adapted to manage cheaply non-static data within non-strictly topological applications, whereas spaghetti model associated with classic spatial indexing provides good performances for all permitted manipulations. Thus, the topological model may be used with most benefits as a secondary structure (secondary index) associated with a spaghetti primary representation model (cf 2.3.).

Note that the integrity constraints implicitly included in a topological model [Meier86] [Laurini91], such as a tessellation constraint for example, may still be defined and enforced by the system, as explicit spatial integrity constraints, if need be.

Geometry Representation

The GEOMETRY domain has been designed to support geometric modeling in spaces of dimensions 2D, 2.5D, or 2.75D. A 2D modeling is a classic planar representation obtained by projecting a real 3D feature according to some reference system. The 2.5D modeling of a given object, as it is poorly but traditionally called, is similar to a planar representation with the addition of a third coordinate to each point (maximum elevation of the object at this point). Note that an object is prevented from having two points belonging to the same vertical line. The result is a representation corresponding to a subset of deformed plane with no fold. Further misusing terminology, we call 2.75D the extension of 2.5D where the planar representation of an object has both a minimum and a maximum elevation for each point. The 2.75D modeling captures the thickness of an object. In 2.75D an object is approximated as a slice between two non-parallel 2.5D representations having the same 2D projection and corresponding to the top and the bottom of the object.

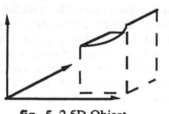   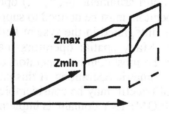

fig. 5. 2.5D Object   **fig. 6.** 2.75D Object

2.5D is well suited for the representation of a "flat" object such as a road or a field. If the thickness of the object has to be represented, as for a forest, or if the object is a volume, such as a building, 2.75D provides a much better representation while keeping most of the simplicity of 2.5D. Full 3D and 4D modeling are still under study in the project and will be implemented later.

Geometry Description

A value of the GEOMETRY domain is a set of elements that are either points, connected lines, or connected regions accepting holes. Elements are described with an approximation of their contour with a set of points taking 2, 3, or 4 coordinates depending on the chosen modeling space dimension. A value combining elements of various types is a complex geometry. Complex geometries are useful to describe, at a given resolution level, objects having parts both over and below the resolution threshold in some direction. An example of such an object is a river that may be in turn narrow (line) or wide (region), and include for example lakes or an estuary (regions with islands).

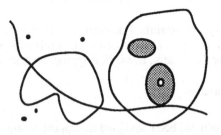

fig. 7. A Complex Geometry Value

Simple GEOMETRY values, composed of a single element, are recognized as special cases and processed as such, in order to keep storage efficiency.

2.2. Spatial Operators

A fourth generation spatial database system should support extensive retrieval possibilities through selection queries combining predicates on both non-spatial and spatial attributes. Traditional predicates on non-spatial data rely on both comparison (=, >, ...) and arithmetic (+, *, ...) operators in most database systems. Similarly, spatial operators must be defined to support spatial predicates. These spatial operators have to be integrated in the system kernel for efficiency, in the same way as other operators. Many spatial operators may be of interest for a given application. However, the most common operators can be simply expressed using a small subset of basic geometric operations. If this subset takes advantage of kernel optimization, the overall benefit may be considerable. Such a subset, defined on the values of the generic GEOMETRY domain, is implemented in GéoSabrina's kernel

Spatial operators in GéoSabrina are of three different kinds: functions, predicates, and aggregates. Spatial functions take geometries as arguments, and return spatial or non-spatial result. Traditional operator notation is supported for most unary and binary operators (+ for union, * for intersection, ...). The main built-in spatial functions compute geometric intersections, unions, differences, area, length, distances, ... Because of the way the GEOMETRY domain is defined, the usual pitfall of function support is avoided: the domain remains closed under all the operations combining geometries. Spatial predicates are either boolean functions or operator expressions whose outermost operator is a comparison operator as in $(g1 - g2) * g3 <> \emptyset$ (precedence rule applies). The main built-in predicates verify inclusion, intersection, adjacency, emptiness, ... Note that the predicate implementation of the intersection is different from its function implementation to avoid a useless computation of large cost with geometries described with many points. Reversibly, the functional versions of the operators can be used to define more complex predicates than in the example above. Spatial aggregates are iterations of (associative) binary operators on all the members of a set of geometries returning a single result. When this paper was written, only the sum aggregate of SQL had been extended with the natural meaning of iterated geometric union.

2.3. Performance of Spatial Data Access

Geographic applications manipulating large data volumes tend to generate substantial access costs (I/Os). Likewise, geometric operator computations incur large algorithmic costs (CPU), often in $O(n^2)$. To limit these costs data clustering and database accelerators such as indexes and join indices must be used.

Techniques for traditional data (alphanumeric) such as hashing or B-Trees are not suited for spatial data: multidimensional techniques are necessary. Spatial indexing is a well developed field with an abundant literature. A method providing for both searching and clustering spatial data is necessary.

Two index categories are implemented in the kernel of GéoSabrina: the first category deals with absolute position searching, such as pointing or windowing, the second deals with topological-based searching by using the relative positions of objects such as overlap, adjacency, inclusion.

Indexes of the first category chiefly reduce access costs, i.e. reduce the number of objects that must be accessed by a given selection request. The choice of an index using a simple approximation of an object, such as its minimum bounding rectangle (parallel to the reference axes), provides for all forms of querying. Such an index quickly preselects a subset of likely candidates for a given searching query. GéoSabrina uses an extension of the R-Tree [Gutman84], the R*-Tree [Beckmann90] with additional in-house improvement for the management of large objects. This index is used both as a clustering and as a non-clustering (secondary) index [Artal92].

Indexes of the second category are also likely to reduce access costs, but more importantly, reduce algorithmic costs. Example of such indexes are the join-indices of the relational model [Valduriez87]. While the second effect remains usually hidden with traditional data for which the cost of tuple comparisons is low and is buried in other costs, it is of utmost significance with $O(n^2)$ comparisons where n is the average number of points necessary to describe a geometry, that is quite large with recent data acquisition technology. In the context of spatial data these join-indexes keep the result of the computation of some costly match-expression and/or basic comparisons. In addition to straightforward extensions of the join-index of the relational model, a topological index has been defined for GéoSabrina. This topological index is a table structure capturing the same information as a topological graph: intersection, adjacency, and inclusion. A topological index can be defined for a couple of relations (in the sense of the relational model) of the database. This is a secondary structure, its creation does not modify the representation of the underlying objects. A topological index is managed in the general framework of indexes in the relational model [David91] [Rascon92].

2.4. Integration with the Relational Algebra

Specific relational algebra operators are provided to compute spatial-based queries or parts of queries. These operators are: the spatial-select, the spatial-project, the spatial-join, and the spatial-group. Spatial-select and spatial-join are able to efficiently evaluate spatial predicates, spatial-project computes functions on each tuples, and spatial-group computes spatial aggregates. They are implemented within the system kernel and their semantics and costs are known by the optimizer.

Several versions of these operators are provided. For each operator, the version using a brute-force geometric algorithm is called the naive version. A semi-naive version takes advantages of the minimum bounding rectangles stored with the geometries to drastically reduce the computation cost by discarding obviously negative or empty results. More advanced versions make use of the various available indexes described above. For the spatial-join, the cost may be such that it justifies the building of an index prior to the computation. Details are provided in [Chretien92].

Because of the various features of the system described in this section, built-in domain, built-in operators, spatial accelerators, spatial-extended algebra, the integration of spatial and non-spatial data management provided by GéoSabrina can be characterized as a strong integration.

3. A Geographic SQL

SQL is the standard interface of all relational database systems. From this point of view, it is natural that the query language of a spatial database system be an extension of SQL.

We don't consider SQL as an end user language, as [Egenhofer92] [Lorie91] [Roussopoul88] did, but rather as an interface language between the database system kernel and the applicative tools.

In our case, extending the data definition, manipulation and protection capabilities of SQL to support spatial data mostly requires the integration of the new spatial domain (s) and the associated operators within the language syntax.

Several proposals of geographic SQL have already been published [Roussopoul88] [Sacks87] [Ashworth92]. In SAND [Aref91], several spatial domains with the corresponding operators are proposed. However, extensions are limited to those compatible with the defined spatial-select and spatial-join operators. This limitation proceeds from the lack of support of the traditional underlying relational database system. Both spatial-select and spatial-join are implemented in the top integration layer (see introduction).

When using an extensible SQL, like XSQL/2 [Lorie91], ESQL2 [Gardarin92] or SQL3 proposal [ISO92] managing geographical data gives birth to peculiar applications. These ones are realized through ADT concept. These domains are seen by the system as long-texts, and are not understood at this level. This limits possible language integration (predicates, aggregates, ...).

GéoSabrina SQL uniformly treats the non-spatial and the spatial attributes of relations. Since the features are built-in, their behaviour is known by the request optimizer. They result in a true geographic query language, assertional, with both the full expressive power of SQL and the conceptual simplicity of the underlying model. No additional clause is necessary in the basic SELECT ... FROM ... WHERE blocks of SQL. Additional features apply to each SQL clause with no restriction. These language features are presented using examples.

3.1. Geographic Data Definition

Geographic information is usually made of several thematic layers. A thematic layer gathers objects of the same kind, with similar characteristics, that can be described by a set of both non-spatial and spatial properties. Hence, such a layer forms a natural basis for the definition of geographic relations (SQL tables). Non-spatial and spatial properties translate to attributes defined on the corresponding domains.

As an example, the administrative layer for (French) cities can be represented by this SQL definition:

```
CREATE TABLE CITY
                (CITY_NUMBER      CHARACTER (5),
                DEPARTMENT        INTEGER,
                NAME              VARCHAR,
                POPULATION        INTEGER,
                GEOM              GEOMETRY)
```

Such a spatial relation is defined as any other relation. It behaves in exactly the same way. As an example, a new spatial attribute may be added later:

```
ALTER TABLE CITY ADD CITY_CENTER GEOMETRY
```

Internal schema definition

Spatial attributes of a geographical relation can be used, as any other attribute, as the basis of indexing and clustering techniques. As an example, if one wishes to index both the numeric value of the CITY_NUMBER with a common B-Tree index and the geometric value of the GEOM attribute with a spatial index, the corresponding SQL is:

```
CREATE BTREE INDEX ON CITY CITY_NUMBER
CREATE RTREE INDEX ON CITY GEOM
```

3.2. Geographic Data Manipulation

Spatial and non-spatial attributes are jointly and uniformly specified in a SQL query. Retrievals and updates are ruled by the usual concepts, semantic and syntactic rules of SQL.

Retrievals

GéoSabrina SQL allows direct access to the values of a spatial attribute; it is simply accessed through its name. To retrieve the geometry and the population of a given city only the following query is needed:

```
SELECT      GEOM, POPULATION
FROM        CITY
WHERE       NAME = 'CORNEBARRIEU'
```

The use of functions using geometric values and/or returning these is possible at any place where in SQL syntax a *value expression* may be provided. The syntax is straightforward as shown in the following example returning the name and boundary length of large cities:

```
SELECT      NAME, LENGTH (GEOM)
FROM        CITY
WHERE       AREA (GEOM) > 10000
```

Operator notation can be used with most GEOMETRY-producing binary functions. This applies as well to the expression in the selection clause which can mix non-spatial and spatial predicates. To find neighbouring cities of our sample city the request is:

```
SELECT      N.NAME
FROM        CITY N, CITY C
WHERE       C.NAME = 'CORNEBARRIEU'
AND         N.NAME <> 'CORNEBARRIEU'
AND         N.GEOM * C.GEOM IS NOT EMPTY
```

In this request, N.GEOM * C.GEOM IS NOT EMPTY is a syntactic sugar to use the same operator notation for both the intersection function and the intersection predicate. The optimizer performs the proper translation to use the cheaper predicate algorithm. As stated earlier, this notation provides for more complex predicates as in:

```
...C.GEOM ** (R1.GEOM * R2.GEOM) IS NOT EMPTY
```

which returns the city (ies) containing (here the overlap operator ** excludes bordering) a crossroad between two specific roads (which may happen to cross several times).

Spatial aggregation can be performed on spatial attributes with this syntax, building department geometries from the component cities:

```
SELECT      DEPARTMENT, SUM (GEOM)
FROM        CITY
GROUP BY    DEPARTMENT
```

Finally, all the expressive power of SQL may apply to spatial properties as in the following request where a FOREST relation is assumed with attributes TYPE and GEOM (at least) and which retrieves cities with no pine forest within city limits:

```
SELECT      NAME, GEOM
FROM        CITY C
WHERE       NOT EXISTS (
            SELECT   *
            FROM     FOREST F
            WHERE    TYPE = 'PINE'
            AND      F.GEOM * C.GEOM IS NOT EMPTY)
```

Updates

Updates are similarly performed with standard SQL commands. The following example creates the DEPARTMENT table from the CITY table:

```
CREATE TABLE DEPARTMENT
            (NUMBER          INTEGER,
            TERRITORY        GEOMETRY)

INSERT INTO DEPARTMENT
            SELECT           DEPARTMENT, SUM (GEOM)
            FROM             CITY
            GROUP BY         DEPARTMENT
```

3.3. Geographic Data Protection

If concurrency control and reliability are transparently enforced by the database system, security rules (access rights) and integrity constraints are specified through the request language. Access rights allocation on spatial attributes is performed with standard GRANT and REVOKE commands combined as usual with proper view definition. Since a view definition uses a basic SELECT block, all the geographic extensions apply to view definition as well.

Using spatial predicates in the definition of integrity constraints applies similarly for simple spatial integrity constraints. More advanced constraints require more syntactic support and are not described in this paper.

This section has shown how easily new built-in operators (functions, predicates, and aggregates) can be added to the existing SQL syntax, by analogy with the syntax already provided for arithmetic. This apparent simplicity relies on a tight integration of these operators within the database system kernel and on the implementation of the corresponding GEOMETRY domain as a basic type.

4. Extensibility

GéoSabrina offers a spatial model based on a fairly generic spatial domain and several built-in common spatial operators. This is expected to cover a large subset of the possible needs. On the other side, there may be some applications whose requirements are poorly, or not-at-all, satisfied by this model. Extensibility is hence necessary to allow users to define their own specific domains and/or their specific operators. Such a mechanism is provided by GéoSabrina, as by Sabrina [Gardarin89]. Any built-in type may be extended by user, including LONGBIN which provides for the definition of almost anything. Application specific spatial domains may be defined as an entirely different ADT package, in a way very similar to that of POSTGRES, or more interestingly defined as an extension of GEOMETRY. The first method, to be used for drastically different requirements than those satisfied by the built-in domains, relies on application programmer skills and will not be further dealt with in this paper. The second method is described in the remainder of this section.

4.1. Application-Specific Spatial Domains

The extensibility mechanism allows for the specialization of the built-in spatial domain GEOMETRY through some additional syntax. This works in a similar way as deriving an integer range type from the built-in integer type. Integer operators still apply: they are inherited; but new operators may be defined on the new type such as a modulo version of the addition or multiplication.

In this framework, a new spatial domain is defined as a specialization of some already existing spatial domain. The specialization is achieved through selection of a subset of all possible values. The selection specification, a user provided procedure in some C-compatible programming language, is used as a type checking procedure by the system. The procedure is separately compiled and statically linked with the system. The following simple request provides for the declaration of a new SURFACE domain within the database system with its corresponding type checking procedure name:

CREATE DOMAIN GEOMETRY:SURFACE check_surface ()

This process is recursive and a user may further declare more restricted domains as in the following, self-explanatory, example:

    CREATE DOMAIN GEOMETRY:SURFACE:SURF_WITHOUT_HOLE
        check_surf_without_hole ()

As soon as it is defined, a new domain can be used in other SQL statements as with this new definition of the CITY relation:

    CREATE TABLE CITY
                (CITY_NUMBER   CHARACTER (5),
                 ...   ...
                 GEOM   SURFACE)

All values used for the GEOM attribute must be valid SURFACE values and must verify the check_surface () procedure. This control is enforced by the system whenever a value assignment is performed on the GEOM attribute. This is equivalent to strong typing. However, the system has no way to verify that the user provided procedure is correct. The newly defined domain is whatever is not filtered out by the supplied procedure.

A full hierarchy of spatial domains can be built in this way, with various levels of refinement. By transitivity, all domains in the hierarchy are sub-domains of GEOMETRY and inherit from the built-in operators. Each sub-domain inherits from the constraints and the operators defined along the entire path from the root to the sub-domain. An example of such a user defined hierarchy is given in the following figure:

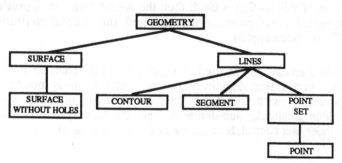

fig. 8. A Sample Sub-Domain Hierarchy

4.2. Non-Standard Methods

The extensibility also allows to define new methods - functions and predicates - for already defined domains, either basic root domains or user defined ones.

The following syntax corresponds to the declarations of the interface for an adjacency predicate, a second predicate overloading the former for the special case of sub-domain comparison, and a function overloading the built-in area function for surfaces (regions):

CREATE PREDICATE [GEOMETRY, GEOMETRY] ADJACENCY
pred_adj_geom ()

CREATE PREDICATE [GEOMETRY:SURFACE,
GEOMETRY:SURFACE]
ADJACENCY pred_adj_surf ()

CREATE FUNCTION [GEOMETRY:SURFACE] AREA: REAL
func_area_surf ()

As soon as they are defined, new predicates and functions are integrated in the language like built-ins are. Overloading is performed at compile time, since the variables of tuple calculus underlying SQL do not support polymorphism. For example a request returning the AREA of a given city may translate into two different queries depending on the schema version of the CITY relation as follows:

```
SELECT      N.NAME, AREA (N.GEOM)
FROM        CITY N, CITY C
WHERE       C.NAME = 'CORNEBARRIEU'
AND         ADJACENCY (N.GEOM, C.GEOM)
```

If the CITY schema version of section 3 is used, then GEOM attributes are defined on the GEOMETRY domain and the built-in version of the AREA function is called, while the first definition of the ADJACENCY predicate applies. If instead the new schema version of this section is used, then the AREA function is overloaded with the user supplied corresponding method and the second definition of the ADJACENCY predicate applies.

This overloading scheme can be used to attach a set of different methods to a single operator name in a spatial domain hierarchy. The scheme is mostly intended to support operations with the same external specification but with simpler implementations on simpler sub-domains. The scheme may also be used in many other ways, under user control, because methods are multi-target.

4.3. Strong Integration of user-defined predicates

GéoSabrina only knows how to optimize a selection query when it recognizes the expression predicates that can benefit from indexation, spatial or not. A join-index or a topological index structure can only be used to speed up the predicates for which they have been designed. A more general index, as a minimum bounding rectangle index, can prove useful for each predicate implying an intersection from its definition.

The extended optimizer knows that built-in predicates in the list (intersection, overlap, adjacency, inclusion) belong to this category. It takes a special command to extend such a knowledge to user defined predicates. The keyword INTERSECTION_LIKE is provided for this purpose. For example:

CREATE INTERSECT_LIKE PREDICATE [GEOMETRY, GEOMETRY]
CORNER_ADJACENCY pred_adj_geom

5. Conclusion

A relational model based, geographic database system, integrating into a single model and a unified architecture non-spatial and spatial data, has been presented. This system, GéoSabrina, provides a built-in spatial domain and built-in operators defined on this domain. Database secondary structures, such as indexes, and new versions of algebra operators are implemented in the kernel of the system, thus resulting in a tight integration with efficient geometric processing.

A uniform access to all data types is provided through an extended version of SQL, superset of standard SQL. All system geometric features are accessible through this language and can be used with no limitation for the various data management aspects, from searching conditions, to view definition or integrity constraint definition.

A further extensibility mechanism is supported to specify user specific spatial domains and/or restrictions on already existing domains. Brand-new operators may be added to the system and new methods can be created for existing ones with an overloading mechanism.

GéoSabrina manages data in a representation model of dimension 2D, 2.5D, or 2.75D. In these modeling spaces only a single approximation of 3D objects is allowed. Spatial objects are static and only evolve through conventional database update commands.

Studies presently carried out are under way to increase the representation power of this system. These studies include: (1) true 3D modeling and manipulation, with a 3D domain and associated operators [Cambray93], (2) data variability with history, versions, active objects, and dynamic objects; also with temporal extensions of SQL [Yeh92], and (3) multimedia extension to transform the database kernel into a multimedia object server.

We wish to thank the members of the GéoTropics research team of the MASI laboratory and the GéoSabrina research and development team of INFOSYS company for their contribution for many of the ideas and implementations presented in this paper.

This work was partially supported by the DRET administration under grants n° 91–344 and 91–349.

6. References

[Abel89]   Abel, D.J., "SIRO-DBMS : a Database Tool-kit for Geographical Information Systems", Int. J. Geographical Information Systems, Vol. 3, Num. 2, 1989, pp 103--116.

[Aref91]   Aref, W., Samet, H., "Extending a DBMS with Spatial Operations", SSD'91, Zürich, Switzerland, August 1991. (also Lecture Notes in Computer Science N° 525)

[Artal92]   Isabelle Artal, "Utilisation de méthodes d'indexation spatiales pour optimiser les opérateurs spatiaux dans un SGBD Géo-Relationnel", Mémoire ingénieur Cnam Paris 92.

[Ashworth92]   M. Ashworth, "The GIS perspective on spatial and object oriented extensions to SQL", Computervision GIS Draft, 1992

[Beckmann90]   Beckmann N., Kriegel H., Schneider R., Seeger B., "The R*-tree: an efficient and robust access method for points and rectangles", ACM SIGMOD'90, pp 322-331.

[Cambray93]   Béatrix de Cambray, "Three Dimensional (3D) objects in Geographical Databases", EGIS'93, Genova Italy, March 1993.

[Chambers89]   Don Chambers, "Overview of GIS Database Design ESRI" Arc News vol 11 No 2 1989

[Chretien92]   Didier Chrétien ,"La jointure spatiale", Technical Report IBP under press

[David91]   Benoît David, "Modélisation, représentation et gestion d'information géographique : une approche en relationnel étendu", Phd Thesis, university of Paris VI, July 1991.

[Egenhofer90]   M. J. Egenhofer, J. R. Herring, "A Mathematical Framework for the Definition of Topological Relationships", Proceedings of the 4th International Symposium on Spatial Data Handling, Zürich Switzerland, 1990, Vol. 2, pp. 803-813

[Egenhofer91]   M. J. Egenhofer, R. Franzosa, "Point-set Topological Spatial Relations" Int. Journal of Geographical Information Systems, 1991, Vol. 5, N° 2, pp 161-174

[Egenhofer92]   Egenhofer, M., "Why not SQL!", Int. J. Geographical
                  Information Systems, 1992, Vol. 6, N° 2, pp 71–85.

[Frank88]   A. U. Frank "Requirements for a Database Management
                  System for a GIS", Photogrammetric Engineering and
                  Remote Sensing, Vol. 54, N°11, November 1988, pp
                  1557-1564

[Gardarin87]   G. Gardarin, M. Jean-Noël, B. Kerhervé, F. Pasquer, D.
                  Pastre, E. Simon, P. Valduriez, Y. Viémont, L.
                  Verlaine, "Sabrina, a relational database system developed
                  in a research environment", Technology and Sciences of
                  Informatics, AFCET-Gauthier Villard-John Willey &
                  Sons Ltd, 1987

[Gardarin89]   G. Gardarin, J. P. Cheiney, G. Kiernan, D. Pastre, H.
                  Stora, "Managing Complex Objects in an Extensible
                  Relational DBMS", Proc. of the fifteenth International
                  Conference on Very Large Data Bases, VLDB'89,
                  Amsterdam, 1989, pp 55-65

[Gardarin92]   G. Gardarin, P. Valduriez , "ESQL2 : An Object-Oriented
                  SQL with F-Logic Semantics", IEEE Data Engineering,
                  Salt Lake City, 1992.

[Güting88]   R.H. Güting, "Geo-Relational Algebra: A Model and
                  Query Language for Geometric Applications",
                  Proceedings of the Int. Conf. on Extending Database
                  Technology, EDBT'88, Venice, March 1988, pp506-527

[Güting89]   R.H. Güting, "Gral: An Extensible Relational database
                  System for Geometric Applications", Proc; of 15th Int.
                  Conf. on Very Large Data Bases VLDB'89, Amsterdam
                  1989

[Gutman84]   Gutman, A., "R-Tree: A Dynamic Index Structure for
                  Spatial Data Searching", SIGMOD'84, Boston,
                  Massachussets USA, June 1984.

[ISO92]   ISO/IEC JTC1/SC21 Information Retrieval Transfert and
                  Management for OSI, ISO Working Draft, Database
                  Language SQL, Juin 1992

[Laurini91]   R. Laurini, F. Milleret-Raffort, "Using integrity
                  constraints for checking consistency of spatial databases",
                  GIS/LIS'91 Atlanta USA 1991

[Lorie91]   Lorie, R., "The Use of a Complex Object Language in Geographic Data Management", SSD'91, Zürich, Switzerland, August 1991. (also Lecture Notes in Computer Science N° 525)

[Meier86]   A. Meier, M. Ilg, "Consistent Operations on a Spatial Data Structure", IEEE Transactions on Pattern Analysis and Machine Intelligence, Vol. 8, N° 4, July 1986, pp. 532-538

[Morehouse85]   Morehouse Scott, "ARC/INFO : A relational model for spatial information", Auto-carto 7 1985

[Morehouse89]   Morehouse Scott, "The Architecture of ARC/INFO", Auto-carto 9, Baltimore, Maryland USA, April 2-7 1989

[Ooi90]   B.C. Ooi, "Efficient Query Processing in Geographic Information Systems" lectures notes in Computer Science N°471, 1990

[Oosterom91]   Peter van Oosterom, Tom Vijlbrief, "Building a GIS on top of the open DBMS 'Postgres".EGIS'91 Brussels, Belgium pp 775-787.

[Osborn86]   S. L. Osborn, T. E. Heaven, "The Design of a Relational Database System with Abstract Data Types for Domains", ACM Transactions on Database Systems, Vol. 11, N° 3,, September 1986, pp 357-373

[Peuquet84]   D.J. Peuquet, "A Conceptual Framework and Comparison of Spatial Data Models" Cartographica vol 21 N°4, 1984, pp66-113

[Rascon92]   Virginie Rascon, "Méthodes d'accélération de la jointure spatiale à base de Pré-jointure et de topologie dans un SGBD Géo-Relationnel", Mémoire ingénieur Cnam Paris 92.

[Roussopoul88]   N. Roussopoulos, C. Faloutsos, T; Sellis, "An Efficient Pictorial Database System for PSQL", IEEE Transaction on Software Engineering, Vol 14 N°5, May 1988, pp. 639-650

[Sacks87]   R. Sacks-Davis, K. J. McDonell, B. C. Ooi, "GEQL: A Query Language for Geographic Information Systems", Australian and New Zealand Association for the Advancement of Science Congress, Townsville Australia 1987

[Scholl89]   M. Scholl, A. Voisard, "Thematic Map Modeling",
                Symposium on the Design and Implementation of Large
                Spatial Databases, July, 1989.

[Sinha88]   Sinha A.K., Waugh T.C., "Aspects of the
                implementation of GEOVIEW design", Int J. of
                Geographical Information Systems Vol. 2 1988 pp 91--
                99

[Spooner89]   R. Spooner, "Advantages and Problems in the Creation
                and Use of a Topologically Structured Database",
                Photogrammetry and Land Information Systems,
                Lausanne, 1989, Presses Techniques Romandes 1990, pp
                73-85

[Stonebraker86] Stonebraker M, Rowe L.A., "The Design of
                POSTGRES", SIGMOD Conf., Washington, District of
                Columbia USA 1986.

[Svensson91]   P. Svensson, Z. Huang, "Geo-SAL: A Query Language
                for Spatial Data Analysis", SSD'91, Zürich, Switzerland,
                August 1991. (also Lecture Notes in Computer Science
                N° 525) pp119-140

[Valduriez87]   Patrick Valduriez, "Join Indices", ACM Trans. on
                Database Systems, Vol. 12, No. 2, June 1987.

[Waugh87]   Waugh T.C., Healey R.G., "The GEOVIEW Design, a
                relational Database Approach to Geographical Data
                Handling", Int.J. Geographical Information Systems,
                1(2), 1987, pp 101--118.

[Yeh92]   T.S. Yeh et Y. Viémont, "Temporal Aspects of
                Geographical Databases", EGIS 92, march 1992,
                Munich

The Transformation Technique for Spatial Objects Revisited*

Bernd-Uwe Pagel, Hans-Werner Six, Heinrich Toben

FernUniversität Hagen

Abstract. The transformation technique is one of the earliest approaches for storing a set of bounding boxes of arbitrary geometric objects such that insertion, deletion and proximity queries can be carried out with reasonable performance. The basic idea is to transform the bounding boxes into points in higher dimensional space in order to apply data structures for points which are better understood and easier to handle. Even though the basic concept of the transformation idea at first glance seems fascinatingly simple and elegant, the majority of the data structure community regard this technique as less appropriate because some of its properties are considered harmful.
Main contribution of this paper is to shed some new light on the transformation technique in a sense that some of these properties can be proven to be harmless while the harmful ones can be overcome by new methods. Furthermore, we demonstrate that new kinds of transformations which take other than pure location parameters into account, provide the transformation technique with new quality.

1 Introduction

In recent years, various efficient data structures for maintaining large sets of multidimensional geometric objects have been developed. First and foremost, these data structures claim to improve the performance of spatial accesses, i.e. to support queries referring to the location or spatial proximity of the objects. The general idea behind all approaches is to cluster the objects according to their spatial location. To this end, the data space is divided into (not necessarily disjoint) subspaces and the objects in a subspace are stored together in a corresponding data bucket (a block of fixed size on secondary storage).

Most data structures have been designed for multidimensional points (see e.g. [1, 5, 10]). In typical applications, however, objects are arbitrarily geometric, i.e. non-point objects. In many situations, it has been proven to be useful to characterize non-point objects by their bounding boxes, i.e. minimal enclosing multidimensional intervals, serving as simple geometric keys. Hence, non-point data structures mostly deal with multidimensional intervals (see e.g. [3, 5, 6]). Only the cell tree [2] does not use this approximation.

---
* This work has been supported by the European Community, ESPRIT Project No. 6881 (AMUSING).

The transformation technique is one of the earliest approaches for storing bounding boxes such that proximity queries are supported. The idea is to map the bounding boxes of geometric objects into points in higher dimensional space in order to directly reuse well-understood point data structures. When this technique came up it was regarded as less appropriate for proximity queries, mainly because proximity is lost in the image space. In addition, the distribution of the resulting points tends to be highly biased and point data structures of that time could not cope with that efficiently. Finally, the transformation of the query range of a simple window query yields a partially unbounded query range in the image space. Other query types cannot meaningfully be transformed at all.

In this paper, we refute the main arguments and demonstrate that the transformation technique can be made competitive to any other data structure maintaining sets of bounding boxes. One reason is due to recent point data structures which are able to handle the image point distribution efficiently (see e.g. the LSD-tree [5]). Second reason is that inherent geometric properties of the domain space can be carried over and drive the actions in the image space. This opens the door for an efficient performance of arbitrary proximity queries. Furthermore, we demonstrate that new kinds of transformations taking other than pure location oriented parameters into account provide the transformation technique with new quality.

2 Concepts of Spatial Data Management

Let us shortly review the basic concepts of the management of geometric objects which are characterized by geometric attributes determining shape and location and by some conventional attributes, e.g. the name of the class an object belongs to. Operations on these objects which have to be performed efficiently are insert, delete, search by location, i.e. exact match, and proximity queries. Concerning proximity queries, we restrict our investigations to window queries, i.e. queries with rectangular query range.

Data structures which support this bundle of operations cluster the geometric objects in data buckets (equally sized blocks on secondary storage) according to their spatial locations. With each data bucket a subspace of the data space, the so-called bucket region, is associated surrounding all objects of the corresponding bucket. Except for the BANG-File [1], the cell tree [2], and the R-File [6], a bucket region is a multidimensional interval.

Point data structures usually create bucket regions which form a partition of the data space (see e.g. [1, 5, 10]). Data structures for bounding boxes either generate bucket regions which may overlap and do not necessarily cover the entire data space (see e.g. [3, 6]), or follow the transformation paradigm, which propagates the transformation of the bounding boxes into higher dimensional points and enables the reuse of point data structures.

Let us end off this section with a more precise definition of the spatial data management problem under concern. Let d be the dimension of the data space we consider, $S_i = [0, 1)$, $1 \leq i \leq d$, and $S = S_1 \times S_2 \times \ldots \times S_d$ be the d-

dimensional data space in which all geometric objects are defined. For sake of simplicity we assume that each geometric object g is a d-dimensional interval $g = [g.l_1, g.r_1] \times \ldots \times [g.l_d, g.r_d]$, $g.l_i, g.r_i \in S_i$, $g.l_i \leq g.r_i$. For a point object $g.l_i = g.r_i$ for $i = 1, \ldots, d$ holds and the representation may be abbreviated to $g = (g.l_1, g.l_2, \ldots, g.l_d)$. Let us assume that for storing the set G of objects the data structure $DS(G)$ currently consumes m consecutive blocks $B_1, B_2, \ldots, B_m$, the so-called data buckets. With each object $g \in G$, a bucket is uniquely associated. The bucket region $R(B_i) \subseteq S$ of a bucket B_i is the minimal d-dimensional interval enclosing all objects in B_i. We call $B = \{B_1, \ldots, B_m\}$ a bucket set and $R(B) = \{R(B_1), \ldots, R(B_m)\}$ the corresponding organization of the data space.

Without loss of generality and only for simplicity reasons, we choose $d = 2$ for further considerations. This reduces bounding boxes, bucket regions, and query windows to two-dimensional rectangles.

3 Excursus: A Performance Measure for User Queries

An investigation and a fair comparision of different approaches of spatial data management requires a comparative measure, which should be independent of data structure and implementation details, and even independent of whether the objects are points or non-point objects. We claim that the expected number of bucket accesses needed to perform a query is such a desirable cost measure, because in practical applications data bucket accesses form the dominating part of query costs (e.g. in particular exceed by far external accesses to the paged parts of the corresponding directory concerning frequency and execution time).

Obviously, this cost measure depends on the actual bucket set B and the query behavior of the user. Since we deal with expected values, we first have to define the underlying probability model. To this end, we introduce a probabilistic query model $\mathcal{QM}$ reflecting the expected query behavior of the user.

For a bucket set $B = \{B_1, \cdots, B_m\}$ and a query model $\mathcal{QM}$, let $P(q \text{ meets } B_i)$ be the probability that performing query q forces an access of bucket B_i, and $P(q \text{ meets } B; j)$ be the probability that performing query q forces exactly j buckets in B to be inspected. Then the expected number of bucket accesses needed to perform query q – we call it the *performance measure $\mathcal{PM}$ for $\mathcal{QM}$* – is given by

$$\mathcal{PM}(\mathcal{QM}, B) = \sum_{j=0}^{m} j \cdot P(q \text{ meets } B; j).$$

The following Lemma facilitates the computation of $\mathcal{PM}$.

Lemma.

$$\sum_{j=0}^{m} j \cdot P(q \text{ meets } B; j) = \sum_{i=1}^{m} P(q \text{ meets } B_i)$$

We omit the proof and refer to [12].

Example 1. In order to illustrate the performance measure $\mathcal{PM}(\mathcal{QM}, B)$ let us take its 'instantiation' derived from the following simple query model $\mathcal{QM}_1$, which is based on window queries where the user may vary the aspect ratio, the location of the query window and the query size. Let us assume square windows on the average, every part of the data space equally likely to be requested, and the query size to be an (area) constant. The assumptions of this query model reflect a behavior which can sometimes be observed with novice and occasional users.

More precisely, $\mathcal{QM}_1$ is defined by a constant aspect ratio of 1:1, a constant window area c_A and a uniform window center distribution $U[S]$. Furthermore, we assume a data structure guaranteeing that $P(q \text{ meets} B_i) = P(q \text{ intersects } R(B_i))$, i.e. unnecessary bucket accesses are avoided. This assumption is fulfilled by any data structure with a directory providing information about the bucket regions of the data buckets (see e.g. the R-tree [3] and the LSD-tree [5]). If we abstain from boundary considerations in favour of readability, then $P(q \text{ meets} B_i)$ is just the bucket region $R(B_i)$ of bucket B_i inflated by a frame of width $\sqrt{c_A}/2$. Let $R(B_i).L$ describe the width and $R(B_i).H$ the height of $R(B_i)$. Then we get (see Fig. 1)

$$\mathcal{PM}(\mathcal{QM}_1, B) = \sum_{i=1}^{m} (R(B_i).L + \sqrt{c_A}) \cdot (R(B_i).H + \sqrt{c_A})$$

$$= \sum_{i=1}^{m} R(B_i).L \cdot R(B_i).H$$

$$+ \sqrt{c_A} \cdot \sum_{i=1}^{m} (R(B_i).L + R(B_i).H) + c_A \cdot m.$$

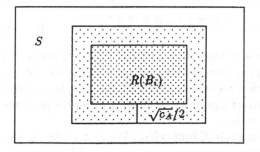

Fig. 1. $P(q \text{ meets} B_i)$

In geometric terms, $\mathcal{PM}(\mathcal{QM}_1, B)$ combines the sum of all region areas, the weighted sum of all region perimeters, and the weighted number of regions. □

In $\mathcal{QM}_1$, one possible user behavior is modelled. For other kinds of user behavior and their corresponding query models the interested reader is referred to [12].

4 First Generation Transformation Technique

The original intention of the transformation technique was to directly reuse well-understood and efficient point data structures for storing extended geometric objects. To this end, each geometric object is transformed into a higher-dimensional point serving as an object-key. A transformation rule is a mapping φ uniquely assigning to each geometric object g in the domain space S a point object $\hat{g}$ in the image space $\hat{S}$. We define the image space in terms of the transformation rule as follows.

$$\hat{S} := \hat{S}_1 \times \hat{S}_2 \times \ldots \times \hat{S}_{\hat{d}}, \ \hat{d} \geq 2d$$

with

$$\hat{S}_i := \{\hat{g}.l_i \ ; \ \hat{g} = \varphi(g), \ g \text{ located in } S\}, 1 \leq i \leq \hat{d}.$$

Assuming φ to be continuous, the image space $\hat{S}$ forms the minimal rectangular parallel-epipedon covering all mapped objects. Furthermore, the uniqueness property implies that the dimension $\hat{d}$ of the image space must be at least twice as large as the original dimension d.

The oldest and most popular transformation rule is the so-called *corner transformation*, which uses the coordinates defining the object boundaries as point coordinates (point notation used for image objects)

$$\varphi_{\text{corner}}(g) = (g.l_1, g.r_1, g.l_2, g.r_2, \ldots, g.l_d, g.r_d)$$

Applying the definition of the image space to mapping φ_{corner}, we get $\hat{d} = 2d$ and $\hat{S}_i = [0, 1), 1 \leq i \leq 2d$.

Another well-known transformation is the center transformation

$$\varphi_{\text{center}}(g) = (\frac{g.l_1 + g.r_1}{2}, \frac{g.l_2 + g.r_2}{2}, g.r_1 - g.l_1, g.r_2 - g.l_2).$$

The image spaces of the center and the corner transformation are identical.

The rest of this section is devoted to a discussion of the basic properties of the transformation technique. We use the simple corner transformation to support a better understanding. All graphical representations are restricted to the hyperplane $\hat{S}_1 \times \hat{S}_2$.

Property 1: Geometric Clustering. We first review a metric $\mathcal{M}$, which defines a popular distance measure on geometric objects. Informally, the distance between two objects is zero, if and only if they have at least one point in common; otherwise the distance is determined by the minimal euclidian distance of the object boundaries. Imposing $\mathcal{M}$ on the interval space of geometric objects yields a metric space.

Main goal of spatial data management is to assign objects to data buckets in such a way that the proximity of the objects is as far as possible preserved in order to achieve maximal selectivity in proximity queries. As depicted examplarily in Figs. 2 and 3, the corner transformation is a mapping which does not preserve distance measure $\mathcal{M}$, i.e. proximity is lost in the image space. Fig. 3 shows the projection of the image space $\hat{S}$ onto $\hat{S}_1 \times \hat{S}_2$. Storing the image points in a spatial data structure yields a clustering of image points and not necessarily a clustering of domain objects. This property has led to the widely accepted opinion that the transformation technique does not provide a sufficient performance of proximity queries with respect to the domain objects. In the next section, we will revert to this argument and refute it partially.

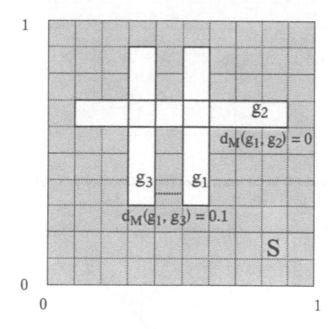

Fig. 2. Object proximity in the domain space

Property 2: Object Distribution. The distribution of the image points in space $\hat{S}$ tends to be rather skew. Some parts of $\hat{S}$ may be privileged, others are not involved at all. Figure 4 shows a typical distribution of image points under the corner transformation. The subspace below the main diagonal is empty because for each original object g the condition $g.l_i \le g.r_i$ holds. If we assume a majority of rather small intervals (relative to the size of S), the density of the image points in the upper subspace decreases when the distance to the diagonal increases. Point objects are exactly transformed onto the diagonal. Hence, almost all objects are transformed nearby the main diagonal of the image space. Unfortunately, common point data structures based on regular or nearly regular grid partitions of the data space (see e.g. [7] or [10]) cannot cope with such an object distribution efficiently.

Property 3: Query Transformation. A consequence of the transformation technique is that the data structure stores information about the image space and

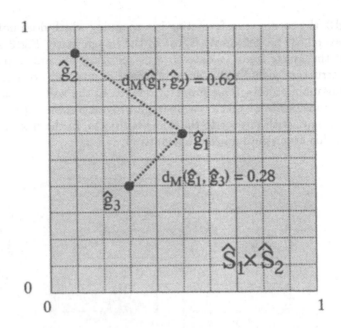

Fig. 3. Object proximity in the image space (projection onto $\hat{S}_1 \times \hat{S}_2$)

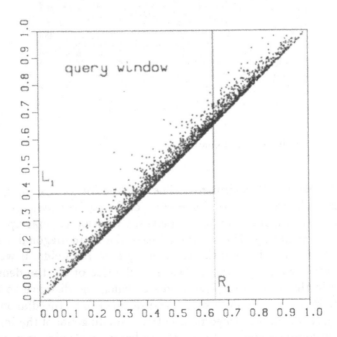

Fig. 4. Typical distribution of image points and the transformation of an intersection query window $[L_1, R_1] \times [L_2, R_2]$ into an unbounded image query window (projection onto $\hat{S}_1 \times \hat{S}_2$)

not about the domain space. Hence, user queries which are defined with respect to domain space must be transformed into corresponding queries in image space.

Exact match queries can easily be transformed, applying the transformation rule to the questioned object. The query performance is optimal, because exactly one bucket has to be accessed (unique transformation assumed). A *window intersection query*, requesting all objects intersecting the query window, is transformed into a query in image space with partially unbounded query range (see Fig. 4). Others than window queries cannot meaningfully be transformed at all.

Since the three properties from above (seem to) induce such severe drawbacks, the transformation technique has been regarded as a non-adequate approach to the spatial management of extended geometric objects. Up to now, the R-tree [3], one of the earliest data structures for extended objects, has been clearly preferred.

5 Second Generation Transformation Technique

In the second generation transformation technique, all drawbacks stemming from the three properties mentioned in the last section can be overcome such that data structures based on this technique can be made competitive to the R-tree. Starting point is the observation that a lost of proximity in the image space does not necessarily lead to a high number of bucket accesses when a proximity query is answered. The invention of flexible point data structures with clever split heuristics which gracefully adapt even to rather skewed object distributions, offers the possibility to cope with the situation in image space efficiently. Since the LSD-tree, for example, in almost all situations provides a high storage utilization, those parts of the image space which contain only few objects are covered by a few buckets with large bucket regions. Hence, an unbounded query in image space does not cause an inappropriate number of bucket accesses.

Concerning the query transformation problem, the second generation transformation technique overcomes this problem by simply avoiding it. This is achieved by keeping track of the situation in domain space thus letting the actual domain situation control the query (and update) algorithms. For a more detailed explanation let us take the LSD-tree as data structure basis for the transformation technique, and let for bucket B_i storing image points domain bucket region $R_{\text{dom}}(B_i)$ be the minimal bounding box of all the objects in domain space which correspond to points in B_i. In the LSD-tree, a k-d directory guides the search to the data buckets. Each directory node represents a split decision and stores the corresponding split dimension and split position. To keep track of the domain situation, each directory node additionally contains the minimal bounding boxes surrounding the domain bucket regions of all buckets of its two subtrees.

Figure 5 depicts an LSD-tree as a basis for the second generation transformation technique. Node v_2 stores the domain bucket regions $R_{\text{dom}}(B_1)$ and $R_{\text{dom}}(B_2)$, v_3 stores the bounding box of $R_{\text{dom}}(B_4)$ and $R_{\text{dom}}(B_5)$ as well as

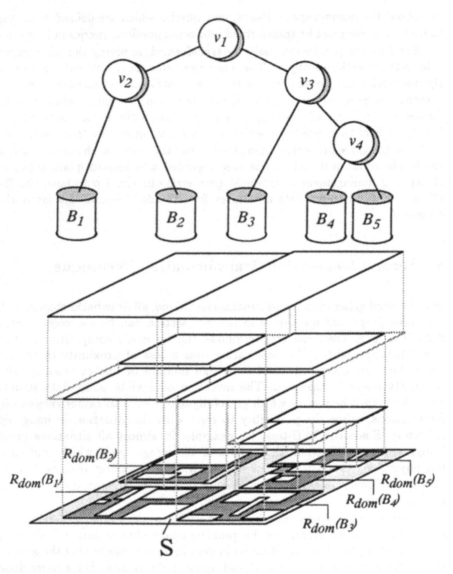

Fig. 5. Second generation transformation technique and the LSD-tree

$R_{\mathrm{dom}}(B_3)$, and v_1 stores the bounding box of the two bounding boxes attached to v_2 and the bounding box of the two bounding boxes attached to v_3.

In a window query, for example, the access to the requested data buckets is now guided by matching the original query range against the bounding boxes in domain space attached to the nodes on the search path. Note that proximity queries need no longer be transformed which allows for the natural application of arbitrary queries.

Exact match queries are treated as usual, i.e. performed in the image space, in order to take advantage of the unique search path.

Experimental results. In order to demonstrate the performance potential of the second generation transformation technique we have compared the R-tree using Guttmans quadratic cost algorithm [3] and the LSD-tree using the corner transformation. Whenever a split has to be performed in the LSD-tree, we have used the radix split choosing the split dimension in a cyclic manner. The R-tree and the LSD-tree have been implemented in Eiffel [9] on a SUN SPARCstation.

During each test run, 10.000 2-dimensional rectangles with an overlapping factor 7.5 (i.e. each point of the data space is covered by 7.5 rectangles, on average) from the data space $[0,1) \times [0,1)$ have been inserted into the initially empty data structures. The bucket capacity was set to 25 objects. The data structures were evaluated with respect to the performance measure for the query model QM_1 assuming constant c_A to be 1%, 0.1%, and 0.01% of the area of the data space.

A β-distribution randomly generates different object distributions, namely a uniform and a 2-heap distribution. The 2-heap distribution is a suitable abstraction of cluster patterns typically occuring in real applications. A representative pattern of the 2-heap distribution is depicted in Fig. 6.

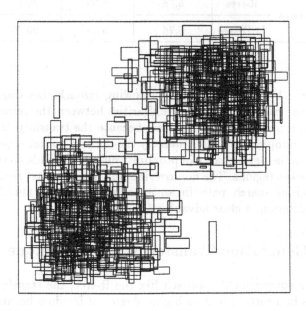

Fig. 6. 2-heap distribution

The experimental results presented in Table 1 exhibit that for any window area the performance of the data structures differ only marginally and hence validate the claim that the transformation technique can be made competitive to the R-tree. Actually, using the more efficient center transformation with an appropriate split heuristic instead of the simple combination of corner transformation and cyclic radix split yields much better performance results which clearly outperform those of the R-tree. However, going into these details is beyond the scope of this paper. The interested reader is referred to [4].

Table 1. $\mathcal{PM}(\mathcal{QM}_1, B)$ for the R-tree and LSD-tree

$\mathcal{PM}(\mathcal{QM}_1, B)$		Window area related to data space		
		0.01%	0.1%	1.0%
uniform	R-tree	6.38	9.22	21.22
	LSD-tree	6.26	8.95	20.23
2-heap	R-tree	5.78	8.59	20.98
	LSD-tree	5.76	8.53	20.70

Let us close the section with the following remark. Looking through the right glasses, one can realize strong similarities between the second generation transformation technique and the R-tree, because the transformation technique also creates overlapping subspaces, namely the domain bucket regions. Hence, in both approaches the performance of proximity queries depends on the patterns of overlapping bucket regions. The non-overlapping image bucket regions, however, allow for a unique search path in an exact match which also facilitates the insertion and deletion, a clear advantage over the R-tree.

6 Third Generation Transformation Technique

Compared to a conventional approach like the R-tree, the transformation technique provides in a certain sense a higher degree of freedom because of the four dimensions of the image space instead of the two dimensions of the domain space. This higher degree of freedom resulting in disjoint image bucket regions is a necessary condition for the unique search path of an exact match query, respectively of an insertion and a deletion. Now the question whether one could take more, respectively other, advantages from the higher degree of freedom than just to improve the exact match operation is coming up rather naturally. For example, if we choose for the image space other than pure location oriented dimensions, the iterated splitting of such a dimension imposes a classification on the objects and therefore supports the selectivity in queries related to this dimension. In other words, are there other transformations than the up to now exclusively used corner- and center transformation which can be used with advantage in a broader application area?

As a first step into that direction, we present the so-called area-sensitive transformation which efficiently supports window queries with a conjunctively added area condition. Such a query requests, for example, all objects intersecting the query range with areas in between a given interval.

Queries of this kind may be posed by an intelligent query processor to restrict the response set to objects of a size which is significant for the size of the query range. Another example is a query optimizer supporting queries which take class attributes into account in the case that the area of objects belonging to the same class is bounded by some upper and lower value. These values can be computed on the fly during the insertion process.

6.1 An Area-sensitive Transformation

We are now going to demonstrate that an area-sensitive transformation together with an appropriate split heuristic significantly improves area-sensitive window queries. Moreover, pure window queries also gain substantially from this approach – an effect we will explain later.

Let $g.A$ denote the area of a geometric object g. An area-sensitive range query is defined analogously to a conventional range query, but an additional filter restricts the response set to objects g satisfying the additional condition $\underline{A} \leq g.A \leq \overline{A}$, $0 \leq \underline{A} \leq \overline{A} \leq 1$. We define the *area transformation* φ_A as

$$\varphi_A(g) = (\frac{g.l_1 + g.r_1}{2}, \frac{g.l_2 + g.r_2}{2}, g.A),$$

using the abbreviated notation for point objects. Note that this mapping is not unique.

Dimensions 1 and 2 of the image space represent the center coordinates of object g and are responsible for geometric clustering. Proximity query processing is still sufficiently supported by the domain bucket region information stored in each directory node. The split decisions with respect to dimension 3 divide objects into classes of different area sizes. Whenever during the query processing a node corresponding to a split position in dimension 3 is met, the split value can be tested against the actual area condition of the query. Such a classification of objects with respect to their area sizes even improves the performance of conventional window queries because a large bucket region which is mainly due to only one large object (among some other smaller ones) can no longer occur (see Fig. 7). Obviously, large bucket regions cause a high overlapping and deteriorate the selectivity of proximity queries.

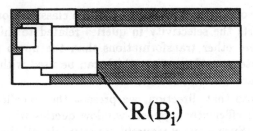

$$R(B_i)$$

Fig. 7. One large object among a lot of smaller ones and its effect on the bucket region

6.2 Excursus: A Performance Measure for Area-sensitive Window Queries

Let us return to the simple query model $\mathcal{QM}_1$ with quadratic windows of constant area and uniformly distributed centers. We now impose an additional area constraint on $\mathcal{QM}_1$ leading to query model $\mathcal{QM}_2$ by assuming the lower bound $\underline{A}$ on the area of the requested objects to be 0 and the upper bound $\overline{A}$ to be uniformly distributed over $[0, 0.01]$. The choice of $\overline{A}$ stems from our experiences with real applications, where an object very rarely exceeds 1% of the data space area and hence queries for objects of a larger area are unlikely. For query model $\mathcal{QM}_2$ and bucket set B, we are interested in the performance measure $\mathcal{PM}(\mathcal{QM}_2, B)$ denoting the expected number of bucket accesses needed to perform an area-sensitive query according to $\mathcal{QM}_2$. The Lemma in Sect. 3 tells us that we have to compute $P(q$ meets $B_i)$ for query q in $\mathcal{QM}_2$ and every bucket B_i in B. Assuming the query window and the area constraints to be independent we get

$$P(q \text{ meets } B_i) = P(q_{\text{window}} \text{ meets } B_i) \cdot P(q_{\text{area}} \text{ meets } B_i),$$

where $P(q_{\text{window}}$ meets $B_i)$ is defined as in $\mathcal{QM}_1$ and $P(q_{\text{area}}$ meets $B_i)$ denotes the probability that requesting objects with an area in between $[0, \overline{A}]$ forces an inspection of bucket B_i.

From $\mathcal{QM}_1$ we know that

$$P(q_{\text{window}} \text{ meets } B_i) = (R_{\text{dom}}(B_i).L + \sqrt{c_A}) \cdot (R_{\text{dom}}(B_i).H + \sqrt{c_A}).$$

(Remember that $R_{\text{dom}}(B_i)$ denotes the domain bucket region of B_i.)

It remains to determine $P(q_{\text{area}}$ meets $B_i)$. Let $\underline{a}_i$, resp. $\overline{a}_i$, be the area of the smallest, resp. largest, element in B_i. Then B_i must be accessed iff $[0, \overline{A}] \cap [\underline{a}_i, \overline{a}_i] \neq \emptyset$. Since $P([0, \overline{A}] \cap [\underline{a}_i, \overline{a}_i] \neq \emptyset) = P(\overline{A} \geq \underline{a}_i)$ and $\overline{A}$ is uniformly distributed over $[0, 0.01]$, we have

$$P(q_{\text{area}} \text{ meets } B_i) = 1 - \min(\frac{\underline{a}_i}{0.01}, 1),$$

and finally

$$PM(QM_2, B) = \sum_{i=1}^{m} (R_{\text{dom}}(B_i).L + \sqrt{c_A})$$
$$\cdot (R_{\text{dom}}(B_i).H + \sqrt{c_A}) \cdot (1 - \min(\frac{\underline{a}_i}{0.01}, 1)).$$

Note that this performance measure determines the average number of bucket accesses needed to perform a query in QM_2 for a given data structure with bucket set B, *only if the data structure guarantees that unnecessary bucket accesses are avoided.* This holds only for data structures with directories providing sufficient information about the domain bucket region $R_{\text{dom}}(B_i)$ as well as the smallest object area $\underline{a}_i$ of each data bucket B_i.

Assuming a realistic situation where concerning the area dimension the directory contains information only about split decisions and not about the $\underline{a}_i$ then for each B_i $\underline{a}_i$ must be estimated on the basis of the split information. For bucket B_i we proceed as follows. Consider the lowest node v in the directory on the search path to B_i which reflects a split according to the area dimension. If B_i is contained in the right subtree of v, then the split value serves as an estimation for $\underline{a}_i$, otherwise the estimation of $\underline{a}_i$ is 0. For a correct evaluation of the data structure in the performance measure $PM(QM_2, B)$ each $\underline{a}_i$ must be substituted by its estimated value.

At the end of this excursus let us shortly mention one further obvious query model QM_3 where the area constraint is given by the upper area bound $\overline{A} = 1$ and the lower area bound $\underline{A}$ being uniformly distributed over $[0, 0.01]$. For QM_3 calculations similar to QM_2 lead to $P(q_{\text{area}} \text{ meets } B_i) = \min(\frac{\overline{a}_i}{0.01}, 1)$.

6.3 Experimental Results

We have compared the R-tree using the quadratic cost algorithm with the LSD-tree using the area transformation φ_A. For a split in the LSD-tree, the split dimension and split position are chosen such that the resulting two domain bucket regions minimize the performance measure for QM_1. Our experiments have exhibited that taking this global cost measure for a local optimization leads to the best results with respect to all global performance cost measures, i.e. the performance measures for query models QM_1, QM_2, and QM_3.

All technical parameters are identical to those of the experiments presented in the previous section except for the object distribution where only the 2-heap distribution is generated.

The experimental results presented in Table 2 demonstrate that the area-sensitive transformation clearly outperforms the R-tree for each of the three query models. Note the improvement of the area-sensitive transformation over the R-tree even for pure window queries without area constraints (see the results for QM_1). For window query model QM_2, resp. QM_3, and each window area, the quotient

$$\frac{PM(QM_2, \text{LSD-tree})}{PM(QM_2, \text{R-tree})}, \text{ resp. } \frac{PM(QM_3, \text{LSD-tree})}{PM(QM_3, \text{R-tree})},$$

Table 2. $\mathcal{PM}(\mathcal{QM}_1, B)$, $\mathcal{PM}(\mathcal{QM}_2, B)$, $\mathcal{PM}(\mathcal{QM}_3, B)$ for different query region sizes

$\mathcal{PM}(\mathcal{QM}_i, B)$		Query window area related to data space			
		0.01%	0.1%	1.0%	10.0%
$\mathcal{QM}_1$	R-tree	5.78	8.59	20.98	88.22
	LSD-tree	4.86	7.39	18.80	82.12
$\mathcal{QM}_2$	R-tree	5.78	8.59	20.98	88.22
	LSD-tree	4.78	7.27	18.50	80.90
$\mathcal{QM}_3$	R-tree	4.50	6.52	15.23	61.42
	LSD-tree	3.15	4.61	10.93	44.54

reflects the quotient

$$\frac{\text{answer size of the area-sensitive window query}}{\text{answer size of the pure window query.}}$$

This indicates that the improvement of the area transformation is optimal within this context.

7 Conclusion

In this paper, we have demonstrated that keeping track of the domain situation together with a flexible point data structure makes the transformation technique competitive to at least the R-tree, but in fact we claim to any other data structure specialized for storing extended objects. The free choice of image dimensions also allows for new kinds of transformations which take other than pure location parameters into account. The area transformation as an example does not only open the door for an efficient performance of area-sensitive queries but also improves the performance of conventional window queries. More important, we regard the area transformation as a first step towards the processing of so-called multi-class range queries. In such a query, the objects of the answer set of a range query must fulfill additional (non-geometric) class attributes specified in the query. Experimental results presented by Ohler [11] demonstrate that an integrated approach where the class attributes to be requested directly flow into the overall data structure design is the only attempt providing reasonable performance. Ohler heavily modifies the multilayer gridfile [8] to cope with the increased requirements. The adaption results in a complex data structure with complicated algorithms. We believe that the transformation technique using a suitable transformation will probably be a conceptually more elegant and more efficient approach to this important application area.

References

1. Freeston, M.W.: The BANG file: a new kind of grid file. In: Proc. ACM SIGMOD Int. Conf. on the Management of Data, pp. 260–169, San Francisco 1987.
2. Günther, O. (ed.): Efficient structures for geometric data management, volume 337 of Lecture Notes in Computer Science. Springer Verlag, Berlin 1988.
3. Guttman, A.: R-trees: a dynamic index structure for spatial searching. In: Proc. ACM SIGMOD Int. Conf. on Management of Data, pp. 47–57, Boston 1984.
4. Henrich, A., Six, H.-W.: How to split buckets in spatial data structures. In: Gambosi, G., Scholl, M., Six, H.-W. (eds.): Geographic Database Management Systems, pp. 212–244, Capri (Italy), May 1991. Esprit Basic Research Series DG XIII, Springer-Verlag.
5. Henrich, A., Six, H.-W., Widmayer, P.: The LSD-tree: spatial access to multidimensional point- and non-point objects. In: 15th Int. Conf. on VLDB, pp. 45–53, Amsterdam 1989.
6. Hutflesz, A., Six, H.-W., Widmayer, P.: The R-file: an efficient access structure for proximity queries. In: Proc. 6th Int. Conf. on Data Engineering, pp. 372–379, Los Angeles 1990.
7. Kriegel, H.-P., Seeger, B.: Multidimensional order preserving linear hashing with partial expansions. In: Proc. Int. Conf. on Database Theory, pp. 203–220, Rome 1986.
8. Krishnamurthy, R., Whang, K.-Y.: Multilevel grid files. Research report, IBM Yorktown Heights (1985).
9. Meyer, B.: Eiffel: The Language. Prentice Hall (1991).
10. Nievergelt, J., Hinterberger, H., Sevcik, K.C.: The grid file: an adaptable, symmetric multikey file structure. ACM Transactions on Database Systems, 9(1):38–71 (1984).
11. Ohler, T.: The multi class grid file: an access structure for multi class range queries. In: Proc. 5th Int. Symp. on Spatial Data Handling, pp. 260–271, Charleston 1992.
12. Pagel, B.-U., Six, H.-W., Toben, H., Widmayer, P.: Towards an analysis of range query performance in spatial data structures. In: Proc. ACM 12th Symposium on Principles of Database Systems (PODS), Washington D.C., May 1993.

A Paging Scheme for Pointer-Based Quadtrees

Clifford A. Shaffer

Department of Computer Science
Virginia Tech
Blacksburg, VA 24061
shaffer@vtopus.cs.vt.edu

Patrick R. Brown

IBM Corporation
Neighborhood Road
Kingston, NY 12401
pbrown@vnet.ibm.com

Abstract: Hierarchical data structures, most notably the quadtree, have become increasingly popular for the indexing of the large databases required by GIS since they support the efficient computation of traditional GIS spatial analysis algorithms. While the quadtree has many representations, the *linear quadtree* has become the standard. Initially thought to be more space efficient than traditional *pointer-based* quadtree representations, its main operational virtue has been its ability to minimize data transfers between main memory and disk. Recent results show that a good pointer-based representation is more space efficient than the linear quadtree. This paper presents a pointer-based representation for quadtrees called the *paged-pointer quadtree*, which partitions the nodes of a pointer-based quadtree into pages and manages the pages using B-tree techniques. A paged-pointer quadtree always requires less space than the corresponding linear quadtree. Our initial implementation provides better performance than a highly optimized system based on linear quadtrees.

1. Introduction

This paper describes the *paged-pointer quadtree*, a disk-based implementation for pointer-based quadtrees. The *quadtree* [Sam90a, Sam90b] is a family of data structures that represent spatial data using recursive subdivision. The quadtree subdivides the unit square into four equal quadrants, which themselves may be further subdivided. Subdivision ceases when some decomposition criteria are met. For example, the *region quadtree* subdivides a $2^n \times 2^n$ array of pixels until all the pixels in each quadrant are of the same color.

The *pointer-based quadtree* is the direct representation of the hierarchy obtained when a quadtree is built (see Figure 1). Each block created by the subdivision corresponds to a node in a pointer-based quadtree. A node corresponding to a block that is subdivided has four children (its quadrants) and is referred to as an *internal node*. A node meeting the decomposition criteria (e.g., a uniform block) has no children and is referred to as a *leaf node*. A traditional pointer-based quadtree explicitly represents both internal nodes and leaf nodes, with pointers in internal nodes explicitly determining the tree structure.

The *linear quadtree* [Gar82] provides a way to represent the tree structure of the quadtree without the space overhead involved with pointers. A linear quadtree consists of a sorted list of records corresponding to the leaf nodes of the quadtree. Stored with each leaf node is a *locational code*. Locational codes represent the location of a leaf within the image space and are usually based on the Morton code [Mor66]. For a given integer coordinate pair, the Morton code is created by bit interleaving the x and y values. In particular, the *FD location code* [Sam90a] stores a fixed length Morton code for some specified pixel within the node (such as the upper left corner) combined with an indication of the size for the node. The linear quadtree representation is simply a sorted list of records consisting of the locational code and the attribute values for each leaf.

The implementation of linear quadtrees on disk is fairly straightforward. The linear quadtree is simply a sorted list of leaves, with the locational code serving as the sort key. This list can be managed easily by a B^+-tree, as described in [Abe84].

Nodes in pointer-based quadtrees have historically been implemented as two distinct types. An internal node stores four pointers, one to each of its children. A leaf node stores the values of its attributes. To identify each node as one of these two types, a tag bit is needed. This can be done in the node itself, but can also be done by reducing the size of each pointer by one bit and using that bit to identify the type of node the pointer points to.

This traditional representation has a subtle space inefficiency. In the parent of each leaf node, a pointer locates the node, while the node stores only the values of its attributes. The *leafless quadtree* (for example, see [DT81, OHS90]) overcomes this problem. A leafless quadtree stores only internal nodes, each of which contains four *child fields*. For each internal node, the corresponding child field in its parent holds a pointer to that node. For each leaf, the corresponding child field in its parent holds the values of the leaf's attributes. Thus, each child field in an internal node contains either a *pointer* or a *leaf*. Not only does this representation save space, but the lack of separate leaf nodes reduces the number of nodes in a leafless quadtree by a factor of four. This allows pointers in a leafless quadtree to be two bits smaller than those of traditional pointer-based quadtrees. In a system with fixed-size pointers, this means images with more nodes can be stored using leafless quadtrees than with traditional representations.

It is often useful to have a pointer to the parent of a node in addition to the children. Access to parent pointers allows an algorithm to directly locate the immediate ancestor of a node. The ancestors of a node can be found without parent pointers by maintaining a stack holding the path from the root of the tree to the node. When parent pointers are used, a pointer to a node is sufficient to access both the ancestors and descendants of that node. Without parent pointers, both a pointer to the node and the stack of ancestors are necessary. Despite this advantage, an implementation with parent pointers increases the amount of storage required for each internal node by 25% in pointer-based quadtrees. While parent pointers are not strictly necessary, the implementation described below supports them despite the space cost. Leafless quadtrees, even with parent pointers, still require less space than linear quadtrees.

2. A Comparison of Quadtree Representations

Because the linear quadtree avoids the overhead involved in representing pointers and internal nodes, it has generally (but incorrectly, as demonstrated in [SW89]) been thought to require less storage space than the pointer-based quadtree. Linear quadtrees are also easy to represent on disk because they reduce the tree structure to a simple sorted list. Several prototype geographic information systems (e.g., [SPMA87, SSN90]) are based on the linear quadtree. QUILT [SSN90] is used later for comparison with our pointer-based implementation.

The pointer-based quadtree representation offers several significant advantages over the linear quadtree. For example, the data stored in a pointer-based quadtree can be accessed in any traversal order by simply following pointers. Linear quadtrees are arranged to allow quick preorder traversals, i.e., visits in a predetermined order such as NW, NE, SW, SE, but require logarithmic-time searches to find the next node for any other order. Back-to-front display of data represented by an octree (the three dimensional analog of the quadtree) is an example in which traversal order is dependent on the viewing position. Such methods can be used to display 3D views of topographic data. Quadtrees are also useful when implementing *progressive refinement* [BFGS86], in which a rough approximation of an image is built quickly and then the image is later refined to its final form. One way of supporting progressive refinement in quadtrees is to store attribute values in internal nodes and traverse the tree only to a certain depth. These techniques are crucial to quadtree-based hierarchical data generalization algorithms. While linear quadtrees can be extended to store internal nodes as well as leaves, each internal node must store both attribute values and a locational code. Pointer-based quadtrees simply add a new field to existing internal nodes, introducing far less overhead than in linear quadtrees.

The DF-expression [KE80] is an alternative quadtree representation that is extremely space efficient. The DF-expression is simply a preorder listing of all nodes of the quadtree (leaf and internal nodes) without pointers. The DF-expression requires less overhead than either linear or pointer-based representations, but does not allow random access to nodes. The S$^+$-tree [JSS91] is a proposed paging scheme for DF-expressions. The S$^+$-tree appears promising and may be more efficient than the paged implementation for pointer-based quadtrees described here. However, to our knowledge S$^+$-trees have not been implemented, and there are several reasons to suspect that they may not be efficient. The S$^+$-tree breaks the DF-expression into pages such that each page contains a complete, self-contained tree structure by adding "dummy" nodes to each page. These require additional overhead, and additional empty space within a page results from the restriction that the nodes on a page form an acceptable tree structure. The S$^+$-tree may also have poor performance under dynamic updates to the tree if they require major adjustments on overflow and underflow of pages. Finally, like the linear quadtree, S$^+$-trees are biased in favor of one predetermined traversal order. We hope to see empirical work on S$^+$-trees in the future that addresses these issues. S$^+$-trees will not be considered further in this paper.

3. Analysis of Space Requirements

In this section we briefly compare space requirements of FD linear quadtrees and leafless pointer-based quadtrees. This is a special case of the analysis of space requirements given in [SW89], where Samet and Webber have shown that contrary to conventional opinion, the pointer-based quadtree often requires less space than the linear quadtree.

For any particular image, the subdivision process is the same for either quadtree representation. Let L and I denote the number of leaves and internal nodes, respectively, in the quadtree. In 2 dimensions, L is slightly less than $3I$. For both representations, each leaf has a set of attribute values to represent, requiring a total of Lb bits to store attribute values. Attribute compaction schemes apply equally to both representations, so are not considered for this analysis. Additional space used to index the leaves is referred to as *overhead*. Let h represent the *height* of the image; if there are 2^h pixels in each dimension, the resulting quadtree has a height of at most h.

Each leaf in an FD linear quadtree consists of two components: its attribute values and its FD locational code. The number of bits required for an FD locational code for a 2D image with h levels is $2h + \lceil \log(h + 1) \rceil$ (two bits for each level of resolution plus representation for the height). Since there are L

leaves, the total number of bits to store an entire FD linear quadtree is simply:

$$S_{lq} = L\left(b + 2h + \lceil \log(h+1) \rceil\right)$$

Leafless quadtrees store only internal nodes; the attribute values of each leaf are encoded in a pointer field of its parent. This analysis assumes that this encoding wastes no space. For example, if leaves only require 8 bits (including the tag field) while pointers require 32 bits, the leaves are actually encoded in a field using only 8 bits. The implementation discussed in the next section satisfies these assumptions, although we do require that each node begin on a byte boundary.

A pointer must be large enough to distinguish among the internal nodes of the quadtree. A single tag bit is also required to indicate that the field holds a pointer rather than a data value. Therefore, each pointer requires $\lceil 1 + \log I \rceil$ bits. Each internal node in a leafless quadtree without parent pointers (except the root) is pointed to exactly once. Thus, the number of bits used to store pointers in a leafless quadtree is $I \lceil 1 + \log I \rceil$. Since each leaf requires b bits for its attribute values and also a tag bit, the number of bits used to store leaves in a leafless quadtree is $L(1 + b)$. Therefore, the total number of bits required to store a leafless quadtree is:

$$S_p = I \lceil 1 + \log I \rceil + L(1 + b).$$

The addition of parent pointers requires an additional pointer in each of the I internal nodes. Although parent pointers do not require a tag bit (since leaves are never stored in this field), the tag bit simplifies implementation. In a leafless quadtree with parent pointers, the number of bits required by the entire quadtree is:

$$S_{pp} = 2I \lceil 1 + \log I \rceil + L(1 + b).$$

By suitable manipulation of these three equations, it is easy to show that $S_p < S_{pp} < S_{lq}$.

In practice (e.g., both the University of Maryland's QUILT system [SSN90] and our implementation), the size of both pointers and locational codes is fixed prior to use. Because it simplifies programming when node structures fall on word boundaries, both pointers and locational codes are typically 32 bits long. With fixed size fields, a comparison of space requirements is simpler and more faithfully reflects implementation results. With pointer size fixed to 32 bits, and since there is one pointer to each internal node, a leafless pointer-based quadtree requires $L(1 + b + 32/3)$ bits, while a linear quadtree requires $L(32 + b)$ bits. Including parent pointers raises the cost for the pointer-based quadtree to $L(1 + b + 64/3)$ bits. In two dimensions, the amount of overhead (i.e., space required beyond b bits per leaf) in a leafless quadtree is a little more than 1/3 that of a linear quadtree (2/3 with parent pointers). For 3D data, the leafless octree requires 1/7 the overhead of a linear octree (2/7 with parent pointers).

The primary drawback of fixing the size of pointers and location codes is the strict limit placed on image size. With 32-bit locational codes, a linear quadtree can represent a resolution of $2^{14} \times 2^{14}$ in two dimensions, and $2^9 \times 2^9 \times 2^9$ in three dimensions. For higher resolution, larger locational codes are necessary. On the other hand, leafless pointer-based quadtrees with 32-bit pointers can represent a resolution of $2^{15} \times 2^{15}$ in two dimensions and $2^{11} \times 2^{11} \times 2^{11}$ in three dimensions. Moreover, substantially higher resolution databases can often be represented as pointer-based quadtrees since the number of nodes required is significantly smaller than in a worst-case image (i.e., where every leaf is one pixel). This advantage can be important, particularly for data sets with large areas of low-resolution data but with pockets of high-resolution data. For such data, linear quadtrees require locational codes large enough to encode leaves at the finest resolution while pointer-based quadtrees only need pointers large enough to distinguish between the actual number of nodes found in the tree [SW89]. Therefore, the restriction of image resolution due to fixed field sizes is far more serious for linear quadtrees than pointer-based quadtrees. When field sizes are fixed, the leafless quadtree is both more compact and can represent substantially larger images than the linear quadtree.

4. The Paging Scheme

We now describe how the paged-pointer quadtree maps quadtree nodes to disk pages. Nodes are shifted between pages as necessary following B-tree split and merge rules. For additional implementation details, as well as extensive comparisons of our page swapping algorithms versus the operating system's virtual memory handler, see [Brown92].

The paged-pointer quadtree is represented on disk as a file broken into a collection of pages. The first page of this file holds global information on the image represented by the quadtree, such as image type, coordinates, scale, orientation, and storage space required for attribute values. Subsequent pages contain a collection of nodes. A pointer in a paged-pointer quadtree has two parts: *page number* and *offset*. The page number identifies the page of the quadtree file containing the node pointed to; the offset identifies the location of the node within that page.

Our implementation uses a buffer pool that caches several pages from the disk-based paged-pointer quadtree, replacing pages as chosen by an algorithm (described below) whose behavior approximates least recently used page replacement.

Child fields may naturally be implemented in one of two ways. The simplest is to make the size of the field be independent of its contents. The advantage is that when child fields are of constant size, both nodes within a page and fields within a node can be found quickly. However, when attribute values and pointers require different amounts of space, fixed-size child fields require more space than necessary. Important examples include binary images (where the data value is much smaller than a pointer value) and lists of line segments or objects (where the data value is much larger than a pointer value). Variable-size fields eliminate such wasted space by representing pointers and leaves in the minimum amount of space needed for each node. The primary drawback of variable-sized nodes is that individual nodes within a page and individual fields within a node cannot be accessed directly.

Our implementation of the paged-pointer quadtree combines these two approaches, using fixed-size child fields in main memory and variable-size fields on disk. Using variable-size fields on disk allows a greater number of nodes to be placed on each page on disk and therefore decreases the number of disk pages required to store a quadtree (in turn reducing the number of page faults). The internal buffers holding pages using fixed-size fields allow direct computation of the location of a node within its page.

This combined approach makes it necessary to convert page representations when I/O is performed. When the disk is accessed, the cost of I/O far exceeds the cost of the computation needed to convert between representations. Our compression algorithm generates a stream of bits to be written to the page on disk. Each node is added to the stream in order. Within a node, the tag bit of each field is written, followed by the contents of that field. For example, if pointers require 31 bits and leaves require one bit (both plus the tag), we add 32 bits to the stream for each pointer and two bits for each leaf. Decompression reads from the stream of bits previously written to a page in the same manner. For each field, the first bit read (i.e., the tag bit) indicates the field type and thus the number of bits used in the remainder of the field.

This combined approach requires buffers in memory larger than the disk page size. Because of the compression, each node will generally require less space on disk than in memory. The amount of free space on a page is defined in terms of the amount of available space when the page resides on disk. Each page stores a count of the amount of available space on the page, and updates this count as the nodes of the page change. An insertion or deletion that would cause the amount of free space to go below zero or above one-third of the page size would leave a page either overfull or underfull. In this case, nodes are moved between pages using traditional B*-tree rules.

One of the most serious limitations of traditional pointer-based quadtrees is that there is no natural mechanism for keeping neighboring nodes nearby in memory under dynamic updates of the tree. Virtual memory systems exploit the fact that memory accesses patterns (e.g., the fetch-execute cycle for instructions) are often sequential in nature so many consecutive accesses all involve a small number of pages. Access patterns in traditional pointer-based quadtrees need not have this sequential nature, even when processing is done in preorder, since trees that have been modified are not likely to remain in preorder within memory. When a pointer-based quadtree is stored on disk or in virtual memory, the resulting lack of locality of node references can cause an unacceptable number of page faults.

Like leaves in linear quadtrees, the nodes in our paged-pointer quadtree are arranged according to a preorder traversal. Storing nodes in this order has several advantages. First, this order is not too difficult to maintain using B-tree techniques. Second, quadtree processing is frequently done in preorder. (Note that the pointer-based quadtree pointer structure still allows direct access to nodes in any traversal order.) Third, the nodes of subtrees deep in the quadtree are grouped together and likely to be on the same page. Thus, random access to specified nodes will require fewer page faults than the depth of the tree, and neighboring nodes are likely to be on the same page. This is significant when performing neighbor-finding operations [Sam90a]. Other approaches to node ordering may lead to different and perhaps more efficient clusterings. However, optimal clusterings methods often require substantial computation whenever the structure changes.

A traditional B-tree stores records in sorted order on a page so that a binary search can be used within the page. When a new record is added to a page, other records on the page are shifted to make room for the new record (this accounts for a significant fraction of total processing time in the QUILT system). The same basic approach is used when overflow or underflow occurs on a page, except records are shifted among a small collection of pages, all in memory.

There is an important difference between the index structures of the paged-pointer quadtree and the B^+-tree storing the linear quadtree. The internal nodes of a B^+- or B^*-tree serve as an index for a sorted list stored at the leaf nodes of the B-tree. In the paged-pointer quadtree, this index for the sorted list is replaced by the pointer-based quadtree's own pointer structure. The concept of internal and leaf pages is lost. In this sense, the paged-pointer quadtree is more like a B-tree than a B^+-tree. Most significantly, there is no need to perform binary search on nodes within a page since the pointer structure of the quadtree explicitly stores the locations of nodes, allowing the location of a child or parent to be found directly. As a consequence, whenever a node is moved (for example, when rebalancing pages), all pointers to that node must also be updated. While the close relatives of many of these nodes are on the same page, updating off-page relatives introduces the possibility of page faults.

As a result, while pages of the paged-pointer quadtree are organized in preorder, the nodes within a page need not and should not be. This reduces the amount of updating required when inserting or deleting nodes. See Figure 1 for an example of a paged-pointer quadtree broken into pages. Each page contains a contiguous section from a preorder traversal of the tree, but the nodes within the page may not be in preorder. For details on the page updating algorithms that reorder and reallocate the nodes onto pages when overflow or underflow occurs, see [Brown92].

The page replacement algorithm in a virtual memory system (whether implemented in hardware or software) significantly affects the performance of the system. Performance suffers if pages are accessed in a manner not matching the page replacement strategy. General-purpose virtual memory systems typically seek to replace the least recently used (LRU) page and are often very effective. Unfortunately, general-purpose LRU algorithms cannot determine which nodes will be revisited during a tree traversal and which will not be used again. However, this information can be maintained by a traversal algorithm. When a traversal visits a node N and continues with N's descendants, N will certainly be revisited later. Our buffer pool implementation provides a locking feature not supported by traditional virtual memory systems, so as to exploit the special characteristics of a tree traversal. Since a traversal returns to each ancestor of the current node in the traversal, the pages containing these nodes are locked into main memory when first visited. Locking indicates to our page replacement algorithm that a page should not be swapped out since it will be accessed later. When the traversal returns to that node for the last time, the page is then unlocked. The number of pages locked at any one time is bounded by the depth of the quadtree. The buffer pool should be large enough to hold a number of pages other than those that are locked; otherwise, the presence of locked pages severely decreases the effective size of the buffer pool. In practice, twice the depth of the tree should be sufficient.

Although our implementation is slightly more complicated than that of the B-tree used to organize linear quadtrees, all the necessary code can be provided in a library defining a quadtree abstract data type. The application programmer need not be concerned with the intricacies of implementation or the fact that these quadtrees are actually stored on disk. In all respects except one, the application code can be written as though a traditional pointer-based quadtree were being used. The one exception relates to explicit pointers to quadtree nodes. It is possible that the position of a node may be changed by the quadtree page management algorithms, invalidating the previous pointer values. Library functions that change the shape of the tree return a pointer to the modified node. Library users must be careful not to rely on the old values of pointers after the tree structure is modified. In practice, this has not been an issue in the implementations of three standard quadtree algorithms described in the next section.

5. Time and Space Performance

The paged-pointer quadtree presented in Section 4 provides a compact disk-based representation for quadtrees. We now compare the efficiency of algorithms using our implementation of the paged-pointer quadtree to similar algorithms using QUILT, an experimental geographic information system based on linear quadtrees developed at the University of Maryland [SSN90]. Three representative application functions are used in our tests: raster to quadtree conversion (a good test of dynamic quadtree updating), quadtree to raster conversion (a good test of random access to a static quadtree) and unaligned intersections (a good test of both search and update in quadtrees).

Our paged-pointer quadtree implementation is written in the programming language C, as was QUILT. Both systems have been implemented on several computers running the Unix operating system, including a DECStation 3100 and a 25 Mhz Commodore Amiga 3000UX.

Our first test algorithm converts a raster image to a region quadtree. The spatial data represented by a quadtree is rarely obtained in quadtree form. The most common sources of pixel data are binary, grayscale, or color images represented in raster-scan order. To use a quadtree to access and manipulate such data, a raster image must first be converted into quadtree form.

Shaffer and Samet [SS87] present algorithms for building linear and pointer-based quadtrees with node accesses proportional to the number of nodes in the final quadtree. The linear quadtree algorithm uses a small buffer holding leaves in which one but not all of its pixels have been visited in the original image. The pointer-based algorithm begins with an "uncolored" quadtree and modifies it as pixels are read. It traverses the tree by *neighbor-finding* [Sam90a], an average-case constant-time operation, to locate the node adjacent to the current one.

QUILT implements the linear quadtree building algorithm of [SS87]. Our paged-pointer quadtree building algorithm is the pointer-based building algorithm based on neighbor-finding given in [SS87], slightly modified to process odd rows from left to right and even rows from right to left. This significantly decreases the number of times that high-level subdivisions of the quadtree being built are crossed during neighbor finding.

The performance of the pointer-based and linear quadtree build algorithms was tested on six raster images. The first three images were generated as test data during the design of QUILT. They consist of maps portraying the flood plain, land usage, and topographical data in a river valley in northern California and are referred to as "floodplain," "landuse," and "topography." Each of these images is 400 pixels wide and 450 pixels high and are represented as 512×512 pixel images by the quadtrees. They contain 5,206, 28,549 and 25,012 leaves, respectively. The other three images, called "big floodplain," "big landuse," and "big topography," are 800×900 and consist of four copies of the corresponding original image. They are represented as 1024×1024 pixel images by their quadtrees and contain 19,426, 112,819 and 98,491 leaves, respectively.

The build algorithms were tested on the three 400×450 pixel data sets on the Amiga, and the three 800×900 data sets on the DECStation. The resulting pointer-based quadtrees are 38-42% smaller than the corresponding linear quadtrees built by QUILT. When these quadtrees are built, nodes are not inserted in order and the B-tree algorithms leave free space within pages. QUILT, whose B-tree splits three pages for four [SSN90], leaves approximately 20% of each page free. Our paged-pointer quadtrees, which splits two pages for three, leave about 25% free. Both implementations provide a compaction operation that eliminates this free space. Our packed pointer-based quadtrees are 44-46% smaller than QUILT's linear quadtrees. Using analysis similar to that of Section 3, we expect our paged-pointer quadtrees to use just over 37 bits per leaf and the linear quadtrees of QUILT to use 64 bits per leaf. This results in an expected space savings of 42%, which does not include the added cost of representing the internal structure of the B-tree used by QUILT. A significant part of this advantage is due to the fact that our paged-pointer quadtree encodes leaves in 16-bit fields, while QUILT uses a fixed-size attribute value field of 32 bits. If we also used 32 bits, we would expect a space savings of only 17%. However, the paged-pointer implementation is also storing parent pointers, which are not strictly necessary. With 32-bit leaves but no parent pointers, our paged-pointer quadtrees would be just over 33% smaller.

Table 1. Quadtree build times (in seconds).				
Image	Pointer-Based		QUILT	
Name	DEC	Amiga	DEC	Amiga
Floodplain	5.6	5.4	7.3	4.5
Landuse	54.9	21.0	104.9	48.8
Topography	47.4	19.4	85.0	34.0
Total (real)	121.5	45.8	222.2	87.3

The average times required to build the quadtrees on our two machines are given in Table 1. On each system, builds are nearly twice a fast using our pointer-based representation.

To display the spatial data represented by a region quadtree, the quadtree is often converted to raster form. This operation has been implemented both by QUILT and our pointer-based system, and performance was measured by reconverting the six test quadtrees. The linear quadtree algorithm implemented by QUILT maintains an array holding those leaf nodes currently part but not completely processed. When a new pixel is processed, the linear quadtree is searched only if the pixel is not contained by a leaf in this array. Several pointer-based algorithms were implemented. Both a direct adaptation of the linear quadtree algorithm and a neighbor-finding approach visiting pixels in the same order used by the quadtree building algorithm were found to be significantly slower than the linear quadtree algorithm. Our new pointer-based algorithm avoids visiting nodes more than once by maintaining a heap holding the internal nodes of the quadtree covering the row being processed and using neighbor-finding to update the heap when a new row is processed. As Table 2 indicates, this algorithm using the paged-pointer quadtree is significantly faster than that of the linear quadtree.

The region quadtree efficiently performs set operations (e.g., area intersection, union) on spatial data sets, since large homogeneous parts of the two images are compared all at once. The algorithms used to perform set operations on quadtrees depends on whether the images represented by the quadtree are *aligned* (same origin and orientation) or *unaligned*.

Set operations on aligned quadtrees [HS79] simply requires traversing the input quadtrees in parallel and performing the proper set operation on pairs of leaves. Because the input quadtrees are traversed in preorder, aligned set operations execute efficiently using both linear quadtrees and paged-pointer quadtrees.

Table 2. Time required for quadtree-to-raster conversion.				
Image	Pointer-Based		QUILT	
Name	DEC	Amiga	DEC	Amiga
Floodplain	4.1	5.9	4.5	6.1
Landuse	12.6	7.0	22.2	10.6
Topography	11.8	6.3	20.6	9.7
Total	28.5	19.2	47.3	26.4

Set operations on unaligned quadtrees are considerably more complex. An efficient algorithm for set operations on unaligned linear quadtrees is presented in [SS90].

Table 3. Time required (in seconds) for unaligned set operations - Amiga.						
Image &	Pointer-Based			QUILT		
Offset	0	1	100	0	1	100
Floodplain	2.3	5.3	2.4	2.1	5.4	2.6
Landuse	4.1	7.2	4.0	5.5	8.1	5.2
Topography	2.7	6.2	3.6	4.7	7.5	4.7
Total	9.1	15.7	10.0	12.3	21.0	12.5

Table 4. Time required (in seconds) for unaligned set operations - DEC.						
Image &	Pointer-Based			QUILT		
Offset	0	1	100	0	1	100
Big floodplain	2.1	4.6	2.4	1.8	4.3	2.8
Big landuse	5.6	7.0	5.3	6.5	6.7	5.6
Big topography	3.2	6.2	5.6	5.2	5.9	5.5
Total	10.9	17.8	13.3	13.5	16.9	13.9

Set operations on unaligned quadtrees require searches in the unaligned quadtree. The need for searching makes unaligned set operations a good test of random access to the pages of the quadtree. Tables 3 and 4 compare the times required to perform unaligned set operations using the nine test cases presented in [SS90]. In each test, a portion of "floodplain" serves as the unaligned quadtree and is intersected at several different offsets with one of the original maps. Relative to each aligned quadtree, the origin of the unaligned quadtree was set at $(0, 0)$ (i.e., aligned), $(1, 1)$, and $(100, 100)$. These tables show that our implementation outperforms QUILT on the Amiga, while execution times are nearly identical on the DECStation. Both systems implement the unaligned set operation of [SS90], which was designed for linear quadtrees. It may be possible to implement a more efficient pointer-based algorithm taking advantage of the internal structure of the quadtree.

To help understand the why the paged-pointer implementation is faster than QUILT, we studied the number of page faults generated by both systems and also profiled various critical sections of the code. On each machine, the linear quadtree system spends substantially more time performing I/O, while our pointer-based quadtrees incur greater computational overhead involved in translating each pointer into an address in the buffer pool. Profiling our code indicates that our address translation code consumes between 20% and 30% of total execution time. At the same time, the paged-pointer implementation generates between 1/2 and 3/4 the number of page faults generated by QUILT (with significant variation between images). However, there is only modest correlation between time improvement and page fault improvement. For more timing details and information on page faults, see [Brown92].

6. Conclusions

The most significant drawback to traditional pointer-based quadtrees is that the structure is not easily stored in pages on disk. While this issue is not important for quadtrees small enough to fit in main memory, it is important for larger data sets. Representing large quadtrees in memory requires the use of disk for swapping and can cause significant performance problems. On the other hand, linear quadtrees can be organized on disk by a B-tree, using the locational codes of the leaves to order the records. We have described the paged-pointer quadtree, a mapping of a leafless pointer-based quadtree to disk pages. The nodes of a paged-pointer quadtree are stored in preorder and its pages are managed by routines similar to those used in a B-tree. This mapping overcomes the problems associated with representing pointer-based quadtrees on disk.

Because of its perceived efficiency, the linear quadtree has historically been used to represent large quadtrees on disk, despite the many other advantages of pointer-based quadtrees. The primary motivation for our work is to produce a disk-based representation that exploits the many advantages of pointer-based quadtrees while providing adequate performance. The tests reported in Section 6 demonstrate that our implementation of the paged-pointer quadtree produces performance comparable to, and in most cases better than, a very efficient disk-based linear quadtree system.

7. Acknowledgements

During the course of this work, we have benefited from discussions with Robert E. Webber. We also wish to thank the reviewers for their comments, which helped us to improve our presentation.

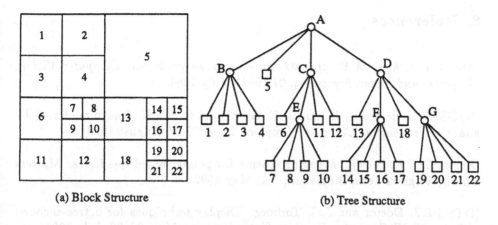

(a) Block Structure   (b) Tree Structure

Page 1	Parent	NW Child	NE Child	SW Child	SE Child
A	➤ NULL	➤ B	5	➤ C	➤ ➤ E
C	➤ A	6	➤ ➤ D	11	12
B	➤ A	1	2	3	4

Page 2	Parent	NW Child	NE Child	SW Child	SE Child
E	➤ ➤ C	13	➤ ➤ F	18	➤ ➤ G
D	➤ ➤ A	7	8	9	10

Page 3	Parent	NW Child	NE Child	SW Child	SE Child
F	➤ ➤ D	14	15	16	17
G	➤ ➤ D	19	20	21	22

(c) Paged Pointer Quadtree Representation. Assumptions: Maximum number of nodes per page is 4; Minimum number of nodes per page is 2; a single arrow is a pointer to a node on this page; a double arrow is a pointer to a node on another page.

Figure 1. Three representations for an example quadtree.

8. References

[Abe84] D.J. Abel. A B$^+$-tree structure for large quadtrees. *Computer Vision, Graphics, and Image Processing*, 27:19–31, July 1984.

[BFGS86] L. Bergman, H. Fuchs, E. Grant and S. Spach. Image rendering by adaptive refinement, *Computer Graphics*, 20(4):29-37, August 1986.

[Brown92] P.R. Brown. A paging scheme for pointer-based quadtrees. Masters Thesis, Virginia Tech, Blacksburg VA, May 1992.

[DT81] L.J. Doctor and J.G. Torborg. Display techniques for octree-encoded objects. *IEEE Computer Graphics & Applications*, 1(3): 29–38, July 1981.

[Gar82] I. Gargantini. An effective way to represent quadtrees. *Communications of the ACM*, 25(12):905–910, December 1982.

[HS79] G.M. Hunter and K. Steiglitz. Operations on images using quad trees. *IEEE Transactions on Pattern Analysis and Machine Intelligence*, 1(2):145–153, July 1979.

[JSS91] W. de Jonge, P. Scheuermann and A. Schijf. Encoding and manipulating pictorial data with S$^+$-trees, in *Advances in Spatial Databases: Proceedings of SSD'91*, Lecture Notes in Computer Science 525, O. Günther and H-J. Schek, eds., Springer Verlag, Berlin, 401-419, 1991.

[KE80] E. Kawaguchi and T. Endo. On a method of binary picture representation and its application to data compression, *IEEE Transactions on Pattern Analysis and Machine Intelligence*, 2(1):27–35, January 1980.

[Mor66] G.M. Morton. A computer oriented geodetic data base and a new technique in file sequencing. Technical report, IBM, Ottowa, Canada, 1966.

[OHS90] D.N. Oskard, T.H. Hong, and C.A. Shaffer. Real-time algorithms and data structures for underwater mapping. *IEEE Transactions on Systems, Man, and Cybernetics*, 20(6):1469–1475, November 1990.

[Sam90a] H. Samet. *Applications of Spatial Data Structures: Computer Graphics, Image Processing, and GIS*. Addison-Wesley, 1990.

[Sam90b] H. Samet. *The Design and Analysis of Spatial Data Structures*. Addison-Wesley, 1990.

[SS87] C.A. Shaffer and H. Samet. Optimal quadtree construction algorithms. *Computer Vision, Graphics, and Image Processing*, 37:402–419, March 1987.

[SS90] C.A. Shaffer and H. Samet. Set operations for unaligned linear quadtrees. *Computer Vision, Graphics, and Image Processing*, 50(1):29-49, April 1990.

[SSN90] C.A. Shaffer, H. Samet, and R.C. Nelson. Quilt: A geographic information system based on quadtrees. *International Journal of Geographic Information Systems*, 4(2):103-131, August 1990.

[SW89] H. Samet and R.E. Webber. A comparison of the space requirements of multi-dimensional quadtree-based file structures. *Visual Computer*, 5(6):349-359, December 1989.

[SPMA87] T.R. Smith, D.J. Peuquet, S. Menon and P. Agarwal. KBGIS-II: A knowledge-based geographical information system. *International Journal of Geographical Information Systems*, 1(2):149–172, April 1987.

A Hierarchical Spatial Index for Cell Complexes

Elisabetta Bruzzone[1] Leila De Floriani[2] Monica Pellegrinelli[2]

[1] Elsag Bailey S.p.A.
Research and Development
Via Puccini, 2 - 16154 Genova (Italy)
[2] Department of Computer and Information Sciences
University of Genova
Viale Benedetto XV, 3 - 16132 Genova (Italy)

Abstract. A new hierachical spatial index for object representation schemes based on three-dimensional cell complexes is introduced. We consider a domain consisting of general n-dimensional spatial objects described by n-dimensional cell complexes. The new hierarchical spatial index, called a cellular n-tree, generalizes similar structures developed for planar maps, and is defined as a recursive subdivision of a universe containing the cell complex into regular blocks. Terminal blocks may be completely inside a cell or outside the complex, or may contain indices to sets of cells within the complex. We briefly review the properties of n-dimensional cell complexes, that we call cellular decompositions, and introduce a few basic atomic operators for building them in the three-dimensional case. We shortly describe algorithms for building a cellular octree from a 3D cellular decomposition and for updating the cellular octree, when the cellular decomposition is modified by applying the atomic constructive operators introduced. Algorithms for solving point location and proximity queries on a cellular decomposition with a cellular octree superimposed are presented.

1 Introduction

The problem of providing a description of geometric objects within a computer system has become more and more important because of the increasing development of application fields dealing with spatial entities, such as geographic data processing, CAD/CAM, computer vision, robotics. Since each application focusses on the object representation, the geometric representations developed have different characteristics. A very powerful description of spatial entities in three or n dimensions is provided by *cell complexes* [3, 9, 10, 15], which represent a spatial entity as a collection of quasi-disjoint cells, together with incidence and adjacency relations between cells and their boundaries. One advantage of cell complexes, often called *cellular decompositions*, with respect to other representation schemes lie in the possibility of describing internal entities, such as internal faces in a solid object, as elements of the model. Such property turns out to be significant, for instance, in applications of geometric modeling to manufacturing automation when non-solid geometric entities describe intersections of solids [17]. The simplest example of a cell complex is a simplicial complex, i.e., a cell complex in which each k-dimensional cell, $0 \leq k \leq n$, is a k-dimensional simplex, i.e., the smallest k-dimensional convex set. Simplicial complexes have been used to describe general spatial entities in a geometric modeling environment [11, 13, 12].

A first generalization of simplicial complexes is to allow a k-dimensional cell to be a topological space homeomorphic to a k-dimensional disk and each k-dimensional cell to be on the boundary of at least a $(k + 1)$-dimensional cell. The boundary of each k-dimensional cell is the union of cells having a dimension lower than k. The cellular decompositions we consider are cell complexes with such properties. Other authors generalize this notion of a cell complex to that of a geometric complex [17, 18]: geometric complexes can have lower dimensional cells that are not bounding any higher dimensional cell. In this way, point sets which are not dimensionally homogeneous can be adequately represented into a single model. Cell complexes and their generalizations provide an object-based decomposition of a spatial entity (in constrast to space-based decomposition schemes, which subdivide the space occupied by the entity).

One of the major drawbacks of cellular decompositions is the conceptual complexity of algorithms for answering spatial queries on them. We can classify spatial queries on a cellular decomposition into three major categories:

(i) *Topological queries*, which are based on the topological incidence and adjacency relations among the entities of a cell complex (for instance, retrieve the edges bounding a given face or, more generally, the $(n-1)$-dimensional cells bounding a given n-dimensional cell)

(ii) *Interference queries*, which are based on intersection, containment or coincidence of entities (for instance, locate the n-dimensional cell containing a given query point or the k-dimensional cells intersecting a given query segment).

(iii) *Proximity queries*, which are based on the geometric distance between a query entity and the entities forming a cellular decomposition (for instance, find the k-dimensional cell which is closer to a given point, edge or face).

Topological queries involve only entities which are present in the cellular model, and, thus, can be answered efficiently by selecting a suitable encoding structure for the cell complex (for instance, the data structure presented in Section 2). On the contrary, interference and proximity queries involve checking a query entity against the cellular model, and, thus, their efficiency can be considerably improved by using a *spatial index*, which provides a subdivision of the space containing the cell complex. Any spatial search can be first carried out on the spatial index, in order to reduce the amount of cells which are to be considered. Thus, a spatial index acts as a pruning device in the search.

In two dimensions, spatial indexing structures (in particular, hierarchical spatial indices, such as *PM-quadtrees*) have been superimposed on planar maps to improve the efficiency of spatial queries and of geometric operations [19, 20]. Indexing structures for planar subdivisions are built by recursively partitioning the space containing the map into square blocks until some simplicity criterion related to the information contained into a terminal block is met.

Apparently similar, but conceptually different, hierarchical models have been developed in the context of solid modeling by two research groups. Such models, called *extended octrees* [4] and *polytrees* [6], combine an octree with a boundary description of an object. Extended octrees and polytrees are basically hierarchical boundary models, since the hierarchical description itself embeds the boundary representation of the object into its terminal nodes. Hierarchical boundary models have been designed as auxiliary representations for solids in order to speed up boolean operations and conversions to other representation schemes.

On the other hand, an indexing structure can be superimposed on an underlying object model in order to speed up spatial searches. Unlike hierarchical boundary models, a hierarchical spatial index alone is not able to describe the topology of the represented object. Octrees have been used as spatial indices in hidden surface elimination and ray tracing techniques [1].

Here we introduce a new spatial indexing structure, called a *cellular n-tree*, which is superimposed on an n-dimensional cell complex, in order to speed up interference and proximity queries on cellular decompositions. The novelty of our approach is in the combination of a hierarchical spatial index, i.e., a space-based decomposition scheme, with a cell complex, i.e., an object-based decomposition scheme; moreover, the proposed structure is suitable to represent entities in any dimension.

A cellular n-tree for a given cell complex is defined by the recursive subdivision of an n-dimensional universe containing it into blocks. We characterize the structure in the more general n-dimensional case, but our interest is in using it in three dimensions, where a cellular n-tree is called a *cellular octree*. A cellular octree is described by a tree in which the root represents the universe, internal nodes represent blocks which are further subdivided. Terminal nodes can be of type *full*, in the case they describe a partition of the space internal to a three-dimensional cell, of type *empty*, if they describe a partition of the universe external to the solid, or of type *face, edge*, or *vertex*, if they have a non-empty intersection with the boundary of the three-dimensional cells. A node of type *vertex* corresponds to a terminal block containing one vertex and intersected by the edges and faces incident at that vertex. A node of type *edge* corresponds to a terminal block containing no vertex and intersected by one or more edges, all incident at the same external vertex. A node of type *face* corresponds to a terminal block containing no edge or vertex and intersected by one or more faces, all incident at an external vertex. Each terminal block is maximal.

We have defined both an algorithm which builds a cellular octree for an existing cell complex by using the classical block classification paradigm and algorithms for updating a cellular octree when atomic modifications are performed on the underlying cellular decomposition. Such modifications of cellular decompositions are performed through a minimally complete set of constructive Euler operators. Thus, the proposed model provides a support to dynamic variations of the described object.

Then, we show the application of a cellular octree in solving two "classical" interference and proximity queries on a three-dimensional cell complex. As examples, we have considered a point location query in a three-dimensional cell of the cell complex and a proximity query consisting of detecting the face of a cellular decomposition which is closest to a given query point.

The remainder of the paper is organized as follows. In Section 2, we review some definitions and properties of cellular decompositions, and we describe four basic constructive operators for the three-dimensional case. Section 3 introduces the cellular n-tree, and discusses its encoding structure and storage requirements. In Section 4, algorithms for building and updating a cellular octree are briefly described. Section 5 and Section 6 present, respectively, an algorithm for solving the point location problem and a neighbour finding algorithm on cellular octrees.

2 Cellular Decompositions

Generally speaking, a cellular decomposition (or cell complex) is a subdivision of a topological n-dimensional space into cells.

A k-cell, with $0 \leq k \leq n$, is a closed connected subset of a variety, homeomorphic to a k-dimensional disk. Given a k-cell c, we denote with $b(c)$ and $i(c)$ the boundary and the interior, respectively, of c. A *cellular decomposition* Σ of $\Re^n$, usually termed a *cell complex* or an *n-complex*, is a finite collection C of cells satisfying the following properties:

(i) for every pair $c, d \in C$, where c is a k-cell (with $k \leq n$) and d an m-cell (with $m \leq n$), $i(c) \cap i(d) = \emptyset$.
(ii) the boundary $b(c)$ of a cell $c \in C$ is union of cells in C.
(iii) if $c, d \in C$ and $c \cap d \neq \emptyset$, then $c \cap d$ is the union of cells of C.

A cell f is said to be a *face* of a cell c if $f \subseteq c$. If $f \neq c$, then f is said to be a *proper face* of c. Two cells c and d are said to be *incident* if c is a proper face of d, or d is a proper face of c. Two k-cells c and d, $0 < k \leq n$, are said to be *adjacent* if there exists a $(k-1)$-cell in C which is proper face of both c and d. Also, two 0-cells c and d are said to be *adjacent* if there exists a 1-cell a in C such that c and d are both proper faces of a.

We define two symmetric topological operators on a cell c, called *boundary* and *coboundary*, as follows:

$$boundary(c) = \{d \in C \mid d \text{ proper face of } c\}$$

$$coboundary(c) = \{d \in C \mid c \text{ proper face of } d\}$$

In an n-dimensional cellular decomposition we can define $(n+1)^2$ ordered topological relations between ordered pairs of cells (i.e., between a k-cell and its adjacent k-cells and between a k-cell and the m-cells incident at it, $m = 0, 1, \ldots, n$, $m \neq k$). A relation R_{kk} between a k-cell c and all k-cells of Σ adjacent to c is called an *adjacency relation*. A relation R_{km} between a k-cell c and all m-cells of Σ incident at c, with $m > k$, is called an *incidence coboundary* relation. A relation R_{km} between a k-cell and all m-cells of Σ incident at c, with $m < k$, is called an *incidence boundary* relation. Note that, for $k = n$, only incidence boundary relations are defined, while, if $k = 0$, only incidence coboundary relations exist.

To describe a cellular decomposition Σ we use an *incidence graph* G_Σ [10], i.e., a graph in which the nodes correspond to the k-cells of Σ, $k = 0, 1, \ldots, n$, and the arcs describe incidence coboundary relations $R_{k(k+1)}$, $k = 0, 1, \ldots, n-1$, and incidence boundary relations $R_{k(k-1)}$, $k = 1, 2, \ldots, n$. In other words, for every pair (c, d) of cells such that c is a k-cell, $k = 0, 1, \ldots, n-1$, and d is a $(k+1)$-cell such that $d \in coboundary(c)$, there exists a directed arc (c, d) in G_Σ. For every pair (c, f) of cells such that c is a k-cell, $k = 1, 2, \ldots, n$, and f is a $(k-1)$-cell such that $f \in boundary(c)$, there exists a directed arc (c, f) in G_Σ.

In the three-dimensional case, 0-cells are *vertices*, 1-cells are *edges*, 2-cells are *faces*, and 3-cells are simply called *cells*. Thus, a three-dimensional cellular decomposition Σ is described by a $4 - tuple$ $\Sigma = (\mathcal{C}, \mathcal{F}, \mathcal{E}, \mathcal{V})$, where $\mathcal{C}$ denotes the set of cells, $\mathcal{F}$ the set of faces, $\mathcal{E}$ the set of edges and $\mathcal{V}$ the set of vertices of Σ. There are sixteen incidence and adjacency relations between topological elements. Six incidence relations are described in the incidence graph, namely *Vertex-Edge*, *Edge-Face*, *Face-Cell*, *Cell-Face*, *Face-Edge* and *Edge-Vertex*.

All relations, except for the Vertex-Edge one, are sortable, i.e., an order can be assigned to the entities involved in the relation. For instance, the faces around an edge can be ordered counterclockwise, while all relations involving a constant number of entities (such as Face-Cell and Edge-Vertex) are always sortable. The only non-sortable relation among the stored ones is the Vertex-Edge relation, since there is no way of ordering all the edges incident at a given vertex. Thus, all the arcs in the incidence graph are sorted around the node from which they emanate, except for those describing the Vertex-Edge relation.

We have defined a minimal set of primitive Euler operators on a cellular decomposition. Such operators involve a constant number of entities and ensure that the necessary validity condition expressed by Euler-Poincarè formula is always satisfied at each update. The Euler-Poincarè formula, in the original extension due to Poincarè, relates the number of simplices in an n-dimensional simplicial complex to its connectivity degree [21]:

$$\sum_{i=0}^{i=n}(-1)^i\alpha_i = \sum_{i=0}^{i=n}(-1)^i p_i$$

where α_i is the number of simplices of dimension i and p_i is the ith Betti number. This formula holds for all n-dimensional complexes with simply-connected faces. Betti numbers are connection numbers; p_0 is the number of connected components within the cell complex; p_1 indicats the number of cuts necessary to make the complex simply-connected; p_2 is the number of cavities included by two-dimensional surfaces. For a 3D cellular decomposition, which describes a solid with no cavities, null genus and with simply connected faces, the Euler-Poincarè formula reduces to:

$$\alpha_0 - \alpha_1 + \alpha_2 - \alpha_3 = p_0$$

The manipulation of such a decomposition can be performed by using the following four *constructive* operators, introduced in [5] for three-dimensional simplicial complexes:

- MVB (*Make_Vertex_and_Body*): it creates a cellular decomposition Σ composed of a single vertex and a single connected component.
- MEV (*Make_Edge_and_Vertex*): it inserts a new vertex v and a new edge e incident at v and at an existing vertex in a cellular decomposition Σ.
- MEF (*Make_Edge_and_Face*): it inserts a new edge e connecting two existing vertices and a new face f bounded by e in a cellular decomposition Σ.
- MFC (*Make_Face_and_Cell*): it inserts a new face f bounded by a set of existing edges and a new cell c bounded by face f in a cellular decomposition Σ.

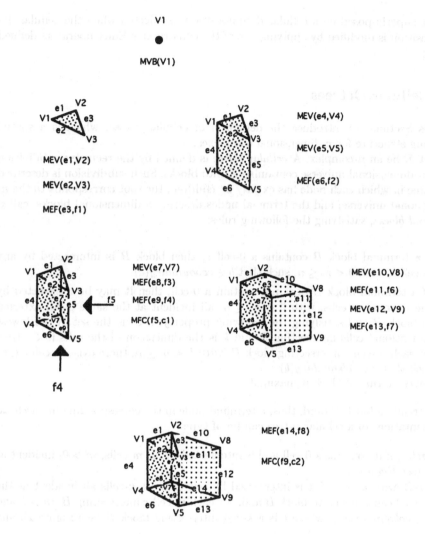

Fig. 1. An example of construction of a cellular decomposition by using Euler operators. For each operator, only the newly created entities are indicated.

Figure 1 shows an example of an application of the four constructive Euler operators to build a simple cellular decomposition.

Four *destructive* operators have also been defined, which perform the inverse operations. The eight operators together allow the creation and the manipulation of a 3D cellular decomposition satisfying Euler-Poincarè formula. Such operators, however, do not ensure other conditions to be satisfied, like each k-cell being homeomorphic to a k-dimensional disk or the absence of dangling edges or faces in the cell complex. The presence of situations violating the definition of a 3D cell complex should be verified algorithmically. In Section 4, we briefly describe how a cellular octree, superimposed on a cellular decomposition, is affected when the cellular decomposition is modified by applying one of the constructive Euler operators defined above.

3 Cellular Octrees

In this Section, we introduce the definition of cellular n-tree, which is a spatial indexing structure for n-dimensional complexes.

Let Σ be an n-complex. A *cellular n-tree* is defined by the recursive subdivision of an n-dimensional universe containing Σ into blocks. Such subdivision is described by a tree in which each node has exactly 2^n children; the root corresponds to the n-dimensional universe, and the terminal nodes describe n-dimensional blocks, called *terminal blocks*, satisfying the following rules:

(i) if a terminal block B contains a 0-cell c, then block B is intersected by any m-cell b, with $0 < m \leq n$, such that $b \in coboundary(c)$

(ii) if a terminal block B does not contain a 0-cell, then it may be intersected by one or more m-cells, with $0 < m \leq n$, all incident at the same 0-cell external to block B and satisfying the following property: if C' is the set of the lowest dimensional cells intersecting B and k is the dimension of the cells in C', then for each m-cell c intersecting block B, with $k < m \leq n$, there exists a cell $b \in C'$ such that $c \in coboundary(b)$

(iii) every terminal block is maximal.

A terminal block B (and, thus, a terminal node in the corresponding hierarchical representation) of a cellular n-tree can be of type:

- *vertex*, if it contains a 0-cell and is intersected by all m-cells, $m > 0$, incident at it (see Figure 2a)
- *k-cell*, with $k > 0$, if it is intersected by one or more k-cells all incident at the same 0-cell external to block B and, for each m-cell c intersecting B, $m > k$ and $c \in coboundary(b)$, where b is a k-cell intersecting block B (see Figure 2b and 2c)
- *full*, if it is not intersected by any k-cell, $0 \leq k < n$, but there exists an n-cell c of Σ such that block B is contained into c
- *empty*, if it is not intersected by any k-cell, $0 \leq k \leq n$ (i.e., block B is external to any cell of Σ).

In two dimensions ($n = 2$), a cellular n-tree reduces to a PM2-quadtree [19]. Terminal blocks in a PM2-quadtree can be of type *vertex, edge, full* or *empty*. A terminal block of type *vertex* contains a single vertex and all the edges of the map incident at it, while a block of type *edge* is intersected by a collection of edges, all incident at the same external vertex, but it does not contain any vertex.

In the three-dimensional case, we have a *cellular octree*, that we use to describe three-dimensional cell complexes. In a cellular octree, we have five kinds of terminal blocks: *vertex, edge* and *face* (see Figure 2), *full* and *empty*. A terminal block of type

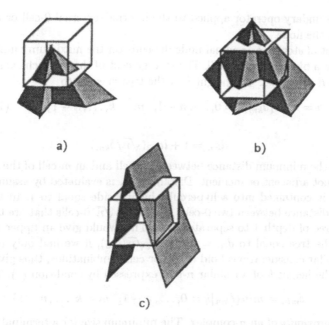

Fig. 2. Examples of terminal blocks of type *vertex* (a), *edge* (b) and *face* (c) in a cellular octree.

vertex contains one vertex and all edges and faces incident at it. A terminal block of type *edge* is intersected by one or more edges (and by the faces incident at them), all incident at the same vertex external to the block. A terminal block of type *face* is intersected only by one or more faces (not by edges or vertices), all incident at the same vertex external to the block.

Being a spatial indexing structure, a cellular octree is conceptually different from exact octree representations developed to describe the boundary of solid objects, like polytrees [6], and extended octrees [2, 4]. In a polytree, the boundary of the object is clipped against the blocks corresponding to the leaves of the tree. Thus, new vertices and edges (called *pseudo-vertices* and *pseudo-edges*) are stored in this representation. This may cause numerical approximation problems. In an extended octree, a set of half-spaces is encoded in each terminal block. The planes, which define the faces having a non-empty intersection with that block, are stored in a way that the boundary of the solid can be locally unambiguously reconstructed from such plane configurations. In both representations, the boundary of the solid is encoded in the leaves of the octree representation, either explicitly, like in a polytree, or implicitly, like in an extended octree. A cellular octree, instead, is a structure superimposed on the underlying topological model (in our case, a cellular decomposition).

The encoding structure for a cellular n-tree is very simple. Each terminal node contains a field indicating its type (*vertex*, k-*cell*, $k = 1, \ldots, n$, *full*, *empty*). If a node is of type *vertex*, it contains a link to the corresponding 0-cell in the data structure storing the cellular decomposition. If a node is of type k-*cell*, it contains a list of pointers to all k-cells intersecting the corresponding block. For a node of type *vertex* and k-*cell*, the other m-cells, with $k < m \leq n$, intersecting the block can be obtained by the coboundary operator applied to the internal/external 0-cell or to the k-cells encoded in the node.

The cost of storing a terminal node depends on the maximum number of k-cells intersecting a block of type k-cell. The storage cost of the hierarchical structure can be evaluated as follows. The height h of the tree is equal to

$$h = max\{d_{km} | k = 0, \ldots, n-1, \quad m = k, \ldots, n-1\} \qquad (1)$$

where

$$d_{km} = 1 + log_2(\sqrt{n}/\delta_{km})$$

and δ_{km} is the minimum distance between a k-cell and an m-cell of the cell complex, which are not adjacent or incident. Distance d_{km} is evaluated by assuming that the n-complex is contained into a hypercube having side equal to 1. In this case, the maximum distance between two 0-cells is at most $\sqrt{n}$. 0-cells that are thus far apart require a tree of depth 1 to separate them. This would give an upper bound to the height of the tree equal to $d_{00} = 1 + log_2(\sqrt{n}/\delta_{00})$, if we had only nodes of type *vertex*. Similar considerations hold for other cell combinations, thus giving an upper bound to the height h of a cellular n-tree expressed by condition (1). The quantity

$$\delta_{min} = min\{\delta_{km} | k = 0, \ldots, n-1, \quad m = k, \ldots, n-1\}$$

is the *cell proximity* of an n-complex. The minimum size for a terminal block is then $\frac{\delta_{min}}{2\sqrt{n}}$. Note that in the three-dimensional case,

$$\delta_{min} = min\{\delta_{vv}, \delta_{ve}, \delta_{vf}, \delta_{ee}, \delta_{ef}, \delta_{ff}\}$$

where v, e and f represent, respectively, a vertex, an edge and a face of the cellular decomposition.

4 Algorithms for Building and Updating a Cellular Octree

In this Section, we present algorithms for building and updating a cellular octree from an existing cellular decomposition, based on the classical block classification paradigm. Note that we consider only cellular decompositions with planar faces. We call the first approach *static*, since it requires that the whole cellular decomposition is a priori known. Then, we describe an algorithm for updating a cellular octree when the underlying cellular decomposition is modified.

4.1 A Static Approach

Given a cellular decomposition $\Sigma = (\mathcal{C}, \mathcal{F}, \mathcal{E}, \mathcal{V})$, the algorithm builds first an initial block (the universe) containing Σ. Then, it subdivides the universe into eight blocks. For each resulting block B, it computes the lists of the cells, faces, edges and vertices of Σ intersecting B and checks the conditions which make B a terminal block. If one of such conditions is met, a terminal node of the corresponding type is created; otherwise, a partial node is created and the block subdivision process is recursively repeated. A high-level pseudo-code description of the algorithm is reported below. Implementating such an algorithm, partial nodes do not have to be created, if an encoding structure based on a locational code is used [19].

Procedure BUILD_OCTREE(B, C, F, E, V, T)

/* B: current octree block; at the first activation, B is the block containing
the cellular decomposition;

C, F, E, V: lists of cells, faces, edges and vertices associated with block B;
at the first activation, they are the set of cells, faces, edges and vertices
of the cellular decomposition;

T: resulting cellular octree; at the first activation, $T = \emptyset$ */

begin

    if ($V = \emptyset$ **and** $E = \emptyset$ **and** $F = \emptyset$) **then**

      /* block B is either of type *full* or *empty* */

      if (B is inside a cell $c \in C$) **then** INSERT_TREE(T, B, *full*)

      else INSERT_TREE(T, B, *empty*)

    else if ($V = \emptyset$ **and** $E = \emptyset$) **then**

        if (all the faces in F are incident at the same external vertex)

          /* block B is of type *face* */

          then INSERT_TREE(T, B, *face*) ;

      else if ($V = \emptyset$) **then**

        if (all the edges in E are incident at the same external vertex

          and all the faces in F are incident at edges in E)

          /* block B is of type *edge* */

          then INSERT_TREE(T, B, *edge*) ;

        else if (V contains a single vertex v) **then**

          if (all the edges in E **and**

            all the faces in F are incident at vertex v)

            /* block B is of type *vertex* */

          then INSERT_TREE(T, B, *vertex*) ;

        else begin /* recursive splitting */

          INSERT_TREE(T, B, *partial*) ;

          Select the cells, faces, edges and vertices which

            intersect the blocks B_i, i=0, ..., 7, into which

            B is subdivided from the lists C, F, E, V;

            for i:=0 **to** 7 **do** BUILD_OCTREE($B_i, C_i, F_i, E_i, V_i, T$)

          /* C_i, F_i, E_i, V_i are the lists of elements

            intersecting block B_i */

        end

end.

The time complexity of algorithm BUILD_OCTREE is given by the sum of the
complexity of each recursive call. Hence, it is

$$\sum_{i=1}^{i=nbcalls} max\{O^i_{face}, O^i_{edge}, O^i_{vertex}, O^i_{select}\}$$

where O^i_{face}, O^i_{edge} and O^i_{vertex} are the complexities associated with the ith iteration
and due to the processes which classify a block into a block of type *face*, *edge*
or *vertex*, while O^i_{select} is the cost for the distribuition of the lists of cells, faces,

edges and vertices from a parent block to its eight children. *nbcalls* depends on the number of nodes in the cellular octree, i.e., on the height h of the final tree and, thus, $nbcalls = \frac{8^{h+1}-1}{7}$. If s is the length of the side of the smallest block, then $h = log_2(1/s)$, provided that a unitary block has been taken as root. In more details, $O^i_{select} = O(N_C + N_F + N_\mathcal{E} + N_V)$, where N_C, N_F, $N_\mathcal{E}$ and N_V are the number of elements in the lists of cells, faces, edges, and vertices attached to the block processed at the ith iteration; $O^i_{face} = O(N_{F_v}(N_{F_v} + N_F))$, where N_{F_v} is the maximum number of faces incident at a vertex in the cell complex; $O^i_{edge} = O(N_F N_\mathcal{E} N_{F_e})$, where N_{F_e} is the maximum number of faces incident at an edge; $O^i_{vertex} = O(N_F N_{F_v} + N_\mathcal{E})$.

4.2 A Dynamic Approach

We have defined algorithms for updating a cellular octree after a cellular decomposition has been modified by applying the four constructive Euler operators defined in Section 2. As an example, in the following we describe the modifications of the cellular octree due to the application of operator MEV. A detailed description of the remaining operators is presented in [7].

Operator MEV adds a new vertex v to a cellular decomposition Σ and a new edge e which connects v to an existing vertex w of Σ. First of all, the terminal blocks which are intersected by e and v must be found. In what follows, we examine how the different types of terminal nodes (blocks) of the cellular octree T_Σ describing Σ are affected by the above modification (see also Figure 3).

If B is a block of type *vertex*, then
 - if v is outside B, but w is the vertex inside B, then no update is performed (see Figure 3a).
 - if edge e intersects B, but both v and w are outside B, then B must be subdivided (see Figure 3b).
 - if v is inside B, then B must be subdivided (see Figure 3c).

If B is a block of type *edge*, then
 - if v and w are both outside B and w is the vertex at which all edges intersecting B are incident, then a new link to edge e must be added to B (see Figure 3d).
 - if edge e intersect B and if v and w are both outside B, but w is not the vertex at which the edges intersecting B are incident, then B must be subdivided (see Figure 3e).
 - if v is inside B, then B must be subdivided (see Figure 3f).

If B is a block of type *face*, then
 - if v is inside B or v is outside but e intersects B, then B must be subdivided (see Figures 3g and 3h).

If B is a block of type *full* or *empty*, then
 - if v is inside B, then B becomes a block of type *vertex*.
 - if v is outside B and e intersects B, then B becomes a block of type *edge*.

When a block B must be subdivided, B is split once and the algorithm is recursively applied to each block arising from such subdivision and not satisfying one of the conditions for terminal blocks.

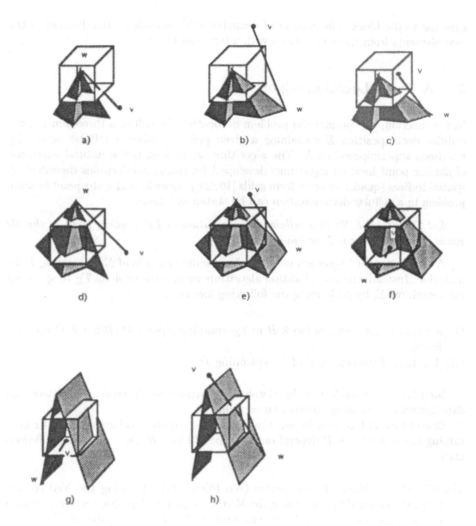

Fig. 3. Situations arising when applying operator MEV to a cellular decomposition.

The complexity of the algorithm is given by the combination of the complexity due to the selection of the terminal blocks which are intersected by the new edge and vertex with that due to the terminal blocks recursive splitting. The terminal blocks intersected by new elements are identified by traversing the cellular octree, and hence the time complexity due to this phase is $\frac{8^{h+1}-1}{7}$, where h is the height of the tree. The operations performed at each recursive call have a constant cost, with the exception of the creation of the lists of cells, faces, edges and vertices intersecting the eight blocks into which a terminal block is subdivided. In this case, the search is restricted to the faces and edges incident at a vertex, which may be internal or external to the block. The number of recursive calls depends on the distance of the new elements from those associated with a terminal block.

5 A Point Location Algorithm

In this Section, we consider the problem of locating the cell of a three-dimensional cellular decomposition Σ containing a given point P, when a cellular octree T_Σ has been superimposed on Σ. The algorithm we present is the natural extension of similar point location algorithms developed for planar subdivisions described by spatial indices (quadtrees or uniform grids [19, 20]). More formally, the *point location problem* in a cellular decomposition can be stated as follows:

Let $\Sigma = (\mathcal{C}, \mathcal{F}, \mathcal{E}, \mathcal{V})$ be a cellular decomposition and P a query point in the 3D space. Find the cell $c \in \mathcal{C}$ containing point P.

A straightforward approach consists of examining all cells of Σ and testing P for inclusion. Instead, the point location algorithm we propose exploits T_Σ to speed up the search on Σ, by performing the following two steps:

(i) location of the terminal block B in T_Σ containing point P (B is called the *base block*)

(ii) location of the cell $c \in \mathcal{C}$ of Σ containing P.

Step (i) can be performed by classical algorithms for traversing an octree and depends on the encoding structure used [19].

Once block B has been found, the operations required to locate the cell c containing the query point P depend on the type of block B. Four different situations arise:

Case 1: B is a block of type *vertex* (see Figure 4a). By using the Vertex-Face relation, obtained by combining the Vertex-Edge and Edge-Face relations stored in the incidence graph of Σ, we can find the list $\mathcal{F}_v$ of the faces of Σ incident at vertex v and intersecting block B. Then, we can compute the face $f \in \mathcal{F}_v$ closest to P and then, through the Face-Cell relation, the cell containing P.

Case 2: B is a block of type *edge* (see Figure 4b). We determine the face f closest to P in the list of the faces $\mathcal{F}_B$ intersecting block B. Such faces are those incident at the edges of Σ associated with block B. Given such edges, $\mathcal{F}_B$ can be found by using the Edge-Face relation. Once f has been found, the cell c containing P is obtained by applying the Face-Cell relation.

Case 3: B is a block of type *face* (see Figure 4c). We have just to locate the face f closest to P among those intersecting B. Then, c can be located by applying the Face-Cell relation.

Case 4: B is a block of type *full* or *empty*. In this case, there must exist at least a sibling of the node corresponding to B, whose associated block B' contains a face bounding the cell c containing the query point. Then, for block B', one of the previous three cases arises.

Note that, when the Face-Cell relation is applied to the face closest to P, two cells are retrieved, if f is not on the boundary of Σ. The cell containing P must be selected. Furthermore, if f lies on the boundary of Σ, then only one cell is returned by the Face-Cell relation, and we have just to check whether P is inside or outside the cell complex.

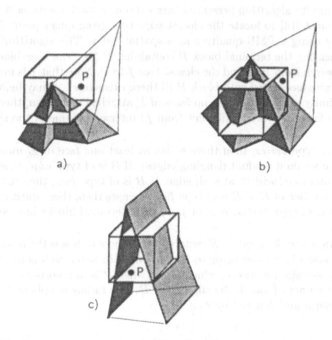

Fig. 4. Base blocks of type *vertex* (a), *edge* (b) and *face* (c) of a cellular octree containing a query point P. The cells containing P are represented.

The time complexity of the block classification algorithm outlined above is linear in the maximal number N_{F_v} of faces incident at a vertex in Σ, provided that the siblings of a given node can be located within T_Σ in constant time. The time complexity of the entire point location algorithm depends on the time complexity of locating the base block containing P and of classifying such block, i.e., on the height of the tree and on the local complexity of the cellular decomposition (expressed by parameter N_{F_v}).

6   A Proximity Algorithm

In this Section, we consider an example of a proximity query on a cellular decomposition, and we present an algorithm for answering such query, which exploits the cellular octree. The proximity problem we consider can be stated as follows:

Let $\Sigma = (\mathcal{C}, \mathcal{F}, \mathcal{E}, \mathcal{V})$ be a cellular decomposition and P a query point. Find the face of Σ closest to P.

A bruteforce approach would lead to consider all the faces of Σ and picking the face with minimum distance from point P.

The proximity algorithm presented here extends a similar approach proposed by Hoel and Samet [14] to locate the closest edge to a given query point P in an edge database by using a PMR-quadtree as a spatial index. The algorithm we propose starts by locating the terminal block B containing P (i.e., the base block). Then, it starts the search from B to find the closest face f to P. Note that f is not necessarily one of the faces associated with block B (if there exists one): it may belong to blocks in the proximity of B. If there are no faces of Σ attached to B then, there must exist at least one face (in general, different from f) intersecting one of the sibling blocks of B.

If B is of type *vertex*, then there exists at least one face of Σ incident at such vertex (since we do not admit dangling edges). If B is of type *edge*, then there must be at least one face incident at such edge. If B is of type *face*, then it is intersected by at least one face of Σ. If B is of type *full* or *empty* then, there must exist a sibling block B' of B of type *vertex, edge* or *face*, since terminal blocks in a cellular octree are maximal.

We define a *searching sphere S* centered at P whose radius is the distance between P and the closest face f belonging to B or to one of its seven sibling blocks. In Figure 5, the worst situation is shown, which arises when P is in a corner of B and f is at the furthest corner of one of the siblings of B. The radius of sphere S is called the *searching radius* and denoted by r.

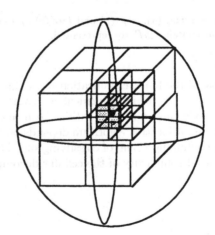

Fig. 5. Searching sphere centered at a given query point P: the siblings of B and those of its parent block are represented.

In order to cover to searching sphere we have to visit not only the seven sibling blocks of the base block B, but also blocks having a dimension equal to or greater than the parent block of B. In the worst case, we have to examine fifty-six blocks of size equal to (or greater than) the parent block of B. Such blocks are the eight blocks internal to the searching sphere S depicted in Figure 5, plus forty-eight blocks which surround the internal ones and that are necessary to cover S completely. The algorithm is essentially a traversal of the subtree of the cellular octree rooted at the block of minimum size containing S. For each block B' associated with a node of the subtree we check first whether B' intersects S: if there is no intersection, B' and its descendants are neglected; if an intersection exists, two different situations arise, depending on whether B' is a partial block or a terminal one; if B' is a terminal block and it is intersected by a face f', the distance r' between P and f' is computed and the searching radius r and closest face f updated if necessary; otherwise the children of B' are processed.

Note that when examining the blocks, the size of S may become smaller and, then, the number of blocks neglected increases. The time complexity of the algorithm depends on the height of the subtree whose root contains S, and on the number of faces intersecting a terminal block, i.e., on the maximum number of faces incident at a vertex or at an edge. The intersection test of a block B' with the current searching sphere S can be simply carried out by evaluating the distance between the four corners of B' and the center P of S and comparing it with the current radius r.

7 Concluding Remarks

Cellular n-trees provide a spatial indexing structure for cell complexes. The application domain of such structures include geographic information systems, CAD/CAM and computer vision systems. In the paper, we have focussed on the three-dimensional case by considering cellular octrees and presenting algorithms for answering spatial queries on them. The novelty of a cellular n-tree lies in the combination of a hierarchical spatial index (which generalizes the octree) with an n-dimensional cell complex.

Cellular n-trees act as a pruning device to make spatial searches more efficient. To show this, we have considered two classical interference and proximity queries on a 3D cell complex: a point location and a point-face proximity query, consisting, respectively, of finding the cell containing a given query point P and the closest face to a point P. The cellular octree allows us to restrict the search to a restricted volume of the cell complex and also, unlike uniform grids, it does not depend on the data distribution. The algorithms presented can be extended to n-dimensions, thus providing an efficient way of answering spatial queries in an n-dimensional space.

An alternative spatial index for n-dimensional cell complexes can be defined by extending the PMR-quadtree [16, 19]. Such spatial index is called a *PMR-tree* and is defined by the recursive subdivision of an n-dimensional hypercube into blocks, according to the following splitting rule: a block, which contains a number of $(n-1)$-cells exceeding a predefined threshold value, is split into 2^n blocks exactly once (even if one of the resulting blocks contains a number of $(n-1)$-cells exceeding the threshold). A PMR-tree is a spatial index for an arbitrary collection of k-cells in an n-dimensional universe, since it does not exploit the incidence and adjacency relations between the cells in a cell complex.

Further developments of our work include: the design and implementation of algorithms for speeding up interference and proximity finding algorithms on cell complexes, according to the classification presented in [8]; the definition of algorithms for performing Boolean operations on cellular decompositions described by cellular octrees; the extension of cellular n-trees to represent n-dimensional geometric complexes (i.e., describing not dimensionally homogeneous point sets in n-dimensions); esperimental comparisons between cellular octrees and PMR-octrees.

References

1. Arvo, J., Kirk, D., "A Survey of Ray Tracing Acceleration Techniques", in *An Introduction to Ray Tracing*, A.S. Glassner editor, 201-262, 1989.
2. Ayala, D., Brunet, P., Juan, R., Navazo, I., "Object Representation by Means of non Minimal Division Quadtrees and Octrees", *ACM Transactions on Graphics*, 4, 1, 41-59, 1985.
3. Brisson, E., "Representing Geometric Structures in d-dimensions: Topology and Order", *Proceedings 5th ACM Symposium on Computational Geometry*, Saarbruchen, 218-227, 1989.
4. Brunet, P., Navazo, I., "Solid Representation and Operation using Extended Octrees", *ACM Transactions on Graphics*, 8, 1989.
5. Bruzzone, E., De Floriani, L., "Two Data Structures for Building Tetrahedralizations", *The Visual Computer*, 6, 266-283, 1990.
6. Carlbom, I., Chakravarty, I., Vanderschel, D., "A Hierarchical Data Structure for Representing Spatial Decomposition of 3-D Objects", *IEEE Computer Graphics and Applications*, 5, 4, 24-31, 1985.
7. De Floriani, L., Pellegrinelli, M., Bruzzone, E., "Building a Hierarchical Representation for Cellular Decompositions", *Technical Report*, DISI, University of Genoa, 1992.
8. De Floriani, L., Marzano, P., Puppo, E., "Spatial Queries and the Hybrid Models", in preparation.
9. Dobkin, D., Laszlo, M., "Primitives for the Manipulation of Three-Dimensional Subdivisions", *Proceedings 3rd ACM Symposium on Computational Geometry Models*, Canada, 86-99, 1987.
10. Edelsbrunner, H., *Algorithms in Combinatorial Geometry*, Springer Verlag, 1987.
11. Egenhofer, M.J., Frank, A.U., Jackson, J.P., "A topological Model for Spatial Database", *Design and Implementation of Large Spatial Database*, SSD 89, Lecture Notes in Computer Science, Springer Verlag, 271-286, 1989.
12. Frank, A., Kuhn, W., "Cell Graphs: A Provable Correct Method for the Storage of Geometry", *Proceedings 2nd International Symposium on Spatial Data Handling*, Seattle, Washington, 411-436, 1986.
13. Ferrucci, V., Paoluzzi, A., "Extension and Boundary Evaluation for Multidimensional Polyhedra", *Computer Aided Design*, 23, 1, 40-50, 1991.
14. Hoel, E.G., Samet, H., "Efficient Processing of Spatial Queries in Line Segment Database", *Computer Science*, 525, Springer Verlag, Berlin, 1991.
15. Lienhart, P., "Topological Models for Boundary Representations: a Comparison with n-dimensional Generalized Maps", *Computer Aided Design*, 23, 1, 59-82, 1991.
16. Nelson, R.C., Samet, H., "A Consistent Hierarchical Representation for Vector Data", *Computer Graphics* 20, 4, 197-206, 1986.

17. Rossignac, J.R., O'Connor, M.A, "SGC: A Dimensional-Independent Model for Pointsets with Internal Structures and Incomplete Boundaries", *Geometric Modeling for Product Engineering*, Wozny, M.J., Turner, J.U., and Preiss, K., editors, Elsevier Science Publishers B.V. (North Holland), 145-180, 1990.

18. Rossignac, J.R., "Through the Cracks of the Solid Modeling Milestone", *Eurographics 91 State of the Art Report on Solid Modeling*, 23-109, 1991.

19. Samet, H., *The Design and Analysis of Spatial Data Structures*, Addison-Wesley, Reading, MA, 1990.

20. Samet, H., *Applications of Spatial Data Structures*, Addison-Wesley, Reading, MA, 1990.

21. Takala, T., "A Taxonomy on Geometric and Topological Models", *Proceedings Eurographics Workshop on Mathematics and Computer Graphics*, S. Margherita, Genova, Italy, October 1991.

On Optimal Multiversion Access Structures *

Bruno Becker[1], Stephan Gschwind[1], Thomas Ohler[2], Bernhard Seeger[3],
Peter Widmayer[2]

[1] Institut für Informatik, Universität Freiburg, Rheinstraße 10–12, D–7800 Freiburg
[2] Institut für Theoretische Informatik, ETH Zentrum, CH–8092 Zürich
[3] Institut für Informatik, Universität München, Leopoldstraße 11b, D–8000 München

Abstract. We propose an asymptotically optimal multiversion B-tree. In our setting, insertions and deletions of data items are allowed only for the present version, whereas range queries and exact match queries are allowed for any version, present or past. The technique we present for transforming a (usual single version) B-tree into a multiversion B-tree is more general: it applies to a number of spatial and non-spatial hierarchical external access structures with certain properties directly, and it can be modified for others. For the B-tree and several other hierarchical external access structures, multiversion capabilities come at no extra cost, neither for storage space nor for runtime, asymptotically in the worst case. The analysis of the behavior of the multiversion B-tree shows that the constant loss of efficiency is low enough to make our suggestion not only a theoretical, but also a practical one.

1 Introduction

The importance of maintaining data not only in their latest version, but also to keep track of their development over time has been widely recognized. Version data in engineering databases [Kat90] and time oriented data [CA86] in geographical information systems [Lan92], e.g. to manage land register data, are two prime examples for situations in which the concepts of versions and time are visible to the user; in multiversion concurrency control [BK91, BHG87], these concepts are transparent to the user, but they are used by the system (e.g. the scheduler) for concurrency control and recovery purposes. In this paper, we are concerned with access structures that support version based operations *on external storage* efficiently. We follow the convention of [BHG87, DSST89] in that each update to the data creates a new version; note that this differs from the terminology in engineering databases, where an explicit operation exists for

---

* Partially supported by the ESPRIT Basic Research Project "AMUSING".

creating versions, and versions of design objects are equipped with semantic properties and mechanisms — such as inheritance or change propagation. Our choice of creating a new version after each update turns out not be restrictive, in the sense that the data structuring method we propose can be easily adapted to create versions only on request, without loss of efficiency.

We are interested in spatial access structures for *external storage* that support at least *insertions, deletions, exact match queries* (associative search) and locality based spatial queries such as e.g. *proximity queries*, in addition to application specific operations like *purging* of old enough versions in concurrency control. We limit our discussion to the situation in which a change can only be applied to the present version, whereas queries can be performed on any version, present or past. Some authors call this a management problem for *partially persistent* data; we call an access structure that supports the required operations efficiently a *multiversion* structure.

The problem in designing a multiversion spatial access structure lies in the fact that data are on external storage. For *main memory*, there is a recipe for designing a multiversion structure, given a single version structure. More precisely, any single version main memory data structure in a very general class, based on pointers from record to record, can be transformed into a multiversion structure, asymptotically at no extra amortized time and space costs, by applying a general technique [DSST89]. For the special case of balanced binary search trees, the extra time bounds hold even in the worst case per operation — clearly a perfect result.

Given quite a general recipe for transforming single version main memory data structures into multiversion structures, it is an obvious temptation to apply that recipe accordingly to external access structures. This can be done by simply viewing a block in the external structure as a record in the main memory structure. At first glance, this models block access operations well; unfortunately, it does not model storage space appropriately: the size of a block is not taken into consideration. That is, a block is viewed to store a constant number of data items, and the constant is of no concern. Even worse, the direct application of the recipe consumes one block of storage space for each data item. In contrast, no external data structure can ever be satisfactory unless it stores significantly more than one data item in a block on average; balanced structures, such as the B-tree variants, actually require to store in each block at least some constant fraction of the number of items the block can hold, the *block capacity b*. As a consequence, at least the space efficiency of this approach is clearly unacceptable.

It is the contribution of this paper to propose a technique for transforming spatial and non-spatial single version *external* access structures into multiversion structures, with no extra cost in space or time asymptotically, where the block capacity b is not considered to be a constant. This result is achieved for a certain class of hierarchical external access structures. It is important to note that this class contains the B-tree and its variants, not only because the B-tree is a ubiquitous external data structure, but also because B-tree variants play a prominent role in the area of spatial data structures. Here they are used e.g. for maintaining quad trees on external storage by means of their quad code, and, more generally, for maintaining any linearly coded spatial arrangement (for a comprehensive introduction and survey, see [Sam89a, Sam89b]). In addition, it is worth noting that our result solves the long-standing open problem of designing multiversion B-trees with asymptotically optimal extra cost.

For the sake of concreteness, we base the presentation of our technique in this paper on B-trees; it is implicit how to apply our technique to other hierarchical structures. Each data item stored in the tree consists of a *key* and an *information* part; access to data items is by key only, and the keys are supposed to be taken from some linearly ordered set (such as locational codes of spatial cells). Let us restrict our presentation to the following operations:

- *insert (key, info)*: insert a record with given *key* and *info* component into the *present* version; this operation creates a new version.
- *delete (key)*: delete the (unique) record with given *key* from the *present* version; this operation creates a new version.
- *exact match query (key, version)*: return the (unique) record with given *key* in the given *version*; this operation does not create a new version.

- *range query (lowkey,highkey,version)*: return all records whose key lies between the given *lowkey* and the given *highkey* in the given *version*; this operation does not create a new version.

Before reviewing the previous approaches of designing a B-tree that supports these operations efficiently, let us state the strongest efficiency requirements that a multiversion B-tree can be expected to satisfy. To this end, consider a sequence of N update operations (insert or delete), applied to the initially empty structure, and let m_i be the number of data items present after the i-th update (we say, in version i), $0 \leq i \leq N$. Then a multiversion B-tree with the following properties holding for each i (all bounds are for the worst case) is the best we can expect:

- for the first i versions, altogether the tree requires $O(i/b)$ blocks of storage space;
- the $(i+1)$-th update accesses and modifies $O(\log_b m_i)$ blocks;
- an exact match query in version i accesses $O(\log_b m_i)$ blocks;
- a range query in version i that returns r records accesses $O(\log_b m_i + r/b)$ blocks.

The reason for the bounds being optimum is the fact that for each version i, the efficiency of all operations is the same as if the data present in version i would be maintained separately in its own B-tree. This paper presents a multiversion B-tree structure satisfying these efficiency requirements. For comparison, the next section reviews previous approaches to the problem of designing multiversion B-trees. Section 3 describes and Section 4 analyzes our multiversion B-tree. Section 5 concludes the paper.

2 Previous approaches for B-trees

In building multiversion structures, there is a general tradeoff between storage space, update time and query time. For instance, building an extra copy of the structure at each update is extremely slow for updates and extremely costly in space, but extremely fast for queries. Near the other extreme, [KS89] view versions (time) as an extra dimension and store 1-dimensional intervals in 2-dimensional space in an R-tree. This gives good storage space efficiency, but query and update efficiency may be as bad as $\Theta(\log_b N)$. That is, the time to answer a query on version i does not depend on the number of items in that version only, but instead on the total number of all updates. Also with the aim of good storage space efficiency, [EWK90] suggest to organize all keys in the leaves of a B$^+$-tree, and for each key maintain a further B$^+$-tree for the set of version-intervals and associated attributes of that key; this results in the same query and update time inefficiency as [KS89].

In a different setting, [LS89] propose the time-split B-tree, based on the write-once B-tree of [Eas86], for storing multiversion data on both, magnetical and optical WORM disks. Under the basic assumption that *deletions do not occur*, the time-split B-tree (as well as the write-once B-tree) yields good space and time efficiency (for an analysis, see [LS90]) by making clever use of two types of block splits, the usual split according to keys and a split according to time. Even under this restriction (which clearly takes away much of the burden in designing multiversion structures), range queries cannot be performed efficiently: a single range query may require $\Theta(r)$ block accesses, since records in a version that are close in key space are not necessarily clustered in blocks. Therefore, the time-split B-tree is efficient only for insertions and exact match operations. For spatial queries and also most other applications, this is not sufficient. If deletions are allowed, retrieval performance can degenerate. For example, an exact match query in version i may require $\Theta(\log_b N)$ block accesses; that is, it does not depend on the number of data items in version i, but on the total number of update operations in the file.

Several variants of multiversion B$^+$-trees that also allow updates in the past have been proposed in [LM91], based on the ideas on full persistence in [DSST89]. This is a more general concept than ours; if simplified for our multiversion situation (in the past only queries, no updates), query efficiency depends only on the number of items that belong to the queried version, as desired. Storage space, however, may be as high as $\Theta(N)$ blocks, because each operation may copy an entire block — a result that is achieved trivially by identifying each node in the *node copying* method of [DSST89] by a block.

As a result, none of the B-trees for multiple versions presented in the literature so far achieve optimum performance in time and space. In the next section, we present an optimum multiversion B-tree; it is suited to spatial applications, because it accomodates multiversion range queries efficiently. Our description suggests a rather general method for transforming hierarchical external data structures into optimal multiversion structures, provided that operations proceed in a certain way along paths between the root and the leaves. But even if the external single version data structure does not precisely follow the operation pattern we request (as in the case of R-trees, for instance), we conjecture that the basic ideas carry over to an extent that makes a corresponding multiversion structure competitive and useful.

3   Optimal Multiversion Access Structures for External Storage

We present our technique to transform single version external access structures into multiversion structures at the example of the B-tree. To achieve the desired behavior, we associate insertion and deletion versions with items, since items of different lifespans need to be stored in the same block. Let < *key*, *in_version*, *del_version*, *info* > denote a data item with a *key* that is unique for any given version, an associated *inf*ormation, and a lifespan from its insertion version *in_version* to its deletion version *del_version*. Similarly, an entry in an inner node of the tree is denoted by < *router*, *in_version*, *del_version*, *reference* >; the *router*, together with the earliest *in_version* and the latest *del_version* of the *referenced* subtree, guides the search for a data item in the obvious way, for exact match queries as well as for range queries.

Each update (insert or delete operation) creates a new version; the i-th update creates version i. An entry is said to be *of version i*, if its lifespan contains i. A block is said to be *live* if it has not been copied, and *dead* otherwise. In a live block, deletion version $*$ for an entry denotes that the entry has not yet been deleted at present; in a dead block, it tells that the entry has not been deleted before the block died. For each version i and each block A except the roots of versions, we request that the number of entries of version i in block A is either zero or at least d, where $b = k \cdot d$ for block capacity b and some constant k (assume for simplicity that b, k, d are all integers and b is the same for directory and data blocks); we call this the *weak version condition*.

Operations that do not entail structural changes are performed in the straightforward way that can be inferred from the single version structure by taking the lifespan of entries into account. That is, an entry inserted by update operation i into a block carries a lifespan of $[i, *)$ at the time of insertion; deletion of an entry by update operation i from a block changes its *del_version* from $*$ to i.

Structural changes are triggered in two ways. First, a *block overflow* occurs as the result of an insertion of an entry into a block that already contains b entries. A block underflow, as e.g. in B-trees, cannot occur, since entries are never removed from blocks. However, the weak version condition may be violated as a result of a deletion; such a *weak version underflow* occurs, if an entry is deleted in a block with exactly d present version entries.

The structural modification after a block overflow copies the block and removes all but the present version entries from the copy. We call this operation a *version split*; it is comparable to a time split at the present time in [Eas86]; equivalently, it may be compared to the node copying operation of [DSST89]. Clearly, if no obsolete information is present, no copy needs to be made. Nevertheless, in general a copy produced by this version split may be an almost full block. In that case, a few subsequent insertions would again trigger a version split, resulting in a space cost of $\Theta(1)$ block per insertion. To avoid this and the similar phenomenon of an almost empty block, we request that at least $\varepsilon d + 1$ insert operations or delete operations are necessary to arrive at the next block overflow or version underflow in that block, for some constant ε (assume for simplicity that εd is integer) to be defined more precisely in the next section. As a consequence, the number of present version entries after a version split must be in the range from $(1 + \varepsilon)d$ to $(k - \varepsilon)d$; we call this the *strong version condition.* If a version split leads to less than $(1 + \varepsilon)d$ entries – we say: a *strong version underflow* occurs –, a merge is attempted with a copy of a sibling block containing only its present version entries. If necessary, this merge must be followed by a version independent split according to the key values of the items in the block – a *key split.* Similarly, if a version split leads to more than $(k - \varepsilon)d$ entries in a block – we say: a *strong version overflow* occurs –, a key split is performed. A similar idea is used for the write-once B-tree [Eas86] to eliminate a time-overflow.

To make these restructuring operations more precise, let us now present the main points in a semi-formal algorithmic notation. In order to present the main idea without obstructing irrelevant details, we assume that an exact match query in the single version structure returns a block in which the searched item is stored if it is present in the structure. For the same reason, we ignore the treatment of the end of the recursion in our operations, when a change propagates up to the root.

To insert a data item, we proceed as follows:

> **insert** key k, present version i, information *info* :
> > {assume k is not yet present}
> > exact match query for k in version i leads to block A;
> > **blockinsert** $< k, i, *, info >$ into A.

Here, **blockinsert** is defined as follows:

> **blockinsert** entry e into block A:
> > enter e into A;
> > **if**   *block overflow* of A **then**
> > > **version split**: copy present version entries of A into B;
> > > **blockinsert** entry referencing B into father of A;
> > > **if**   *strong version underflow* of B **then**
> > > > **merge** B

> **elsif** *strong version overflow* of B **then**
>> **treat strong version overflow** of B.

Note that after a version split, the deletion version stored in the entry referring to the dead block must be adjusted to represent the version of the version split, in order to guide subsequent searches correctly.

Merging a block makes use of the fact that a suitable sibling can always be found in the access structure:

> **merge** block B:
>> identify a sibling D of B to be merged;
>>
>> **version split:** copy present version entries of D into E;
>>
>> unite B and E into B and discard E;
>>
>> **if** *strong version overflow* of B **then**
>>> **treat strong version overflow** of B
>>>
>>> {no weak version underflow possible in father of B}
>>
>> **else**
>>> adapt router to B in father of B;
>>>
>>> **check weak version underflow** of father of B.

Essentially, a strong version overflow is treated by a key split of the entries according to their key or router values:

> **treat strong version overflow** of block A:
>> **key split:** distribute entries of A evenly among A and B;
>>
>> adapt router to A in father of A;
>>
>> **blockinsert** entry referencing B into father of A.

A weak version underflow leads to a version split and a merge:

> **check weak version underflow** of block A:
>> **if** *weak version underflow* of A **then**
>>> **version split:** copy present version entries of A into B;
>>>
>>> **blockinsert** entry referencing B into father of A;
>>>
>>> **merge** B.

This completes the description of the insertion of an item into a block. To delete an item, we proceed as follows:

> **delete key** k, present version i {assume k is present}:
> exact match query for k in version i leads to block A;
> **blockdelete** k, i from A.

> **blockdelete key** k, version i from block A:
> change entry $< k, i', *, info >$ into $< k, i', i, info >$ in A;
> **check weak version underflow** of A.

This completes the more detailed presentation of update operations. Let us mention that the multiversion structure defined in this way is not a tree, but a directed acyclic graph; the same is true also for other multiversion access structures, like e.g. the time-split B-tree [LS89]. In general, more than one *root* block may exist. Since the number of root blocks to be expected is very small, maintaining these blocks is not a major data organization problem. We simply propose to maintain references to root blocks with associated version numbers as data items in a B-tree, where keys are the version numbers alone. It is easy to calculate that the B-tree of version numbers will rarely have depth two and never exceed it, and for all practical purposes can be kept in main memory.

In the next section, we show in an analysis that the basic operations actually do lead to the desired behavior.

4 Efficiency Analysis

Recall that a block is *live* if it was not copied up to the present version, *dead* otherwise. N is the number of update operations performed on the data structure from the beginning up to the present version, m_i is the number of data items present in version i.

What are the restrictions for the choice of k and ε? First, after a *key split*, the resulting blocks must fulfill the strong version condition. Before a *key split* on a block A is performed, A contains at least $(k - \varepsilon) \cdot d + 1$ entries. After the *key split* operation that distributes the entries of A among two blocks, both blocks must contain at least $(1 + \varepsilon) \cdot d$ entries. Therefore, the following inequality must hold:

$$(\star) \qquad (k-\varepsilon) \cdot d + 1 \geq \tfrac{1}{\alpha} \cdot (1+\varepsilon) \cdot d \qquad \text{or, equivalently,} \qquad k \geq \tfrac{1}{\alpha} + (1 + \tfrac{1}{\alpha}) \cdot \varepsilon - \tfrac{1}{d}.$$

Here, α depends on the underlying access structure. It denotes the constant fraction of data entries that are guaranteed to be in a new node. For example, $\alpha = 0.5$ is fulfilled for B-trees, i.e. inequality $(\star)$ is equivalent to $k \geq 2 + 3\varepsilon - \tfrac{1}{d}$.

Second, no strong version underflow is allowed for a block A resulting from a *merge* operation. Before a *merge* operation is performed, together there are at least $2d - 1$ present version entries in the blocks which have to be merged. Therefore we have:

$$(\star\star) \qquad 2d - 1 \geq (1 + \varepsilon) \cdot d \qquad \text{or, equivalently,} \qquad \varepsilon \leq 1 - \tfrac{1}{d}.$$

4.1 Runtime analysis

Recall that our multiversion structures are based on leaf oriented balanced access structures. The data blocks are on *level 0*, the directory blocks are on level 1,2,.... Assuming that the valid *root* reference can be found for each version i with at most one block access – an extremely conservative count, as in [LM91] –, the number of block accesses for searching a data item x in version i is at most $2 + \lceil \log_d m_i \rceil$, because each directory block on the path from the *root* of version i to the leaf where x is stored has at least d references of i. Therefore, we conclude:

Theorem 1 *The number of block accesses for searching a data item in version i is $2 + \lceil \log_d m_i \rceil$ in the worst case.*

The arguments above can be extended to range queries that are answered by traversing the corresponding umbrella-like part of a subtree of the tree for the queried version:

Theorem 2 *The number of block accesses for answering a range query in version i that returns r data items is $O(\lceil \log_d m_i \rceil + r/b)$ in the worst case.*

For comparison, the data structure in [LM91], when updates in the past are disallowed, yields a worst case complexity for exact match queries of $2 + 2 \cdot \lceil \log_{d'} m_i \rceil$ with $b = 2 \cdot d' - 1$ (note that in that case, only entries with constant length need to be handled in the directory of [LM91]). The asymptotic efficiency of exact match queries is, hence, the same, and for realistic choices of k and d (e.g. $d \geq 10, k \leq 5$), our access paths are shorter by at least 25 %, a certain fringe benefit.

The $(i+1)$-th update operation first performs an exact match query in version i and then modifies at least one data block A. If A violates the weak version condition, up to three other data blocks have to be created or modified. In this case, the parent of A – say A' – has to be modified. Again, this can lead to a violation of the weak version condition of A'. In the worst case, this situation occurs on each directory level up to the *root* of version i. On each directory level, at most four directory blocks have to be modified or created. Therefore we have:

Theorem 3 *The number of block accesses and modifications for the $(i+1)$-th update operation is $2 + 5 \cdot \lceil \log_d m_i \rceil$ in the worst case.*

In contrast to the write-once B-tree [Eas86] and the time-split B-tree [LS89], the results of our structure (presented in Theorems 1, 2 and 3) depend on m_i, the number of data entries in the i-th version. Whenever deletions would be allowed, both, the time-split B-tree and the write-once B-tree, would require $1 + \log_{b/2} N$ block accesses in the worst case for an exact match query. Thus, retrieval performance would actually depend not on m_i, but on N instead.

4.2 Space analysis

We analyze the worst case space utilization over the sequence of the N update operations. The crucial factor in the analysis is the fact that a *version split*, if necessary followed by a *merge* or a *key split* leads to new blocks which fulfill the strong version condition. Therefore we need a certain number of update operations on these blocks, before the next underflow or overflow situation on these blocks can occur. To be more precise, we consider the utilization of data blocks and of directory blocks separately.

For data blocks, one update operation can lead to at most one overflow or underflow situation. We distinguish four types of situations:

- *Version split only:* One block A becomes *dead* and one new *live* block B is created. A was the first data block in the data structure or has fulfilled initially –after its creation– the strong version condition. If it becomes over- or underfull, at least $\varepsilon \cdot d + 1$ operations must have taken place on A since its creation. So the amortized space cost for each of these operations is at most $\frac{k \cdot d}{\varepsilon \cdot d + 1}$.

- *Version split and key split:* One block A becomes *dead* and two new *live* blocks $B1$ and $B2$ are created. Again, at least $\varepsilon \cdot d + 1$ operations must have taken place on A and therefore the amortized space cost for each of these operations is at most $\frac{2 \cdot k \cdot d}{\varepsilon \cdot d + 1}$.

- *Version split and merge without key split:* Two blocks $A1$ and $A2$ become *dead* and one new *live* block B is created. On $A1$ or $A2$ at least $\varepsilon \cdot d + 1$ operations must have taken place. So the amortized space cost for each of these operations is at most $\frac{k \cdot d}{\varepsilon \cdot d + 1}$.

- *Version split and merge with key split:* Two blocks $A1$ and $A2$ become *dead* and two new *live* blocks $B1$ and $B2$ are created. Again, on $A1$ or $A2$ at least $\varepsilon \cdot d + 1$ operations must have taken place. The amortized space cost for each of these operations is at most $\frac{2 \cdot k \cdot d}{\varepsilon \cdot d + 1}$.

In all cases the amortized data block space cost per update operation S_{dat} is at most

$$\frac{2 \cdot k \cdot d}{\varepsilon \cdot d + 1} < \frac{2 \cdot k}{\varepsilon} = O(1)$$

For directory blocks, one update operation can lead to at most one *block overflow* or *version underflow* situation on each directory level up to the directory level of the *root* in the present version. Let L denote the maximum level that occurs during the N operations. To look precisely at the different underflow and overflow situations, we distinguish between directory blocks that are *roots* at their lifetime and inner blocks.

Let A^l denote an *inner directory block* of level l. We call a reference in A^l *dead*, if it is a reference to a *dead* block, *live* otherwise. The following situations can cause a *weak version underflow* or a *block overflow* of A^l:

- One reference in A^l becomes *dead* and one new reference has to be inserted into A^l. This can cause a *block overflow* with the creation of two new directory blocks.

- One reference in A^l becomes *dead* and two new references have to be inserted into A^l. This can cause a *block overflow* with the creation of two new directory blocks.

- Two references in A^l become dead and one new reference has to be inserted into A^l. This can cause a *weak version underflow* or a *block overflow*. In the case of a *weak version underflow*, a sibling of A^l becomes also *dead*, and up to two new directory blocks are created.

- Two references in A^l become *dead* and two new references have to be inserted into A^l. This can cause a *block overflow* with the creation of two new directory blocks.

Note that if a directory block is the *root* of the data structure in version i, a *weak version underflow* does not lead to a new copy of the block. A *block overflow* of a *root* block is treated in the same manner as a *block overflow* of an inner block.

We explain the amortized space cost per operation for the first case. The extension to the other cases and the *root* blocks is straightforward and yields the same result. Because A^l is the only *live* parent for the *live* blocks referenced from A^l, and A^l has initially fulfilled the strong version condition, in the subtree of A^l on level $l-1$ at least $\varepsilon \cdot d + 1$ new blocks have been created between the creation of A^l and the *block overflow* of A^l. Therefore at least $(\varepsilon \cdot d + 1) \cdot k \cdot d$ space was used since then. As an induction hypothesis, assume that the amortized space cost per update on level $l-1$ is at most C^{l-1}, with $C^0 = \frac{2 \cdot k}{\varepsilon}$. Then it follows that at least $\frac{(\varepsilon \cdot d + 1) \cdot k \cdot d}{C^{l-1}}$ operations have taken place in the subtree of A^l between the creation of A^l and the *block overflow*. The space cost for the *version split* and the subsequent *key split* of A^l is $2 \cdot k \cdot d$. Therefore, the amortized space cost for the operations in the subtree of A^l is at most

$$\frac{2 \cdot k \cdot d \cdot C^{l-1}}{(\varepsilon \cdot d + 1) \cdot k \cdot d} < \frac{C^{l-1} \cdot 2}{\varepsilon \cdot d},$$

for $l = 1, .., L$.

Therefore, the total amortized directory block space cost S_{dir} per operation is at most

$$\left(\frac{2}{d \cdot \varepsilon}\right) \cdot \frac{2 \cdot k}{\varepsilon} + \left(\frac{2}{d \cdot \varepsilon}\right)^2 \cdot \frac{2 \cdot k}{\varepsilon} + \dots + \left(\frac{2}{d \cdot \varepsilon}\right)^L \cdot \frac{2 \cdot k}{\varepsilon}.$$

For $d \geq \frac{4}{\varepsilon}$, we have $(\frac{2}{d \cdot \varepsilon})^l \leq (\frac{1}{2})^l$ for $l \geq 1$.

Hence,

$$S_{dir} \leq \frac{2 \cdot k}{\varepsilon} \cdot \sum_{l=1}^{L} \left(\frac{1}{2}\right)^l \leq \frac{2 \cdot k}{\varepsilon} = O(1).$$

Theorem 4 *The worst case amortized space cost per update operation* $S = S_{dat} + S_{dir}$ *is* $O(1)$ *if* $d \geq \frac{4}{\varepsilon}$.

This is in contrast to the mechanism of [LM91], were the amortized space cost per update operation can be as high as $\Theta(b)$. Note that the condition that $d \geq \frac{4}{\varepsilon}$ can be easily satisfied in all practically relevant circumstances. In total, we get:

Theorem 5 *The multiversion B-tree constructed in the described way from the single version B-tree is asymptotically optimal in the worst case in time and space for all considered operations.*

The analysis shows that for a given block capacity b it is useful for the time complexity to choose d large and k small. To guarantee a good space utilization it is useful to choose ε maximum, that is equal to $1 - \frac{1}{d}$, and k as small as possible without violating inequality $(\star)$. Choosing $\varepsilon = 1 - \frac{1}{d}$ gives bounds for the strong version condition of $2d - 1$ and $(k-1) \cdot d + 1$.

5   Conclusion

In this paper, we have presented a technique to transform spatial and non-spatial single version hierarchical external storage access structures into multiversion structures. We have shown that our technique delivers multiversion capabilities asymptotically free of charge for B-trees. The properties of B-trees that we have used include the following characteristics of access structures:

1. the access structure is a rooted tree of external storage blocks;
2. data items are stored in the leaves (data blocks) of the tree; the inner nodes (directory blocks) store routing information;
3. the tree is balanced; typically, all leaves are on the same level;
4. the tree can be restructured by splitting blocks or by merging blocks with siblings along a path between the root and a leaf;
5. a block split can be balanced; that is, each of the two resulting blocks is guaranteed to contain at least a constant fraction α, $0 < \alpha \leq 0.5$, of the entries.

Single version access structures satisfying these requirements are therefore the prime candidates for carrying over and applying our technique. A prominent example of such an access structure is the B^+-tree; other examples that are important in spatial applications include the cell-tree [GB91], the BANG-File [Fre87], and the R-tree family [Gut84, Gre89, BKSS90], whenever reinsertion of data items can be replaced by block merge without loss of geometric clustering. Note that the data items are not limited to one-dimensional points, but may even be multidimensional geometric objects of non-zero size.

For B-trees, the number of block accesses for insertion, deletion, exact match query and range query increases only by a small constant in the worst case; the same holds for the number of blocks needed to store the data. That is, our suggestion is not merely of theoretical, but also of practical interest. Previously, asymptotically optimal multiversion behavior had not even been achieved for B-trees.

While in our model, each update creates a new version and hence version numbers are consecutive integers, our technique still works whenever version numbers are monotonically increasing. For instance, associating a (real-valued) point in time with each version – e.g. its creation time – makes it possible to pose queries referring to the data present at any given point in time.

It should be clear that the multiversion structures designed according to our technique are not limited to the basic operations we considered explicitly. Furthermore, the multiversion structures are flexible enough to sustain even structural additions. As an example case, consider the possibility that a multiversion database may run out of space as the number of versions keeps growing. In some applications, old versions can be moved to an archival storage medium, such as an optical WORM disk; in others, such as multiversion concurrency control, versions older than the time stamp of the oldest active operation can be deleted from the database. Our structures can be made to support these *purge* operations by maintaining a *purge queue* that contains all the dead blocks in the order of increasing time stamps. After a version split, the block that became dead is enqueued; a purge operation with a given time stamp dequeues all dead blocks of lower time stamp and simply frees their storage space, without performing any other changes in the multiversion structure. As a consequence, the multiversion structure may be left with references to blocks that have been purged. This is not a problem in the described setting, since the validity of a reference can be determined by comparing it with the time stamp of the oldest version that has not been purged yet. Additionally, when a block overflow occurs, entries with references to purged blocks can be deleted, such that a version split may be unnecessary.

We conjecture that our technique may be useful also for spatial and non-spatial access structures that do not satisfy all of our requirements, such as hierarchical grid files. In that case, the derived performance guarantees do not carry over without change. This is clearly due to the fact that the performance guarantees do not hold for the single version structure in the first place. However, we do not know in sufficient generality how the performance of an arbitrary external access structure changes if it is transformed into a multiversion structure along the lines of our technique.

References

[BHG87] P.A. Bernstein, V. Hadzilacos, and N. Goodman. Concurrency control and recovery in database systems. *Addison Wesley Publ. Co., Reading, Massachusetts*, 1987.

[BK91] N.S. Barghouti and G.E. Kaiser. Concurrency control in advanced database applications. *ACM Computing Surveys*, 23(3):269–317, 1991.

[BKSS90] N. Beckmann, H.P. Kriegel, R. Schneider, and B. Seeger. The R*-tree: An efficient and robust access method for points and rectangles. *ACM SIGMOD International Conf. on Management of Data*, 19:322–331, 1990.

[CA86] J. Clifford and G. Ariav. Temporal data management: models and systems. *New directions for database systems, Eds. Ariav, G. and Clifford, J. Ablex, Publishing Co., Norwood, N.J.*, pages 168–186, 1986.

[DSST89] J.R. Driscoll, N. Sarnak, D.D. Sleator, and R.E. Tarjan. Making data structures persistent. *Journal of Comp. and System Sci.*, 38:86–124, 1989.

[Eas86] M. Easton. Key-sequence data sets on indelible storage. *IBM J. Res. Development 30, 3*, pages 230–241, 1986.

[EWK90] R. Elmasri, G. Wuu, and Y.-J. Kim. The time index: An access structure for temporal data. *ACM SIGMOD International Conf. on Management of Data*, 19:1–12, 1990.

[Fre87] M.W. Freeston. The BANG-file: a new kind of grid file. *ACM SIGMOD International Conf. on Management of Data*, 16:260–269, 1987.

[Gre89] D. Greene. An implementation and performance analysis of spatial access methods. *Fifth IEEE International Conference on Data Engineering, Los Angeles*, 5:606–615, 1989.

[GB91] O. Günther and J. Bilmes. Tree-based access methods for spatial databases: implementation and performance evaluation. *IEEE Trans. on Knowledge and Data Eng.*, pages 342–356, 1991.

[Gut84] A. Guttman. R-trees: A dynamic index structure for spatial searching. *ACM SIGMOD International Conf. on Management of Data*, 12:47–57, 1984.

[Kat90] R.H. Katz. Towards a unified framework for version modeling in engineering databases. *ACM Computing Surveys*, 22(4):375–408, 1990.

[KS89] C. Kolovson and M. Stonebraker. Indexing techniques for historical databases. *IEEE Trans. on Knowledge and Data Eng.*, pages 127–137, 1989.

[Lan92] G. Langran. Time in Geographical Information Systems. *Taylor and Francis*, 1992.

[LM91] S. Lanka and E. Mays. Fully persistent B^+-trees. *ACM SIGMOD International Conf. on Management of Data*, 20:426–435, 1991.

[LS89] D. Lomet and B. Salzberg. Access methods for multiversion data. *ACM SIGMOD International Conf. on Management of Data*, 18:315–324, 1989.

[LS90] D. Lomet and B. Salzberg. The performance of a multiversion access method. *ACM SIGMOD International Conf. on Management of Data*, 19:353–363, 1990.

[Sam89a] H. Samet. The design and analysis of spatial data structures. *Addison-Wesley*, 1989.

[Sam89b] H. Samet. Applications of spatial data structures: computer graphics, image processing, and GIS. *Addison-Wesley*, 1989.

Concurrent Accesses to R-Trees*

Vincent Ng and Tiko Kameda

School of Computing Science, Simon Fraser University,
Burnaby, British Columbia, Canada. V5A 1S6

Abstract. Access to spatial objects is often required in many non-standard database applications, such as GIS, VLSI and CAD. In this paper, we examine the R-tree as an index structure, and modify it to allow concurrent accesses. We investigate three different locking methods for concurrency control. The first method uses a single lock to lock the entire tree, allowing concurrent searches but only sequential updates. The second method locks the whole tree only when the splitting or merging of nodes in the tree is required. The third method uses the lock-coupling technique to lock individual nodes of the tree.

We discuss in detail three common user operations, *search*, *insert*, and *delete*, on the R-tree. A system operation, *maintain*, which may be invoked when there is overflow or underflow at some nodes is also discussed. Concurrency control algorithms using the three locking methods mentioned above are described in this paper. They have also been implemented in the SR distributed programming language. We report on our preliminary results comparing their relative performance.

1 Introduction

In databases for geographic, CAD, VLSI and other non-standard applications, large sets of spatial objects with geometric attributes have to be stored. A typical database query refers to a spatially clustered subset of objects. Perhaps, the most common query is a **window query**, which selects the objects overlapping a given search window. Even though there has been a lot of work done in organizing spatial data [9], there is no published work on concurrency control of accesses to them. Kamel and Faloutsos have recently tried to exploit parallelism with multiple disks to obtain better search performance, but has not reported any concurrent updating algorithms [7].

The **R-tree** proposed by Guttman [6] is a hierarchical data structure derived from the B-tree. Each non-leaf node in an R-tree represents the smallest d-dimensional rectangle that encloses the rectangles represented by its child nodes. The leaf nodes contain pointers to the actual geometric objects in the database. In an R-tree, rectangles associated with different nodes may overlap. An object may be spatially contained in the rectangles associated with several nodes, yet

---

* This work was supported in part by the Natural Sciences and Engineering Research Council of Canada under the Networks of Centres of Excellence Program and in part by the Advanced Systems Institute of British Columbia.

it can only be represented by one leaf node. This means that processing a query often requires traversing several search paths before ascertaining the presence or absence of a particular object. An example of an R-tree is shown in Figure 1.

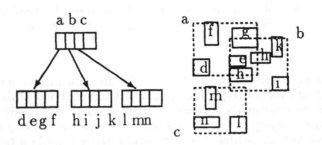

Fig. 1. An R-tree.

More formally, it is a height-balanced tree with all the leaf nodes at the same level. Each node in the tree has at least m entries and at most M entries ($1 \leq m < M$), with the exception of the root, which may have fewer than m entries. In Figure 1, $M = 4$ and $m = 3$. The root has at least two entries if it is a non-leaf node. Each non-leaf node of the tree contains entries of the form ($RECT,P$), where $RECT$ is the **minimum bounding rectangle**[2] (MBR, for short) associated with a child node P.[3] A leaf node contains entries of the form ($RECT,O$) where $RECT$ is the MBR associated with object O.

In applications with spatial indices, an entire index structure is often locked. This limits access to the index information to one process at a time. In this paper, we study ways to modify the R-tree data structure to allow concurrent operations. Three different approaches based on locking have been suggested. The "simple-lock" approach locks the whole tree with a single lock. The "modify-lock" approach locks the whole tree only when the splitting or merging of nodes in the tree is required. The "lock-coupling" allows access to a node in the tree by locking the node and its parent.

We will study three operations in this paper. The first is the **search** operation which finds the objects overlapping a given search window. The second operation is the **insert** operation which inserts an object into an R-tree. The third operation, **delete**, is to remove an object from an R-tree. To simplify the discussion of our algorithms given in later sections, we now introduce a few short-hand notations.

$RECT(P)$ The MBR of node or object P.

---

[2] A minimum bounding rectangle of a node is the smallest rectangle which contains all the rectangles pointed to by the node.

[3] To be precise, P is a pointer to a child node. We often identify the node and a pointer to it.

PARENT(P)	Node identifier or pointer referencing the parent of P.
FULL(P)	Predicate indicating if node P is full.
OVERFL(P)	Predicate indicating if node P has overflowed.
UNDERFL(P)	Predicate indicating if node P has underflowed.
PUSH(P,Q)	Push node P onto stack Q.
POP(Q)	Remove and return the first element of Q.
	If Q is empty, return *NULL*.
APPEND(Q, P)	Append node P to the end of queue Q.
NEXT(Q)	Return the next item in queue Q.
FREE(Q)	Empty queue Q.
NULL	Null referencing pointer.

2 Concurrent Search Algorithms

Concurrency control is the activity of preventing inconsistency among data in a database. Algorithms have been developed that produce conflict-preserving serializable histories [3] for data structures such as a B-tree [4] and a binary tree [5]. We frequently make use of two standard types of locks: a share lock, denoted by ρ, and an exclusive lock, denoted by ϵ. The compatibility among these two types of locks is shown in Figure 2. A ρ lock (ϵ lock) on a data item I is denoted by $\rho(I)$ ($\epsilon(I)$).

	ρ	ϵ
ρ	1	0
ϵ	0	0

Fig. 2. Lock compatibility matrix.

The **R-simple** tree is a modified R-tree to be used with the **simple-lock** locking method. With this method, only the root of the tree has a lock associated with it. (This is equivalent to associating a lock with the entire tree.) The lock management is very simple. The only difference from sequential access is that multiple search operations are allowed using a share-lock. But for an insert or a delete operation, an exclusive lock must be acquired,[4] which disallows any other operation. This locking method is used as the benchmark for comparisons with the two other approaches.

Locking the entire tree whenever an updating operation is invoked reduces concurrency. Note that, when there is no splitting or merging of nodes in the tree, the tree remains in a consistent state if individual nodes are locked while

---

[4] To acquire a share (exclusive) lock on a node means to lock the node in share (exclusive) mode.

being accessed by different types of operations. The granularity of locking now becomes at the node level rather than the entire tree. This is the second locking method, called the **modify-lock** method, and the **R-lock** tree is a modified R-tree to be used with this method. It allows multiple concurrent operations accessing the tree. Insert and delete operations can proceed if they do not cause any overflow or underflow at nodes. If such a situation arises, we lock the whole tree until a splitting and/or merging process has been completed.

The **R-couple** tree is a modified R-tree to be used with the third locking method, which also locks individual nodes rather than the whole tree. Bayer and Schkolnick proposed the **lock-coupling**[2] protocol that takes advantage of the B-tree structure. We adapt their protocol to the R-tree. With this locking method, a search or an update operation locks children of a node before releasing its lock on the node itself. Thus, a process always holds at least one lock while accessing an R-tree, but locks are acquired locally in different sub-trees of the R-tree. Multiple search, insert, and delete operations can be taking place concurrently in different parts of the same tree, regardless of overflows and underflows at nodes. It is true that, in the worst case, the whole tree may be locked, but this is no worse than the other two locking methods. For B-trees, Otoo further improved lock-coupling by having a third type of locking mode (in addition to the share and exclusive modes) to allow more concurrent operations on the same node [8]. We will adopt a similar method for the R-couple tree.

3 Simple-Lock Method and R-Simple Tree

With no modification at all to an R-tree data structure, we can allow concurrent accesses to it by associating a single lock with its root. If an R-tree is used this way, we call it an **R-simple** tree, to distinguish it from modified R-trees we will introduce later. In order to invoke a certain operation, an appropriate lock on the root must be obtained. A search operation requires a ρ lock, but since the ρ locks are compatible with each other, multiple search operations can run together. An insert and a delete operation require an ϵ lock to block any conflicting access to the tree.

We now show how search, insert, and delete operations can be carried out on an R-simple tree.

3.1 Search

Search(W, R) starts at the root of the tree and descends to the leaf level. When a search operation is in progress in an R-tree, updates to the tree are prevented by a ρ lock.

R1.Search(W, R)

1. Acquire $\rho(R)$.
2. *R1.DoSearch*(W, R).
3. Release $\rho(R)$.

R1.DoSearch(W, P)

- **if** P is a non-leaf node **then**
  - Let $\{E_i = (RECT(P_i), P_i) \mid i = 1, \ldots, k\}$ be the entries in P such that $RECT(P_i) \cap W \neq \phi$.
  - **if** $(k > 0)$ **then**
    - * For each entry E_i found above, continue the search in parallel invoking *R1.DoSearch(W $\cap$ RECT(P_i),P_i)*.
- **if** P is a leaf node **then**
  - For all entries in P whose MBR's overlap with W, return their object ids.

3.2 Insert

Insert(O, R) first acquires an ϵ lock on the root. Once it holds an ϵ lock, no other operation can access the tree. Let E_O be the entry representing the object O.

R1.Insert(O, R)

1. Acquire $\epsilon(R)$.
2. $L = R1.Select(RECT(O), R)$, which selects a leaf node where object O is to be placed.
3. Add entry E_O to L.
4. *R1.Update(L)*.
5. Release $\epsilon(R)$.

R1.Select(W, P)

1. **if** P is a non-leaf node **then**
   - Find an entry $E_s = (RECT(P_s), P_s)$ in P, where $RECT(P_s)$ requires the smallest enlargement to include W. Resolve ties by choosing E_s with the smallest $RECT(P_s)$.
   - **if** $RECT(P)$ does not contain W **then** enlarge $RECT(P)$ to accommodate W.
   - Continue the selection with *R1.Select(W, P_s)*.
2. **if** P is a leaf node **then** returns P.

R1.Update(L)

1. **if** not $FULL(L)$ **then** return.
2. Split L into L and L', and update their MBR's. Add entry $(RECT(L'),L')$ to $PARENT(L)$ and update the MBR of $PARENT(L)$. (If L was the root, create a new root first and make it $PARENT(L)$.)
3. *R1.Update(PARENT(L))*.

3.3 Delete

Delete(O, R) can be carried out in a manner similar to the insert operation. It first acquires an ϵ lock on the root to block all other operations, and then carries out its steps in two phases. The first phase is to locate the object with the *FindLeaf*(O) procedure. This procedure is similar to a search operation, except that it returns the leaf node which contains the object, O, to be deleted. The second phase removes the object, and reorganizes the tree if an underflow occurs.

4 Modify-Lock Method and R-Lock Tree

In the modify-lock method, we lock the whole tree only when a node needs to be split or two nodes need to be merged. We let search, insert, and delete operations proceed concurrently, using locks on individual nodes, as long as no overflow or underflow occurs at nodes in the R-tree.

When an overflow occurs at a node, there may be other concurrent operations in the tree. One could delay the splitting of the node and reorganization of the tree until those operations had completed. However, this might lead to a deadlock, since there might be several concurrent insert operations which might result in overflows at several nodes in the tree. In order to solve this problem, we permit temporary overflows and underflows at nodes in the tree. To manage overflows and underflows, we introduce the **R-lock** tree, which is a slightly modified R-tree. The only modification is the addition of a buffer space in each node to accommodate overflowed entries.

Together with the R-lock tree, we make use of the *maintenance queue*, denoted Q, which records the nodes at which an overflow or underflow has occurred, until the tree is re-organized. We also use the *delete queue*, denoted DQ, which records the deleted nodes in the tree until the next reorganization.

We will need to keep track of and control the number of concurrent search, insert, or delete operations operating on the tree. For this purpose, we introduce the *in-transaction counter*, denoted TC_{in}, which is incremented whenever a transaction invokes an operation on the R-tree. We also introduce the *out-transaction counter*, denoted TC_{out}, which is incremented whenever an operation on the tree is completed. Therefore, the difference, $TC_{in} - TC_{out}$, indicates the number of operations currently accessing the tree. We check for $TC_{in} - TC_{out} = 0$ to see if the whole tree can be locked for reorganization explained below.

A system process, *Maintain*, is used to reorganize the R-tree. It checks for entries in the maintenance queue Q and performs the splitting and merging of nodes. The *Maintain* process gets activated after overflows have occurred as a result of insert operations, or underflows have occurred as a result of delete operations.

We lock individual nodes using a ρ lock or an ϵ lock. Each operation must request locks on nodes in a top-down and left-to-right fashion; i.e., after locking a node, it cannot request a lock on a node that is closer to the root in the above order. This order of lock requests guarantees deadlock freedom.

4.1 Search

As in the simple-lock method, a search operation starts at the root of the tree and descends to the leaf level. In order to access a node, a ρ lock on the node must be obtained to avoid any modification to it by an update operation (i.e., insert or delete). In Figure 3, the search operation S_1 holds a ρ lock on node A. It reads the content of A and starts two sub-search operations, S_{11} and S_{12}. The ρ-lock on A can now be released because there cannot be any split or merge in nodes A, B or F, while S_{11} and S_{12} are in progress. At most one ρ-lock is needed at each branch of the search operation.

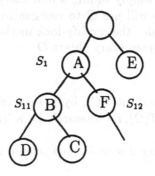

Fig. 3. Search operations using the modify-lock method.

More formally, $Search(W, R)$ under the modify-lock method is carried out as follows.

R2.Search(W, R)

1. Acquire $\epsilon(TC_{in})$, increment TC_{in} by 1, then release $\epsilon(TC_{in})$.
2. R2.Look(W, R).
3. Acquire $\epsilon(TC_{out})$, increment TC_{out} by 1, then release $\epsilon(TC_{out})$.

R2.Look(W, P)

- Acquire $\rho(P)$.
- if P is a non-leaf node **then**
  - Let $\{E_i = (RECT(P_i), P_i) \mid i = 1, \ldots, k\}$ be the entries in P such that $RECT(P_i) \cap W \neq \phi$.
  - Release $\rho(P)$.
  - For all entries E_i found above, continue the search in parallel invoking $R2.Look(W \cap RECT(P_i), P_i)$.
- if P is a leaf node **then**
  - For all objects whose MBR's overlap with W, return their object ids.
  - Release $\rho(P)$.

4.2 Insert

Insertion under the modify-lock method can be carried out much as under the simple-lock method, except for the locking operations involved. In descending the tree in the first phase, at each visited node, we first acquire an ϵ lock, update the MBR of the node if needed, then choose the next node to visit, and finally release the lock. The reason why we update the MBR of a visited node in the first phase is to allow subsequent search operations to find the newly inserted object.

If no overflow occurs at the leaf node, the second phase is not necessary. As we mentioned earlier, we permit temporary overflows and delay the second phase of an insert operation by simply adding a new entry to the maintenance queue, Q. The *Maintain* process will use Q to reorganize the tree periodically. More formally, *Insert*(O, R) under the modify-lock method is carried out as follows, where E_O be the entry representing object O.

R2.Insert(O, R)

1. Acquire $\epsilon(TC_{in})$, increment TC_{in} by 1, then release $\epsilon(TC_{in})$.
2. $L := R2.Select(RECT(O), R)$ to search for a leaf node to which to add the object O.
3. Acquire $\epsilon(L)$, add entry E_O to L, then release $\epsilon(L)$.
4. **if** $OVERFL(L)$ **then**
   - Acquire $\epsilon(Q)$, $APPEND(Q, L)$, then release $\epsilon(Q)$.
5. Acquire $\epsilon(TC_{out})$, increment TC_{out} by 1, then release $\epsilon(TC_{out})$.

R2.Select(W, P)

1. Acquire $\rho(P)$.
2. **if** $RECT(P)$ does not contain W **then**
   - Upgrade $\rho(P)$ to $\epsilon(P)$.
   - Enlarge $RECT(P)$ to accommodate W.
   - Downgrade $\epsilon(P)$ to $\rho(P)$.
3. **if** P is a leaf node **then** release $\rho(P)$ and return P
   else
   - Find an entry $E_s = (RECT(P_s), P_s)$ in P, where $RECT(P_s)$ requires the smallest enlargement to include W. Resolve ties by choosing E_s with the smallest $RECT(P_s)$.
   - Release $\rho(P)$.
   - Continue the selection with $R2.Select(W, P_s)$.

4.3 Delete

We carry out the delete operation using the 'mark-and-remove' technique. If we imitate the way this technique is used in the B-tree, we should shrink bounding rectangles during the first phase of the delete operation, as we search for the object to be deleted. However, this cannot be done, since, while we are searching for the object to be deleted, we don't know which search path will lead to that object. On the other hand, if we don't shrink them, the bounding rectangles associated with some nodes may no longer be their MBR's and may contain a great deal of dead space, degrading subsequent search performance. To resolve this dilemma, we delay updating bounding rectangles, but not too long. We use a queue, DQ, to record the deleted nodes whose effect on some bounding rectangles has not been reflected. Let DC denote the number of objects in DQ. If DC exceeds a certain limit, $MAX_{deleted}$, then the $Maintain$ process recomputes the affected MBR's.

A reorganization of the R-tree may be necessitated by underflows. When an underflow occurs at some node, we append the node to the maintenance queue, Q. As we discuss in the next subsection, this will be detected by the $Maintain$ process, which is constantly checking if Q is empty.

More formally, $Delete(O, R)$ under the modify-lock method is carried out as follows.

$R2.Delete(O, R)$

1. Acquire $\epsilon(TC_{in})$, increment TC_{in} by 1, then release $\epsilon(TC_{in})$.
2. $L := R2.Find(RECT(O), R)$[5] to search for the leaf node containing the object O.
3. $RECT.old := RECT(L)$.
4. Acquire $\epsilon(L)$, remove the entry representing object O from L, and set $RECT(L)$ to the MBR of the resulting L.
5. Acquire $\epsilon(DC)$.
6. **if** ($UNDERFL(L)$) or ($DC \geq MAX_{deleted}$) **then**
   - Acquire $\epsilon(Q)$, $APPEND(Q, L)$, then release $\epsilon(Q)$.
   else if ($RECT.old \neq RECT(L)$) **then**
   - Acquire $\epsilon(DQ)$, $APPEND(DQ, L)$, then release $\epsilon(DQ)$.
   - Increment DC by 1.
7. Release $\epsilon(DC)$ and $\epsilon(L)$.
8. Acquire $\epsilon(TC_{out})$, increment TC_{out} by 1, then release $\epsilon(TC_{out})$.

4.4 Maintain

The system process $Maintain$ checks the maintenance queue Q periodically. When Q becomes non-empty, $Maintain$ prepares for reorganization of the R-tree by waiting until no operation is accessing the tree. For this purpose, it first acquires and holds an exclusive lock on TC_{in}. This prevents other transactions from starting a new access to the R-tree. It then compares the values of TC_{in} and TC_{out}. If they are the same, then all previous operations accessing the tree have

---

[5] The operations of $R2.Find$ is the same as $R2.Look$ except it returns the node which contains object O.

completed and it can proceed to do the reorganization. Otherwise, it releases the lock on TC_{out} and try again later.

When all previous operations have completed, *Maintain* appends DQ to Q. *Maintain* then takes nodes from Q one after another and processes them accordingly to the reason why they are in the queue (overflow, underflow, shrunken MBR). When all the nodes in Q have been processed, *Maintain* releases the locks on TC_{in} and TC_{out} to allow resumption of operations on the R-tree.

R2.Maintain()

- **while** (*TRUE*) **do**
    1. Acquire $\rho(Q)$.
    2. **while** (Q is empty) **do**
       {Release $\rho(Q)$, Sleep a while, Acquire $\rho(Q)$} End **do**
    3. Release $\rho(Q)$.
    4. Acquire $\epsilon(TC_{in})$.
    5. Acquire $\epsilon(TC_{out})$.
    6. **if** $TC_{in} = TC_{out}$ **then**
        - Reset $TC_{in} := TC_{out} := 0$.
        - Append DQ to Q and empty DQ.
        - $P :=$ The first node in Q.
        - **while** ($P \neq NULL$) **do**
            * **if** $UNDERFL(P)$ then re-distribute entries of P into its siblings.
              if $PARENT(P)$ underflows as a result **then** $APPEND(Q,PARENT(P))$.
            * **if** $OVERFL(P)$ then split P into P and P'. Add a new entry for P' to $PARENT(P)$.
              if $PARENT(P)$ overflows **then** $APPEND(Q,PARENT(P))$.
            * Update the MBR's of P, its siblings and $PARENT(P)$, if necessary.
            * $P := NEXT(Q)$.
        - End **do**.
       else
        - Release $\epsilon(TC_{out})$.
        - Sleep a while.
        - Go back to step 5.
    7. Release $\epsilon(TC_{in})$ and $\epsilon(TC_{out})$.
- End **do**.

5   Lock-Coupling Method and R-Couple Tree

The lock-coupling method, the third and the last method we investigate, was originally developed for the B-tree by Bayer and Schkolnick [2]. In this method, a search or an update operation locks children of a node before releasing its lock on the node itself. Recently, Otoo has suggested to use the "warning lock", called the ω lock, for update operations to improve concurrency [8]. We adopt his idea in carrying out insert and delete operations. The ϵ lock is an exclusive lock which allows an operation to modify a node and is not compatible with any other locks. The compatibility among the three locks we use is shown in Figure 4. An ω lock allows its holder a read but not write access. However, unlike a ρ lock, an ω lock is not compatible with another ω lock. We require that all locks be requested in a top-down, left-to-right (among the children of a node) fashion. This order of lock acquisition guarantees deadlock freedom.

	ρ	ω	ϵ
ρ	1	1	0
ω	1	0	0
ϵ	0	0	0

Fig. 4. Lock compatibility matrix.

5.1 Search

As always, a search operation starts at the root of a tree and descends to the leaf level. At each visited node, a ρ lock on it must be acquired and held until the ρ locks on the child nodes to be visited are acquired. If the ρ lock on the parent is released after a ρ lock on the first child is acquired, the parent may be updated before a ρ lock on the second child is acquired. This will cause an incorrect result. To implement this rule, we introduce a lockable variable, $Count$, which is initialized to the number of subsearch operations initiated at a node. It is decremented by one whenever a child node is ρ-locked. When it reaches 0, the ρ lock on the parent is released.

More formally, $Search(W, R)$ under the lock-coupling method is carried out by calling $R3.Search(W, R, Count)$ given below, after setting $Count := 0$. $Count$ in the following procedure is a call-by-reference parameter.

$R3.Search(W, P, Count)$

1. Acquire $\rho(P)$.
2. **if** $PARENT(P) \neq NULL$ (i.e., $P \neq root$) **then**
   - Acquire $\epsilon(Count)$.
   - Decrement $Count$ by one.
   - **if** $(Count = 0)$ **then** release $\rho(PARENT(P))$.
   - Release $\epsilon(Count)$.
3. **if** P is a non-leaf node **then**
   - Let $\{E_i = (RECT(P_i), P_i) \mid i = 1, \ldots, k\}$ be the entries in P such that $RECT(P_i) \cap W \neq \phi$.
   - **if** $(k > 0)$ **then**
     • $MyCount := k$.

- For all entries E_i found above, continue the search in parallel invoking $R3.DoSearch(W \cap RECT(P_i), P_i, MyCount)$.
  else release $\rho(P)$.
4. **if** P is a leaf node **then**
   - For all objects whose MBR's overlap with W, return their object ids.
   - Release $\rho(P)$.

5.2 Insert

As with the insert operation in the simple-lock method, we carry out an insert operation in two phases. During the first phase, we locate the leaf node to which to add the new object. The path in the tree we take is called the **insertion path**. After adding the entry representing a new object to a leaf node (i.e., in the second phase), we may have to perform some maintenance operations by tracing back the insertion path to

1. reorganize the tree, and/or
2. enlarge the MBR's of some nodes.

In the modify-lock method discussed in the previous section, we delegated these maintenance chores to a system process, called *Maintain*, which periodically carried them out. This meant that they were carried out after some delays. In this section, we take a different approach and carry them out as a part of the insert operation without help from a system process.

Let us examine in more detail the maintenance action 1. stated above. If a node visited in the first phase is full, then there is a possibility that it may be split during the second phase. If a split does occur, the parent of the node will have a new entry. This information must be available to the subsequent operations. This situation also occurs in performing an insert operation on a B-tree. So we can use a similar solution. Namely, in the first phase of an insert operation, we ω-lock the first full node encountered in the insertion path, and its parent, if any. Thereafter, we ω-lock consecutive full nodes. Once a non-full node is encountered along the insertion path, we release all the existing ω-locks and restart the above procedure from scratch. So, when we reach a full leaf, we will have ω-locked a string of nodes at the end of the insertion path. This string starts with a non-full node (with one exception mentioned below) and is followed by one or more full nodes including the full leaf. During the second phase, splitting will propagate upwards up to that only one ω-locked non-full node, but will terminate there. If the root node is full, it is possible that this string consists only of full nodes, and a new root will be created in the second phase.

Let us call a node **unsafe** if (with the currently available information) there is a possibility that maintenance operations in the second phase may reach that node. What we described above can be restated as the following rule:

Safety rule: In the first phase, ω-lock the unsafe nodes along the insertion path, and release ω-locks from nodes as they become safe (i.e., not unsafe.)

There is another reason why a node may be unsafe; it is due to the possibility of maintenance action 2. mentioned above. In the first phase, the MBR's of some nodes will change if the object to be inserted covers additional area. If the bounding rectangle of a node is updated in the first phase, it may be changed by a subsequent delete operation (see the subsection on delete operation), which may cause a later search operation to have an incorrect answer. This problem is solved by delaying the update; instead of updating the MBR of the visited node immediately, we record the MBR of the object to be inserted in a data structure, called *Pending*, associated with the node. We call the MBR stored in *Pending* a **pending MBR**. The pending MBR is read during the second phase to enlarge the node's bounding rectangle. In the mean time, before the second phase of the insertion is completed, subsequent search operations look at both the bounding rectangle and the pending MBR of the node. (The search procedure described in the previous section should be modified accordingly.) During the second phase, we backtrack and enlarge the MBR's of those nodes with a pending MBR. In order to do this without interference, these nodes need to be ω-locked in the first phase. Incidentally, observe that, if a node has a pending MBR, then all its descendants along the insertion path will also have the same pending MBR. The safety rule we stated above covers all unsafe nodes. Note that once a node obtains a pending MBR, the node will remain unsafe until its MBR is updated.

As an illustration, consider Figure 5, where an insert operation, I_1, is visiting node B in its first phase. It first acquires an ω-lock on B to prevent other operations from changing B. If B's MBR will expand as a result of I_1, the ω-lock on B is upgraded to an ϵ-lock, to update B's *Pending* information. Before I_1 visits node C, it downgrades the lock on B to an ω-lock. If B's MBR will not expand, on the other hand, B is safe when C is non-full and the ω-lock on B is simply released. If B's MBR will not expand but node C is full, then node B is unsafe. In this case, an ω-lock on it must be maintained.

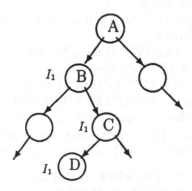

Fig. 5. Insert operation using the lock-coupling method.

During the second phase, after inserting the entry representing a new object into the selected leaf node, the insert operation backtracks along the insertion path to update MBR's and/or to split nodes. In Figure 5, suppose node D overflows, after a new object has been added to a leaf node. Before splitting D, we upgrade the ω-locks on nodes C and D to ϵ-locks. If D is a non-leaf node, we also ϵ-lock D's children,[6] because their parent pointers need to be updated due to the split. After the split, we release the ϵ-locks on nodes C, D, and D's children, if any. We continue the update, level by level, until we reach the first unsafe node on the insertion path.

More formally, $Insert(O, R)$ under the lock-coupling method is carried out as follows, where $E_O = (RECT(O), O)$.

R3.Insert(O, R)

1. $FREE(\pi)$. (π is a stack.)
2. $L := R3.Select(RECT(O), R, \pi)$, which returns an ω-locked leaf node, L, in which to place the entry E_O. Stack π is changed by call-by-reference and, on return, gives a stack of unsafe nodes, which forms a subpath of the insertion path.
3. Upgrade $\omega(L)$ to $\epsilon(L)$, and add entry E_O to node L.
4. Downgrade $\epsilon(L)$ to $\omega(L)$.
5. $R3.Update(L, \pi)$.

In the following procedure, the parameter $Path$ is a stack, and we define $RECT(NULL) = \phi$. Note that, when $R3.Select(W, P, Path)$ is recursively called, $PARENT(P)$ is ω-locked, and on exit, P is ω-locked and either $PARENT(P)$ is placed on $Path$ or $\omega(PARENT(P))$ has been released.

R3.Select(W, P, Path)

1. Acquire $\omega(P)$.
2. if $PARENT(P) \neq NULL$ then
   - $unsafe := 0$.
   - if $FULL(P)$ then $unsafe := 1$.
   - if $W \not\subseteq RECT(PARENT(P))$ then $unsafe := unsafe + 2$.
   - if $(unsafe \geq 2)$[7] then
     - Upgrade $\omega(PARENT(P))$ to $\epsilon(PARENT(P))$.
     - Put W in $PARENT(P).Pending$.
     - Downgrade $\epsilon(PARENT(P))$ to $\omega(PARENT(P))$.
   - if $unsafe \geq 1$ then $PUSH(PARENT(P), Path)$.
   - if $(unsafe = 0)$ then release ω-lock on $PARENT(P)$.
   - if $(unsafe = 0)$ and $(Path \neq \Lambda)$ then release all ω-locks on nodes which do not have a pending MBR in $Path$, and remove them from $Path$.

---

[6] The top-to-bottom, left-to-right locking order should be used here in upgrading the ω-locks on C, D, and D's children to prevent deadlock.

[7] As commented earlier, once a node has a pending MBR, all its descendants along the insertion path will have the same pending MBR.

3. **if** P is a non-leaf node **then**
   - Find an entry $E_s = (RECT(P_s), P_s)$ in P, where $RECT(P_s)$ requires the smallest enlargement to include W. Resolve ties by choosing E_s with the smallest $RECT(P_s)$.
   - Continue the selection with $R3.Select(W, P_s, Path)$.
   else return P.

When the following procedure is called, unless $P = NULL$, P is ω-locked, and when $PARENT(P) \neq NULL$ (i.e., $P \neq root$) or $Path \neq \Lambda$, $PARENT(P)$ is ω-locked.

$R3.Update(P, Path)$

1. **if** $P = NULL$ **then** return.
2. **if** $OVERFL(P)$ **then**
   - **if** $PARENT(P)$ exists **then** upgrade $\omega(PARENT(P))$ to $\epsilon(PARENT(P))$
     else
     - Create a new root.
     - ϵ-lock the new root.
     - Make it $PARENT(P)$.
     - Add entry E_P representing P to $PARENT(P)$.
   - Upgrade $\omega(P)$ to $\epsilon(P)$.
   - Split P into P and P', and update their MBR's.
   - Add entry $E_{P'}$ representing P' to $PARENT(P)$ and update its MBR.
   - **if** P and P' has k children together, $P_1 \ldots, P_k$ **then**
     - acquire $\epsilon(P_i)$ for $i = 1, \ldots, k$.
     - Update the parent pointer in P_i for $i = 1, \ldots, k$.
     - Release $\epsilon(P_i)$ for $i = 1, \ldots, k$.
3. **if** $P.Pending \neq \phi$ **then**
   - **if** not $OVERFL(P)$ **then** $\epsilon(P)$.
   - Update the MBR of P and empty $P.Pending$.
4. Release $\epsilon(P)$.
5. $P := POP(Path)$.
6. $R3.Update(P, Path)$.

5.3 Delete

We use two phases to carry out a delete operation. The first phase is to locate the leaf node which points to the object to be deleted. This phase is almost identical to $R3.Search$. (Note that the condition $W \subseteq RECT(P_i)$ should now be used here in Steps 3 and 4, instead of $RECT(P_i) \cap W \neq \phi$.) Only ρ locks are held on at most two levels of non-leaf nodes, and MBR's are not shrunk in this phase. Once the object has been found, it is removed and the tree is reorganized in the second phase.

In the second phase, we backtrack the R-tree if needed. We now face two problems. The first is how to deal with concurrent insertions and changing parent pointers. The delete operation needs to be able to find the path along which to propagate the change up the tree. The second problem is the potentially conflicting lock requests with other updating operations. We need to ensure lock requests do not cause deadlocks.

To solve the first problem, we maintain another piece of information at each node of the R-tree, i.e., the parent pointer. The pointer is updated whenever its parent is involved in splits or merges. The second problem is solved by ordering the nodes to be locked and have the *Delete* algorithm release all of its locks from time to time. The ordering ensures the serializability among delete operations, and the releasing of locks permits insert operations to acquire locks which may be held by a delete operation. During deletion, a node is not removed immediately because there can be other delete operations referencing it. They are marked as deleted and are later garbage-collected periodically.

More formally, *Delete*(O, R) under the lock-coupling method is carried out as follows.

R3.Delete(O, R)

1. $L := R3.Find(RECT(O), R, 0)$[8] to locate the leaf node which contains entry E_O pointing to object O to be deleted.
2. Acquire $\epsilon(L)$, delete entry E_O which points to object O, and release $\epsilon(L)$.
3. *R3.Condense*(L).

R3.Condense(L)

1. Acquire $\rho(L)$.
2. **if** L is marked as deleted **then** release $\rho(L)$ and return.
3. $P := PARENT(L)$.
4. Release $\rho(L)$.
5. **if** $(P = NULL)$ **then**
   - Acquire $\epsilon(L)$.
   - Update the MBR of L.
   - **if** $((L$ has only one child$)$ and $(L$ is a non-leaf node$))$ **then**
     - Let L_c be the node of the single child.
     - Make L_c the new root of the tree.
     - Mark L as deleted.
   - Release $\epsilon(L)$ and return.
6. Acquire $\epsilon(P)$.
7. Acquire $\epsilon(L)$.
8. **if** $(P \neq PARENT(L))$ **then**
   - Release $\epsilon(L)$ and $\epsilon(P)$
   - Goto Step 1.
9. **if** $($not $UNDERFL(L))$ and $(RECT(P - L)$ [9] $= RECT(P))$ **then**

---

[8] Its operations are similar to *R3.Search* except it returns the node containing entry E_O pointing to object O.

[9] $RECT(P - L)$ represents the change in the bounding rectangle when a child node L is removed from node P.

- Release $\epsilon(L)$ and $\epsilon(P)$, and return.
10. if (not $UNDERFL(L)$) then
    - Update the MBR of P.
    else
    - Acquire $\epsilon(L^j)$ for $j = 1, 2, \ldots, m$, where L^j's are the m siblings of L.
    - if L is a non-leaf node then acquire $\epsilon(L_i)$ for $i = 1, 2, \ldots, k$, where L_i's are the k children of L.
    - Merge the nodes by re-distributing the entries of L among L^j's.
    - Update the MBR's of P and L^j's.
    - Update the parent pointers in L_i's.
    - Mark L as a deleted node.
    - Release $\epsilon(L^j)$ for $j = 1, \ldots, m$.
    - if L is a non-leaf node then release $\epsilon(L_i)$ for $i = 1, \ldots, k$.
11. Release $\epsilon(L)$ and $\epsilon(P)$.
12. $R3.Condense(P)$.

6 Implementations

To assess the performance of the three concurrency control methods for R-trees described in the previous three sections, we have implemented the algorithms in SR[1], which is a language for writing distributed programs. A resource in SR is similar to a class in an object-oriented language like C++. SR also supports dynamic process creation, message passing, multicast, and semaphores.

In our implementations, we use the client-server paradigm. The server is implemented as a set of multi-threaded processes to serve *insert*, *search*, and *delete* requests on an R-tree. A new process is created to provide a service whenever a request is received. The scheduling of the processes is handled by the runtime library of the SR language.

We ran our simulation programs on a SUN SPARC 2 Workstation with 32 Mbytes of main memory. In our simulations, we generated only search and insert requests. The reason for this decision is because we thought deletions and insertions required much the same service. We were mainly interested in measuring the search performance under different locking methods, since, presumably, they comprise the majority of operations in most applications. Batches of pre-generated requests, composed of different numbers of insertions and searches, were tested against R-trees of different sizes. For each batch, we calculated the average response time (*atime*) of all the search operations.

In each simulation run, initially, an R-tree was created with a data file containing only insert requests. The locations and sizes of the inserted rectangles were generated randomly within a 2-dimensional space which measured 1000 × 1000. The width and the height of each rectangle were generated using a uniform distribution over the range $[1, 10]$. The maximum number of entries in each node, M, was set to 3, so that there would be sufficient levels in the tree without too many nodes. In splitting a node, the *linear splitting strategy* of [6] was used in all three programs.

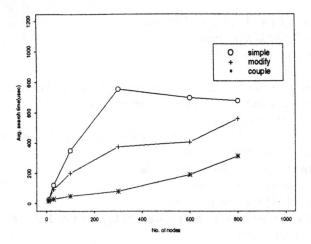

Fig. 6. Search performance with one insert operation (Avg. search time in μseconds versus no. of nodes).

For each of 6 different initial trees (of sizes 10, 30, 100, 300, 600 and 800), we ran simulations with two different request batches, yielding 12 values of *atime* for each locking method. The first batch consisted of one insert operation followed by 9 search operations. The width and the height of the inserted object as well as the search windows of the search operations were generated using a uniform distribution over the range [1, 10]. As expected, the results in Figure 6 show that the **lock-coupling** method performed best and the **modify-lock** method performed better than the **simple-lock** method. The second batch we tested consisted of 5 insert operations followed by 5 search operations. The results shown in Figure 7 indicate that the search times for this batch are generally shorter than those in Figure 6. Among the three locking methods, the **lock-coupling** again performed best.

The third set of simulation experiments were carried out with a fixed initial tree containing 500 objects. Seven batches, which consisted of 1 to 7 insertions among 10 operations, were tested. Every insert operation added an object at the same location with the same bounding rectangle. With these experiments, we intended to find search performance when nodes in tree are being split or merged. Figure 8 shows the results. Again, the **lock-coupling** outperformed the other two methods. The relative performance of the **lock-simple** method and the **lock-modify** method was not clear-cut, especially when a small number of insertions were involved. It could be due to the extra overhead of lock management and the *Maintain* process in the **lock-modify** method.

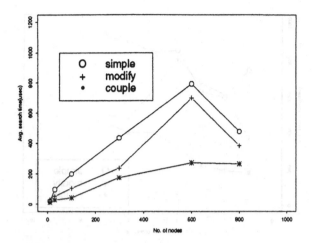

Fig. 7. Search performance with 5 insert operations. (Avg. search time in μseconds versus no. of nodes).

7 Conclusion

In this paper, we have investigated concurrency control for accesses to the R-tree. We examined three different locking methods. The first uses a single lock to lock the entire tree; this is a slight extension to the sequential access method, since more than one search operation can access the tree by locking it in the share mode. The second method locks the whole tree only when the splitting or merging of nodes in the tree is required; otherwise, individual nodes of the tree are locked to avoid conflicting operations on them. The third method adapts the **lock-coupling** technique often used for the B-tree.

In connection with the above three locking methods, we have discussed in detail three common user operations, **search**, **insert**, and **delete**, on the R-tree. System operations which handle node overflows and underflows were also discussed. We have implemented our algorithms in the SR distributed programming language and carried out a number of simulation experiments. Simulation results indicate that, for the data that we used, the **lock-coupling** method has the best search performance.

References

1. G.R. Andrew. *The distributed programming language SR*, Software-Practice and Experience, Vol. 12, No. 8 (Aug. 1982), pp. 719-754.
2. R. Bayer and M. Schkolnick. *Concurrency of operations on B-trees*, Acta Inf., Vol. 9(1977), pp. 1-21.
3. P. Bernstein, et al., *Concurrency Control and Recovery in Database Systems*, Addison-Wesley, 1987.

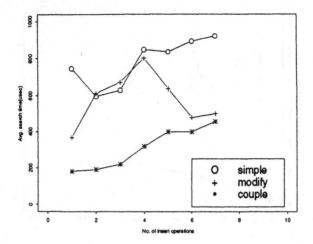

Fig. 8. Search performance with an R-tree containing 500 objects (Avg. search time in μseconds versus no. of insert operations).

4. D. Comer. *The ubiquitous B-tree*, ACM Computer Surveys, Vol. 11, No. 2 (1979), pp. 121-138.
5. C.S. Ellis. *Concurrent search and inserts in 2-3 trees*, Acta Inf. Vol. 14, No. 1 (1980), pp. 63-86.
6. A. Guttman. *R-Trees: A dynamic index structure for spatial searching*, SIGMOD Record, Vol. 14, No. 2 (June 1984), pp. 47-57.
7. I. Kamel and C. Faloutsos. *Parallel R-trees*, CS-TR-2820, UMIACS-TR-92-1, Computer Science Technical Report Series, University of Maryland, College Park, MD, 1992.
8. E.J. Otoo. *Efficient concurrency control protocols for B-tree indexes*, SCS-TR-166, Jan. 1990, School of Computer Science, Carleton University, Ottawa, Canada.
9. H. Samet. *Hierarchical representations of collections of small rectangles*, ACM Computing Surveys, Vol. 20, No. 4 (Dec. 1988), pp. 271-309.

A Spatial Data Model and a Topological Sweep Algorithm for Map Overlay

Ulrich Finke, Klaus Hinrichs

FB 15, Informatik, Westfälische Wilhelms-Universität
Einsteinstr. 62, D - 48149 Münster, Germany
E-Mail: finke, hinrichs@math.uni-muenster.de

Abstract. One of the most general query problems in spatial information processing is the map overlay operation that computes from one or more thematic map layers a new map by using an overlay function. Existing algorithms for vector-based map overlay operations suffer from one or more of the following disadvantages: lacking generality, inefficiency or poor adaptability to existing GIS-Systems. Furthermore only few proposals for parallel implementations of this operation have been made. In this paper we present a model for planar subdivisions similar to the well-known arc model. This model can be easily adapted to existing spatial access methods. Our overlay algorithm uses an overlay function and includes a fine-grain parallelism. The homogeneous structure of input and output maps allows pipelining of map overlay operations (coarse-grain parallelism).

Keywords: Geographic information systems, cartographic modeling, map overlay, computational geometry, topological plane sweep, parallel processing.

1   Introduction

The computation of new scenes or maps from existing information is a kernel operation in every spatial information system. The most general operation for this task is the map overlay [13]: Given one or more thematic map layers the overlay operation computes a new map in which the thematic attribute of each location is a function of the thematic attributes of the corresponding locations in the input maps. This overlay function enables manifold applications of the map overlay operation. Besides composing, overlaying or superimposing thematic maps it is also possible to update maps by inserting, deleting or merging given regions [3] or to perform simple queries like window- and region-queries.

In the following we give some criteria which we will use for classifying existing map overlay algorithms and their underlying data models.

Data Format: Map overlay algorithms can be raster or vector based. For raster data the overlay operation can be easily computed. However, its efficiency depends crucially on how far redundant function evaluations can be avoided. Degenerate configurations and limited accuracy make the computation of the overlay for vector data difficult. In the following we will only consider algorithms for vector data.

Dimension: The simplest overlay operation is one-dimensional and intersects one or more interval sets. The overlay problem can be extended to arbitrary dimensions, but in most applications only the two- or three-dimensional cases are of interest.

Overlay Function: Map overlay algorithms which do not use an overlay function only have to compute intersections of spatial subdivisions given by different map layers. Each resulting region inherits its thematic attributes from all its defining regions in the different map layers. Map overlay algorithms applying an overlay function do not only have to compute intersections of spatial subdivisions, but also have to merge resulting regions which have been assigned the same attribute value by the overlay function.

Flexibility: An important role in the design and implementation of algorithms for map operations plays the underlying spatial data model. On one hand, this data model has to support efficient map operations, on the other hand it should facilitate the integration of these algorithms in different environments, i.e. the model should easily adapt to different access structures for secondary storage. These requirements seem hard to realize, since many algorithms access data in a way not supported by the underlying secondary storage structure and therefore require many redundant time-consuming disk accesses.

Efficiency: The complexity of map overlay algorithms is defined by using different parameters describing the amount of input data, i.e. the input map layers, and the output overlay map. Since our primitive geometric objects in the input map layers can be defined by points we use the total number n of points as parameter to capture the size of the input data. To simplify the determination of the output size we assume that the overlay function is information preserving and therefore no merging of regions occurs. Furthermore we assume that the time and space needed to evaluate the overlay function is constant. Since all n input points are included in the output the total complexity of a map overlay algorithm is measured in terms of n and the size of the additionally generated information contained in the output which is given by the number k of intersection points between the region boundaries of the input map layers. In the worst case k may grow quadratically in n, i.e. $k = O(n^2)$.

Parallelism: The increase of remote sensing data and the growing number and complexity of problems to be solved require more and more computing power. This increasing demand for more computing power and the already foreseeable limits for a further increase of computing speed using conventional architectures more and more lead to a departure from sequential program execution towards parallel solutions. The parallelization of raster based map overlay algorithms is straightforward. Unfortunately this is not true for vector based algorithms since the inhomogenous structure of vector based data makes it difficult to partition the data and requires more communication between interacting parallel processes.

In the following we discuss some well-known algorithms which can be used to solve the map overlay problem.

The algorithm described in [2] can be applied to solve the map overlay problem for vector based data. It is based on the plane sweep principle and computes the intersections of n line segments in time $O((n+k) \cdot \log n)$ and space $O(n+k)$ where k denotes the number of intersecting pairs of line segments.

In [9] Nievergelt and Preparata apply the plane sweep technique to solve the map overlay problem for planar maps that consist of simply connected regions. The algorithm uses $O((n+k) \cdot \log n)$ time and $O(n+k)$ space. If all the regions are convex, their complexity is reduced to $O(n \cdot \log n + k)$ and $O(n)$, respectively. Guibas and Seidel [6] present a topological plane sweep to process the overlay of two convex subdivisions if the subdivisions are represented by some suitable planar graph structure, e.g. the quad edge structure. Their algorithm runs in optimal time $O(n+k)$. Neither [9] nor [6] consider overlay functions, integration in spatial information systems and parallelization.

In [11] a plane sweep algorithm is suggested which uses the method of attribute propagation and line segment classification. This technique works with a boolean overlay function. The time complexity is unfortunately worse than that of [6].

In [7] and [8] Kriegel et al. show how to generalize the algorithm presented in [9] to support an overlay function and how to integrate it in a geographic data base system. The maps are partitioned in strips and stored on secondary storage by using spatial access methods (e.g. buddy tree, R^*-tree). The authors suggest a synchronised parallel strip processing of the plane sweep. Their algorithm uses time $O((n+k) \cdot \log n)$. The static subdivision of maps in strips may lead to a loss of performance for worst case data distributions.

Orenstein proposes in [10] another technique to apply spatial access methods. In a preprocessing step all regions of a map are approximated by axis parallel boxes according to a space filling Z-curve. Every box is uniquely identified by one Z-value which can be inserted into a one-dimensional index structure, e.g. B-tree. The map overlay is similar to merging of linear sorted lists; it uses the Z-order as a filter to minimize the number of tuples of non-intersecting regions. This technique is a hybrid: it applies raster methods to vector data and can be applied to an arbitrary number of dimensions. Because of the decomposition the performance depends on the redundancy of region representations and can only be expressed empirically.

Our algorithm is similar to a topological sweep algorithm for which the sweep line corresponds to the y-maximum of the unprocessed boundary curves. In a single step our algorithm processes a local part of the maximum by transferring it to the overlay map and replacing it by a new local y-maximum of unprocessed boundary curves.

The paper proceeds as follows. In section 2 we explain the spatial data model, which is a slight modification of the well-known arc model. In section 3 we give a description of our map overlay algorithm. Section 4 shows how to parallelize the algorithm. Section 5 concludes the paper.

2   Spatial Data Model

A spatial data model serves to represent spatial objects which are given by geometric properties, e.g. shape, location, orientation, as well as non-geometric properties, e.g. color, material, name [3].

Our data model is a slight modification of the well-known arc model for the representation of maps: The boundary curves (e.g. polygonal lines, Bezier-curves or B-splines) of all regions are divided into *arcs* which are *monotone* in the x-direction, i.e. any vertical line may intersect such an arc at most once. Arcs may intersect only in their end points. We assume that the left end point belongs to an arc but not the right end point. Each arc obtains a thematic attribute variable which is assigned the value of a thematic attribute or a reference to the region lying below the arc. In the following we assume that the attribute variable allows to access the arguments needed for computing the overlay function in constant time. In addition we assign to each arc four references to neighboring arcs. These references allow to determine all the *direct ancestors* and *descendants* of an arc: An arc *d* is a *direct descendant* of another arc *a* if there exists a vertical line *V* intersecting *d* below *a*, and no other arc intersects *V* between its intersections with *a* and *d*. Arc *a* is a *direct ancestor* of *d* if *d* is *direct descendant* of *a*.

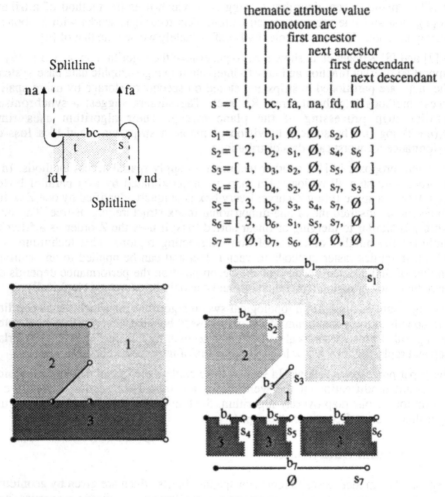

thematic attribute value
  monotone arc
    first ancestor
      next ancestor
        first descendant
          next descendant

$s = [\ t,\quad bc,\quad fa,\quad na,\quad fd,\quad nd\ ]$

$s_1 = [\ 1,\quad b_1,\quad \emptyset,\quad \emptyset,\quad s_2,\quad \emptyset\ ]$
$s_2 = [\ 2,\quad b_2,\quad s_1,\quad \emptyset,\quad s_4,\quad s_6\ ]$
$s_3 = [\ 1,\quad b_3,\quad s_2,\quad \emptyset,\quad s_5,\quad \emptyset\ ]$
$s_4 = [\ 3,\quad b_4,\quad s_2,\quad \emptyset,\quad s_7,\quad s_3\ ]$
$s_5 = [\ 3,\quad b_5,\quad s_3,\quad s_4,\quad s_7,\quad \emptyset\ ]$
$s_6 = [\ 3,\quad b_6,\quad s_1,\quad s_5,\quad s_7,\quad \emptyset\ ]$
$s_7 = [\ \emptyset,\quad b_7,\quad s_6,\quad \emptyset,\quad \emptyset,\quad \emptyset\ ]$

Fig. 1. Spatial data model

More specifically, the four references assigned to an arc *a* are defined as follows:

fd specifies the *first descendant*, which is the direct descendant below the left end point.

fa specifies the *first ancestor*, which is the direct ancestor above the right end point.

nd specifies the *next descendant* of *fa* to the right of *a*.

na specifies the *next ancestor* of *fd* to the left of *a*.

An arc together with its four references is called a *sector*. The example of Fig. 1 illustrates our data model using a simple map and shows that verticals are represented implicitly by change of thematic attribute value.

The list *LD* of all direct descendants of a sector can be determined from left to right by starting with *fd* and then following the sequence of *nd* references. The list *LA* of direct ancestors can be determined from right to left by starting with *fa* and then following the sequence of *na* references.

If a direct ancestor or descendant of a sector *s* is not contained in *s*'s ancestor list *LA* or descendant list *LD* then the sector *s* must be split. Fig. 2 shows the worst case that a sector triggers a split of two other sectors.

The storage requirement for this data model grows linearly with the number of points *n* since the number of sectors n_s is bounded by *n*.

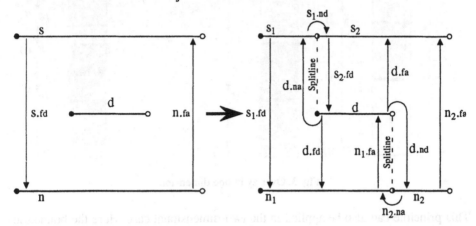

Fig. 2. Splitting a sector

3 A Topological Sweep Algorithm for Map Overlay

We will first present the principles underlying our map overlay algorithm for the one-dimensional case; this algorithm will then be extended to two dimensions.

3.1 Principle of the Overlay Algorithm

Assume that a set of one-dimensional intervals is given as a singly linked linear list of pairs consisting of a thematic attribute value and an upper interval boundary (Fig. 3).

The overlay algorithm for one-dimensional interval sets extends the merge algorithm for sorted lists by taking into account the overlay function. The resulting interval set is computed iteratively from top to bottom by adding the topmost item to the result set. A next interval item *n* is determined by

- an interval boundary *b* which is given as the maximum of the upper boundaries of all top-most intervals in the interval sets which have not yet been passed by the merge process, and by
- a thematic attribute value which is obtained by applying the overlay function to the attribute values valid directly below *b* in the different interval sets.

This item is added to the output list if its interval boundary *b* is necessary, i.e. its attribute value is different from the attribute value of the last interval item which has been added to the output list. The process terminates after a pair (∅, ...) has been added to the output list. Fig. 3 shows the resulting interval set C when applying this algorithm to interval sets A and B using the overlay function 'maximum'.

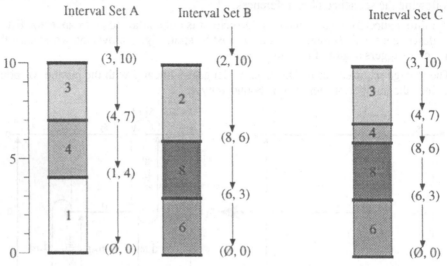

Fig. 3. Overlay in one dimension

This principle can also be applied in the two-dimensional case. Here the boundaries are not scalar values but the arcs defined in Section 2, i.e. they consist of polygonal line, Bezier-curve or B-spline segments in the plane. In each input map we consider the *map maximum*, i.e. the maximum with respect to the y-coordinate of all those arcs or parts of the arcs in the input map which have not yet been processed. The maximum with respect to the y-coordinate of all these map maxima is called the *overlay maximum* (Fig. 4). Each arc in the overlay maximum is part of a unique arc in one of the input maps. The thematic attribute value of an arc in this overlay maximum is obtained by applying the overlay function to the attribute values valid for the corresponding arcs in the different input maps.

The map overlay algorithm for two-dimensional maps works as follows:

- Transfer the overlay maximum to the overlay map:
  Insert the arcs of the current overlay maximum as descendants of the previously transferred arcs. Arcs which have the same attribute value as their ancestor are not necessary and can therefore be ignored.

- Compute the new overlay maximum:
  We consider all arcs of the previous overlay maximum as being processed. For each map the new map maximum is obtained from the old map maximum by replacing those parts which are equal to the processed arcs of the old overlay maximum by their direct descendants. The new overlay maximum can now be computed from these updated map maxima.

This algorithm produces the correct results but may be quite inefficient as the example in Fig. 5 shows.

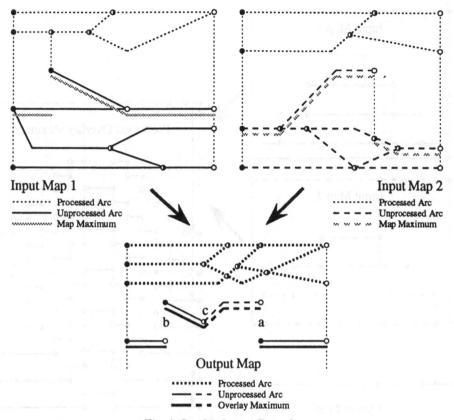

Input Map 1

········· Processed Arc
———— Unprocessed Arc
wwwwwww Map Maximum

Input Map 2

········· Processed Arc
– – – – Unprocessed Arc
∿ ∿ ∿ ∿ Map Maximum

Output Map

·········· Processed Arc
— – – Unprocessed Arc
▬▬▬ ▬ ▬ Overlay Maximum

Fig. 4. Overlay in two dimensions

The overlay maxima transferred in successive steps lead to an unnecessary partitioning of the arcs in the overlay map. This partitioning can be avoided by not transferring the complete overlay maximum to the overlay map but only special parts as will be shown in the following.

Three different cases can be distinguished at the *cut* between two arcs of the overlay maximum; examples are shown in the output map of Fig. 4:

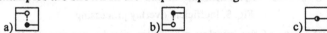

a) The left arc L ends in a point lying above the start point of the right arc R. Since R may be part of an arc in one of the input maps which extends below L we defer the processing of R, i.e. R may not yet be transferred to the output map. We say that R is *blocked* by its left end point.

b) Similar as in the previous case. Here the processing of L is deferred, i.e. L is blocked by its right end point.

c) Both arcs could be processed. However, we defer processing of R, i.e. we block R, to enforce that an arc in a map maximum is replaced by its direct descendants in the input map from left to right, i.e. in the order defined by the references *fd* and *nd* to access its list of descendants.

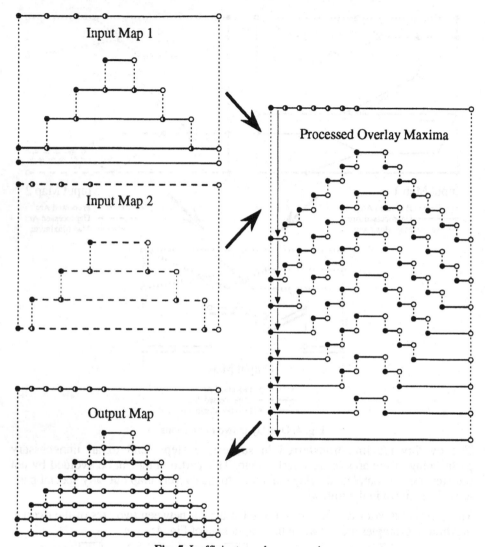

Fig. 5. Inefficient overlay processing

Only unblocked arcs of the overlay maximum can be processed. By definition an outer-most arc cannot be blocked by its outer-most end point. Deadlocks cannot occur, i.e. there is always at least one unblocked arc. All unblocked arcs are stored in a queue. An arc from this queue is processed as follows:

- Transfer the arc into the overlay map if necessary.
- Compute the new overlay maximum for the x-interval covered by the arc and replace the arc by this maximum.
- Update the queue by storing new unblocked arcs.

This algorithm is similar to a topological sweep algorithm for which the sweep line corresponds to the overlay maximum. In a single step our algorithm sweeps locally across an unblocked arc. The sequence of these local sweeps is illustrated by the example in Fig. 6.

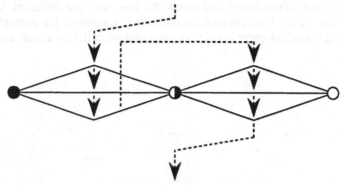

Fig. 6. Sequence of sweeps

Before we obtain a practical algorithm we still have to solve the following problems:

- How can we detect whether two arcs can be merged?
- How can unblocked arcs of the overlay maximum be transferred efficiently such that no searching for their point of insertion in the output map is necessary?
- How can the map maxima and the overlay maximum be updated efficiently after each local sweep?

The last question will be answered in Section 3.3, the remaining questions in Section 3.2. The basic idea is to make full use of the available information and to represent it in simple data structures, e.g. lists. Hence all operations can be performed locally; sorting which is usually necessary in plane sweep algorithms is not needed.

3.2   The Cuts

We define a *cut* as a vertical C which separates two arcs L and R in the overlay maximum such that the right end point of L and the left end point of R lie on C.

At a cut C a merge of two arcs is possible if the thematic attribute values above both arcs and the thematic attribute values below both arcs are the same, and if no other arc ends in their common end point on C.

In order to detect pairs of arcs which can be merged we will model a cut as a finite state machine. The state of a cut determines whether two arcs in the overlay maximum or the output map which meet in this cut can be merged. Each time an arc in the overlay maximum is replaced the bounding cuts of this arc may change their state. The state transitions of a cut depend on a predicate and an icon which is determined by a *classification tree*.

Let L and R be two arcs defining a cut as described above. Let L_y be the y-coordinate of L's right end point and R_y the y-coordinate of R's left end point. Denote by L_a, R_a, L_b and R_b the thematic attribute values above and below L and R, respectively. In addition we need for each end point a predicate *Merge?* which is true if the end point separates exactly two arcs, and false otherwise.

The classification tree shown in Fig. 7 assigns each cut an icon. If an icon contains a vertical on the left, for example 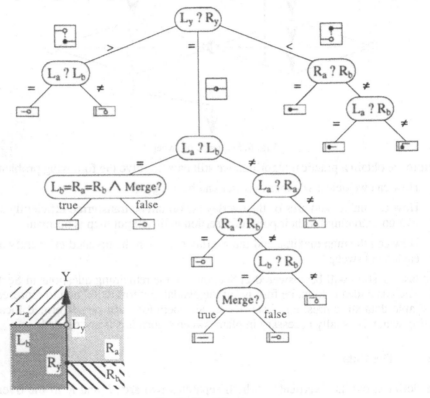, then the corresponding arc is necessary, e.g. the thematic attribute values above and below the boundary are different. We call it a *necessary* icon. If the icon contains no additionally vertical, for example ⌐-○⌐, the corresponding boundary curve is not necessary and we call it an *unnecessary* icon.

Fig. 7. Classification tree

Initially each cut is in the start-state. If one of the arcs determining a cut is replaced by a local sweep the cut processes its input icon according to the state transition diagram shown in Fig. 8. This processing also depends on a predicate p which is true if the y-value of the end point at this cut, i.e. L_y or R_y, has changed by the local sweep.

Classification is performed for each of the $m+1$ cuts after an arc in the overlay maximum has been replaced by m new arcs and after the two outermost cuts have processed their icons. The initial state of the $m-1$ newly created inner cuts is the start-state.

State transitions are performed according to the following rules:

- If no transition is shown for a given input icon the cut remains in its old state.

- If a transition shown in the diagram contains a ⊟ it can only be performed if the predicate p is false. ⊠ denotes a transition that can only be performed if p is true.

- ⌐—⌐ represents all necessary input icons, ⌐—⌐ all unnecessary input icons.

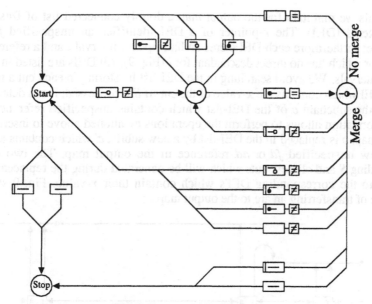

Fig. 8. State transition diagram

A cut may assume the following states:

(Start) Start state. In this state the cut is waiting for a left merge partner indicated by ⌷ or a merge icon ⌷, ⌷ which transfers the cut to the stop state.

(-o) Left merge state. The cut stores the arc which has caused the transition to this state because this is a possible left merge partner. The cut is waiting for a right merge partner indicated by the icon ⌷ or any other necessary icon which prevents a merge by transferring the cut into the start state.

(-o-) Possible merge state. In the output map a merge is possible between the stored left merge partner and the arc which has caused the transition to this state. The merge is performed if p is true in the next transition. If a necessary arc is processed which starts or ends at the merge point (⌷), the merge is rejected.

(Stop) Stop state. The left and right arc of the cut are merged in the overlay maximum, and the cut can be deleted.

The finite state machine for cuts executes all possible merges.

The following basic mechanism allows to transfer arcs into the output map efficiently without any searching for the point of insertion: During any local sweep the map overlay algorithm first transfers a necessary arc S from the overlay maximum to the output map, and then updates the overlay maximum.

If I is the x-interval covered by S, then S can be inserted into the output map by

- possibly splitting its ancestor in the output map above S's left end point,
- splitting S for all unspecified nd-references of sectors in the output map in I and
- setting all unspecified references in the output map for the interval I to the corresponding parts of S.

To do this we maintain for the output map a doubly connected list of **Descendant Entry Items** (DEI). The r-pointer of a DEI identifies an unspecified *fd* or *nd* reference; furthermore each DEI stores an half-open x-interval i and a reference a to the sector which has no direct descendant for i (Fig. 9). All DEIs are listed in order of their i intervals. We avoid searching in the DEI-list by storing in each cut a reference to the DEI which contains the x-value of the cut. If S is processed, it can determine by its cuts the subchain c of the DEI-list which contains unspecified references for I. This information allows to perform the operations mentioned above to insert S in the output map. c is replaced in the DEI-list by a new sublist c' which contains a DEI for each new unspecified *fd* or *nd* reference in the output map. The two old cuts surrounding S and all new cuts which will be generated during the replacement of S are set to the corresponding DEI's which contain their x-value. Fig. 9 shows an example of transferring an arc to the output map.

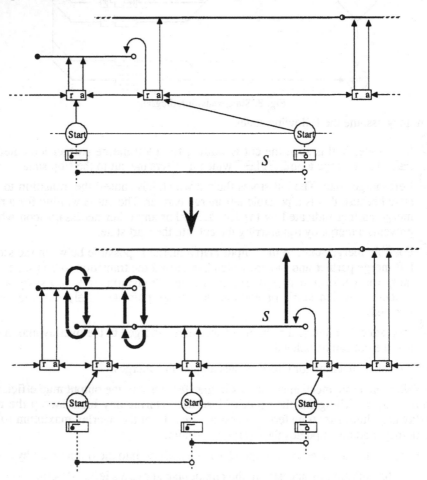

Fig. 9. Transferring an arc to the output map

3.3 Components of the Map Overlay Algorithm

Our map overlay algorithm consists of the following components which interact as shown in Fig. 10:

- Map managers,
- Subdivider,
- Topological sweep line.

A map manager loads and stores the sectors of a thematic map according to the data model defined in Section 2. This can be achieved by using different well-known file structures, e.g. R- [4], R$^+$- [12], R*-tree [1] or Cell-tree [5]. Since the data model provides all the necessary references the descendants of a sector can be accessed in constant time; therefore it is even possible to store the sectors in a sequential file without using any supporting index structure. The performance of the map managers for the input maps is improved by buffering input sectors which are not yet used. The performance of the map manager for the output map is improved by buffering output sectors which still have to wait until their descendant references are set.

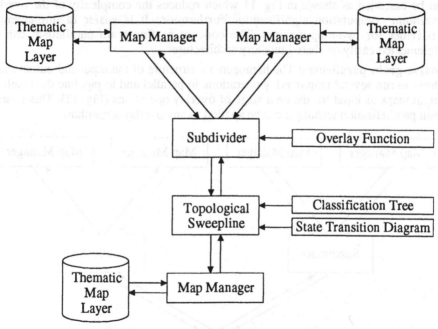

Fig. 10. Components of map overlay algorithm

The subdivider stores all map maxima with references to the corresponding sectors in the map managers. After an unblocked arc S of map m has been processed the subdivider replaces S in m's map maximum by the direct descendants of S in m. The subdivider computes the new overlay maximum for the x-interval covered by S from the corresponding arcs of the map maxima. Furthermore the subdivider applies the overlay function to compute the thematic attribute values in the overlay map.

The topological sweep line represents the core of the algorithm. It replaces an unblocked arc S of the overlay maximum by new arcs obtained from the subdivider. If S is necessary it is transferred to the output map manager by using the DEI-list.

These components are reflected in the parallel version of this map overlay algorithm which is discussed in the next section.

4   Parallelization

The map overlay algorithm can be parallelized in two different ways:

Fine-grain parallelism: Conventional plane-sweep algorithms cannot be easily parallelized since they are based on the sequential processing of events contained in an event queue. In contrast, our map overlay algorithm exploits the fact that usually there exists more than one unblocked arc in the queue. Since unblocked arcs are independent and do not interfere with each other we can process them in parallel. To avoid that the subdivider becomes a bottleneck we can apply two orthogonal methods. Each process corresponding to an unblocked arc creates a subdivider process which generates the new local overlay maximum. Furthermore subdividers can be cascaded as shown in Fig. 11 which reduces the complexity of the overlay maximum computation significantly. Furthermore it is easier to implement a subdivider for two-map-maxima. The concept of fine-grain parallelism can be implemented easily on shared-memory architectures.

Coarse-grain parallelism: The homogenous structure of the input and output maps allows to run several map overlay operations in parallel and to pipeline the resulting output maps as input for the next stage of overlay operations (Fig. 12). This coarse-grain parallelization technique can be applied to any overlay algorithm.

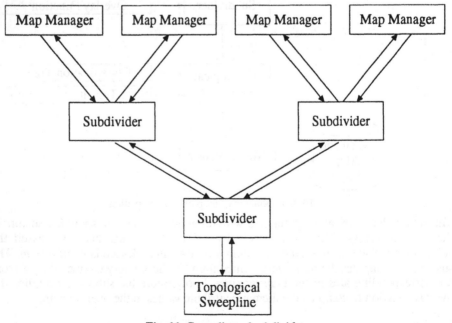

Fig. 11. Cascading of subdividers

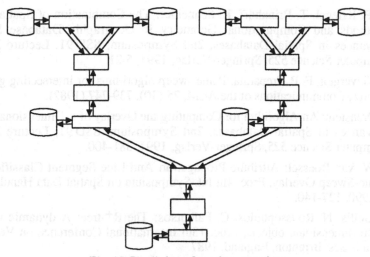

Fig. 12. Pipelining of overlay operations

5   Conclusion

This paper presents a new map overlay algorithm for vector data and its underlying spatial data model. The algorithm avoids expensive searching and sorting operations by making extensive use of locality inherent in the problem. This locality is reflected in the underlying data model and therefore allows to apply straightforward and efficient techniques to parallelize the time consuming map overlay operation. We are currently implementing a prototype of this algorithm in C++.

References

1. N. Beckmann, H. P. Kriegel, R. Schneider, B. Seeger: The R*-tree: An Efficient and Robust Access Method for Points and Rectangles, Proc. of ACM SIGMOD Conference on Management of Data, 1990, 322-331.

2. J. L. Bentley, T. A. Ottmann: Algorithms for reporting and counting geometric intersections, IEEE Transactions on Computers, C-28 (9), 643-647 (1979).

3. A. U. Frank: Overlay Processing in Spatial Information Systems, Proc. 8th Int. Symposium on Computer-Assisted Cartography (AUTO-CARTO 8), 1987, 16-31.

4. A. Guttman: A dynamic index structure for spatial searching, Proc. of ACM SIGMOD Conference on Management of Data, Boston, 1984, 47-57.

5. O. Günther: Efficient Structures for Geometric Data Management, Lecture Notes in Computer Science 337, Springer-Verlag, 1988.

6. L. J. Guibas, R. Seidel: Computing Convolutions by Reciprocal Search, 2nd ACM Symposium on Computational Geometry, 1986, 90 - 99.

7. H. P. Kriegel, T. Brinkhoff, R. Schneider: An Efficient Map Overlay Algorithm Based on Spatial Access Methods and Computational Geometry, Proc. Int. Workshop on DBMS's for geographical applications, Capri, May 16-17, 1991.

8. H. P. Kriegel, T. Brinkhoff, R. Schneider: The Combination of Spatial Access Methods and Computational Geometry in Geographic Database Systems, Advances in Spatial Databases, 2nd Symposium, SSD'91, Lecture Notes in Computer Science 525, Springer-Verlag, 1991, 5-21.

9. J. Nievergelt, F. P. Preparata: Plane sweep algorithms for intersecting geometric figures, Communications of the ACM, 25 (10), 739-747 (1982).

10. J. Orenstein: An Algorithm for Computing the Overlay of k-Dimensional Spaces, Advances in Spatial Databases, 2nd Symposium, SSD'91, Lecture Notes in Computer Science 525, Springer-Verlag, 1991, 381-400.

11. J. W. van Roessel: Attribute Propagation And Line Segment Classification in Plane-Sweep Overlay, Proc. 4th Int. Symposium on Spatial Data Handling, Vol. 1, 1990, 127-140.

12. T. Sellis, N. Roussopoulos, C. Faloutsos: The R^+-tree: A dynamic index for multi-dimensional objects, Proc. 13th International Conference on Very Large Data Bases, Brighton, England, 1987.

13. C. D. Tomlin: Geographic Information Systems and Cartographic Modeling, Prentice Hall, Englewood Cliffs, NJ, 1990.

An Optimal Quadtree Translation Algorithm

Chuan-Heng Ang

Department of Information Systems and Computer Science
National University of Singapore
SINGAPORE

ABSTRACT. Many operations on maps such as windowing and map overlaying require the maps to be translated. Therefore an efficient algorithm used to translate a map is very important in any application dealing with maps, GIS in particular. In this paper, an optimal algorithm that runs in $O(s_{in} + s_{out})$ is described and analyzed where s_{in} and s_{out} denote the number of nodes in the quadtree of the map and that of the translated map.

1. Introduction

Geographic information systems is widely used in managing natural resources and map production. In these applications, a large number of spatial objects such as cities, transport network, lakes, and land parcels are involved. When they are represented using raster images, they need a huge space to store. To reduce the space requirement, the images are usually compressed with the use of certain encoding method and stored in some data structures such as quadtrees.

Given a black and white image I, the *quadtree* T used to describe I can be constructed as follows. If I is of one color, then it is represented by the root node R of T with that color. Otherwise, R is colored grey and I is subdivided equally into four quadrants, namely the NW, NE, SW, and SE quadrants. Each of them is represented by one of the four son nodes of R. The decomposition process is repeated for each of these quadrants until they are of one color or they have become pixels that cannot be divided any more. This is called the *regular decomposition* process and the resulting quadtree is called a *region quadtree*, or simply a quadtree. We make no difference between a quadtree node and the part of the image, called *block*, that the node represents. We use the terms node or block freely to mean either one. We also use the terms quadtree and image interchangeably. Figure 1 shows an image array, its decomposition into blocks, and its quadtree. Note that a block of size $2^i \times 2^i$ is placed at level i of the quadtree.

Using a quadtree to encode an image of size $2^n \times 2^n$ reduces its space requirement from $O(4^n)$ to $O(p)$ where p is the perimeter of the black region [1,4]. The encoding also makes many operations on an image more efficient. These operations include neighbor finding, map union, map intersection, and the computation of various geometric properties such as the area or the perimeter of a region in a map.

When a quadtree is stored within a file, following the pointers in accessing the nodes becomes very inefficient if the nodes are not properly organized. Gargantini [2] proposes to use a pointerless quadtree called *linear quadtree* in which all the leaf nodes are being stored in the ascending order of their locational codes together with their level numbers. Assuming that the origin of a map is at its top left corner with the positive x and y directions to the right and bottom respectively, the *locational code* of a node is obtained by interleaving the x and y coordinates of the top left corner of the node. The list of locational codes are usually organized using a B-tree structure. It provides sequential access that is equivalent to a quadtree depth first traversal. It also allows

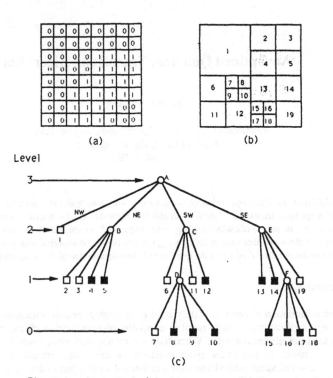

Figure 1. An example (a) a binary array, (b) its maximal blocks (blocks in the region are shaded), and(c) the corresponding quadtree

random access to any quadtree node through the *B*-tree index structure.

One major disadvantage of quadtree encoding is its sensitivity to the map's position. A map slightly shifted from its original position will need a completely different quadtree to represent. Nevertheless, quadtree has been regarded as a very common data structure in computer graphics, image processing, and geographic information systems. It has been equipped with many efficient algorithms and useful operations. More details about quadtree can be found in [8,9]. From now on, it is assumed that all maps are encoded in linear quadtrees.

Maps are frequently translated, either because they are to be overlaid, compared, or extracted. Thus an efficient translation algorithm is essential to the manipulation of maps. In our discussion, the translation of a map is restricted to an integral number of units along the *x* or the *y* directions. No attempt will be made to consider rotation of a map.

The paper is organized as follows. In Section 2, some works related to image translation are briefly mentioned before Touir's work [12] is being discussed. An example is given to show the worst case for Touir's algorithm that was purported to run in $O(n)$ where *n* is the resolution of an image. We describe Shaffer's algorithm on the conversion from an image array to its quadtree in Section 3 to prepare the groundwork for the description of our new translation algorithm. The new algorithm is then described and analyzed in Section 4. In Section 5, an example is used to illustrate how the new algorithm works on a simple map. We draw our conclusion in Section 6 and acknowledge the reviewers' comments in section 7.

2. Touir's Translation Algorithm

Let the size of the given pattern I be $2^n \times 2^n$ and the size of the encoding quadtree be s_{in}. We call the quadtree of the translated image as the *translated quadtree*. Let the size of the translated quadtree be s_{out}. It is noted in [5] that to translate an image of size $2^n \times 2^n$, it is not necessary to shift beyond the rectangular area of size $2^{n+1} \times 2^{n+1}$ that encloses the image in its NW quadrant. In other words, the translations to be considered are those with values (t_x, t_y) such that $0 \le t_x, t_y < 2^n$ where t_x and t_y represent the number of units of translation made in the x axis and y axis respectively.

The size of the translation (t_x, t_y) is defined to be the size of the largest quadtree block with (t_x, t_y) as its upper leftmost corner. For example, the size of the translation (8,4) is 4 because the largest quadtree block with (8,4) as its upper leftmost corner is of size 4x4. Similarly, the size of the translation (8,5) is 1. In general, the size of a translation (t_x, t_y) is equal to the largest power of 2 that can divide both t_x and t_y. When either t_x or t_y is odd, the size of the translation is 1.

Let us first consider a quadtree block which is to be translated only in the x direction. Figure 2 shows the results of different translations. It is noted that when the size of a quadtree block is smaller than that of a translation, the quadtree block remains intact after being moved. Otherwise the block is decomposed into smaller blocks. The worst situation occurs when $t_x = 1$ and $t_y = 1$. In this case, all blocks have to be decomposed into pixels.

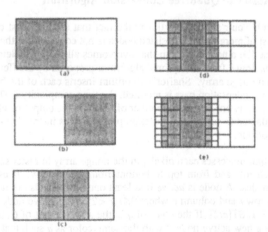

Figure 2. Results of translating (a) an image, by (b) 8 pixels,
(c) 4 pixels, (d) 2 pixels, and (e) 1 pixel.

Conceptually, translation of an image encoded in a quadtree can be realised easily by first converting the quadtree to an image array, performing the translation, and converting the array back to a quadtree. This is what has been proposed in [3]. Translation of an image array is a low cost operation since it can be done by adding t_x columns of white pixels to the left and t_y rows to the top of the image array logically. Unfortunately, the two conversions involved have time complexities that depend on the size of the array.

Touir and Kerherve [12] bypass the use of the image array and perform the translation directly on the quadtree blocks as follows:

> For each quadtree block
>   if its size <= the translation's size
>   change its locational code as a result of the translation and done
>   else
>   decompose it and process each quadrant

This algorithm is very efficient for those blocks of sizes not greater than the translation's size since modification of locational code is simple. We are more concerned about the effort needed to decompose those blocks of size greater than the translation's size.

Figure 3 shows an image that will reveal the inefficiency of the decomposition phase of Touir's algorithm. When the image is translated by (1,1), although all the black nodes can be merged into one big node as a result of the translation, all blocks which are not pixels have to be decomposed. A condensation pass is required to merge all the nodes produced by the decomposition. Therefore the worst case time complexity is $O(4^n)$. The claim in [12] that the algorithm takes $O(n)$ is not true.

3. Shaffer's Raster to Quadtree Conversion Algorithm

The problem with Touir's algorithm lies in the fact that the high cost of decomposition is overlooked. The cost of merging the translated nodes is not considered either. In the next section, we are going to describe a new algorithm that overcomes all these problems. The basic idea of the new algorithm is drawn from the optimal algorithm proposed by Shaffer [10] to construct a quadtree from a given image array. Shaffer's algorithm inserts each of the blocks in the output quadtree once and no condensation pass is required. Its time complexity is $O(4^n + s_{out})$ where 4^n is the size of the image array and s_{out} is the number of nodes in the output quadtree. In order to illustrate how it can be adapted to solve the translation problem, it is instructive to give a brief description of Shaffer's algorithm.

Shaffer's algorithm processes each pixel q in the image array in raster scan order, i.e., from left to right within each row and from top to bottom from row to row. It uses LIST$[0:2^{n-1}]$ to keep track of active nodes. A node is *active* if at least one of its pixels but not all has been processed. Suppose q is in row r and column c where $0 \le r, c < 2^n$. The active node Q that q falls into can be accessed through LIST$[c/2]$. If the color of q is the same as that of Q, proceed to the next pixel; otherwise insert a new active node R with the same color as q such that R is the biggest quadtree block that contains q as its first pixel. If q happens to be the last pixel of Q, then Q is no longer active. In this case, Q has to be written to the output quadtree*. In addition, all nested active

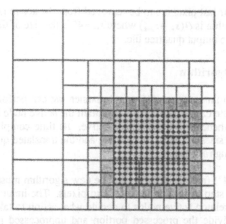

Figure 3. An image that requires decomposition and
condensation by Touir's algorithm when the
translation is (1,1). Nodes to be decomposed
are shaded with

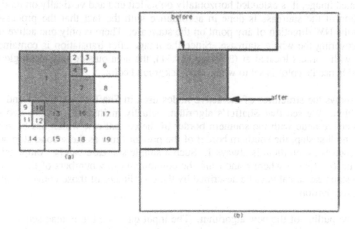

Figure 4. (a) An image, (b) the initial staircase and that
after node 1 is translated.

nodes containing q as their last pixel are to be removed from the active node list. The time complexity of Shaffer's algorithm is $O(s_{in} + s_{out})$ where $s_{in} = 4^n$ is the size of the image array and s_{out} is the number of nodes in the output quadtree file.

4. New Translation Algorithm

To adapt Shaffer's algorithm in a straightforward manner, we can perform a raster scan through the input quadtree, translate each row of pixels, maintain the active node list, and create a node in the translated quadtree whenever it is no longer active. Its time complexity is $O(s_{in} + 4^n + s_{out})$ where s_{in} and s_{out} are the sizes of the input quadtree and the translated quadtree, and $O(4^n)$ is the effort needed in performing raster scan.

To get rid of the term $O(4^n)$ from the complexity, the new algorithm must handle a quadtree node as a whole, avoiding the step to convert the nodes to pixels. The input nodes will be translated and checked against the related active nodes to decide what action to take next. A staircase like structure is formed to divide the processed portion and unprocessed portion in the translated image with the processed portion containing those nodes, black or white, which have been translated. Each active node must be the largest quadtree node straddling the portion of staircase which has its processed portion of single color, either black or white, whereas the unprocessed portion is always white. The staircase is partitioned by the list of active nodes into many smaller portions that make the updating of staircase structure more efficient.

Figure 4b shows how the staircase is adjusted after node 1 of Figure 4a has been translated (3,3). Initially, the western and northern borders of the image will form part of the staircase before they are translated. In order to have the staircase touched the sides of the big square which encloses the translated image, it is extended horizontally on its left end and vertically on its right end. The initialization of the staircase is done in accordance with the fact that the processed portion is always in the NW direction of any point on the staircase. There is only one active node Q which is white covering the whole staircase. Since the image after translation is contained within the rectangle with corners located at (3,3) and (11,11), the area outside this rectangle is never processed and hence its color is set to white, the background color.

Figure 5 shows the structures of the active nodes used in Shaffer's algorithm and those used in our algorithm. We see that Shaffer's algorithm actually maintains a simple two-step staircase within an active node with the southern border of the current row which has been partially processed as the first step, the southern border of the previous row as the second step, and the difference in height between them is always 1. Such a simple staircase can be completely determined by the point $(c+1, r+1)$ where c and r are the column and row numbers of the current pixel. In general, a staircase can always be described by the coordinates of those convex angles formed by the processed portion.

Below is the outline of the new algorithm. The input quadtree file is read sequentially and each node is processed as follow. Let P be an input node and its first pixel be q. After the translation, q is used to index into the active node list to retrieve the containing active node Q.

> If P is a subset of Q,
>> then the staircase structure in Q is updated to include P.
>> If Q and P are of the same color,
>>> If the last pixel of Q has not been processed,
>>>> then we are done with P and the next input node will be read.
>>> else
>>>> output Q and process the next node.
>> else
>>> a regular decomposition will be carried out within Q

When P is not a subset of Q, then P may be divided into not more than four parts, namely $P \cap Q$, the eastern portion of P, the southern portion of P, and the corner portion of P, denoted by PE, PS, and PC respectively as shown in Figure 6 and they will be processed in this order.

The regular decomposition on Q is carried out in such a way that a node is always decomposed unless

(1) it is completely within the staircase (the processed portion), and the node is output with the color of Q; or

(2) it straddles the staircase of single color. If the processed portion of the staircase is white and the unprocessed portion is beyond the translated range, then it can be output as a white node. Otherwise it becomes a new and smaller active node nested within Q; or

(3) it is completely out of the staircase, that is, it is in the unprocessed portion. In this case, if the node is found to be out of the translated range (e.g. the rectangle bounded by (3,3) and (11,11) in our working example), then it can be output as a white node. Otherwise, there is no action for this node.

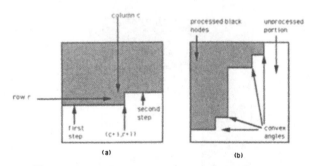

(a)   (b)

Figure 5. (a) The staircase within an active node in Shaffer's algorithm, and
(b) the staircase within an active node in the new translation algorithm.

In the implementation, we need the array $LIST[0:2^{n+1}]$. For each u, $0 \leq u < 2^{n+1}$, $LIST[u]$ points to the smallest active node which contains u in its x projection. Whenever active nodes overlap in their x projection, they are linked in the ascending order of their y values. When the last pixel of an active node has been processed, it is replaced by its successor in its active node list.

Since LIST is used and the number of active nodes is $O(2^n)$ [10], the space requirement is $O(2^n)$. As for the time complexity, it consists of the time to read the input quadtree, to write the output quadtree, and to update the staircase structure. The maintenance of the staircase can be done through the use of a binary search tree constructed from the SE vertexes of the translated input nodes and hence it takes $O(s_{in} \log s_{in})$ time. Reading and writing of quadtrees takes $O(s_{in})$ and $O(s_{out})$ respectively. Since the I/O time of this algorithm is dominant, the algorithm takes $O(s_{in} + s_{out})$ time. Similar arguments have been used in deriving the time complexity of Shaffer's algorithm [10].

5. An Example

To understand how the translation algorithm works, we shall translate some nodes of the quadtree shown in Figure 4a. The result of translating the whole quadtree by (3,3) is shown in Figure 7 and those of translating individual nodes are shown in Figure 8. Nodes in a quadtree are denoted by numbers whereas active nodes are denoted by alphabets. For example, nodes 2_{in} and 26_{out} represent input node 2 and output node 26 respectively, and A represents the first active node created. We will describe the translation of 1_{in} in more details, following which the translations of nodes 2_{in} to 7_{in} are briefly described.

(1) 1_{in}: (Figure 8a)
         Initially we have only one active node which is white and it is denoted by Q. After the translation, node 1_{in} falls within Q. Since its color is different from that of Q, a regular

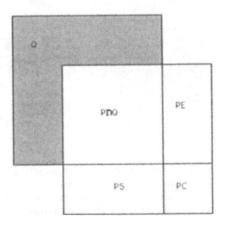

Figure 6. Decomposition of an input node.

decomposition is performed on Q. Nodes 1_{out} to 25_{out} are created in the translated quad-tree in ascending order and new active nodes A to E are also created in that order. In Table 1 we show the active nodes that cover various portions of the x axis. Notice that nodes E and B both cover $x=3$. Since B has smaller y, LIST[3] is set to point to B. Similarly, LIST[7] points to node A instead of C. There are 3 active node lists, namely $A{\to}C{\to}E{\to}Q, B{\to}E{\to}Q$, and $D{\to}Q$. In Table 2 we describe the staircases for each active node. Each active node is determined by the coordinates of its top left corner and bottom right corner.

(2) 2_{in}: (Figure 8b)
Active node A is removed and node 26_{out} is output.

(3) 3_{in}: (Figure 8c)
Staircase in D is changed to $\{(9,4),(11,3)\}$.

(4) 4_{in}: (Figure 8d)
Staircase C is changed to $\{(7,7),(8,5)\}$.

(5) 5_{in}: (Figure 8e)
Staircase D is changed to $\{(9,5),(11,3)\}$.

(6) 6_{in}: (Figure 8f)
Staircase D is changed to $\{(11,5)\}$.

(7) 7_{in}: (Figure 8g)
Since 7_{in} is not a subset of C, it is divided into $7_{in} \cap C$ and $7_{in}E$. $7_{in} \cap C$ causes the staircase in C to be changed to $\{(8,7)\}$ whereas $7_{in}E$ causes a regular decomposition to be performed on D due to the difference in color. As a result, nodes 27_{out} to 32_{out} are written to the output quadtree and 3 active nodes, namely $F((9,5),(10,6))$,$G((10,4),(12,6))$, and $H((8,6),(10,8))$ are created. Node 27_{out} is output because its processed portion is white and its unprocessed portion, the rectangle $((11,0),(12,4))$, is also white as it is beyond the range of the image translation. Node 28_{out} and 32_{out} are created since both of them are beyond the range of the image translation. Node D is removed since its last pixel $(15,7)$ has been processed although certain part of D is still unprocessed. As a result, D is replaced by those smaller active nodes.

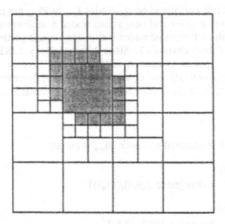

Figure 7. Result of translating the image in Figure 4a
by (3,3).

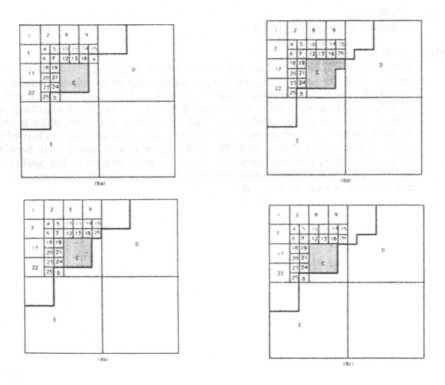

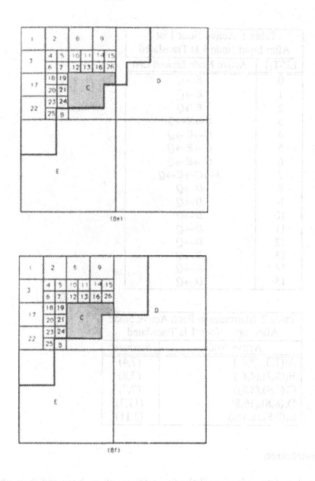

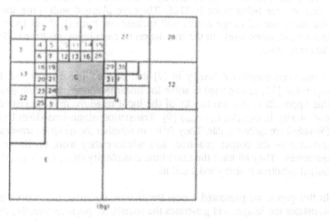

FIGURE 8. The quadtree nodes output and active nodes
created when the input nodes are translated in the order of
(a) node 1,(b) node 2, (c) node 3, (d) node 4, (e) node 5, (f)
node 6, and (g) node 7

Table 1. Active Node List After Input Node 1 Is Translated	
LIST[]	Active Node Linked List
0	$E \rightarrow Q$
1	$E \rightarrow Q$
2	$E \rightarrow Q$
3	$B \rightarrow E \rightarrow Q$
4	$C \rightarrow E \rightarrow Q$
5	$C \rightarrow E \rightarrow Q$
6	$C \rightarrow E \rightarrow Q$
7	$A \rightarrow C \rightarrow E \rightarrow Q$
8	$D \rightarrow Q$
9	$D \rightarrow Q$
10	$D \rightarrow Q$
11	$D \rightarrow Q$
12	$D \rightarrow Q$
13	$D \rightarrow Q$
14	$D \rightarrow Q$
15	$D \rightarrow Q$

Table 2. Staircases in Each Active Node After Input Node 1 Is Translated	
Active Node	Staircase
A((7,3),(8,4))	(7,4)
B((3,7),(4,8))	(3,8)
C((4,4),(8,8))	(7,7)
D((8,8),(16,8))	(11,3)
E((0,8),(8,16))	(3,11)

6. Conclusion

How to translate an image efficiently is not a new problem and there are a few solutions with the latest attempt being made in [12]. They are plagued with some shortcomings. Those solutions that make use of image arrays will include the term $O(4^n)$ in their time complexities. On the other hand, those work on the translation of each input quadtree node will incur the high cost of decomposition.

It has been mentioned briefly in [9] that the rectilinear unaligned linear quadtree intersection algorithm [11] can be used to solve the linear quadtree translation problem. The shortcomings of this approach is that the blocks of the input quadtree may be visited more than once. Its time complexity is $O(s_{in} \log s_{in} + s_{out})$ [9]. Translation algorithms described in [Pete85], [Lier86], and [Wals88] are quite similar. They differ in whether the quadtree traversal is to be done on the input quadtree or the output quadtree, and whether they work on linear quadtrees or pointer-based quadtrees. They all have the same time complexity $O(s_{out}(n + \log s_{in}))$ where s_{out} is the size of the output quadtree before condensation.

In this paper, we presented a new translation algorithm that works on an input image quadtree, translates the image, and generates the translated quadtree directly, bypassing the step to convert the image into an image array, and at the same time avoiding all the unnecessary decomposition and subsequent condensation steps. With these improvements, we are able to control its time complexity to be bounded by $O(s_{in} + s_{out})$ where s_{in} and s_{out} are the sizes of the input quadtree and the translated quadtree respectively. Although the new translation algorithm seems to be optimal according to the asymptotic analysis, its superiority has yet to be demonstrated through empirical results that compare its performance with others. The experiment is going to be an interesting project to be embarked on in the future.

7. Acknowledgement

The author would like to thank the reviewers for their useful comments.

References

1. C.R. Dyer, The space efficiency of quadtrees, *Computer Graphics and Image Processing 19*, 4(August 1982), 335-348.
2. I. Gargantini, An effective way to represent quadtrees, *Communications of the ACM 25*, 12(December 1982), 905-910.
3. I. Gargantini, Translation, rotation, and superposition of linear quadtrees, *International Journal of Man-Machine Studies 18*, 3(March 1983), 253-263.
4. G.M. Hunter, Efficient computation and data structures for graphics, Ph.D. dissertation, Department of Electrical Engineering and Computer Science, Princeton University, Princeton, NJ, 1978.
5. M. Li, W.I. Grosky, and R. Jain, Normalized quadtrees with respect to translation, *Computer Graphics and Image Processing 20*, 1(September 1982), 72-81.
6. M.L.P. van Lierop, Geometrical transformations on pictures represented by leafcodes, *Computer Vision, Graphics, and Image Processing 33*, 1(January 1986), 81-98.
7. F. Peters, An algorithm for transformations on pictures represented by quadtrees, *Computer Vision, Graphics, and Image Processing 32*, 3(December 1985), 397-403.
8. H. Samet, *The Design and Analysis of Spatial Data Structures*, Addison Wesley, Reading, Massachusetts, 1990.
9. H. Samet, *Applications of Spatial Data Structures: Computer Graphics*, Image Processing, and GIS, Addison Wesley, Reading, Massachusetts, 1990.
10. C.A. Shaffer, Application of alternative quadtree representations, Ph.D. dissertation, TR-1672, computer science Department, University of Maryland, College Park, MD, June 1986.
11. C.A. Shaffer and H. Samet, Set operations for unaligned linear quadtrees, *Computer Vision, Graphics, and Image Processing 50*, 1(April 1990), 29-49.
12. A. Touir and B. Kerherve, Pattern translation in images encoded by linear quadtree, *Modeling in Computer Graphics*, Proceedings of the IFIP WG 5.10 working conference, Tokyo, Japan, April 8-12, 1991.
13. T.R. Walsh, Efficient axis-translation of binary digital pictures by blocks in linear quadtrees representation, *Computer Vision, Graphics, and Image Processing 41*, 3(March 1988), 282-292.

Database Support
for Multidimensional Discrete Data

Peter Baumann[*]

Softlab GmbH
Zamdorfer Str. 120
D-8000 München 80
email: bmp@softlab.Germany.EU.net

Abstract. Current image database systems either treat images as pure byte sequences where the database system does not have any knowledge about the semantics of the image, or they are designed as specialized systems providing sophisticated imaging functionality, but no general data modeling and retrieval capabilities; none of them provides full modeling support for arbitrary pixel data types. Still more important, no system offers enough data independence to query an image in another format than exactly the byte stream as which it has been stored.

In this paper, a small set of language constructs is proposed which facilitates *multidimensional discrete data* (MDD) management in databases. Its special contribution is the *array abstraction* together with appropriate operations on arrays of arbitrary size over arbitrary data types. This allows to formulate powerful operations on images in a concise and optimizable way. A MDD storage mechanism is outlined which provides efficient access to such kind of data.

Implementation of the approach presented is currently in progress to enhance the object-oriented database system APRIL with MDD management capabilities.

Keywords. multidimensional discrete data, multimedia database system, image database system, image manipulation language, data modeling, data independence, image tiling, spatial index, APRIL

1. Introduction

Imagine database systems do not support real numbers, and there is no unifying, commonly accepted floating point standard like IEEE 488. Reals, therefore, have to be encoded into byte streams, and each application (and especially each machine type) tends to employ its own encoding rules. Even simple queries like

```
select r*r*3.14 from Circles where r>5.0
```

cannot be stated, as two important things are missing:

- Real numbers cannot be part of the search condition. The only convenience is, say, preselection according to the sign of a number, because it is agreed that the first bit is set to zero iff the value is nonnegative; the exact query result has to be determined by the application program.

---

[*] This work has been performed at the Fraunhofer Computer Graphics Research Group in Darmstadt, sponsored by DFN Assoc. (German Research Net Association) under grant no. TK558-VA014

- No arithmetic operations are provided on the byte streams representing reals in a query result; at best, we have bit operations available to extract mantissa and exponent from real valued byte containers.

This scenario comes quite close to the state of the art in image database systems (in the sequel, *image* will always mean *raster image*). Current practice in office information systems [Feli-88] and multimedia database systems [MwLW-89] is to regard images as bit streams; for example, in [MwLW-89] where the relational model is extended with a new attribute domain for images, the authors first state that *"raw image data consist of a matrix of pixels"*, and then conclude (quite surprisingly) *"the raw data appear just as a string of bits"*. A similar approach is reported in [Gros-84].

In all these cases, images cannot be involved in search criteria, e.g. *"select all X-ray images where in the region specified by a given bit mask, intensity exceeds a certain threshold value"*, and they cannot be processed in a fashion like *"extract the infrared channel from a given multispectral satellite image"* or *"retrieve only the upper right 200 by 200 part of a several Megabyte image"*.

Moreover, such systems can deliver images only as exactly the same byte stream as which they have been written before, a. they lack data independence. Consequently, such systems cannot be used in heterogeneous networks coming up with open multimedia environments.

Another class of image database systems provides more semantics by viewing images as arrays of some pixel type. The number of available pixel types varies; IQ [LiHa-80] solely knows integer pixels, PICDMS [ChCK-84] offers integer, float and bit/char strings; the system described in [MwLW-89] augments the bit stream image with two attributes DEPTH telling the number of bits per pixel and ENCODING specifying the color model used (e.g., RGB or IHS). In any case, however, the set of available pixel types is predefined and fixed.

The same holds for the operators on images. Usually a fixed set of basic image processing functions is provided [ChFu-80], including scaling, translation, rotation, or thresholding; some sophisticated systems [KaAl-88, OrMa-88] provide geometric operations on points, lines, and areas which, however, require the raster image to be interpreted first and hence cannot be regarded as pure raster operations.

Advanced systems allow to combine operators to construct more complex ones. IQ [LiHa-80] offers functional composition to formulate complex operations on images. PICDMS [ChCK-84] employs a command language which exhibits procedural elements, but also a QBE-like frontend called PICQUERY [JoCa-88].

Some recent semantic and object-oriented models indeed support array data types both structurally and operationally. The R2D2 system [KeWa-87] knows the array constructor, but these arrays are constrained to very small sizes, such as 4x4 matrices; sizes of millions of elements cannot be handled. Moreover, advanced array functionality like subarray extraction is missing. The EXTRA/EXCESS system [VaDe-91] relies on an algebraic framework which, among others, introduces fixed-length and variable-length arrays in a formal manner. From the nine array operations available, two are of special importance. ARR_APPLY applies a function to all array members; this corresponds to induced operations in our model - see Section 3.3. The SUB_ARR operator extracts a rectangular part from an array, yielding a new array with appropriate boundaries, something which in our approach is covered by the trimming operator. On the conceptual level, the EXTRA/EXPRESS array facilities are equally powerful as our approach; however, the algebraic framework is not paired by appropriate storage techniques to cope with really huge arrays efficiently.

In summary, it can be stated that current systems either do not offer modeling flexibility and data independence on discrete data to a degree comparable with the classical database types, or they do not complement such concepts with storage mechanisms suited for huge arrays.

To remedy this, an (image) database system must offer comprehensive *multidimensional discrete data* (MDD) management facilities. On the conceptual level, this means definition of *arrays over arbitrary pixel types*, not just a predefined selection of pixel types like integer and real. A *coherent, orthogonal set of operations* must be available on such array types which allows for enough modeling flexibility to express MDD retrieval and manipulation. The physical database layer must support the array concept by providing *efficient access methods* for n-dimensional arrays of basically arbitrary size. Concealment of these internal storage structures, i.e., *data independence*, is an essential prerequisite for cooperative, open multimedia environments distributed over heterogeneous networks, as only then image structures can be transmitted and reassembled appropriately according to the target machine's representation needs.

Please note that we do not demand to embed a fully-fledged imaging system into the database machine - this is an inadequate solution anyway, but first of all contradicts modularity. To stress our introductory example again: Certainly nobody will perform number crunching tasks in a database system; yet it is feasible not just to store and load real numbers, but to use them in query expressions, too.

In this contribution, we propose an extension to an existing data model, namely that of the object-oriented database system APRIL [BaKö-89], which allows to define, retrieve, and manipulate arbitrary MDD structures. The concept stems from a well-founded algebraic framework developed for image and signal processing. Our approach obeys data independence, which opens up a good potential for storage and query optimization. The conceptual outline is complemented with a proposal for efficient secondary storage management based on a combination of tiling techniques and spatial indexes.

The remainder of this paper is organized as follows. In the next section, we develop a set of requirements on MDD modeling in databases. After that, we propose a set of language concepts in Section 3 which allows for flexible MDD definition, retrieval, and manipulation according to the above stated requirements. An architecture suitable for this conceptual model is presented in Section 4, and finally we summarize our findings in Section 5.

2. Requirements

In this section, we derive structural and operational requirements on MDD management in databases.

2.1 Image Structure

Today available image sources (satellite sensors, renderers, telefax devices, etc.) come with a variety of different image types. Table 1 lists the characteristics of some of the most important image types.

Usually, images form n-dimensional arrays over some base type, called the *pixel type*. Non-rectangular images like sonograms are embedded into a minimal enclosing rectangle, hence it is no undue limitation to stick with the rectangularity imposed by arrays.

	geometric resolution	color resolution	pixel data type	data volume (uncompressed)
G3 fax (DIN A4)	1728x1083	1 bit	binary	500 kB
HDTV still image (Eureka format)	1920x1152	4+2+2 bit	YC_hC_r	210 MB
VGA	640x300 - 1024x768	e.g. 16 bit	RGB, color table	e.g. 480 kB
scanned slide	3000x2000	24 bit	RGB	18 MB
medicine:				
- tomogram	$256^2 - 512^2$	12 bit	gray-scale	98 kB - 392 kB
- X-ray image	$\leq 2048^2$	12 - 16 bit	gray-scale	8,4 MB
satellite images:				
- Landsat MSS	3240x2340	4x8 bit	multispectral	30 MB
- Landsat TM	7020x5760	7x8 bit	multispectral	283 MB
- MOMS	6912 per line	2x8 bit	multispectral	variable
- SPOT	6000^2	1x8 bit	panchromatic	36 MB
resp.	3000^2	3x8 bit	RGB	27 MB
prepress	2000x3000 - 15000^2 and more	4x1 - 4x8 and more	CMYK and others	24 - 900 MB and more

Table 1: Image types in different application areas

The underlying pixel type remains constant over the lifetime of an image. Image size, on the contrary, shows too much variation to introduce a separate type for each geometry, and sometimes even may vary during the lifetime of an image. It seems, therefore, adequate to fix the pixel type in a type definition, but it should be possible to leave open the actual image size (i.e., dynamic arrays should be supported).

A selection of common pixel types is presented in Table 2. Binary, gray-scale, and RGB are well-known color representations. However, pixel information does not necessarily denote a color value; an arbitrary semantics, for example a reference to an entity somewhere else in the database, can be associated with a pixel. PICDMS [ChCK-84] exploits this to mark regions making up a country in image based geographic maps. Matrix valued pixels are frequently used in the prepress (printing) area to describe color values through binary subpixels (this corresponds to the physical process of composing color spots by aggregating several small fixed size ink drops). In graphics systems, subpixel techniques serve to reduce aliasing effects.

pixel data type	application
enum (BLACK, WHITE)	binary images
Natural	gray-scale and color table images
record r, g, b: Natural end	RGB coded color values
COUNTRY_ID	references
array [1..8,1..8] of enum (BLACK, WHITE)	subpixel techniques

Table 2: Various pixel data types

2.2 Image Operations

As for the operators on such images, existing image processing calculi like the *AFATL Image Algebra* [RiWD-90] provide useful insights. Image Algebra provides a mathematically elegant, precise and unambiguous algebraic framework for the formulation of image and signal processing algorithms. It has been proven [RSFW-87] that all image processing transforms can be expressed in this calculus. In the following, we give a sketchy overview of Image Algebra; for more details, the reader is referred to the previously cited papers.

An image (MDD element in our terminology) is a function

$$b: X \rightarrow C$$

from a coordinate set $X \subseteq \mathbf{R}^n$ into some color space C; note that X is not necessarily discrete and finite, although in practice X will usually be something like $\{1..640\} \times \{1..480\}$.

The most basic access operation beside querying the current image boundaries is subimage extraction. For some cutout domain Y, this is mathematically described as

$$e_Y(b) = \{ (x,c(x)): c(x) = b(x), x \in X \cap Y \}$$

Next the natural induced operations of the algebraic system C are provided. On real valued pixels, for example, these are the unary and binary operations like addition, multiplication, and maximum. Thus, the addition of two images b and c for $C = \mathbf{R}$ is given by

$$b + c = \{ (x,d(x)): d(x) = b(x) + c(x), x \in X \}$$

In general, any unary function f: $R \to R$ induces a function F: $R^X \to R^X$ defined as

$$F(b) = \{ (x,c(x)): c(x) = f(b(x)), x \in X \}$$

The extension to binary functions is straightforward. The same way, predicates on pixel level can be lifted to characteristic functions on images:

$$c_{\leq b}(c) = \{ (x,d(x)): d(x) = \text{if } c(x) \leq b(x) \text{ then } 1 \text{ else } 0 \text{ fi, } x \in X \}$$

This is an example for an operation where the resulting pixel type differs substantially from the input pixel type.

This brief glance at the basics of Image Algebra is sufficient for our purpose, as the remaining constructs serve for image manipulation purposes that go beyond the tasks of an image database management system.

2.3 Summary of the Requirements

The data structure underlying a raster image always can be viewed as a homogeneous n-dimensional array over some arbitrary pixel data type. Whereas it is feasible to fix the pixel type at definition time, the large number of different image sizes suggests open array boundaries which can vary dynamically. Access operations can be classified into three basic schemes:

1) Retrieve current array boundaries,
2) retrieve a rectangular part of an image, and
3) retrieve an image where for each pixel p in the original image some value f(p) is substituted.

All these access schemes can occur in combination. The third scheme can be refined according to the presumed sequence of iteration over the pixels (i.e., the order in which the result is built): Traversal sequence is

a) irrelevant (e.g., store/load image or filter operations),
b) relevant and known in advance (e.g., line by line access in ray tracing algorithms), or
c) random and not predictable (e.g., stochastic texture generation algorithms or contour finders in image recognition systems).

It is very important that traversal sequence is not prescribed unnecessarily, because only then an optimizer has the chance of finding an optimal sequence with minimal disk access. Obviously, access schemes 3a) and 3b) offer a good potential for optimization, whereas scheme 3c) is unlikely to benefit from optimizations.

3. The MDD Sublanguage

We now introduce a MDD definition and manipulation language which forms a database sublanguage suitable for the description and manipulation of images and other MDD types. We use the type definition and query language of the object-oriented database system APRIL [BaKö-89] to tie the concepts to some concrete language. The embedding of an extended MDD language variant into another object-oriented model - COISINHA - is outlined in [Baum-93]; basically, any conceptual model could be augmented this way.

3.1 The APRIL Object Model

To provide a context for our approach to MDD treatment in databases, we give a brief outline of the APRIL object model.

Attribute and object type definition deliberately has been kept close to the C language, extended with a new relationship concept and (multiple) inheritance.

Objects are identified by an externally visible object key. The extension of a type is a set of object keys plus a set of operations; the generic operation set is augmented with type-specific attribute operations which accomplish transformation to and from the application program structure. Attribute access operations are generated as C source code which is compiled together with the application program.

An object type describes the following object constituents:

- A set of attributes. All C base types and constructors, such as enumerations, records and arrays with arbitrary nesting, are available, except for bitfields and pointers; the latter ones have been substituted by the safer and more expressive successors clause (see below).
- One optional long field per instance, the so-called *object contents*. In the original version, the contents was viewed as the usual byte string with no further semantics imposed.
- A *successors clause* [ZhBa-92] describing the set of admissible object references wrt. referenced object types, cardinality, and possible variants. Both object hierarchies and general object graphs are modelled this way.

Example: A stereo image consists of two raster images which are described by their geometric resolution and pixel type; the pixel matrix itself is stored in the object contents. This is specified as

```
typedef object
{   unsigned int xResolution, yResolution;
    enum { BINARY, GRAYSCALE, RGB } colorType;
    contents;
} RasterImage;

typedef object
{   successors 2 RasterImage;
} StereoImage;
```

The APRIL query language leans itself towards standard SQL. In the `select` clause, the query result structure is described which in the first version allows only lists of object keys to be returned, as the issue of host language data coupling is being tackled right now. The `where` clause allows the usual predicates known from SQL, enhanced with path expressions to state conditions on the object graph. Note that no `from` clause is necessary, as the types involved can be deduced from the other query parts.

Example: *"Retrieve the keys of those stereo images which contain grayscale images"* is expressed as

```
select StereoImage
where  StereoImage downto
       RasterImage.colorType = GRAYSCALE
```

For the modeling of MDD structures as APRIL object constituents, two alternatives were available, attributes and the contents. Attributes offer sufficient structuring capabilities, but are intended to hold only small amounts of data compared to image sizes. The contents, on the contrary, up to now has been a byte stream of potentially arbitrary size, but with no further semantics. We decided to overlay the contents with a structure definition to implement huge arrays; syntactically, the single keyword `contents` is extended to become an array definition for the special attribute named `contents`.

3.2 Structure Definition of MDD

Any attribute type known in the schema is allowed as array base type. Whereas in the relational model only simple types would be possible, more recent models like APRIL can support arbitrary user-defined array base types. Array boundaries are indicated by the number of elements; as usual in C, the lower bound is zero. The symbol ' # ' instead of an index range denotes variable array limits. Arrays can be arbitrarily nested.

Examples:

```
typedef unsigned int GrayscaleMatrix[640][480];
```

describes the structure of a 640x480 gray-scale image.
A G3 telefax with a fixed number of pixels per line, but a variable number of lines, is expressed as

```
typedef enum { WHITE, BLACK } BinaryPixel;
typedef BinaryPixel G3FaxMatrix[1728][#];
```

Such a template can be used to define an image valued contents, e.g.

```
typedef object
{   char description[80];
    GrayscaleMatrix contents;
} GrayscaleImage;

typedef object
{   char sender[80], sendingSite[20];
    G3FaxMatrix contents;
} G3Fax;
```

3.3 Operations on MDD

We introduce three sorts of operations on MDD data, namely the builtin function family `range`, trimming, and induced operations.

The current array limits of an MDD attribute can be queried through a family of builtin functions where each one returns the index range of one array dimension. Function `range1(a)` returns array a's current first dimension size, `range2(a)` the upper bound of a's second dimension, and so on. By convention, `range` is synonymous with `range1`.

Extraction of a rectangular part of an array is called *trimming*. Let a be a d-dimensional array, d>0, of fixed or variable size over some base type T. Let further $(m_1, n_1), \ldots, (m_d, n_d)$ be pairs of integer numbers with $0 \leq m_i \leq n_i < range_i(a)$ for $i \leq d$. Then, image a trimmed to $(m_1, n_1), \ldots, (m_d, n_d)$, denoted as

```
a[ m₁..n₁, …, m_d..n_d ]
```

is that array a' defined as a fixed-size array A of type

```
typedef T A[n₁-m₁+1]…[n_d-m_d+1];
```

where

$$a'[i_1,…,i_d]=a[m_1+i_1,…,m_d+i_d] \text{ for } 0≤i_1≤n_1-m_1 \text{ and } 0≤j≤n_d-m_d.$$

The next language element is that of operations induced by pixel operations. We show the definition for the one-dimensional case only; it is straight-forward to extend the concept to higher dimensions. Let f be some function

```
f: T, U → V
```

where T, U and V are arbitrary (not necessarily different) data types. TArray shall be a variable size or fixed size array over the data type T, and VArray shall be an array over V. Then, by default the operation

```
F: TArray, U → VArray
```

is available where F is defined as follows. For $t \in TArray$, $u \in U$, and $v \in VArray$,

```
F(t,u) = v   where v[i] = f(t[i],u)
                for all  0≤i<min(range(t),range(v)).
```

If VArray has variable limits, they will be adapted appropriately to the source array boundaries, otherwise excessive array elements will be cut away.

Induction of operations allows to state operations on multidimensional arrays by indicating only the base type operation without prescribing the sequence of element access in any way. In Section 4, we will propose a storage structure for such operations.

3.4 Examples

Some further examples will demonstrate both expressive power and practical use of the array operations.

Color Images. Suppose RGB images are stored in *pixel-interleaved* mode, i.e., as a pixel matrix where each pixel consists of three components for the red, green, and blue intensity, respectively:

```
typedef object
{    struct
     {    unsigned int red, green, blue;
     }    contents[1024][768];
} RGB_Image;
```

A certain application, however, may require to obtain an image in *channel-interleaved* representation where for each color the intensity values are collected in a separate gray-scale image. This requires conversion from a matrix of records to a record of matrices. As the record access operator '.' can be induced, the corresponding query is denoted as

```
select RGB_Image.contents.red,
       RGB_Image.contents.green,
       RGB_Image.contents.blue
where  RGB_Image = r
```

Now let us assume that image acquisition has been done with a decalibrated sensor generating too high red values. This can be corrected by the following query which uses induced subtraction:

```
select RGB_Image.contents.red - 5,
       RGB_Image.contents.green,
       RGB_Image.contents.blue
where  RGB_Image = r
```

Color lookup tables (CLUTs) serve to significantly reduce storage space for images by replacing the actual color values by entries into a table stored separately. Color images with a 16 entry color map can be specified as

```
typedef object
{   struct
    {   unsigned int red, green, blue;
    }   colorTable[16];
    unsigned int contents[1024][768];
} CLUT_Image;
```

Telefax. The task *"The first 100 lines of all G3 telefaxes"* is answered by the query

```
select G3Fax.contents[#][0..99]
```

The number of lines of all faxes sent from Germany is returned by

```
select range2(G3Fax.contents)
where  G3Fax.sendingSite like '0049*'
```

With aggregate functions similar to those in SQL, the query language can be extended to compute derived information. To make the aggregation run over array indices, the using clause introduces typed index variables. As an example, *"Count all blank lines in fax f"* looks as follows:

```
select count(i)
using  unsigned int i
where  G3Fax.contents[#][i] = WHITE
       and i < range2(G3Fax.contents)
       and G3Fax = f
```

Pixel comparison is an induced operation extending comparison over a whole line (note the '#'!). By convention the results of Boolean operations are ANDed together in the induced operation to yield a single Boolean value instead of a Boolean array, hence a line is selected only when it contains nothing but white space.

Computer Tomogram Series. The last example is taken from the application field Hospital Information System (HIS). Let us call a series of computer tomograms (CTs) a *volume tomogram* (VT). A VT can be defined as

```
typedef object
{   unsigned int contents[256][256][256];
} VolumeTomogram;
```

Insertion of the ith of all 256 slices into a VT object v is done by statements like

```
update VolumeTomogram
set     contents[0..255][0..255][<i>] = <scan data>
where   VolumeTomogram = v
```

Now suppose we want a cut through the volume along the x/z plane at a certain position y0. The query *"extract all pixels in the x/z plane with y position y0   of VolumeTomogram v"* is written as

```
select VolumeTomogram.contents[#][y0][#]
where   VolumeTomogram = v
```

y0 is short for y0..y0. Note that this query produces a data ordering orthogonal to the way the CTs have been stored before.

4. Implementation

An intricate description of array structures is useless unless it is supported by corresponding storage mechanisms such that, for instance, column access is not more expensive than row access. For this reason and because images are not unlikely to be too big to fit into main memory as a whole (remember Table), tiling techniques must be used where arrays are decomposed into rectangular units of access called *tiles*. Such techniques are well-known in image processing (e.g., [Tamu-80]).

A tiling concept should be supported by an appropriate spatial index [SeKr-88], a technique which has successfully been used for geometric entities like lines and regions. In our particular case the situation is much simpler than in those applications, because image tiles are by definition axis-parallel rectangles, they never overlap, they altogether cover the image, and the complete image is a finite region with known axis-parallel boundaries. After reviewing several spatial indexing techniques [Furt-93], we decided to choose the R+-Tree [SeRF-87] as one of the most efficient spatial indexes [FaSR-87].

4.1 Architecture

The resulting architecture for the MDD management subsystem of APRIL is shown in Fig. 1. The general APRIL application interface must support two ways of accessing MDD attributes. First, the *query interpreter* offers the array facilities previously introduced. One of its main tasks is to expand induced operations to complete the parse tree with the necessary loops. Second, the *MDD import and export facility* serves as a bulk loader for those cases when the whole data set is addressed. This is useful, for instance, to generate or load image files formatted in some image exchange format like TIFF, GIF, or JPEG.

The *query optimizer* tries to rearrange the parse tree in such a way that disk access is minimized. For example, the optimizer exploits knowledge about the tiles affected by the query to rearrange loops in a way that each tile is read no more than once.

The *Basic MDD Access* module is the virtual machine on which the query interpreter executes the parse tree. It maintains MDD tiles and the spatial index on them and performs extraction of the desired data subset.

The *MDD Storage* module finally is in charge of storing and retrieving tiles and index nodes, accessed by their primary key.

In our implementation, we store both MDD tiles and the index in relational tables. The reasons were the following. First, APRIL is implemented on top of a relational database system. Already in its current status, the object contents is stored in relations by partitioning the byte sequence into chunks small enough to fit into one relational long field attribute. (The current implementation relies on ORACLE where the maximum long field size is 64 kB; on other systems, this could be adapted appropriately.) The results of this approach were promising and made us continue this way. Second, an approach for storing geoindex information in relational tables has been reported for geometric applications in [HHSW-91], where it has been shown that a spatial index on top of a relational system is still more efficient than a conventional non-spatial index internal to the RDBMS. Nevertheless, we agree that the ultimate goal should be a specialized storage manager not relying on a relational system.

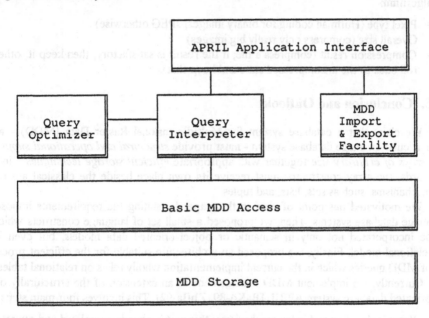

Fig. 1. Architecture of the MDD management subsystem

The resulting table structure for a tile relation looks as follows:

```
TileRel(oid:raw,tid:number,comp:char,bucket:long raw)
```

The `oid` attribute contains the APRIL object identifier, `tid` is the tile identifier, `comp` is a flag indicating the compression technique used (this is currently not used, but has been incorporated for future use), and `bucket` is a character string attribute containing the raw tile data. On `oid` and `tid`, a conventional index is maintained. All tile relation queries are prepared in advance with the search keys. Physical clustering of the tile relation serves to minimize disk head movement during retrieval of consecutive tiles.

Quite a similar approach was adopted for the spatial index. Each tree node of the R+-Tree is stored in one relational tuple, with a tuple identifier maintained by APRIL establishing the tree reference structure. As index tree nodes again can contain up to 64 kB, in most cases the tree has depth one and can be fetched with one disk access.

4.2 Discussion

The approach described so far leaves open several degrees of freedom for different tiling policies. We think about the following alternatives:

- Split into regular units when the image is inserted (regular gridding).
- Split and merge dynamically, e. g. to preserve a given minimum and maximum tile size.
- Determine maximal homogeneous areas.

The last case is especially interesting with respect to compression, because homogeneous areas yield the best compression factors. Note that compression now does not involve the whole image uniformly, but is performed on each tile independently, thus yielding more flexibility. Again, several criteria can guide the decision for the appropriate compression algorithm:

- Pixel type (Huffman coding for binary images, JPEG otherwise).
- Overall size (compress only really big images).
- Compression result (compress a tile; if the result is satisfactory, then keep it, otherwise roll back to the uncompressed state and keep that).

5. Conclusion and Outlook

We claim that a database system for Multidimensional Raster Data (MDD) - and in particular an image database system - must provide *structural and operational support for arrays of arbitrary size* together with appropriate *efficient storage techniques* - in other words, the array constructor must receive its own place beside the classical abstraction mechanisms, such as sets, lists, and tuples.

We motivated this point of view in this paper by stating the requirements imposed on image database systems. Then, we proposed a small set of language constructs which can be incorporated not only in semantic or object-oriented data models, but even in the relational model. Finally, we proposed an architecture suitable for the efficient processing of MDD queries which in the current implementation wholly relies on relational tables.

Currently, we implement MDD management as an extension of the structurally object-oriented database system APRIL [BaKö-89, ZhBa-92]. This involves four main steps:

- Provide the tiling and index mechanisms; this part is already completed and operational.
- Extend the data dictionary to keep the structure definition of object contents.
- Build the language interpreter and lateron the optimizer on top of the image store.
- Develop efficient MDD encoding and decoding components for the transmission of MDD data in heterogeneous networks.

When finished, this extended version of APRIL will be used to provide a public image database service in the wide area High Speed Data Networks (HDN) of the German Research Net (DFN).

However, MDD is not just two-dimensional images. Although our first and main application is image management, many new applications like multimedia, remote sensing, environmental planning and control, require general database support for multidimensional discrete data. In fact, any by nature analog data finally appear as MDD of some specific dimensionality when sampled, as the examples in Table 3 show.

Acknowledgement

The MDD storage facility has been implemented by Paula Furtado during a research stay at Fraunhofer Computer Graphics Research Group. It was a fruitful cooperation, and she contributed many good ideas.

dimension	application
1	time series (audio data, environmental data, etc.)
2	2D images
3	2D animation; 3D data sets (simulation results, etc.)
4	time-variant volumetric data
5	PIKS generic image type [ISO-92]

Table 3: MDD of different dimensionality

Special thanks to an unknown referee who helped to improve this paper considerably through his/her outstanding accuracy.

References

[BaKö-89]
Baumann, P.; Köhler, D.: APRIL - Another PRODAT ImpLementation. Fraunhofer Computer Graphics Research Group Darmstadt, FhG Report FAGD-89i007, June 1989

[Baum-93]
Baumann, P.: Ein konzeptuelles Informationsmodell für Visualisierungsdatenbanken. PhD Thesis, Darmstadt Technical University 1993

[ChCK-84]
Chock, M.; Cardenas, A.: Klinger, A.: Database Structure and Manipulation Capabilities of a Picture Database Management System (PICDMS). IEEE ToPAMI, Vol 6, No. 4, July 194, pp. 484 - 492

[ChFu-80]
Chang, S.; Fu, K. (ed.): Pictorial Information Systems. Lecture Notes in Computer Science Vol. 80, Springer 1980

[FaSR-87]
Faloutsos, C.; Sellis, T.; Roussopoulos, N.: Analysis of Object Oriented Spatial Access Methods. Proc. ACM SIGMOD 1987 Annual Conference, San Francisco, June 1987, pp. 426-439

[Feli-88]
Felician, L.: Image Database Management System: A Promising Tool in the Large Office System Environment. Proc. DATABASE Fall/Winter 1987/1988, pp. 29 - 36

[Furt-93]
Furtado, P.: A Storage Manager for Raster Images Based on a Relational Database System. Master's Thesis, Universidade de Coimbra (in preparation)

[Gros-84]
Grosky, W.: Towards a Data Model for Integrated Pictorial Databases. Computer Vision, Graphics, and Image Processing, Vol. 25, 1984, pp. 371 - 382

[HHSW-91]
Henrich, A.; Hilbert, A.; Six, H.-W.; Widmayer, P.: Anbindung einer räumlich clustern-
den Zugriffsstruktur für geometrische Attribute an ein Standard-Datenbanksystem am
Beispiel von Oracle. Proc. BTW 91, Kaiserslautern/Germany 1991, Springer 1991, pp.
161 - 177

[ISO-92]
International Organization for Standardization (ISO): Information technology - Comp-
uter Graphics and Image Processing - Image Processing and Interchange - Functional
Specification - Part 2: Programmer's Imaging Kernel System - Application Program
Interface. ISO/IEC JTC1 SC24 Document IM-157, Draft International Standard
(DIS), October 1992

[JoCa-88]
Joseph, T.; Cardenas, A.: PICQUERY: A High Level Query Language for Pictorial
Database Management. IEEE ToSE Vol. 14, No. 5, Mai 1988, pp. 630 - 638

[KaAl-88]
Kasturi, R.; Alemany, J.: Information Extraction from Images of Paper-Based Maps.
IEEE Transactions on Software Engineering, Vol. 14, No. 5, May 1988, pp. 671 - 675

[KeWa-87]
Kemper, A.; Wallrath, M.: An Analysis of Geometric Modeling in Database Systems.
ACM Computing Surveys, Vol. 19, No. 1, March 1987, pp. 47 - 91

[LiHa-80]
Lien, E.; Harris, S.: Structured Implementation of an Image Query Language. Lecture
Notes in Computer Science 80, Springer 1980, pp. 416 - 430

[MWLW-89]
Meyer-Wegener, K.; Lum, V.; Wu, C.: Image Management in a Multimedia Database.
Proc. Working Conference on Visual Database Systems, Tokyo/Japan, April 1989,
Springer 1989, pp. 497 - 523

[OrMa-88]
Orenstein, J.; Manola, F.: PROBE Spatial Data Modeling and Query Processing in an
Image Database Application. IEEE ToSE Vol. 14, No. 5, Mai 1988, pp. 611 - 629

[RiWD-90]
Ritter, G.; Wilson, J.; Davidson, J.: Image Algebra: An Overview. Computer Vision,
Graphics, and Image Processing, Vol. 49, 1990, pp. 297 - 331

[RSFW-87]
Ritter, G.; Shrader-Frechette, M.; Wilson, J.: Image Algebra: A Rigorous and Trans-
lucent Way of Expressing All Image Processing Operations. Proc. 1987 SPIE Tech.
Symp. Southeast on Optics, Elec.-Opt., and Sensors, Orlando, May 1987

[SeKr-88]
Seeger, B.; Kriegel, H.P.: Design and Implementation of Spatial Access Methods. Proc.
14th Int. Conf. on Very Large Databases (VLDB), 1988, pp. 360 - 371

[SeRF-87]
Sellis, T.; Roussopoulos, N.; Faloutsos, C.: The R+-tree: A Dynamic Index for Multi-
Dimensional Objects. Proceedings of the 13th VLDB Conference, Brighton, 1987, pp.
507-518

206

[Tamu-80]
Tamura, H.: Image Database Management for Pattern Information Processing Studies. In: [ChFu-80], pp. 198 - 227

[VaDe-91]
Vandenberg, S.; DeWitt, D.: Algebraic Support for Complex Objects with Arrays, Identity, and Inheritance. Proc ACM SIGMOD Conf. 1991, pp. 158 - 167

[ZhBa-92]
Zhou, J.; Baumann, P.: Evaluation of Complex Cardinality Constraints. Proc. 11th Int. Conf. on Entity-Relationship Approach, Karlsruhe/Germany 1992, LNCS 645, Springer 1992, pp. 24 - 40

From Extensible Databases to Interoperability between Multiple Databases and GIS Applications

Hans-J. Schek and Andreas Wolf
Swiss Federal Institute of Technology
Department of Computer Science - Databases
{schek,wolf}@inf.ethz.ch

Abstract

One of the key concepts for the support of geographical objects in GIS is the extensibility of database management systems. In this paper, we will show that its generalisation in an open distributed environment well supports the exchange of either (foreign) data or of (foreign) operations between multiple geo-databases and several GIS application systems and in particular between databases and application-specific computation services. This is a step towards the interoperability of several (semi-) autonomous GIS specific services with database services in a global GIS environment (GGIS). We will elaborate on the advantages of externally defined types for an improved exchange of objects between a geo-database system and several application systems in a multi-lingual environment. This includes the support of multiple representations often required for the same object. We will describe how remote computation services follow the same principle. Heterogeneity in both aspects, in the system platform as well as in the data representation can be overcome in a systematic and explicit way. At the same time the protection issue, hindering the conventional extensibility, is addressed. By using our Geo DASDBS prototype system we are able to present measurements that confirm that the cost overhead by external remote computation services is well invested in view of the increased flexibility we gain.

1. Introduction and Motivation

Database research in the last decade was strongly influenced by the so-called non-standard applications, including engineering, office, multimedia, and geographical information systems. In particular, the support of geographical information systems (GIS) applications by future database systems is considered as the convincing test case for *extensible database management systems.* Extensibility has been proposed for all systems layers, from the language [Gü89,SRH90], query optimiser (e.g. Exodus [GDW87]), down to index management [Sto83,SW86,WWH88], and storage structures (e.g. Starburst). The notion of extensibility is independent of the data model. It is useful for the relational model as well as for any object model. Object-oriented database management specifically addresses extensibility by their inherent property of including methods on their objects. Nobody doubts the usefulness of an extensible object-oriented database system, open for the inclusion of new types and their methods, open for new indices, and for different storage managers.

Consequently, it seems that - even more than in the past - the DBMS is the central integrated and integrating component, responsible for everything and under the control of which everything is executed. The DBMS community seems to give the impression that all application programs that ever need some data must be executed in the control sphere of a DBMS, or, in other words, as a method on some object in the spirit of object-oriented databases. This ranges from simple methods on simple objects like polygon clipping up to complex operations like the overlay of several maps, the adjustment of large geodetic networks, or the optimisation of electric network load. Even if we admit that the objects and/or the methods may be foreign ones, we nevertheless assume that they are known to the central DBMS and they are processed on its behalf.

What is wrong with this perception? What is wrong if we bring ourselves as DBMS people in the foreground to such an extent? Apart from the obvious asymmetry between application systems and database systems, and apart from the unjustified expectation we raise that the new DBMS concepts can solve any application problem, many aspects are not covered and we must reconsider the role of the database systems in the context of a global geographic information system (GGIS) as we try to show by the following hypothetical traffic accident analysis scenario:

Assume an environmental engineer wants to analyse the accidents on the highways and come up with a map that visualizes the important facts of the accidents. For every accident it should show a ranked list of hypotheses of the cause and their justification.

As everybody can easily see without being an expert in this field a lot of various data and different evaluations using various kinds of computations on these data are necessary. Note that most of the data needed may already be stored in some files or in a database system of some public authority or private institution (see Appendix). Accidents certainly are registered and described by various attributes. Further there is a database that describes all highways, i.e. the geometry of the highway, the crossings, signals etc., and the responsibility for maintenance and control. Measurements on the traffic density may have been collected, some evaluations may have been performed already in order to redesign the highway net and in order to improve its capacity. Insurance companies have information on the accidents and further information may be found in some hospital information systems for the more severe accidents. Topographic information is available from digital terrain models in a GIS maintained by the surveying departement and information on the weather conditions, such as rainfall or fog certainly is kept in a GIS of the weather forecast institution.

Note further that not only the data are already available in various GISs or other databases, but also tools for processing data exist in the one kind or the other. As opposed to a database system, a today's GIS (e.g. Gradis, ArcInfo, Grass, ...), has a rich set of operations for point, line and area data, for map production, e.g. map overlays, for generating 3D views of a landscape etc. Moreover, many libraries exist that contain algorithms for computational geometry or for statistical analysis They are successfully used in institutions that process GIS data. Nevertheless the environment engineer in the example above has three major problems, namely to

(1) *find the information and the methods,*

(2) *get authorization, do the integration, and solve semantic mismatches, and*

(3) *combine the data with the methods.*

Problem (1), the functionality, design and realization of directory services ("yellow pages service") where information retrieval methods have to be combined with metadata administration is an interesting and challenging research topic that will not be discussed in this paper. For more information see e.g. [FML92]. Problem (2), the specification and the management of those parts of an information system that can be exported for the establishement of a federated schema and so made available to a global application is an extremely urgent problem too that has been investigated e.g. in [SL90, LMR90]. It will only be discussed briefly in this paper. Rather we will concentrate on problem (3), the combination of data with operations. This by itself is a large research area and the following aspects deserve more attention

- **Heterogeneity:** The practical reality is heterogeneous. There has always been a choice between different kinds of data base management systems from different manufacturers on different system platforms. As is the case with programming languages, the variety of data models in use is a consequence both of the historical development process and also of fundamental differences in principle. Data sources are heterogeneous because of different units, coordinate systems and because of different exchange format standards (TIGER vs ADALIN).
- **Legacy:** From the past we need to take over existing and well-maintained systems. It looks like waste of resources if a new (and a possibly better) model or programming environment requires new application programming of existing software.
- **Re-usability:** Similarly, it is desirable that systems that have been developed for one environment could be used within another without spending much effort for data or method translation and conversion.
- **Delegation:** The decomposition of a large task into smaller sub tasks is an approved principle. Subtasks can be clearly defined, controlled, and variants can be defined. We may think of negotiations between the contractor and potential subcontractors in order to find the best subcontractor for taking over a specific sub task. We can use parallelism in the execution of sub tasks.
- **Autonomy:** The more independent the execution of a sub task can be performed the higher is the potential for local optimisation and for the provision of dedicated and specialised services. On the other hand this introduces heterogeneity because data representations and operations are chosen autonomously to optimize the local tasks.

As a consequence we must consider the database system in its environment and we must reconsider its role in the environment. We are interested in the mechanisms which are needed if geographical application systems must be linked with one or several databases for the management of a complex task. We have to be concerned about how the complex task may be decomposed, what the responsibility of an application system is, what sub-tasks remain for the database systems, and how they co-operate.

Note that these questions are not relevant for end-users. They will utilise canned programs through window managers and enter required parameters. Rather we are interested in the support of GIS application programmers and GIS engineers who are responsible for the realisation of such programs. Our concern is the support of an environmental sciences specialist who tries to prove a hypothesis by analysing data from different GIS sources and by performing computations on them. And, last not least, we are interested in supporting the data base administrator who wants to customise an extensible database system by application-specific geographical objects. The objective of this paper therefore is a description of concepts which might be relevant in this general scenario.

Several other research groups are working on similar issues [IMS91,IMS93]. Closest to the work presented in our paper is the *Remote Exchange* project [FHML*91] that studies the cooperation of multiple (heterogeneous) object bases via e.g. remote method invocation [FHML*92] and the *Distributed Object Management* project [MHG*92] that concentrates more on the aspect of integrating existing databases and data repositories in a distributed environment. Another related project is the *Sequoia* project [SD91,Sto91]. There the main emphasis is put on the further extension of the extensible POSTGRES [SK91] prototype. As opposed to our COAX project [SW92b], there is less emphasis on the interoperability between database systems and special external computation and storage services. The aspect of translation between data representations in heterogeneous information systems is discussed e.g. in the *Mediator* project [Wie92] and in the work on *Information Brokers* [BC92].

We see our main contribution in the interoperability between databases and geo-application systems. As opposed to many in the field of multi-database systems, this paper explicitly includes the co-operation between databases and multiple application systems as well.

In the following we will describe the general framework and we will introduce an example that is repeatedly used through the rest of the paper. The presentation is mainly driven by this running example. In section 3 we discuss the extensibility by external types and show how this improves the exchange between application objects and database objects. This allows a direct application of external computation services. Section 4 extends section 3 in that different kinds of multiple representations necessary for the cooperation between several application systems and multiple databases are discussed. In section 5 we show results of experiments run in our prototype environment. We close with a discussion of the main results and an outlook into further work.[1]

2. The General Problem and a Case Study

2.1 General Framework

We follow [OV91] and state that distribution, autonomy, an heterogeneity are orthogonal properties of databases (see Fig. 1). Specifically we are interested in the degrees of autonomy. According to [DE89] we let *design autonomy* to a subsystem if it may choose its own object schema, i.e. its own representation and its own operations. With *execution autonomy* we characterize a subsytem if it can choose the way in which it executes a request submitted to it, and with *communication autonomy* the right of a system to choose what type of information it wants to communicate to other partners. In addition [SKS91] define *control autonomy* as the right to reject all attempts of other systems to influence the execution of a task (which is somehow related to execution autonomy). We will use this terminology not only for database systems but also for application systems.

---

[1]Parts of this paper have been adopted from [SW91]. The measurements in section 5 are more precisely described in [SW92b]

211

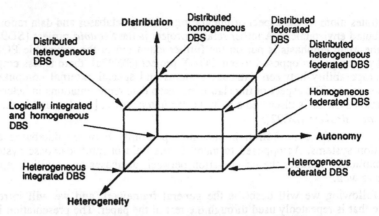

Figure 1: Architectures of DBS adopted from [OV91]

A global geo-information system (GGIS), on a high level of abstraction, consists of a network of different service nodes. A service node in this context and for the following presentation is either a geographical application system, denoted by *A* system in the following, or it is a (geo-)database system, abbreviated by *D* system for short, containing geographical and/or other objects. A directed link between two nodes *A* and *D*, or between two *D*s means that the two nodes exchange data and/or operations, in the sense that first controls the second one that in turn provides service for the first. An *A* system processes data from one or several *D*s, a *D* system provides database functionality, i.e. in particular persistency to one or several *A*s. There is no exchange, i.e. no link between two *A* nodes. In order to link two *A*s we need to link them via a *D*. Figure 2 shows an example environment. *A1* processes objects from *D1* and *D2*; it may store the result in one of these. Node *D2* is a multi-database node that imports from *D3* and *D4*. Node *A2* only works with *D4*. In the terminology of federated databases *A2* is local to *D4* while *A1* is global and accesses *D4* only via the part exported to *D2*. The node A3 is connected to D1 and D2 and it might be an example of a subordinated A service only accessed via D1 or via D3.

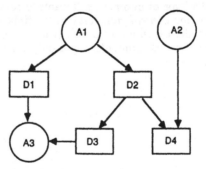

Figure 2: Several geo-specific application nodes A coupled with several geo-databases D.

For the following discussion a node is characterized by the data model (M), i.e. by the data structures which can be constructed and by the operations available on them, and by the system platform (S) on which data model is realized, i.e. the hardware, operating system etc. We denote with M_A the data model and with S_A the system platform of A and with M_D and S_D the ones of D. While the term data model is quite usual for D we use it also for A in the application environment. There we mean the data structures and the generic operations of an application programming language. In essence, we assume two different type systems, called M_A and M_D in the following. Roughly D is responsible for persistence and A does application-specific computations on data from D.

We concentrate on the case where D needs to be extended by (some) A methods. More precisely, we assume that main internal D components need to call an A method in order to process a selection operation or to create an index. We distinguish the following main cases

- *Externally Defined Types (EDTs)*: In this case we assume $M_A \neq M_D \wedge S_A = S_D$.

  Although we have different data models we are able to run the methods on the same systems. Note that we need data model conversions in this case.

- *External Operation Service (EOS)*: In this case we assume $M_A \neq M_D \wedge S_A \neq S_D$.

  This case no longer assumes compatibility in the system platforms and supports heterogeneity in the most general sense.

We will discuss these two cases in the following section. Before doing so, we will introduce a simple GGIS example to be used as a running example throughout this paper.

2.2 An Example GIS Scenario

Our scenario consists of several geographical information systems and databases that are established and maintained by different public and private institutions.

A first GIS, the property database PDB, is administered by the land registry office. It contains the land ownership information for the properties of a given region. Figure 3 gives an example of a plan that can be created from this database.

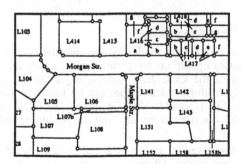

Figure 3: Example plan created from the PDB database

A second IS, the tax database TADB, is maintained by the tax department. It containes data about tax-payers and taxes classified according to the different kinds of taxes e.g. income tax and property tax.

A third GIS, the 'facility' management database FDB, is maintained by the electric power company. It contains data sets about the electricity cables, high tension lines and their pylons, the transformers, as well as electricity meters in the houses. A second data set in the FDB contains the information about the consumers of the electricity. Although independently managed the two data sets are related via the electricity meters which are part of both databases.

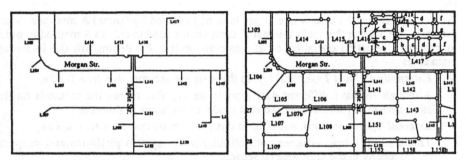

Figure 4: Example plans created from a) the FDB database and b) FDB and PDB databases

Figure 4a) shows a plan representing the electricity cable information that is maintained by the electric power company. On the other hand for many applications running in the electric power company, this is not sufficient. They will always use a plan like the one in figure 4b) that combines the cable information with the property information of the PDB database.

The Appendix contains a short description of a real community GGIS scenario [Mes90] from which our running example GGIS and the related object database were derived. While our example is rather naive and still not realistic enough to a GIS expert, it serves the purpose of introducing GIS problems to database people who are not yet aware of the GIS area.

2.3 The Example Object Database

We will introduce our object data model by showing the schema of our sample object classes and the (generic) operations by giving typical query and update examples. We will use the notation of the COCOON generic object model [SLR*92] but we will restrict ourselves only to those features that can be found in almost any object model e.g. IRIS [WLH90], O2 [Deu91], UniSQL [Uni], BROOM [Nor91,Nor92], DOM [Man89]. Most of the considerations are, not surprisingly, independent of the data model.

Figure 5 introduces the essential part of the object schema of the property database PDB. Note that we do not distinguish types from classes here for the sake of simplicity.

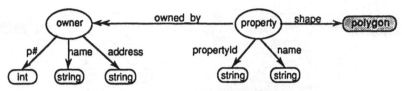

Figure 5: The schema of the property database PDB

The schema of the PDB contains two object types. Type owner is an *object* type with three *functions*, namely p# mapping to integers and name and address mapping to character strings. Type property is defined as an object type with four functions, namely propertyId and name mapping to a character string, shape mapping to type polygon, and owned_by mapping to sets of owners. The most interesting type for the following is polygon because it is an externally defined type (EDT). It is graphically presented similar to the standard basic types but using shadowed boxes. We will discuss EDTs later in section 3.

The tax authorities database shown in Fig. 6 contains information about tax payers and taxes. It does not contain geo-objects and could as well be a standard relational database. The schema in Fig. 6 could then be read as the design of such a database.

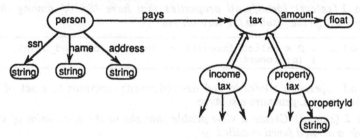

Figure 6: The schema of the tax authorities database TADB

Again there is a type person representing tax payers here. The function pays returns a set of tax objects, i.e. all the different taxes a person has to pay. Type tax has two subtypes income_tax and property_tax and possibly other special taxes as subtypes of tax. These allow to distinguish the different kinds of taxes. As can be seen by the function propertyId defined for property_tax we will be able to refer to information on properties in the context of the property tax for some global application, i.e. we will have to link the two databases PDB and TADB.

The third object schema is part from the FDB. It is almost self-explaining according to the previous descriptions. Two types are worth noting. polyline, another EDT describes the geometrical line of a cable between two nodes. A node has a function location that returns an instance of the (EDT) type point.

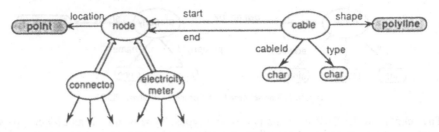

Figure 7: The schema of the electricity cable database FDB

The objects in a COCOON database can be manipulated via a generic data manipulation language. Objects can be created and deleted, updated and re-classified, and retrieved by an object preserving algebra. An algebra expression can also be used to define a view. For the purpose of this paper we will only need the *select* and the *extend* operation in the following examples. In addition we will need one object-generating operation called *extract*. A complete description of all operations can be found in [SLR*92].

The *select* operation supports the identification of objects by means of a selection predicate. It returns objects that satisfy the predicate query expression. An example is

Example 1 *(select): Identify all properties that have 'Smith' among the owners; temporarily assign the result to the variable res:*

```
res := select [ Ø ≠ select [name(o) = 'Smith'] (o:owned_by(p))
              ] (p:property)
```

The *extend* operation allows to add new (derived) functions to a set of objects. It extends the type, i.e. generates a subtype

Example 2 *(extend): Create a view pcable that shows the start point of every cable directly via a derived function called sp:*

```
create view pcable:= extend [sp(c):= location(start(c))] (c:cable)
```

The result of this view definition is shown in Fig. 8.

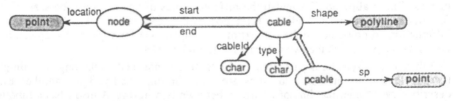

Figure 8 : The result type of the extend view pcable

While *select* and *extend* are object preserving i.e. they return existing objects, the operation *extract* creates (nested) sets of tuples by repeatedly applying functions to each object in the input sets

Example 3 *(extract): Generate a data structure that shows the 'MortonHouse' property-ids called p_id. For each such property it shows the p# and name of its owners called owner:*

```
tres := extract [ p_id:=propertyId(p),
                  owners:=extract[ p#(o), name(o) ] (o:owned_by) ]
                ( select [ name(p) = 'Morton House' ] (p:property))
```

The above query creates a nested relation with two attributes, the p_id and the set valued attribute owners. Owner itself is a subrelation with two attributes, p# and name of the owner. We will need this functionality later in sections 3 and 4 when talking about the extraction of data into the application environment.

3. Coupling of a Database with Application Objects

In this section we will re-consider the traditional host language coupling and summarize proposals for (complex) object buffers. The other, in our opinion more important step, are externally defined types.

3.1 Host Language Coupling

The most primitive data exchange between an application A and a database system D, called 'host language coupling' in SQL systems, is based on the exchange of variables of the basic types that exist in both environments e.g. via the SQL SELECT ... INTO clause. The values of the basic types are automatically converted e.g. between D integers (SQL NUMBER(8)) and A integers (C int) and vice versa. Extracting larger data sets therefore requires many data moves through the D interface and an important computational effort for the restructuring of the data. The first extension, in the meantime also available in some commercial systems, is known as the 'database portals' approach [SR84]. Relations (query results) in the D environment are mapped to array-of-record structures in the A environment. Later, this idea has been generalized to so called 'Object Buffers' as introduced e.g. in the PRIMA [HMMS87], AIM [KDG87], and DASDBS [SPSW90] projects. Object buffers contain arbitrary complex objects in a main memory representation e.g. as multiply linked lists. They allow the direct use of a complex object in the A environment. Since the structure is typically derived from the query sent to the D system, different representations can easily created to support different A systems. In DASDBS an object buffer would be generated by the specification given in example 3. A cursor is used to move through the property data and, by moving the cursor downward all owner data is available.

3.2 Externally Defined Types

The need for extending the set of base types with user-defined new types has been proposed already in [OH86], and it became known as the *support of abstract data types* (ADTs) in a database system. Since then several authors e.g. [Sto86,SW86,LKD88, Gü89,LNE89,HSWW88] have pointed out its usefulness and have introduced various forms of generalisation. However it seems that the importance in connection with the improved co-operation between application systems and databases has not been recognised. Therefore we will elaborate on that aspect and explain the approach of "externally defined types" (EDTs) that explicitly improves the support of application objects to be embedded directly into the database.

The principle of this architecture is shown in Fig. 9. As opposed to the standard host language coupling (Fig. 9a), now a "piece" is moved from A and is linked to D (Fig. 9b)

a)   b)

Figure 9: Cooperation between an application and (a) a relational database, and (b) an extensible DBMS with the EDT concept

According to the classification in section 2 we deal with the case where the database environment D needs to be extended by methods which are written in a model M_A different from M_D. However we do assume that the system platforms S_A and S_D are identical. We do not want to re-implement an existing A method. The EDT concept [HSSW88] allows the A methods to use data structure definitions and operation implementations in "arbitrary" M_A environments. The main idea consists of

- factoring out the conversion functions and making them explicitly known to M_D together with the type definition, and
- generating the conversion function automatically whenever possible.

First we utilize two conversion functions defined as

$A\_D(a:X@A)$ returns $b:Y@D$ ... converts from A to D

$D\_A(b:Y@D)$ returns $a:X@A$ ... converts from D to A

where parameter a of A_D (and result a of D_A) is of type X in the type system M_A of the application A and parameter b of D_A (and result b of A_D) is of type Y in the databases type system M_D. These two functions are inverse, i.e. they convert back and forth between the two environments[2].

$$A\_D \cdot D\_A = D\_A \cdot A\_D = id \qquad\qquad (1)$$

The A_D and D_A conversion functions are critical with respect to system correctness. In an efficient implementation, the routines fill variables of running programs without using the standard programming language assignment methods and thus bypassing the runtime checks of the programming environment for validating variable values. Correctness of the database system may be undermined by wrong conversion functions. Therefore we have investigated possibilities to generate correct A_D and D_A conversion routines automatically [Wo89].

If these functions are available to M_D, all instances a of type X can be stored in D and retrieved from D without any knowledge of the A representation. Further, and more

---

[2]By $F \cdot G$ we mean the sequence of the functions, i.e. G applied to the result of F or $G(F(x))$.

importantly, utilizing these conversion functions, any A method F_A implemented on the A type X can also be called from D, abbreviated as F_D, by using the obvious equality

$$F_D = D\_A \cdot F_A \cdot A\_D \qquad (2)$$

meaning that a (virtual) function F_D is obtained by converting the D representations of all input parameters of F_D to their corresponding A representations, executing F_A, and then converting the result(s) back to the D representation(s). When finding a reference to F_D in a query, the algebraic optimizer has to transform the operation tree according to formula (2). Moreover the optimizer knows equation (1). Assume a sequence of external operations $F_D \cdot G_D$ appears in a query. The optimizer then should not generate the sequence $D\_A \cdot F_A \cdot A\_D \cdot D\_A \cdot G_A \cdot A\_D$ but optimize this into $D\_A \cdot F_A \cdot G_A \cdot A\_D$. This clearly shows the advantage of factoring out the conversion functions and making them known to the DBMS. Otherwise the unnecessary conversions could not be eliminated.

Example 4: *Determine the properties which have an area larger than a given constant c. Create a view prop_c of these properties.*

```
create view prop_c:= select [area(shape(p)) > c] (p:property)
```

We assume that *polygon* includes a function *area* returning the area of the *polygon* instance. Internally the predicate expression is executed using the A_D_p function for polygons and the A_D_f for the result type float of area.

```
D_Af(area(A_Dp(shape(p)))))>c
```

The view generated is introduced into the object schema as shown in Fig. 10

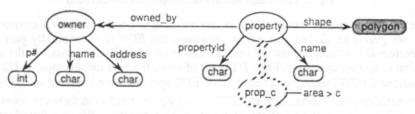

Figure 10: The result class of the select view in example 4

3.3 Foreign Computation Services

There are two main concerns with the EDT concept, namely *protection* and *heterogeneity*. The first, the protection issue, is considered so serious that real extendibility in the sense described above has been forbidden [LLPS91]. The major point of criticism still is in the integration of `foreign' code into the database system. Even when the conversion functions are correctly generated automatically, the A method called afterwards may corrupt the database. Since it is application programmers code representing a potentially difficult algorithm it is almost impossible to check it for correctness. This opens the database system for possible failures and may create security leaks.

The second issue, the heterogeneity, is not taken into account with EDTs because of the restrictive assumption that the runtime environments SA and SD are compatible in the sense that the conversion functions and the A methods can be linked to the D code and run together. Note that this assumption caused the protection problem above.

The approach which solves both problems mentioned above looks simple. We propose the creation of a special "operation service" which consists of all those A methods that are called from D. Fig. 11 shows the types of processes. The application process(es) A exchange(s) data with the D process(es). The D process, in order to satisfy the request from A, calls the operation service O_A. This process provides the service in terms of A-specific computations for D. It consists of the set of procedures identified to be necessary for the DBMS to manage EDT data. The procedures are integrated into a single code module that is extended with a (synchronous) RPC like interface. In their Remote Cooperation System (RCS) project [GGS93] propose a similar but more flexible integration via an asynchronous communication protocol.

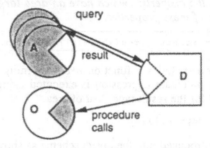

Fig. 11: Cooperation with an external operation service (EOS)

The external operation service (EOS) is implemented and operates in an A environment, i.e. we guarantee *design autonomy*. However, the EOS is conceptually part of D. Therefore D has complete control over the execution of service requests, i.e. the service has no *execution autonomy*. From D's point of view, the type management in O_A looks similar to the EDT management except that EDT operations are executed remotely.

In generalizing the execution of an EDT method F_A we need to include the conversions to a transfer representation of the communication subsystem. We will introduce D_T and T_D for conversions between D and the transfer representation and similarly the functions A_T and T_A for the conversion between A and the transfer representation. Further we denote by T the transfer of data. We still use the abbreviation 'A' for the environment O_A since we assume that it is the same as for A. Using these conventions we can represent the A_D conversion and its inverse introduced in the previous section more precisely as

$$D\_A = D\_T \cdot T \cdot T\_A \qquad (3)$$
$$D\_A = A\_T \cdot T \cdot T\_D$$

Therefore, instead of executing F_D according to formula (2) we now execute F_D as a sequence according to

$$F_D = D\_T \cdot T \cdot T\_A \cdot F_A \cdot A\_T \cdot T \cdot T\_D \qquad (4)$$

The input parameter(s) for the function F_A must be converted from D to the transfer representation using D_T. The actual transport of data is performed by T, the conversion to the A representation occurs (T_A), and the operation F_A is executed. Afterwards the output parameter(s) are converted back to the transfer representation (A_T), transferred (T), and converted to a D representation (T_D).

Optimizing EOS calls

Again we have to introduce this extended semantics to the optimizer. If we look at the example $F_D \cdot G_D$, where F_A and G_A are the 'real' (EDT) implementations in S_A, the standard transformation is

$$D\_T \cdot T \cdot T\_A \cdot F_A \cdot A\_T \cdot T \cdot T\_D \cdot D\_T \cdot T \cdot T\_A \cdot G_A \cdot A\_T \cdot T \cdot T\_D$$

The most simple optimization uses only $T\_D \cdot D\_T = id$. A better optimization does not restrict itself to the database side where D_T and T_D takes place but tries to eliminate unnecessary data transfer and data conversion on the operation service side too. An optimal expression would be

$$D\_T \cdot T \cdot T\_A \cdot F_A \cdot G_A \cdot A\_T \cdot T \cdot T\_D$$

This however assumes that the operation service allows to issue a *sequence* of operations and that the optimizer knows about that.

Cost factors for EOS calls

Even if we eliminate redundant conversions and data transfer we apparently have more operations to execute than just executing F_A or G_A. Therefore we are interested in the cost factors, especially we want to know the increase in execution costs for an F_D compared to F_A. Three kinds of costs can be distinguished, namely data *conversion* cost, data *transfer* cost, and operation *execution* cost.

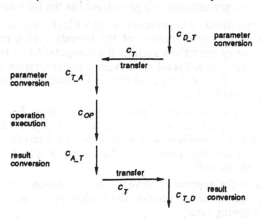

Fig. 12: General cost schema for operation service calls

Figure 12 summarizes the costs arising. Data conversion cost is imposed by the change of the data model ($M_A \neq M_D$). Data transfer cost appears whenever the operation is executed in a different system environment ($S_A \neq S_D$).

In the general model (see equation 4) data conversion costs appear in four different situations during an operation call. Parameters of a procedure have to be converted from the D representation to the A representation in two steps via the intermediate data transfer format and the results have to be converted back to the D representation in the same two steps. Data transfer cost appears twice, for the parameters and for the results. The resulting cost formula is

$$C_{FD} = C_{D\_T} + C_T + C_{T\_A} + C_{FA} + C_{A\_T} + C_T + C_{T\_D} \tag{5}$$

The cost model in Fig. 12 and formula 5 are applicable to the pure EDT implementation too. If there is no longer a data transfer and the data conversion is done in one step without the need for an intermediate representation the following costs arise

$$C_{FD} = C_{D\_A} + C_{FA} + C_{A\_D} \tag{6}$$

In any case this shows that additional costs occur which must be justified by other benefits. We will quantify these additional costs by measurements on realistic data in section 5 below.

4. Multiple Representations and Multi-Object Databases

4.1 Multiple Application Representations

So far we have shown that it is possible to embed complicated geo-objects into the database. There is a well-defined interface known to D as well as to A. All applications A must agree on this interface. Further, since an EDT is an abstract data type only for the database, not for the application to which the object is delivered, there is only one single represention that is generated by the corresponding D_A function. However the agreement on a single representation of a geo-object has the following disadvantages.

First, different algorithms that process a geo-object often need it in several representations. A vector representation of the boundary of a parcel object may be preferable for elementary operations such as the computation of the area or the length of the along to a neighbour. A hybrid raster/vector representation [Sam90] of the same parcel objects might be desired if a parcel map is intersected or overlayed with another map showing agricultural land utilization.

Second, we want to support a multi-lingual environment. For every programming language that needs D service and wants to process a geo-object a D_A conversion must be provided. Note that this requirement is to be expected. Conversions for all base types must be provided in the traditional host language coupling between D and any programming language as well.

Both aspects require the support of several representations and "exchange format" processing. The D system has to provide the book-keeping as we will elaborate by a distinction of the following cases.

Two Different Representations in Homogeneous A's

In this case we assume that a geo-object g is needed in different representations G1 and G2 because different algorithms processs it. But we assume that G1 and G2 are expressed in the type system M_A of a single A environment, i.e. the two algorithms are implemented in the same programming language. In particular we may assume that, again in M_A, we have available two conversion functions C_{12} and C_{21} that convert from the G1 representation to G2 and vice versa. Let us now assume that only one representation should be used in D, and let us further assume that $A1\_D$ and D_A1 have been generated from the G1 type declarations, then the other two obviously are expressed by

$$D\_A2 = D\_A_1 \cdot C12 \qquad (7)$$
$$A2\_D = C21 \cdot A1\_D$$

Fig. 13a shows this scenario. Note thet the conversions are executed in the $A2$ environment which is possible because $S_A = S_D$.

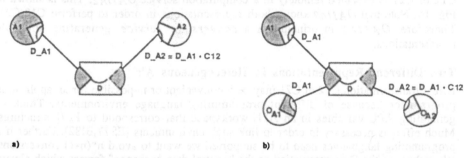

a)   b)

Fig. 13: Coupling two application environment via a single D representation

Similarly, in Figure Fig. 13b we have an A system coupled with a D system that in turn needs two operation services O_{A1} and O_{A2}. For example O_{A1} may be a clip computation service requiring a vector representation of a line object and of O_{A2} as the intersection computation service that requires a hybrid raster-vector representation of the same line object. If the two different representations are frequently used, we may introduce two different D representations.The advantage now is that both conversions between $A1$ and D and $A2$ and D are generated form the G1 and G2 specifications respectively. In order to keep both D representations consistent in case of updates we need to derive the conversion functions between the two D representations as follows

$$C12' = D1\_A1 \cdot C12 \cdot A2\_D2 \qquad (8)$$
$$C21' = D2\_A2 \cdot C21 \cdot A1\_D1$$

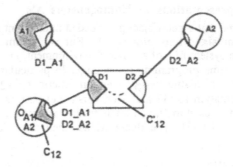

Fig. 14: Using two D representations with a conversion service

Using (8) enables us to enforce consistent updates. Note that D-internally we do not need to know anything about the D representations. We could even admit that the conversion C12 or C21 is executed remotely in a computation service $O_{A1/A2}$. This is shown in Fig. 14. Note that $O_{A1/A2}$ knows both representations in order to perform C12/C21. Therefore $O_{A1/A2}$ in principle is a *conversion service* generating multiple representations.

Two Different Representations in Heterogeneous A's

Direct transformation C12 or C21 may be inconvenient or impossible for an application programmer because of different programming language environments. Think of generating APL variables in an APL workspace that correspond to PL/1 structures. Much effort is necessary in order to link such environments [ES77,B182]. Further if n programming languanges need to be supported we want to avoid n*(n-1) conversions. We rather see the D representation as the "neutral data exchange" format which always has to be used if geo-objects are stored from an $A1$ and retrieved into $A2$. Note however that in this case an automatic generation of the A_D conversion and its inverse are no longer possible. Rather the D representation must be carefully selected as to support the conversion into all desired A environments equally well. But this is an advantage. The D-representation is not visible to any A user. There will always be a transformation between D and A. The D-representation can therefore be optimised according to cost considerations and it even may change over time without causing any change to an A system.

A D system therefore plays the role of an "object exchange" administrator. It knows what format has to be generated in response to an A client and it knows where a required object has to be taken from and where the required conversion has to be computed. But there is more than a simple object exchange. The D system also performs computations on geo-object on behalf of an A client. Again the administration function of the D system becomes obvious. After locating the corresponding geo-object(s) it knows where the computation can be performed and what representation has to be generated first. After performing the computation the result is handed over to the client in the right fomat and the A system, the client, takes over the reponsibility and performs other specific computations. The result of these may again be handed over to the previous D system or to another D system that is available. We will come to the question of managing several D systems shortly below.

4.2 Dual Object Types

In the previous subsection we have discussed several A representations and have pointed out that the D representations were solely internal. This changes when we now introduce "dual" object types.

Dual objects are EDT objects i.e. they have an explicit A type and they have a D representation that is generated by the conversion functions. In addition now a dual object has also an explicit "dual" D type. It is structured explicitly using the functionality of the model MD. This is important for the following reason. In the pure EDT approach all operations must be realised as A methods. We cannot utilise operations provided for explicit D types other than the primitives create, extract, and delete. We cannot use a filter and we cannot make EDT internal relationships explicit by the D model.

Let us look back into the property example. The important design decision was that the border of any property was introduced by the function shape that returns a value of the EDT polygon. This allowed us to consider functions like extension or display as foreign EDT functions. If we now explicitly wish to support the neighbour relationship telling us which property is a adjacent to which other property a different model is required. In our current schema two neighboured properties have two independent polygon values when the shape function is used.. Therefore, it becomes obvious that in our schema we have to cope with redundancy since one border line always occurs in two parcels. In our current model it is the responsibility of the user to take care of the right updates in case of changes of the border of a parcel. The database system cannot handle this kind of referential integrity because it has not been modelled explicitly in MD. Therefore a better schema is Fig. 15.

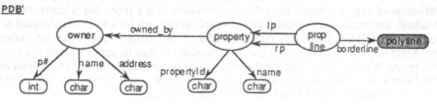

Fig. 15: Revised schema of Figure 5

We now have two object types property and propline that are related by the functions lp and rp that refer to the left (lp) and right (rp) neighbour property. The function borderline returns a value of the EDT polyline as a geometrical description. The type polyline represents the line object that separates two properties. Now the relationship between the property and the border is made explicit. A border line appears only once. A change in a border line is visible and effective to both neighbours.

How can we now, using this schema instead of the one given in Fig. 5, utilize a computation service that needs shape as a polygon type? Note that we want to utilize the existing functions extension or display. We will do this in two steps: First, let us define a subtype PV as a view that defines a new function plines which returns the border lines to every property. The corresponding view definition is

```
create view PV := extend [ plines :=
                  select [ rp(l)=p or lp(l)=p ] (l:propline) ] (p:property)
```

According to our preparations for an improved host language coupling we can also extract and transfer the set of border lines. While this transfers data to the A environment and also takes care of the conversion of the polyline objects by the appropriate D_A function for this line type, we still need the polygon type representation. But now we arrive at the problem we have dealt with in the previous section. We need a transformation between two different A representations. The one is generated by extract, the other one is the desired polygon representation. Let us call this conversion Clg. It converts the object buffer representation to the type polygon. Using Clg we can now define a view PV' that defines the new and desired function shape returning an instance of polygon as follows

```
create view PV' := extend [ shape :=
                    Clg( extract [ l#(l) , borderline(l) ]
                                  (l:plines(p)) ] (p:PV)
```

Dual types again have two different representations, but now there is one in the A system and there is another one in the D system, and therefore there exists also a different representation if it is extracted from the D representation to an A environment.

4.3 Coupling Multiple Object Databases

The interoperability of multiple object bases is a central research subject in the database area. We will need the results from these efforts for the GGIS area, specifically the definition of export schema, the schema integration into a federated schema, and multi-database transaction management (see several survey articles and books devoted to this subject e.g. [HM85,SL90,LMR90,El91,BGS92]). We believe that these are extremely important but not GGIS- specific and a discussion of these issues is beyond the scope of this paper. We will only point out the importance of view definitions over several object databases and we will show how the support of several A representations carries over to the case of multiple object bases. As before the presentation is example driven.

For the further discussion we assume, that we have homogeneous object databases or at least homogeneous export schemas. Further we assume that only the lowest degree of schema integration [SST92] is applied, i.e. the (exported) schema of the local object base is globally available. No object unification is defined. We will use the names qualified by the database name, e.g. property@PDB, as is common in existing products.

Oviously, in our running example the amount of tax to be payed for a property is related to that property. Assume now the tax authorities want to verify the amount of tax for a property by looking at the property's data and applying some taxation formula to calculate the property tax. Then they need to have access to the PDB. The following view definition extends the schema of the TADB.

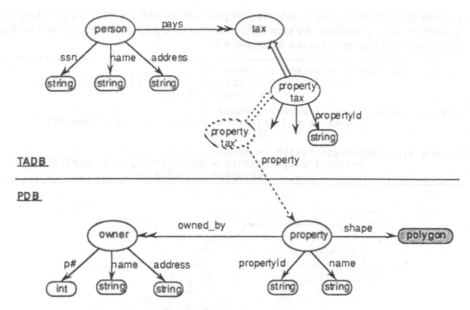

Figure 16: TADB extended by a multi-database view

```
create view propertytax' :=
    extend [ property :=
            select [ propertyId(p) = propertyId(pt) ] (p:property@PDB)
        ] (pt:propertyTax@TADB)
```

It introduces a (virtual) subtype called propertytax' with a function property that refers to the property in the PDB directly (see Fig. 16).

Using this view a user could access the owner of a property and check whether it is the same as the person paying tax for it. As views in the sense of COCOON are updatable [SLT91] he technically could even update the owner's address through this view if the corresponding authorization has been specified in PDB's export schema definition.

Note that we assume in this view definition, that there is an easy (formal) way of identifying the property object in PDB that is related to the propertytax object with a given propertyId value.

4.4 Linking Multiple Applications with Multiple Object Databases

In this last case we can profit from the preparations in the last sections. Section 3.3 described the support for multiple *A* representations within a single database. Section 3.4 described the generic transformation operations necessary to allow multiple *D* views and dual representations. Together with the views over multiple object bases sketched in the previous section, we can easily set up an environment that allows us to link multiple applications using different object representations with multiple object bases.

Assume now in continuing with our previous example, that within the TADB we often want to compute the extension of a property and display it. In order to conveniently process this we need a (view) schema that provides us with the EDT type `polygon`. Therefore we can combine the view definition we have prepared in section 4.2 with a view definition similar to the one in section 4.3.

```
create view PV@PDB := extend [ plines :=
            select [rp(l)=p or lp(l)=p ] (l:propline@PDB) ]
                        (p:property@PDB)

create view PV'@TADB := extend [ shape :=
            Clg(extract [ l#(l), borderline(l) ] (l:plines(p)) ]
                        (p:PV@PDB)

create view propertytax'@TADB := extend [ property :=
            select [ propertyId(p) = propertyId(pt) ] (p:PV'@TADB) ]
                        (pt:propertyTax@TADB)
```

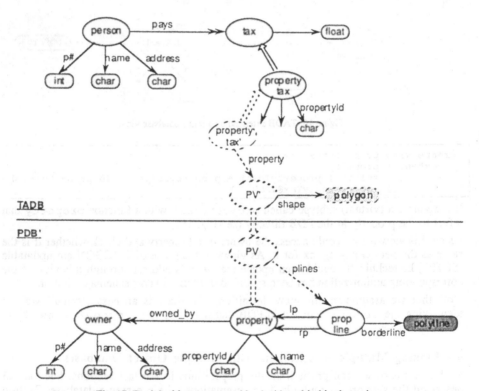

Fig. 17: Dual A object types combined with multi-objectbase views

Fig. 17 shows the result of the view definition. The PDB is extended with view PV as shown in section 4.2. TADB is first extended with a dual representation `polygon` of the PDB' object representation `set of polyline`. The method is similar to the one described in section 4.2 for PDB' but now affecting both databases. Finally the TADB is extended as in section 4.3, but now referring to `PV'` view instead of `property`. Note that the question of whether views are materialized or supported by additional redundant (index) structures is not discussed at that level and is left open.

5. Evaluation and Experimental Results

5.1 The Prototype Systems

In order to evaluate the concepts we have set up an experimental environment that couples DASDBS [SPSW90] with the geometrical computation service XYZ-GeoBench [NSDL*91].

The Geo DASDBS [SW86,Wo89,SW92a] is an extensible database kernel system. Special attention has been given to basic type extensibility and to the extension by generic access methods [HSWW88]. The kernel implements the EDT mechanism ($MA \neq MD$, $SA = SD$). Several versions of primitive geometric data types have been implemented together with some basic operations. One reference implementation is an implementation of the types polyline and polygon. polylines describe lines as list of point to point line segments. The area type polygon is derived from the line type by representing the surrounding lines (the borders) of the area in a polyline (see details in [SW92b]). polyline and polygon are implemented in a Modula-2 system that provides basic inter-language communication with the standard C system used for DASDBS.

A second prototype is the XYZ-GeoBench [NSDL*91]. It is a toolbox of computational geometry algorithms and a front-end to acquire and display 2D (and partially 3D) data. GeoBench is implemented in Object Pascal [THINK] on a Macintosh system. Therefore linking these two gives us an example for the case $MA \neq MD$ and $SA \neq SD$[3]. The GeoBench serves as both the application program and the operation service for the Geo DASDBS which in turn serves as the storage system for the data manipulated in the GeoBench. Figure 18 shows the principle cooperation architecture.

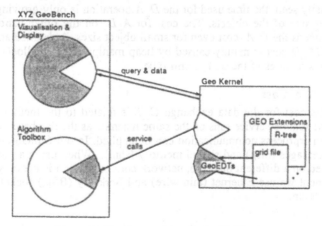

Figure 18: The Cooperation with the GeoBench

---

[3]It requires some "tricks" to make Macintosh applications callable from outside.

5.2 Measurements

In the following section we measure the different costs in detail. The hardware platform for these measurements was a Sun cluster with Sun 3/60 machines under SunOS Release 4.1.1 running Geo DASDBS and a Macintosh FX using the Object Pascal environment running the XYZ-Geobench. The data sets used in both tests are realistic and have been gathered by cartographers by digitizing map sheets. The data has been used to build up the initial data set for automatic map construction.

Conversion Cost

The data conversion cost highly depends on the internal representation of the data structure to be converted. Data structures that are pointer free can easily be mapped to database representations while heap oriented representations with pointer references have to be restructured by either linearizing with pointer elimination or mapping programming language pointers (addresses) to logical ones such as object IDs.

As an example we show the cost for the D_A/A_D conversions for the data type polyline. M_A is the Modula-2 type system. The representation in M_D is a linearization of the M_A representation with elimination of pointers, i.e. a simple bytestring. The data objects are polylines with 2 to 196 points each. The conversion times given in the table are the averages over the objects classified according to their size.

#points	#bytes	D_A (msecs)	A_D (msecs)
2-50	16-400	0.5	0.7
50-100	400-800	0.6	2.0
100-200	800-1600	0.7	2.6

Table 1: Data conversion times for polylines

As can be easily seen, the time used for the D_A operation is only growing slightly with an increasing size of the objects. The cost for A_D on the other hand grows much faster and exceeds the D_A cost even for small object sizes. A detailed analysis showed that the D_A/A_D cost is mainly caused by heap manipulation (malloc()/free()) for the dynamic data structures of the polyline type.

Communication Cost

Obviously the cost for the data exchange C_T is related to the method used for data transfer. If the remote service runs on the same machine as the database system different methods of interprocess communication can be applied. In our SunOS environment we used both, messages (msg) and shared memory (shm). When using a remote operation service located on a different machine, network communication is the only possibility In our environment we use Ethernet (thin wire) and Berkeley (BSD) sockets for this kind of communication.

method	transfer time (msecs/kbyte)
Ethernet / TCP/IP	10-50
unix messages	1-10
unix shared memory	0.1-1

Table 2: Data exchange cost

Table 2 shows the communication cost for the different communication methods. Times for Ethernet transfer heavily depend on the network load. In the tests shown here we had a medium network load with only few conflicts (overnight experiments). The speed of (socket based) Ethernet communication also depends on the amount of data sent with one request. Optimal results require request sizes of more than 1 kByte. Our results match those found in the RAID project [MB91]. The Ethernet throughput measured in the Sequoia 2000 project is smaller [PPFK91]. This reflects their wide area network environment and with a much higher load.

5.2.4. Operation cost

In the GEO Kernel basic operations on geometries have been tested with several data sets. Table 3a gives examples of operation costs for polyline and table 3b for polygon operations.

	polyline operations		polygon ops.
#points	intersects (msec)	clip (msec)	clip (msec)
2-50	0.55	2.7	20
50-100	1.6	7.5	68
100-200	2.7	12.6	142

Table 3: Basic operations for a) polylines and b) polygons

Since polygon areas are implemented by surrounding lines of type polyline, they share major parts of the intersects rectangle operation. Table 3b therefore only shows the CPU times for the clip operation. Compared to the clip operation for lines the cost is significantly higher because of the increased complexity of areas compared to lines[4].

In the cooperation, the GeoBench deals with the more complex operations on geometric objects. The algorithms of the GeoBench are a good example for the usability of the operation service approach in several ways. They are complicated and cannot be recoded. For example a Voronoi calculation is about eight pages of code. Specific data structures are needed, for example Delauny triangulation requires a Voronoi representation of the point set.

In Tables 4 a set of sample runs of different algorithms is given to illustrate their CPU-time complexity. The algorithms selected may occur in a join between two spatial relations, i.e. they are called by the most inner D components.

---

[4]Lines have much more special cases where an empty result can easily be detected (e.g. line outside rectangle). Therefore the average cost is lower but the worst case cost is equivalent.

#points	polygon intersect (sec)	polygon union (sec)
40 * 60	0.31	0.33
100 * 100	27	30
200 * 200	136	120

Table 4: Sample runtimes for simple CG algorithms

Table 5 shows the results for a different class of algorithms. The calculation of a Voronoi representation of a point set may be seen as result preparation step that can be performed either in the application or in the database system. The same is true for the spanning tree calculation. However, if a nearest neighbour search or the minimum spanning tree is a frequent operation, the calculation of the Voronoi representation can be seen as the preparation of a precomputed intermediate result (like an access path) and therefore it could also be an important algorithm inside the database system.

algorithm	100 points (sec)	500 points (sec)	1000 points (sec)
Voronoi / plane sweep	1.4	7.3	15.7
nearest neighbour	0.5	2.8	6.0
minimum spanning tree	2.1	14.3	41.3
nearest neighbour of Voronoi	0.1	0.5	1.1
minimum spanning tree of Voronoi	0.4	2.6	5.1
triangulation of Voronoi	0.1	0.5	1.6

Table 5: Sample runtimes for complex CG algorithms

As can easily be seen even simple algorithms such as intersecting two polygones need several seconds whenever the polygons have a realistic size (100 or more points). More complex calculations like the Voronoi polygon calculation require significantly more time.

5.5. Discussion

The main question we wanted to answer with the experiments sketched in the previous sections was: 'How much do we have to pay when we execute operations remotely?'

Table 6 gives the detailed cost analysis for the (simple) `polygon clip` operation executed on a remote machine. As we can see the operation cost is between 50 and 60 percent of the total cost. Data conversion time (1-3% of execution time) can be ignored, i.e. the EDT concept does not introduce significant additional cost to the necessary operation cost. The data transfer cost even with a slow network is less than the computation cost. It should not be ignored but is surprisingly small in view of the relatively simple operations executed remotely.

#points	time (msecs)	% conv.	%transf.	% oper.
2-50	41.2	3.0	48.5	48.5
50-100	110.6	2.5	36.0	61.5
100-200	220.3	1.5	34.0	64.5

Table 6: Cost factors of remote `polygon clip`

If we extrapolate the same data for a more complex operation like the Voronoi calculation we can see that the additional is no longer significant. Table 7 shows this time analysis based on data from tables 1, 2, and 5.

#points	time (sec)	% conv.	%transf.	% oper.
100	1.5	~ 0.0	6.6	93.4
500	7.8	~ 0.0	6.4	93.6
1000	16.6	~ 0.0	5.4	94.6

Table 7: Cost factors of remote Voronoi / plane sweep

6 Conclusions and Open Questions

In the previous sections we have concentrated on co-operation between several application systems and one or multiple database systems. We have shown that extensibility by EDTs is a key concept for object exchange and remote computation using specialized services. It can also be conveniently combined with object views and supports several representations. We have presented them in detail and by a series or examples because we felt that they are somehow neglected in current research. In particular the role of application systems that are connected to but not subordinated to database systems must be re-considered with the consequence that data conversion and exchange formats must be made known to the database system in order to make optimization possible.

The examples we have chosen may look too simple as to justify the overhead of external operation services. However, the measurements in our prototype system confirm that the gain in increased flexibility and higher protection pays off already in the simple examples. This will be the more the case the complexer the computations are like map overlay or generalization of map representations. Further it looks like the technological development will support the fast communication between many powerful workstations with large main memories. In the following let us comment on some critical questions that may arise:

The Impedance Mismatch Problem: The need for various conversion functions, i.e. the impedance mismatch, was one of the driving forces for OODBMS technology. OODBMS provide an integrated homogeneous application development environment, often by a persistent programming language. However, it turns out that a GGIS environment requires to deal with system heterogeneity and with the distribution of data and of functions in local and global networks in an explicit manner. As a consequence we must provide tools that deal with the impedance mismatch on a higher level of abstraction rather than hide it in an ideal but unrealistic environment. Note however that for the end-user it may look like providing such and integrated system.

Foreign Functions a Trojan Horse? As we discussed the protection issue was considered so serious that extensibility of the DBMS was converted to the opposite, i.e. extension of the application system [LLPS91]. They proposed that a function implemented by the a database type implementor (such as clip or intersect) is also made available to the application environment. However, we feel that this is not the problem to be solved for GIS support. As we have shown by the measurements interprocess, communication, and data conversion adds almost no overhead even to relatively simple external function executions but ensures protection. In case of heterogeneous system platforms where the overhead by network transfer is too high, we may think of recoding some basic functions but still would keep them in a separate address space. Whether or not bringing an external function "near" to the DBMS is a question of the implementation effort versus the performance gains and so it is an open optimization problem.

Do we Need a Data Model? In view of foreign objects, it looks like we should manage GIS objects by "sophisticated database blobs", i.e. by EDTs and EOSs. The role of a database system in the context of GGISs consists in the administration of larger units and the control of computations done by EOSs. But we also have shown that for basic integrity constraints we often want to model objects in several ways. This has led us to dual object types as a special case of multiple object representations. Therefore, we do need a simple object model that takes care of the basic integrity constraints such as existential dependencies for identical objects in different representations or for derived objects. A GGIS needs what has been called a "RISC" object model [MH92] or what others called a generic core object manager (such as COCOON [SLR*92], BROOM [Nor91], GOM [KMWZ91], McLeod [FMGL*93]).

Does the database contain data? This seems to be a purely rhetorical question at a first glance. In the approach we described so far we certainly stored all data in one or several object base systems but we proposed to have serious computation done externally. The question now arises whether we should not also store the objects externally and have specialized storage and index managers. Going into this direction means that the database system more and more is a managing service that knows something about its clients, the application systems and it knows also what services are available at what dependencies exist among them.

We are convinced that these questions will deserve much more research, especially the last one seems interesting because it comes up in other global information systems as well such as computer integrated manufacturing. We will investigate some of these questions in the framework of our COSMOS project [SSPW90].

Acknowledgement

We would like to thank Moira Norrie, Andrew Deacon, and Lukas Relly for their helpful comments that significantly improved the presentation of this paper.

234

Bibliography

BC92   Barbara, D., Clifton, C., Information Brokers: Sharing Knowledge in a Heterogeneous distributed System, Matsushita Information Technology Laboratory, Technical Report MITL-TR-31-92, 1992

BGS92   Breitbart, Y., Garcia-Molina, H., Silberschatz, A., Overview of Multidatabase Transaction Management, VLDB Journal, 1(2), 1992

Bl82   Blaser, A., et al., Integrated Data Analysis and Management System Feature Description, in: Brodie, M.L., Schmidt, J.W. (eds.), Relational Data Base Management Systems, Springer, 1982

BLN86   Batini, C., Lenzerini, M., Navathe, S.B., A Comparative Analysis of Methodologies for Database Schema Integration, ACM Computing Surveys, 18(4), 1986

Deu91   Deux, O. et al., The O_2 System, Communications of the ACM, 34(10), 1991

DE89   Du, W., Elmagarmid, A.K., Quasi-Serializability: A Correctness Criterion for Global Concurrency Control in InterBase, Proc. 15th VLDB Conf., 1989

El91   Elmagarmid, A.K. (ed.), Database Transaction Models for Advanced Applications, Morgan Kaufmann, 1991

ES77   Eberle, H., Schmutz, H., Calling PL/1 or FORTRAN Subroutines Dynamically from VSAPL, IBM Heidelberg Scientific Center, Technical Report 77.11.007, 1977

FHML*91   Fang, D., Hammer, J., McLeod, D., Si, A., Remote Exchange: An Approach to Controlled Sharing Among Autonomous, Heterogeneous Database Systems, Proc. IEEE Spring Compcon, 1991

FHML*92   Fang, D., Hammer, J., McLeod, D., A Mechanism for Function-Based Sharing in Federated Databases, Proc. DS-5 Semantic on Interoperable Database Systems, 1992

FGML*93   Fang, D., Ghandeharizadeh, S., McLeod, D., Si, A., The Design, Implemetation, and Evaluation of an Object-Based Sharing Mechanism for Federated Database Systems, Proc. IEEE Data Engineering, 1993 (to appear)

FML92   Fang, D., McLeod, D., Seamless Interconnection in Federated Database Systems, in: Kambayashi, Y. (ed.), Database Systems for Next Generation Applications: Principles and Practize, World Scientific, 1992

GDW87   Gräfe, G., DeWitt, D.J., The EXODUS Optimizer Generator, Proc. ACM SIGMOD Conf. on Management of Data, 1987

GGS93   Gesmann, M., Grasnickel, A., Schöning, H., A Remote Cooperation System Supporting Interoperability in Heterogeneous Environments, in: [IMS93]

Gü89   Güting, R.H., GRAL: An Extensible Relational Database System for Geometric Applications, Proc. 15th VLDB Conf. 1989

HM85   Heimbigner, D., McLeod, D., A Federated Architecture for Information Management, ACM TOIS, 3(3), 1985

HMMS87   Härder, T., Meyer-Wegener, K., Mitschang, B., Sikeler, A., PRIMA - A DBS Prototype Supporting Engineering Applications, Proc. VLDB Conf., 1987

HSSW88   Haas, L.M., Schwarz, P.M., Schek, H.-J., Wilms, P.F., Incorporating Data Types in an Extensible Database Architecture, in Proc. of the 3rd Int. Conf. on Data and Knowledge Bases, Jerusalem, June 1988

HSWW88   Horn, D., Schek, H.-J., Waterfeld, W., Wolf, A., Spatial Access Paths and Physical Clustering in a Low-Level Geo-Database System, in: Niedersächsisches Landesamt für Bodenforschung (ed.), Construction of Geoscientific Maps Derived from Databases (Proc. of an Intern. Colloquium), Geologisches Jahrbuch, Sonderband, Hannover 1988

IMS91   International Workshop onResearch Issues in Data Engineering: Interoperability in Multidatabase Systems, 1991 (Kyoto), IEEE Computer Society Press

IMS93   International Workshop onResearch Issues in Data Engineering: Interoperability in Multidatabase Systems, 1993 (Vienna), IEEE Computer Society Press

KDG87   Küspert, K., Dadam, P., Günauer, J., Cooperative Object Buffer Management in the AIM Prototype, Proc. VLDB Conf., 1987

KDWZ91   Kemper, A., Mörkotte, G., Walter, H.-D., Zachmann, A., GOM: A Strongly Typed Persistent Object Model With Polymorphism, Proc. 4th GI Conf. on Database Systems for Office, Engineering, and Scientific Applications (BTW), Springer IFB, 1991

LH90   Lindsay, B., Haas, L.M., Extensibility in the Starburst Experimental database System, in: Blaser, A. (ed.), Database Systems of the '90s Springer, LNCS 466, 1990

LKD88   Linneman, V., Küspert, K., Dadam, P., The Design and Implementation of an Extensible Database Management System Supporting User-Defined Types and Functions, Proc. VLDB Conf., 1988

LLPS91   Lohman, G.M., Lindsay, B., Pirahesh, H., Schiefer, K.B., Extensions to Starburst: Objects, Types, Functions, and Rules. Communications of the ACM, 34(10):94-109, October 1991

LNE89   Lohmann, F., Neumann, K., Ehrich, H.-D., Design of a Database Prototype for Geoscientific Applications, in [BTW89], (in German)

LMR90   Litwin, W., Mark, L., Roussopoulos, N., Interoperability of Multiple Autonomous Databases, ACM Computing Surveys, 22(3), 1990

Mai89   Maier, D., Why isn't there an Object-Oriented Data Model?, Oregon graduate Center Technical Report CS/E-89-002

Man89   Manola, F., Obect Model Capabilities for Distributed Object management, GTE Laboratories Technical Report TM-0149-06-89-165, 1989

MB91   Mafla E., Bhargava, B., Communication Facilities for Distributed Transaction Processing, IEEE Computer, 1991

Mes90   Messmer, W., Organisattiondes données dans le cadre d'une administration, in: Kölbl, O. (ed.), Photogrammetry and Land Information Systems, Presses polytechniques romandes, Lausanne, 1990 (in French)

MH92   Manola, F., Heiler, S., An Approach to Interoperable Object Models, Proc. Intern. Workshop on Distributed Object Management, 1992

MHG*92   Manola, F., Heiler, S., Georgakopoulos, D., Hornick, M., Brodie, M., Distributed Object management, International Journal of Intelligent and Cooperative Information Systems, 1(1), June 1992

NSDL*91   Nievergelt, J., Schorn, P., DeLorenzi, M., Ammann, C., Brüngger, A., eXperimental geometrY Zurich - software for geometric computation, Department of Computer Science, ETH Zurich, Technical Report 163, 1991

Nor91   Norrie, M.C., A Specification of an Object-Oriented Data Model with Relations, in: Harper, D.J., Norrie, M.C. (eds.), Specification of Database Systems, Springer, 1991

Nor92   Norrie, M.C., A Collection Model for Data Management in Object-Oriented Systems, Ph.D. Thesis, Dept. of Computer Science, University of Glasgow, 1992

OH86   Osborne, S., Heaven, T.E., The design of a Relational database System with Abstract Data Types for Domains, ACM Trans. on Database Systems, 11(3):357-373, September 1986

ORA   Oracle RDBMS Administrators Guide Version 6.0, Oracle Cooperation, 1988

OV91   Oszu, M.T., Valduriez, P., Principles of Distributed Database System, Prentice-Hall, 1991

PPFK91   Pasquale, J.C., Polyzos, G.C., Fall, K.R., Kompella, V.P., Internet Throughput and Delay Meusurements Between Sequoia 2000 Sites, Univ. of California, San Diego, Sequoia 2000 Technical Report 91/7

Sam90   Samet, H., The Design and Analysis of Spatial Data Structures, Addison Wesley, 1990

SD91   Stonebraker, M., Dozier, J., Sequoia 2000: Large Capacity Object Servers to Support Global Change Research, Univ. of California, Berkeley, Sequoia 2000 Technical Report 91/1

SK91   Stonebraker, M., Kemnitz, G., The POSTGRES Next-Generation Database Management System, Communications of the ACM, 34(10), 1991

SKS91   Soparkar, N., Korth, H.-F., Silberschatz, A., Trading Control Autonomy for Relieability in Multidatabase Transactions, Department of Computer Science, Univ. of Texas, Technical Report TR-91-05, 1991

SL90   Shet, A.P., Larson, J.A., Federated Database Systems for Managing Distributed, Heterogeneous, and Autonomous Databases, ACM Computing Surveys, 22(3), 1990

SLR*92   Scholl, M., Laasch, C., Rich, C., Schek, H.-J., Tresch, M., The COCOON Object Model, Department of Computer Science, ETH Zurich, Technical Report 193, 1992

SLT91   Scholl, M., Laasch, C., Tresch, M., Updatable Views in Object-Oriented Databases, Department of Computer Science, ETH Zurich, Technical Report 148, 1991

SPSW90   Schek, H.-J., Paul, H.-B., Scholl, M., Weikum, G, The DASDBS Project: Objectives Experiences, and Future Prospects, IEEE Transactions on Knowledge and Data Engineering, 2(1), 1990

SRH90   Stonebraker, M., Rowe, L.A., Hirohama, M., The Implementation of Postgres, IEEE, Transactions on Data and Knowledge Engeneering, 2(1), 1990

SSPW90   Schek, H.-J., Paul, H.-B., Weikum, G, From the KERNEL to the COSMOS - The database Research Group at ETH Zurich, Department of Computer Science, ETH Zurich, Technical Report 136, 1990

SST92   Scholl, M., Schek, H.-J., Tresch, M., Object Algebra and Views for Multi-Objectbases, Proc. Intern. Workshop on Distributed Object Management, 1992

Sto83   Stonebraker, M., Application of Abstract Data Types and Abstract Indiuces to CAD Databases, Proc.

Sto86   Stonebraker, M., Inclusion of New Types in Relational Database Systems, Proc. IEEE Data Engineering, February 1986

Sto91   Stonebraker, M., An Overview of the Sequoia 200 Project, Univ. of California, Berkeley, Sequoia 2000 Technical Report 91/5

SW86   Schek, H.-J., Waterfeld, W., A Database Kernel System for Geoscientific Applications, Proc. 2nd Symp. on Spatial data Handling, 1986

SW91   Schek, H.-J., Weikum, G, Extensibility, Co-operation, Federation of Database Systems, Proc. 4th GI Conf. on Database Systems for Office, Engineering, and Scientific Applications (BTW), Springer IFB, 1991 (in German)

SW92a   Schek, H.-J., Waterfeld, W., The DASDBS GEO-Kernel - An Extensible Database System For GIS, in: Turner, A.K. (ed.), Three-Dimensional Modelling with Geoscientific Information Systems, Kluwer Academic Publishers, 1992

SW92b   Schek, H.-J., Wolf, A., Cooperation between Autonomous Operation Services and Object Database Systems in a Heterogeneous Environment, Proc. DS-5 Semantic on Interoperable Database Systems, 1992

THINK   THINK Pascal Version 4.0, Product of Symantec Coorporation

Uni   UniSQL, Product of UniSQL Corporation

Wie92   Wiederhod, G., Mediators in the Architecture of Future Information Systems, IEEE Computer, 1992

WLH90   Wilkinson, K., Lyngbæk, P., Hasan, W., The Iris Architecture and Implementation, IEEE transactions on Knowledge and Data Engneering, 2(1), 1990

WWH88   Waterfeld, W., Wolf, A., Horn, D., How to make Spatial Access Methods Extensible, in Proc. of the 3rd Int. Symp. on Spatial Data Handling, Sydney, August 1988

Wo89   Wolf, A., The DASDBS Geo-Kernel, Concepts, Experiences, and the Second Step, Proc. 1st Int. Symp. on the Design and Implementation of Large Spatial Databases SSD89, Springer LNCS 409, July 1989

Appendix

Within the city of Basel (Switzerland) a number of different authorities independently run a set of partally related information systems. One of these information systems is the Information System for the Administration of the City of Basel (BAIS, Basel Administration IS). It consists of five major databases, *person*, *finance*, *property*, *buildings*, and *survey*. Three of these databases, *property*, *buildings*, and *survey* manage geographic and alphanumeric data, the others purely alphanumeric data. Except the *survey*-database these databases build the basic reference data set for all the different authorities and their administrational tasks. Again with the exception of *survey*, all the data in these databases is gathered by one of the cities authorities. Obviously and as shown by the arrows in the figure, all the data is related through different applications. E.g. tax maintenance requires access to either person data and finance data and land registry requires access to property, survey, person and sometimes building data. The survey data is somehow special since the responsibility for gathering and maintaining this database is with the surveying department that is independent from the cities administration. The BAIS only keep copies of the original database of the surveying department.

Similar to the BAIS other information systems of similar complexity and size exist autonomously in independent departments on the city or the state level and in companies e.g. for electricity, gas, and water supply. All these independent ISs, graphically depicted by small circles in the following figure are somehow related to at least one of the datasets in the BAIS. Mostly the relationship is expressed in getting the relevant data as a more or less 'up to date' copy from the BAIS. The power supply company for example gets copys from cadastrial maps from the surveying department and ownership information from the property and the buildings database from the land registry.

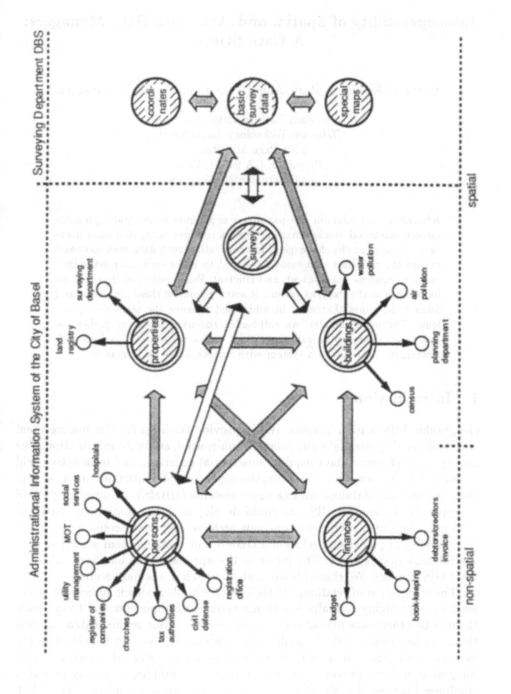

Interoperability of Spatial and Attribute Data Managers: A Case Study

Curtis P. Kolovson, Marie-Anne Neimat, and Spyros Potamianos

Hewlett-Packard Laboratories
Database Technology Department
1501 Page Mill Road
Palo Alto, CA 94304, USA
E-mail: lastname@hpl.hp.com

Abstract. We relate in this paper our experience in integrating a commercial relational storage manager and a commercial spatial data manager. We present the challenge of interoperating such data managers and expose the problems that must be solved to make such interoperability feasible, painless, transparent, and efficient. We present the approach we have taken in the Papyrus system at solving some of these problems, and discuss the issues that must be addressed to solve the remaining problems. Through examples, we emphasize the need for a comprehensive cost-based query optimization strategy, and show that the lack of such a strategy can result in a system with unacceptable performance.

1 Introduction

Geographic Information Systems (GIS) provide facilities for the management and analysis of spatial data and related, non-spatial, attribute information. The management of spatial data requires substantial expertise, and is an active field of research in its own right. Similarly, the management of attribute data, as typified by relational database management systems (DBMS), requires specialized expertise. In designing a GIS, one could develop both the spatial and attribute data management capabilities in one new architecture, or one could leverage the functionality of preexisting relational DBMS and combine them somehow with spatial data management. The latter is the approach that has been taken by most GIS vendors. We elaborate on that approach in the next section.

The integration of relational DBMS in GIS applications is indicative of the need to reuse highly-specialized data management components and to integrate them with other data management components so that sophisticated applications can be constructed. A similar example can be found in hypertext applications where image management systems and text retrieval systems can be integrated and can provide a better alternative to building a new system that combines features of both. Other such examples can be found in CAD/CAM, office systems, CIM, etc.

The approach taken by the Papyrus project [8] has been to focus on the interoperability of preexisting, specialized data managers so that new applications can be easily constructed. We assume that these data managers were developed by experts, that the algorithms and data structures they use were carefully chosen, and that high performance has often dominated and motivated their design. Thus, we focus on integrating these specialized data managers while preserving their performance requirements. In integrating this class of data managers, we assume that preserving their autonomy is not the primary requirement, but rather preserving the performance of the integrated system is the dominant factor. This work focuses on the system issues related to interoperability. Integration at the semantic level and data models that facilitate such integration have been addressed elsewhere [7].

In our terminology, a *data manager* is a set of specialized methods that manage persistent data. A collection of *functions* defines the interface to a data manager. A data manager has exclusive access to its data and permits access to its data only through the functions that define its interface.

A simple GIS was chosen as a "driving application" for the Papyrus prototype, since GIS is an application that typically requires spatial and attribute data management. In building the prototype GIS application, we integrated a commercial relational storage manager and a commercial spatial data manager. We present the challenge of interoperating such data managers and expose the problems that must be solved to make such interoperability feasible, painless, transparent, and efficient. We present the approach we have taken in the Papyrus system at solving some of these problems, and discuss the issues that must be addressed to solve the remaining problems. Through examples, we emphasize the need for a comprehensive query optimization strategy, and show that the lack of such a strategy can result in a system with unacceptable performance.

The remainder of the paper is organized as follows. Section 2 presents the approaches that have been used to develop GIS applications. Section 3 discusses the issues that must be addressed to properly handle the interoperability of preexisting data managers. Section 4 elaborates on our experience in integrating two commercial data managers and stresses the need for a comprehensive query optimization strategy. Related work is presented in Section 5, and we conclude in Section 6.

2 Approaches to GIS Architectures

Standard DBMS, in particular relational DBMS (RDBMS), excel at managing attribute data, but are not well-suited to deal with spatial data, such as interconnected line segments forming complex lines and polygons. Therefore, GIS designers have taken the approach of integrating the spatial processing component of their systems with a DBMS in some manner. The system architectures of most commercial GIS software packages may generally be categorized as one of the following three types [33]: *dual*, *layered*, or *integrated*. This taxonomy is not always mutually exclusive, as some systems fall within more than one category. The distinguishing characteristics of these approaches, as well as some of their advantages and disadvantages are discussed below. We also contrast the approach taken by the Papyrus system with these three approaches.

2.1 Dual Architecture

The *dual* architecture is the most common approach taken by commercial GIS. It is also known as the *geo-relational* architecture as it typically consists of a geographic (or geometric) data manager combined with a RDBMS. One logical object may have attribute information stored in the RDBMS, and spatial data stored in the geographic data manager. Typically, the object's components or "parts" are linked by a common identifier. To retrieve an object, the data managers must be separately queried and the answer constructed from the combined results. Examples of GIS that employ the dual architecture are ARC/INFO [12], MGE [23], and GENAMAP [16].

The advantage of this approach is that it is partly based on standard RDBMS, and is therefore highly portable. The chief disadvantages are threefold. First, since the two data managers are "loosely coupled", query optimization is typically ignored for queries that span both data managers. Such optimization would require taking into account the performance characteristics of both data managers, and reordering queries to minimize the cost of execution. Second, storing spatial data outside the DBMS can result in the loss of integrated transaction support. The geographic data manager may or may not be transactional. In either case, the coordination of transactions that span the two data managers is ignored. Third, integrity constraints can be violated, as logical objects that have components in both data managers often require that one component be updated or deleted whenever its corresponding component in the other data manager is modified or deleted.

2.2 Layered Architecture

In contrast to the dual architecture, which is composed of two separate data managers, the *layered* architecture stores both the spatial and non-spatial data in a RDBMS. To facilitate operations on the spatial data, a layer of translation software is introduced between the query language interface and the RDBMS. This translation layer transforms a GIS-oriented query language into the standard RDBMS query language, namely SQL. Spatial access methods are sometimes implemented using relations in the RDBMS. Examples of GIS that employ the layered architecture are System 9 [28], GEOVIEW [34], and SIRO-DBMS [1].

The main advantage of the layered architecture is that it is based on only one data manager, a RDBMS. It has several disadvantages, however. First, the mapping of the user data model to the relational model introduces inefficiencies with respect to both storage requirements and query processing - the latter since the transformed queries may involve a large number of joins to reconstruct the spatial data objects. Second, the translator that converts the high-level GIS-oriented query language to SQL is likely to be complicated, thus making it difficult for the application builder to extend the functionality offered by the intermediate translation layer. Third, implementing spatial access methods as relations is not nearly as efficient as an implementation based on more appropriate data structures and algorithms.

2.3 Integrated Architecture

The *integrated* architecture requires the use of an Extensible Database Management System (EDBMS) such as one of the systems described in [9] and surveyed in [6, 20]. These systems provide extensibility at one or more levels. Of particular relevance to the integrated architecture are EDBMS that accept user-defined data types and that provide a complete DBMS with "hooks" for extensions to be added to the actual DBMS engine. These hooks permit the registration of operators or functions that extend the query language, and of access methods that speed up the execution of some of these operators. Ideally, the new operators and access methods should become known to the optimizer. Their costs and properties should be taken into account by the optimizer and should affect the plans it generates.

Gral [4], POSTGRES [32], Probe [10], Sabrina [15], and Starburst [19] are EDBMSs that provide extensibility at one or more levels of the system. The two systems that go the farthest in permitting users to install new code are POSTGRES and Starburst. POSTGRES has facilities for defining abstract data types and for registering and installing new operators and access methods on the data types. It allows the installer to specify that an operator behaves like one of the access methods that are already well-understood by the system. For example an R-tree implementation speeds up the execution of an "overlap" operator in the same way a B+-tree speeds up the execution of a range predicate. Furthermore, the R-tree has similar performance characteristics to that of a B+-tree. Starburst goes further in optimizing user-installed access methods and operators. The cost of user-installed operators is taken into account by the Starburst optimizer. Rewrite rules involving user-installed operators can be registered in the system and are used by the preprocessor to the optimizer as heuristics for reordering queries.

Some of the disadvantages of the dual and layered architectures are eliminated in the integrated architecture. The main advantage offered by this architecture is improved query processing performance. Other advantages are that the implementation of a user data model is made easier, since appropriate geometric types can be registered as user-defined data types. Spatially-oriented queries may be supported by an extensible query language, since spatial operators may be added. One disadvantage of this approach is that adding new data types, operators, and particularly access methods may be a complicated and cumbersome chore. Another disadvantage is that the spatial data must be loaded in the EDBMS and must be managed by the EDBMS. Data types that require their own buffer management techniques, special storage devices or special transaction models must be made to conform to the model imposed by the EDBMS.

Since EDBMS have been mostly limited to research prototypes, the use of the integrated architecture has not been pervasive in commercial GIS. An example of a system that has used the integrated architecture approach is the research-oriented system GEO++ [33], which is based on POSTGRES.

2.4 Papyrus Approach

Rather than attempt to extend a preexisting DBMS or to build a EDBMS with hooks for extensibility, the Papyrus approach is to treat each data manager as a first-class entity, and to focus on their efficient interoperability. Special attention is given to the properties, costs and operational characteristics of data managers' functions so that queries that span data managers can be adequately optimized. This approach combines the benefits of the dual architecture and the integrated architecture. Like the dual architecture, each data manager preserves its interface, implementation and the management of its persistent data. Like the integrated architecture, much is conveyed to the system about the cost of the methods implemented by a data manager, their properties and their behavior so that their efficient integration can be possible. This approach preserves the independence of each data manager while addressing the optimization of queries that span the data managers. It also addresses numerous interoperability issues such as data format conversions, query processing, and transaction management. These issues are further examined in the next section.

3 Challenge of Interoperability

While the specialization of data managers is driven by functionality and improved performance, their subsequent integration may be difficult and could result in performance degradation. We focus in this section on the issues that must be addressed to support the interoperability of data managers, and to ensure high-performance for the integrated system. These issues are listed below.

3.1 Interface Language

To facilitate the interoperability of data managers, it is necessary to have a common interface language to the data managers. This language is needed to invoke data managers' functions, and to provide mechanisms for processing data between functions. A desirable characteristic of this language is that it permit optimization of expressions that span data managers.

The Papyrus Interface Language (PIL) [21] is the common interface to all Papyrus-registered data manager functions. It supports the invocation of functions, and the communication of data between functions. It is a functional language with declarative constructs that permit the optimization of data-intensive applications. Experience with Iris [13] applications showed the need for procedural extensions to database query languages [2]. Hence PIL also supports the efficient combination of data-retrieval and general computation.

PIL makes no assumptions about the semantic model presented by each data manager, or the model of the integrated system that is presented to the end-user. It serves as an intermediate language at which optimization takes place. A PIL program will typically be generated by a software translator from a data model-dependent language. An OSQL [13] to PIL translator [24] was developed with a modest amount of effort.

In PIL, a *database* is a named collection of persistent variables. These variables may be managed by different data managers and must be registered with Papyrus. For example, a geographic database may have some of its persistent variables managed by an attribute data manager, others managed by a spatial data manager, and yet others managed by an image data manager. A *program* is an expression which, when evaluated in the environment of the database, returns a value and potentially modifies the bindings of variables. Expressions are constructed using literals, variables, function application, conditionals, sequencing, assignment and function definition.

PIL provides a minimal set of built-in data types that are deemed essential to support effective optimization. These are *atomic* and *aggregate* data types. PIL provides the atomic data types *integer, float, string, boolean,* and *function;* and the aggregate data types *bags, sequences,* and *tuples.* In addition, a data manager may define new atomic data types as well as specify alternate implementations for aggregate data types. This extensibility is essential to enable the integration of preexisting data managers.

Special functions are provided in PIL to query over aggregate objects. Although such queries can be expressed procedurally in PIL, these functions are provided so they can be detected and optimized. Two forms of queries are supported. The first is *iteration* and is a generalization of select-project-join queries. The second is *reduction* and is a form of iteration which permits communication between iterations so that aggregates over bags can be easily computed. Iteration and reduction are higher order functions. They are presented here with syntactic sugaring to be more intuitively understandable.

To iterate over bags, the following syntax is used:

for each bag element v_1 **in** b_1, ... , v_n **in** b_n
where $pexpr(v_1, ..., v_n)$
apply $fexpr(v_1, ..., v_n)$

The semantics of this expression is that for each element in the cartesian product of the bags $b_1, ..., b_n$, the expression $pexpr$ is evaluated. If the expression evaluates to *true*, the function $fexpr$ is evaluated. Note that arbitrary predicates $pexpr$ can be used instead of selection and arbitrary functions $fexpr$ can be used instead of projection.

The syntax for reduction over bags is:

for each bag element e **in** b
with initial $v_1 := c_1, ..., v_m := c_m$
reduceby $expr(e, v_1, ..., v_m)$

The semantics of this expression is that for each element of the bag b, the function $expr$ is evaluated. Each iteration returns the values of the variables $v_1, ..., v_m$ to be used in the following iteration. The initial binding of the variables $v_1, ..., v_m$ is $c_1, ..., c_m$.

Examples of GIS queries given throughout the paper will be given in PIL.

3.2 Operational Aspects (Glue)

Since data managers are constructed independently of one another, their internal data formats are likely to differ. Requests that combine the results of different data managers or that pass data from one data manager to another must handle the various conversions. We chose one internal, self-describing data format for the Papyrus engine. It is flexible enough to support a variety of data representations. We expect the installer of a data manager to supply conversion routines to translate the data manager representation to/from the Papyrus internal representation.

As described in the previous section, one of the main roles of PIL is to invoke data managers' functions. Functions that return bags may present one of two interface styles. RDBMSs typically support a *factored* style where a function presents *open*, *next*, and *close* entry points. This factored style is efficient for data processing because it permits pipelining. But since data managers are preexisting entities, it is important for an integrating system to also accept a *monolithic* interface whereby the function returns an entire bag result at once. The Papyrus system accepts both styles of interfaces.

Another operational aspect of interoperability is whether a data manager's functions should execute in their own address space or whether they can execute in a common address space with other data managers. For protection reasons, a data manager may choose to always execute in a separate or protected address space. This characteristic of a data manager should be registered with an integrating system. It should be taken into account by the optimizer and should be properly handled by the runtime environment. This aspect has not been addressed by the current Papyrus implementation. In our prototype, all data managers execute in the same address space.

3.3 Efficient Integration

We discuss below some characteristics of functions that should become known to an integrating system so that an adequate performance level can be achieved. Knowledge of these characteristics is not essential to interoperability but is essential to achieving good performance.

Multiple Function Implementations: A data manager may have multiple implementations of the same function. We refer to a *function* as the signature of a certain operation, and to a *method* as an actual implementation. A function may have multiple implementations where each implementation is appropriate under a certain set of circumstances. For example, the *sort* function has multiple methods that implement it: *bubble sort* if the input data is almost sorted, *quicksort* if the amount of data is large and not sorted at all, etc. Papyrus accepts multiple implementations of the same function.

A function might also have different implementations for different bindings of its arguments. For example, the function $plus(x, y, z)$, where z is the sum of x

and y, might have one implementation to be used when x and y are bound and z is free, and another to be used when x and z are bound and y is free.

Method Cost: Knowing the cost of executing different methods is essential to being able to produce an efficient query execution plan. For example, a query that requests all the elements of a bag that satisfy a number of predicates should evaluate the cheap predicates first thus filtering out as many of the bag elements as possible, and should postpone the evaluation of the expensive predicates to the end. In this context, the number of times an expensive predicate is invoked is also very important. This number will depend on the selectivity of the predicates that were evaluated prior to its own evaluation. The LDL system [14] developed an extended cost model for foreign functions. The cost model takes into account: the cost of an individual function invocation, the selectivity of functions, and their fanout, i.e. the cardinality of the result of each invocation.

Some methods have a fixed cost of invocation, while for others, the cost of an invocation depends on the argument that is passed to the function. For example, the cost of finding the shortest path between two points is not a constant. It depends on the absolute distance between the two points and on the density of the network connecting the two points. In the current Papyrus implementation, the optimizer assumes a fixed cost of invocation. However we are planning to extend our cost model, and allow the optimizer to take into account statistical information about function arguments.

The relative cost of the different data managers must also be calibrated so that the cost of a method is meaningful within a global context.

Method Properties / Behavior: Many aspects of method behavior or properties are relevant to optimization and interoperability. We mention some of them below.

We discussed earlier how a method may have a factored or a monolithic interface. Independently of the actual interface, the method may have a factored or a monolithic behavior. A method that returns a bag may for example have a factored interface, but may actually compute and cache its entire bag result when its *open* entry point is called. It would then return bag elements as needed when its *next* entry point is invoked. Such a behavior indicates that, for this method, the response time for returning the first result is almost the same as returning the entire result.

Another method property that is of interest to the optimizer is if the method has *side-effects*. Reordering method invocations across a method with side-effects can only be done if the optimizer can guarantee that the expression will preserve its semantics.

Whether a method is *clonable* or not is relevant to the optimizer in a multi-processor environment. A method is said to be clonable if its input can be partitioned, passed to clones of the method so that all the clones execute in parallel, and finally the results combined to produce the same output as a single method invocation with the original input.

Knowing that a method is a *sorting* method or an *order-preserving* method is also relevant to the optimizer.

In addition to the properties listed above, it is important to be able to convey more elaborate relationships between methods. We are particularly interested in equivalence of expressions containing data managers' methods. These equivalent expressions should be considered by a cost-based optimizer and the least expensive expression, within the context of a query, should be chosen for the query execution plan. Consider for example the expression:

$$f(x, y) \text{ and } g(y, z) \leftrightarrow g(x, w) \text{ and } f(w, z)$$

This expression states that the methods f and g are commutative. The input to the composition of the two functions is x and the output is z. f may be executed first, passing its output, y, to g. Conversely, g may be executed first, passing its output, w, to f. f and g may represent *transmit* and *decompress* methods where x is a compressed image and z is the corresponding decompressed and transmitted image. Whether an image is first decompressed and then transmitted to a client or first transmitted and then decompressed does not affect the final result. However, one approach may be preferable to the other depending on the cost of transmission and the load on the server.

We refer to these equivalent expressions as *rewrite rules*. They convey semantics of methods. We stress that the optimizer should not consider them as reordering heuristics but as equivalent expressions where the choice it makes should be cost-based. This is a different approach than the one taken in [19] where rewrite rules are used as reordering heuristics that are always applied.

An interesting type of rules are the ones that convey "indexing" information to the optimizer. For example if we have a bag *StBlk* with information about streets, and an index on their names, then we can use the following rule:

StBlk(stBlkID, stname, ...) and EQ(stname, X)
$\leftrightarrow$ StBlkByName(stBlkID, X, ...)

to specify that if we are interested in retrieving information about a street given its name, we can use the special call *StBlkByName* which takes advantage of the appropriate index. In general it will be more efficient to handle indexing information as a special case, thus reducing the number of rewrite rules that the optimizer must consider. On the other hand the rewrite rule approach gives a simpler (although less efficient) alternative.

In the current Papyrus prototype we have implemented a simple rewrite rule system. The rules supported are "one-time" rules and symbols appearing in their right hand side can not appear in the left hand side of other rules. However we are already designing and implementing a more elaborate system that can handle more complicated rules.

Data Passing Between Methods: The way data is passed between methods should depend on where the methods execute. Methods may execute in the same address space; they may execute in different address spaces on the same computer; and they may execute on different computers. A method implementation should not be affected by the consumer of its output or by the producer of its input.

In the Papyrus system, the Execution Engine [31] handles data passing between methods. It chooses the appropriate way of passing data and it buffers data between producers and consumers.

Format Conversions: When passing data between two methods from different data managers, format conversions may be required. As stated in Section 3.2, we have taken the approach of converting different data manager representations to a Papyrus internal representation. However, when passing data between two methods from the same data manager, the format conversion can be avoided. Furthermore, assuming that everything else is equal, the optimizer should group methods that belong to the same data manager together so that format conversions are avoided as much as possible.

At this point, the Papyrus system ignores any optimizations that deal with format conversions.

3.4 Data Dependencies between Data Managers

When building an application that uses the services of several specialized data managers, it is very likely that the same object will have different components or attributes stored in different data managers. It is important that related data between data managers be consistent and remain so as the database evolves. For example a road could have its coordinates stored in a spatial data manager, and its name and other attributes stored in an attribute data manager. If the road is deleted, the related data should be deleted from both data managers.

Techniques that have been used in active databases such as rules, triggers, monitors, etc. can be used to guarantee that such consistency is maintained. At this point, the Papyrus system does not address these issues.

3.5 Transaction Management

Some data managers may be transactional, and others may not. Data managers may also support different transaction models. For data managers to be truly interoperable, transaction management across data managers must be properly handled.

In Papyrus, we have taken the approach that data managers that are already transactional should be XA compliant [36]. For data managers that are not transactional, we have used the Encina Toolkit from Transarc Corp. [11] to make them transactional. [29] provides a detailed description of how to convert a nontransactional data manager to a transactional one. To coordinate transactions across XA compliant data managers, we have again used the Encina Toolkit. In this context, it is used to manage two-phase commit across data managers.

4   Case Study

A simple GIS[1] was chosen as a "driving application" for the Papyrus prototype. To build the application, we integrated a commercial relational storage manager and two spatial data managers. The relational storage manager is similar to System R's RSS [5]. It is the storage component of Hewlett Packard's Allbase relational DBMS [22], known as DBCORE. We used DBCORE to store attribute data and refer to it as the Attribute Data Manager (ADM). The first spatial data manager was obtained from Etak Inc.[2] and is known as the MapEngine. We used the MapEngine to store spatial objects representing streets. We refer to it as the Street Data Manager (SDM). We prototyped the second spatial data manager, and used it to store point spatial objects representing businesses. We refer to it as the Business Data Manager (BDM).

4.1   Database

The database was derived from two sources of data, both obtained from Etak. The first consists of a map file and the second of business listings.

The map file contains spatial and attribute data representing all streets and highways covering the greater San Francisco Bay Area. It also contains other line-oriented features such as political boundaries and hydrography. The spatial object types are points, lines, and polygons. The attribute data is stored as "annotations" and contains information such as street names, address ranges on both sides of each block, street types, etc. Examples of street types are *freeway, light duty road, arterial road*, etc. The attribute data for each road is similar to that found in TIGER files from the US Census Bureau.

The basic unit of information is a "block" of a street, which is a meaningful unit of demographic data collection for the Census Bureau. The spatial data is organized as *0-cells* (points), *1-cells* (lines), and *2-cells* (polygons)[3], with topological relationships fully represented. Each block corresponds to a single 1-cell, which is composed of two endpoints (two 0-cells which form the *boundary* of the 1-cell) and a set of *shape points* which are a sequence of connected points that form the 1-cell. That is, a 1-cell is a multi-segment that is either a straight line (has no shape points) or else approximates an arbitrary curve. The map file contains information about roughly 265,000 blocks.

The business listings contain information about businesses in the greater San Francisco Bay Area. The data includes business name, street address, business

---

[1] It is somewhat of an overstatement to call our prototype application a "GIS", as the spatial analysis capabilities of the system are quite limited. However, we have provided a realistic solution to the standard GIS database problem of efficiently managing the relationships between spatial objects and their associated attribute data.

[2] Etak Inc. is a company that designs vehicle navigation devices and produces digital map databases. It is located in Menlo Park, California.

[3] In general, an arbitrary spatial object in the Etak Map file will hereafter be referred to as a k-cell, $k = 0$, 1, or 2.

type, phone number, and latitude/longitude coordinates. Examples of business types are *restaurant, gas station, pharmacy, bank,* etc. The spatial object type associated with each business is a point that represents the location of that business. The business listings contain information about roughly 16,000 businesses.

4.2 Schema

We have partitioned information related to street blocks between the ADM and SDM, and information related to businesses between the ADM and BDM. This partitioning was performed to take advantage of the specialized operations of each data manager. The ADM is efficient for attribute searches but not for spatial operations, while the SDM and BDM are efficient for spatial operations but not for attribute searches.

Each record in the SDM contains an identifier made up of two components. The first is its own cell identifier (cellID) in the SDM and the second is an *external reference key*, consisting of the tuple identifier (TID) of the corresponding attribute tuple in the ADM. Similarly, each tuple relating to street attributes in the ADM has an identifier composed of its own TID and the cellID of the corresponding record in the SDM. A one-to-one correspondence exists between related records in the ADM and SDM. Similarly, each record in the BDM has an identifier composed of its point identifier (pntID) in the BDM and of the TID of the corresponding business attribute tuple in the ADM; each business attribute tuple has an identifier composed of its TID and the corresponding pntID in the BDM; and a one-to-one correspondence exists between related records in the ADM and BDM. This concatenation of identifiers is useful in many contexts. For example, the identifier may be passed to a function that can use it to either directly access a record in the ADM or the SDM. Another use of such identifiers is to perform a join based on common identifiers for efficiency in query processing, as discussed in [3].

The data collections described above had to be registered as *persistent bags* in Papyrus. Their full definition is given in Appendix A. The two persistent bags managed by the ADM are *StBlk* and *Biz*. The persistent bags managed by the SDM are *StBlkMap* and *StBlkMapAttr*, and the persistent bag managed by the BDM is *BizMap*. *StBlk* has indexes associated with the attributes *stname* and *sttype*, while *Biz* has indexes on *bizname* and *biztype*.

StBlkMap contains the entire set of 1-cells that make up the map. Although the original map file from Etak contained 0-, 1-, and 2-cells, for our application we have chosen to extract only 1-cells, and among them only the 1-cells that represent streets. In other words, we ignore 1-cells that represent political boundaries, hydrography, etc. *StBlkMapAttr* contains the same information as *StBlkMap* and a copy of all the attribute data stored in *StBlk*. The reason for this data duplication is that the SDM does not support indexes on attribute data (as opposed to the ADM). On the other hand if an index is not required, retrieving the data directly from the SDM avoids the need for a join with the ADM. *BizMap* contains the entire set of points that represent the locations of all the business listing data.

4.3 Data Managers

The ADM is implemented by DBCORE, which provides basic storage, retrieval, and maintenance of relations. In particular, it provides optional B-tree and hash-based indexing on attributes of a relation. The method that returns the content of a relation (or persistent bag in our terminology) is the *sequential scan*. Additional methods that are relevant to our application are *index scan*, and *fetch-by-TID*. Sequential scan retrieves all the tuples in a relation. Selections (predicates) and projections can be pushed into a sequential scan. Index scan uses an index to retrieve, from a relation, all the tuples that satisfy a given predicate. Projections can also be pushed into an index scan. Both sequential scan and index scan have a factored interface. The fetch-by-TID retrieves a tuple given its unique TID.

The SDM is implemented on top of the Etak MapEngine. The SDM can store, retrieve, and update 0-cells, 1-cells, and 2-cells. The SDM can be used to retrieve all the k-cells in a map. This is equivalent to the relation scan of the ADM. Like the sequential scan method, it supports a factored interface. The SDM also provides a spatial access method that retrieves all k-cells within a *window*. This access method has a factored interface. The SDM does not support efficient searches based on attribute values. To find a k-cell with a given attribute, all k-cells must be retrieved, and the attribute of each k-cell must be examined outside the MapEngine. The SDM also supports a *fetch-by-cellID* function which, given a cellID, retrieves a k-cell.

The BDM is implemented by a simple grid partitioning data structure, which is used to store the points that represent the locations of the business listing data items. Each record entry in the BDM includes the coordinates of a point. The grid partitions the space representing the greater San Francisco Bay area into a set of mutually disjoint cells, and points are assigned to buckets that contain records whose point coordinates lie within the boundaries representing the cell. The reason that a separate data manager was required for the business listing spatial objects was that the SDM does not directly support the addition of "landmark" point objects. In particular, it is not efficient to add them as 0-cells, as the purpose of 0-cells is to represent the topological intersection of streets and other line-oriented features. While it would have been possible to add point objects to the SDM as annotations to 1-cells, the SDM does not support efficient spatial search queries based on the content of annotations. Like the SDM, the BDM supports the retrieval of all points in a map, and it also supports the retrieval of all points within a window. Both of these access methods have a factored interface. The BDM also provides an access method for the retrieval of a point given its pntID.

Appendix B describes the interface to the data managers.

4.4 Rewrite Rules

Section 3.3 stressed the importance of rewrite rules in conveying the semantics of methods to the optimizer. The rewrite rules used in our prototype application are listed in Appendix C. Rewrite rules are used by the optimizer in conjunction with variable binding constraints and method costs to construct an optimal query plan.

4.5 Architecture

Figure 1 illustrates the architecture of the Papyrus prototype. Programs are

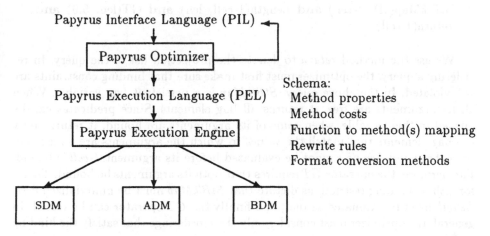

Fig. 1. GIS Prototype Architecture

submitted to Papyrus in PIL. The programs contain expressions that may span multiple data managers. A PIL program is submitted to the Papyrus optimizer where it undergoes numerous transformations to equivalent PIL programs. The final (optimal) PIL program generated by the optimizer is passed to a translator before being handed over to the Execution Engine. This translator converts the program into the Papyrus Execution Language (PEL). PEL [31] is fairly close to PIL but has many annotations necessary to execute a program. The Execution Engine manages the execution of the program. It handles the control flow features of PIL such as conditionals and loops, as well as the data passing between methods. Throughout these steps, various aspects of the database schema are relevant. These include method properties, method costs, function to method mappings, rewrite rules and format conversion methods.

4.6 Optimization Strategy

We now illustrate, through a series of examples, the need for a comprehensive query optimization strategy.

Example 1 (binding constraints): The following example requests all 1-cells whose length is greater than 5.0 miles.

for each bag element sm **in** StBlkMap
where Length(sm.1-cell) > 5.0
apply sm.1-cell;

Note that this is a declarative query where the user does not have to specify the order in which different methods are executed. The predicates that must be satisfied by the above query are:

StBlkMap(ID, 1-cell) **and** Length(1-cell, len) **and** GT(len, 5.0) **and** return(1-cell)

We use the method *return* to denote the projection list of the query. In reordering a query, the optimizer must first make sure that binding constraints are not violated. In the above query, *StBlkMap* is a persistent bag variable. When all its arguments are free, it returns all bag elements. Since predicates can be pushed in this variable, when some of its arguments are bound, it returns only the bag elements that match the values to which the arguments are bound. On the other hand *Length* cannot be evaluated before its argument *1-cell* is bound. Furthermore, the operator *GT* requires that both its arguments be bound. Therefore, these binding restrictions dictate that *StBlkMap* must be materialized first, *Length* must be evaluated second, and finally the *GT* operator can be tested. In general, the optimizer must consider only the reorderings that satisfy the binding restrictions.

Example 2 (reordering based on cost): Another important point is that, apart from considering the possible join reorderings, the optimizer must also consider reordering "expensive" functions. For example, consider the function *ShortestPath*, which given two points on the map, returns the shortest path between them (in the form of a 1-cell).

function ShortestPath (coordType pnt1,
　　　　　　　　　　　coordType pnt2)
$\longrightarrow$　　　　　　　 1-cellType path

This function requires complicated calculations, and has a non-trivial cost. In the following example, we use this function to find all the restaurants that are inside a given window $wndw, are reachable from a given point $pnt, and for which the shortest path from that point to the restaurant is less than 5 miles long.

for each bag element bd **in** Biz, bm **in** BizMap
where bm.bizID = bd.bizID **and** Inside(bm.pnt, $wndw) **and**
　　　bd.biztype = "Restaurant" **and**
　　　Length(ShortestPath($pnt, bm.pnt)) < 5.0
apply bd.bizname

The predicates that must be satisfied by the above query are:

$Biz(ID_1, bizname, ..., biztype)$ **and** $BizMap(ID_2, pnt)$ **and** $EQ(ID_1, ID_2)$
and $EQ(biztype,$ "Restaurant") **and** $Inside(pnt, \$wndw)$ **and**
$ShortestPath(\$pnt, pnt, 1\text{-}cell)$ **and** $Length(1\text{-}cell, len)$ **and** $LT(len, 5.0)$
and $return(bizname)$

The optimizer needs not only to consider the order in which *Biz* and *BizMap* will be ordered, but also when to evaluate the predicate *Length(ShortestPath($pnt, bm.pnt)) < 5.0* . For example, if *BizMap* is materialized first, and then joined with *Biz*, it is possible to evaluate this expensive predicate either before or after the materialization of *Biz*. In the first case, this predicate will cut down the number of tuples that will participate in the join. However, the function *ShortestPath* must be evaluated once for each business inside the window *$wndw*. In the later case, the join with *Biz* along with the predicate *EQ(biztype, "Restaurant")* will reduce the number of calls to *ShortestPath*. Either of these two possibilities can be plausible depending on the cardinalities of the bags, the selectivities of the operators etc. So, the optimizer must consider both of them.

Example 3 (rewrite rules): The following query requests the names of all streets of a given type within a given window. Note that {} represents the empty bag.

> **for each bag element** sb **in** StBlk, sm **in** StBlkMap
> **where** sb.sttype = $sttype **and** sb.stBlkID = sm.stBlkID **and**
>   Clip(sm.1-cell, $wndw) ≠ {}
> **apply** sb.stname;

The predicates that must be satisfied by the above query are:

$StBlk(ID_1, stname, ..., sttype)$ **and** $EQ(sttype, \$sttype)$ **and**
$StBlkMap(ID_2, 1\text{-}cell_1)$ **and** $EQ(ID_1, ID_2)$ **and**
$Clip(1\text{-}cell_1, \$wndw, 1\text{-}cell_2)$ **and** $NE(1\text{-}cell_2, null)$ **and** $return(stname)$

In this query, the predicate *EQ(sttype, $sttype)* acts as a filter on elements of *StBlk*. A second predicate, *Clip(1-cell₁, $wndw, 1-cell₂)* acts as a filter on elements of *StBlkMap*. There are many candidate plans for executing this query.

For example, we can materialize elements of *StBlk* that satisfy the predicate *EQ(sttype, $sttype)*. Use of the index on *sttype* is recommended in this case. The ID of each materialized element is then used to materialize the matching element from *StBlkMap*. According to Rule 3 of Appendix C, we can use *StBlkMapByID* to materialize these elements more efficiently. This rule is an "indexing" rule, and allows the optimizer to consider an efficient implementation of retrieving cells from *StBlkMap* if their cell ID is known. Finally the predicate *Clip(1-cell₁, $wndw, 1-cell₂)* is applied to those elements.

Alternatively, we can materialize elements of *StBlkMap* that satisfy the predicate *Clip(1-cell₁, $wndw, 1-cell₂)*. According to Rule 1, *StBlkMapClip* may be used to materialize these elements. The ID of each materialized element is then used to materialize the matching element from *StBlk*. Finally the predicate *EQ(sttype, $sttype)* is applied to those elements.

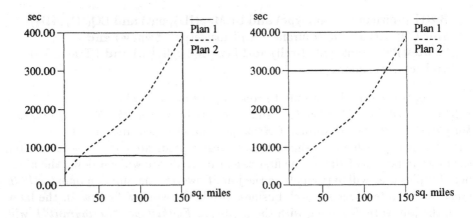

Fig. 2. Execution times for query of example 3

The best plan depends on the selectivity of the predicates *EQ(sttype, $sttype)* and *Clip(1-cell$_1$, $wndw, 1-cell$_2$)*. These selectivities in turn depend on the values of variables *$sttype* and *$wndw*. For example, if the window *$wndw* is very big (and therefore the selectivity of the *Clip* function is small), and there are few roads of type *$sttype* in our database, the first plan will be more efficient than the second. If however the window is small, and *$sttype* is a very common street type, then the second plan will be preferable.

At this point we have to stress that the rules are not blindly applied, but the optimizer considers all the alternatives and chooses the one with the smallest cost. In our example, the two rules that apply (Rule 1 and Rule 3) are exclusive. If we apply Rule 1 we cannot use Rule 3 and vice versa. It is not possible to choose one of them based on simple heuristics. Instead the choice must be cost-based.

Figure 2 shows the query execution time as a function of the window area (in square miles) for two different street types. In the graph on the left, the street type is *Super Freeway*, which has a selectivity of 2.6%, while for the graph on the right, the street type is *Arterial*, with a selectivity of 8.2%. As we can see the execution time for the first plan discussed above, does not depend on the window size, but it depends on the street type. The execution time for the second plan depends on the window size, but is independent of the street type. It is clear that neither of these two plans is always better than the other. The optimizer must consider the original query, all the rewrite rules that may apply, and chose the optimal plan based on a cost analysis.

Example 4 (more rewrite rules): The following query retrieves the names and 1-cells of all streets that are inside a given window *$wndw*.

for each bag element sb **in** StBlk, sm **in** StBlkMap
where sb.stBlkID = sm.stBlkID **and** Clip(sm.1-cell, $wndw) ≠ {}
apply sb.stname, sm.1-cell;

However, if we use the variable *StBlkMapAttr* instead, we can rewrite this query as:

for each bag element sma **in** StBlkMapAttr
where Clip(sma.1-cell, $wndw) ≠ {}
apply sma.stname, sma.1-cell;

This second form is more efficient, because it avoids the join between *StBlkMap* and *StBlk*. However the user must explicitly choose between these forms. A better solution is for the user to write the query in any form, and let the optimizer rewrite it if necessary to a more efficient one. This can be achieved by the following rewrite rule:

StBlkMap($cellID_1$, 1-cell) **and** StBlk($cellID_2$, stname, ..., sttype) **and**
EQ($cellID_1$, $cellID_2$)
↔ StBlkMapAttr($cellID_1$, 1-cell, stname, ..., sttype)

Although in this particular example application of this rule will always result in a more efficient query execution, there are other cases where this rule might not be beneficial. For example, if this query had an extra qualification on one of the street attributes e.g. *sb.name = "Page Mill Rd"*, we would like to retain the join with *StBlk* so we can use the index defined on this attribute.

5 Related Work

In recent years, several research projects have attempted to combine DBMS functionality with spatial data processing, particularly GIS. These attempts have taken several forms. Some researchers have incorporated spatial access methods as part of their DBMS. Others have built extensible DBMSs and have taken spatial data management as an instance of an extension to their system. Yet others have looked at the explicit needs of spatial data management. We briefly survey some of these efforts.

Probe [10, 25, 26, 27] is an extensible object-oriented DBMS that handles spatial data in a special way. An object class *point-set* is predefined in the system. All spatial objects must belong to this class. Users can define new spatial classes, but they must be subclasses of *point-set* and they must support a predefined set of operators. The query optimizer understands these operators and knows how to optimize them. Hence extensibility is provided for a very specific context.

The Gral system [17, 4] is based on an algebraic data model with an extensible type system. The system allows different relation representations, different access methods, and different atomic types. Gral has an extensible query optimizer that uses a rule-based approach. A query is transformed from a non-procedural expression to an executable expression by applying a series of transformations or rules. The emphasis of the optimizer is on using heuristics that are known to improve a query plan. Little emphasis is put on making optimization choices based on cost.

The GEO-kernel [35] is a GIS database that was built using the DASDBS [30] extensible DBMS. DASDBS allows the definition of new data types and of new access methods. Several spatial data types and access methods are part of the GEO-kernel. Query optimization has not yet been addressed, but the intent is to explore numerous techniques, in particular techniques for optimizing geometric operations.

The Starburst project [19] is an extensible RDBMS. *Database customizers* can extend the system with new storage organizations, and new access methods. Integrity constraints and trigger extensions can also be specified on the extensions. The Starburst cost-based optimizer takes the new access methods into account. Rewrite rules are allowed on installed methods. These rules are used as reordering heuristics by the optimizer preprocessor. They are not considered by the cost-based optimizer.

The SAND Project [3] integrates a spatial data manager with an attribute data manager. In [3], a number of feasible query plans are presented for a set of queries that access both spatial and non-spatial data collections, and various trade-offs related to the alternative plans are discussed.

POSTGRES [32] is an extensible DBMS. In addition to the extensibility aspects that were described in Section 2.3, POSTGRES provides some geometric data management capabilities. For example, it has an integrated R-tree [18] spatial access method, and it supports the built-in data types: *point, line-segment, path,* and *box.* Some simple operators are also provided such as *box-overlap, point-inside-box,* and *distance.* The GEO++ system [33] is implemented using POSTGRES. It uses the POSTGRES geometric data types, and implements complex two dimensional and three dimensional spatial object types, as well as a number of operators on those types.

6 Conclusion

We have presented in this paper a simple GIS application that was developed by integrating a commercial spatial data manager and a commercial relational storage manager. We have exposed the interoperability challenge posed by such an integration and have presented the solutions that have been adopted in the Papyrus system. We have stressed the need for a comprehensive cost-based query optimization strategy to make such integrations efficient.

The Papyrus system is operational and the status of various components of the system has been described throughout the paper. Efforts are under way in experimenting with various query optimization techniques. Of particular interest is the tradeoff of using rewrite rules to describe all legal query transformations versus treating index push-down as a special case. The former approach simplifies the implementation of the optimizer but results in a larger number of rewrite rules that the optimizer must consider.

Acknowledgements: We have benefited from numerous useful discussions with Surajit Chaudhuri, Waqar Hasan, Michael Heytens, Ravi Krishnamurthy, and Donovan Schneider. We are indebted to Ravi Krishnamurthy for explaining the treatment of foreign functions in LDL and for sharing his insight in query optimization strategies.

References

1. D. J. Abel. SIRO-DBMS: A Database Tool-kit for Geographical Information Systems. *International Journal of Geographical Information Systems*, vol. 3, no. 2, 1989.
2. J. Annevelink. Database Programming Languages: A Functional Approach. *Proc. of the ACM SIGMOD Conference*, Denver, Colorado, May 1991.
3. W. Aref and H. Samet. Optimization Strategies for Spatial Query Processing. *Proc. of the 17th International Conference on Very Large Databases*, Barcelona, September 1991.
4. L. Becker and R. H. Güting. Rule-Based Optimization and Query Processing in an Extensible Geometric Database System. *ACM Transactions on Database Systems*, vol. 17, no. 2, June 1992.
5. M.W. Blasgen and K.P. Eswaran. Storage and Access in Relational Databases. *IBM Syst. J.*, vol. 16, no. 4.
6. M. Carey and L. Haas. Extensible Database Management Systems. *ACM SIGMOD Record*, vol. 19, no. 4, December 1990.
7. *Computing Surveys*, vol. 22, no. 3, Special Issue on Heterogeneous Databases, S. March, ed., September 1990.
8. T. Connors, W. Hasan, C. Kolovson, M.-A. Neimat, D. Schneider, K. Wilkinson. The Papyrus Integrated Data Server. *Proc 1st International Conference on Parallel and Distributed Information Systems*, December 1991.
9. *Database Engineering*, vol. 10, no. 2, Special Issue on Extensible Database Systems, M. Carey, ed., June 1987.
10. U. Dayal, J. Smith. Probe: A Knowledge-Oriented Database Management System. In *On Knowledge Base Management Systems: Integrating Artificial Intelligence and Database Technologies*, (eds.) Brodie & Mylopoulos, Springer Verlag, 1986.
11. *Encina Toolkit Server Core: Programmer's Reference.* Transarc Corporation.
12. Environmental Systems Research Institute. The Georelational Model Revisited. *ARC News Winter*, vol. 11, no. 1, 1989.
13. D.H. Fishman, et al. Overview of the Iris DBMS. In *Object-Oriented Concepts/Applications and Databases*, (ed.) W. Kim, E. Lochovsky, Addison/Wesley, 1989.
14. R. Gamboa, D. Chimenti, and R. Krishnamurthy. Towards an Open Architecture for LDL. *Proc. 15th International Conference on Very Large Databases*, Amsterdam, August 1989.
15. Gardarin, G., et al. Managing Complex Objects in an Extensible Relational DBMS. *Proc. 15th International Conference on Very Large Databases*, Amsterdam, August 1989.
16. Genasys II, Inc. The Genasys System Overview. Brochure. November 1991.

17. R. H. Güting. Gral: An Extensible Relational Database System for Geometric Applications. *Proc. 15th International Conference on Very Large Databases*, Amsterdam, August 1989.

18. A. Guttman. R-Trees: A Dynamic Index Structure for Spatial Searching. *Proc. of ACM SIGMOD Conference*, Boston, MA, June 1984.

19. L. Haas, et al. Starburst Mid-Flight: As the Dust Clears. *IEEE Trans. on Knowledge and Data Engineering*, vol. 2, no. 1, March 1990.

20. L. Haas and W. Cody. Exploiting Extensible DBMS in Integrated Geographic Information Systems. *2nd Symposium on Large Spatial Databases*, Lecture Notes in Computer Science, vol. 525, Springer Verlag, Zürich, Switzerland, August 1991.

21. W. Hasan and R. Krishnamurthy. PIL: An Optimizable Functional Language for Data Intensive Applications. *Fifth International Workshop on Persistent Object Systems Design, Implementation, and Use*, Pisa, Italy, October 1992.

22. Hewlett-Packard Company. *HP-SQL Reference Manual*. Part Number 36217-9001.

23. Intergraph Corp. MGE - The Modular GIS Environment. Brochure. 1990.

24. K. Lew and W. Hasan. *Translation of OSQL to PIL*. Technical Memo HPL-DTD-92-9, Aug 24, 1992.

25. F. Manola and J. Orenstein. Toward a General Spatial Data Model for an Object-Oriented DBMS. *Proc. 12th International Conference on Very Large Databases*. Kyoto, Japan. 1986.

26. J. Orenstein. Spatial Query Processing in an Object-Oriented Database System. *Proc. of the ACM SIGMOD Conference*. 1986.

27. J. Orenstein and F. Manola. Probe Spatial Data Modeling and Query Processing in an Image Database Application. *IEEE Trans. on Software Engineering*, vol. 14, no. 5. 1988.

28. L.-O. Pedersen, R. Spooner. Data Organization in System 9. WILD Heerbrugg. 1988.

29. R. Rastogi and M.-A. Neimat. *On Using the Encina Toolkit to Provide Recovery Support for Data Managers*. Technical Memo HPL-DTD-92-21, Nov 19, 1992.

30. H.-J. Schek, et al. The DASDBS Project: Objectives, Experiences, and Future Prospects. *IEEE Trans. on Knowledge and Data Engineering*, vol. 2, no. 1. March 1990.

31. D. Schneider and T. Connors. Managing Query Execution for an Advanced Database Programming Language. To appear *2nd Int'l. Conf. on Parallel and Distributed Information Systems*, San Diego, January 1993.

32. M. Stonebraker, L. Rowe, M. Hirohama. The Implementation of POSTGRES. *IEEE Trans. on Knowledge and Data Engineering*, vol. 2, no. 1, March 1990.

33. T. Vijlbrief, P. van Oosterom. The GEO++ System: An Extensible GIS. *5th International Symposium on Spatial Data Handling*, Charleston, SC, August 1992.

34. T. C. Waugh, R. G. Healy. The GEOVIEW Design. A Relational Data Base Approach to Geographical Data Handling. *International Journal of Geographic Information Systems*, vol. 1, no. 2, 1987.

35. A. Wolf. The DASDBS GEO-Kernel, Concepts, Experiences, and the Second Step. *Design and Implementation of Large Spatial Databases, First Symposium SSD Proceedings*. Springer-Verlag. 1989.

36. X/Open CAE Specification (Co. Review draft, 1991). *Distributed Transaction Processing: The XA Specification*.

Appendix

The following notational convention is used. $\{ e_1, \dots , e_n \}$ is used to denote a bag with elements $e_1, \dots , e_n$; $< f_1, \dots , f_n >$ is used to denote a tuple with fields $f_1, \dots , f_n$; $\rightarrow$ is used to denote the result of a function; and $\leftrightarrow$ is used to denote an equivalence relationship.

The types *1-cellType*, *bizIDType*, *coordType*, *stBlkIDType*, and *wndwType* are user-defined and must be registered with Papyrus. The type *bizIDType* consists of two concatenated identifiers. The first is an Attribute Data Manager (ADM) tuple identifier and the second a Business Data Manager (BDM) identifier. Similarly, the type *stBlkIDType* consists of two concatenated identifiers. The first is an ADM tuple identifier and the second a Street Data Manager (SDM) identifier.

A. Persistent Variables

The persistent bag variables *StBlk* and *Biz* are managed by the ADM. Each of these variables is a bag of tuples. The persistent bag variables *StBlkMap* and *StBlkMapAttr* are managed by the SDM. They are also bags of tuples, which contain all the streets in the map. Each street is decomposed into a set of "blocks", each corresponding to a portion of a street between intersections. In topological terms, a block corresponds to a 1-cell. Variable *StBlkMap* contains the geometrical information about these 1-cells, while *StBlkMapAttr* also contains a duplicate copy of the attribute data stored in ADM. The persistent bag variable *BizMap* is managed by the BDM. Again, this variable is a bag of tuples. The bag contains all the businesses in the map. Persistent variables that are managed by data managers must be registered with Papyrus. It is assumed that each data manager has a function that returns the content of its persistent variables. These functions may be *factored* or *monolithic* (see Section 3.2). They, also, are registered with Papyrus. These functions are not shown here. We refer to the function that returns the bag B as simply B.

```
bag StBlk {< stBlkIDType stBlkID,        /* street block ID */
             string stname,              /* name of street */
             integer leftaddrlo,         /* lo left side addr */
             integer leftaddrhi,         /* hi left side addr */
             integer rightaddrlo,        /* lo right side addr */
             integer rightaddrhi,        /* hi right side addr */
             string sttype           >} /* street type */

bag Biz   {< bizIDType bizID,            /* ID of business */
             string bizname,             /* business name */
             integer stnum,              /* street addr no. */
             string stname,              /* street name */
             string city,                /* city name */
             string phonenum,            /* phone number */
             string biztype              /* business type */
```

```
bag StBlkMap        {< stBlkIDType stBlkID,      /* street block ID */
                       1-cellType 1-cell       >} /* street block cell */


bag StBlkMapAttr {< stBlkIDType stBlkID,        /* street block ID */
                    1-cellType 1-cell,          /* street block cell */
                    string stname,              /* name of street */
                    integer leftaddrlo,         /* lo left side addr */
                    integer leftaddrhi,         /* hi left side addr */
                    integer rightaddrlo,        /* lo right side addr */
                    integer rightaddrhi,        /* hi right side addr */
                    string sttype             >} /* street type */

bag BizMap          {< bizIDType bizID,          /* ID of business */
                       coordType pnt           >} /* coordinates */
```

B. Data Managers Functions

In addition to functions that return the persistent bag variables defined above, the data managers support the following functions.

Functions supported by the ADM: We do not list the functions supported by the ADM because they are standard functions found in traditional relational storage manager. The ADM supports the retrieval of a tuple by its ID, the pushing of predicates (selections) into scans, the specification of projection lists, the use of B-tree indices to speed up the execution of range predicates, and the use of B-tree and hashed indices to speed up the execution of equality predicates.

Functions supported by the SDM: The function *Clip* clips a 1-cell by a window (or rectangle). The result is a possibly empty bag of 1-cells. The function *Intersect* computes the intersection of two windows. The result is a window with possibly null coordinates if the two windows do not overlap. The function *Length* computes the length of a 1-cell and returns the result in miles. The function *StBlkMapByID* retrieves an instance of a street block using its ID. The function *StBlkMapClip* returns all streets in a window. This function returns a bag of tuples representing the streets that fall in the input window. If the input window has null coordinates, the output bag will be empty. The function *StBlkAttrMapClip* is similar to *StBlkMapClip* but also returns attribute information about the streets. The function *NearestSt* finds the nearest street to a point.

```
func Clip ( 1-cellType 1-cell,      /* cell to clip */
            wndwType wndw     ) /* clip window */
    →        { 1-cellType new1-cell } /* clipped cell */
```

```
func Intersect          (   wndwType wndw₁,        /* 1st wndw */
                            wndwType wndw₂    )    /* 2nd wndw */
    →                       wndwType wndw₃         /* intersection */

func Length             (   1-cellType 1-cell  )   /* input cell */
    →                       real len               /* length */

func StBlkMapByID       (   stBlkIDType stBlkID )   /* st block ID */
    →                       1-cellType 1-cell

func StBlkMapClip       (   wndwType wndw      )   /* input wndw */
    →                       {< stBlkIDType stBlkID,
                            1-cellType 1-cell      >}

func StBlkMapAttrClip   (   wndwType wndw      )   /* input wndw */
    →                       {< stBlkIDType stBlkID,
                            1-cellType 1-cell,
                            string stname,
                            integer leftaddrlo,
                            integer leftaddrhi,
                            integer rightaddrlo,
                            integer rightaddrhi,
                            string sttype          >}

func NearestSt          (   coordType pnt      )   /* point */
    →                   <   stBlkIDType stBlkID,   /* st block ID */
                            real distance      >   /* nearest st dist */
```

Functions supported by the BDM: The function *Inside* takes a point and a window for arguments and returns true if the point falls inside the given window; otherwise, it returns false. The function *BizMapByID* retrieves an instance of a BizMap record having a specified ID. The function *BizMapClip* returns a bag of all BizMap records that intersect a specified window.

```
func Inside          (   coordType pnt,         /* point to test */
                         wndwType wndw )         /* window */
    →                    boolean                /* falls in wndw? */

func BizMapByID (   bizIDType bizID, )           /* ID of business */
    →                coordType pnt               /* coordinates */

func BizMapClip (   wndwType wndw )              /* query window */
    →                {< bizIDType bizID,         /* ID of business */
                     coordType pnt    >}         /* coordinates */
```

C. Rewrite Rules

To simplify the notation in the following equivalence expressions, we denote all arguments and results of functions as arguments. Specifications of bindings (not shown here since they are understood) should indicate which are input arguments and which are results. Note that persistent variables behave like functions where all combinations of argument bindings are acceptable. In relational terms, bindings on these variables are equivalent to selections. As stated earlier, we use the simplified notation *StBlkMap* to denote the function that returns the bag *StBlkMap*, and *BizMap* to denote the function that returns the bag *BizMap*. The function *EQ* is the equality predicate. The ADM has similar rules. They are not listed here because they are well-understood in RDBMSs.

1. StBlkMap(..., 1-cell$_1$, ...) **and** Clip(1-cell$_1$, wndw, 1-cell$_2$) ↔
   StBlkMapClip(..., wndw, 1-cell$_2$, ...)
2. BizMap(..., pnt, ...) **and** Inside(pnt, wndw) ↔
   BizMapClip(..., wndw, pnt, ...)
3. StBlkMap(..., cellID, ...) **and** EQ(cellID, stBlkID) ↔
   StBlkMapByID(..., stBlkID, ...)
4. BizMap(..., pntID, ...) **and** EQ(pntID, bizID) ↔
   BizMapByID(..., bizID, ...)
5. StBlkMapAttr(..., 1-cell$_1$, ...) **and** Clip(1-cell$_1$, wndw, 1-cell$_2$) ↔
   StBlkMapAttrClip(..., wndw, 1-cell$_2$, ...)
6. Clip(1-cell$_1$, wndw$_1$, 1-cell$_2$) **and** Clip(1-cell$_2$, wndw$_2$, 1-cell$_3$) ↔
   Intersect(wndw$_1$, wndw$_2$, wndw$_3$) **and** Clip(1-cell$_1$, wndw$_3$, 1-cell$_3$)
7. Inside(pnt, wndw$_1$) **and** Inside(pnt, wndw$_2$) ↔
   Intersect(wndw$_1$, wndw$_2$, wndw$_3$) **and** Inside(pnt, wndw$_3$)

GeO2: Why objects in a geographical DBMS ?

Benoit DAVID, Laurent RAYNAL, Guylaine SCHORTER
IGN / COGIT & CNRS / Cassini, 2 Avenue Pasteur, BP 68
F-94160 Saint-Mandé, France
E-mail: {david,raynal,schorter}@cogit.ign.fr

Véronique MANSART
FLEXIMAGE / BDG, 43 rue de la Brèche-aux-Loups
F-75012 Paris, France
E-mail: vero@inf.enst.fr

Abstract. This paper proposes a semantic geographical data model. Localization of geographical entities is defined using an abstract data type. The geographical entities' semantic is expressed through high level concepts in an entity-relationship model extended by both inheritance and propagation mechanisms.

The system's implementation is described. It takes advantage of the object-oriented aspect of the O_2 DBMS, and in particular of the inheritance mechanism. Three different data structures allow to implement geographical entities' localization. They correspond to the topology description levels described in modern exchange formats. A principle of independence between data structures and operations is defined. This principle allows avoiding the re-questioning of the definition of a process if the data structure must be modified.

Lastly the described system has been effectively developed and is used with sets of a large volume of real data produced by the French Institut Géographique National (IGN).

1 Introduction

To date, most of the Geographical Information Systems (GIS) available on the market are built above a Relational Data Base Management System (RDBMS). The RDBMS manages the entire set of classical data types - which we call facts. At the same time, a proprietary file management system takes care of geometrical and/or topological data. A complex pointer mechanism translates links between facts and geometry. As a first consequence, this system is a single-user one since the file manager is single-user. Furthermore, there is an impedance mismatch between the two manager levels and the two query languages are not homogeneous. Arc/Info from ESRI Corp. [25] and MGE from Intergraph Corp. are such systems.

A more recent approach consists in building a GIS by extending a RDBMS. As a first step the RDBMS is extended to manage geographical objects by adding spatial data types and associated spatial functions and predicates. This architecture is more suitable for geographical data management. It eliminates previous disadvantages such as single-user, impedance mismatch and non-homogeneous query languages. System 9 from Computer Vision [12], Smallworld [6], GEO++ [29] and GeoSabrina [24] are such systems. Nevertheless, the RDBMSs are still poor regarding several aspects: concepts are simple ; the data type system is weak ; data have to be normalized in first normal form while hierarchical structures are needed ; semantic links are lost and need to be rebuilt through integrity constraints ; and the data access system is very expensive because of joins. Furthermore, relational query languages (such as SQL) are not complete and therefore must be merged in more classical programming languages. Thus there is also an impedance mismatch between system and developers [10].

A third very recent approach consists in building the GIS around an Object-Oriented DBMS (OODBMS). All Object-Oriented (OO) programming benefits are available such as object identity, complex objects, property inheritance and methods. However, even if the OODBMS architecture seems to be more appropriate, it is still necessary to extend the system for managing geographical data. Specifically, geometrical data types (i.e., point, line and area) must be added to its basic structure and associated functions (union, distance, rectangle, ...), and predicates (cross, adjacency, overlapping,...) must be added to the query language.

The work presented in this paper belongs to this approach. The objective was to add the necessary functions to make a GIS using a commercially available OODBMS. We chose O_2 from O_2Technology [2] as a basis of our work. Similar works have been described in [20, 28] for example. But our work has unique aspects.

First of all, this system, we name: GeO_2, is truly operational and has been used with sets consisting of large volumes of real geographical data containing several tens of thousands of lines and several hundreds of thousands of points (40 Megabytes). Performance was therefore a main objective of our work.

On the other hand, since different data sets may be structured differently, a GIS must be capable of handling the different data structures. A GIS should not mandate its own data structure because a change of structure is never neutral, either more information is necessary, or information is lost. The described system offers different data structures and induces independence between data structures and the operations. This independence allows the operations not to be modified if data structures must. The operations need to be programmed only once, even if they must be computed with different data structures.

This paper is organized as follows. Section 2 reviews the numerous studies about the benefits of OO in geographical DBMS and describes the specific points of our work. Section 3 introduces our data model and section 4 gives a detailed description of the different data structures developed in this system. Section 5 presents the conclusion and our future plans.

2 Background and Focus

This section reviews papers focussing on the benefits of OO concepts in geographical data management and presents the unique aspects of our work.

2.1 State of the art

The term "object", as applied to geographical data management, has generated numerous papers these past years. Topics addressed in these papers, associated with this fashionable word, can be classified in four different categories. In the first category, the papers highlight the various needs of geographical data management and then explain what the OO concepts can offer [15, 19, 18].

In the second category of papers [23, 16, 6, 26], the benefit of OO languages for geographical DBMS software development is discussed. Because OO concepts have originated from programming languages, it is understandable to see, as a first objective, the use of software engineering techniques.

In the third category, authors exhibit the benefit of semantical or OO models for geographical database development [17, 31, 22]. From this perspective, [17] clearly demonstrates the benefit of two mechanisms in order to specify the geographical data schema semantic. The first mechanism, *inheritance,* enables the use of *specialization* and *generalization* concepts. The second mechanism, *propagation,* determines a complex-entity property originating from the property of its components. These two mechanisms are described in section 3.1.

In the last category, papers present projects using either extended RDBMS [21, 29] or management systems with object-oriented characteristics [20, 28].

From these papers, one may think that OO techniques can solve all geographical data management problems. Some of the work such as described in [20] describes a set of tools to be used for application development and not ready-to-use systems. Other works such as those described in [28] lead to completely redevelop the data structures without being able to use the original ones. The authors, for example, redefine the tuple and relation data structures and then implement the join operator. This approach is not realistic, not only because of the amount of software development necessary but also because of the foreseeable lack of performance. These drawbacks and others are partially due to a certain confusion around the word "object".

2.2 Conceptual or internal object ?

The word "object" is used to describe conceptual models as well as to define software development techniques or tools. If some OO concepts such as generalization are useful for geographical data schema conception, this does not mean that one could easily implement a geographical database with an OODBMS. Geographical data management requires complex data structures. This is the case, for example in topological data management or for spatial indices which should not be described at the same conceptual level as the user-defined geographical data schema. In order to avoid confusion between conceptual and internal levels, one should consider the benefit of what we call OO from two different points of view. First, from the point of view of the semantic model targeted to the user for him/her to express his/her data semantic, and secondly from the point of view of the software development environment and of the extensibility of the system.

Furthermore, since the internal mechanisms will change quickly with the evolution of database and programming language technologies, and since the conceptual level should be stabilized to preserve the huge investments realized in data capture, it is absolutely mandatory to provide independence between the conceptual level and the internal level. Therefore, we find it necessary to define and differentiate between the conceptual model (section 3.1) and the internal OO data structures used for the implementation of the system (section 4).

2.3 Which internal data structure ?

The choice of the internal data structure is particularly important and may alter functionality and performances. Different geometrical and topological data structures have been formalized by the results of recent work on exchange format standardization, such as EDIGéO [13], NTF, SDTS and DIGEST-VPF [30]. For example, in DIGEST-VPF, four topological levels are described and each one defines a way of structuring and managing the information. The first level called "Cartographic Spaghetti" is a spaghetti data structure in which there is no topology. The "Non Planar Graph" level describes a topological graph which is not necessarily a planar graph. The "Planar Graph" level mandates that the graph be planar (i.e., the creation of a node is mandatory when two arcs intersect). In the last level, called "Full Topology", the graph is planar and faces are managed. The need to standardize and differentiate between these different levels indicates that the levels are not compatible and that conversion of a data set from one level to a higher one cannot be performed automatically.

Therefore, to provide a full range of functionalities, it is necessary to implement several data structures. This approach is very expensive for the implementation of spatial operators, such as overlay operator or display operator. For example, for each non-symmetric binary operator, the number of implementations is the square of the number of defined data structures.

For this reason, we describe in section 4 an internal data structure that is able to manage concurrently the different topological levels. The three levels defined in this paper are called *Spaghetti*, *Network* (corresponding to Non Planar Graph and Planar Graph) and *Map* (corresponding to Full Topology). Using the inheritance mechanism provided by the OODBMS, the internal data structure allows having only one implementation for each spatial operator. Furthermore, with this original technique a user is able to update his/her data when he/she has new information about topology and he/she can also transparently integrate heterogeneous data sets into a unique GIS.

3 The GeO$_2$ conceptual data model

The GeO$_2$ conceptual data model is made of a semantic data model which is an extension of the Entity-Relationship (ER) data model and a localization data model which is defined by an Abstract Data Type (ADT).

3.1 The Semantic Geographical Data Model

The need for independence between the conceptual and internal levels led us to correctly separate the semantic model definition from the implementation techniques used in the O_2 DBMS. The semantic model should allow a user not to have to deal with the internal mechanisms, especially for localization management. This localization is a very important property of geographical entities and can be considered as an ADT as in [1, 3, 9, 29]. To provide independence between the conceptual and internal levels, topology management is included in the ADT. Thus, it is no longer necessary for the user to represent complex data structures as those needed for topology.

Regarding the semantic model, our experience with geographical information, at the IGN, showed us that the ER model [7] allows a correct representation of most data schemas. However, we add to the ER model the two already cited mechanisms introduced in [17].

The first mechanism, *inheritance*, is added with two concepts: generalization and specialization relationships. *Generalization* allows to group several type entities with common properties into a supertype, while *specialization* allows the opposite: to extend or refine properties of a type into subtypes.

The second mechanism, *propagation*, is added to the model with new information on attributes and with a specific kind of relationship called aggregation relationship. This is a binary relationship and allows definition and management of complex entities. Independently, each entity attribute is eventually associated with an aggregate function for this attribute. If there is no aggregate function, then the attribute cannot be aggregated. With aggregate relationships and aggregate functions, attributes on complex entities can be automatically computed from attributes on simple entities.

3.2 The Localization Data Model

The goal of such a model is mainly to allow processing the localization of entities. This processing is defined by the operations of the localization ADT. To allow powerful expressions, composition of operations should be allowed. For example, the intersection test between one line and two areas cannot be computed using a binary intersection predicate. On the contrary, it can be calculated using a binary intersection function: first compute the intersection between the two areas and then the intersection between the result and the line. This example shows that a predicate based model as in GEOQL [27] is not powerful enough. Therefore, an operation on the ADT should be defined as a function taking one or several parameters and giving a new value as a result which can eventually be a localization value. Geometrical intersection and union functions are part of the operations.

The choice of a function based model gives the necessary flexibility for the query resolution but imposes constraints on the ADT definition: it is necessary that the ADT be closed for the defined functions, that is to say the resulting value for a function pertains to the ADT. Furthermore, this ADT should allow the depiction of punctual, linear and areal figures. The smallest closed domain that verify these two constraints is defined as a set of primitives of either point, line or polygon types [9, 24]. This ADT is named Geometry.

So, any entity defined in the semantic data model may have an attribute of type Geometry. Even, an entity may carry several localization attributes. Finally, localization attributes may be aggregated as other attributes in order to define the localization of complex objects.

3.3 Implementation of GeO$_2$

The semantic schema given by a user has to be translated into classes in the OODBMS. Some of these classes do not depend on the semantic schema, and for the most part implement the geometrical and topological internal data structure. The other classes, however, only implement entity and relationship types as they are defined in the semantic schema.

Implementation of entity types and relationship types. Each entity or relationship type is implemented as one class in the OODBMS. Each factual attribute is implemented as an attribute of similar type. Relationships are implemented with mutual references between objects, implementing the relationship and the entity. Localization attributes are implemented by attributes referencing an object of the class: Geometry.

The Geometry ADT. The Geometry ADT is implemented by a Geometry class. The data structure of the class is a set of geometrical or topological primitives. Operations on the Geometry ADT, such as intersection or union are implemented by methods of the Geometry class. New operations may be added very easily.

The geometrical or topological primitives. To represent punctual (0D), linear (1D), and areal (2D) data, three kinds of primitives are defined. The definition of primitives also depends on topological levels. New primitives may eventually be added to extend the system. The following table gives the name of the default primitives depending on the dimension and on the topological level (Spaghetti, Network and Map).

	0D	1D	2D
Spaghetti	Point	Line	CompPoly
Network	Node	Dart	CompArea
Map	Node	DartF	Zone

The definition of these primitives is given in the following section.

4 Three data structures

An enhanced management of geographical entities requires efficient and appropriate structures to store geographical coordinates and spatial relationships between entities. This is extremely important since a poor internal storage model would strongly affect response time to queries. For this reason we have considered three levels of data structures that may match the user's needs.

The simplest data structure is defined by the Spaghetti level in which the primitives are defined independently of each other. This is meant for graphical data, for which no or little analytical processing is foreseen. The Network level corresponds to a non planar network model. It is appropriate for networks in which the navigational aspect is essential. Lastly, the Map level corresponds to the topological map model [4, 9]. It is meant for parceled data users for whom the concepts of adjacent zones and boundary sharing between parcels are rather important. However GeO_2's critical factor consists of preserving in the structure, a hierarchy between the three levels. As a matter of fact, due to the inheritance mechanism, it is possible to use, in a transparent way, either of these structures. This leads to a unique internal model.

4.1 The Spaghetti data structure

This is the simplest data structure. Each element of this structure is stored independently from the others according to a wire representation. No relationship is kept between the geometrical primitives. The Spaghetti structure is therefore limited to the persistence of objects with their coordinates. The geometrical primitives are implemented using the following classes:

- the *Point* class implement the punctual primitive, its data structure is a pair of coordinates (x,y);

- the *Line* class is a generic class corresponding to two possible data structures for the linear primitive: either, for the class *Vpt*, an array of pairs of coordinates giving the intermediate points of the line, or, for the *Inv* class, a reference to an object of the Vpt class that means that the line should be followed in the opposite direction ;

- lastly, the *SimpPoly* class implements a simple polygon. Its data structure is a list of objects of the Line class which corresponds to the external contour of the polygon that has to be closed. Complex polygons (i.e., polygons with holes) are implemented by the *CompPoly* class which is defined as a SimpPoly (this is why it inherits from it) with an additional list of objects of the SimpPoly class for the list of holes.

The Figure class is introduced to generalize the Point, Line, and SimpPoly classes, so that general geometric operations (e.g., bounding rectangle, intersection test) may be defined on this generalized class. The inheritance hierarchy for the Spaghetti primitives is described by fig. 1.

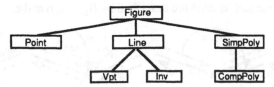

Fig. 1. Inheritance hierarchy for the Spaghetti primitives

4.2 The Network data structure

Network managers, regardless of their field of interest (road, electricity, sanitation,...), have more specific requirements for which the spaghetti model is inadequate. Moving navigational aspect through the network is a very important topic in most of the applications. The connectivity topological relationship must not be computed each time from geometry but kept in a data structure so as to achieve better performances. The initial topological data structures are based on graph theory [5]. We have chosen as the basis of our data structure modeling, another theory called "combinatorial map theory" [14, 8]. It is a variation of the graph theory that has been adapted to geographical applications [11, 4].

The combinatorial map theory. A combinatorial map is defined by two permutations, α and σ, on a set of darts. Adapted to geographical data, a dart corresponds to an oriented line. Therefore, for one line we have two opposite darts, one for each direction of the line. The α permutation goes from one dart to its opposite one and is illustrated by fig. 2a.

To relate contiguous darts, i.e., darts sharing a common endpoint, we apply a σ permutation which performs a positive trigonometric rotation around the common endpoint which yields the succeeding incoming dart as a result. Consequently, the endpoint which corresponds to a *node*, is entirely defined by the σ cycle, i.e., all the incoming darts. The σ function is illustrated by fig. 2b. With the dart set and the α and σ permutations the graph can be covered.

The two main benefits of the combinatorial map theory compared to the graph theory are: first, the ability to easily define faces (addressed below); and second, the efficiency of the implementation in an OO framework. In fact, each permutation is implemented by a reference from one object to another.

The Network data structure. Darts and nodes are implemented as two classes: *Dart* and *Node*. Darts are either positive darts or negatives darts which are implemented as two classes: *DartPos* and *DartNeg*. Both inherit from the Dart class. A dart references its opposite dart (using attribute inv) and the succeeding dart corresponding to the application of permutation σ (attribute sigma). A dart also references the node to which it belongs (attribute node), that is its final node. Inversely, a node references one of its incoming darts (attribute dart). The sigma attribute is used to find the other darts of the node. These relationships between darts and between a node and its darts are described by fig. 2 a, b and c.

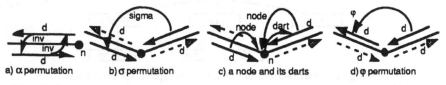

a) α permutation   b) σ permutation   c) a node and its darts   d) φ permutation

Fig. 2. Topological relationships between darts and between a node and its darts

Because a positive dart carries its own geometry, the DartPos class inherits from the Vpt class. A negative dart references its opposite dart and therefore the DartNeg class inherits from the Inv class. Similarly, the Node class inherits from the Point class.

For areas, because user networks are not planar and because the network data structure does not force the creation of a node for each dart intersection, faces are not defined in the graph and do not describe areal primitives. This is the reason why areas are defined by their external contour. This primitive is implemented by two classes: *SimpArea* and *CompArea*. The SimpArea class defines a simple area (i.e., with no holes) by a list of darts. The CompArea class defines a complex area that additionally contains holes which are defined as SimpArea. SimpArea and CompArea classes inherits from SimpPoly and CompPoly classes, respectively.

The inheritance hierarchy for the Network primitives is shown in fig. 3.

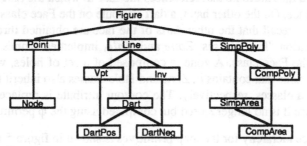

Fig. 3. Inheritance hierarchy for the Network primitives

4.3 The Map data structure

Thematic data such as land cover or wards make up a partition of space and require the automatic generation of faces from the existing limits. The corresponding users have therefore specific needs which are not completely covered by the preceding structures. In fact, the requested topology level must take into account the concept of adjacency between faces and constitutes an evolution of the Network level. Such a management requires the representation of a planar graph. Lastly, to manage non connected graphs, an extension of the combinatorial map theory, called topological map, has been used.

The topological map theory. The structure of combinatorial maps is ideal for nodes and dart management. To describe the graph faces, a third permutation, called φ, is defined by composition of α and σ ($\varphi = \alpha \circ \sigma$). For a given dart, φ gives the following dart in the face. The φ permutation is illustrated by fig. 2d.

However, a face, defined by the φ permutation, only describes its external boundary and does not acknowledge the holes potentially included. To fulfil this requirement, topological map theory proposes to manage the relationship between a face and the connected components geometrically included in the face [4, 9]. Each connected component has a unique external boundary, which is a φ cycle, and therefore a face, called *hole*. A face which is not a hole is called *zone*. For higher level connected components, a virtual infinite zone is created and includes these components. The concepts of zone and hole are illustrated by fig. 4.

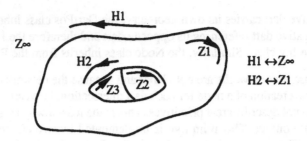

Fig. 4. Relationship between a zone and its holes

Structure of a topological map. Bringing this extension in operation does not modify relationships between darts and nodes made explicit for the Network structure. A *Face* class implements faces. A new class, *DartF*, inherited from the Dart class allows to add a face attribute that references the face to which the dart belongs, that is its right-side face. On the other hand, a dart attribute on the Face class references one of its darts. We recall that the other darts of the face are obtained through the use of the φ permutation. Two classes: *Zone* and *Hole*, implement zones and holes and inherit from the Face class. A zone is composed of a set of holes, while each hole references the zone that contains it. Zone and Hole classes also inherit from SimpArea and CompArea classes, respectively. The contour attribute is replaced by a contour method because it is no longer stored but computed using the φ permutation.

The inheritance hierarchy for the map primitives is shown in figure 5 which gives the complete schema of geometrical and topological primitives.

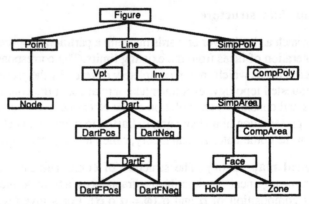

Fig. 5. Inheritance hierarchy for the geometrical and topological primitives

The aforementioned principle of independence between data structures and operations is actually achieved using inheritance provided by the OODBMS. For example, a display operator implemented on the Point, Line, and CompPoly classes will automatically work on the other primitives.

5 Conclusions and future plans

This work enabled, among other things, to assess the OO techniques for the management of geographical information and in particular the O_2 DBMS. The advantage of the OO is obvious, as shown by the extensive use of the inheritance and overriding mechanisms. Thanks to these mechanisms, the system is efficient and extensible. However, our experiment leads us to formulate various remarks.

The complete schema of classes we end up with is complex: it contains several tens of classes, even more inheritance arcs. This structure has been the end of a long process, of many steps backwards and many hesitations. It is indeed difficult to choose the schema of classes because the choice depends on many parameters such as the ease of conception, the restrictions imposed on inheritance, or the performance goal. The conception would have been easier by using an appropriate conception method.

On the other hand, we have met some difficulties to properly use the inheritance mechanism. This is due to the fact that, in the OO approach, inheritance is used to implement mechanisms that are rather different from one another. One finds essentially three mechanisms:

- the first one is the general refinement mechanism which enables to add to a subclass new properties or new behaviors. This mechanism does not require any particular explanation ;

- the second mechanism attempts to use, in a given class, services defined in another class. The inheritance defined between the DartPos class and the Vpt class illustrates this mechanism. It allows a positive dart to use services defined in the Vpt class. This approach seems to have the advantage of being more efficient than the aggregation of two objects. One sees here that a performance oriented choice imposes one solution rather than another on the conception of the schema ;

- the third mechanism consists of implementing different classes with similar external behaviors but with different internal implementations. A common super class between different implementations, defining the common behavior, is mandatory in order to be able to define a variable that may contain an object from one of the classes. This mechanism is illustrated by the example of the Figure class already mentioned.

These different inheritance types could be eventually combined. For instance, it may be useful to refine a class that corresponds to several implementations. It is then necessary to refine the super class as well as each of the preceding implementations. The mechanism becomes rather heavy and consuming in terms of number of classes. One ends up with a very complex schema and may even exceed the limitations of multiple inheritance imposed by the O_2 model. We are currently trying to better formalize this aspect of our conception.

Lastly we have met limitations related to the O_2 DBMS, in particular the absence of an array constructor (important to manage intermediate points in polylines and polygons) and an association constructor (which could handle inverse references between two objects). Finally, the major drawback of the O_2 DBMS, from a performance point of view, is the inability to define a spatial clustering of objects.

Future plans. Many developments are being undertaken with the GeO$_2$ prototype. We have already implemented various spatial indices and their performances have been compared. An operator to overlay layers, taking into account the geometrical accuracy, has been designed and implemented. We are also studying the definition of an assertional manipulation language of SQL type, to operate the processes in the system. At last, we also intend to compare different data structures to implement our model, and to adapt our prototype on various OO DBMS's, in order to compare them.

The universality of the data model we have defined allows us to use the GeO$_2$ system for numerous studies. Work has been started to assess the coherence between geographical data input at various scales. We believe that this problem will soon become a major consideration for all users who use data at different scales and want either to assess their coherence, or to integrate data in a unique database. We consider the OO concept as a promising approach on this topic.

Acknowledgements. The work stated in this paper has been partially financed by the ESPRIT BRA AMUSING. It also has been done in collaboration with the CEDRIC Department of the CNAM-PARIS. The authors wish to thank Professor Michel SCHOLL, for the discussions we had with him, and the students who worked in building and evaluating the system.

References

1. W. Aref, H. Samet: An approach to information management in geographical applications. In: Symp. on Spatial Data Handling, Zürich, July 1990.

2. F. Bancilhon, C. Delobel, P. Kanellakis (eds): Building an oject-oriented database system: the story of O$_2$. Morgan Kaufman Pub., 625 pages, 1992.

3. Bennis, David, Quilio, Viémont: GéoTROPICS: Database support alternatives for geographic applications. In: Symp. on Spatial Data Handling, Zürich, 1990.

4. Bennis, David, Quilio, Thévenin, Viémont: GéoGraph: A topological storage model for extensible GIS. In: Auto-Carto 10, Baltimore, pp 349-367, 1991.

5. C. Berge: Graphes. Gauthier Villars, 1983.

6. A. Chance, R. Newel, D. Theriault: An object-oriented GIS - Issues and solutions. In: EGIS'90, Amsterdam, pp 179-188, April 1990.

7. Chen: The entity-relationship model: Toward a unified view of data. In: ACM Transaction on Database Systems, Vol. 1, no 1, March 1976.

8. R. Cori: Un code pour les graphes planaires et ses applications. Astérisque, Société Mathématique de France, Vol. 27, 1975.

9. B. David: Modélisation, représentation et gestion d'information géographique: une approche en relationnel étendu. Thèse de l'université Paris 6, juillet 1991.

10. C. Delobel, C. Lécluse, P. Richard: Bases de données: des systèmes relationnels aux systèmes objets. InterEditions, 1991.

11. J.F. Dufourd, C. Gross, J.-C. Spehner: A Digitisation Algorithm for the Entry of Planar Maps. In: 7th Int. Conf. on Computer Graphics, Leeds, June 1989.

12. J W van Eck, M Uffer: A Presentation of System 9. In: Photogrammetry and Land Information Systems, Lausanne (Switzerland), pp 139-178, March 1989.

13. Norme EDIGéO AFNOR Z-13-150, 1992.

14. J Edmonds: A Combinatorial Representation for Polyhedral Surfaces. Notices of American Mathematic Society, no. 7, 1960.

15. M. Egenhofer, A. Frank: Object-oriented databases: database requirements for GIS. In: Int. Geographic Information Systems Symp, Crystal City, Nov. 1987.

16. M. Egenhofer, A. Frank: Why object-oriented software engineering techniques are necessary for GIS. In: Int. GIS Symp., Baltimore, March 1989.

17. M. Egenhofer, A. Frank: Object-oriented modelling in GIS: inheritance and propagation. In: Autocarto 9 Conference, Baltimore, pp 588-598, April 1989.

18. M. Feuchtwanger: Geographic logical database model requirements. In: Auto-Carto 9 Conference, Baltimore, pp 599-609, April 1989.

19. A. Frank: Requirements for a database management system for a GIS. In: Photogrammetric Engineering and Remote Sensing, vol. 54, no. 11, Nov. 1988.

20. M. Halstead, H. Mackenzie, P. Milne, S. Milton, J. Smith: A spatial object toolkit. In: URPIS 18, Canberra, Nov. 1990.

21. S. de Hoop, P. van Oosterom: Storage and manipulation of topology in Postgres. In: EGIS'92, München, pp 1324-1336, March 1992.

22. Z. Kemp: An object-oriented model for spatial data. In: Symp. on Spatial Data Handling, Zürich, vol. 2, pp 659-668, 1990.

23. D. Kjerne, K.J. Dueker: Modeling cadastral spatial relationships using an object-oriented language. In: Symp. on Spatial Data Handling, Seatle, 1986.

24. T. Larue, D. Pastre, Y. Viémont: Strong integration of spatial domains and operators in relational database systems. In: SSD'93, Singapore, 1993.

25. S. Morehouse: The Architecture of ARC/INFO. In: Auto-Carto 9 Conf., Baltimore, pp 266-277, April 1989.

26. J. A. Orenstein: An object-oriented approach to spatial data processing. In: Symp. on Spatial Data Handling, Zürich, vol. 2, pp 669-678, 1990.

27. Sacks-Davis, McDonell, Ooi: GEOQL: A query language for geographic information systems. In: Australian assoc. for science, Townsville, 1987.

28. M. Scholl, A. Voisard: Geographic applications: an experience with O_2. In: [Bancilhon 92], pp 585-618, 1992.

29. T. Vijlbrief, P. van Oosterom: The GEO++ system: an extensible GIS. In: Symp. on Spatial Data Handling, Charleston, pp 40-50, August 1992.

30. Military Standard Vector Product Format (VPF). Defense Mapping Agency, MIL-STD-600006, April 1992.

31. Worboys, Hearnshaw, Maguire: Object-oriented data modelling for spatial databases. In: Int. Journal of Geographical Information Systems, 4, 369-384, 1990.

A Small Set of Formal Topological Relationships Suitable for End-User Interaction

Eliseo Clementini[1], Paolino Di Felice[1], and Peter van Oosterom[2]

[1] Università di L'Aquila, Dipartimento di Ingegneria Elettrica,
67040 Poggio di Roio, L'Aquila, Italy
Email: clementini@vaxaq.cc.univaq.it
pdifelice@vxscaq.aquila.infn.it
[2] TNO Physics and Electronics Laboratory,
P.O. Box 96864, 2509 JG The Hague, The Netherlands
Email: oosterom@fel.tno.nl

Abstract. Topological relationships between spatial objects represent important knowledge that users of geographic information systems expect to retrieve from a spatial database. A difficult task is to assign precise semantics to user queries involving concepts such as "crosses", "is inside", "is adjacent". In this paper, we present two methods for describing topological relationships. The first method is an extension of the geometric point-set approach by taking the dimension of the intersections into account. This results in a very large number of different topological relationships for point, line, and area features. In the second method, which aims to be more suitable for humans, we propose to group all possible cases into a few meaningful topological relationships and we discuss their exclusiveness and completeness with respect to the point-set approach.

1 Introduction

In the context of geographic information systems (GISs), the spatial relationships existing between the geographic objects play a central role both at the query definition level and at the query processing level. In fact, the easiest way for users to define spatial queries is based on the possibility of expressing spatial conditions among geographic objects (e.g., adjacency of regions) inside the query statement.

The need to refer to spatial relationships arises a second time when the database management system (DBMS) tries to process a spatial query. Obviously, spatial queries can be easily processed if all the geometric relationships between the objects of interest are explicitly stored; however, such a choice is unsatisfactory since it requires a tremendous amount of disk space and, furthermore, it implies the execution of time-consuming maintenance procedures. It follows that instead of storing all spatial relationships among the objects of interest it is more convenient to compute them. To that purpose, a deep understanding of how to evaluate spatial relationships is needed.

The need for developing a sound mathematical theory of spatial relationships to overcome the shortcomings of almost all geographic applications was clearly stated by Abler several years ago [1]. Nevertheless, the exploration/formalization of spatial relationships is still an open problem, and a multi-disciplinary effort involving linguists and psychologists besides geographers and computer scientists is probably the best approach to get good results.

So far there is a good, but still incomplete, understanding of *topological relationships*, that is the subset of spatial relationships characterized by the property of being preserved under topological transformations, such as translation, rotation, and scaling. In the literature, we find several attempts to describe a set of meaningful topological relationships (see, among others [2, 4, 11, 12]), but it is difficult to find a formal definition of them. A good formal approach can be found in [6], that has been extended in [7], where the authors adopt a method to give exact semantics to the binary topological relationships based on the point-set theory. A drawback of this method is that they distinguish only between empty or non-empty intersections of boundaries and interiors of geometric objects, and also the method results in too many different relationships to be used by end-users. This will become even worse if the method of Egenhofer is extended in order to take into account the dimension of intersections. The list of cases that results from this approach is not directly related to the user interpretation of topological facts. In [10], after a testing experience with human subjects, the authors conclude that there is a significant connection between human interpretation of spatial relationships and the Egenhofer method. However, a way of grouping relationships is needed in order to map concepts from a geometric level to a higher (user-oriented) level.

In the present contribution, we take into account the dimension of the result of the intersection (*dimension extended method*); furthermore, our objective is to keep the resulting number of potential topological relationships as small as possible. To achieve the latter goal, we grouped together the relationships (that are somehow similar) into a few more general topological relationships: *touch*, *in*, *cross*, *overlap*, and *disjoint*. We called this approach the *calculus-based method*, since it uses the constructs of the Object-Calculus introduced in a previous paper [3]. The five relationships are overloaded concepts in the sense that they may be used for point, line, and area type of features. Further, more detailed distinctions among topological situations are possible by introducing operators on the *boundary* of features. Specifically, it is possible to use directly circular lines (coming from the boundaries of areas) and end-points (coming from the boundaries of lines).

The paper is structured as follows. Section 2 contains general definitions for the Object-Calculus and for the geometric point-set theory approach. Section 3 first recalls the original Egenhofer method and hence it discusses the dimension extended method. In Section 4, we give the exact semantics to the five basic topological relationships and several examples of usage of them; then we prove that the five relationships are mutually exclusive (e.g., it cannot be the case that two features are involved in an *in* and *overlap* relationship with each-other) and that there are no cases that fall outside them. Furthermore, we prove that a combination of these terms, together with a boundary operator for line and area features, is expressive enough to represent all possible cases in the dimension extended method. Section 5 contains a discussion about the possible extensions.

2 General Definitions

The notations P, L, and A are used for point, line, and area features. If it is necessary to distinguish between two features of the same type, then numbers are used; e.g. A_1 and A_2. The symbol λ is used in situations where it may represent one of the three feature types.

In [3], we proposed the Object-Calculus, which is a formal query language suitable for querying geographical databases. In such a calculus, the notation $\langle \lambda_1, r, \lambda_2 \rangle$ means that the features λ_1 and λ_2 are involved in the relationship r; we call this triplet a *fact*. Facts can be combined through the *and* ($\wedge$), *or* ($\vee$) Boolean operators. Besides stating facts, the Object-Calculus allows the usage of methods (operations) inside a query statement. Let m be a method and I a specific instance of a feature type λ, the pair (I, m) means that the method m operates on the instance I, and returns a new instance, say I_1. We overload the notation (I, m) to denote also the resulting instance I_1.

Formal definitions of geometric objects (features) and relationships are based on the point-set approach, where features are sets and points are elements of these sets (see [9]) for a general topology reference). The subject of the relationships are the "simple" points, lines, and areas commonly used in GISs: the topological space is $\mathbb{R}^2$; all kinds of features are closed sets, that is, each feature contains all its accumulation points (also called limit points); also all features are connected, that is, they are not the union of two separated features. Specifically:

1. area features are only connected areas with no holes;
2. line features are lines with no self intersections and either circular (closed curves) or with only two end-points;
3. point features may contain only one point.

We consider a function "dim", which returns the dimension of a point-set. In case the point-set consists of multiple parts, then the highest dimension is returned. Note that this can only be the case for intermediate point-sets as our features always consist of one part. In the following definition, S is a general point-set, which may consist of several disconnected parts:

$$dim(S) = \begin{cases} - & \text{if } S = \emptyset \\ 0 & \text{if } S \text{ contains at least a point and no lines or areas} \\ 1 & \text{if } S \text{ contains at least a line and no areas} \\ 2 & \text{if } S \text{ contains at least an area .} \end{cases}$$

The boundary and the interior of features are used in the Egenhofer method for describing the topological relationships. The same is true for our approach;

therefore, we give definitions of boundary and interior for the three types of features that are slightly different from the pure mathematical theory, but lead to consistent definitions for relationships. The boundary of a feature λ is denoted by $\partial\lambda$. It is defined for each of the feature types as follows:

1. ∂P: we consider the boundary of a point feature to be always empty;
2. ∂L: the boundary of a line is an empty set in the case of a circular line while otherwise is the set of the two separate end-points;
3. ∂A: the boundary of an area is a circular line consisting of all the accumulation points of the area.

The interior of a feature λ is denoted by λ°. It is defined as:

$$\lambda^\circ = \lambda - \partial\lambda \ .$$

Note that the interior of a point and of a circular line is equal to the feature itself.

3   The Dimension Extended Method

Egenhofer [6] originally described his method for classifying topological binary relationships between area features. The classification is based on the intersections of the boundaries and interiors of the two features. These are represented by the four sets:

$$S_1 = \partial A_1 \cap \partial A_2$$
$$S_2 = \partial A_1 \cap A_2^\circ$$
$$S_3 = A_1^\circ \cap \partial A_2$$
$$S_4 = A_1^\circ \cap A_2^\circ \ .$$

Each of these four sets may be empty ($\emptyset$) or non-empty ($\neg\emptyset$). This results in a total of $2^4 = 16$ combinations (Table 1), which may not all result in a valid topological relationship, because of the properties of area features. As there are 8 impossible cases (proved in [6]) and 2 pairs of converse relationships, the number of different types of relationships is 6: disjoint, in, touch, equal, cover, and overlap. Figure 1 gives a pictorial representation of these six relationships. One of the good aspects of this approach is that it gives an exact definition of the mentioned relationships. Also, it takes into account all possible combinations of intersections (a form of completeness).

The first extension to the standard approach is to add also point and line features, resulting in 6 major groups of binary relationships: area/area (as described above), line/area, point/area, line/line, point/line, and point/point. This approach has been described in [5, 7, 8]. A drawback of the approach is the large number of different relationships, of which each has its own name. As it may be hard to remember all these names, the users might become confused.

Another drawback of this method is that it is impossible to distinguish between certain cases, which are usually regarded as different by users. For example,

Table 1. The range of area/area situations as in the original Egenhofer method

case	S_1	S_2	S_3	S_4	relationship name
	$\partial A_1 \cap \partial A_2$	$\partial A_1 \cap A_2^\circ$	$A_1^\circ \cap \partial A_2$	$A_1^\circ \cap A_2^\circ$	
1	$\emptyset$	$\emptyset$	$\emptyset$	$\emptyset$	A_1 disjoint A_2
2	$\emptyset$	$\emptyset$	$\emptyset$	$\neg\emptyset$	
3	$\emptyset$	$\emptyset$	$\neg\emptyset$	$\emptyset$	
4	$\emptyset$	$\emptyset$	$\neg\emptyset$	$\neg\emptyset$	A_2 in A_1
5	$\emptyset$	$\neg\emptyset$	$\emptyset$	$\emptyset$	
6	$\emptyset$	$\neg\emptyset$	$\emptyset$	$\neg\emptyset$	A_1 in A_2
7	$\emptyset$	$\neg\emptyset$	$\neg\emptyset$	$\emptyset$	
8	$\emptyset$	$\neg\emptyset$	$\neg\emptyset$	$\neg\emptyset$	
9	$\neg\emptyset$	$\emptyset$	$\emptyset$	$\emptyset$	A_1 touch A_2
10	$\neg\emptyset$	$\emptyset$	$\emptyset$	$\neg\emptyset$	A_1 equal A_2
11	$\neg\emptyset$	$\emptyset$	$\neg\emptyset$	$\emptyset$	
12	$\neg\emptyset$	$\emptyset$	$\neg\emptyset$	$\neg\emptyset$	A_1 cover A_2
13	$\neg\emptyset$	$\neg\emptyset$	$\emptyset$	$\emptyset$	
14	$\neg\emptyset$	$\neg\emptyset$	$\emptyset$	$\neg\emptyset$	A_2 cover A_1
15	$\neg\emptyset$	$\neg\emptyset$	$\neg\emptyset$	$\emptyset$	
16	$\neg\emptyset$	$\neg\emptyset$	$\neg\emptyset$	$\neg\emptyset$	A_1 overlap A_2

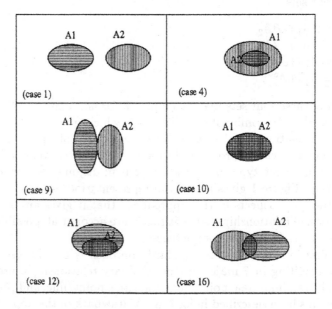

Fig. 1. A visualization of the six different relationships in Table 1

two areas that have one point in common, and two areas that have a complete line in common, do both fall under the same "touch" relationship, because the intersection of their boundaries (S_1) is non-empty and the other intersections $(S_2, S_3, \text{and } S_4)$ are all empty (case 9 in Table 1).

In the dimension extended method, we take into account the dimension of the intersection, instead of only distinguishing empty or non-empty intersections. In order to illustrate this extension, the line/area type of topological relationships will be elaborated on. In two-dimensional space, the intersection set S can now be either $\emptyset$ (empty), 0D (point), 1D (line), or 2D (area). At first sight, these 4 possibilities might result into $4^4 = 256$ different cases. Fortunately, a lot of cases are impossible and only the following are possible:

$$
\begin{aligned}
S_1 &= \partial A \cap \partial L : \emptyset, \text{or 0D} && \text{(2 cases)} \\
S_2 &= \partial A \cap L^\circ : \emptyset, \text{0D, or 1D} && \text{(3 cases)} \\
S_3 &= A^\circ \cap \partial L : \emptyset, \text{or 0D} && \text{(2 cases)} \\
S_4 &= A^\circ \cap L^\circ : \emptyset, \text{or 1D} && \text{(2 cases)} .
\end{aligned}
$$

This is due to the fact that the dimension of the intersection cannot be higher than the lowest dimension of the two operands of the intersection; $dim(\partial A) = 1$, $dim(A^\circ) = 2$, $dim(\partial L) = 0$, and $dim(L^\circ) = 1$. Further, the definitions of line and area features exclude the option that $dim(S_4) = 0$. Therefore, instead of 256, there are only $2 * 3 * 2 * 2 = 24$ possible cases. Table 2 shows that only 17 out of these 24 cases are really possible.

Cases 3, 7, 11, 15, 19, and 23 are impossible because, if the intersection of the interior of an area with the boundary of a line (S_3) results in a point (0D), then it is impossible that the intersection of the interiors (S_4) is empty. Case 2 is impossible because if the intersection of the interiors (S_4) results in a line, then the other sets $(S_1, S_2, \text{and } S_3)$ cannot all be empty. Note that in Table 2, we did not even bother anymore to give names to all the 17 different topological relationships. Figure 2 is a visualization of these relationships.

A similar analysis for the other groups of topological relationships results in a total of 52 real cases (see Table 3).

4 The Calculus-based Method

The grand total of 52 relationships is far too much for humans to be used in a reasonable manner. It is better to have an overloaded set of just a few basic relationships which the user understands well. The dimension extended method uses various results of feature intersections (empty, 0D, 1D, and 2D) together with the boundary and interior operators to describe the required relationships. It may be clear that it is not a very user-friendly method, as the user is not (directly) interested in the intersections of the boundaries and the interiors. Furthermore, though the concept of boundary may be familiar to users, the concept of interior may be less well understood because it is based on the mathematical point-set theory (open/closed sets).

Table 2. The line/area situations in the dimension extended method

case	S_1	S_2	S_3	S_4	possible
	$\partial A \cap \partial L$	$\partial A \cap L^\circ$	$A^\circ \cap \partial L$	$A^\circ \cap L^\circ$	
1	-	-	-	-	yes
2	-	-	-	1	no
3	-	-	0	-	no
4	-	-	0	1	yes
5	-	0	-	-	yes
6	-	0	-	1	yes
7	-	0	0	-	no
8	-	0	0	1	yes
9	-	1	-	-	yes
10	-	1	-	1	yes
11	-	1	0	-	no
12	-	1	0	1	yes
13	0	-	-	-	yes
14	0	-	-	1	yes
15	0	-	0	-	no
16	0	-	0	1	yes
17	0	0	-	-	yes
18	0	0	-	1	yes
19	0	0	0	-	no
20	0	0	0	1	yes
21	0	1	-	-	yes
22	0	1	-	1	yes
23	0	1	0	-	no
24	0	1	0	1	yes

Table 3. A summary of the analysis for all relationship groups

relationship groups	# possible cases	# real cases
area/area	24	9
line/area	24	17
point/area	4	3
line/line	24	18
point/line	4	3
point/point	2	2
		Grand total 52

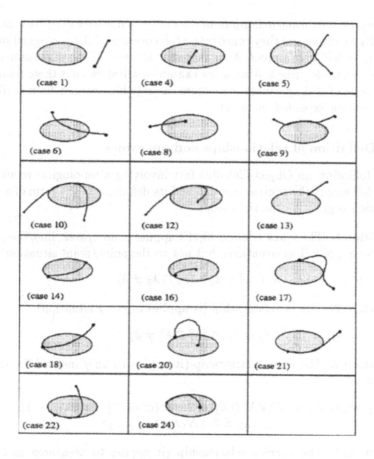

Fig. 2. The 17 different line/area cases in the dimension extended method

At the query language level, we take into account the considerations above by making available to the users only boundary operators (for area and line features) together with the five topological relationships: *touch, in, cross, overlap,* and *disjoint*. Therefore, in the generic object-calculus fact $\langle \lambda_1, r, \lambda_2 \rangle$, r may be one of the five relationships, while λ_1 and λ_2 may be either features or boundaries of features. We refer to the use of such operators and relationships as the calculus-based method. Formal definitions of these terms will be given in the next subsection. The definitions are general in the sense that they apply to point, line, and area features (unless stated otherwise). It is our conjecture that this is the smallest set of relationships capable of representing all cases of the dimension extended method under the condition that only the additional boundary operators for area and line features are available. The set of topological relationships is close to the normal human use of these concepts and still powerful enough to represent a wide variety of cases.

Based on the formal definitions of the relationships we will prove that they are mutually exclusive and they constitute a full covering of all topological situations. Further, we will give a proof of the fact that all cases of the dimension extended method can be described. Also, a few examples will show that these relationships are capable of distinguishing even more cases (which cannot be described with the dimension extended method).

4.1 Definition of relationships and operators

In the following, an Object-Calculus fact involving a topological relationship is on the left side of the equivalence sign and its definition in the form of a point-set expression is given on the right side.

Definition 1. The *touch* relationship (it applies to area/area, line/line, line/area, point/area, point/line situations, but not to the point/point situation):

$$\langle \lambda_1, touch, \lambda_2 \rangle \Leftrightarrow (\lambda_1^o \cap \lambda_2^o = \emptyset) \wedge (\lambda_1 \cap \lambda_2 \neq \emptyset) \ .$$

Definition 2. The *in* relationship (it applies to every situation):

$$\langle \lambda_1, in, \lambda_2 \rangle \Leftrightarrow (\lambda_1 \cap \lambda_2 = \lambda_1) \wedge (\lambda_1^o \cap \lambda_2^o \neq \emptyset) \ .$$

Definition 3. The *cross* relationship (it applies to line/line and line/area situations):

$$\langle \lambda_1, cross, \lambda_2 \rangle \Leftrightarrow dim(\lambda_1^o \cap \lambda_2^o) = (max(dim(\lambda_1^o), dim(\lambda_2^o)) - 1) \wedge$$
$$(\lambda_1 \cap \lambda_2 \neq \lambda_1) \wedge (\lambda_1 \cap \lambda_2 \neq \lambda_2) \ .$$

Definition 4. The *overlap* relationship (it applies to area/area and line/line situations):

$$\langle \lambda_1, overlap, \lambda_2 \rangle \Leftrightarrow (dim(\lambda_1^o) = dim(\lambda_2^o) = dim(\lambda_1^o \cap \lambda_2^o)) \wedge$$
$$(\lambda_1 \cap \lambda_2 \neq \lambda_1) \wedge (\lambda_1 \cap \lambda_2 \neq \lambda_2) \ .$$

Definition 5. The *disjoint* relationship (it applies to every situation):

$$\langle \lambda_1, disjoint, \lambda_2 \rangle \Leftrightarrow \lambda_1 \cap \lambda_2 = \emptyset \ .$$

A relationship r is symmetric if and only if $\langle \lambda_1, r, \lambda_2 \rangle \Leftrightarrow \langle \lambda_2, r, \lambda_1 \rangle$. A relationship r is transitive if and only if $\langle \lambda_1, r, \lambda_2 \rangle \wedge \langle \lambda_2, r, \lambda_3 \rangle \Rightarrow \langle \lambda_1, r, \lambda_3 \rangle$. It comes from the definitions that all relationships are symmetric with the exception of the *in* relationship. It can be easily proved that only the *in* relationship is transitive.

In order to enhance the use of the above relationships, we define operators able to extract boundaries from areas and lines. With regard to a non-circular line, the boundary ∂L is a set made up of two separate points. Since the 0-dimensional features that we consider are limited to single points, we need to have operators able to access each end-point. We call the end-points f (from) and t (to) respectively, though we do not consider a direction on the line.

Definition 6. The boundary operator b for an area A: The pair (A, b) returns the circular line ∂A.

Definition 7. The boundary operators f, t for a non-circular line L: The pairs (L, f) and (L, t) return the two separate points belonging to the set ∂L.

4.2 Examples

An important advantage of this approach is to provide relationship names that have a reasonably intuitive meaning for users of spatial applications. In the following, we try to substantiate such a claim through several examples.

Intuitively, we say that two geometric elements *touch* each other, if the only thing they have in common is contained in the union of their boundaries. It may be verified easily that all cases in Fig.3 are covered by the formal definition of the *touch* relationship.

One feature is *in* another one if the former is completely contained in the latter. The examples of Fig.4 illustrate this relationship.

We say that two lines *cross* each other if they meet on an internal point (note that it could not be a *touch* because in that case the intersection is only on the boundaries). Similarly, a line crosses an area if the line is partly inside the area and partly outside. See Fig.5 for examples of the *cross* relationship.

Informally, two features *overlap* each other if the result of their intersection is a third feature of the same dimension, but different from both of them. It comes from the definition that this relationship can apply only to homogeneous cases (area/area and line/line, see Fig.6 for a visualization of these cases).

Two features are *disjoint* if their intersection is void; this case is quite obvious to understand: see the examples in Fig.7.

4.3 Mutual exclusiveness and full covering of relationships

In this section, we will prove that the five relationships are mutually exclusive, that is, it cannot be the case that two different relationships hold between two features; furthermore, we will prove that they make a full covering of all possible topological situations, that is, given two features, the relationship between them must be one of the five.

Theorem 1. *Given two geometric entities* λ_1, λ_2 *and a relationship* r *between them, if* $\langle \lambda_1, r, \lambda_2 \rangle$ *holds, then* $\langle \lambda_1, r_i, \lambda_2 \rangle$ *does not hold for every* $r_i \neq r$, *and there does not exist a topological situation that falls outside the five relationships of the calculus-based method.*

Proof. Every internal node (see Fig.8) in the "topological relationship decision" tree represents a boolean predicate; if for a certain topological situation, the predicate evaluates to "true" then the left branch is followed, otherwise the right branch is followed. This process is repeated until a leaf node is reached which will indicate to which of the 5 (or 6 if the asymmetric *in* is counted for

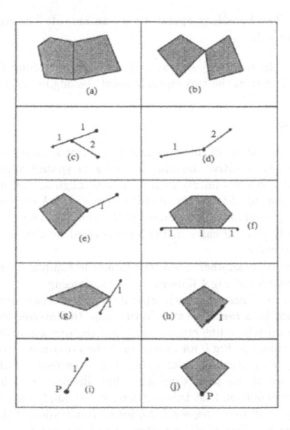

Fig. 3. Topological situations illustrating the *touch* relationship between two areas (a,b), two lines (c,d), a line and an area (e–h), a point and a line (i), a point and an area (j)

two different relationships) basic relationships this situation belongs. Now, two different relationships cannot hold between two given features, because there is only one path to be taken in the topological relationship decision tree. Furthermore, there can be no cases outside the calculus-based method, because (a) every internal node has two branches, so for every value of the predicate there is an appropriate path; and (b) every leaf node has a label that corresponds to one of the five topological relationships. □

Note that the "topological relationship decision" tree is a general tree that can be used for all situations: area/area, line/area, point/area, line/line, point/line, and point/point. From the definition of a point and the predicates it follows that a point can never "travel down" the decision tree below the second level. At this level the relationship (either *touch*, *disjoint*, or *in*) is decided on. In order to evaluate the predicate at the lowest level, one has to take into account the fol-

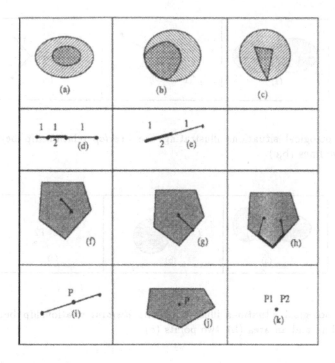

Fig. 4. Topological situations illustrating the *in* relationship between two areas (a–c), two lines (d,e), a line and an area (f–h), a point and a line (i), a point and an area (j), two points (k)

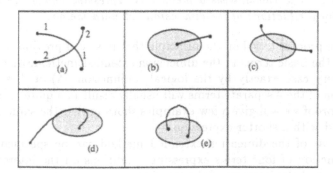

Fig. 5. Topological situations illustrating the *cross* relationship between two lines (a), a line and an area (b–e)

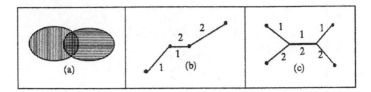

Fig. 6. Topological situations illustrating the *overlap* relationship between two areas (a), two lines (b,c)

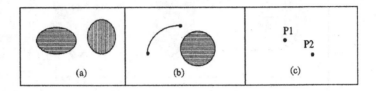

Fig. 7. Topological situations illustrating the *disjoint* relationship between two areas (a), a line and an area (b), two points (c)

lowing situations: area/area, line/area, and line/line, because of the use of the dimension function dim in the predicate.

4.4 The calculus-based method versus the dimension extended method

Theorem 2. *The calculus-based method is expressive enough to represent all the topological situations of the dimension extended method.*

Proof. The proof is based on the principle that if we can provide the equivalents of each of the basic terms in the dimension extended method, then we can also specify every case exactly by the logical conjunction ($\land$) of these terms. The conjunction of the 4 separate terms will usually result in a quite long expression. After the proof we will give a few examples showing that the same case can also be specified with a shorter expression.

Each case of the dimension extended method can be specified by the logical conjunction of four terms expressing conditions on the intersection of the boundaries and the interiors of the two features; in general:

$$T_1(\partial\lambda_1 \cap \partial\lambda_2) \land T_2(\partial\lambda_1 \cap \lambda_2^o) \land T_3(\lambda_1^o \cap \partial\lambda_2) \land T_4(\lambda_1^o \cap \lambda_2^o) \ . \tag{1}$$

It is possible to give the equivalences for every term T_i admissible in the dimension extended method. On the right of each equivalence we have a logic expression P_i making use of the five relationships between features and between

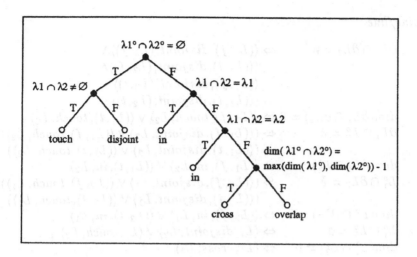

Fig. 8. The topological relationships decision tree

their boundaries. Each equivalence can be easily tested by applying the definitions given for the five relationships. By substituting each T_i with the corresponding P_i, we obtain an expression $P_1 \land P_2 \land P_3 \land P_4$ that is equivalent to (1). Therefore, the calculus-based method is able to express each situation of the dimension extended method. □

In the following, for each term of the dimension extended method, an equivalent term in the calculus-based method is given:

Area/area

$$\partial A_1 \cap \partial A_2 = \emptyset \quad \Leftrightarrow \langle (A_1, b), disjoint, (A_2, b) \rangle$$
$$dim(\partial A_1 \cap \partial A_2) = 0 \Leftrightarrow \langle (A_1, b), cross, (A_2, b) \rangle$$
$$dim(\partial A_1 \cap \partial A_2) = 1 \Leftrightarrow \langle (A_1, b), overlap, (A_2, b) \rangle \lor \langle (A_1, b), in, (A_2, b) \rangle$$
$$\partial A_1 \cap A_2^\circ = \emptyset \quad \Leftrightarrow \langle A_2, in, A_1 \rangle \lor \langle A_2, touch, A_1 \rangle \lor \langle A_2, disjoint, A_1 \rangle$$
$$dim(\partial A_1 \cap A_2^\circ) = 1 \quad \Leftrightarrow (\langle A_1, in, A_2 \rangle \land (\langle (A_1, b), disjoint, (A_2, b) \rangle \lor$$
$$\langle (A_1, b), cross, (A_2, b) \rangle \lor$$
$$\langle (A_1, b), overlap, (A_2, b) \rangle)) \lor \langle A_1, overlap, A_2 \rangle$$
$$A_1^\circ \cap \partial A_2 = \emptyset \quad \Leftrightarrow \langle A_1, in, A_2 \rangle \lor \langle A_1, touch, A_2 \rangle \lor \langle A_1, disjoint, A_2 \rangle$$
$$dim(A_1^\circ \cap \partial A_2) = 1 \quad \Leftrightarrow (\langle A_2, in, A_1 \rangle \land (\langle (A_2, b), disjoint, (A_1, b) \rangle \lor$$
$$\langle (A_2, b), cross, (A_1, b) \rangle \lor$$
$$\langle (A_2, b), overlap, (A_1, b) \rangle)) \lor \langle A_2, overlap, A_1 \rangle$$
$$A_1^\circ \cap A_2^\circ = \emptyset \quad \Leftrightarrow \langle A_1, touch, A_2 \rangle \lor \langle A_1, disjoint, A_2 \rangle$$
$$dim(A_1^\circ \cap A_2^\circ) = 2 \quad \Leftrightarrow \langle A_1, in, A_2 \rangle \lor \langle A_2, in, A_1 \rangle \lor \langle A_1, overlap, A_2 \rangle$$

Line/line

$$\partial L_1 \cap \partial L_2 = \emptyset \quad \Leftrightarrow \langle (L_1, f), disjoint, (L_2, f)\rangle \wedge$$
$$(\langle (L_1, t), disjoint, (L_2, f)\rangle \wedge$$
$$\langle (L_1, f), disjoint, (L_2, t)\rangle \wedge$$
$$(\langle (L_1, t), disjoint, (L_2, t)\rangle$$

$$dim(\partial L_1 \cap \partial L_2) = 0 \Leftrightarrow \langle (L_1, f), touch, L_2\rangle \vee \langle (L_1, t), touch, L_2\rangle$$

$$\partial L_1 \cap L_2^\circ = \emptyset \quad \Leftrightarrow (\langle (L_1, f), disjoint, L_2\rangle \vee \langle (L_1, f), touch, L_2\rangle) \wedge$$
$$(\langle (L_1, t), disjoint, L_2\rangle \vee \langle (L_1, t), touch, L_2\rangle)$$

$$dim(\partial L_1 \cap L_2^\circ) = 0 \Leftrightarrow \langle (L_1, f), in, L_2\rangle \vee \langle (L_1, t), in, L_2\rangle$$

$$L_1^\circ \cap \partial L_2 = \emptyset \quad \Leftrightarrow (\langle (L_2, f), disjoint, L_1\rangle \vee \langle (L_2, f), touch, L_1\rangle) \wedge$$
$$(\langle (L_2, t), disjoint, L_1\rangle \vee \langle (L_2, t), touch, L_1\rangle)$$

$$dim(L_1^\circ \cap \partial L_2) = 0 \Leftrightarrow \langle (L_2, f), in, L_1\rangle \vee \langle (L_2, t), in, L_1\rangle$$

$$L_1^\circ \cap L_2^\circ = \emptyset \quad \Leftrightarrow \langle L_1, disjoint, L_2\rangle \vee \langle L_1, touch, L_2\rangle$$

$$dim(L_1^\circ \cap L_2^\circ) = 0 \quad \Leftrightarrow \langle L_1, cross, L_2\rangle$$

$$dim(L_1^\circ \cap L_2^\circ) = 1 \quad \Leftrightarrow \langle L_1, overlap, L_2\rangle \vee \langle L_1, in, L_2\rangle \vee \langle L_2, in, L_1\rangle$$

Line/area

$$\partial A \cap \partial L = \emptyset \quad \Leftrightarrow \langle (L, f), disjoint, (A, b)\rangle \wedge \langle (L, t), disjoint, (A, b)\rangle$$

$$dim(\partial A \cap \partial L) = 0 \Leftrightarrow \langle (L, f), in, (A, b)\rangle \vee (\langle (L, t), in, (A, b)\rangle$$

$$\partial A \cap L^\circ = \emptyset \quad \Leftrightarrow \langle L, disjoint, (A, b)\rangle \vee \langle L, touch, (A, b)\rangle$$

$$dim(\partial A \cap L^\circ) = 0 \Leftrightarrow \langle L, cross, (A, b)\rangle$$

$$dim(\partial A \cap L^\circ) = 1 \Leftrightarrow \langle L, overlap, (A, b)\rangle \vee \langle L, in, (A, b)\rangle$$

$$A^\circ \cap \partial L = \emptyset \quad \Leftrightarrow (\langle (L, f), disjoint, A\rangle \vee \langle (L, f), touch, A\rangle) \wedge$$
$$(\langle (L, t), disjoint, A\rangle \vee \langle (L, t), touch, A\rangle)$$

$$dim(A^\circ \cap \partial L) = 0 \Leftrightarrow \langle (L, f), in, A\rangle \vee \langle (L, t), in, A\rangle$$

$$A^\circ \cap L^\circ = \emptyset \quad \Leftrightarrow \langle L, touch, A\rangle \vee \langle L, disjoint, A\rangle$$

$$dim(A^\circ \cap L^\circ) = 1 \Leftrightarrow \langle L, cross, A\rangle \vee \langle L, in, A\rangle$$

Point/line

$$\partial L \cap P = \emptyset \quad \Leftrightarrow \langle P, disjoint, L\rangle \vee \langle P, in, L\rangle$$

$$dim(\partial L \cap P) = 0 \Leftrightarrow \langle P, touch, L\rangle$$

$$L^\circ \cap P = \emptyset \quad \Leftrightarrow \langle P, disjoint, L\rangle \vee \langle P, touch, L\rangle$$

$$dim(L^\circ \cap P) = 0 \Leftrightarrow \langle P, in, L\rangle$$

Point/area

$$\partial A \cap P = \emptyset \quad \Leftrightarrow \langle P, disjoint, A\rangle \vee \langle P, in, A\rangle$$

$$dim(\partial A \cap P) = 0 \Leftrightarrow \langle P, touch, A\rangle$$

$$A^\circ \cap P = \emptyset \quad \Leftrightarrow \langle P, disjoint, A\rangle \vee \langle P, touch, A\rangle$$

$$dim(A^\circ \cap P) = 0 \Leftrightarrow \langle P, in, A\rangle$$

Point/point

$$P_1 \cap P_2 = \emptyset \quad \Leftrightarrow \langle P_1, disjoint, P_2\rangle$$

$$dim(P_1 \cap P_2) = 0 \Leftrightarrow \langle P_1, in, P_2\rangle$$

An example may help to understand the proof of Theorem 2: let us consider case 5 of Table 2, which is expressed by:

$$(\partial A \cap \partial L = \emptyset) \wedge (dim(\partial A \cap L^\circ) = 0) \wedge (A^\circ \cap \partial L = \emptyset) \wedge (A^\circ \cap L^\circ = \emptyset) \ ;$$

by making all the substitutions with the equivalences given above, it can be expressed by:

$\langle (L, f), disjoint, (A, b) \rangle \wedge \langle (L, t), disjoint, (A, b) \rangle \wedge$
$\langle L, cross, (A, b) \rangle \wedge$
$(\langle (L, f), disjoint, A \rangle \vee \langle (L, f), touch, A \rangle) \wedge$
$(\langle (L, t), disjoint, A \rangle \vee \langle (L, t), touch, A \rangle) \wedge$
$\langle L, touch, A \rangle \vee \langle L, disjoint, A \rangle \ .$

Of course, this is a long expression, valid in general, but not so practical. An "ad hoc" expression much more effective for the same case is the following:

$$\langle L, touch, A \rangle \wedge \langle L, cross, (A, b) \rangle \wedge \langle (L, f), disjoint, A \rangle \wedge \langle (L, t), disjoint, A \rangle.$$

Other examples of some situations in Fig.3 are simply expressed by:

$\langle A_1, touch, A_2 \rangle \wedge \langle (A_1, b), overlap, (A_2, b) \rangle$ (Fig.3.a)
$\langle A_1, touch, A_2 \rangle \wedge \langle (A_1, b), cross, (A_2, b) \rangle$ (Fig.3.b) ,

and some situations in Fig.4 by:

$\langle (L_2, in, L_1) \rangle \wedge \langle (L_2, f), in, L_1 \rangle \wedge \langle (L_2, t), in, L_1 \rangle$ (Fig.4.d)
$\langle L, in, A \rangle \wedge \langle L, overlap, (A, b) \rangle \wedge \langle (L, f), in, A \rangle \wedge \langle (L, t), in, A \rangle$ (Fig.4.h).

Theorem 2 states that all the cases in the dimension extended method can be expressed with the calculus-based method. But is the converse true? It is easy to see that there are some topological situations that are undistinguishable in the dimension extended method, but that can be represented with the calculus-based method.

For example, the two situations between the lines L_1 and L_2 in Fig.9.a both fall in the following case in the dimension extended method:

$$(\partial L_1 \cap \partial L_2 = \emptyset) \wedge (\partial L_1 \cap L_2^\circ = \emptyset) \wedge (dim(L_1^\circ \cap \partial L_2) = 0) \wedge (L_1^\circ \cap L_2^\circ = \emptyset),$$

while we can make a distinction with the primitives of the calculus-based method:

   I. $\langle L_1, touch, L_2 \rangle \wedge ((\langle (L_2, f), in, L_1 \rangle \wedge \langle (L_2, t), disjoint, L_1 \rangle) \vee$
      $(\langle (L_2, t), in, L_1 \rangle \wedge \langle (L_2, f), disjoint, L_1 \rangle));$
   II. $\langle L_1, touch, L_2 \rangle \wedge \langle (L_2, f), in, L_1 \rangle \wedge \langle (L_2, t), in, L_1 \rangle.$

Another example is depicted in Fig.9.b, where both situations correspond to the line/area case no. 20 in Table 2. The first situation is a *cross*, while the second one is an *in*; in detail:

   I. $\langle L, cross, A \rangle \wedge \langle L, cross, (A, b) \rangle \wedge ((\langle (L, f), in, (A, b) \rangle \wedge \langle (L, t), in, A \rangle) \vee$
      $(\langle (L, t), in, (A, b) \rangle \wedge \langle (L, f), in, A \rangle));$
   II. $\langle L, in, A \rangle \wedge \langle L, cross, (A, b) \rangle \wedge ((\langle (L, f), in, (A, b) \rangle \wedge \langle (L, t), in, A \rangle) \vee$
      $(\langle (L, t), in, (A, b) \rangle \wedge \langle (L, f), in, A \rangle)).$

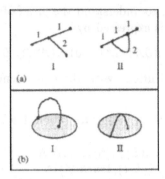

Fig. 9. Comparison between the calculus-based method and the dimension extended method

This additional expressive power comes with the *in* relationship and the *f* and *t* operators. In fact, the *in* relationship allows to say (see Definition 2) that the result of the intersection of the two entities is equal to one of them (not only the dimension of the result like in the dimension extended method); furthermore, the *f* and *t* operators allow to specify conditions on the single end-point of a line (in the dimension extended method, the boundary of a line is a unitary concept).

5 Discussion

In conclusion, we proposed a formal way of modeling topological relationships adopting a calculus-based method, suitable for the definition of an actual query language towards GISs, and close to the way users think about topological relationships. We defined the calculus-based method starting from a point-set theory approach, which is the most recent one adopted in the literature (e.g. [6]) to model topological situations.

The cases that are left out during this first presentation of the calculus-based method are:

1. complex area or line features (that is, in case of an area: a non-connected boundary, and in case of a line: more than two end-points and self-intersections) (Fig.10.a-b);
2. distinguishing the number of simple features that can characterize the intersection of two features (Fig.10.c-d);
3. ordering of the different parts of crossing lines (Fig.10.e-f);
4. line features crossing above/below each-other; this is left out because it is a 3D problem (we will need a 3D variant of the method) (Fig.10.g).

We plan to extend the calculus-based method to encompass also the cases above. Another point in our wish list is related to test if the calculus-based

294

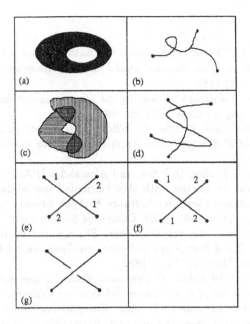

Fig. 10. Extensions left out in our modeling

method is really suitable for end-users. This will lead to some experiments on human subjects to check if the way we grouped topological situations is close to the way people do the same and, therefore, check the usefulness of our query language.

The proposed operators b, f, and t (boundary, from, and to respectively) and the topological relationships have been all implemented as functions (and operators) in the Postgres [13, 14] extendible DBMS environment on a Sun workstation. It is implemented in a manner similar to (and compatible with) the standard geometric extension used in GEO++ [15, 16]. When using the topological relationships in the Postgres/GEO++ environment, one should be aware that due to the Postquel query language, the syntax is a little different from the Object-Calculus. However, the semantics of the implemented relationships and methods are exactly the same.

Acknowledgments

This work has been supported by "Progetto Finalizzato Sistemi Informatici e Calcolo Parallelo" of the Italian National Council of Research (C.N.R.) under grant no. 92.01574.PF69 and by the division "Software Development and Information Technology" of the TNO Physics and Electronics Laboratory.

Special thanks go to Max Egenhofer for his help and suggestions.

References

1. Ronald F. Abler. The national science foundation national center for geographic information and analysis. *International Journal of Geographical Information Systems*, 1(4):303–326, 1987.
2. K. Bennis et al. GéoGraph: A topological storage model for extensible GIS. In *Auto-Carto 10*, pages 349–367, March 1991.
3. Eliseo Clementini and Paolino Di Felice. An object calculus for geographic databases. In *ACM Symposium on Applied Computing*, pages 302–308, Indianapolis, February 1993.
4. Eliseo Clementini, Paolino Di Felice, and Alessandro D'Atri. A spatial data model underlying human interaction with object-oriented spatial databases. In *Fifteenth Annual International Computer Software & Applications Conference*, pages 110–117, Tokyo, September 1991. IEEE Computer Society Press.
5. Sylvia de Hoop and Peter van Oosterom. Storage and manipulation of topology in Postgres. In *Third European Conference on Geographical Information Systems*, pages 1324–1336, Munich, March 1992.
6. Max J. Egenhofer and Robert D. Franzosa. Point-set topological spatial relations. *International Journal of Geographical Information Systems*, 5(2):161–174, 1991.
7. Max J. Egenhofer and John R. Herring. Categorizing binary topological relationships between regions, lines, and points in geographic databases. Technical report, Department of Surveying Engineering, University of Maine, Orono, ME, 1992. submitted for publication.
8. Thanasis Hadzilacos and Nectaria Tryfona. A model for expressing topological integrity constraints in geographic databases. In *Theories and Methods of Spatio-Temporal Reasoning in Geographic Space*, Lecture Notes in Computer Science no. 639, pages 252–268. Springer-Verlag, 1992.
9. John L. Kelley. *General Topology*. Springer-Verlag, New York, 1955.
10. David M. Mark and Max J. Egenhofer. An evaluation of the 9-intersection for region-line relations. In *GIS/LIS Conference*, San Jose, CA, November 1992.
11. Sudhakar Menon and Terence R. Smith. A declarative spatial query processor for Geographic Information Systems. *Photogrammetric Engineering and Remote Sensing*, 55(11):1593–1600, November 1989.
12. Nick Roussopoulos, Christos Faloutsos, and Timos Sellis. An efficient pictorial database system for PSQL. *IEEE Transactions on Software Engineering*, 14(5):639–650, May 1988.
13. Michael Stonebraker and Lawrence A. Rowe. The design of Postgres. *ACM SIGMOD*, 15(2):340–355, 1986.
14. Michael Stonebraker, Lawrence A. Rowe, and Michael Hirohama. The implementation of Postgres. *IEEE Transactions on Knowledge and Data Engineering*, 2(1):125–142, March 1990.
15. Peter van Oosterom and Tom Vijlbrief. Building a GIS on top of the open DBMS "Postgres". In *Proceedings EGIS'91: Second European Conference on Geographical Information Systems*, pages 775–787, Utrecht, April 1991. EGIS Foundation.
16. Tom Vijlbrief and Peter van Oosterom. The GEO system: An extensible GIS. In *Proceedings of the 5th International Symposium on Spatial Data Handling*, pages 40–50, Charleston, South Carolina, August 1992. International Geographical Union IGU.

Qualitative and Topological Relationships in Spatial Databases *

Z Cui 1, A G Cohn 2 and D A Randell 3

1 Advanced Computation Laboratory, Imperial Cancer Research Fund
London WC2A 3PX, England { cui@acl.lif.icnet.uk}
2 School of Computer Studies, University of Leeds, LS2 9JT
England {agc@scs.leeds.ac.uk}
3 School of Dentistry, The University of Birmingham
Birmingham B4 6NN, England { randelda@ibm3090.bham.ac.uk}

Abstract. In this paper, we present a spatial logic which can be used to reason about topological and spatial relationships among objects in spatial databases. The main advantages of such a formalism are its rigorousness, clear semantics and sound inference mechanism. We also show how the formalism can be extended to include orientation and metrical information. Comparisons with other formalisms are discussed.

1 Introduction

A formal theory of space and time has always been an important issue in Artificial Intelligence. Recently, its importance in spatial databases has been recognized (Egenhofer 1989, 1991, Egenhofer and Herring 1990, and Pullar and Egenhofer 1988). Advances of database technology have required a database not only to store, to retrieve and to update data, but also to reason about the relationships among its data, and to have production rules and triggers. A formal theory of data models is important in securing the data consistency in such situations. A deductive database should allow its users to formulate complex queries based on simple facts (relations), otherwise it is difficult to meet the requirements of many applications.

Geographic information systems, image data bases, and CAD/CAM systems are often based upon the relationships among spatial objects. Although some query languages support queries with some spatial relationships; however, the diversity, semantics, completeness and terminology of these relationships vary dramatically (eg Egenhofer and Frank 1988, Roussopoulos, Faloutsos and Sellis 1988, Guenther and Buchmann 1990, Güting 1988). In general, the underlying basis of most existing spatial databases seems to be that of point set geometry, perhaps with some application specific ontology in addition (eg Rawlings 1985).

However, many explanations of phenomena and descriptions of the relationship between objects in informal discourse appeal to relatively high level qualitative spatial information, in particular, topological information. Much of this

---

* This work has been partially funded by the SERC under grant no. GR/G36852

appears to be done unconsciously, but little reflection on our use of language (particularly the use given to prepositions and prepositional phrases) reveals how important this information is. While we need not assume that linguistic descriptions necessarily uncover those entities represented and exploited by the brain in all such activity (eg. in the encoding and representation of perceptual information), the design of formal spatial query languages which mirror the ontology used in informal discourse may ease the use of such a language. Thus there is a need to develop a unified theory on topological relations. Egenhofer(1991, 1989) has proposed a topological relationships based on point set combinatorical topology. However, it relies on relatively sophisticated mathematics concepts such as open and closed regions. The main purpose of this paper is to present a higher level, axiomatic approach (Randell and Cohn 1989, Randell et al 1992) to representing and reasoning about qualitative (including topological) spatial information and to discuss the application of the language to spatial databases. A distinguishing feature of our approach is that our basic ontology is that of a *region*, thus abstracting away from point set semantics, which may indeed be a model for our formalism but is not presupposed.

The other main advantages of this approach are its logical rigorousness and its foundation in first order predicate calculus allowing well investigated inference rules and many different theorem proving technologies to be readily used to prove theorems, make inferences and test consistency and constraints of the databases. Moreover the ontological commitments required are few: two basic primitive notions allow an arbitrarily complex taxonomy of qualitative spatial relationships and concepts to be defined (Cohn, Randell and Cui 1993).

The remainder of this paper is structured as follows: first we present the extant formalism and discuss how the calculus can be easily used to check database consistency and constraints. Then we show how the formalism can be extended to incorporate notions of orientation and direction. Related works are discussed, mainly in the context of the formalisms developed by Egenhofer (1991) and Freksa (1991); finally we mention some current and future work and summarise the paper.

2   The Extant Formalism

The basic ontological entity we consider[4] is a *region*; note that boundaries, lines and points are not regions.[5]. Regions are non empty. Regions in the theory support either a spatial or temporal interpretation, though we will only consider the spatial interpretation here. Informally, these regions may be thought to be

---

4 Most of the material in this section can be found in (Randell, Cui and Cohn 1992) but we review it here for convenience and to make this paper more self contained. Previously we have also considered a temporal interpretation of the formalism (Randell and Cohn 1989, 1992) but we concentrate on the spatial case here.

5 However we believe that from a modelling point of view at least for commonsense reasoning, such mathematical abstractions are not necessary and one can use special kinds of regions such as *skins* and *atoms* – see (Randell, Cui and Cohn 1992)

potentially infinite in number, and any degree of connection between them is allowed in the intended model, from external contact to identity in terms of mutually shared parts. The formalism supports two or three dimensional interpretations (or higher dimensions!) and is based upon Clarke's (1981, 1985) calculus of individuals based on "connection"; it is expressed in the many sorted logic LLAMA (Cohn 1987).[6]

The basic part of the formalism assumes one primitive dyadic relation: $C(x, y)$ read as 'x connects with y'. The relation $C(x, y)$ is reflexive and symmetric. We can give a topological model to interpret the theory, namely that $C(x, y)$ holds when the topological closures of regions x and y share a common point.[7] Two axioms are introduced.

(1) $\forall x C(x, x)$

(2) $\forall x y[C(x, y) \rightarrow C(y, x)]$

Using $C(x, y)$, a basic set of dyadic relations are defined: '$DC(x, y)$' ('x is disconnected from y'), '$P(x, y)$' ('x is a part of y'), '$PP(x, y)$' ('x is a proper part of y'), '$x = y$' ('x is identical with y'), '$O(x, y)$' ('x overlaps y'), '$DR(x, y)$' ('x is discrete from y') '$PO(x, y)$' ('x partially overlaps y'), '$EC(x, y)$' ('x is externally connected with y)', '$TPP(x, y)$' ('x is a tangential proper part of y') and '$NTPP(x, y)$' ('x is a nontangential proper part of y'). The relations: P,PP,TPP and NTPP being non-symmetrical support inverses. For the inverses we use the notation Φ^{-1}, where $\Phi \in \{P, PP, TPP \text{ and } NTPP\}$. In order to save space we will not give the definitions for any of the inverse predicates as they are all of the form $\Phi^{-1}(x, y) \equiv_{def} \Phi(y, x)$. Of the defined relations, DC,EC,PO,=,TPP,NTPP and the inverses for TPP and NTPP are provably mutually exhaustive and pairwise disjoint.

(3) $DC(x, y) \equiv_{def} \neg C(x, y)$

(4) $P(x, y) \equiv_{def} \forall z[C(z, x) \rightarrow C(z, y)]$

(5) $PP(x, y) \equiv_{def} P(x, y) \wedge \neg P(y, x)$

(6) $x = y \equiv_{def} P(x, y) \wedge P(y, x)$

(7) $O(x, y) \equiv_{def} \exists z[P(z, x) \wedge P(z, y)]$

(8) $PO(x, y) \equiv_{def} O(x, y) \wedge \neg P(x, y) \wedge \neg P(y, x)$

(9) $DR(x, y) \equiv_{def} \neg O(x, y)$

(3) $TPP(x, y) \equiv_{def} PP(x, y) \wedge \exists z[EC(z, x) \wedge EC(z, y)]$

(10) $EC(x, y) \equiv_{def} C(x, y) \wedge \neg O(x, y)$

(11) $NTPP(x, y) \equiv_{def} PP(x, y) \wedge \neg \exists z[EC(z, x) \wedge EC(z, y)]$

---

6 Although we use a sorted logic, for the most part this need not concern us here; important sortal restrictions will be mentioned as appropriate.

7 In Clarke's theory and in our original theory (Randell and Cohn 1989, 1992), when two regions x and y connect, they are said to share a point in common; thus the interpretation of the connects relation here and in (Randell, Cui and Cohn 1992) is weaker. Alternative models for the C relation not relying explicitly on point set semantics are that it is true when the distance between the two regions is zero, or that no other region can be 'fitted' between them.

A pictorial representation of the relations defined above is given in Figure 1.

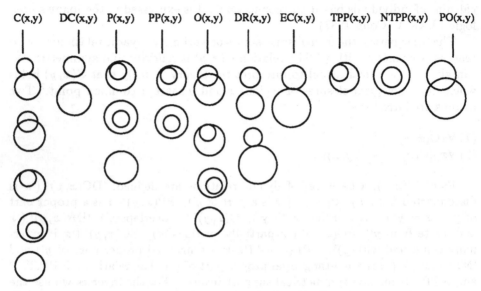

C(x,y) DC(x,y) P(x,y) PP(x,y) O(x,y) DR(x,y) EC(x,y) TPP(x,y) NTPP(x,y) PO(x,y)

Fig. 1. A set of sample configurations (in 2D) modelling the defined relations.

The Boolean functions[8] are: 'sum(x,y)' which is read as 'the sum of x and y', 'us' as 'the universal (spatial) region', 'compl(x)' as 'the complement of x', 'prod(x,y)' as 'the product (i.e. the intersection of x and y' and 'diff(x,y)' as 'the difference of x and y'. The functions: 'compl(x)', 'prod(x,y)' and 'diff(x,y)' are partial but are made total in the sorted logic by simply specifying sorts restrictions and by introducing a new sort called NULL. The sorts NULL and REGION are disjoint.

$\text{sum}(x,y) =_{def} \iota y[\forall z[C(z,y) \leftrightarrow [C(z,x) \vee C(z,y)]]]$
$\text{compl}(x) =_{def} \iota y[\forall z[[C(z,y) \leftrightarrow \neg NTPP(z,x)] \wedge [O(z,y) \leftrightarrow \neg P(z,x)]]]$
$\text{us} =_{def} \iota y[\forall z[C(z,y)]]$
$\text{prod}(x,y) =_{def} \iota z[\forall u[C(u,z) \leftrightarrow \exists v[P(v,x) \wedge P(v,y) \wedge C(u,v)]]]$
$\text{diff}(x,y) =_{def} \iota w[\forall z[C(z,w) \leftrightarrow C(z,\text{prod}(x,\text{compl}(y)))]]$
$\forall xy[\text{NULL}(\text{prod}(x,y)) \leftrightarrow DR(x,y)]$

An additional axiom is also required which stipulates that every region has a nontangential proper part:[9]

---

8 $\alpha(\overline{x}) =_{def} \iota y[\Phi[\alpha(\overline{y})]]$ means $\forall \overline{x}[\Phi(\alpha(\overline{x}))]]$; thus, e.g., the definition for prod(x,y) is translated out (in the object language) as: $\forall xyz[C(z,\text{prod}(x,y)) \leftrightarrow \exists w[P(w,x) \wedge P(w,y) \wedge C(z,w)]]$.
9 A consequence of this axiom is that there can be no *atomic* regions, i.e. regions which

(12) $\forall x \exists y [\text{NTPP}(y, x)]$

This axiom mirrors a formal property of Clarke's theory, where he stipulates that every region has a nontangential part, and thus an interior (remembering that in Clarke's theory a topological interpretation is assumed).

2.1 One piece regions

Clarke's theory supports a model where regions may topologically connected (i.e. in one piece) or disconnected (in more than one piece). This naturally arises given the above definitions for Boolean functions: the sum of two regions will be disjoint unless they are connected. Such scattered regions may be used to model, for example, a cup broken into several pieces. The definition CON(x) (x is connected one piece region) simply states that an individual region is connected if it cannot be split into parts whose union is that region, and where these parts are not connected to each other.

$$\text{CON}(x) \equiv_{def} \forall yz[\text{sum}(y, z) = x \rightarrow C(y, z)]$$

2.2 Concavity and Convexity

A primitive function 'conv(x)' ('the convex-hull of x') is defined and axiomatised.[10] Informally this function generates the region of space that would arise by completely enclosing a body in a taught 'cling film' membrane. This function provides a very intuitive notion for describing objects that may be considered inside, partially inside or outside another object without forming part of that object. Figure 2 gives sample configurations. We also can define a predicate CONV(x) which is true for convex regions.

$\forall x P(x, \text{conv}(x))$
$\forall x P(\text{conv}(\text{conv}(x)), \text{conv}(x))$
$\forall x \forall y \forall z [[P(x, \text{conv}(y) \wedge P(y, \text{conv}(z))] \rightarrow P(x, \text{conv}(z))]$
$\forall x \forall y [[P(x, \text{conv}(y)) \wedge P(y, \text{conv}(x))] \rightarrow C(x, y)]$
$\forall x \forall y [[\text{DR}(x, \text{conv}(y)) \wedge \text{DR}(y, \text{conv}(x))] \leftrightarrow \text{DR}(\text{conv}(x), \text{conv}(y))]$
$\text{CONV}(x) \equiv_{def} x = \text{conv}(x)$

Note that a consequence of these axioms is that the universal region, us, is convex since us is not a proper part of any other region and thus conv(us)=us.

---

contain no subparts. For a discussion of how such regions can be introduced into the language, see Randell, Cui and Cohn (1992).

10 The fourth of these axioms is different to our previous publication (Randell, Cui and Cohn 1992), as we have recently discovered a counterexample to the old axiom – originally the axiom was $\forall x \forall y[[P(x, \text{conv}(y)) \wedge P(y, \text{conv}(x))] \rightarrow O(x, y)]$. Also, it should be noted that whereas we previously assumed (eg Randell, Cui and Cohn 1992) that conv is only well sorted when defined on one piece regions, we have now dropped this restriction since on consideration the axioms for conv are also clearly true for non one piece regions.

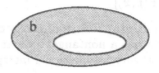

Fig. 2. Illustrations of the convex hull: a is a region (shaded area), its convex-hull is the area enclosed by outer line including the dotted line; b is the shaded area and its convex-hull is the area enclosed by the outer oval.

We use conv to define a set of relations which describe regions being inside, partially inside and outside, e.g. 'INSIDE(x, y)' (x is inside y'), 'P-INSIDE(x,y)' ('x is partially inside y') and 'OUTSIDE(x,y)' ('x is outside y'), each of which also has an inverse. Two functions[11] capturing the concept of the inside and the outside of a particular region are also definable (where 'inside(x)' is read as 'the inside of x', and 'outside(x)' as 'the outside of x' respectively.

INSIDE$(x, y) \equiv_{def} DR(x, y) \wedge P(x, \mathrm{conv}(y))$
P-INSIDE$(x, y) \equiv_{def} DR(x, y) \wedge PO(x, \mathrm{conv}(y))$
OUTSIDE$(x, y) \equiv_{def} DR(x, \mathrm{conv}(y))$
inside$(x) =_{def} \iota y[\forall z[C(z, y) \leftrightarrow \exists w[\mathrm{INSIDE}(w, x) \wedge C(z, w)]]]$
outside$(x) =_{def} \iota y[\forall z[C(z, y) \leftrightarrow \exists w[\mathrm{OUTSIDE}(w, x) \wedge C(z, w)]]]$

This particular set of relations refines $DR(x, y)$ in the basic theory. In (Randell, Cui and Cohn 1992, Randell, Cohn and Cui 1992) we generated a pairwise disjoint and mutually exhaustive set of relations by taking the relations given above, their inverses, and the set of relations that result from non-empty intersections. The set of base relations for this particular set were then finally generated by defining an EC and DC variant for each of these relations.

A new set of base relations (using the relations defined immediately above) are constructed according to the following schema:

$$\alpha\_\beta\_\gamma(x, y) \equiv_{def} \alpha(x, y) \wedge \beta(x, y) \wedge \gamma(x, y)$$

where: $\alpha \in$ {INSIDE, P-INSIDE, OUTSIDE}, $\beta \in$ {INSIDE^{-1}, P-INSIDE^{-1}, OUTSIDE^{-1}}, and $\gamma \in$ {EC, DC} excepting where $\alpha =$ INSIDE and $\beta =$ INSIDE^{-1} This give a total of 22 base relations instead of the original 8.

2.3 Bodies v. Regions

We make an ontological distinction between physical objects (bodies) and the regions of space they occupy. Bodies and regions are represented in the formal theory as disjoint sorts. The mapping between the two is done by introducing

---

11 Note that it does not really make much sense to define a functional analogue of P-INSIDE as this would simply be the sum of the inside and the outside, i.e. the complement of x!

a transfer function 'space(x, y)' read as 'the space occupied by x at y', which takes a body at a given moment in time, and maps this to the region of space it occupies. If the body does not exist at a particular moment, then it will be mapped to the sort NULL.

3 Inferences and Constraints

Efficient inferences can be made by exploiting the structures of the formalism. The computational cost of using uncontrolled inference within computational logics for non-trivial domain problems is well known. Various hybrid representation and reasoning systems have recently gained much interest among AI research workers in an attempt to meet such difficulties (see eg. Frisch and Cohn 1990). The basic idea involves factoring out distinct ways to represent knowledge structures and assigning each "factor" to a subsystem in which specialised inference is done. It should be apparent that our representation is naturally hybrid. Although keeping (sorted) first order logic as the main language, we have knowledge about sorts, subsumption relationships (of both sorts and sets of relations) and continuity restrictions, all of which may be represented and reasoned about by special means. In (Randell and Cohn 1992) we discuss various inference mechanisms for our spatial logic. We review and discuss the most important of these here and relate them to databases.

The first point to note is that the relations naturally form a lattice structure (Figure 3) which can be exploited by any 'clash' based inference mechanism (such as a resolution based deductive engine) via *theory resolution* (Stickel 1990, Randell and Cohn 1992).[12] Moreover, both facts and queries can be expressed at the most appropriate level of abstraction with respect to the hierarchy. Such a lattice can be used to derive relations efficiently. At its simplest, such a lattice can be used to answer queries such as 'is b connected to c?' (ie $C(b, c)$) given that the database contains the entry $TPP(c, b)$, very efficiently (the answer being 'yes' in this case, since $TPP(c, b)$ is equivalent to $TPP^{-1}(b, c)$ and TPP^{-1} is below C in the hierarchy. Similarly the lattice can also be used for integrity checking when entering new data. For example it may already be known that $P(b, c)$; an update of $TPP(b, c)$ would be consistent with this but an update of $EC(c, b)$ would not, because the greatest lower bound in the latter case is $\perp$ but is not $\perp$ in the former case.

3.1 Composition Tables

For the temporal interval logic (Allen 1983), a composition table[13] has been used extensively for many purposes. Such a table has also been constructed for the

---

12 We have extended the LISP implementation of LLAMA in this way, using a bit-encoding of the lattice to allow lattice operations to be efficiently implemented – cf (Aït-Kaci 1989).

13 Allen originally used the term *transitivity* table.

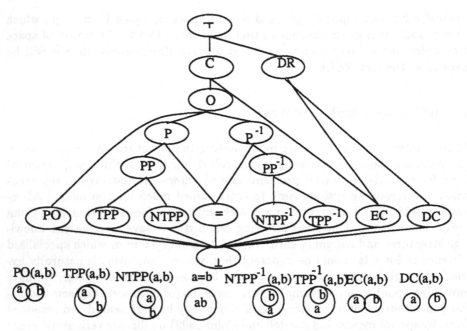

Fig. 3. A lattice defining the subsumption hierarchy of the dyadic relations defined solely in terms of the primitive relation $C(x, y)$.

initial eight[14] base relations in our spatial logic (Randell 1991, Randell, Cohn and Cui 1992) – see Table 1 and, independently, by Egenhofer (1991) for his closely related formalism.

Each entry of the form $R_1(a, b)$ and $R_2(b, c)$ is mapped to a disjunctive set of base relations, corresponding to a theorem and no redundant base relations are given (ie. there is a model for each of the disjunctions). Although the composition table is only given for the base relations, non-base relations may appear in the target set (eg. $PP(a, b)$ and $PP(b, c)$) so in these cases the following calculation is performed. Firstly we use the lattice L (see figure 3) to compute the set of base relations each relation covers (in this case $\{TPP(a, b)$, $NTPP(a, b)\}$ and $\{TPP(b, c), NTPP(b, c)\}$ – remembering that $\forall xy[PP(x, y) \leftrightarrow [TPP(x, y) \vee NTPP(x, y)]]$). Next we take each $R_1(a, b)$, $R_2(b, c)$ pair, where $R_1(a, b) \in \{TPP(a, b), NTPP(b, c)\}$ and $R_2(b, c) \in \{TPP(b, c), NTPP(b, c)\}$ and form the union of all disjunctive sets of base relations each $R_1(a, b)$, $R_2(b, c)$ pair yields using the composition table. In this case this would be $[TPP \vee NTPP](a, c)$ or simply $PP(a, c)$. So given $PP(a, b)$ and $PP(b, c)$ we deduce $PP(a, c)$.

An interesting open question is whether and when the composition table is

14 See later for our progress in building tables for the extended set of relations.

R2(b,c) R1(a,b)	DC	EC	PO	TPP	NTPP	TPP⁻¹	NTPP⁻¹	=
DC	no.info	DR,PO,PP	DR,PO,PP	DR,PO,PP	DR,PO,PP	DC	DC	DC
EC	DR,PO,PP⁻¹	DR,PO TPP,TP⁻¹	DR,PO,PP	EC,PO,PP	PO,PP	DR	DC	EC
PO	DR,PO,PP⁻¹	DR,PO,PP⁻¹	no.info	PO,PP	PO,PP	DR,PO,PP⁻¹	DR,PO PP	PO
TPP	DC	DR	DR,PO,PP	PP	NTPP	DR,PO TPP,TP⁻¹	DR,PO PP	TPP
NTPP	DC	DC	DR,PO,PP	NTPP	NTPP	DR,PO,PP	no.info	NTPP
TPP⁻¹	DR,PO,PP⁻¹	EC,PO,PP⁻¹	PO,PP⁻¹	PO,TPP,TP⁻¹	PO,PP	PP⁻¹	NTPP⁻¹	TPP⁻¹
NTPP⁻¹	DR,PO,PP⁻¹	PO,PP⁻¹	PO,PP⁻¹	PO,PP⁻¹	O	NTPP⁻¹	NTPP⁻¹	NTPP⁻¹
=	DC	EC	PO	TPP	NTPP	TPP⁻¹	NTPP⁻¹	=

Table 1. Composition table for the 8 basic relations. If $R_1(a,b)$ and $R_2(b,c)$, it follows that $R_3(a,c)$ where R_3 is looked up in the table. "no info." means that no base relation is excluded. Multiple entries in a cell are interpreted as disjunctions. Note that DR stands for DC and EC, PP for TPP and NTPP, PP^{-1} for TPP^{-1} and $NTPP^{-1}$, TP^{-1} for TPP^{-1} and =, and O for PO, TPP, NTPP, TPP^{-1}, $NTPP^{-1}$, and =.

sufficient to check for consistency. For example in our qualitative spatial simulation program (Cui, Cohn and Randell 1992a) a state is a conjunction of $n^2/2$ ground atoms whose predicates are the relation symbols presented here, and where there is exactly one atom $R(a,b)$ or $R(b,a)$ for each pair of regions a, b where n is the total number of regions in the state. Potential new states are generated by 'envisioning rules' (see below) and these must be checked for consistency with respect to our spatial theory. At present this is done simply by checking all triples of atoms of the form $R_1(a,b)$, $R_2(b,c)$, $R_3(a,c)$ in the state against the composition table. We believe that this is sufficient in that despite extensive search we cannot find a counterexample. If one restricts the intended interpretation then it is clear that such 'triangle checking' is not sufficient in general; for example if all regions are intended to be circles of the same size, then at most six distinct circles can EC with a particular circle, but this fact will not be detected by triangle checking. Similarly, also in two dimensions, the maximum number of regions that can be mutually partially inside each other (a relationship defined in a following section) is four, and again this cannot be verified by triangle checking. However in the general case, it would appear that triangle checking is sufficient, but we have been unable, despite extensive effort, to formally verify this conjecture to date. Formally stated, the conjecture is as below; readers are invited to contact any of the authors with a counterexample or proof! The conjecture is stated just for the simple case of the 8 basic pairwise disjoint and mutually exhaustive predicates, but we believe the result also holds for the extended case where the relations defined in terms of conv(x) are included.

Conjecture

    $\Gamma, \Psi \models$ False iff $\Psi, \Pi \models$ False where Γ is the set of axioms and definitions (1) to (12) in section 2 above (including the implicit definitions for the inverse relations), Ψ is a conjunction of ground atomic formulae whose predicate symbols are only drawn from the set of eight base relations and whose arguments are constants, and Π is the set of theorems expressed by table 1.

3.2 Continuity Constraints

Assuming continuous motion, there are constraints which can be imposed upon the way the base relations of L can change over consecutive moments in time for any pair of spatial regions. Intuitively, this is best illustrated by the pictorial representation in figure 4.[15] These transitions are alternatively expressed as 'envisioning axioms' (Randell 1991).[16] These continuity networks have been used as the basis of a qualitative spatial simulation program (Cui, Cohn and Randell 1992a), or in the present context of spatial databases could be used to perform consistency checks on the movement of regions in a spatio-temporal database. The construction of such continuity networks for the extended sets of relations is discussed in (Cohn, Randell and Cui 1993). It may also be noted that Egenhofer and Al-Taha (1992) have independently formulated topological change diagrams very similar to ours. They also consider various specialisations where further information is known about the regions in question, as does Galton (1993).

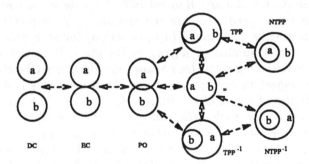

Fig. 4. A pictorial representation of the base relations and their direct topological transitions.

We now turn to consider the continuity network required when we include the predicates defined in terms of conv(x). It is easiest to specify the possible

---

15 These continuity networks are closely related to what Freksa (1992) calls *conceptual neighbourhoods*.

16 Each link in the diagram corresponds to an axiom which expresses that if R1(x,y) is true then either R1(x,y) will continue to be true for ever, or x or y will disappear (become NULL) or R2(x,y) will be the next relationship to be true of x and y in the future.

transitions using relatively high level predicates rather than in terms of the base predicates. First we will consider the transitions whose name includes OUTSIDE, P-INSIDE, INSIDE. The transition network for these predicates is displayed in figure 5.

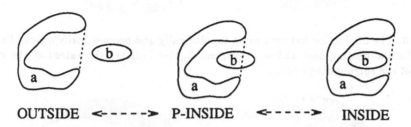

OUTSIDE <-----> P-INSIDE <-----> INSIDE

Fig. 5. The transition network for the 3 high level inside/outside relations.

In order to determine the possible transitions for a predicate with a multipart name (such as OUTSIDE_P-INSIDE^{-1}_EC) one simply determines the allowable transitions for each part of the name; thus in the above example, OUTSIDE can only transition to P-INSIDE, P-INSIDE^{-1} to INSIDE^{-1} or to OUTSIDE^{-1} and EC to PO or DC. In the case that a sub-name transitions from EC to PO, then of course the rest of the sub-names are dropped, e.g. OUTSIDE_CONT-INSIDE^{-1}_EC can transition to EC.

4 Extensions to the Expressive Power

4.1 Refining Inside and Outside

In a previous section the DR relation was specialised to cover relations describing objects being either inside, partially inside or outside other objects. However this ignores some useful distinctions that can be drawn between different cases of bodies being inside another. In this case we can separate out the case where one body is topologically inside another, and where one body is inside another but not topologically inside – this we call being geometrically inside (Randell, Cui and Cohn 1992). The important point of one body being topologically inside another is that one has to 'cut' through the surrounding body in order to reach and make contact with the contained body. In the geometrical variant this is not the case – see figure 6.

TOP-INSIDE$(x, y) \equiv_{def}$
    INSIDE$(x, y) \land \forall z[[\text{CON}(z) \land \text{C}(z, x) \land \text{C}(z, \text{outside}(y))] \rightarrow \text{O}(z, y)]$
GEO-INSIDE$(x, y) \equiv_{def}$ INSIDE$(x, y) \land \neg$TOP-INSIDE(x, y)

It is also possible to specialise the relation of being geometrically inside – in this case setting up definitions to distinguish between the pictorial representations in Figure 7.

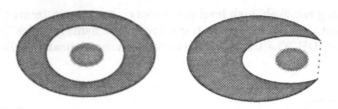

Fig. 6. The distinction between being topologically and geometrically inside. The dotted lines appearing here and in subsequent figures indicate the extent of the convex hull of the surrounding bodies.

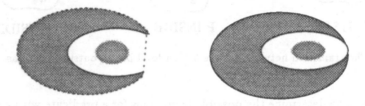

Fig. 7. Two variants of being geometrically inside. In the right hand figure the two 'arms' meet at a point.

In order to make this formal distinction we first set up a stronger case of a connected or one-piece region to that assumed above. The important part of the following definition is the $P(\mathrm{conv}(\mathrm{sum}(v, w)), x)$ literal in the consequent of the definiens. This condition ensures that the connection between any two parts of a region whose sum equals that region, is not point or edge connected. That is to say it ensures a 'channel' region exists connecting any two connected parts. This notion of being connected mirrors and simplifies our previous definition of a quasi-manifold – in this case we use the concept of a convex body rather than use topological and Boolean concepts in the earlier definition – see Randell and Cohn (1989).

$$\mathrm{CON}'(x) \equiv_{def} \mathrm{CON}(x) \wedge$$
$$\forall yz[[\mathrm{sum}(y, z) = x \rightarrow \mathrm{C}(y, z)] \rightarrow$$
$$\exists vw[\mathrm{P}(v, y) \wedge \mathrm{P}(w, z) \wedge \mathrm{P}(\mathrm{conv}(\mathrm{sum}(v, w)), x)]]$$

Now we give the formal distinction between the two cases of being geometrical inside. In the first case a 'channel' region exists connecting the outside of the surrounding body with the contained body, in the second case the surrounding body has closed forming (in this case) a point connection. In both cases we can see how in contrast with the notion of being topologically inside, it is possible to construct a line segment that connects with both the surrounding body and the contained body without cutting through the surrounding body. Definitions distinguishing between the two cases are as follows, where the open and closed variants respectively refer to the first and second cases described above.

$$\mathrm{GEO\text{-}INSIDE\text{-}OPEN}(x, y) \equiv_{def} \mathrm{GEO\text{-}INSIDE}(x, y) \wedge$$

$$\text{CON}'(\text{sum}(\text{inside}(y), \text{outside}(y)))$$
$$\text{GEO-INSIDE-CLOSED}(x, y) \equiv_{def}$$
$$\text{GEO-INSIDE}(x, y) \wedge$$
$$\text{CON}(\text{sum}(\text{inside}(y), \text{outside}(y))) \wedge$$
$$\neg\text{CON}'(\text{sum}(\text{inside}(y), \text{outside}(y)))$$

This technique of refining a base relation into a set of finer grained mutually exhaustive and pairwise disjoint specialised relations can be continued as often as required for a particular application. In Cohn, Randell and Cui(1993) we show how the set of base relations can be expanded to some 100 relations and point to ways in which the process can be continued. We also discuss criteria to help decide when such refinements are worthwhile.

4.2 Orientations and Directions

Thus far we have only considered the relationship between two regions based on essentially topological notions. However, it is often useful to be able to express and reason about the relative or absolute orientation of two regions. In the temporal version of our calculus (Randell and Cohn 1989, 1992) we introduce an additional primitive $B(x, y)$ which is true when the temporal region (*period*) x is entirely before y. Of course it is natural to introduce this to the spatial calculus as well, although we have thus far not done this. We therefore introduce three more primitives: B_1, B_2 and B_3. These are analogues of the three axes of the Cartesian coordinate scheme and are axiomatized below. Conventionally, we will arbitrarily associate B_1 and B_2 with the horizontal axes and B_3 with the vertical axis (though other interpretations are of course possible apart from this intended interpretation).

$$\forall x \neg B_i(x, x)$$
$$\forall xyz[B_i(x, y) \wedge B_i(y, z) \rightarrow B_i(x, z)]$$
$$\forall xy[B_i(x, y) \rightarrow \forall x_1 y_1[(P(x_1, x) \wedge P(y_1, y)) \rightarrow B_i(x_1, y_1)]]$$

These relationships are transitive, but one often requires a non transitive relation (eg 'directly below' in the sense that a gravity vertical would intersect both regions). We can thus define $\text{D-}B_1(x, y)$, $\text{D-}B_2(x, y)$, $\text{D-}B_3(x, y)$:[17]

$$\text{D-}B_i(x, y) \equiv_{def} B_i(x, y) \wedge \neg B_{j+1}(x, y) \wedge \neg B_{j+1}(y, x) \wedge \neg B_{j+2}(x, y) \wedge \neg B_{j+2}(y, x)$$

These relationships are illustrated in Figure 8.

Related to these notions are the functional terms denoting the extremities of an object in a particular direction[18] eg the top or bottom of a region. Thus we may define a set of monadic function symbols extreme_1, extreme_1^{-1}, extreme_2, extreme_2^{-1}, extreme_3, extreme_3^{-1}. To do this we define a set of corresponding binary relations, Extreme_1, Extreme_1^{-1}, Extreme_2, Extreme_2^{-1}, Extreme_3, Extreme_3^{-1}.

---

17 In the definition 'j+1' and 'j+2' denote modulo arithmetic, eg 3+1=1, 3+2=2.

18 Remember that we allow multipiece regions and the extremity of a concave region may well be a multipiece region.

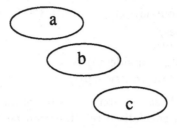

Fig. 8. The following are true in the above figure: $B_3(a,b)$, $B_3(b,c)$, $B_3(a,c)$, D-$B_3(a,b)$, D-$B_3(b,c)$, but ¬D-$B_3(a,c)$.

$\text{Extreme}_i(y,r) \equiv_{def} P(y,r) \wedge \forall x[[P(x,r) \wedge \neg(x=y)] \rightarrow B_i(y,x)]$
$\text{extreme}_i(r) =_{def} \iota y[\text{Extreme}_i(y,r) \wedge \forall x[\text{Extreme}_i(x,r) \rightarrow P(x,y)]]$
$\text{Extreme}_i^{-1}(y,r) \equiv_{def} P(y,r) \wedge \forall x[[P(x,r) \wedge \neg(x=y)] \rightarrow B_i(y,x)]$
$\text{extreme}_i^{-1}(r) =_{def} \iota y[\text{Extreme}_i^{-1}(y,r) \wedge \forall x[\text{Extreme}_i^{-1}(x,r) \rightarrow P(x,y)]]$

Note that it is not difficult to see that these definitions presuppose a notion of atomic region, i.e. a region which has no proper subparts. The calculus as presented thus far does not admit atomic regions because of the axiom $\forall x \exists y[\text{NTPP}(y,x)]$. However, in Randell, Cui and Cohn (1992), we discussed a number of ways to modify the calculus to allow atomic regions.

Given our intended interpretation, more natural names for $\text{extreme}_3(x)$ and $\text{extreme}_3^{-1}(x)$ would be top(x) and bottom(x). In a particular context one may wish to rename the other relations and functions just defined as well. For example, one might want to name B_1 as EastOf, B_1^{-1} as WestOf, B_2 as NorthOf and B_2^{-1} as SouthOf. Or if one assumes a particular viewpoint, then these four relations may be more naturally named LeftOf, RightOf, Behind and InFrontOf. Of course, rather than regard the viewpoint as fixed, one may want to add an extra argument to give the viewpoint and define, eg, LeftOf(x,y,z), meaning x is to the left of y when viewed by/from z. In this case we do not need to assume a fixed cartesian coordinate scheme. Interestingly, Behind(x,y,z) and InFrontof(x,y,z) are actually definable from C(x,y) and conv(x) alone, without recourse to the additional B_i primitives (see Figure 9). However, the other 3 place relative relations do seem to require the relevant additional primitives.

$\text{InFrontof}(x,y,z) \equiv_{def} \text{DR}(x,y) \wedge \text{DR}(y,z) \wedge \text{DR}(x,z) \wedge$
$\quad \exists w \; \text{EC}(w,z) \wedge \text{EC}(w,y) \wedge \text{CONV}(w) \wedge \text{O}(x,w) \wedge \text{P}(w,\text{inside}(\text{sum}(z,y)))$
$\text{Behind}(y,x,z) \equiv_{def} \text{InFrontof}(x,y,z)$

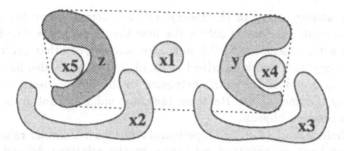

Fig. 9. Defining a relative notion of InFrontof. x1, x2 and x3 are all in front of y when viewed from z. The definition rules out the possibility that x4 and x5 are in front of y when viewed from z because w has to be convex (one piece) region touching both y and z. Arguably x2 and x3 should not be regarded as being in front of y when viewed from z; to achieve this the definition should be strengthened so that the conjunct $O(x, w)$ is replaced by $P(x, w)$

4.3 Integrating metric and scalar information

So far we have principally concentrated on developing a purely qualitative calculus. However this can never be a replacement for metric information, but rather should complement a metric representation. Indeed Forbus et al (1991) have argued that there is no purely qualitative representation of space – their so called 'poverty conjecture'. Joskowicz (1992) has also argued that there is no general purpose commonsense spatial reasoning and representation mechanism and that a hybrid representation is necessary. We do not have space here to describe our approaches to integrating metric information with our qualitative calculus. Some of our initial ideas can be found in (Randell and Cohn 1989, Randell 1991). We have also recently integrated our purely qualitative spatial simulator (Cui, Cohn and Randell 1992a) with QSIM (Kuipers 1986) which allows both region based spatial knowledge and scalar quantities (eg the qualitative distance between two regions) to be reasoned about together (Cui, Cohn and Randell 1992b).

5 Related Work

We have already mentioned Clarke's calculus of individuals, our earlier work on which this present theory is based, and Allen's work on interval logics. The other work of which we are aware, that uses Clarke's theory for describing space, is Augnague(1991) and Vieu(1991). Other work on the description of space using a body rather than a point based ontology, can be found in Laguna(1922), Tarski (1965) and Whitehead (1978). There have been some attempts in the qualitative spatial reasoning literature to employ Allen's interval logic for describing space, see for example Freska (1990), Mukerjee and Joe (1990) and Hernandez(1990,1992), but here a stronger primitive relation is used, which does not allow the full range of topological relationships to be formally described as given in both Clarke's and our original and new theories. Apart from the question raised by adding atoms to the theory, we are currently working on the question as to what a decidable subset the new theory supports. We have already indicated some extensions to this new logic above. For other extensions to the spatial theory itself, work described in Randell (1991) can also be included. For example, we could add a metric extension to the theory, using a ternary relation (along the lines of Van Benthem 1982, appendix A) that gives comparative distances between objects.

Egenhofer's work (1991) on topological relations has similar relations to ours, though we have an extended set owing to the relations defined in terms of conv(x). However, we draw distinction between physical objects and regions; intuitively, a region of space may be likened to a space that could be conceivably occupied by a physical body. We restrict our interpretation of time and space so that time is treated as a one-dimensional region, and space a three-dimensional region. In Egenhofer's work, the usual concepts of point-set topology with open and closed sets are assumed. For the corresponding part of his theory, we only use one primitive C. Open, closed, etc concepts can be defined in our theory (see Randell et al 1989, 1992) although in the theory presented above, we assumed no distinctions between open and closed regions because we believe that applications, and reasoning about physical objects and commonsense reasoning in particular, do not need to differentiate between open and closed regions. Another difference is that we do not have a notion of points in the theory,[19] nor do we view an arbitrary set of points as a region. Finally we introduce the convex hull operator allowing many more base relations to be defined.

In both theories, eight disjoint base relations are defined. There is a one to one correspondence between the base relations: DC (disjoint), EC (meet), = (equal), TPP (coverBy), PO (overlap), NTPP (inside) TPP^{-1} (covers) and NTPP^{-1} (contain). One minor difference is between EC and meet. In our theory, if the sum of two regions equals the universe (assuming universe is continuous), the two regions EC, whereas the two regions do not meet in Egenhofer's (as they did not in our original theory which distinguished between open and closed regions).

The composition table in both theories is the same although we used a combination of theorem proving and model building (Randell, Cohn and Cui 1992b) to derive the composition table whilst Egenhofer used exhaustive search by PROLOG. Egenhofer used matrix representations of the base relations in the theory and this obviously provides a model for his theory. We have investigated a linear bitmap representation in calculating and constructing the composition tables (Randell, Cohn and Cui 1992b). In Randell, Cohn and Cui (1992), we proposed calculating an extended composition table. The task is formidable. We have in fact constructed the table for 22 × 22 case. This took some 2 days of cpu time on a Sparc IPC. For an even larger table (Cohn, Randell and Cui 1993), this becomes more difficult. It would be very interesting to investigate whether an

---

19 In the earliest version we did include points (Randell and Cohn 1989) but have since abandoned them as pragmatically unnecessary (Randell et al 1992) though they could be reintroduced if necessary (Randell, Cui and Cohn 1992a).

extension of Egenhofer's matrix method could be used.

Perhaps the most important work in qualitative spatial orientation is that of Freksa(1991), who also surveys the existing work in this area. The principal tenets of his approach are that he just treats points rather than regions[20], orientations are relative and are terms in his language rather than relations as outlined in our approach above; he then uses qualitative relations to compare orientations (eg he would say same(ab,cd) meaning that the directions from a to b and from c to d are identical). Other relations include additional *exact* directions (such as 'opposite') and inexact relations (such as 'left', which cover a segment of directions. Further refinements of these relations allow a notion of relative qualitative distance to be expressed as well. He also defines a composition table on his qualitative directions.

The inferential power of his approach relies crucially on having some exact directions (as compared eg to Hernadez (1990, 1992)). An interesting question arises as to whether it is possible to integrate Freksa's calculus with a region based approach (whilst retaining Freksa's inferential power). We speculate that this may be possible using either atomic regions (Randell, Cui and Cohn 1992a) or by defining 'strong' versions of D-B_i. The relations defined in this paper are 'weak' in the sense that, for example, D-$B_3(b,c)$ is true if some part of b is directly above some part of c. A strong version would only be true if every part of b was directly above some part of c (or, perhaps, some part of b was above every part of c). These ideas need further investigation but should allow a sufficient notion of transitivity to be gained (the transitivity of exact directions are most important to Freksa's calculus). Also worthy of investigation is the extension of Freksa's calculus to 3D (at present he only considers the 2D case).

We conclude this discussion of qualitative orientation by noting that the purpose of the exposition of qualitative orientation in the body of this paper was not to give a definitive axiomatisation, but rather to show how such information might be axiomatised, defined and related to the rest of the calculus.

6   Conclusion

We have presented a spatial logic based on a primitive notion of connection. Eight mutually exclusive and pairwise disjoint relations were defined giving an alternative formulation of Egenhofer's calculus. By introducing a further primitive, more expressive calculi can be defined. A number of inference techniques, dealing with both static and dynamic spatial configurations were outlined which may be efficiently implemented and their relevance to databases was discussed. Of course many questions remain unanswered and deserve further research. We have mentioned some of these above.

---

20 Freksa does remark that regions may be treated as points at a certain level of abstraction.

References

1. H. Aït-Kaci, et al: "Efficient Implementation of Lattice Operations," *ACM Trans. on Programming Languages and Systems,* 11(1), 1989
2. J. F. Allen: "Maintaining Knowledge about Temporal Intervals," Comm. ACM26(11), 1983.
3. M. Aurnague: " Contribution a l'etude de la semantique formelle de l'espace et du raisonnement spatial: la localisation interne en francais, semantique et structures inferentielles", PhD thesis, l'Universite Paul Sabatier de Toulouse, 1991.
4. Van Benthem: *The Logic of Time,* Synthese Library vol 156, Reidel, London, 1982
5. B. L. Clarke: "A Calculus of Individuals Based on Connection," *Notre Dame Journal of Formal LOGIC,* vol. 2, No. 3, 1981.
6. B. L. Clarke: "Individuals and Points", *Notre Dame Journal of Formal Logic* Vol. 26, No. 1, 1985.
7. A. G. Cohn: "A More Expressive Formulation of Many Sorted Logic," J. Autom. Reasoning., Vol. 3(2), pp. 113–200, 1987
8. A. G. Cohn, D. A. Randell and Z. Cui: "A Taxonomy of Logically Defined Qualitative Spatial Relations," Proc International Workshop on Formal Ontology in Conceptual Analysis and Knowledge Representation, Padova, Ladseb-CNR Internal Report 01/93, ed N Guarino and R Poli, pp 149-158, 1993
9. Z. Cui, A. G. Cohn and D. A. Randell: " Qualitative Simulation Based On A Logical Formalism Of Space And Time", Proc AAAI, 1992a.
10. Z. Cui, A. G. Cohn and D. A. Randell: "Qualitative Simulation Based On A Logic Of Space And Time", Proc. of QR92, 1992b.
11. M. Egenhofer: "A Formal Definition of Binary Topological Relationships," In: W Litwin and H J Schek, editors, Third International Conference on Foundations of Data Organization and Algorithms, Paris, France, Lecture Notes in Computer Science, Vol. 367, pages 457–472, Springer-Verlag, New York, NY, June 1989
12. M. Egenhofer:"Reasoning about Binary Topological Relations," In: Proceedings of the Second Symposium on Large Spatial Databases, SSD'91 (Zurich, Switzerland, 1991), O. Gunther and H. J. Schek, Eds. Lecture Notes in Computer Science 525, pp 143-160.
13. M. Egenhofer and J. A. Herring: "A Mathematical Framework for the Definition of Topological Relationships," In: Proceedings of Fourth International Symposium on Spatial Data Handling (Zurich, Switzerland, 1990), K. Brassel and H. Kishimoto, Eds.
14. M. Egenhofer and A. Frank: "Towards a Spatial Query Language: user interface considerations," In: Proceedings of 14th International Conference on Very Large Data Bases (Los Angeles, CA, 1988) D. DeWitt and F. Bancilhon, Eds.
15. M. Egenhofer and K K Al-Taha: "Reasoning about Gradual Changes of Topological Relationships", in Theoreies and Methods of Spatio Temporal Reasoning in Geographic Space, LNCS 639 Springer Verlag, 1992
16. K. D. Forbus, P. Nielsen and B. Faltings: "Qualitative spatial reasoning: the CLOCK project," *Art. Int.* 51, pp. 417–471, Elsevier, 1991
17. C. Freksa: "Using Orientation Information for Qualitative Spatial Reasoning", Berick Nr 11, Kognitionswissenschaft, Univ. Hamburg, 1992a.
18. C. Freksa: "Temporal Reasoning based on Semi-intervals," *Artificial Intelligence,* 54, Elsevier, 1992b
19. A. M. Frisch and A. G. Cohn: "Thought and Afterthoughts on the 1988 Workshop on Principles of Hybrid Reasoning," *AI Magazine* 1990

20. A Galton, Towards an integrated logic of space, time, and motion, to appear in Proc IJCAI93, Morgan Kaufmann, 1993.
21. D. Guenther and A. Buchmann: "Research Issues in Spatial Databases," *SIGMOD RECORD* 19 (4), 1990
22. R. Güting: "Geo-Relational Algebra: A Model and Query Language for Geometric Database Systems," Advances in Database Technology, 1988.
23. D. Hernandez: "Using Comparative Relations to represent Spatial Knowledge", Workshop RAUM, Univ. of Koblenz, 1990.
24. D. Hernandez: "Qualitative Representation of Spatial Knowledge", PhD Dissertation, Fakultaet fuer Informatik, Technischen Universitaet Muenchen, Germann, 1992.
25. L. Joskowicz: "Commonsense Reasoning about Moving Objects: an Elusive Goal", IBM T J Watson Research Center, Yorktown Heights, 1992.
26. B. Kuipers: "Qualitative Simulation," *Artificial Intelligence* 29: 298–338, 1986
27. T. de Laguna: "Point, Line and Surface as sets of Solids" *The Journal of Philosophy.*, Vol 19., pp. 449–461, 1922.
28. A. Mukerjee and G. Joe: "A Qualitative Model for Space", Proc AAAI, 1990.
29. D. Pullar and M. Egenhofer: "Towards Formal Definitions of Topological Relations among Spatial Objects," In: proceedings of Third International Symposium on Spatial Data Handling (Sydney, Australia, 1988), D. Marble, Ed.
30. D. Randell, A. G. Cohn and Z. Cui: "Naive Topology: modeling the force pump," *in Recent Advances in Qualitative Reasoning,* ed B Faltings and P Struss, MIT Press, in press, 1992a.
31. D. A. Randell: "Analysing the Familiar: Reasoning about space and time in the everyday world," *PhD Thesis,* Univ. of Warwick, UK 1991.
32. D. A. Randell, A. G. Cohn and Z. Cui: "Computing Transitivity Tables: a Challenge for Automated Theorem Provers," Proc CADE11, 1992b.
33. D. A. Randell and A. G. Cohn: "Modelling Topological and Metrical Properties in Physical Processes," in *Principles of Knowledge Representation and Reasoning,* ed. R. J. Brachman, H. Levesque and R. Reiter, Morgan Kaufmann, Los Altos. 1989.
34. D. A. Randell and A. G. Cohn: "Exploiting Lattice in a Theory of Space and Time," *Computers and Mathematics with Applications,* 1992.
35. D. A. Randell, Z. Cui and A. G. Cohn: "A Spatial Logic based on Regions and Connection", Proc 3rd Int Conf on the Principles of Knowledge Representation and Reasoning, Morgan Kaufmann, 1992a.
36. D. Randell, Z. Cui and A. G. Cohn: "An Interval Logic for Space based on "Connection"," *in proc. of ECAI92, 1992b*
37. C. J. Rawlings, W. R. Taylor, J. Nyakairu, J. Fox and M. J. E. Sternberg: "Reasoning about Protein Topology using the Logic Programming Language PROLOG," *J. Mol. Graphics 3(4),* 1985
38. N. Roussopoulos, C. Faloutsos and T. Sellis: "An Efficient Pictorial Database System for PSQL," IEEE Transactions on Software Engineering 15 (5), 1988
39. M. Stickel: "Automated Deduction by Theory Resolution," *J. Automated Reasoning,* 1, 1985
40. A. Tarski: "Foundations of the geometry of solids," in Logic, Semantics, Metamathematics, trans. J. H. Woodger, Oxford Uni. Press, 1956
41. L. Vieu: "Semantique des relations spatials et inference spatio-temporelles: Une contribution a l'etude des structures formelles de l'espace en Language Naturel.", PhD thesis, l'Universite Paul Sabatier de Toulouse, 1991.

42. A. N. Whitehead: "Process and Reality: Corrected Edition," eds. D.R. Griffin and D.W. Sherburne, The Free Press, Macmillan Pub. Co., New York, 1978

Topological Relations
Between Regions in $\mathbb{R}^2$ and $\mathbb{Z}^{2*}$

Max J. Egenhofer and Jayant Sharma

National Center for Geographic Information and Analysis
and
Department of Surveying Engineering
Department of Computer Science
University of Maine
Orono, ME 04469-5711, U.S.A.
max@mecan1.maine.edu
jayant@thrush.umesve.maine.edu

Abstract. Users of geographic databases that integrate spatial data represented in vector and raster models, should not perceive the differences among the data models in which data are represented, nor should they be forced to apply different concepts depending on the model in which spatial data are represented. A crucial aspect of spatial query languages for such integrated systems is the need mechanisms to process queries about spatial relations in a consistent fashion. This paper compares topological relations between spatial objects represented in a continuous (vector) space of $\mathbb{R}^2$ and a discrete (raster) space of $\mathbb{Z}^2$. It applies the 9-intersection, a frequently used formalism for topological spatial relations between objects represented in a vector data model, to describe topological relations for bounded objects represented in a raster data model. We found that the set of all possible topological relations between regions in $\mathbb{R}^2$ is a subset of the topological relations that can be realized between two bounded, extended objects in $\mathbb{Z}^2$. At a theoretical level, the results contribute toward a better understanding of the differences in the topology of continuous and discrete space. The particular lesson learnt here is that topology in $\mathbb{R}^2$ is based on coincidence, whereas in $\mathbb{Z}^2$ it is based on coincidence and neighborhood. The relevant differences between the raster and the vector model are that an object's boundary in $\mathbb{Z}^2$ has an extent, while it has none in $\mathbb{R}^2$; and in the finite space of $\mathbb{Z}^2$ there are points between which one cannot insert another one, while in the infinite space of $\mathbb{R}^2$ between any two points there exists another one.

1 Introduction

Spatial relations are significant ingredients of query languages for geographic information systems (GISs), where they are used to describe constraints among spatial objects to be retrieved or updated. Relations among spatial objects are less well understood than the commonly used relations among integers or strings [18] and

---

* This work was partially supported by grants from Intergraph Corporation. Jayant Sharma was supported by a University Graduate Research Assistantship (UGRA) from the University of Maine. Additional support from NSF for the NCGIA under grant No. SES 88-10917 is gratefully acknowledged.

attempts to formalize them have been rare. Recently, progress has been made on selected topics such as cardinal directions between point objects [14, 20] and some combinations of relations such as topological and direction relations [2, 25, 28].

Topological relations have been studied extensively in the past and there exists a comprehensive formalism [7, 8]. This model has become popular in the GIS community and has been used extensively for a variety of purposes. Svensson and Zhexue [37] incorporated it into a spatial-analysis query language. De Hoop and van Oosterom [27] designed a topological query language around these operators. Herring [26] discussed possible extensions of the model to cover topological relations between lines in $\mathbb{R}^2$. Egenhofer and Al-Taha [12] used the model to investigate various aspects of temporal changes of topological relations. Pigot [32] and Hazelton *et al.* [23] showed how the model applies to 3-dimensional objects; Hadzilacos and Tryfona [22] and Clementini *et al.* [4] showed how the model for regions behaves when applied to model topological relations between regions, lines, and points; and Egenhofer and Herring [9] extended the principle of boundary and interior intersections to include intersections with the exterior as well as a generic model for topological relations involving n-dimensional objects embedded in higher-dimensional spaces. Parts of these extensions are now being tested with human subjects to identify how closely the formalism models human cognition [30]. The sound model also enabled a number of advanced theoretical studies such as the formal derivation of the composition table for this set of relations [6] and comprehensive reasoning systems to detect inconsistencies in topological descriptions [11, 35]. A derivative of the method has also been successfully implemented in a commercial GIS [26].

This paper extends the scope of this model by investigating its usefulness for modeling topological relations among bounded objects embedded in the discrete space $\mathbb{Z}^2$. Its goal is to answer such questions as, "Are the topological relations between bounded objects in $\mathbb{R}^2$ and $\mathbb{Z}^2$ the same?" and if they are different then, "What are their differences?" By basing the investigations of raster relations on the same model as vector relations, we expect to make formal comparisons in the model, rather than giving intuitive interpretations.

Such an approach is a significant contribution towards designing spatial information systems that integrate what is usually called a "vector" and "raster" representation of spatial objects [16, 21], which is a topic that has gotten considerable attention through the discussions of integrating remotely sensed data with GIS data in vector format [13]. Much of this discussion has been at the level of data structures. The actual problems faced as one attempts to merge a data model for continuous space with a model of discrete space, are deeper in nature. To date, there exist only a few approaches that try to combine the two views at a conceptual level [31]. In order to come up with an integrated model it is definitely necessary to formalize the differences at the conceptual level, rather than the level of particular data structures or implementations. This paper contributes towards such an integrated data model for geographic databases, as it identifies topological properties that are common or different between the two views. As such, the results of this paper will help in gaining a better understanding of the differences between raster and vector space.

The remainder of this paper is structured as follows. Section 2 briefly summarizes the basic concepts of the 9-intersection applied for topological relations between regions in $\mathbb{R}^2$. Following an introduction of a data model for spatial regions in $\mathbb{Z}^2$ (Section 3), we derive formally the existing topological relations based on the 9-intersection (Section 4). Section 5 compares the two sets of topological relations by analyzing the differences of $\mathbb{R}^2$ and $\mathbb{Z}^2$ that caused them, and by giving a cognitive interpretation in terms of their conceptual neighborhoods. Conclusions in Section 6 show how the results also apply to "coarse" spatial reasoning.

2 The 9-Intersection as a Model for Topological Relations in $\mathbb{R}^2$

The usual concepts of point-set topology with open and closed sets are assumed [1, 36]. The interior of a set A, denoted by $A°$, is the union of all open sets in A. The closure of A, denoted by $\overline{A}$, is the intersection of all closed sets of A. The exterior of A with respect to the embedding space $\mathbb{R}^2$, denoted by A^-, is the set of all points of $\mathbb{R}^2$ not contained in A. The boundary of A, denoted by ∂A, is the intersection of the closure of A and the closure of the exterior of A. The spatial objects of concern are called spatial regions. A *spatial region* is defined as 2-dimensional point-set that is homeomorphic to a 2-disk, i.e., each of the three object parts of a region—its interior, boundary, and exterior—is non-empty and connected.

For two regions A and B, the binary topological relation between them is characterized by comparing A's boundary (∂A), interior ($A°$), and exterior (A^-) with B's boundary (∂B), interior ($B°$), and exterior (B^-). These six object parts are combined such that they form nine intersections that represent the topological relation between the two regions. They are:

- the boundary-boundary intersection, denoted by $\partial A \cap \partial B$,
- the boundary-interior intersection, denoted by $\partial A \cap B°$,
- the boundary-exterior intersection, denoted by $\partial A \cap B^-$,
- the interior-boundary intersection, denoted by $A° \cap \partial B$,
- the interior-interior intersection, denoted by $A° \cap B°$,
- the interior-exterior intersection, denoted by $A° \cap B^-$,
- the exterior-boundary intersection, denoted by $A^- \cap \partial B$,
- the exterior-interior intersection, denoted by $A^- \cap B°$, and
- the exterior-exterior intersection denoted by $A^- \cap B^-$.

The topological relation between regions A and B, is concisely represented as a 3×3 matrix, called the *9-intersection*.

$$\mathbf{R}\,(A, B) = \begin{pmatrix} \partial A \cap \partial B & \partial A \cap \partial B & \partial A \cap B^- \\ A° \cap \partial B & A° \cap \partial B & A° \cap B^- \\ A^- \cap \partial B & A^- \cap \partial B & A^- \cap B^- \end{pmatrix}$$

Topological relations are characterized by *topological invariants* of the 9-intersections, i.e., properties that are preserved under topological transformations. The *content* of the nine intersections was identified as the simplest and most general topological invariant [7], though others may be useful as well such as the components of an intersection and their dimensions [17]. The content invariant characterizes each of the nine intersections by the value empty ($\emptyset$) or non-empty ($\neg\emptyset$). With the empty/non-empty distinction of the nine intersections, one can distinguish $2^9 = 512$ different topological relations. Exactly one of these topological relations holds true between any two regions, because the nine empty/non-empty intersections describe a set of relations that are mutually exclusive and provide a complete coverage—the three object parts boundary, interior, and exterior cover the entire universe as a complete partition of space; and the contents of their intersections are such that any set is either empty or non-empty. The actual number of realizable relations depends on the dimension of the space with respect to the dimension of the objects—there are more topological relations if objects are embedded in higher-dimensional space—and on topological properties of the objects embedded in that space. For example, the boundary of a (non-cyclic) line—the set of its start and end points—is a separation, whereas the boundary of a region without holes is connected, and the difference in these topological properties influences what topological relations can be realized.

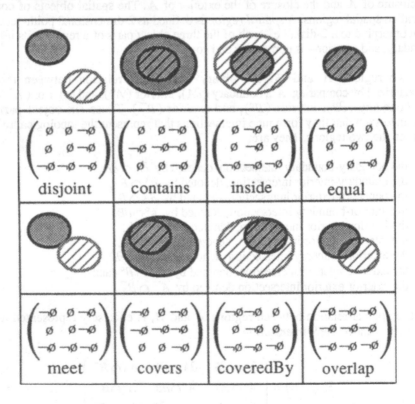

Fig. 1. The eight relations between two regions in $\mathbf{R}^2$.

From the 512 possible relations, only eight can be realized if the objects are spatial regions in $\mathbb{R}^2$. We call these eight relations *disjoint, meet, equal, inside, contains, covers, coveredBy,* and *overlap* (Fig. 1). Recently, these results were verified using an independent method [33] that is based on an interval logic about connections rather than set theory with intersections.

3 Spatial Data Model for Objects in $\mathbb{Z}^2$

The present investigations concentrate on topological relations in raster space. Raster space, or the digital plane $\mathbb{Z} \times \mathbb{Z}$, is defined as a rectangular array of points or pixels. Each point is addressed by a pair of integer valued coordinates (x, y). We will briefly review the concepts most relevant for the subsequent discussions. More extensive and detailed treatments of digital topology can be found in [24, 34].

Given a point in the plane, the neighboring points can be classified as 4-neighbors or 8-neighbors. The 4-neighbors of a point P are the vertically and horizontally adjacent points. Along with the diagonally adjacent points, they form the 8-neighbors. Fig. 2 gives an example of the 4- and 8-neighbors of a point.

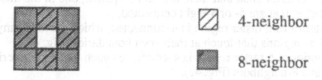

4-neighbor

8-neighbor

Fig. 2. A point with its 4- and 8-neighbors.

A finite proper subset of $\mathbb{Z}^2$ is called an extended spatial object. Any two points P and Q that belong to an extended object R are connected if there exists a connected path between them, i.e., a sequence of adjacent points, all in R, that starts at P and ends at Q. If all adjacent points in the path are 4-neighbors then P and Q are connected by a 4-path. R is 4-connected if for any pair of points P, Q in R there exists a 4-path of finite length between them. The corresponding definition holds for 8-connectedness.

The objects of concern are *raster regions*, i.e., extended objects that are bounded. The boundary of a raster region is a simple closed curve C, which divides the background into two components and every point on C is adjacent to both these components; therefore, the boundary of a raster region is a Jordan Curve [38], which separates the region into an interior and an exterior (Fig. 3).

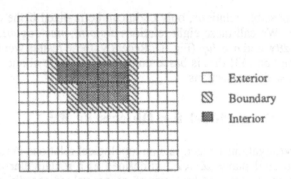

Fig. 3. The boundary, interior, and exterior of a region.

Raster regions have the following properties:

- Boundary and interior are non-empty (Fig. 4a). (The non-emptiness of the exterior is already guaranteed by R being a proper subset of $\mathbb{Z}^2$.)
- The boundary is 4-connected such that each boundary point has exactly two 4-neighbors (Fig. 4b and c). This implies that the boundary separates the interior from the exterior such that there are no two points, one in the interior and one in the exterior, that are 4- or 8-eight connected.
- The exterior of a raster region is 4-connected, which excludes any interior holes as well as regions that touch at their own boundaries (Fig. 4d).
- The interior of a raster region is 4-connected such that each interior point has at least three 8-neighbors (Fig. 4e).

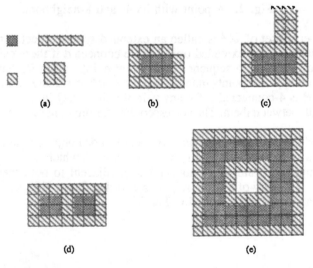

Fig. 4. Disallowed raster regions: (a) empty interior or boundary; (b) the boundary is not 4-connected; (c) a boundary point with more than two 4-neighbors; (d) disconnected interiors; and (e) disconnected exteriors.

Furthermore, we exclude some degenerate cases—very small and very large objects—by limiting the raster regions to have the following properties:

- Each point in the interior of a raster region has at least three 8-neighbors.
- The union of no pair of raster regions can occupy $\mathbb{Z}^2$ completely.

4 Realizable 9-Intersections in $\mathbb{Z}^2$

This section examines the binary topological relations between raster regions in $\mathbb{Z}^2$. As the underlying model, we use the 9-intersection whose empty/non-empty invariant gives rise to 2^9, i.e., 512 different relations. Here, we will determine which 9-intersections represent feasible topological relations between raster regions embedded in $\mathbb{Z}^2$. The result will enable us to compare raster-region relations with vector-region relations.

The identification of 9-intersections for which topological relations exist in $\mathbb{Z}^2$ is a four-step process:

(1) Describing the conditions that must hold among interiors, boundaries, and exteriors in order to guarantee consistency within the data model of raster regions. The conditions are based upon the mathematical properties of the objects and the underlying space, such as the Jordan-Curve-Theorem, and restrictions on objects, e.g., a region must have a non-empty interior and a non-empty exterior.

(2) Formalization of all conditions such that they can be integrated and compared. Rather than finding all constraints that describe the *valid* configurations among interiors, boundaries, and exteriors, we pursue the opposite, that is, we collect a set of constraints that describe *invalid* configurations and infer as candidates for valid configurations those that do not violate any constraint. This is achieved by translating all conditions among boundaries, interiors, and exteriors into *consistency violations* and expressing them as templates of 9-intersections for non-existing relations.

(3) Determining the set of 9-intersections that represent existing relations. This is done by applying the templates for non-existing conditions and removing matching patterns from the set of all 512 possible 9-intersections. Note that the conditions are not mutually exclusive and therefore, a particular 9-intersection may match more than one template.

(4) Verifying the existence of corresponding topological relations for this set of 9-intersections by finding geometric configurations for them.

Subsequently, we present a set of conditions that lead to the set of binary topological relations between two regions in a raster space.

4.1 Consistency Constraints among Interiors, Boundaries, and Exteriors

Raster regions are 2-dimensional and embedded in $\mathbb{Z}^2$, therefore, any part of a region—its interior, boundary, or exterior—constrains the location of the other two parts. Thus, one can infer from the fact that two parts of a raster region coincide that the other corresponding parts must coincide as well:

Condition 1a:	If the interiors of two raster regions coincide, then the regions' exteriors and boundaries must coincide as well.
Condition 1b:	If the boundaries of two raster regions coincide, then the regions' interiors and exteriors coincide equal as well.
Condition 1c:	If the exteriors of two raster regions coincide, then the regions' interiors and boundaries must coincide as well.

The boundary of a raster region forms a Jordan Curve, separating the interior from the exterior such that any connected path from the interior to the exterior has to intersect with the boundary. This leads to the following six conditions for connected object parts:

Condition 2a:	If A's interior intersects with B's interior *and* exterior then it must also intersect with B's boundary and vice versa.
Condition 2b:	If A's boundary intersects B's interior *and* exterior then it must also intersect with B's boundary and vice versa.
Condition 2c:	If A's exterior intersects with B's interior *and* exterior then it must also intersect with B's boundary and vice versa.
Condition 2d:	If A's boundary intersects with the boundary, interior, *and* exterior of B then A's interior must intersect with B's boundary, and vice versa.
Condition 2e:	If A's boundary is a subset of B's closure, then A's interior must be a subset of B's interior, and vice versa.
Condition 2f:	If both interiors are disjoint, then each interior must intersect with the other regions' exterior.

Since the regions are small with respect to the embedding space, we can claim that no two regions will cover the entire universe.

Condition 3:	The exteriors of two regions must intersect with each other.

4.2 Translating Consistency Constraints into 9-Intersection Templates

In order to compare the conditions among interiors, boundaries, and exteriors it is necessary to represent them in a unifying model. The 9-intersection serves as the basis for such a model. Since the content of some intersections may be irrelevant for some consistent configurations, we introduce a "wild card" (_) to denote intersections whose content may be either empty or non-empty [9]. A *9-intersection template* is a pattern of empty, non-empty, or arbitrary intersections which represent constraints among interiors, boundaries, and exteriors. The following example illustrates how a constraint among boundary and interior can be formalized as a 9-intersection template. If A's boundary is disjoint from B's interior then $\partial A \cap B^\circ$ must be empty, while the values of the other eight intersections do not matter:

$$\mathbf{R}\,(A, B) = \begin{pmatrix} \_ & \varnothing & \_ \\ \_ & \_ & \_ \\ \_ & \_ & \_ \end{pmatrix}$$

A constraint about a valid configuration can be transformed into a constraint about an invalid configuration, because empty/non-empty 9-intersections are a closed system providing complete coverage. For example, "the interior must intersect with at least one part of the other object" is equivalent to the expression, "it is invalid if all three intersections of the interior with the boundary, interior, and exterior of the other object are empty." In terms of the 9-intersection this means:

$$\mathbf{R}\,(A, B) = \begin{pmatrix} \_ & \_ & \_ \\ \varnothing & \varnothing & \varnothing \\ \_ & \_ & \_ \end{pmatrix}$$

Such translations may be applied for all conditions, transforming a consistency constraint that must hold for all valid configurations into a consistency constraint that cannot hold for any valid configuration. Appendix A shows the complete set of 9-intersection templates for non-existing relations.

4.3 Realization of Region Relations in $\mathbb{Z}^2$

The set of 9-intersection templates for non-existing relations serves two purposes: (1) to find the smallest set of constraints and (2) to find the 9-intersections that are candidates for relations that may be realized in $\mathbb{Z}^2$.

Multiple conditions may be correlated because the same non-existing relation, described by two patterns of 9-intersections, can be a member of different conditions. By determining a minimum set-cover [3] of all 9-intersection templates for non-existing relations one can eliminate such redundant constraints. We found that condition (1b) is implied by the other constraints and, therefore, can be left out. The minimum set cover shows also that conditions (1a) and (1c) can be simplified into what is shown as conditions (1a') and (1c') in the Appendix.

By successively eliminating the 9-intersections for invalid configurations from the set of all 512 possible empty/non-empty intersections, one determines the set of 9-intersections that are expected to be realized in $\mathbb{Z}^2$. We programmed this stepwise elimination. It leaves a set of sixteen 9-intersections. For each of these we found a geometric interpretation, shown in Fig. 5 together with their corresponding

9-intersections. In lieu of assigning them names, we have chosen to number them 1...16. We can, therefore, conclude that these sixteen topological relations are the complete set of region relations that can be realized with empty/non-empty 9-intersections in $\mathbb{Z}^2$.

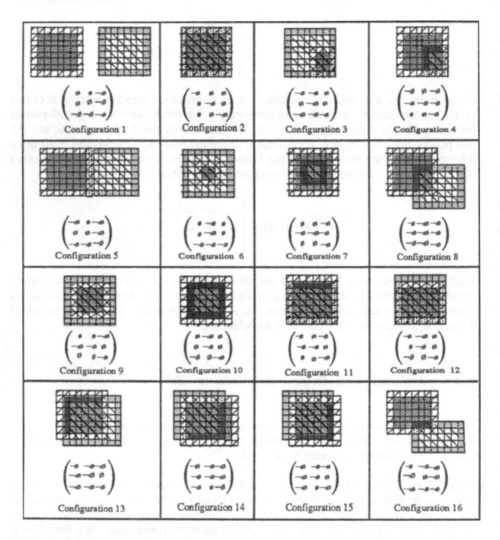

Fig. 5. The sixteen relations between two raster regions.

4.4 Beyond the Content Invariant

The 9-intersection may be analyzed using criteria other than the content of the intersections to describe more detailed topological relations [8, 26]. Examples of such additional criteria applied to regions in $\mathbb{R}^2$ are the dimension, the type of boundary-

boundary intersection (touching from outside, touching from inside, or crossing), and the sequence of the components (i.e., the largest connected subset) of boundary-boundary intersections [17].

For relations between raster regions, it is most important to determine whether two boundaries are neighbors or not. This criterion is special for relations in $\mathbb{Z}^2$, as it represents a particular property of a discrete space (see Section 5.1). Two boundaries, ∂A and ∂B, are neighbors if $\partial A \cap \partial B$ is empty and there exist at least two points, $a \in \partial A$ and $b \in \partial B$, such that a is a 4- or 8-neighbor of b. In general, such refinements are possible for all 9-intersections with empty boundary-boundary intersections. Exceptions are the 9-intersections for which a different boundary neighborhood would change their empty/non-empty specifications. This is the case with configurations 9 and 10, which have empty boundary-boundary intersections, but all boundary points must be 4- or 8-neighbors. If they were not neighbors, then their 9-intersections were the same as configurations 6 and 7, respectively. Therefore, only for configurations 1 and 6—and its converse configuration 7—can one find more detailed relations if the neighborhood criterion of boundary-boundary intersections is considered. These detailed relations will be called 1a, 6a, and 7a (Fig. 6).

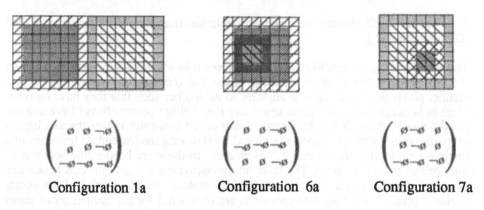

$$\begin{pmatrix} \emptyset & \emptyset & \neg\emptyset \\ \emptyset & \emptyset & \neg\emptyset \\ \neg\emptyset & \neg\emptyset & \neg\emptyset \end{pmatrix}$$

Configuration 1a

$$\begin{pmatrix} \emptyset & \emptyset & \neg\emptyset \\ \neg\emptyset & \neg\emptyset & \neg\emptyset \\ \emptyset & \emptyset & \neg\emptyset \end{pmatrix}$$

Configuration 6a

$$\begin{pmatrix} \emptyset{-}\emptyset & \emptyset \\ \emptyset & \neg\emptyset & \emptyset \\ \neg\emptyset{-}\emptyset & \neg\emptyset \end{pmatrix}$$

Configuration 7a

Fig. 6. Detailed raster region relations for 9-intersections with empty boundary-boundary intersections.

5 Comparing Existing Topological Relations in $\mathbb{R}^2$ and $\mathbb{Z}^2$

The comparison of topological relations in $\mathbb{R}^2$ and $\mathbb{Z}^2$ can be discussed at three different levels: (1) the pure comparison of 9-intersections that can be realized in the two spaces; (2) an analysis of the conditions that lead to the different sets; and (3) a cognitive assessment of the two sets of relations through their conceptual neighborhoods. The first discussion will identify particular topological properties that result from the 9-intersection. The comparison of the different constraints will contribute to a better understanding of the differences between continuous and discrete space. Finally, from the cognitive analysis we expect to learn what kinds of relations may be necessary in a spatial query language of an integrated raster-vector system.

5.1 Additional 9-Intersections and Conditions for Relations in $\mathbb{R}^2$

Comparing the sixteen raster relations with the eight vector relations, one finds that all 9-intersections of the vector relations are a subset of the raster relations; therefore, the set of constraints in $\mathbb{Z}^2$ may be obtained as an extension of the set of constraints in $\mathbb{R}^2$. The following two constraints among interiors, boundaries, and exteriors of regions in $\mathbb{R}^2$ reduce the set of sixteen raster relations to the set of eight relations that can be realized in $\mathbb{R}^2$. They hold only for relations between vector regions, not for raster regions, and have to be applied *in addition* to conditions (1-3).

Condition 4: If A's interior intersects with B's boundary then it must also intersect with B's exterior, and vice-versa.

This condition eliminates seven of the sixteen raster relations (Configurations 9–15).

Condition 5: If both interiors are disjoint then A's boundary cannot intersect with B's interior, and vice-versa.

This condition eliminates the last raster relation that cannot be realized in $\mathbb{R}^2$ (Configuration 16).

These two additional conditions can be interpreted in several ways. First, they reflect the difference between (discrete) raster space and (continuous) vector space: Two distinct pixels in a raster may be adjacent to each other such that they have no other pixel in between, while in vector space any two distinct points always have another point between them. A second interpretation of the two rules is that the topological properties of a vector space can be achieved by shrinking the (extended) boundary of a raster region so that the boundary "disappears" to the mere border line between an interior and an exterior pixel. The latter interpretation leads also to the conclusion that the topology of a raster space is obtained by making the boundaries of the vector regions "broad." All these interpretations are only valid for the limited set of raster regions considered, i.e., that each pixel in the region's interior must have at least three 8-neighbors.

5.2 Conceptual Neighborhoods

While the differences between the two sets of relations are relevant for the processing of spatial queries, they are also significant for the use of these spatial concepts in spatial query languages. The questions arises, "should the query language of a raster-based GIS have a different set of topological relations than a vector-based GIS?" From the perspective of a system designer, the previous results may suggest that it is necessary to do so. On the other hand, users should not be made aware of the particular data model of a GIS when they query about spatial relations. Since we found that the set of region relations in $\mathbb{R}^2$ is a subset of the ones in $\mathbb{Z}^2$, the relations in

$\mathbf{R}^2$ may be considered as the "integral set." Our goal here is to find the mappings from raster relations onto vector relations that would be most reasonable. Certainly these mappings should conform with cognitive measures, i.e., the "most similar" relations should be mapped onto a single relation.

For this goal, we are comparing the *conceptual neighborhoods* [19] of both sets of relations. Conceptual neighborhoods identify those relations that are close to each other and yield information about cognitive aspects of the relations, such as their behavior under specific deformations. They have been successfully applied to relations between 1-dimensional intervals [19], cardinal directions in 2-D [20], and topological relations between regions in $\mathbf{R}^2$ [12]. Two topological relations are *conceptual neighbors* if the transition from one relation to another will be "smooth," such that no other relation is between the two relations when applying a gradual change. Such gradual changes may be deformations to one of the two regions involved, such as scaling, rotation, and translation, that do not change the topology of the region.

For topological relations, the *topology distance* has been proposed as a measure to determine conceptual neighbors [12]. The topology distance is the number of differences in corresponding values of two 9-intersections. Informally the topology distance between two 9-intersections is the smallest number of "bits" that must be flipped to convert one 9-intersection into the other. The topology distance between a relation and itself is 0, and it is between 1 and 9 for any other pair of topological relations. For example, the topology distance from *disjoint* to *meet* is 1. The shorter the topology distance between two relations, the smaller is their conceptual difference. Pairs of raster relations with topology distance 1 and 2 provide a connected graph in which each node corresponds to a topological relation and each edge, linking two relations, denotes that these relations are conceptual neighbors.

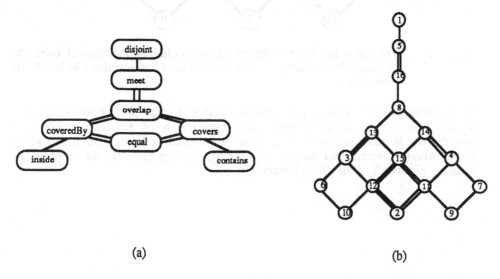

(a)   (b)

Fig. 7.   The conceptual neighbors of topological relations in (a) vector and (b) raster space. (Single lines indicate neighbors with topology distance 1, while double lines stand for neighbors with topology distance 2 or more.)

The three additional raster relations obtained from considering 4- and 8-neighbors of non-empty boundary-boundary intersections (Section 4.4) can be added into the conceptual neighborhoods: Configuration 1a is located between 1 and 5; 6a is equally close to 3 and 10 from 6; and 7a is equally close to 4 and 9 from 7 (Fig. 8). This addition to the conceptual neighborhood graph adds edges whose topology distance is 0 (from 1 to 1a; 6 to 6a; and 7 to 7a).

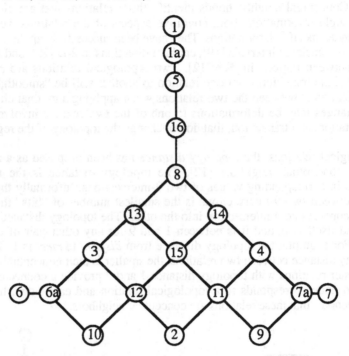

Fig. 8. The extended raster relation graph, including topological relations obtained from empty boundary-boundary intersections being 4- or 8-neighbors.

A *conceptual neighborhood cluster* groups together all relations that are transitively within 1 topology distance unit. The comparison of the two conceptual neighborhoods reveals that both sets of topological relations have the same neighborhood clusters and that corresponding clusters have the same links (of topology distance 2) with other clusters (Fig. 9).

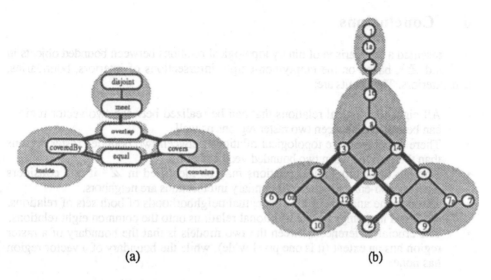

Fig. 9. The conceptual neighborhood clusters for (a) vector relations and (b) raster relations.

With the help of these five common neighborhood clusters, we find the following mappings from raster relations onto vector relations:

- In each space, there is one (topological) equivalence relation, therefore, the raster configuration 2 maps onto the vector configuration *equal*.
- The four "new" raster relations 13, 14, 15, and 16, which are grouped around configuration 8, map onto the vector relation *overlap*.
- Configurations 3, 6, 6a, 10, and 12 map onto *inside/coveredBy*. The analysis of how the neighborhood clusters are interrelated reveals that 3 and 12 correspond to *coveredBy*, while 6 maps onto *inside*. This leaves the question where 6a and 10 belong. One can make a case for either grouping—putting them with *inside* or with *coveredBy*. The corresponding mappings can be done for the cluster with *contains/covers*.
- Configurations 1, 1a, and 5 map onto the cluster *disjoint/meet*. Within this cluster, 1 corresponds to disjoint—they are both at the end of the graph. More difficult is the assessment of where 1a belongs, as it can be grouped with either *disjoint* or *meet*. It might even be argued that 5 belongs into the *overlap* cluster and 1a is the only raster relation that corresponds to *meet*.

The ambiguities in some of these mappings may indicate that both situations may occur, depending on the spatial concept used. For example, if individual objects, such as buildings, are represented in a raster model, then two buildings may *meet* according to configuration 1a; whereas two objects in a partition of space (e.g., land parcels) would *meet* according to configuration 5.

6 Conclusions

We presented a comparison of binary topological relations between bounded objects in $\mathbb{R}^2$ and $\mathbb{Z}^2$, based on the empty/non-empty intersections of interiors, boundaries, and exteriors. The results are:

- All eight topological relations that can be realized between two vector regions can be realized between two raster regions as well.
- There are eight more topological relations between two bounded raster regions than there are between two bounded vector regions.
- Another three topological relations may be identified in $\mathbb{Z}^2$ if one considers whether non-empty boundary-boundary intersections are neighbors.
- Through the analysis of the conceptual neighborhoods of both sets of relations, we found mappings for the additional relations onto the common eight relations.
- The crucial difference between the two models is that the boundary of a raster region has an extent (it is one pixel wide), while the boundary of a vector region has none.

The results are germane to the integration of raster and vector GISs [13]. The approach chosen is significantly different from previous integration attempts [31] as it identify common properties at the level of spatial data models, rather than comparing implementation aspects of data structures [10, 15].

The results are also significant for reasoning in geographic (large-scale) space, which has to account for imprecise information. A particular category of geographic objects are those whose boundaries are not well-defined such as the Rocky Mountains, the Gulf of Mexico, or the Great Lakes region. Despite a lack of precision, humans can effectively reason about such objects—Aspen is in the Rockies; Hurricane Andrew crossed the Gulf of Mexico; or a storm front is approaching the Great Lakes. Current spatial data models for geographic information systems do not account for the representation of and reasoning about such "imprecise" objects. There have been attempts, however, to describe the boundaries through "fuzzy" lines [5, 29]. The results may be considered as a new approach to "coarse" topological reasoning, where objects are represented as "big blocks" whose boundaries have an extent. Such a representation corresponds to a raster model in which each object's boundary is made up of cells or pixels, rather than being the (invisible) separation between the interior and the exterior of the object.

Appendix A: Consistency Constraints for Non-Existing Topological Relations in $\mathbb{Z}^2$

Condition 1a:

$$R(A,B) = \begin{pmatrix} - & \varnothing & - \\ \varnothing & \neg\varnothing & \varnothing \\ - & \varnothing & \varnothing \end{pmatrix} \vee \begin{pmatrix} \varnothing & \varnothing & - \\ \varnothing & \neg\varnothing & \varnothing \\ - & \varnothing & - \end{pmatrix} \vee \begin{pmatrix} - & \varnothing & \neg\varnothing \\ \varnothing & \neg\varnothing & \varnothing \\ - & \varnothing & - \end{pmatrix} \vee \begin{pmatrix} - & \varnothing & - \\ \varnothing & \neg\varnothing & \varnothing \\ \neg\varnothing & \varnothing & - \end{pmatrix}$$

Condition 1a':

$$R(A,B) = \begin{pmatrix} \varnothing & \varnothing & - \\ \varnothing & \neg\varnothing & \varnothing \\ - & \varnothing & - \end{pmatrix} \vee \begin{pmatrix} - & \varnothing & \neg\varnothing \\ \varnothing & \neg\varnothing & \varnothing \\ - & \varnothing & - \end{pmatrix} \vee \begin{pmatrix} - & \varnothing & - \\ \varnothing & \neg\varnothing & \varnothing \\ \neg\varnothing & \varnothing & - \end{pmatrix}$$

Condition 1b:

$$R(A,B) = \begin{pmatrix} \neg\varnothing & \varnothing & \varnothing \\ \varnothing & - & - \\ \varnothing & - & \varnothing \end{pmatrix} \vee \begin{pmatrix} \neg\varnothing & \varnothing & \varnothing \\ \varnothing & \varnothing & - \\ \varnothing & - & - \end{pmatrix} \vee \begin{pmatrix} \neg\varnothing & \varnothing & \varnothing \\ \varnothing & - & \neg\varnothing \\ \varnothing & - & - \end{pmatrix} \vee \begin{pmatrix} \neg\varnothing & \varnothing & \varnothing \\ \varnothing & - & - \\ \varnothing & \varnothing & - \end{pmatrix}$$

Condition 1c:

$$R(A,B) = \begin{pmatrix} - & - & \varnothing \\ - & \varnothing & \varnothing \\ \varnothing & \varnothing & \neg\varnothing \end{pmatrix} \vee \begin{pmatrix} \varnothing & - & \varnothing \\ - & - & \varnothing \\ \varnothing & \varnothing & \neg\varnothing \end{pmatrix} \vee \begin{pmatrix} - & \neg\varnothing & \varnothing \\ - & - & \varnothing \\ \varnothing & \varnothing & \neg\varnothing \end{pmatrix} \vee \begin{pmatrix} - & - & \varnothing \\ \neg\varnothing & - & \varnothing \\ \varnothing & \varnothing & \neg\varnothing \end{pmatrix}$$

Condition 1c':

$$R(A,B) = \begin{pmatrix} - & \neg\varnothing & \varnothing \\ - & - & \varnothing \\ \varnothing & \varnothing & \neg\varnothing \end{pmatrix} \vee \begin{pmatrix} - & - & \varnothing \\ \neg\varnothing & - & \varnothing \\ \varnothing & \varnothing & \neg\varnothing \end{pmatrix}$$

Condition 2a:

$$R(A,B) = \begin{pmatrix} - & - & - \\ \varnothing & \neg\varnothing & \neg\varnothing \\ - & - & - \end{pmatrix} \vee \begin{pmatrix} - & \varnothing & - \\ - & \neg\varnothing & - \\ - & \neg\varnothing & - \end{pmatrix}$$

Condition 2b:

$$R(A,B) = \begin{pmatrix} \varnothing & \neg\varnothing & \neg\varnothing \\ - & - & - \\ - & - & - \end{pmatrix} \vee \begin{pmatrix} \varnothing & - & - \\ \neg\varnothing & - & - \\ \neg\varnothing & - & - \end{pmatrix}$$

Condition 2c:

$$R(A, B) = \begin{pmatrix} - & - & - \\ - & - & - \\ \emptyset & \neg\emptyset & \neg\emptyset \end{pmatrix} \vee \begin{pmatrix} - & - & \emptyset \\ - & - & \neg\emptyset \\ - & - & \neg\emptyset \end{pmatrix}$$

Condition 2d:

$$R(A, B) = \begin{pmatrix} \neg\emptyset & \neg\emptyset & \neg\emptyset \\ \emptyset & - & - \\ - & - & - \end{pmatrix} \vee \begin{pmatrix} \neg\emptyset & \emptyset & - \\ \neg\emptyset & - & - \\ \neg\emptyset & - & - \end{pmatrix}$$

Condition 2e:

$$R(A, B) = \begin{pmatrix} - & \neg\emptyset & \emptyset \\ \neg\emptyset & - & - \\ - & - & - \end{pmatrix} \vee \begin{pmatrix} - & \neg\emptyset & - \\ \neg\emptyset & - & - \\ \emptyset & - & - \end{pmatrix}$$

Condition 2f:

$$R(A, B) = \begin{pmatrix} - & \emptyset & \emptyset \\ - & - & - \\ - & - & - \end{pmatrix} \vee \begin{pmatrix} - & \emptyset & - \\ - & \emptyset & - \\ - & - & - \end{pmatrix}$$

Condition 3:

$$R(A, B) = \begin{pmatrix} - & - & - \\ - & - & - \\ - & - & \emptyset \end{pmatrix}$$

Condition 4:

$$R(A, B) = \begin{pmatrix} - & - & - \\ \neg\emptyset & - & \emptyset \\ - & - & - \end{pmatrix} \vee \begin{pmatrix} - & \neg\emptyset & - \\ - & - & - \\ - & \emptyset & - \end{pmatrix}$$

Condition 5:

$$R(A, B) = \begin{pmatrix} - & - & - \\ \neg\emptyset & \emptyset & - \\ - & - & - \end{pmatrix} \vee \begin{pmatrix} - & \neg\emptyset & - \\ - & \emptyset & - \\ - & - & - \end{pmatrix}$$

References

1. P. Alexandroff (1961) *Elementary Concepts of Topology*. Dover Publications, Inc., New York, NY.

2. S. K. Chang, Q. Y. Shi, and C. W. Yan (1987) Iconic Indexing by 2-D Strings. *IEEE Transactions on Pattern Analysis and Machine Intelligence* PAMI-9(6): 413-428.

3. V. Chávtal (1979) A Greedy Heuristic for the Set-Covering Problem. *Mathematics of Operations Research* 4(3): 233-235.

4. E. Clementini, P. di Felice, and P. van Oosterom (1993) A Small Set of Formal Topological Relationships Suitable for End-User Interaction. in: D. Abel and B. Ooi (Eds.), *Third International Symposium on Large Spatial Databases, SSD '93*, Singapore. *Lecture Notes in Computer Science*. Springer-Verlag, New York, NY.

5. S. Dutta (1991) Topological Constraints: A Representational Framework for Approximate Spatial and Temporal Reasoning. in: O. Günther and H.-J. Schek (Eds.), *Advances in Spatial Databases—Second Symposium, SSD '91*, Zurich, Switzerland. *Lecture Notes in Computer Science* 525, pp. 161-180, Springer-Verlag, New York, NY.

6. M. Egenhofer (1991) Reasoning about Binary Topological Relations. in: O. Günther and H.-J. Schek (Eds.), *Advances in Spatial Databases—Second Symposium, SSD '91*, Zurich, Switzerland. *Lecture Notes in Computer Science* 525, pp. 143-160, Springer-Verlag, New York, NY.

7. M. Egenhofer and R. Franzosa (1991) Point-Set Topological Spatial Relations. *International Journal of Geographical Information Systems* 5(2): 161-174.

8. M. Egenhofer and J. Herring (1990) A Mathematical Framework for the Definition of Topological Relationships. *Fourth International Symposium on Spatial Data Handling*, Zurich, Switzerland, pp. 803-813.

9. M. Egenhofer and J. Herring (1991) *Categorizing Binary Topological Relationships Between Regions, Lines, and Points in Geographic Databases*. Technical Report, Department of Surveying Engineering, University of Maine, Orono, ME (submitted for publication).

10. M. Egenhofer and J. Herring (1991) High-Level Spatial Data Structures for GIS. in: D. Maguire, M. Goodchild, and D. Rhind (Eds.), *Geographical Information Systems, Volume 1: Principles*. pp. 227-237, Longman, London.

11. M. Egenhofer and J. Sharma (1992) Topological Consistency. *Fifth International Symposium on Spatial Data Handling*, Charleston, SC, pp. 335-343.

12. M. J. Egenhofer and K. K. Al-Taha (1992) Reasoning About Gradual Changes of Topological Relationships. in: A. U. Frank, I. Campari, and U. Formentini (Eds.), *Theories and Models of Spatio-Temporal Reasoning in Geographic Space*, Pisa, Italy. *Lecture Notes in Computer Science* 639, pp. 196-219, Springer-Verlag, New York.

13. M. Ehlers, G. Edwards, and Y. Bedard (1989) Integration of Remote Sensing with Geographic Information Systems: A Necessary Evolution. *Photogrammetric Engineering & Remote Sensing.* 55(11): 1619-1627.

14. A. Frank (1992) Qualitative Spatial Reasoning about Distances and Directions in Geographic Space. *Journal of Visual Languages and Computing* 3(4): 343-371.

15. A. Frank (1992) Spatial Concepts, Geometric Data Models and Data Structures. *Computers and Geosciences* 18(4): 409-417.

16. A. Frank and D. Mark (1991) Language Issues for GIS. in: D. Maguire, M. Goodchild, and D. Rhind (Eds.), *Geographical Information Systems, Volume 1: Principles.* pp. 147-163, Longman, London.

17. R. Franzosa and M. Egenhofer (1992) Topological Spatial Relations Based on Components and Dimensions of Set Intersections. *SPIE's OE/Technology '92—Vision Geometry*, Boston, MA.

18. J. Freeman (1975) The Modelling of Spatial Relations. *Computer Graphics and Image Processing.* 4: 156-171.

19. C. Freksa (1992) Temporal Reasoning Based on Semi-Intervals. *Artificial Intelligence* 54: 199-227.

20. C. Freksa (1992) Using Orientation Information for Qualitative Spatial Reasoning. in: A. U. Frank, I. Campari, and U. Formentini (Eds.), *Theories and Models of Spatio-Temporal Reasoning in Geographic Space*, Pisa, Italy. *Lecture Notes in Computer Science* 639, pp. 162-178, Springer-Verlag, New York.

21. M. Goodchild (1992) Geographical Data Modeling. *Computers and Geosciences* 18(4): 401-408.

22. T. Hadzilacos and N. Tryfona (1992) A Model for Expressing Topological Integrity Constraints in Geographic Databases. in: A. U. Frank, I. Campari, and U. Formentini (Eds.), *Theories and Models of Spatio-Temporal Reasoning in Geographic Space*, Pisa, Italy. *Lecture Notes in Computer Science* 639, pp. 252-268, Springer-Verlag, New York.

23. N. W. Hazelton, L. Bennett, and J. Masel (1992) Topological Structures for 4-Dimensional Geographic Information Systems. *Computers, Environment, and Urban Systems* 16(3): 227-237.

24. G. Herman (1990) On Topology as Applied to Image Analysis. *Computer Vision, Graphics, and Image Processing* 52: 409-415.

25. D. Hernández (1991) Relative Representation of Spatial Knowledge: The 2-D Case. in: D. Mark and A. Frank (Eds.), *Cognitive and Linguistic Aspects of Geographic Space.* pp. 373-385, Kluwer Academic Publishers, Dordrecht.

26. J. Herring (1991) The Mathematical Modeling of Spatial and Non-Spatial Information in Geographic Information Systems. in: D. Mark and A. Frank (Eds.), *Cognitive and Linguistic Aspects of Geographic Space.* pp. 313-350, Kluwer Academic Publishers, Dordrecht.

27. S. de Hoop and P. van Oosterom (1992) Storage and Manipulation of Topology in Postgres. *Third European Conference on Geographical Information Systems, EGIS '92*. Munich, Germany, pp. 1324-1336.

28. S.-Y. Lee and F.-J. Hsu (1992) Spatial Reasoning and Similarity Retrieval of Images Using 2D C-String Knowledge Representation. *Pattern Recognition* 25(3): 305-318.

29. Y. Leung, M. Goodchild, and C.-C. Lin (1992) Visualization of Fuzzy Scenes and Probability Fields. *Fifth International Symposium on Spatial Data Handling*, Charleston, SC, pp. 480-490.

30. D. Mark and M. Egenhofer (1992) An Evaluation of the 9-Intersection for Region-Line Relations. *GIS/LIS '92*, San Jose, CA.

31. D. Peuquet (1988) Representations of Geographic Space: Toward a Conceptual Synthesis. *Annals of the Association of American Geographers* 78(3): 375-394.

32. S. Pigot (1991) Topological Models for 3D Spatial Information Systems. in: D. Mark and D. White (Eds.), *Autocarto 10*, Baltimore, MD, pp. 368-392.

33. D. Randell, Z. Cui, and A. Cohn (1992) A Spatial Logic Based on Regions and Connection. *Principles of Knowledge Representation and Reasoning, KR '92*, Cambridge, MA, pp. 165-176.

34. A. Rosenfeld (1979) Digital Topology. *American Mathematical Monthly* 86: 621-630.

35. T. Smith and K. Park (1992) Algebraic Approach to Spatial Reasoning. *International Journal of Geographical Information Systems* 6(3): 177-192.

36. E. Spanier (1966) *Algebraic Topology*. McGraw-Hill Book Company, New York, NY.

37. P. Svensson and H. Zhexue (1991) Geo-SAL: A Query Language for Spatial Data Analysis. in: O. Günther and H.-J. Schek (Ed.), *Advances in Spatial Databases—Second Symposium, SSD '91*, Zurich, Switzerland. *Lecture Notes in Computer Science* 525, pp. 119-140, Springer-Verlag, New York, NY.

38. A. Vince and C. Little (1989) Discrete Jordan Curve Theorems. *Journal of Combinatorial Theory Series B* 47: 251-261.

Query-Adaptive Data Space Partitioning using Variable-Size Storage Clusters

Gisbert Dröge and Hans-Jörg Schek

Information Systems - Databases, ETH Zürich
CH-8092 Zürich, Switzerland
droege@inf.ethz.ch, schek@inf.ethz.ch

Abstract. All spatial access methods decompose the data space into a number of subspaces or cells. The size of a cell is determined by the capacity of a *single* disk page. Here we present considerations on data space partitions which use large *multi-page* storage clusters of variable size rather than single pages. Its main motivation is given by real complex geographical objects ranging from 100 Bytes to 10 KBytes in storage size. For such objects it does not make sense to insist on the one-page-per-cell paradigm. The problem of determining "good" multi-page storage clusters is attacked by introducing a cost model. In the ideal case an expected query is satisfied by accessing only one storage cluster of appropriate size. To get near to this optimum we adapt the data space partition to query ranges. We call this approach a *query driven partitioning strategy*. Initial evaluation studies show the feasibility of this approach.

1 Introduction

The handling of spatial data in geographic information systems (GIS) is an important and complex problem of high significance. There is a need to be able to manage geographical objects like highways, rivers or cities within maps, or streets, parcels and buildings in an urban planning environment. Every geographical object consists of spatial and non-spatial or thematic description parts. The spatial description itself is a complex information in structure and storage size and is often much more space consuming than the thematic information. The structure of spatial description may consist of multiple discontinuous subparts or may have areas with holes. For example (see Figure 1) discontinuous subparts appear at a river line, that is interrupted by a lake or a river with several springs. A lake containing islands is an example of an area with holes.

The storage size of such spatial descriptions out of a collection of spatial objects ranges e.g. from simple triangles up to sophisticated polygons with several hundreds of points [2]. Accordingly the storage space needed for a single spatial object may vary from a few bytes to tens of thousands of bytes. The great variety and the overall large storage requirements for spatial objects necessitates a redesign of storage management components in spatial databases to support GIS applications [11]. Special storage managers must be involved to support the varying size of spatial objects. Moreover the execution of spatial

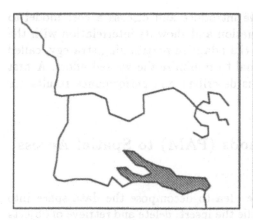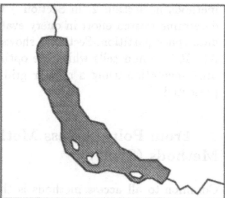

Fig. 1.: Complex Data Items

range queries enforces an efficient access to the qualified spatial objects, so that spatial clustering is needed.

While existing point access methods with fix-size storage cluster are useful for simple objects like points or rectangles, our new storage manager is designed under the following main criteria:

- It supports small and large geometrical objects and their spatial clustering.
- It uses multi-page storage cluster, whose size is determined by cost considerations.
- It provides efficient execution of spatial range queries and adapts the data space partition to query ranges.

In our previous work on the design and implementation of DASDBS Geo-Kernel we described various possibilities of mappings between geographical objects and the complex record interface of the DASDBS storage kernel [16, 7]. Specifically the clustering of the spatial part of geograhpical objects was considered and the main decision was to put access mechanisms on top of the storage manager. However we did not address the problem of determining "good" multi-page storage cluster through a suitable adaptable space partitioning. Finding solutions to this problem is the main objective of this paper.

We are not aware of directly related work, with the exception of [5], which will be shortly discussed in Section 2. Adaptive data structures for multidimensional spaces (dynamically quantized spaces (DQS) and pyramids (DQP)) have been proposed by [13]. However these approaches are applied only to point data and single-page storage clusters and their purpose is to detect peaks through a high density of small subspaces in multidimensional histogramming.

The structure of the paper is the following. We start with a review of the problems arising with the extension of point access methods to spatial access methods in Section 2. In Section 3 we introduce and discuss a cost model to determine wasted effort in query evaluation and show its interrelation with the data space partition. Section 4 shows the adaptive partitioning strategy, called APART, to find cells which are optimal to minimize the wasted effort. A first implementation using a regular grid is described and performance results are presented.

2 From Point Access Methods (PAM) to Spatial Access Methods (SAM)

Common to all access methods is the idea to decompose the data space into subspaces or logical cluster and to handle the insert, delete and retrieve of objects locally in those subspaces. The set of objects within each subspace forms a *bucket* [10, 15], that is stored in a physical cluster or *storage cluster*, and which can be read and written in one I/O operation [10]. A lot of access method implementations decided the cluster size to be the same as the physical I/O-unit or disk page size [15]. The data space partition is determined by bucket overflows and therefore we may call these approaches *storage driven partitioning strategies*.

A classification of spatial access methods is given in [9] which serves as a useful framework for evaluating the various approaches. They distinguish between point access methods (PAM) like kdB-tree [14] and the grid file [12] and spatial access methods (SAM) like R-tree [6] and the cell tree [4]. PAMs have been invented to store and access multidimensional point objects, whereas SAM capture multidimensional, extended non-point objects. In the above classification a severe restriction has been introduced with the approximation and simplification of arbitrary spatial objects by their minimal bounding rectangles (MBR). The most convincing argument to use MBR is the reduction of storage complexity to a small and fix number of bytes for each object, along with the preservation of spatial extent and location. So PAMs can still be used, because objects are of small and fix size. The main drawback of this simplification is the lack of exactness when only approximated data is indexed. Especially there is a doubtful quality of that rectangle approximation, e.g. the approximation of a polyline by its MBR is really bad, in the case of a diagonal line segment. Moreover the access method only serves as a first filter and yield a number of *candidate* references.

The only SAM supporting more complex objects like polygons is the cell tree. Cell trees combine a hierarchical disjoint decomposition of the data space into convex polyhedra with a clipping approach (see also [9]) that decomposes spatial objects on insert. Unfortunately the decomposition of objects into cells leads to an increasing population of the cell tree leaves, which tend to be split earlier. This again causes additional decompositions of objects [3] and may end up in an endless loop that has to be avoided definitely. The increased growth of the cell tree directory increases the search path in length and breadth and thereby increases the average search time. After having found the qualifying spatial objects the numerous cells of each object have to be composed. But the composition of objects is quite a CPU cost intensive operation and the CPU cost becomes an important cost factor. The idea to avoid these drawbacks is to add overflow buckets (oversize shelves) to internal cell tree nodes and to stop the decomposition of objects at some tree level [5]. However, it is difficult to decide when to use an overflow bucket or to decompose an object at insertion time. During the search each overflow bucket has to be loaded and inspected in addition to the descended walk through the cell tree.

Variable-Size Storage Clusters

To avoid the decomposition of objects and the growth of the directory we propose a different approach. We relax the requirement to store each tree leave on a single disk page. The obvious solution is to use *multiple continuous* pages.

In general for all SAM the spatial objects within a single or multi-page cluster are not sorted and the inner cluster search becomes expensive, because the spatial selection condition is applied on each object. Moreover the spatial selection condition is not as simple as the test on equality of numbers or strings. It is some test on intersection with, containment in or coverage of a spatial query range and it is, with respect to the object's complexity, really expensive. Appendix A shows time measurements on the intersection and inside test of polylines and polygons with a (query) rectangle. Up to now all performance comparisons of access methods are based on I/O cost and they are expected to be I/O bound. But now the CPU cost to apply a spatial selection condition and to compose the spatial objects becomes a significant part of the query cost.

The enlargement of storage cluster actually brings up countercurrent performance issues. On the one hand if we use a small cluster size we get high I/O cost from the large directory structure and the loading of numerous storage cluster and we get high CPU cost from the composition of highly decomposed objects. On the other hand, if we increase the cluster size too much in order to reduce object decomposition and index size, we may end up with increased I/O cost due to the large cluster size and increased CPU cost due to increased cost for the search within the storage cluster and its increased number of objects.

The question of optimal cluster size arises. Simply using larger fix-size storage clusters is not a solution because of low storage utilization. Most of the PAM/SAM have a low storage utilization like the 60% on average in the kdB-tree [14] or they have no guaranteed storage utilization at all like R-tree or cell tree. To overcome wasted space problem we suggest storage clusters with variable size, i.e. multi-page clusters with a varying number of pages. The problem of storage utilization becomes much less important in variable-size clusters, as now the wasted space is guaranteed to be less than one page.

3   Cost Model for Optimal Storage Clusters

The major goal of spatial partitioning is the support of query evaluation at minimal cost. For performance issues it is desirable to avoid scanning all the data. The typical queries we have in mind are spatial selection queries like

- Give me all hospitals in a distance of 20 miles from an accident.
- Find all the buildings that are less than 1 mile away from a given river line.
- Find all the medium-size cities within a given state.
- Select everything intersecting a given window and display the clipped part.

In these examples, the query ranges differ in shape from a circle, a band, a polygon and a rectangle as shown in Figure 2.

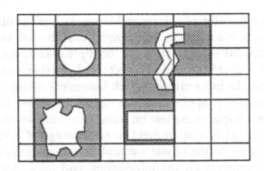

Fig. 2.: Sample Query Ranges and their Approximation by Cells

It is important to note that the costs for processing these kinds of queries, regardless of what specific technique for space partitioning is used, depend mainly on the granularity of the cells, and on the contents of the cells. First, the granularity is important because it determines the degree of approximation of a query range by the cells. If the approximation is bad the cells to be accessed contain many objects which are not relevant (false drops). Second, the contents of a cell determines the costs in that it may consist of spatial objects of one or of several types. If in the latter case only one type of objects is desired the access to a cell storage cluster may transfer many objects that are not required. As an example, while the partitioning in Figure 2 looks reasonable for the circular, rectangular and polygonal range, it is bad for the band-shaped range. If in this case we would not be able to exclude transfer of objects other than buildings the situation could become even worse.

3.1 General Assumptions

In order to present these kinds of considerations in a more quantitative manner we will develop a simple cost model under the following general assumptions:

Spatial Partitions Whatever partitioning strategy is selected we assume that the cells of the partition subdivide the data space in a complete and disjoint manner. If a spatial object is inserted, the cells that cover the spatial object are determined and the object is clipped at these cell boundaries if necessary. This technique is superior to the complex object decomposition approach [8] because it is independant of the details of spatial object representation and requires only the availability and applicability of a clip function among a few other functions (see the EDT approach in [1]).

Spatial Objects The interface of our storage and access manager provides us with a set SO of spatial objects o of different type. Usually there are other sets of stored objects needed for the thematic description but they are not important in the following. We might well distinguish also several different sets of spatial objects SO_1, SO_2, etc. but for the following we only will consider one single SO at a time. SO is a set of (abstract) objects in the sense that any o from SO understands a type check and a collection of (generic) spatial methods like intersect, inside, clip, compose etc. as described in the EDT approach in [1, 20].

Although we do not (want to) know about the details of the realisation of these methods, we do assume that we know about the costs of a method execution. The following costs are assumed to be the most important (c is the spatial description of a cell, and o is a spatial object):

c_{int} : costs for an intersection test between c and o,

c_{comp}: costs for composing two parts of o along a common c boundary,

c_{clip}: costs for clipping o at c

Query Type The query type we admit is of the general form

$$q = filter_{pred}(SO)$$

that "filter out" the matching objects o from SO using a predicate $pred$ applicable on any single o. The predicate $pred$ consists of a spatially related condition and may contain additional restrictions with respect to the type of the spatial object, i.e. whether we want river lines and city boundaries for example. Spatially related conditions are constructed using the above methods intersect, inside, and the like. We only allow a query of the *single scan* kind, i.e. a decision whether an object qualifies is made on the basis of a single object. Consequently *spatial join* type queries are currently excluded.

Query Processing We assume that a partition P has already been created for the set of spatial objects SO and is given and fixed. Note that the analysis of costs is valid for any kind of partition, resulting from different strategies. For the following discussion we will talk about the query range as an abbreviation for the spatially related condition of the query predicate $pred$. We do not assume a specific kind of predicate but we will often use a predicate like o *intersects* r, where r is a rectangle (query window) as a typical example.

Any query is processed in sequence of the following steps:

(S 1) find the cells that intersects the query range, i.e. the cells that form a minimal covering of the query range

(S 2) load the clusters associated with these cells

(S 3) test each of the spatial objects or object parts of those clusters on intersection with the query range and eliminate the false drops objects

(S 4) compose parts of spatial objects to reconstruct the spatial objects

(S 5) clip the resulting spatial objects with the query range to get only that part inside the query range

Let us consider the costs in the different steps. The first step, the partition directory lookup, loads and scans the directory part and determines the intersecting cells and get the addresses of the related storage clusters. We expect the directory to remain quite small and the related pages may be resident in main memory for several queries. Therefore we will assume that the lookup is done at constant cost and is not taken into account in our cost model. The second step causes I/O cost when loading the storage cluster. In the third step the intersection test may consume CPU time at a significant rate, because a possibly complex intersect operation is evaluated for each spatial object. The compose step again may be quite expensive. Finally the clip method has to be applied anyway, independent of the previous steps and we cannot save cost in that step. So the main query costs are the I/O cost $C_{I/O}$ of step (S2) and the CPU costs C_{CPU} of step (S3) and (S4). However, the CPU costs cannot be ignored when complex spatial objects are processed with expensive methods. (see Appendix A for time measurements of representative methods)

3.2 A Simple Cost Model: Avoiding Wasted Effort

We will develop a simple cost model that is based on *wasted effort*. In order to see where effort may be wasted let us re-consider the previous steps when we now vary the spatial partition. First we observe that a spatial query is answered at minimal cost if there is a single subspace of the partition that exactly matches the query range. Then, (S2) loads one cluster containing exactly the spatial objects of the result set. The step (S3) can be omitted as no false drops need to be eliminated and (S4) can be omitted as no spatial objects are split at cell boundaries. Note that (S5) takes advantage of the partition as the clip is already precomputed at insert time. In the general case, an arbitrary query range touches a number of subspaces, but does not cover them exactly. So, wasted effort arises as a result of *false drops*, i.e. objects that are contained in the cells but do not intersect the query range. They cause I/O cost in (S2) and CPU cost for detection and elimination in (S3). A second kind of wasted effort is introduced by cell boundaries that clip spatial objects which have to be composed at query time (S4). In addition loading several smaller clusters instead of one larger cluster produces additional I/O cost in (S2) (see [18]).

It is obvious that the effort for false drops is smaller the finer the partition is made. On the other hand this leads to an increase in cluster accesses and in compose efforts of decomposed objects (see Figure 3). Let N be the number of cells c_i ($i = 1, \cdots N$) intersecting the query range and denote by $c_{I/O}(c_i)$ the I/O cost for reading the storage cluster of cell c_i. Let S be the total number of

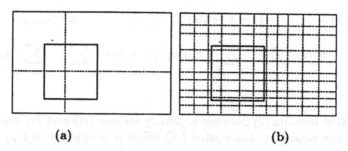

(a)   **(b)**

Fig. 3.: Wasted effort: (a) coarse partition leads to many false drops (b) fine partition leads to many unnecessary small storage cluster accesses and compose effort of clipped subobjects therein

(sub)objects o_j ($j = 1, \cdots S$) in the selected clusters and let M be the number of composed spatial objects o_l ($l = 1, \cdots M$) of the result set which are composed from the subobjects so_{l_s} ($s = 1, \cdots k_l$). Then we may represent the total execution cost $C(q, p)$ for query q dependent on the partition p as follows

(1)
$$C(q, p) = \sum_{i=1, \cdots, N} c_{I/O}(c_i) + \sum_{j=1, \cdots, S} c_{int}(o_j, q)$$
$$+ \sum_{l=1, \cdots, M} \sum_{s=1, \cdots, k_l} c_{comp}(o_l, so_{l_s})$$

Formula (1) consists of three parts. The first roughly measures the cost of accessing the storage clusters and the second of testing the (sub)objects with the query range. Access costs are linear in N and intersection costs are linear in S, the number of (sub)objects found in the cells c_i. In the ideal case all (sub)objects are *matches*, i.e. no cost occurs for false drops detection. In this case the query range approximation by cells is fine enough to exclude false drops and the compose cost in the third part of formula (1) will be high in general because many objects may be highly decomposed through the fine partitioning. On the other hand if the compose cost is zero none of the objects must be composed ($k_l = 1$ for all $l = 1, \cdots M$). In this case the partition is coarse enough that no partition boundary intersects the query range and therefore no qualified objects are clipped. It is obvious that there is an optimal partition $\hat{p}$ to a given query that minimizes (1). However in order to simplify (1) let us restrict the optimization criterion to the wasted effort only. To determine the wasted effort in formula (1) we distinguish intersection cost for matches and false drops. Note that only the false drops intersection cost are wasted. Let S_{fd} be the number of false drops and assume that o_f ($f = 1, \cdots S_{fd}$) are the false drops.

Then the wasted effort consists of the weighted sum of the false drops cost C_{fd} and compose cost C_{comp} for the query q evaluated on partition p. The factor α is a positive constant value with $0 < \alpha < 1$.

$$(2)\, C_w(q,p) = \qquad (1-\alpha) * C_{fd} \qquad + \qquad \alpha * C_{comp}$$

$$= (1-\alpha) * \sum_{f=1,\cdots,S_{fd}} c_{int}(o_j,q) + \alpha * \sum_{l=1,\cdots,M} \sum_{s=1,\cdots,k_l} c_{comp}(o_l,so_{l_s})$$

Note that formula (2) does not explicitly include I/O cost for loading storage clusters. The reason is that wasted I/O effort is coupled with C_{fd} and C_{comp}. The less false drops occur the less objects have been loaded unnecessarily which reduces the I/O cost. This goes along with small cells in a fine partition of the data space resulting in a good approximation of the query range by cells. On the other hand a more coarse partition saves I/O cost due to the reduced number of larger clusters and by using a set-oriented multi-page I/O for large storage clusters. Currently we have no analytic model that specifies the amount of coupled I/O cost. But we introduce a weight factor α that allows to reduce one kind of the wasted effort or the other. Having $\alpha = \frac{1}{2}$, we assume that the minimal wasted effort occurs if false drops and compose costs are about the same size. If we increase α, we try to avoid more compose cost than false drop cost and the cells tend to be larger and the I/O cost is more reduced using set-oriented I/O. On the other hand if we decrease α, we assume that wasted effort is more strongly reduced by avoiding false drops in the I/O.

Clearly we do not want to optimize the partition for a single query but for a set of (observed or given) queries $Q = \{ q_r \mid r = 1, \cdots R \}$. Therefore our optimization problem is the determination of the optimal partition $\hat{p}$ to minimize the wasted costs $\hat{C}$ of the query set Q according to

$$(3) \qquad \hat{C}(\hat{p}) = \min_{p \epsilon P} \left(\sum_{r=1,\cdots,R} C_w(q_r,p) \right)$$

In principle all complete and disjoint partitions are admitted. But the set P of possible data space partitions is too large to enumerate in order to find the best or at least a better partition. In addition, the complexity of a partition directory administration must be taken into consideration. Examples of simple directories for a disjoint partition are the grid file directory, the kdB-tree, the quadtree, the R$^+$-tree or the cell tree directory. The data space partitions resulting from the different directories contain rectangular or polyhedral cells and the partition layout is related to a directory type. Figure 4 shows partitions of a flat grid directory (a) and a kdB-tree directory (b) together with a sampling set of overlapping rectangular query ranges.

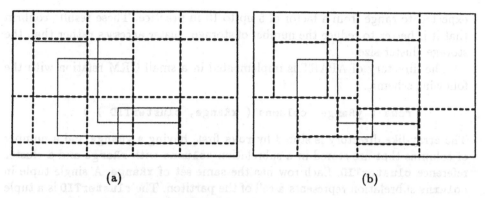

(a)   (b)

Fig. 4.: Examples of a Regular (a) and a Hierachical Directory (b)

4 APART - Regular Adaptive Partitioning and First Evaluations

APART, the Adaptive PARTitioning, is our first implementation of a partitioning strategy that is able to determine storage clusters of appropriate size. The APART partitioning strategy uses a flat grid directory. The APART access and storage method provides operations to insert, delete and retrieve spatial objects. However we do not consider the insert and delete operations for spatial objects here. We rather concentrate on the description of the adaptation aspect. Subsection 4.1 gives a description of the storage manager and how we have implemented the grid directory and the storage clusters. Query evaluation and the adaptation strategy are presented in Subsection 4.2 and first results are discussed in Subsection 4.3.

4.1 Directory and Clusters on Top of a Storage Manager

For our implementation we use the complex record manager (CRM) of the DAS-DBS database system prototype [17]. The CRM is able to handle relations of *Non First Normal Form* (NF^2), i.e. the attributes in the relational schema may be of atomic or relation type. Relations at attribute position are called subrelations and a relation containing subrelations is called a nested relation. The CRM stores complex records of such nested relations in a clustered manner, i.e. each complex record is a variable-size storage cluster. The storage utilization of variable-size multi-page storage cluster is optimal in the sense that storage fragmentation is less than one page. This is much better than the storage fragmentation of a fix-size multi-page cluster. To load n contiguous pages in one I/O is much cheaper than to load n times a single page because of the seek time overhead of each disk access as presented in [19, 18]. The improvement of multi-page I/Os compared to several single-page I/Os can be up to 25 times and is expected to range from a factor of 5 up to 10 in practice. These results confirm that it is better to reduce the number of storage cluster accesses rather than the storage cluster size.

The directory of APART is implemented in a small CRM relation with the following schema

```
rows ( yRange, columns ( xRange, clusterTID ) ) .
```

The array-like directory is stored by **rows** first, having a **yRange** and a number of columns that are stored in a subrelation **columns** with **xRange** and a cluster reference **clusterTID**. Each row has the same set of **xRange**. A single tuple in **columns** subrelation represents a cell of the partiton. The **clusterTID** is a tuple identifier pointing in the **clusters** relation (see below), that allows direct access to the associated cluster. Here **yRange** and **xRange** have interval data types. The size of the directory is expected to become relatively small using variable-size storage clusters compared to a directory for single page storage clusters.

The main part of the APART data, the variable-size storage clusters, take advantage from the nested relation storage structure of a CRM relation. A single complex record of the cluster relation contains the spatial objects of a cell. The following relation schema expresses the storage structure layout:

```
clusters ( cell, type1_entries ( spatialObj, reference ),
                 type2_entries ( spatialObj, reference ),
                 . . .                                    )
```

The field **cell** is a rectangle describing the cell extension and each of **type1_-entries**, **type2_entries** etc. is a subrelation containing a set of cluster entries of a specific type. The field **spatialObj** within each subrelation contains spatial objects of one type and **reference** is a pointer into another storage structure, where the thematic data of that object is stored.

The spatial objects we consider have data types like point, rectangle, polyline or polygon. The data types may be implemented using various data structures and in possibly different programming languages. APART is able to handle any of those spatial datatypes through an abstract type interface of a 2-dimensional spatial datatype. The interface is already described in the context of externally defined datatypes (EDT) [1, 20]. The most important operations are *intersects*, *clip* and *compose* (see Section 3.1).

4.2 The Adaptation Step

The adaptation step is executed to reorganize the partition at specific points in time (see below). It uses a current query set, consisting of queries executed since the last adaptation step. We choose the current query set under the reasonable assumption that queries similar to those from the recent past will be executed again in the near future and benefit from the adapted partition.

During query execution the wasted effort is measured in terms of CPU time calling an operating system function within each query evaluation. We collect the CPU time for the intersection test and for the composition of spatial object parts. The false drops cost C_{fd} is calculated from the intersection test cost C_{int} and from the ratio of matches and false drops. The compose cost C_{comp} is measured directly. Additionally we measure the I/O cost $C_{I/O}$ for comparison purposes.

In the first experiments we set $\alpha = \frac{1}{2}$ and thereby try to *balance* the cost such that $C_{fd} \simeq C_{comp}$ in most queries, i.e. the partition is fine enough to limit the false drops and coarse enough to avoid expensive composes. As long as the deviation $|(1 - \alpha) * C_{fd} - \alpha * C_{comp}|$ is small enough in query execution the partition remains unchanged. However if we find that a significant number of queries (20% in the following experiments) have either too high cost C_{fd} in *false drops dominated* ("*f-dominated*") queries, or too high cost C_{comp} in *compose dominated* ("*c-dominated*") queries, the current partition is changed by an adaptation step.

The f-dominated queries will benefit from *additional* partition boundaries, especially from those matching the query range boundary. For each f-dominated query the range boundary defines up to four so called *weighted boundary segments* that would like to be included in a new partition boundary. Without discussing details, we calculate the weights as the wasted effort from the false drops cost and the surrounding area up to the next cell boundaries, i.e. where the false drops occur. The adaptation step attempts to find repartitioning candidates for new partition boundaries when it combines several of the boundary segments for one new partition boundary and accumulates their weights to the weight of the new partition boundary.

On the other hand, c-dominated queries would benefit from a *deletion* of existing partition boundaries that intersect their range. For each c-dominated query a number of weighted boundary segments occur where existing partition boundaries intersect their range. The weights, describing the wasted effort, are calculated from the compose cost and the length of the boundary segments. The adaptation step accumulates the weights for each existing partition boundary to determine repartitioning candidates that should be deleted. The repartitioning candidates for insertion or deletion are ranked on their weights which corresponds to the wasted effort that could be avoided if that repartition is executed. The most expensive repartitions in the ranked list are (tentatively) realized.

4.3 Evaluation

In the following we present two measurements using APART. The data we use serves as a small test data set[1]. It contains realistic data and is relatively small, containing 281 spatial objects each with on average 4 points. This looks like an insufficient test sample but well enough for the first experiments where we wanted to check wheather the objective function in our cost model and the adaptation heuristic will produce storage clusters of reasonable size. The data

---

[1] We like to thank the "Centre for Spatial Information Systems" within the Australian Research Center CSIRO in Canberra, Australia for providing us with that data set.

space extension is 0-5000 in X and Y. The objects are disjoint and show a dissection of the data space into parcels as depicted in Figure 5 (a). The data distribution is highly non uniform. There is a small area of high data density in the upper left quadrant near the data space center. The spatial objects are inserted into an initially equidistant partition of 9 x 9 cells as shown in Figure 5 (b). As the data is not equally distributed we get a wide range of cluster sizes from an empty cluster with size 0 up to a cluster with 121 (sub)objects and 10KByte size in the initial partition.

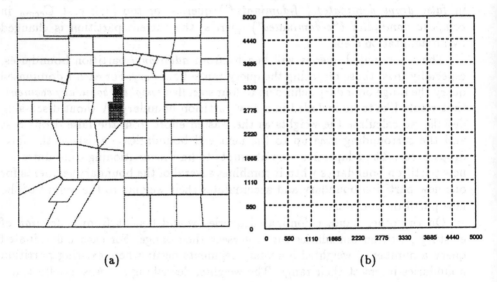

(a) (b)

Fig. 5.: The Sample Data Set

For the evaluations we consider two queries the ranges of which intersect the area of high data density. The first query q_1 is a kind of "overview query" that covers the whole area and query q_2 is a "specialized query" zooming into a more localized area that is about a third of the area of query q_1. The query range of query q_1 has an extension of 2000-2600 in X and 2400-3500 in Y which is 2.64% of the data space and the result set contains 218 spatial objects. q_2 delivers 126 objects in a query range of 2100-2500 in X and 2700-3200 in Y which covers 0.8% of the data space. From the queries q_1 and q_2 we build up two different query sets. Query set $Q_{1:1}$ consists of an equal number of queries q_1 and q_2, i.e. overview and specialized queries occur at the same frequency. Query set $Q_{1:5}$ contains 5 specialized queries q_2 for one overview query q_1.

Our adaptation is a heuristic iterative process. We must consider a sufficiently long sequence of adaptation steps until we get a balanced partition. The query sets remain unchanged during that sequence. For the first query set $Q_{1:1}$ three adaptation steps are needed and the intermediate results, with respect to a single query, are summarized in Table 1. Figure 6 depicted the associated data space partitions and the query ranges.

$msec$/query	data space partitions							
	9 x 9		11 x 9		7 x 8		9 x 8	
	q_1	q_2	q_1	q_2	q_1	q_2	q_1	q_2
$C_{I/O}$	480	480	560	300	480	440	480	240
C_{int}	640	560	720	320	780	620	680	340
C_{fd}	24	219	25	8	24	273	25	8
C_{comp}	120	80	200	80	0	0	40	0
$C_{I/O} + C_{int} + C_{comp}$	1240	1120	1480	700	1260	1060	1200	580
average query	1180		1090		1160		890	
#cluster	6	4	10	4	1	1	3	1
#(sub)object	270	248	291	155	225	225	246	129
#false drops	10	97	10	4	7	99	9	3

Table 1.: Evaluation Cost and Results for Query Set $Q_{1:1}$

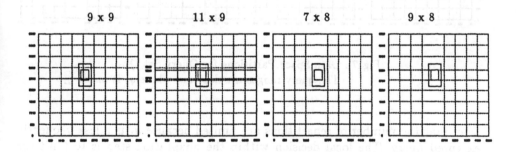

Fig. 6.: Data Space Partitions for Query Set $Q_{1:1}$
The query ranges are depicted where q_2 is inside q_1

Each adaptation step is driven by at most one of the two queries which is f-dominated or c-dominated. After the third adaptation step the queries are almost balanced and query q_2 has less than half the cost and for the average query we gain an improvement of 25% in the average query evaluation time.

The second query set $Q_{1:5}$ performs similarly as shown in Table 2 and Figure 7. Only the second adaptation step differs in the number of repartitions. The adaptation step is mainly driven by q_1 and supported by q_2 as both queries are c-dominated. But query q_1 has only a fifth of the number of query q_2 and

$msec$/query	data space partitions							
	9 x 9		11 x 9		9 x 8		10 x 8	
	q_1	q_2	q_1	q_2	q_1	q_2	q_1	q_2
$C_{I/O}$	480	440	580	300	460	360	480	260
C_{int}	640	560	720	320	720	460	660	300
C_{fd}	24	219	25	8	24	150	24	7
C_{comp}	120	80	200	80	20	0	60	0
$C_{I/O} + C_{int} + C_{comp}$	1240	1080	1500	700	1200	820	1200	560
average query	1107		833		883		667	
#cluster	6	4	10	4	3	1	4	1
#(sub)object	270	248	291	155	238	187	250	129
#false drops	10	97	10	4	8	61	9	3

Table 2.: Evaluation Cost and Results for Query Set $Q_{1:5}$

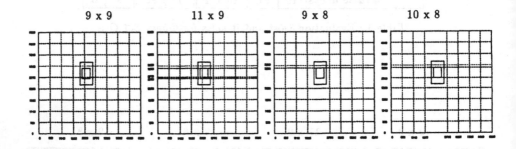

Fig. 7.: Data Space Partitions for Query Set $Q_{1:5}$
The query ranges are depicted where q_2 is inside q_1

from that the number of repartitions are limited because q_1 is a less frequently executed query. The local decision within the adaptation step is to limit the number of repartitions by a ratio between the number of over-average unbalanced queries and the total number of queries. Thus only 3 partiton lines are deleted. Finally in the balanced partition of query set $Q_{1:5}$ we have one more horizontal partition line. Although compose cost occur in q_1 from this partition line, it is not removed because q_2 dominates the query set and the number of unbalanced queries q_1 is only 16.6% which is less than the 20% needed to trigger the adaptaion step. Nevertheless the balanced partition improves the query evaluation time by 40% for an average query, because the improvement of q_2 is multiplied by the frequency of its occurence.

In addition to the detailed analysis of the two simple examples above we started some tests on more complex data and with mutually overlapping query ranges which are shown in Figure 8.

The data set consists of 853 polylines of different complexity from 2 to 172

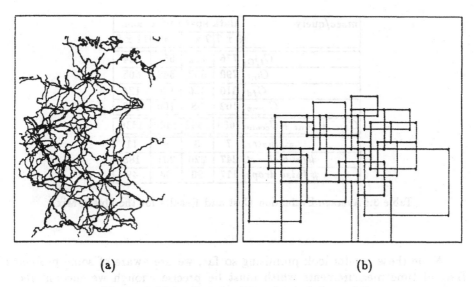

(a)   (b)

Fig. 8.: A More Complex Data Set and Query Mix

points within one polyline. The polylines represent highways, railways, and state borders of Western Germany. The query mix is drawn from 22 different queries, where each query appears between 1 and 24 times in a set of totally 134 queries. The query range extension varies from 0.35% to 12.36% of the data space and the result sets range from 1 to 358 spatial objects. The results presented are restricted to the *average* values of the complete query mix. Figure 9 shows the changes in partitioning starting with partition of 8x7 and ending with an adapted partition of 11x9. Table 3 shows the associated costs and the number of accessed clusters and eliminated false drops. Even in this example with a number of conflicting queries the adaptation improves the evaluation time by about 20% .

8 x 7   9 x 7   9 x 9   11 x 9

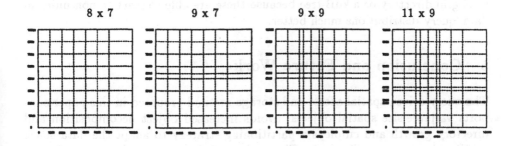

Fig. 9.: Data Space Partitions for Query Mix

$msec$/query	data space partitions			
	8 x 7	9 x 7	9 x 9	11 x 9
$C_{I/O}$	776	702	651	624
C_{int}	790	692	649	605
C_{fd}	310	226	168	124
C_{comp}	102	98	100	107
$C_{I/O} + C_{int} + C_{comp}$	1668	1492	1400	1336
#$cluster$	7	8	9	11
#$(sub)object$	247	220	201	185
#$false\ drops$	117	90	66	49

Table 3.: Average Evaluation Cost and Results for the Query Mix

While these results look promising so far, we are aware of some problems. Beyond time measurements which must be precise enough we encountered a problem with cyclic repartitions, i.e. if one adaptation step deletes some partition boundaries and the next adaptation step inserts just that partition boundaries like an inverse operation. This situation could arise with query set $Q_{1:1}$ if one more adaptation step is performed. In this situation we skip repartitions if its avoidable cost is rather low. As this is actually true for query set $Q_{1:1}$ as can be seen from the last two columns of Table 1 and consequently no repartition is performed. On the other hand we use a *constant* query set $Q_{1:1}$ in the sequence of adaptation steps which is rarely met in practice. Therefore in future evaluations we will have experiments with a slowly changing query set, that benefits from the adaptation and changes partially at the same time.

A further problem is a consequence of the simple directory structure. A partition boundary always divides the whole data space and a repartition that reduces costs in one or several cells may increase costs in other cells for other query ranges. For that reason we decide to investigate other directory structures that allow the insertion and deletion of local partition boundaries such as a multi-level grid directory or a kdB-tree because these are able to react to non-uniform data/query distributions much better.

5 Conclusion and Future Work

The query driven spatial access and storage method proposed in this paper supports variable-size spatial objects, avoids increased object decomposition and directory growth and employs a partitioning strategy to adapt the data space partiton to query requirements. The update of the partition is seperated from insertion and deletion of data and simplifies the data update operations because no subsequent directory updates occur. Our first implementation, the APART access and storage manager is included in the Geo-Kernel of the DASDBS prototype system.

In addition to the evaluation of different directory structures, future work will support spatial joins. As we already have different sets of spatial objects SO_1, SO_2 etc. within each storage cluster we may combine them in a spatial join condition. The spatial join can be evaluated locally on each storage cluster to reduce the $O(m * n)$ complexity. Moreover an additional spatial selection condition may reduce the number of storage clusters that have to be evaluated.

The generalization of our approach to the 3-dimensional space is straightforward if we use appropriate directory structures. For example it is feasible that cuboid range query can be evaluated in a three-dimensional data space with hyperplane partition boundaries.

6 Acknowledgements

The implementations and measurements are made during two master theses and by additional student's work. We like to thank Giovanni Moggi, Andreas Allenspach and Massimo Sarti for their work on the first implementation and their discussions on heuristics to use in APART. We want to acknowlegde Andreas Wolf for his support on the DASDBS Kernel system and Andrew Deacon for carefully reading early drafts and helping to improve the readability of this paper.

References

1. Gisbert Dröge, Hans-Jörg Schek, and Andreas Wolf. Extensibility in DASDBS. *Informatik Forschung und Entwicklung*, 5:162–176, 1990. (in German).
2. Andrew U. Frank. Properties of Geographic Data: Requirements for Spatial Access Methods. In Oliver Günther and Hans-Jörg Schek, editors, *Advances in Spatial Databases, 2nd Symposium, SSD '91*, LNCS 525, pages 225 – 234. Springer-Verlag, August 1991.
3. O. Günther and A. Buchmann. Research Issues in Spatial Databases. *ACM SIG-MOD RECORD*, 19(4):61–68, December 1990.
4. Oliver Günther. The Design of the Cell Tree: An Object-Oriented Index Structure for Geometric Databases. In *Proc. of the 5th IEEE Int. Conf. on Data Engineering*, pages 598–605, February 1989.
5. Oliver Günther and Hartmut Noltemeier. Spatial Database Indices for Large Extended Objects. In *Proc. of the 7th IEEE Int. Conf. on Data Engineering*, pages 520–526, April 1991.
6. A. Guttman. R-trees: A Dynamic Index Structure for Spatial Searching. *ACM SIGMOD Proceedings of Annual Meeting*, 14(2):47–57, June 1984.
7. Dagmar Horn, Hans-J. Schek, Walter Waterfeld, and Andreas Wolf. Spatial Access Paths and Physical Clustering in a Low-Level Geo-Database System. In Geological Survey of Lower Saxony, editor, *Construction of Geoscientific Maps derived from Databases*, Geologisches Jahrbuch, pages 123–138, 1988.
8. Hans-Peter Kriegel, Holger Horn, and Michael Schiwietz. The Performance of Object Decomposition Techniques for Spatial Query Processing. In O. Günther and H.-J. Schek, editors, *Advances in Spatial Databases, 2nd Symposium, SSD*

'91, *Proceedings*, number 525 in LNCS, pages 257–276. Springer Verlag, August 1991.

9. Hans-Peter Kriegel, Michael Schiwietz, Ralf Schneider, and Bernhard Seeger. Performance Comparison of Point and Spatial Access Methods. In A. Buchmann, O. Günther, T.R. Smith, and Y.-F. Wang, editors, *Design and Implementation of Large Spatial Databases, First Symposium, SSD '89, Proceedings*, LNCS 409, pages 89–114. Springer Verlag, July 1989.

10. David B. Lomet. Partial Expansions for File Organizations. *ACM Trans. on Database Systems*, 12(1):65–84, March 1987.

11. Hongjun Lu, Beng Chin Ooi, Ashvin D'Souza, and Chee Chin Low. Storage Management in Geographic Information Systems. In Oliver Günther and Hans-Jörg Schek, editors, *Advances in Spatial Databases, 2nd Symposium, SSD '91*, LNCS 525, pages 451– 470. Springer-Verlag, August 1991.

12. J. Nievergelt, H. Hinterberger, and K.C. Sevcik. The Grid File: An Adaptable, Symmetric Multikey File Structure. *ACM Trans. on Database Systems*, 9(1):38–71, March 1984.

13. Joseph O'Rourke and JR. Kenneth R. Sloan. Dynamic Quantization: Two Adaptive Data Structures for Multidimensional Spaces. *IEEE Trans. on Pattern Analysis and Machine Intelligence*, 6(3):266–280, May 1984.

14. John T. Robinson. The K-D-B-Tree: A Search Structure for Large Multidimensional Dynamic Indexes. In *Proc. of ACM SIGMOD Conf.*, pages 10–18, 1981.

15. Hanan Samet. *The Design and Analysis of Spatial Data Structures*. Addison Wesley, 1990.

16. H.-J. Schek and W. Waterfeld. A Database Kernel System for Geoscientific Applications. In *Second International Symposium on Spatial Data Handling, Proceedings*, pages 273– 288. International Geographical Union IGU, Commission on Geographical Data Sensing and Processing, July 1986.

17. Hans-Jörg Schek, H.-Bernhard Paul, Marc H. Scholl, and Gerhard Weikum. The DASDBS Project: Objectives, Experiences and Future Prospects. *IEEE Transactions on Knowledge and Data Engineering*, 2(1), March 1990.

18. Gerhard Weikum. Set-Oriented Disk Access to Large Complex Objects. In *Proc. of the 5th IEEE Int. Conf. on Data Engineering*, pages 426–433, February 1989.

19. Gerhard Weikum, Bernd Neumann, and Hans-Bernd Paul. Design and Realization of a Set-Oriented Page Server Interface to Support Efficient Access to Complex Objects. In H.-J. Schek and G. Schlageter, editors, *Proc. of the GI Conf. on Database Systems in Office Automation, Engineering and Scientific Applications*, Informatik Fachberichte 136, pages 212–230. Springer, April 1987. (in German).

20. Andreas Wolf. The DASDBS GEO-Kernel, Concepts, Experiences, and the Second Step. In Alejandro P. Buchman, Oliver Günther, Terry R. Smith, and Yuan-F. Wang, editors, *Design and Implementation of Large Spatial Databases, First Symposium SSD '89, Proceedings*, LNCS 409, pages 67–88. Springer Verlag, July 1989.

A   Polyline and Polygon Operation Cost

We have measured the cost of the intersect and inside predicate for the spatial datatypes polyline and polygon. The comparison operand is a rectangle in each case. We choose different rectangles from the minimal bounding rectangle (mbr), the half mbr in left, right, upper and lower position, a quarter of the rectangle in each of the quarter positions and a disjoint neighbouring rectangle. The spatial objects are taken from a map of western Germany containing polylines for borders, rivers, railways and highways and polygons for cities, conurbations, forests and lakes. The hardware platform for these measurements was a Sun 3/60 workstation. The results for polylines are shown in Table 4 and for polygons in Table 5. To interpret the time measurements in the right way, it should be mentioned that an integer comparison take about 2 μsec on a Sun 3/60.

μsec/object						
#objects	576	923	159	78	1736
#points	2 - 9	10 - 49	50 - 99	100 - 196	2 - 196
intersects	mbr	188	188	188	182	188
	half mbr	243	542	1132	1666	507
	quarter mbr	347	909	2138	3333	946
	disjoint	296	931	2516	4487	1037
	average	269	643	1494	2417	670
inside	mbr	312	1235	3082	5897	1376
	half mbr	174	412	755	1026	415
	quarter mbr	174	206	314	384	242
	disjoint	156	154	151	154	155
	average	204	502	1076	1865	547

Table 4.: Polyline Operations

μsec/object						
#objects	368	207	31	18	624
#points	2 - 9	10 - 49	50 - 99	100 - 242	2 - 242
intersects	mbr	147	116	129	111	131
	half mbr	130	174	387	666	173
	quarter mbr	196	272	516	1555	301
	disjoint	391	831	2581	5111	782
	average	216	348	903	1861	347
inside	mbr	152	386	1290	2444	333
	half mbr	43	58	129	222	71
	quarter mbr	43	48	65	111	45
	disjoint	38	39	37	38	38
	average	69	133	380	704	122

Table 5.: Polygon Operations

A Storage and Access Architecture for Efficient Query Processing in Spatial Database Systems

Thomas Brinkhoff, Holger Horn, Hans-Peter Kriegel, Ralf Schneider

Institute for Computer Science, University of Munich
Leopoldstr. 11 B, W-8000 München 40, Germany

e-mail: {brink,holger,kriegel,ralf}@dbs.informatik.uni-muenchen.de

Abstract: Due to the high complexity of objects and queries and also due to extremely large data volumes, geographic database systems impose stringent requirements on their storage and access architecture with respect to efficient query processing. Performance improving concepts such as spatial storage and access structures, approximations, object decompositions and multi-phase query processing have been suggested and analyzed as single building blocks. In this paper, we describe a storage and access architecture which is composed from the above building blocks in a modular fashion. Additionally, we incorporate into our architecture a new ingredient, the scene organization, for efficiently supporting set-oriented access of large-area region queries. An experimental performance comparison demonstrates that the concept of scene organization leads to considerable performance improvements for large-area region queries by a factor of up to 150.

1 Introduction

During the last decade, the management, representation and evaluation of spatial data in information systems gained increasing importance. *Geographic information systems* (GIS) are increasingly used in public administration, science and business. The nucleus of a GIS is the *geographic database system*. Contrary to business applications based on standard database systems, such systems are not suitable for geographic applications [Wid 91]. The insufficient expressive power e.g. of relational systems, leads to unnatural data models and to poor efficiency in query processing.

Therefore, various research groups have developed a large number of concepts and techniques for improving single aspects of a geographic database system. Examples are the design of spatial data models or efficient access methods for managing large sets of spatial objects.

In this paper, we will present our *geo architecture*, a new storage and access architecture for spatial objects integrating several concepts and techniques. It is not our goal to present a new spatial database *system* or a kernel of a system such as DASDBS [SW 86], EXODUS [CDRS 86], GRAL [Güt 89] and POSTGRES [SR 86]. Instead, we would like to assemble suitable concepts and techniques to a spatial query processing mechanism. One of the most important building blocks of our architecture is the *scene organization*, a new technique for supporting large range queries. Its performance improvement by up to two orders of magnitude is demonstrated.

The paper is organized as follows. First, we take a closer look at the objects and operations commonly used in geographic information systems. This leads to a set of basic queries which should be efficiently supported by our architecture. A model of spatial query processing using different phases is described in section three. In section four, we present different algorithms and methods for supporting these phases. The new scene organization is described in section 4.4. The integration of the algorithms and methods leads to our geo architecture. The rest of the paper contains an investigation of the performance of this architecture. In particular, we present a detailed performance evaluation of our new scene organization for real world data. The paper concludes with a brief statement of our findings and some suggestions for future work.

2 Objects and operations of a spatial database system

In this paper, we present a conceptional architecture for storing objects and processing queries in a geographic database system. To develop such an architecture, we first need an exact specification of the objects and queries. This is presented in the following subsections.

2.1 Objects

The objects stored in a geographic database are used for modeling specific parts of the surface of the earth with respect to one or several properties. Therefore, the objects are characterized by a *spatial* and a *thematic component*. The spatial component describes the spatial locality and the shape of the modeled part of reality whereas the thematic component contains the thematic information.

The spatial component

The spatial component of an object is represented by one of the basic topological elements of the plane: point, line or area. Points are described by specifying their coordinates with respect to a given coordinate system. For modeling lines, both polylines as well as free-form curves are used. In this paper, we concentrate on representing areas. From the literature two main concepts for representing areas are known: the raster and the vector model. Because of its favorable scaling capabilities, its lower demand of storage and its "object orientation", the vector model has been preferred over the last few years for application in geographic database systems. The type of spatial objects we consider in this paper is the class of *simple polygons with holes* (SPH for short) (see figure 1). A polygon is called simple if there is no pair of nonconsecutive edges sharing a point. A SPH is a simple polygon where simple polygonal holes may be cut out. The class of SPHs is well suited for geographic applications (see [Bur 86]). It allows representing areas with arbitrary precision and explicitly takes holes into account.

Fig. 1. Simple polygon with holes

The thematic component

The thematic component characterizes an object with respect to one or several thematic properties. We distinguish between *qualitative properties* such as land use and *quantitative properties* such as amount of precipitation. For representing thematic values, simple data types such as strings or real numbers are used.

The object model

The geo architecture to be developed should be able to store *sets* of objects consisting of a spatial (SPH) and a thematic component (vector of simple data types). Figure 2 gives a typical example of a map which is represented by a set of SPHs.

Fig. 2. Map of the European counties modeled by a set of SPH

Both components require a completely different handling by the geo architecture. For managing vectors of simple data types, e.g. in a relational database system, a lot of well known data structures and algorithms are available. However, organizing the spatial component demands for new structures and algorithms. They should organize the objects in such a way that spatial queries referring to location and shape of the objects are processed efficiently.

Additional to these fundamental properties of the spatial objects, two more aspects are important for the design of the geo architecture. First, we need a characterization of the objects from real applications as accurate as possible. Second, we need a specification of the queries and operations to be performed on these objects.

2.2 Characteristics of the objects

In this paper, it is not our goal to present a general characterization of the object sets occurring in geographic applications. From our point of view this is impossible because of the very wide application spectrum geographical information systems are used in. Instead, we outline some general properties of the data which influence the design of our geo architecture considerably.

Complexity and variation of the data

- *Number of objects and data volume*

  In real applications, the number of data objects may be as high as 10^9. The data volume may occupy up to 1 TerraByte (see [Fra 91] and [Cra 90]).

- *Variation of objects and sets of objects*

  Data from real world applications vary extremely with respect to single objects and whole object sets [Fra 91]. This particularly refers to the following aspects:

  - *Object extensions*
    It varies in a range of $1 : 10^6$ [Fra 91], where the largest objects may occupy the whole data space.

  - *Object shape*

  - *Amount of storage*
    As an example, in the World Data Bank II [GC 87] the amount of storage for one polygonal object varies between 0.5 KB and more than 1.1 GB.

- *Distribution of the objects in the data space*
  The number of objects per unit (density) varies in a range of $1 : 10^4$ in real world applications [Fra 91].

In particular, we have to consider that there are no upper bounds neither for the extension of objects, the complexity of object structure, the amount of storage, nor for the density of the objects.

Persistent storage of the objects in a weak dynamic environment

Recording the data of a geographic information system is an expensive task. Very often, data from paper maps as well as satellite pictures have to be integrated into a seamless database. This work is often a source of inaccuracy and inconsistency, which has to be revealed and removed by using time consuming consistency check mechanisms. Altogether recording the data and preserving consistency of the data account for approximately 80% of the operating costs of a geographic database system [Aro 91].

After recording the database, it is persistently stored and used on a long term basis. However, the database is not static because correcting mistakes, removing inconsistencies and adapting to changes in the real world leads to updates of the data. All in all, the database is weakly dynamic.

The properties of spatial objects mentioned above and the queries and operations described in the following section form a requirement definition for the geo architecture which is described in detail in section 4.

2.3 Queries and operations

Geographic database systems are used in very different application environments. Therefore, it is not possible to find a compact set of spatial queries and operations fulfilling all requirements of geographic applications [SV 89]. Instead, we present four basic classes of operations each with a number of typical representatives which should be supported by our architecture.

1) Modifications

Analogously to standard database systems, there are operations for insertion, deletion and update of records in a geographic database system.

2) Selections

We can distinguish between two types of selections: those referring to the spatial and those referring to the thematic component of an object.

a) Spatial selections:

- *Point Query*
  Given a query point P and a set of objects M. The point query yields all the objects of M geometrically containing P (see figure 3(a)).

- *Region Query*
  Given a polygonal query region R (of type SPH) and a set of objects M, the region query yields all the objects of M sharing points with R. A special case of the region query is the *window query*. The query region of a window query is given by a rectilinear rectangle (see figure 3(b)). Both, the window query and the region query are often called *range queries*.

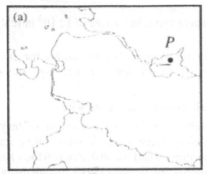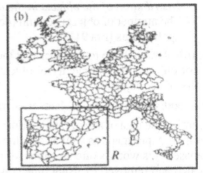

Fig. 3. Examples for a point and a window query

b) Thematic Selections:

When performing a thematic (relational) selection the objects are selected with respect to properties of their thematic component. Within this section, we pay attention only to the spatial component of the objects. In section 4.5 we will describe how to support thematic selections.

3) Combinations

- *Spatial Join*
  For two given object sets A and B the spatial join operation yields all pairs of objects (a, b), $a \in A$, $b \in B$ whose spatial components intersect. More precisely, for each object $a \in A$ we have to look for all objects in B intersecting with a. Note, that for efficient processing of the spatial join a selective spatial access to the objects is necessary.

- *Map Overlay*
  The map overlay is one of the most important operations in a geographic information system [Bur 86]. It combines two or more sets of spatial objects. This combination is controlled by the overlay function determining in which way intersecting objects have to be handled. The map overlay is completely based on variants of the spatial join operation. In addition to the spatial join, the intersection of a pair of overlapping objects has to be computed. Neighboring objects with identical values of their thematic component should be merged [KBS 91].

4) Analyzing sets of objects

Selections or combinations of existing sets of objects are often followed by further processing steps in practical applications. The operations and algorithms used for these steps are very specific for a particular application and, therefore, are not supported by a general storage and access architecture. Without considering the details, we can distinguish two classes of these operations and algorithms.

- *Automatic analysis*
  Analyzing functions applied to the spatial and/or the thematic component of the objects are part of this class. Typical representatives are: calculating the average of the area or perimeter of a set of objects, calculating the minimum and maximum of thematic attributes etc.

- *Visualization*
  In many cases the automatic analysis of a database is not possible and manual inter-

mediate steps performed by a user are necessary to complete the analysis. For this purpose, a visualization of the data on a graphic device is necessary.

The above mentioned facts clearly demonstrate that spatial selections are of great importance within the set of spatial queries and operations. They do not only represent an own query class, but also serve as a very important basis for the operations of the classes 2 - 4. Therefore, an efficient implementation of spatial selections is an important requirement for good performance of the complete geographic information system.

3 A phase model for geometric query processing

After the description and specification of objects and queries, we will design an architecture for storing spatial objects and efficiently processing queries. The main task of the architecture is the efficient processing of *spatial* queries and operations. Therefore, in this section, we take a closer look at this type of queries, distinguish different phases in their processing and specify algorithms and data structures for their processing.

As mentioned in the last section, spatial selections are the most important basic operation in spatial query processing. Their execution can be described abstractly as a sequence of steps:

Step 1: Scaling down the data space

Considering spatial selections in more detail, it turns out that only a local part of the complete data space has to be investigated. Only this area contains candidate objects that *may* fulfill a selective query.

For an efficient scaling down of the data space, it is essential to use data structures organizing the objects with respect to their spatial locality and shape. Obviously, objects jointly fulfilling a query condition lie close together in the data space. Therefore, a physical clustering of the objects with respect to their spatial locality and shape is essential for providing efficient spatial query processing.

Due to the arbitrary complexity of real geographic objects, it is not possible to build up an index considering the complete information on the extension of the objects. Thus, the access method is not able to yield the *exact* result of a query. Instead, it excludes a large subset of objects from the result. A set of *candidate objects* that *may* fulfill the query condition remains and has to be passed on to step 2 of the query processing mechanism. Orenstein established in [Ore 89] the terms *filtering and refinement* for this type of query processing.

Step 2: Exact investigation of the objects

Step 2 of the query processing tests whether a candidate object actually fulfills the query condition or not. For that purpose, a spatial predicate, e.g. "polygon contains point" or "rectangle intersects polygon", has to be checked. Similar to step 1, this test consists of different phases. First, the test has to be restricted to only that part of the object that is really relevant for the test. Figure 4 gives an example: To evaluate whether the query window R overlaps Lake Volta, only its northern west peak has to be examined.

Due to the complexity of the objects on the one hand and the selectivity of spatial queries on the other hand, it is useful to *structure the objects locally*. The resulting structure elements have to be organized in a data structure referring to their spatial locality and extension. Using this data structure, we can efficiently decide which parts of the object are actually relevant to the query. Only this small number of local parts is further examined using computational geometry algorithms, which finally decide whether an object fulfills the query or not.

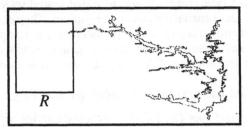

Fig. 4. Test of a query window against Lake Volta

Step 3: Output of objects for further processing

After identifying an object as part of the result, it is usually passed on to further processing e.g. analyzing steps, output operations etc. Therefore, a physically connected storage of all parts of the objects is necessary to support a fast access to the complete object.

4 An architecture for query processing in spatial database systems

After the abstract description of the phase model for spatial query processing, we present algorithmic techniques for supporting the individual phases. Later on in this section, these techniques are used as building blocks within our geo architecture.

4.1 Spatial access methods

Access methods as an essential part of the internal level of a database system are used to organize a dynamic set of objects on secondary storage. One-dimensional access methods like *B-trees* or *linear hashing* are not suitable for spatial database systems. For these systems, we have to look for data structures which organize the polygonal objects with respect to their location and extension in the data space. The arbitrary complexity of the spatial objects (simple polygon with holes) makes it very difficult to develop a structure considering the whole object description. Instead, we consider access methods for simpler two-dimensional objects. Surveys of spatial access methods can be found e.g. in [Sam 90] and [Wid 91].

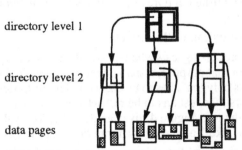

directory level 1

directory level 2

data pages

Fig. 5. Schematic presentation of an R*-tree

The simplest class of two-dimensional objects are rectilinear rectangles. For this class of objects, a number of index structures already exists. A popular representative is the *R-tree* [Gut 84]. The R-tree stores as many spatially close objects (rectangles) on one data page as it accommodates and surrounds them by their minimum bounding box. A set of such bounding boxes is stored on a (directory) page. Again, their minimum bounding box is computed and stored in a directory page one level above and so on. In this way, the whole object set is stepwise spatially clustered and a tree-like directory is created (see figure 5).

A very efficient version of the R-tree is the *R*-tree* [BKSS 90]. Within this data structure sophisticated algorithms for page splitting and local reorganizations are used. The overlap of page regions and the length of their margin are minimized as well as the dead space, i.e. the space occupied unnecessarily by page regions.

This idea of organizing rectangles leads to an efficient processing of point queries and small window queries [BKSS 90]. Unfortunately, this is restricted to rectangles or other simple spatial objects, not larger than a data page. In real applications, it is absolutely necessary to store more complex objects and to process large window queries efficiently. Later on in this section, we will present an access architecture for managing arbitrary simple polygons with holes and processing large window queries efficiently.

4.2 Approximations

The set of results to a spatial query consists of all the objects fulfilling a geometric predicate e.g. containing a query point. As mentioned in the last section, spatial access methods are used for excluding a large subset of the objects from the result as early as possible. The remaining candidate objects have to be investigated by computational geometry algorithms. Considering complex objects (polygons with large numbers of vertices), this is a time consuming task. This leads to the idea of a *geometric pretest*. Such a test should be easy to process and should decide for a large number of objects whether they fulfill the query condition or not.

For implementing the idea of a geometric pretest, the concept of object approximations is an adequate approach. In [Kri 91a] a detailed classification of different approximation techniques is given. The description of an approximation should be simple and its quality should be high, two obviously competing criteria. To make object approximations useful for a geometric pretest, the object has to be contained completely in its approximation (*conservative approximation*) [Sch 92]. Examples for conservative approximations are minimal bounding boxes, convex polygons, ellipses etc. (figure 6).

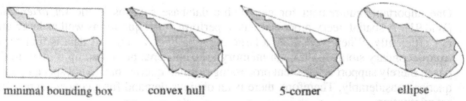

minimal bounding box   convex hull   5-corner   ellipse

Fig. 6. Various conservative approximations

Let us have a closer look at the processing of a point query using object approximations. First, for all candidate objects it is tested, whether their approximation contains the query point or not. In case of a negative result, the object does not contain the query point either. The object is discarded and a time consuming point-in-polygon test could be saved. Only in case of a positive pretest, the object itself has to be tested.

[BKS 93a] contains a detailed examination of object approximations used for spatial query processing in a real data environment. It turned out that the convex 5-corner is the best compromise between the approximation quality and storage amount. Using the

R*-tree, it is shown that other approximations than the minimal bounding box can efficiently be organized in a spatial access method originally designed for bounding boxes.

4.3 Object decompositions

Object approximations are applied to avoid complex geometric tests. Object decomposition techniques, however, are used to simplify and speed up their processing.

Consider again a point-in-polygon test. For processing this test an algorithm with linear runtime complexity is necessary [PS 88]. This examination of complex polygons i.e. polygons with thousands of vertices consumes a considerable amount of CPU time. On the other hand, only a small local part of the object is actually relevant for the decision whether an object contains a point or not. This leads to the idea of object decomposition. Applying this idea, the objects are divided into a number of simple and local components, e.g. triangles, convex polygons etc.. During spatial query processing, only one or a small number of these components has to be checked. In [KHS 91] and [Kri 91a] the decomposition approach for simple polygons with holes is presented and discussed in detail.

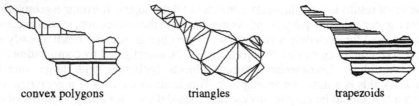

convex polygons   triangles   trapezoids

Fig. 7. Three decomposition techniques for simple polygons

Using object decompositions geometric tests are applied only to components, e.g. trapezoids, which is much more efficient than testing the whole polygon. To decide *which* components are relevant for a particular test, we use again an R*-tree to organize the components of one object with respect to their location and shape. The resulting tree is called a *TR*-tree*. In [SK 91] we demonstrated that the TR*-tree efficiently supports various types of spatial queries and operations.

4.4 Scene organization

One important requirement for geographic database systems is the *set orientation* [Wid 91]. A spatial query processor has to perform small queries as well as large queries efficiently. When processing a large query, a large amount of data is transferred from secondary storage into main memory. The concepts presented up to now in this paper, merely support an efficient processing of small queries but do not speed up large queries considerably. Therefore, there is an obvious demand for a concept supporting set orientation.

Considering the existing storage organization and the type of objects to be stored, we can observe the following points:

- The objects are very large in comparison to the size of the pages they are stored in. Even in the case of large pages (e.g. 4 KByte), the number of objects per page is usually small and often we need several pages for storing just one single object.

- The pages used for storing objects are distributed on the secondary storage device independently from spatial aspects, i.e. pages lying adjacent in space lose their neighborhood on the storage device. Large region queries transfer a large amount of spatially adjacent pages into main memory. Therefore, an arbitrary distribution of these pages on the disk leads to very high access costs during query processing.

The concepts presented in the sections before preserve only a *local ordering* within the pages [Wid 91]. To support the set orientation in an appropriate way, a *global order preservation* i.e. a physical clustering of larger storage units, is required.

Different approaches are conceivable to handle larger storage units. In [Wei 89] *using larger pages, pages of variable length, various buffering strategies* and *physical clustering of pages combined with a set-oriented interface* are discussed in detail to handle large complex objects. In this paper, physical clustering of pages is favored and naturally offers itself as an adequate approach to store scenes within our geo architecture. To translate this approach into action, we need a set-oriented interface between the database system and the secondary storage device [Wei 89]. Such an interface allows an efficient transfer of physically adjacent pages from secondary storage to main memory. The implementation of such an interface is not the subject of this paper.

In [HSW 88] an idea based on dynamic z-hashing for implementing physical clustering of pages is presented. This idea is applied to rectangles in [HWZ 91]. However, the global order is preserved only for approximations of objects. Furthermore, this hash approach is not applicable to access methods with an arbitrary space partitioning scheme. Therefore, we have developed a concept based on the partitioning scheme of the R*-tree.

Building up the scene organization

As mentioned before, we use the R*-tree as a major component of our geo architecture, due to its good performance and its robustness. The R*-tree uses a very efficient scheme for space partitioning neither clipping nor transforming the spatial objects. These facts lead to the idea of using the partitions i.e. subtrees of the R*-tree as basic units for physical clustering. In the following, a *scene* is defined as a subtree of the R*-tree physically clustered on secondary storage. One scene consists of a large set of physically adjacent pages containing all corresponding objects. Using this approach, no additional data structure for handling scenes is necessary.

An object larger than one page is stored on several pages such that all of them are physically clustered within one scene. Thus, also the transfer of such a large object into main memory is supported by the scene organization (see step 3 of the phase model). Note that no order has to be preserved within each scene.

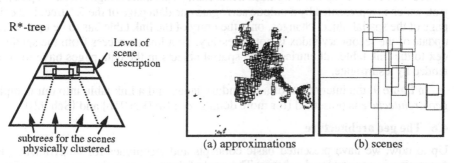

(a) approximations   (b) scenes

Fig. 8. Scene organization

In addition to a schematic structure of the scene organization, figure 8 presents the particular scene organization for the counties of the European Community (see figure 1 also). The R*-tree contains the polygons representing the counties, their decomposition components and their approximations (figure 8 (a)). Figure 8 (b) depicts the partitioning of the R*-tree on a higher directory level. The rectangles describe the scenes, the corresponding subtrees are physically clustered.

Query processing

Using our scene architecture, small queries as well as large queries are processed efficiently. Small queries are processed by single page accesses as described before. If a range query specifies a larger query region, all scenes intersecting the query region, i.e. subtrees of the R*-tree, are transferred into the main memory. For each scene just one search operation on secondary storage is necessary. Without a scene organization, we need one search operation for each page which is much more expensive. Unfortunately, a scene may contain a number of objects not fulfilling the query condition (*false hits*). Nevertheless, the false hits are also transferred into main memory. A relatively small number of false hits does not affect performance considerably, since the time needed for searching a page drastically exceeds the time for transferring a page [PH 90]. In addition, the degree of intersection between the scene and the query region may be used as a measure to decide whether the scene is transferred completely or whether the query is answered without using the scene organization. A detailed performance evaluation of the scene organization is presented in section 5.1.

After transferring the scene into main memory, a query is processed as usual, i.e. using approximations and decomposition techniques (see section 4.2 and section 4.3). A detailed algorithmic description of the dynamic organization of the scene architecture is presented in [Sch 92] and [BKS 93b]. Supplementing the presented query processing techniques by a scene organization allows an efficient query processing for queries of arbitrary size.

4.5 Integration of thematic attributes

The techniques presented up to now are completely dedicated to *spatial* queries. Queries referring to thematic attributes of the stored objects are also important in geographic information systems (see section 2.1).

For an efficient support of thematic queries, an additional index, i.e. a *secondary index* (e.g. a B-tree) is necessary for the relevant thematic attributes. The R*-tree in cooperation with the scene organization determines the location of physical storage of the objects. For connecting both, we need a *link table*. This table assigns to each spatial object, which is represented by a unique surrogate one data page of the R*-tree. If the data page of the spatial object changes, only the entry of the link table has to be updated. An update of the secondary index is not necessary. To allow an access from the spatial index to the link table, all entries of the spatial objects in the data pages have to be extended by a surrogate.

In figure 9, the integration of a secondary index and a link table into our complete *geo architecture* is presented (for more details see also [Kri 91b] and [Sch 92]).

4.6 The geo architecture

Up to now, we have presented basic concepts and techniques for an efficient query processing in geographic databases. The goal of this section is the integration of these concepts into our *geo architecture*. This architecture is presented in figure 9.

The basic building block of our architecture is the R*-tree. It organizes the objects on secondary storage pagewise and allows an efficient spatial indexing. Starting with the root, a spatial query passes through the R*-tree, thereby locating one or several scene descriptions. If the intersection of the query region and the scene exceeds a given threshold, the scene is completely transferred into main memory where query processing proceeds. Otherwise, the required data regions are transferred page by page.

The next ingredient of the architecture are approximations. They support a first preselection to determine whether an object fulfills the query or not. For that purpose, the approximations, e.g. minimal bounding 5-corners, of the objects are stored in the entries of the data pages. If the approximation of a spatial object fulfills the query, the object itself has to be further investigated. Therefore, each object entry contains a pointer to its exact geometric representation managed by a TR*-tree. The TR*-tree organizes all decomposition components and helps exploiting spatial selectivity in query processing. Instead of applying time consuming computational geometry algorithms to complete spatial objects, the query condition is evaluated just considering simple components.

The architecture is completed by secondary indices for thematic attributes. A thematic query traverses the B-tree yielding one or more surrogates. These surrogates are used for accessing to the link table providing the number of the data page storing the object entry.

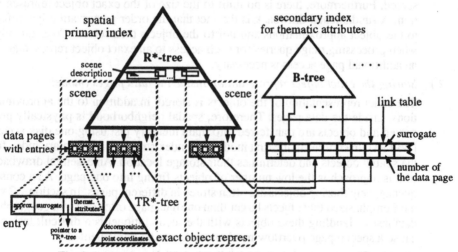

Fig. 9. Integration of efficient building blocks into our geo architecture

5 Evaluation

The techniques integrated in our architecture for spatial databases have been investigated and tested extensively. The basic component of the architecture is the R*-tree. In [BKSS 90] a detailed performance evaluation is presented and it turns out that the R*-tree outperforms the other R-tree variants. A performance comparison of the R*-tree, the R+-tree and the PMR-Quadtree is presented in [HS 92]. Various approximations are compared in [BKS 93a]. The minimum bounding 5-corner turns out to be best suited for spatial query processing.

The decomposition approach is examined in [Kri 91a] and [KHS 91]. Especially small queries are processed much faster using the convex and the trapezoid decomposition instead of the undecomposed representation. The integrated representation of a polygon decomposed into trapezoids using a TR*-tree is considered in [SK 91].

The combination of spatial objects to scenes is introduced in this paper for the first time. As mentioned before, we expect a considerable performance improvement by using this approach. This expectation is confirmed by a detailed performance evaluation of the scene architecture presented in the following subsection.

5.1 Evaluation of the scene organization

Basically, there are three different models for storing spatial objects:

1.) *Storing the exact object representations outside of the data pages (model 1)*

In the data pages of the index structure, we store the approximations and the pointers to the exact representations of the objects. The exact representation is stored outside the index structure, e.g. in a sequential file. This approach is used in quadtrees for instance [HS 92]. In other words, the spatial index structure is a primary index for the approximations and a secondary index for the spatial objects. This model is shown schematically in figure 10. The main advantage of this scheme is the large number of approximations stored together in one data page, i.e. a maximum degree of local ordering of the approximations is preserved. Furthermore, there is no limit to the size of the exact object representation. A fundamental drawback is the fact that the order preservation just refers to the object approximations and not to the objects themselves. Consequently, when processing range queries for each access to an exact object representation an additional page access is necessary.

2.) *Storing the exact object representation inside the data pages (model 2)*

The exact representation of the objects is stored, in addition to the approximations, inside the data pages. Therefore, spatial neighborhood is physically preserved and objects are transferred into main memory just using one disk access [Wid 91]. In contrast to the first model, the index structure is a primary index for the spatial objects and determines their storage location. An essential drawback of this approach is the low number of objects fitting into one page. As a consequence, neighboring objects are often stored in different pages. In section 2.2 we have emphasized that objects larger than one data page often occur in geographic databases. Handling these objects with the second model is a difficult task because a special page overflow mechanism has to be implemented.

3.) *Storing objects in a scene organization (model 3)*

This model has already been presented in section 4.4. Larger parts of the data are physically clustered within so called scenes and organized in an R*-tree.

In figure 10 the three models are depicted.

The scene organization has been designed for supporting large region queries. Considering such set-oriented queries, we have to take a closer look to two important problems:

- Which performance is gained by the three models ? Is the performance of the scene organization superior to the other two models ?
- Which size of the scenes leads to the best query performance ? Does this size significantly depend on the size of the range queries ?

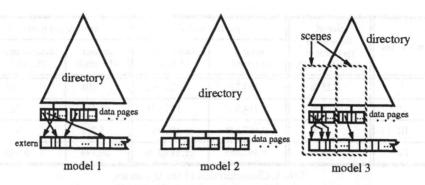

model 1   model 2   model 3

Fig. 10. Models for storing spatial objects

Test environment

To find an answer to these questions, we have carried out a detailed empirical performance comparison of the three models. We used real test data from the US Bureau of the
Census [Bur 89] containing county borders, highways, railway connections and rivers
of four Californian counties. This database consists of 119.151 lines, each consisting of
2 to 349 points. Each co-ordinate is represented by a real number of 8 Bytes. Altogether
the database has a size of 15.9 MByte. The lines were approximated by using minimal
bounding boxes. For the representation of these boxes 16 Bytes are available. These
boxes are depicted in figure 11 (a).

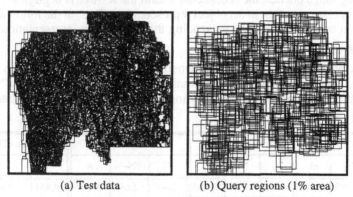

(a) Test data   (b) Query regions (1% area)

Fig. 11. Data and queries used for the tests

Using this data set we built up three R*-trees referring to the three different models. The
page capacity was 4 KByte.

To investigate the performance of the models for large query regions, we carried out
four test series with different sizes of the query regions. Each series consists of 464
quadratic window queries uniformly distributed over the data space covered by the objects. The area of the query regions varies between 0.25% and 16% of the data space.
In figure 11 (b) the 1% queries are shown. Table 1 presents the query specification of
the four test series.

test series	size of the queries (per cent of the data space)	per test series		average per query	
		number of records	data volume (KByte)	number of records	data volume (KByte)
I	0.25 %	189,229	29,392	408	63
II	1 %	714,937	105,521	1,541	227
III	4 %	2,687,648	382,483	5,792	824
IV	16 %	9,462,455	1,315,236	20,393	2,835

Tab. 1. Characteristics of the test series

To evaluate the performance of the three models, we need a measure for the access cost. The time necessary for reading one page into main memory consists of the search time, i.e. the time needed for locating the page on secondary storage, and the transfer time, i.e. the time needed to transfer the data from secondary into main memory. Normalize the cost for a transfer operation to 1. Then in real magnetic disk drives the cost for a search operation is approximately 10 [PH 90]. If N_S denotes the number of search operations and N_T denotes the number of transfer operations then the complete access cost A is given by:

$$A = 10N_S + N_T$$

Considering range queries, the access cost within the R*-tree is negligible in comparison to the access cost of the exact object representation. Thus, in the following, we take into account only the access cost for reading the exact object representation.

Test results:

In table 2, we present the access cost when storing the lines outside the data pages (model 1). The number of search operations (N_S), the number of transfers (N_T) and the access cost A are presented (in the following table, A is not directly calculated from N_S and N_T due to rounding).

test series I (0,25 %)			test series II (1 %)			test series III (4 %)			test series IV (16 %)		
N_S	N_T	A	N_S	N_T	A	N_S	N_T	A	N_S	N_T	A
189	189	2,082	715	715	7,864	2,688	2,689	29,585	9,462	9,463	104,088

Tab. 2. Access cost for model 1 (in thousand, rounded)

Storing the exact object representation outside the data page, requires at least one (expensive) search operation for each answer, because of the missing spatial organization of the exact object representations.

Table 3 contains the results for model 2, i.e. for storing the lines inside the data pages.

test series I (0,25 %)			test series II (1 %)			test series III (4 %)			test series IV (16 %)		
N_S	N_T	A	N_S	N_T	A	N_S	N_T	A	N_S	N_T	A
16	16	175	52	52	573	180	180	1,985	610	610	6,710

Tab. 3. Access cost for model 2 (in thousand, rounded)

Compared to model 1, model 2 needs considerably less search operations. The reason for this behavior is the fact that many neighboring objects are stored in just one data page and read into main memory by one access. The improvement only marginally depends on the size of the query ranges. N_T has basically the same size as N_S, because in the test data only a few records are larger than one page.

In the scene organization (model 3), the results considerably depend on the average size of the scenes. Using model 1, the exact object representation is only accessed if it is necessary for query processing. Contrarily, in the second model exact object representations are read into the main memory if they are close to the margin of the query region, but do not intersect the query region (*false hits*). Large scenes need only a small number of search operations but a high number of transfers from the secondary to the main memory due to the large number of false hits. On the other hand, the smaller the scenes, the higher the effort for searching and the lower the number of transfers. To examine this effect in more detail and to determine the optimal scene size, we varied the scene size in our comparisons. The results are presented in table 4 where the best results are shaded.

average scene size (Byte)	test series I (0.25 %)			test series II (1 %)			test series III (4 %)			test series IV (16 %)		
	N_S	N_T	A	N_S	N_T	A	N_S	N_T	A	N_S	N_T	A
1,852,750	1.1	698	709	1.2	781	794	1.6	943	959	2.1	1,666	1,188
757,943	1.2	275	287	1.6	343	345	2.4	505	529	4.1	837	877
273,357	1.5	128	144	2.3	185	208	4.2	324	365	8.6	638	725
140,124	1.8	78	96	3.0	123	153	6.0	238	298	14.1	528	669
91,619	2.2	62	84	3.9	103	142	8.5	214	299	20.8	503	711
79,027	2.1	51	72	3.9	90	130	8.8	191	280	22.7	474	701
63,402	2.3	46	70	4.5	85	130	10.4	187	291	27.5	467	742
33,283	3.2	36	68	6.7	70	137	17.3	167	340	48.8	447	936
18,610	4.2	26	68	10.0	57	158	27.8	151	429	82.8	432	1,260
10,716	6.1	23	84	15.4	54	209	45.6	153	609	140	452	1,853
8,367	6.8	21	87	18.2	52	235	55.6	152	708	175	460	2,210

Tab. 4. Access cost for the scene organization (model 3) (in thousand, rounded)

As expected, with increasing scene size N_S decreases and N_T increases. Scene sizes between 25 and 100 KByte lead to minimum access cost, depending on the size of the queries. The larger the queries, the larger the optimal scene size. However, this dependency is not as strong as expected. There is a factor of 64 in the size of the queries between test series I and IV, but only a factor of 4 in the resulting optimal scene sizes. Additionally, the graphs for the cost functions are very flat close to their minimum. Thus, we chose 77 KByte as a nearly optimal scene size for all test series.

Conclusion

In table 5, the access cost for all three models is presented. The cost for model 1 is standardized to "1". For the other two models the numbers describe the speed up factor for query processing using these models. The average scene size for model 3 is 79,027 Bytes.

model	speed up factors for query processing			
	I (0.25 %)	II (1 %)	III (4 %)	IV (16 %)
1: Geometry outside of the data pages	1.0	1.0	1.0	1.0
2: Geometry inside the data pages	11.9	13.7	14.9	15.5
3: Scene organization	28.9	60.5	105.7	148.5

Tab. 5. Speed up factors for query processing using model 2 and 3 in comparison to model 1

In conclusion, we would like to point out the following statements:

- Storing the exact object representation inside the data pages (model 2) speeds up query processing by a factor of 12 to 15 in comparison to model 1 (using separate pages). The size of the query regions has only a small influence on this factor. For the interpretation of the results one remark is important: The objects used for the tests are relatively small in comparison to the size of the data pages. Using larger objects, i.e. objects larger than one data page, requires storing the exact representation outside of the data pages. As a consequence, query performance of model 2 comes closer to the performance of model 1.

- The new scene organization is the clear winner of the performance comparison. Even the processing of small queries is performed considerably faster by this storage model. For small queries, we have a speed up factor of about 30 (in comparison to model 1) which is increasing to the impressive value of 148 for large queries.

  Another important result is the fact that the optimal scene size is almost independent of the query sizes. Therefore, using the scene architecture with a fixed scene size is beneficial to queries of very different size.

  Furthermore, the flat form of the cost function guarantees a considerable speed up of the query processing, even if the average size of the scene is varying caused by insertions and deletions of objects.

6 Conclusion

We proposed a *storage and access architecture for geographic database systems*. This architecture integrates a number of various concepts and techniques for efficient query processing.

The *R*-tree* is the basic component of our geo architecture. It organizes the data on secondary storage with respect to their spatial location and shape. In this way, the search region of spatial queries can be quickly narrowed down. The next ingredient of our architecture are *object approximations*. They support an efficient preselection to decide whether an object fulfills the query or not. In comparison to the usually used minimum bounding box, the minimum 5-corner is a good compromise between the quality of the approximation and the amount of required storage. The exact geometric representation of an object is managed by a *TR*-tree*. The polygonal objects are decomposed into simpler components and organized with respect to their spatial location and shape. This allows a selective access to the components needed to process a spatial query. Due to the simplicity of the components, the application of time consuming computational geometry algorithms to complex objects is avoided. Thematic queries are supported by secondary indices for thematic attributes. These secondary indices are connected to the primary index, i.e. the R*-tree, using a link table.

The parts of our architecture mentioned above support efficient processing of queries with high spatial selectivity, i.e. point queries and small window queries. To speed up the set-oriented object access of large range queries, we added a new ingredient to our architecture: the *scene organization*. Using this new approach, large parts of the data are combined in scenes and spatially clustered on secondary storage. These scenes are organized within the primary R*-tree. We investigated the performance of this approach in a detailed performance comparison. For large range queries, the scene organization is superior in performance to ordinary storage models with a speed up factor up to two orders of magnitude.

The use of our architecture is not restricted to geographic information systems. With only slight modifications it can also be used in systems for computer aided design (CAD) or computer integrated manufacturing (CIM).

In our future work, we plan to incorporate our geo architecture into an existing extensible database system for spatial applications. Promising candidates for this idea are DASDBS, GRAL and POSTGRES. Performance evaluations of our geo architecture after incorporating it into such a system will be very interesting.

Furthermore the design of *a parallel geo architecture* is an interesting challenge for future research activities. Parallelism should be exploited in two ways. First, we want to use a multi processor system to process queries in main memory in a massively parallel way. Using object decomposition techniques in a parallel environment promises a considerable performance improvement. Second, we want to use multi disk systems to organize the large data volume of geographic applications more efficiently. The main problem to solve is, to determine an appropriate distribution of the data over the different disk drives.

The application of the presented techniques to *3D-objects* is another interesting field of research activities for the future. For example, bio-computing is an important field of application for 3D-spatial objects. The first step in this direction is the development and implementation of 3D-approximation and decomposition techniques.

References

[Aro 91] Aronoff S.: *'Geographic Information Systems'*, WDL Publications, 1991.

[Bar 88] Bartelme N.: *'GIS Technology: Geographic information systems, land information systems and their fundamentals'* (in German), Springer, 1988.

[BKS 93a] Brinkhoff T., Kriegel H.-P., Schneider R.: *'Comparison of Approximations of Complex Objects used for Approximation-based Query Processing in Spatial Database Systems'*, Proc. 9th Int. Conf. on Data Engineering, Vienna, Austria, 1993.

[BKS 93b] Brinkhoff T., Kriegel H.-P., Schneider R.: *'Scene Organization: A Technique for Global Clustering in Spatial Database Systems'*, 1993, submitted for publication.

[BKSS 90] Beckmann N., Kriegel H.-P., Schneider R., Seeger B.: *'The R*-tree: An Efficient and Robust Access Method for Points and Rectangles'*, Proc. ACM SIGMOD Int. Conf. on Management of Data, Atlantic City, NJ., 1990, pp. 322-331.

[Bur 86] Burrough P.A.: *'Principles of Geographical Information Systems for Land Resources Assessment'*, Oxford University Press, 1986.

[Bur 89] Bureau of the Census: *'TIGER/Line Percensus Files, 1990 Technical Documentation'*, Washington, DC., 1989.

[CDRS 86] Carey M. J., DeWitt D. J., Richardson J. E., Shekita E. J.: *'Object and File Management in the EXODUS Extensible Database System'*, Proc. 12th Int. Conf. on Very Large Data Bases, Kyoto, Japan, 1986, pp. 91-100.

[Cra 90] Crain I.K.: *'Extremely Large Spatial Information Systems - A Quantitative Perspective'*, Proc. 4th Int. Symp. on Spatial Data Handling, Zürich, Switzerland, 1990, pp. 632-641.

[Fra 91] Frank, A.U.: *'Properties of Geographic Data'*, Proc. 2nd Symp. on Large Spatial Databases, Zürich, Switzerland, 1991, in: Lecture Notes in Computer Science, Vol. 525, Springer, 1991, pp. 225-234.

[GC 87] Gorny A.J., Carter R.: *'World Data Bank II: General users guide'*, Technical report, U.S. Central Intelligence Agency, Washington, 1987.

[Gut 84] Guttman A.: *'R-trees: A Dynamic Index Structure for Spatial Searching'*, Proc. ACM SIGMOD Int. Conf. on Management of Data, Boston, MA., 1984, pp. 47-57.

[Güt 89] Güting R. H.: *'Gral: an extensible relational database system for geografic applications'*, Proc. 15th Int. Conf. on Very Large Data Bases, Amsterdam, Netherland, 1989, pp. 33-44.

[HS 92] Hoel E.G., Samet H.: *'A Qualitative Comparison Study of Data Structures for Large Line Segment Databases'*, Proc. SIGMOD Conf., San Diego, CA., 1992, pp 205-214.

[HSW 88] Hutflesz A., Six H.-W., Widmayer P.: *'Globally Order Preserving Multidimensional Linear Hashing'*, Proc. 4th Int. Conf. on Data Engineering, Los Angeles, CA., 1988, pp. 572-579.

[HWZ 91] Hutflesz A., Widmayer P., Zimmermann C.: *'Global Order Makes Spatial Access Faster'*, Int. Workshop on Database Management Systems for Geographical Applications, Capri, Italy, 1991, in: Geographic Database Management Systems, Springer, 1992, pp. 161-176.

[KBS 91] Kriegel H.-P., Brinkhoff T., Schneider R.: *'An Efficient Map Overlay Algorithm based on Spatial Access Methods and Computational Geometry'*, Int. Workshop on Database Management Systems for Geographical Applications, Capri, Italy, 1991, in: Geographic Database Management Systems, Springer, 1992, pp. 194-211.

[KHS 91] Kriegel H.-P., Horn H., Schiwietz M.: *'The Performance of Object Decomposition Techniques for Spatial Query Processing'*, Proc. 2nd Symp. on Large Spatial Databases, Zürich, Switzerland, 1991, in: Lecture Notes in Computer Science, Vol. 525, Springer, 1991, pp. 257-276.

[Kri 91a] Kriegel H.-P., Heep P., Heep S., Schiwietz M., Schneider R.: *'An Access Method Based Query Processor for Spatial Database Systems'*, Int. Workshop on Database Management Systems for Geographical Applications, Capri, Italy, 1991, in: Geographic Database Management Systems, Springer, 1992, pp. 273-292.

[Kri 91b] Kriegel H.-P., Heep P., Heep S., Schiwietz M., Schneider R.: *'A Flexible and Extensible Index Manager for Spatial Database Systems'*, Proc. 2nd Int. Conf. on Database and Expert Systems Applications, Berlin, Germany, 1991, pp. 179-184.

[Ore 89] Orenstein J. A.: *'Redundancy in Spatial Databases'*, Proc. ACM SIGMOD Int. Conf. on Management of Data, Portland, USA, 1989, pp. 294-305.

[PH 90] Paterson D., Hennessy J.: *'Computer Architecture: A Quantitative Approach'*, Morgan Kaufman, 1990.

[PS 88] Preparata F.P., Shamos M.I.: *'Computational Geometry'*, Springer, 1988.

[Sam 90] Samet H.: *'The Design and Analysis of Spatial Data Structures'*, Addison Wesley, 1990.

[Sch 92] Schneider R.: *'A Storage and Access Structure for Spatial Database Systems'*, Ph.D.-thesis (in German), Institute for Computer Science, University of Munich, 1992.

[SK 91]   Schneider R., Kriegel H.-P.: *'The TR*-tree: A New Representation of Polygonal Objects Supporting Spatial Queries and Operations'*, Proc. 7th Workshop on Computational Geometry, Bern, Switzerland, 1991, in: Lecture Notes in Computer Science, Vol. 553, Springer, 1991, pp. 249-264.

[SR 86]   Stonebraker M., Rowe L.: *'The Design of POSTGRES'*, Proc. ACM SIGMOD Conf. on Management of Data, Washinton D.C., 1986.

[SV 89]   Scholl M., Voisard A.: *'Thematic Map Modelling'*, Proc. 1st Symp. on the Design and Implementation of Large Spatial Databases, Santa Barbara, CA., 1989, in: Lecture Notes in Computer Science, Vol. 409, Springer, 1990, pp. 167-190.

[SW 86]   Schek H.-J., Waterfeld W.: *'A Database Kernel System for Geoscientific Applications'*, Proc. 2nd Int. Symp. on Spatial Data Handling, Seattle, Washington, 1986, pp. 273-288.

[Wei 89]   Weikum G.: *'Set-Oriented Disk Access to Large Complex Objects'*, Proc. 5th Int. Conf. on Data Engineering, Los Angeles, CA., 1989, pp. 426-433.

[Wid 91]   Widmayer P.: *'Data Structures for Spatial Databases'* (in German) in: Vossen G., Witt K.-U. (eds.): 'Entwicklungstendenzen bei Datenbank-Systemen' (Future Trends in Database Systems), Oldenbourg, 1991, pp. 317-361.

Query Processing of Spatial Objects: Complexity versus Redundancy

Michael Schiwietz and Hans-Peter Kriegel

Institute for Computer Science, University of Munich
Leopoldstr. 11B, D-8000 Munich 40, Germany
e-mail: {michael,kriegel}@dbs.informatik.uni-muenchen.de

Abstract: The management of complex spatial objects in applications, such as geography and cartography, imposes stringent new requirements on spatial database systems, in particular on efficient query processing. As shown before, the performance of spatial query processing can be improved by decomposing complex spatial objects into simple components. Up to now, only decomposition techniques generating a linear number of very simple components, e.g. triangles or trapezoids, have been considered. In this paper, we will investigate the natural trade-off between the complexity of the components and the redundancy, i.e. the number of components, with respect to its effect on efficient query processing. In particular, we present two new decomposition methods generating a better balance between the complexity and the number of components than previously known techniques. We compare these new decomposition methods to the traditional undecomposed representation as well as to the well-known decomposition into convex polygons with respect to their performance in spatial query processing. This comparison points out that for a wide range of query selectivity the new decomposition techniques clearly outperform both the undecomposed representation and the convex decomposition method. More important than the absolute gain in performance by a factor of up to an order of magnitude is the robust performance of our new decomposition techniques over the whole range of query selectivity.

1 Introduction

The trend of digitizing the wide field of graphic and geographic real world objects results in a strongly growing amount of spatial data with no end in sight. The handling of spatial data is an essential feature in a wide range of applications, such as geographic information systems, image databases, multimedia databases, engineering (CAD/CAM/CAE), as well as geographic and medical applications. Furthermore, the same set of data such as maps often has to be provided for different application areas and different access patterns. Due to data centralization efforts supporting different applications by one central database system, these data have to be managed by a flexible and extensible query processing system which can be extended regarding application specific requirements. Therefore, the demand for a support by a global integrated spatial database system is considerably increasing.

One important characteristic of most spatial applications is the occurrence of complex spatial objects and their algorithmic treatment including query processing. In a relational database system, spatial objects would artificially spread over serveral relations. As a consequence, they have to be rebuilt on an operational level. Thus, spatial query processing is inefficient and unflexible. Therefore, the management of complex spatial objects imposes stringent new requirements on integrated spatial database systems and particularly, on an efficient processing of spatial queries.

An important class of objects occurring in spatial applications are two-dimensional spatial objects. A spatial object is embedded within a global spatially oriented data space. Points, lines, and rectangles are known as simple spatial objects, because their complete geometry and structural description is given by a small and fixed number of parameters. In contrast, complex spatial objects with an application specific complexity, such as contour lines, limits of lots, and contours of CAD objects are often shaped in the form of simple polygons. Complexity properties of such polygonal objects, such as the shape, the number of vertices, the area or the smoothness of the contour are difficult to predict.

Spatial objects occurring in real applications are typically not homogeneous with respect to the number of vertices, the smoothness of the shape, or the object-area. As outlined in [Fra 91] these parameters underly an extreme variance even for objects of one and the same application. Because simple and complex spatial objects are heterogeneously stored within the same set of data, an object-oriented organisation and query processing is essential.

Spatial queries combine the requirements of a spatial locality search and an exact evaluation of complex geometric properties. Therefore, the handling of complex spatial objects concerns their management on secondary storage as well as the evaluation of main memory algorithms from the field of computational geometry. The traditional approach uses bounding box approximations representing their spatial location clustered by spatial access methods (SAMs; see e.g. [NHS 84], [See 89]) and applies complex computational geometry algorithms to their exact representation. This appoach reveals strong disadvantages caused by the coarse approximation and the expensive computational geometry algorithms. These drawbacks are avoided by object decomposition techniques introduced in [KHS 91]. However, object decomposition techniques use a set of simple components representing a complex spatial object. The number of components, called *redundancy* in the remainder of this paper, results in a storage and query processing overhead. Due to the high amount of redundancy of the traditional object decomposition techniques, e.g. triangulations, the storage overhead is unacceptable and the efficiency of spatial queries decreases with an increasing size of the query region. Therefore, the development of new object decomposition techniques is essential for providing a locality based object treatment and for strongly limiting the amount of redundancy.

In this paper, we will in detail examine the correlation between spatial clustering given by SAMs and computational geometry techniques (e.g. [PS 88]). We will introduce new object-oriented decomposition methods that combine both a locality based representation and a small amount of redundancy. An evaluation of spatial query processing shows the superiority of our new decomposition methods compared to known approaches for typical queries of spatial applications.

The paper is organized as follows: the next section contains an overview of known techniques combining spatial clustering and computational geometry using object decomposition techniques for the improvement of geometric algorithms. Section 3 discusses complexity and redundancy aspects. Our new locality based spatial object decomposition techniques regarding object and application oriented requirements are introduced and evaluated in the sections 4 and 5. In section 6, we present a performance comparison between these new representation schemes and the traditional methods. Section 7 concludes the paper.

2 Spatial query processing based on object decomposition

A typical property of spatial queries is their strictly restricted spatial location within the global data space. Only that location and some limited neighboring area can contribute to the query result. Depending on its restricted spatial locality, a query is called *selective* or *non-selective*. Selective queries limit the area of concern and, therefore, the number of objects relevant to the query, whereas non-selective queries require the examination of large portions of the data space.

Obviously, spatial queries are order-preserving. Objects lying close together in the data space are often accessed together. Therefore, a physical clustering of objects with respect to their spatial location is essential for providing an efficient locality based and selective access to the objects. A good spatial clustering is maintained by SAMs commonly known from the literature. In the absence of such spatial clustering, no spatial locality can be exploited by the query processing algorithm. Each stored object has to be explicitly evaluated against the query condition often requiring very time consuming algorithms. This causes a poor query performance which is further decreasing with an increasing number of objects and object complexity. Therefore, one essential ingredient of a spatial database system with respect to an efficient locality based spatial query processing is a good spatial clustering of the objects with respect to their natural spatial location.

A direct handling of complex spatial objects requires a high amount of algorithmic complexity in managing spatial accesses. For this reason, no SAM is available for complex spatial objects and for the class of simple polygons particularly.

For providing efficient handling and query processing of spatial objects traditionally the following approach is applied. Every complex spatial object is placed within a rectilinear rectangle of minimum area forming a simple *container*. A simple spatial object is called container iff any point inside the contour of the object is also contained in the contour of the container. This yields a so-called conservative approximation. For any closed spatial object, a unique minimum rectangular container can be generated. The container object substitutes the original object with respect to its spatial clustering, representing its approximate location and extension within data space.

As simple containers just provide a coarse approximation of arbitrary spatial objects, query processing is performed in a two step approach. The first step, called filter step, reduces the entire set of spatial objects to a subset of candidates applying a process of spatial locality search. This process exploits the SAM facilities in managing simple containers. It is based on the following property:

If the container does not fulfill the query condition, then this is also true for the corresponding spatial object.

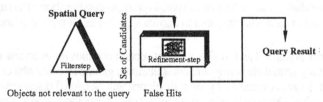

Fig. 1. The two-step approach of a spatial query processing

Therefore, a spatial query on the file of container objects yields a subset of objects definitely including the set of answers to the query. However, the filter step does not exactly evaluate the query, but only yields a set of candidates which potentially may fulfill the query condition. Therefore, those candidates have to be further examined in a second step, the refinement step. The refinement step applies complex spatial algorithms known from the field of computational geometry to the candidates. It detects those objects, actually belonging to the set of answers to the query. Due to these tasks, the filter step is based on a spatial indexing scheme for simple spatial objects, e.g. rectilinear rectangles, representing object containers. The filter step is I/O-intensive, whereas the refinement step using main-memory based computational geometry algorithms is CPU-intensive.

For many years, it was a common agreement that the query performance within database systems is determined by the time necessary for secondary storage accesses. This was due to the fact that main memory operations remained cheap and thus could be neglected. Therefore, minimizing the number of disk accesses was the main goal heading for good performance in a query system. However, if the complexity of the objects and, therefore, the time consumed by main memory algorithms is high, accesses to secondary storage are still important but are definitely no longer the major factor determining query performance. Therefore, in the case of spatial database systems, the more complex spatial objects are, the more dominating are the spatial algorithms performed within main memory. A ´Point in Object´-test, for example, performed on a polygon with 10,000 vertices, occurring in real world geographic applications, consumes the same amount of time as a few 100 secondary storage accesses, with the exact break-even-point depending on the underlying hardware. Therefore, not only the filter step, but also and more important the refinement step determines the overall performance of complex spatial queries.

At first glance, the conservative approach of directly coupling a SAM and computational geometry algorithms seemed to provide a good and general method for a spatial query processing on arbitrary spatial objects. However, more detailed considerations reveal considerable disadvantages:

- examinations of real world geographic object files turned out the bad approximation provided by rectangular containers with some 100% additionally covered area ([Schi 93]). This leads to roughly twice the number of candidates with respect to the cardinality of the answers for point queries.

- the refinement of one single object is very costly, particularly if the object complexity is high. Complex and time-consuming geometric algorithms evaluating the global shape of the objects have to be applied. Generally, no local restriction can be found limiting the evaluation to local aspects of the object.

The first effort to optimize the performance of the refinement step is obviously an optimization of the underlying spatial algorithms using sophisticated techniques from the field of computational geometry. In fact, this isolated tuning of the algorithms for the refinement step will lead to a considerable enhancement in comparison to ad hoc implementations, but is obviously constrained. The main disadvantage of computational geometry algorithms is that complete spatial objects are handled even if only some local aspects of those objects are relevant to a given query.

The next step for improving query processing concerns the approximation quality. The approximation quality of spatial containers can be enhanced by two ways: using a more complex container or using a set of simple objects as a container. More complex containers introduced in [Schi 93] require more complex SAMs ([Gün 89], [Jag 90], [Schi 93]) and do not affect the complexity of the spatial object itself. In contrast, object decompositions combined with set-oriented containers based on the set of components result in a tuning of both the filter step and the refinement step.

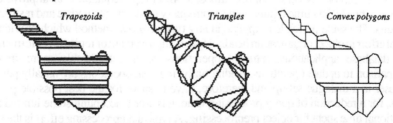

Trapezoids   *Triangles*   *Convex polygons*

Fig. 2. Decomposition of spatial objects into simple components

In [KHS 91] the spatial and algorithmic overhead of object decomposition techniques have been evaluated and shown to be worthwhile. Following the algorithmic concept of ‘*divide and conquer*’, the decomposition of complex spatial objects into triangles, trapezoids, rectangles, or even convex polygons leads to both a better performance of the filter step and simpler spatial algorithms on simple components. The main drawback is given by the huge amount of components. For triangles and trapezoids (see figure 2), the number of components grows linearly in the number of vertices of the original object. This is due to the fact that the particular components are characterized by topological and not by spatial aspects. Surprisingly, this is also true for the convex decomposition. The reason can be found in the typically high number of 'notches' or reflex angles in the contour of geographic objects violating the condition of convexity caused by digitalization aspects. The large number of components leads to a high amount of redundancy and thus results in a slow performance of low-selectivity spatial queries.

A computational geometry structure providing a spatially restricted search on an object decomposed into a number of trapezoids is given by the trapezoid tree ([PS 88]). Decomposing a spatial object into an $O(n \cdot \log n)$ number of components leads to a totally ordered decomposition scheme. This allows an efficient refinement evaluation of point queries based on binary search over the object shape. However, the high amount of storage, the insufficient handling of extended query regions as well as the applicability to other types of queries prevent the use of this scheme in real world applications.

Similarly, the TR*-tree ([SK 91], [Schn 92]) tunes the refinement step by introducing a spatial locality on the object shape based on a decomposition into trapezoids. The set of components is organized by the hierarchical index of the R*-tree ([BKSS 90]). Spatial queries are processed by a tree search directed by the object shape. Because of the locality based definition of the trapezoid decomposition ([KHS 91]), their overlap is small. However, the large amount of components and structural pointers implies that the index needs about the same amount of storage as the original object description. This high amount of additional storage as well as the fact that no spatial storage scheme is provided and complete objects have to be transmitted into main memory is the main drawback of this approach.

However, all these decomposition approaches including the large number of grid based representation schemes (e.g. [Sam 90], [Ore 89], [OM 86]) provide no flexibility for object or application specific requirements to the shape or the complexity of the original object. This is due to the strict condition of the partitioning process given by a predefined constraint to the shape and structure of the components. Therefore, no object-oriented paradigm is applicable controlling the decomposition algorithm.

In the next section, we consider the main aspects of the number and the complexity of the components in spatial object representations.

3 Complexity versus redundancy

The basic idea of any persistent decomposed object representation is to improve query performance by shifting time requirements from query processing to update and restructuring operations. The same principle is applied in any type of access method which provides an additional effort in object organization heading for an improvement of retrieval performance. In typical database applications, retrieval operations occur considerably more frequently in comparison to update operations. Additionally, retrieval operations are usually performed by the user in a dialogue set-up and therefore, have to strive for the best possible performance. Thus, for a reduction of query processing time, it is worth accepting some limited amount of additional time spent for object preprocessing. A typical preprocessing effort is the precomputation of computational geometry aspects.

The persistent handling of such precomputations causes a storage overhead in the object representation as compared to the handling of an object as a linear sequence of vertices. Some additional storage is required for maintaining geometric and topologic locality. Typically for the representation of spatial objects, a preprocessing step is used transforming complex spatial objects into a set of simpler components where the number of components determines the degree of redundancy.

Up to now, two main approaches of structural object representation schemes are known for spatial databases:

- the conservative approach inducing no structural redundancy at all (no decomposition)
- a linear number of components as a result of structural decompositions into very simple spatial components.

As shown before, both approaches are not best suitable for a global spatial retrieval system. The conservative approach avoids redundant object representation at all. Therefore, it is lacking of any spatial object structuring. The whole object geometry has to be transmitted into main memory even if resulting in a false hit. Geometric operations are dependent on the global shape and therefore, perform rather slow, particularly for very complex objects.

In contrast, structural object decompositions define a spatial structure on the object shape. However, the object decomposition into components of a simple shape with constant complexity results in a high number of components. As every component independent of the object represents a constant measure of complexity, the cardinality of the set of components grows linearly in the object complexity. Caused by this high redundancy, spatial query processing is burdened by the following problems and deficiencies:

- time consuming filter step in the case of low-selectivity queries
- high amount of structural redundancy and thus high amount of storage
- complex and expensive inversion of the decomposition process, i.e. generation of the original object from the components
- very expensive update- and delete-operations (e.g. updating or deleting one or a few vertices of a spatial object)

The principal intention of any structural decomposition is replacing retrieval complexity by preprocessing and representational redundancy. Considering the drawbacks listed above, the central question is now:

Which degree of redundancy is best suitable for efficient spatial query processing?

Both representations considered up to now reveal an extreme imbalance between the number and the complexity of their components. While the conservative representation (called 'identity' in the remainder of this paper) combines a redundancy free representation with a linear complexity, structural decompositions shift the whole amount of complexity to a linear number of components each incorporating a constant complexity.

According to the results of our experimental analysis in [KHS 91], both approaches, caused by their unbalanced object representations, obviously reveal weaknesses depending on the query selectivity. In the case of high-selectivity queries, the high structural complexity determines the performance of the identity which can frequently be fully answered based on the container-object for low-selective spatial query conditions. The clustering mechanism of SAMs provides a good filtering of redundancy for structural decompositions in the case of high-selectivity queries, whereas low-selectivity queries degenerate due to the high amount of redundancy (see [KHS 91]). From this observation, we conclude the following statement:

A balanced ratio between complexity and redundancy is essential for efficient spatial query processing.

This ratio is determined using an interaction of both steps of query processing. The handling of an adapted degree of redundancy within the filter step is justified by a gain in efficiency within the refinement step. The main criteria are given by an increased approximation quality, i.e. a decreased number of false hits, and particularly by simpler and more efficient geometric operations on local parts of the object.

These considerations lead to the development of newly designed structural decomposition methods that show a good performance for both selective queries because of a good approximation and simple geometric operations, as well as for non-selective queries because of a strongly reduced amount of redundancy. The main issue is the combination of the following opposing criteria:

- geometric and topologic locality in object representation
- low amount of redundancy

In order to fulfill both demands, the goals of structural object decompositions have to be newly defined. Contrary to the traditional object decomposition methods, there are strongly increased degrees of freedom compared to the strict definition of the shape, the complexity, and the topology of the components. This yields a lot of criteria for designing efficient decomposition algorithms which could not be considered by the rigid definition of the component properties in traditional object decompositions.

4 Object-orientied partitioning methods

The central idea of the class of structural decompositions of spatial objects considered below is the complete and disjoint partitioning of a simple polygon into a set of spatial components each of them representing a locally restricted part of the original object with a given complexity. A characterization of this amount of complexity is given by a suitable *constraint of simplicity* (see figure 3). Up to now, for object decompositions this constraint was limited to the shape of a very simple spatial object or was given by the topological convexity property and thus, extremely restrictive. Contrarily, for the identity it is given by the shape of an arbitrary simple polygon and thus, represents no restriction at all.

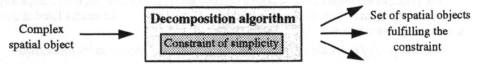

Fig. 3. General scheme of the decomposition algorithm

The correspondence between the number of components, i.e. the redundancy, and their complexity can be expressed by the following formula:

$$Red = \frac{c_{Obj} + a \cdot Red}{c_{comp}} \quad \text{which implies: } Red = \frac{c_{Obj}}{c_{comp} - a}$$

where c_{Obj} and c_{comp} represent the complexity, i.e. the number of vertices, of the original object and of one decomposition component, respectively, and a denotes the structural overhead induced by one step of partitioning. Typical values are $a = 2$ if the partitioning process is restricted to the vertices of the original object, i.e. two original vertices are combined, and $a = 3$ in the case of Steinerpoints.

The constraint of simplicity directly affects both the complexity of the components and the redundancy and therefore, has to be carefully selected. One essential criterion neglected in previous approaches is given by application specific constraints to spatial objects. Such criteria like the existence of holes or the restriction of spatial objects to a maximum number of vertices depending on the application system can be expressed by a corresponding constraint to the partitioning process.

By the instantiation of this constraint, an approximate goal of the decomposition process is established. However, no algorithmic designs are specified. Thus, there remains a lot of flexibility for the decomposition process to be filled by the implementation. In the following, we will first investigate these algorithmic flexibilities before examining the constraint of simplicity with respect to the criteria of redundancy and complexity.

Algorithmic degrees of freedom

The constraint of simplicity defines what type of components have to be generated while the algorithmic instantiation describes *how* to derive them. Thus, the instantiation of the decomposition method is bound to some optimization criteria determining the performance of spatial query processing.

- axis parallel or free oriented partitioning

  Any partitioning with lines parallel to the axes of the data space typically induces Steiner-points. Therefore, as a result, there is a higher amount of structural overhead. Contrarily, free oriented methods with a more flexible selection of partitioning lines may join vertices and thus avoid those drawbacks. However, the container approximation is strongly affected by the orientation of the partitioning lines. Vertical and horizontal lines provide a good bounding box approximation, whereas partitioning lines with angles in $\{k \cdot \pi / 4, \; k \in \{1, 3, 5, 7\}\}$ maximize dead space. Therefore, even for orientation free approaches a 'nearly' axis parallel partitioning is advisable.

- geometric and topologic locality

  The central idea of object decompositions is a local and selective processing of complex spatial objects. Therefore, geometric locality is the crucial property of structural decompositions. With regard to applications such as the organization of versioned objects or geographic and topologic maps with neighboring areas expressed by common polylines, the preservation of a topologic locality is essential as well.

- regularity of the components

  A basic requirement to the representation of spatial objects in real applications is a guarantee for stability and the exclusion of degenerations. This demand is important with respect to spatial, redundancy, and structural aspects. It affects the partitioning process by strict conditions concerning the extension, the number and the complexity of the components. These criteria strongly depend on the object topology and partially describe opposing requirements. Therefore, for designing the partitioning process an integrated consideration of those requirements is necessary. Between opposing parameters, a weighting with a sufficient variability has to be determined for a global consistency and applicability.

  An example for a spatial criterion of regularity can be found in the Delauney-triangulation of simple polygons. It is the *'Lawson-criterion'* ([Law 72]) incorporating a regularity condition on the angles of the triangles. Contrarily, the trapezoid decomposition ([AA 83]) is not bound to any regularity in the shape of the trapezoids and thus, may create degenerated 'line-shaped' components. The decomposition methods investigated in [KHS 91] do not fulfill all regularity criteria outlined above as shown in table 1.

- small number of components (minimum decompositions)

  Beside those degeneration aspects there is the demand for a manageable number of components regarding certain complexity constraints. A minimum number of components generally imposes very expensive algorithms typically with NP-complete or NP-hard time complexity ([Kei 83], [KS 85]). Particularly, for a dynamic decomposition method meeting some regularity conditions, it is inevitable to relax the strict minimality criterion. Instead an algorithmically more simple, suboptimal method with more flexibilities has to be designed.

	shape	redundancy	complexity
trapezoid decomposition	-	+	+
convex decomposition	-	+	، -
identity	-	+	-

Table 1: Regularity of spatial object representations

Having surveyed the general aspects concerning the partitioning process of structural decompositions, we next investigate an appropriate degree for the number of components and their structural complexity. As there is no general answer for an arbitrary type of spatial objects and applications, we develop a set of criteria serving as a basis to an adequate redundancy instantiation for a given application. However, topologic aspects remain unconsidered in this context.

The amount of redundancy

Based on the variety and heterogeneity of geometric applications as well as on the structural variance of spatial objects, applicational and object-oriented aspects have to be considered defining the measure of redundancy in object representation. A global and flat rated instantiation is not possible. It rather depends on a set of factors influenced by the conditions of the underlying application. In the following, the important factors determining redundancy are explained.

- *object-oriented aspects*

  - *structural complexity*
    The complexity of a spatial object strongly influences the number of components. Obviously, an object with say 10 vertices, needs no partitioning at all, whereas a complex object consisting of 50,000 vertices should be partitioned into several hundreds of components.

  - *geometric shape and geometric complexity*
    For a simply shaped object, e.g. a convex polygon, less and simpler components are generated than for a strongly meandering object (see figure 5). This is due to the fact that the spatial locality of the components depends on the geometric complexity of the object

  - *object area relative to the data space*
    The strong variance of the area of spatial objects exerts a bad influence on the clustering and therefore, on the selectivity properties of SAMs. Thus, one goal is to homogenize the area and extension of spatial objects. Large objects are partitioned more distinctly than small objects.

- query oriented aspects
  Depending on the selectivity of application oriented spatial queries, a stronger preference for the number of components or for their complexity may be adequate. In the case of high-selectivity queries, e.g. point queries, a higher amount of redundancy is useful and vice versa (see the results in section 6 and [KHS 91]).

- hardware aspects
  The given hardware environment determines the ratio of the time for one secondary storage access to the time for one typical CPU-operation. Because redundancy is I/O-intensive, whereas complexity is CPU-intensive, the best possible balance between redundancy and complexity has to be tuned for a given hardware environment.

- application specific aspects
  Requirements to object complexity may be imposed by the application system. For example, a polygonal object has to fit in a single page on secondary storage and therefore, only a limited number of vertices are allowed.

- general aspects
  - *data page as clustering unit*
    The term of a data page represents the atomic unit of transfer between main memory and secondary storage. This observation leads to a component complexity approximately meeting the space of a data page. In this case, the redundancy corresponds to the number of data pages. As the structural overhead of the partitioning is low, the number of actual data pages is most likely not increased with respect to the linear sequence of pages, necessary for storing the complex object. However, a spatially organized and accessible set of pages takes the place of the sequentially organized traditional representation.

  - *dynamic balancing between redundancy and complexity*
    A 'fair' balance between redundancy and complexity is provided by the *root criterion*:

    A structural decomposition method fulfills the *root criterion*, if the complexity of the components is in the range of $[c \cdot \lceil \sqrt{n} \rceil, 2 \cdot c \cdot \lceil \sqrt{n} \rceil +1]$, where c is a real constant and n denotes the complexity of the original object. A typical measure of the constant c is given by $c \approx 1$.

    As an example, for a polygon with 100 (50,000) vertices the complexity of the 5-10 (112-223) components is in the range [10, 21] ([224, 449]).

Fig. 4. Examples of object-oriented decompositions

These aspects describe different starting-points for an adaptive selection of the number of components. We have shown that the number of components depends on various application specific aspects. Our goal within this paper is not an evaluation of all those aspects and their mutual affects but to present a number of different decomposition methods under the criterion of a constrained redundancy.

The next section will introduce several structural decomposition methods defining a simultaneous restriction of complexity and redundancy. Two basic methods will be introduced: composition methods are based on an object decomposition into very simple spatial components suitably merging those components to more complex components. However, fragmentation methods directly construct the components by a sophisticated definition of partitioning lines.

5 Object-oriented decomposition methods

Composition methods

Within this section, we generalize the decomposition methods into convex polygons, trapezoids, and heterogeneous components as described in [KHS 91] by merging a number of components to more complex component objects resulting in a decreased amount of redundancy.

Convex composition method

Convex decompositions are based on the treatment of notches, i.e. vertices violating the convexity property. Recursively introducing partitioning lines, in every step of the 'naive' partitioning process, components with a smaller number of notches are generated (see [CD 85]). This process finishes up with convex components containing no notches.

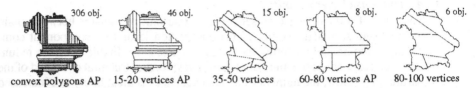

| 306 obj. | 46 obj. | 15 obj. | 8 obj. | 6 obj. |

| convex polygons AP | 15-20 vertices AP | 35-50 vertices | 60-80 vertices AP | 80-100 vertices |

Fig. 5. Examples of the convex composition method

The generalized approach imposes a new criterion on the break off of the partitioning process. Components are partitioned only if their complexity exceeds a predefined constant even if they contain notches. On the logical level, this constraint partitioning process corresponds to a merge of neighboring convex components. Figure 5 depicts the result of the partitioning process with a constraint number of vertices for the axis-parallel (AP) and the orientation free convex composition. The axis-parallel method is one of the competitors in the performance comparison given in section 6.

Trapezoid composition

The main drawbacks of the decomposition into trapezoids originate in the linear number of components and in their degenerated shape inducing a lacking spatial locality. However, the demand for axis parallelism in one dimension causes a partial order on the trapezoids characterizing a neighborhood relation on the components. Thus, a merging process on the set of trapezoids is simple and leads to still axis parallel but less degenerated components. This constrained merging process, however, hinders the definition of locality based components.

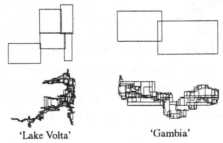

'Lake Volta'   'Gambia'

Fig. 6. First and second directory-level of an R^*-tree for heterogeneously decomposed objects

Heterogeneous composition

The heterogeneous decomposition (see [Schi 93], [KHS 91]) is based on a separation of the contour and the interior of a spatial object. The principal building block of a heterogeneous composition is given by a merge of components describing a locality based part of the object. Joining neighboring edges leads to a topologic locality, whereas their merge with suitable interior components preserves a geometric locality.

One possible instantiation of this merge process is given by the data pages of a clustering SAM. A merge of the components clustered, for example, in one data page of an R^*-tree, while checking some connectivity and integrity constraints yields a good spatial locality of the components (see figure 6).

Fragmentation methods

An alternative approach of object-oriented spatial decompositions of simple polygons is given by the class of fragmentation methods. Fragmentation methods directly decompose a spatial object with respect to a given simplicity constraint. The paradigm of a binary space partition is applied. As there is no preceding decomposition into simple components, a much more flexible partitioning process is available with respect to topologic, geometric, or structural object properties.

A wide range of different partitioning methods is available, all based on the fragmentation approach. We do not want to present all those variants, but describe one selected fragmentation method, which is efficient for a number of reasons.

Within the following, $p_i = (p_{i_x}, p_{i_y})$, $1 \leq i \leq m$, denotes the vertices of a simple polygon $P = (p_1, p_2, ..., p_m)$, where the edges of the polygon are given by pairs of consecutive vertices (p_1, p_2), (p_2, p_3), ..., (p_{m-1}, p_m), (p_m, p_1). Let $\langle p_i, p_j \rangle$ denote the line connecting the points p_i and p_j. Then $dist_{ind}(i,j) := min\{ (i-j+n) \text{ MOD } n, (j-i+n) \text{ MOD } n\}$ denotes the *index-distance* of p_i and p_j. The term of an index-distance describes the number of edges between two given vertices of P.

In the partitioning process, we connect vertices which have a minimum distance from each other under some constraints. Using the Euclidean distance, the following minimization function has to be solved for a polygon $P = (p_1, p_2, ..., p_m)$ and a predefined constant d_{min}:

$$\min_{1 \leq i \leq m} \left(\min_{i < j \leq m, \, dist_{ind}(i,j) \geq d_{min}, \, \langle p_i, p_j \rangle \subset P} (\sqrt{(p_{i_x} - p_{j_x})^2 + (p_{i_y} - p_{j_y})^2})\right).$$

Obviously, the primary effect of this procedure is a minimization of the unnatural contour and therefore, of the contour of the components. However, there are a number of advantageous consequences to the spatial and topological properties of the components.

- spatial and topologic locality of the components
- no Steinerpoints, i.e. no new vertices induced by the components
- small contact of the components defined by single edges and not by polylines
- object-oriented and not component-oriented approach

The realization of this decomposition method necessitates some additional examinations as described in the following:

- using the Euclidean metric for determining the minimum distances, we can make no statement with respect to the orientation of the partitioning lines. We expect uniformly distributed orientations in the range of $[-\pi/2, \pi/2)$. For approximation and regularity reasons, however, axis parallel lines, i.e. lines close to the orientation values of $\{-\pi/2, 0, \pi/2\}$, are desirable. Therefore, we apply the Manhattan metric instead, penalizing a non-axis-parallel orientation: $dist_{sum}(p_i, p_j) = |p_{i_x} - p_{j_x}| + |p_{i_y} - p_{j_y}|$.
- as introduced above, we use the root-criterion determining the complexity of the components. Therefore, the complexity as well as the number of the components is $O(\sqrt{n})$. To avoid a degeneration in the case of objects with a small number of vertices, we define a lower bound of 10 for the number of vertices of one component, therefore: $Min_{Compl}(n) = max\{\lceil \sqrt{n} \rceil \cdot c, 10\}$. The value of c is defined as $c = 2.0$.
- a major problem of the partitioning process is the preservation of regular components. Thus, partitioning lines must be completely included within the object and may not have an intersection with the object border. Principally, any computation of minimum distances has to check for some visibility constraints resulting in a high computational effort. To re-

duce this effort, we choose a 'suboptimal' way to proceed. For this purpose, we define two strict visibility conditions (see figure 7).

Two Points P_1 and P_2 of a simple polygon P are called *locally visible*, if:

$$\exists \; \varepsilon_1, \varepsilon_2 > 0 \text{ with } (\{P_1 + \delta \cdot (P_2 - P_1), 0 \le \delta \le \varepsilon_1\} \subset P) \wedge (\{P_2 + \delta \cdot (P_1 - P_2), 0 \le \delta \le \varepsilon_2\} \subset P)$$

Particularly, two interior points of P are locally visible by definition.

P_1 and P_2 are called *globally visible* or *visible*, if: $\{P_1 + \delta \cdot (P_2 - P_1), 0 \le \delta \le 1\} \subset P$.

While checking for the global visibility constraint takes linear time in the number of vertices, the local visibility is evaluated in constant time. Therefore, within the minimization phase for every vertice we only check the local visibility. Instead, the process of searching pairs of vertices of minimum distance checks the global visibility to maintain correctness. This approach, not guaranteeing the global minimum distance of two points joined by a partitioning line, reduces the time complexity by a linear factor.

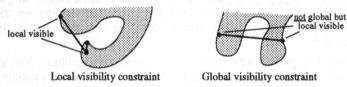

| Local visibility constraint | Global visibility constraint |

Fig. 7. Global and local visibility condition

- releasing the strict structural constraint

Based on the arbitrarily but fixed defined constant of the minimum component complexity, a reduction of the natural locality may be the consequence. In order to prevent this, at least partially, we define a range of fussiness $\vartheta(n)$ and a fixed upper bound Δ. Now, we introduce a relaxation of the strict minimum complexity constraint:

If, for two points P_i and P_j, the following condition holds:

$$dist_{sum}(P_i, P_j) \le (1 - \Delta) \cdot \left(\min_{1 \le k \le n, \; dist_{ind}(i, k) \ge Min_{Kompl}(n)} (dist_{sum}(P_i, P_k)) \right) \text{ with },$$

$$Min_{Kompl}(n) > dist_{ind}(i, k) \ge Min_{Kompl}(n) - \vartheta(n)$$

then a partition line is introduced between P_i and P_j neglecting the low component complexity. A careful selection of the values of $\vartheta(n)$ and Δ is necessary. If $\vartheta(n)$ is too large or Δ is too small, the above defined criteria become annulled. In our instantiation, we define $\vartheta(n) = 0.05 \cdot n$ and $\Delta = 0.25$.

Properties of the fragmentation method

The effect of the algorithm strongly depends on the shape of the object justifying the name of an object-oriented method. We distinguish two basic treatments (see figure 8):

- the join of two dents
- the cut of bulges

If an object includes distinct dents, the minimum distance of a pair of points occurs between those dents under the predefined constraints. This treatment results in a spatial and topologic localized and more regular shape of the components, both underlying a further recursive partitioning. If no such dents exist, i.e. if there is an obvious kernel (see figure 8), parts of the object 'sticking out' in the form of bulges will be cut. Successively, the object is reduced to a topologically simple kernel and a set of components along the object border. As every step of the partitioning treats one bulge, two unsimilar components are generated. One represents the bulge yet fulfilling the complexity property, whereas the other describes the rest of the object which is further partitioned.

This decomposition process for spatial objects is particularly determined by the object shape and topology. The two basic treatments guarantee for a high locality with respect to spatial and topological aspects. In particular, the difficult problem of defining an adequate kernel is solved in a direct and pragmatic way. The existence of a distinct kernel preserves spatial locality and supports answering spatial queries by only considering the kernel.

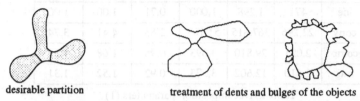

desirable partition   treatment of dents and bulges of the objects

Fig. 8. Instantiation of the object-oriented decomposition method

In the following section, we will evaluate this method of decomposing a complex spatial object with respect to the filter and the refinement step of spatial query processing comparing it to presently known methods.

6 Secondary memory organization and spatial query processing

As outlined in section 2, spatial query processing on complex spatial objects is performed in a two step approach: based on an approximation oriented object representation, the filter step reduces the set of objects to a set of candidates most likely fulfilling the query condition. The refinement step exactly evaluates the query condition. Within this section, we will examine the decomposition methods introduced above, i.e. the convex composition (comp) and the fragmentation method (frag), with respect to this two step approach of spatial query processing. In the performance comparison, we use the identity representation (ide) as well as the convex decomposition (conv) introduced in [KHS 91] as a measuring stick.

This comparison utilizes three different datafiles, two of them corresponding to real geographic objects that do not overlap (county regions of 'Europe' (see figure 9)) and 'Baden-Württemberg' (BW), and the third representing a set of synthetic objects with some 85 vertices and two holes on the average ('sph_85'). 'Europe' and 'BW' mainly differ with respect to the number of objects as well as the average object complexity influencing the amount of decomposition redundancy. The average object complexity of the strongly homogeneous 'sph_85'-file meets the object complexity of 'Europe', while the number of vertices in 'BW' is about six times higher.

The following tables depict the major parameters of the particular representations. They include the number of components and their average and total complexity, the storage needed for the representation and spatial organisation of the decomposition components compared to a linear organization of the objects, each within one or more 2 KByte-secondary memory pages, and the bounding box approximation characterizing the efficiency of the filter step expressed by the number of false hits (see also [BKS 93]).

The convex decomposition turns out to generate a extremely high number of components (about 1/2 the total number of vertices) and a low and constant component complexity (4.5-5 vertices on the average). The overall complexity factor of about 2.5 is a measure for the strong structural overhead caused by a multiple storage of identical vertices within different components and by Steinerpoints. However, this overhead is small for our new decomposition methods. The convex composition method shows a constant component complexity. Due to the merge of convex components, their complexity is much higher and thus, their number is much lower compared to the convex decomposition. The component complexity of the object-oriented decomposition by definition strongly depends on the complexity of the original objects.

	number of components			relative storage space		
	Europe	BW	sph_85	Europe	BW	sph_85
ide	471	1,298	1,000	0.71	1.00	1.00
conv	22,296	367,815	51,183	2.56	4.41	3.74
comp	2,091	29,810	3,093	0.96	1.68	1.36
frag	1,410	12,602	3,573	0.92	1.52	1.31

Table 2: Decomposition parameters (1)

	medium comp. complexity			overall complexity			bounding box approx.		
	Europe	BW	sph_85	Europe	BW	sph_85	Europe	BW	sph_85
ide	94.9	572.5	83.3	1.00	1.00	1.00	2.15	2.00	1.72
conv	4.94	5.01	4.57	2.46	2.48	2.81	1.31	1.05	1.16
comp	23.7	27.8	29.0	1.11	1.12	1.08	1.92	1.30	1.74
frag	33.1	60.8	24.8	1.04	1.03	1.06	1.93	1.54	1.84

Table 3: Decomposition parameters (2)

Now, our goal is to perform spatial queries based on these representation schemes measuring the performance of the particular methods. For that purpose the objects and the components are organized in an R^*-tree, an efficient SAM for rectangles using the concept of overlapping regions ([BKSS 90]). We define a 'one-path' page buffer supporting query processing.

The main criteria determining query efficiency are (see also [KHS 91]):

- disc accesses and main memory page search operations, i.e. *'point in rectangle'* operations and rectangle intersections, performed by the SAM (filter step) and
- exact spatial operations performed on the original objects or their decomposition components (refinement step)

In the case of a decomposed object representation an additional filter of redundancy has to be incorporated within the refinement step to avoid redundant spatial operations. Our instantiation is a temporary main memory binary search tree structure, implemented as an AVL tree.

The tables below present the performance results of point queries and window queries depending on the size of the query window. The percentage values describe the extension of the query window in each dimension of the data space, i.e. a 10%-window query corresponds to a window covering 1% of the data space. As the performance of the access method is independent of the object distribution, the query windows are evenly distributed in the space covered by the data objects. Thus, only successful queries are performed for a good simulation of application specific requirements. The performance values are divided into filter and refinement performance, parametrized as follows:

$$filter = number\ of\ accesses \cdot t_{access} + number\ of\ comparisons \cdot t_{comp}$$
$$ref = number\ of\ duplicates \cdot t_{tree\_search} + spatial\ operations \cdot t_{spatial\_operation}$$

Fig. 9. Partitionings of the 'Europe' file

The time parameters are averaged over the corresponding values measured in numerous experiments on HP 720 RISC workstations under GP MODULA-2. We instantiate the values $t_{access} = 0.12ms$, $t_{comp} = 0.002ms$, and $t_{tree\_search} = 0.015ms$ averaged. $t_{spatial\_operation}$ strongly depends on the type of the spatial operation. In the case of a query region which is large compared to the average object area, the refinement operation is performed by a small number of comparisons, whereas point queries require for the evaluation of the complete shape of the spatial objects. Therefore, this time parameter cannot be globally defined. However, for point queries and small window queries we have approximately: $t_{spatial\_operation} = n \cdot 0.01\,ms$, where n denotes the object complexity.

The following table 4 depicts the average time required for the evaluation of one single query. Due to space limitation, the results for thr 1%-window queries are not presented in the table. The values are given in microseconds. For a clearer evaluation they are divided into the time for the filter step and the refinement step. In the table, we have shadowed the best performing method for each type of query. A summation of both values resulting in the total time needed for the processing of one spatial query is represented in figure 10.

	point queries		0.5 % - window qu.		2 % - window qu.		5 % - window qu.		10 % - window qu.		25 % - window qu.	
	filter	ref.	filter	ref.	filter	ref.	filter	ref.	filter	ref.	filter	ref.
Europe - file (471 objects / 44,716 vertices)												
ide	0.79	3.05	0.83	2.53	0.97	1.06	1.32	0.64	2.08	0.35	5.6	0.1
conv	0.69	0.05	0.83	0.13	1.33	0.52	2.67	1.84	5.78	5.31	21.2	23.2
comp	0.48	0.29	0.55	0.25	0.75	0.16	1.26	0.21	2.35	0.48	7.6	1.8
frag	0.50	0.47	0.55	0.38	0.73	0.17	1.18	0.15	2.20	0.28	7.1	1.0
BW - file (1,297 objects / 743,137 vertices)												
ide	6.98	11.2	7.55	14.0	9.67	13.8	14.8	13.0	26.0	8.31	75.4	2.2
conv	1.01	0.05	1.76	0.60	5.91	4.54	21.7	22.5	65.6	75.0	302	370
comp	0.81	0.32	1.14	0.76	2.73	1.85	8.26	2.21	23.7	6.50	101	29.5
frag	0.78	1.32	1.04	1.47	2.37	1.63	7.13	1.78	20.0	4.06	88.1	11.7
sph_85 - file (1,000 objects / 83,291 vertices)												
ide	2.70	14.7	2.88	15.1	3.46	17.6	4.74	22.3	7.3	17.8	17.7	11.3
conv	1.78	0.55	2.07	0.78	3.09	1.62	5.86	2.84	12.6	9.4	47.3	49.5
comp	2.12	5.17	2.31	4.84	2.91	3.75	4.32	3.63	7.3	2.2	20.2	2.7
frag	2.12	4.69	2.30	4.07	2.88	3.71	4.32	3.15	7.1	2.1	19.6	3.2

Table 4: Average time per query (in ms)

These results reveal strong differences in query performance. As expected, for each of the test files the decomposition based representations perform good for high selectivity queries, whereas for queries with low-selectivity, i.e. for extremely large window queries, their performance gets poorer. In principle, for very large queries a spatial clustering is not supportive anymore. Then, a sequential scan over the objects may turn out to be the best choice. Typical application-oriented queries extract small portions of the objects and therefore, are restricted to small query windows. In this case, any of the object decomposition methods clearly outperforms the identity representation up to an order of magnitude. The identity representation is superior to the decomposition methods only for very large queries when the performance of the decomposition methods degenerates.

The break-even point of the performance curves depends on the characteristics of the underlying objects. The identity representation performs considerably worse than the decomposition methods for a wide range of the window sizes, if the overlap of the objects is strong and the average object area is high (see file 'sph_85'). However, for small objects and for large window queries, the average computational geometry cost becomes cheap in comparison to the cost for handling the high amount of redundancy. Thus, window queries exceeding a break-even point which is in the range of $[0.1, 0.35]$ of the size of the data space in each dimension, are performed most efficiently by the identity representation. However, in most applications these very large window queries rarely occur.

Caused by the reduced amount of redundancy and still a small complexity of the components, the two new methods outperform the convex decomposition already for small window queries and improve their superiority with increasing query size. Only for point queries, where the whole amount of redundancy is neutralized by the clustering effect of the SAM, due to its bounding box approximation quality and its simple refinement operations, the convex decomposition displays the best performance. However, in a wide range of small and medium sized window queries decomposition methods based on a balance between complexity and redundancy take advantage of much less redundancy, and, nevertheless, a reasonably small object complexity (see figure 10). To be more precise, the following table 5 normalizes the total query time for each method and each type of query with respect to the most efficient method. The table clearly shows that for small and medium sized window queries (window sizes in the range of 0.5% to 10% of the data space in each dimension) our new methods are superior to the traditional methods by a factor which varies between 1.24 and 11.34. Possibly even more important, our new methods are very robust in performance over the whole range of queries. For the BW-file there is no query type where their performance is worse than the best method by a factor of more than 2. Since it has been demonstrated that the performance of the R^*-tree is basicaly independent of the object parameters, the above results reflect the performance of the decomposition and not the performance of the access method. .

	point queries	0.5 % - window	1 % - window	2 % - window	5 % - window	10 % - window	25 % - window
	BW - file						
ide	17.15	11.34	8.82	5.87	3.12	1.43	1.00
conv	1.00	1.24	1.68	2.61	4.96	5.84	8.66
comp	1.07	1.00	1.00	1.15	1.18	1.26	1.68
frag	1.98	1.32	1.13	1.00	1.00	1.00	1.29

Table 5: Performance of spatial queries normalized with respect to the most efficient method

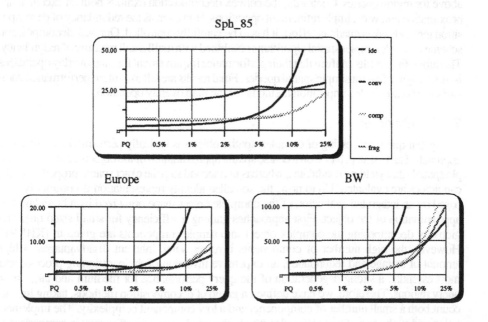

Fig. 10. Total query time (in ms) depending on the window size of spatial queries

Due to the strict axis-parallel partitioning process of the convex composition method, its approximation is superior to the fragmentation method. This property is particularly influencing the performance of small sized window queries. For larger query windows the spatial locality of the fragmentation method inducing a better clustering results in a better performance. However, the performance of the two methods is very similar which is due to the similar complexity and redundancy.

These trends come out even clearer for region queries where the query is specified by a polygonally shaped object. Region queries are typically performed by the sequence of a window query using the query window formed by the bounding box of the query region followed by refinement operations based on the exact shape of the query region. Particularly for the new decomposition methods inducing a low amount of redundancy, a decomposition of the query region combined with an iterated query processing of simple and local query regions becomes a promising approach.

Generally, the refinement operation of the identity representation strongly suffers from an increase of the query region complexity. Typically, the algorithmic complexity is $O(r \cdot n)$, where r and n denote the complexity of the query region and the complexity of the refined object, respectively. As the decomposed spatial objects are considerably less complex, their refinement complexity is much lower, particularly for complex query regions.

A map overlay of two object files (e.g. [KBS 91]), an essential operation for geographic applications, results in a set of object pairs, one of each file, fulfilling a predefined join condition. Again, a two step approach is applied by first computing a set of candidate pairs based on their bounding box approximation, followed by the evaluation of the overlay condition on the exact object shapes. The identity representation as a first approach reveals two strong drawbacks with respect to its performance: as a result of the bad approximation, a high number of object pairs has to be considered and their evaluation takes the same quadratic effort as outlined above for region queries. Contrarily, the convex decomposition exhibits both an excellent approximation and very simple refinement operations. However, as the redundancy of decomposition methods takes quadratic effort, it has to be carefully controlled. Our new decomposition schemes provide simpler spatial algorithms combined with a still small measure of redundancy. Therefore, first results confirm that their performance improvement for map overlay operations is much higher than for simple spatial queries. Final results are left to a future performance comparison of our new decomposition methods for the map overlay operation.

7 Conclusions

Spatial query processing of complex spatial objects is typically performed by a two step approach. The first step, based on a coarse spatial approximation of the objects embodies a simple spatial filter yielding candidates, whereas in a second step the exact spatial properties of the candidates are evaluated. Up to now, the so-called identity representation is commonly used based on an integrated evaluation of the complete object shape organized by a bounding box approximation of the object. First approaches gaining in efficiency for small sized query regions by decomposing the complex object into simple components are given in [KHS 91]. However, the high number of components involves some inherent disadvantages: a high amount of storage and redundancy, an expensive inversion of the partitioning process, and, most essential, a strong degeneration of the query performance for medium and large sized query regions. Therefore, we have defined a group of decomposition methods, taking into account both a small number of components and a low component complexity. The implementation and evaluation of two selected methods show a clear gain in efficiency in comparison to the identity representation and the convex decomposition method, the winner in [KHS 91]. For small and medium sized window queries (window sizes in the range of 0.5% to 10% of the data space in each dimension) this gain in performance is by a factor in the range of 1.24 to 11.34. Possibly even more important, our new methods are very robust in performance over the whole range of window queries. Furthermore, for spatial queries more complex than window queries, this gain will be even higher. Thus, for all applications where extremely large queries do not occur, in other words for most practical applications, our new decomposition methods turn out to be a good choice.

References

[AA 83]   Ta. Asano and Te. Asano, *Minimum partition of polygonal regions into trapezoids*, Proc. 24th IEEE Annual Symp. on Foundations of Computer Science, 1983, 233-241.

[BKS 93]   T. Brinkhoff, H.-P. Kriegel, and R. Schneider, *Comparison of approximations of complex objects used for approximation-based query processing in spatial databases*, in Proc. 9th Int. Conf. on Data Engineering, Vienna, Austria, 1993.

[BKSS 90]   N. Beckmann, H.-P. Kriegel, R. Schneider, and B. Seeger, *The R*-tree: An efficient and robust access method for points and rectangles*, Proceedings ACM SIGMOD Int. Conf. on Management of Data, Atlantic City, NJ, 1990, 322-331.

[Bra 92]   A. Braun, *A graphic-oriented tool for analyzing spatial objects: 'its design and application to real world data'*, Master thesis, Institute for Computer Science, University of Munich, Germany, 1992, (in German).

[CD 85]   B. Chazelle and D.P. Dobkin, *Optimal convex decompositions*, in *computational geometry*, Proceedings Comp. Geometry, Elsevier Science, Netherland, 1985, 63-134.

[Fra 91]   A.U. Frank, *Properties of geographic data*, Proceedings 2nd Symp. on Large Spatial Databases, SSD'91, ETH Zurich, 1991, 225-234, in: Lecture Notes in Computer Science, Vol. 525, Springer, 1991.

[Kei 83]   J.M. Keil, *Decomposing polygons into simpler components*, Ph.D. thesis, Department of Computer Science, University of Toronto, 1983.

[KS 85]   J.M. Keil and J.R. Sack, *Minimum decomposition of polygonal objects*, in *Computational Geometry*, G.T. Toissant (Ed.), Amsterdam, Netherland, 1985, 197-216.

[KBS 91]   H.-P. Kriegel, T. Brinkhoff, and R. Schneider, *An efficient map overlay algorithm based on spatial access methods and Computational Geometry*, Int. Workshop on Database Management Systems for Geographical Applications, Capri, Italy, 1991, in: Geographic Database Management Systems, Springer, 1992, 194-211.

[KHS 91]   H.-P. Kriegel, H. Horn, and M. Schiwietz, *The performance of object decomposition techniques for spatial query processing*, Proceedings 2nd Symp. on Large Spatial Databases, SSD'91, Zurich, 1991, 257-276.

[Law 72]   C.L. Lawson, *Generation of a triangular grid with application to contour plotting*, CIT Jet Propulsion Laboratory, Technical Memorandum 299, Pasadena, CA, 1972.

[NHS 84]   J. Nievergelt, H. Hinterberger, and K.C. Sevik, *The Grid File: an adaptable, symmetric multikey file structure*, ACM Transactions on Database Systems, Vol. 9, 1, 1984,38-71.

[Ore 89]   J. Orenstein, *Redundancy in spatial databases*, Proceedings 1st International Symposium on Large Spatial Databases, SSD'89, Santa Barbara, CA, 1989.

[OM 86]   J. Orenstein and F.A. Manola, *Spatial data modeling and query processing in PROBE*, Technical Report CCA-86-05, Xerox Advanced Inform. Technology Devision, 1986.

[PS 88]   F.P. Preparata and M.I. Shamos, *Computational Geometry*, Springer, New York, 1988.

[Sam 90]   H. Samet, *The Design and Analysis of Spatial Data Structures*, Addison-Wesley, 1990.

[Schi 93]   M. Schiwietz, *Storage and Query Processing of Complex Spatial Objects*, Ph.D. thesis, (in German), Inst. for Computer Science, University of Munich, Germany, 1993.

[Schn 92]   R. Schneider, *A Storage and Access Structure of Spatial Database Systems*, Ph.D. thesis, (in German), Institute for Computer Science, University of Munich, Germany, 1992.

[SK 91]   R. Schneider and H.-P. Kriegel, *The TR*-tree: a new representation of polygonal objects supporting spatial queries and operations*, Proceedings 7th Workshop on Computational Geometry, Bern, Switzerland, 1991, in: Lecture Notes in Computer Science, Vol. 553, Springer, 1991, 249-264.

[See 89]   B. Seeger, *Design and implementation of multidimensional access methods*, Ph.D. thesis, (in German), Depart. of Computer Science, University of Bremen, Germany, 1989.

THE SEQUOIA 2000 Project

Michael Stonebraker and James Frew †
Jeff Dozier ‡

† Computer Science Division
Department of Electrical Engineering and Computer Science
University of California
Berkeley, California 94720

‡ Center for Remote Sensing and Environmental Optics
University of California
Santa Barbara , California 93106

Abstract. This paper describes the objectives of the SEQUOIA 2000 project and the software development that is being done to achieve these objectives. In addition, several lessons relevant to Geographic Information Systems (GIS) that have have been learned from the project are explained.

1. Introduction

The purpose of the SEQUOIA 2000 project is to build a better computing environment for global change researchers, hereafter referred to as SEQUOIA 2000 "clients." Global change researchers investigate issues of global warming, the Earth's radiation balance, the oceans' role in climate, ozone depletion and its effect on ocean productivity, snow hydrology and hydrochemistry, environmental toxification, species extinction, vegetation distribution, etc., and are members of Earth science departments at universities and national laboratories. A cooperative project among five campuses of the University of California, government agencies, and industry, SEQUOIA 2000 is Digital Equipment Corporation's flagship research project for the 1990s, succeeding Project Athena. It is an example of the close relationship that must exist between technology and applications to foster the computing environment of the future [NRC92].

There are four categories of investigators participating in SEQUOIA 2000:

This research was sponsored by Digital Equipment Corporation under Research Grant 1243, DARPA Contract #DABT63-92-C-007,NSF Grant #RI-91-07455, and ARO Grant #DAAL03-91-6-0183

Computer science researchers are affiliated with the Computer Science Division at UC Berkeley, the Computer Science Department at UC San Diego, the School of Library and Information Studies at UC Berkeley, and the San Diego Supercomputer Center (SDSC). Their charge is to build a prototype environment that better serves the needs of the clients.

Earth science researchers are affiliated with the Department of Geography at UC Santa Barbara, the Atmospheric Science Department at UCLA, the Climate Research Division at the Scripps Institution of Oceanography, and the Department of Land, Air and Water Resources at UC Davis. Their charge is to explain their needs to the computer science researchers and to use the resulting prototype environment to do better Earth science.

Government agencies include the State of California Department of Water Resources (DWR), the Construction Engineering Research Laboratory (CERL) of the U.S. Army Corps of Engineers, the National Aeronautics and Space Administration, and the United States Geological Survey. Their charge is to steer SEQUOIA 2000 research in a direction that is applicable to their problems.

Industrial participants include DEC, Epoch, Hewlett-Packard, Hughes, MCI, Metrum Corp., PictureTel Corp., Research Systems Inc., Science Applications International Corp. (SAIC), Siemens, and TRW. Their charge is to use the SEQUOIA 2000 technology and offer guidance and research directions. They are also a source of free or discounted computing equipment.

The purpose of this paper is to explain the objectives of SEQUOIA 2000 and the research focus that we have adopted in support of these objectives. Therefore, Section 2 first motivates the computer science objectives of Sequoia 2000. Then, Section 3 continues with an overview of the projects we are pursuing. Section 4 then explores four different themes that cross most elements of the SEQUOIA 2000 research plan. We close in Section 6 with some comments relevant to large Geographic Information Systems (GIS) that we have learned from our experiences to date.

2. SEQUOIA 2000 MOTIVATION

The SEQUOIA 2000 architecture is motivated by four fundamental computer science objectives:

　　　　1) big fast storage
　　　　2) an all-embracing DBMS
　　　　3) integrated visualization tools
　　　　4) high-speed networking

which we discuss in turn.

2.1. High Performance I/O on Terabyte Data Sets

Our clients are frustrated by current computing environments because they cannot effectively manage, store, and access the massive amounts of data that their research requires. They would like high-performance system software that would effectively support assorted tertiary storage devices. Collectively, our Earth science clients would like to store about 100 terabytes of data now. Many of these are common data sets, used by multiple investigators.

Unlike some other scientific computing users, much of our clients' I/O activity is random access. For example, several investigators use image data from the Landsat Thematic Mapper. Sometimes they want the most current image for a specific area, sometimes they want to examine a time sequence of mosaicked images for a larger area. Similarly, DWR is digitizing the agency's library of 500,000 photographic slides, and will put it on-line using the SEQUOIA 2000 environment. This data set will have some locality of reference but will have considerable random activity.

2.2. All Data in a DBMS

Our clients agree on the merits of moving all their data to a database management system. In this way, the metadata that describe their data sets can be maintained, assisting them with the ability to retrieve needed information. A more important benefit is the sharing of information it will allow, thus enabling intercampus, interdisciplinary research. Because a DBMS will insist on a common schema for shared information, it will allow the researchers to define this schema; then all must use a common notation for shared data. This will improve the current confused state, whereby every data set exists in a different format and must be converted by any researcher who wishes to use it.

2.3. Better Visualization Tools

Our clients use visualization tools such as AVS, IDL, Khoros, and Explorer. They are frustrated by aspects of these products and are anxious for a next-generation visualization toolkit that:

1) allows better management, use, and manipulation of large data sets and model output;

2) provides better interactive data analysis tools, including comparison of data sets and integration and composition of disimilar data;

3) fully exploits the capabilities of a distributed, heterogeneous computing environment, including workstations, large vector machines, and massively parallel processors;

4) produces presentation materials that effectively convey information about the data sets presented;

5) uses "computational steering" techniques to guide models during execution.

2.4. High-Speed Networking

Our clients realize that 100 terabyte storage servers will not be located on their desktops; instead, they are likely to be at the far end of a wide-area network (WAN). Their visualization scenarios often make heavy use of animation, (e.g., "playing" the last 10 years of ozone hole imagery as frames of a movie), which requires ultra-high-speed networking.

3. THE SEQUOIA 2000 TECHNICAL PROJECTS

SEQUOIA 2000 is an interconnected collection of 6 projects in:
> storage
> file systems for tertiary memory
> DBMS
> networking
> visualization
> electronic repositories

In this section we discuss each of these projects

Our environment is a collection of DECstation 5000's which are deployed as both client and server machines. Systems at a single site are interconnected by FDDI networking, and the individual machines will be migrating to Alphas over the next year. The SEQUOIA 2000 sites are interconnected by the SEQUOIA network, a dedicated set of T1 (soon to be T3) lines donated to the project by the University of California. Deep storage consists of a collection of 6 robotic storage devices at Berkeley, with an aggregate capacity of 10 Tbytes. The robotic storage devices and their associated CPUs and secondary storage are collectively called **Bigfoot**, after the legendary gigantic ape-man of the Pacific Northwest.

3.1. The Storage Project

The Berkeley hardware group has pioneered the development of Redundant Arrays of Inexpensive Disks (RAID) [PATT88]. RAID requires a sophisticated I/O controller be placed between the CPU and the collection of disk devices. This I/O controller must keep the redundant parity information up to date and map logical blocks to physical locations on the media.

The same group is now focused on the possible construction of a better I/O controller that might control data migration between secondary and tertiary storage as well as play a part in any end-to-end compression scheme [KATZ91]. We are also considering striping and redundancy over media in a jukebox, robot arms in a jukebox, whole jukeboxes and even whole systems. Also, we are concerned with the issue of backup and A last area of possible research is the design of a backup scheme for tertiary storage. It is impossible to take a dump of a 10-terabyte storage system. At 1 Mbyte/sec, $10^{**}7$ seconds, about 4 months, would be needed. Obviously a new idea for data reliability is required.

3.2. The File System Projects

We are building two files systems for Bigfoot, and plan to run three additional commercial ones. All file systems will support a standard UNIX file system interface.

The first file system is **Highlight** [KOHL93]. It is an extension of the Log-structured File System (LFS) pioneered for disk devices by Rosenblum and Ousterhout [ROSE92]. LFS treats a disk device as a single continuous **log** onto which newly-written disk blocks are appended. Blocks are never overwritten, so a disk device can always be written sequentially. In particular problem areas, this may lead to much higher performance [SELT93]. LFS also has the advantage of rapid recovery from a system crash: potentially damaged blocks in an LFS are easily found, because the last few blocks that were written prior to a crash are always at the end of the log. Conventional file systems require much more laborious checking to ascertain their integrity.

Highlight extends LFS to support tertiary storage by adding a second log-structured file system, plus migration and bookkeeping code that treats the disk LFS as a cache for the tertiary storage one. Highlight should give excellent performance on a workload that is "write-mostly." This should be an excellent match to the SEQUOIA 2000 environment, whose clients want to archive vast amounts of data.

The second file system is **Inversion** [OLSO93, STON93], which is built on top of the POSTGRES DBMS. Like most DBMSs, POSTGRES supports binary large objects (blobs), which can contain an arbitrary number of variable-length byte strings. These large objects are stored in a customized storage system directly on a **raw** (i.e. non-file-structure) storage device. It is a straightforward exercise to have the DBMS make these large objects appear to be conventional files. Every read or write is turned by the DBMS front end into a query or update, which is processed directly by the DBMS.

Simulating files on top of DBMS large objects has several advantages. First, DBMS services such as transaction management and security are automatically supported for files. In addition, novel characteristics of POSTGRES, including **time travel** and an extensible type system for all DBMS objects [STON91b], are automatically available for files. Of course, the possible disadvantage of files on top of a DBMS is poor performance, but our experiments show that Inversion performance is exceedingly good when large amounts of data are read and written [OLSO93], a characteristic of the SEQUOIA 2000 workload.

We plan to conduct a "bakeoff" of our two file systems against the three commercial ones we are using on as many of our robotic devices as possible. Moreover, we plan to drive the bakeoff using two large benchmarks. The first is the national version of the SEQUOIA 2000 benchmark, a 25-Gbyte dataset and associated queries, specified as a project standard [STON93b]. The second benchmark is a scientific and engineering workload derived from a tracing study of the Cray supercomputer at the National Center for Atmospheric Research [MILL92]. The purpose of the bakeoff is to ensure that both SEQUOIA 2000 file systems are robust, and to help SEQUOIA 2000 clients identify the file system that would best serve their particular applications.

The above file systems are traditional **single-site** systems, i.e. each file has a home location but can be remotely assessed through an NFS-like protocol. However, our clients expect that their data will be remotely stored on **multiple** SEQUOIA 2000 systems. Moreover, they expect frequently used data to be cached locally on the disk of their client machine or on a local server in their immediate vicinity. In addition, the clients do not want to know the name or location of the SEQUOIA 2000 server where their data are stored. Similarly, any data redundancy through multiple copies of objects should be likewise transparent. In short, they want a **distributed** file system, that supports location transparency. Several file systems have been designed that begin to serve this need. The most robust is arguably the Andrew File System [HARR91], developed at CMU. The improvements that we expect to make to the Andrew design are [ANDE92]:

1) optimizing for network bandwidth instead of server CPU load;

2) caching of file blocks, instead of caching whole files;

3) the ability to disable caching, when data being fetched are too large to fit in local cache;

4) "write back" cache coherence, so that when temporary files are created they are not immediately sent over the wide area network;

5) data structures designed to scale to terabytes of local cache and millions of cached files;

6) application control (when needed) over the file system's caching and migration policies.

We are embarking on a prototype effort in this direction, known internally as The SEQUOIA 2000 File System. In keeping with the project goal of naming all software systems after California places, it is called **Shasta**.

3.3. The DBMS Project

Some users will simply run application programs against the file system, and will have no use for DBMS technology. Others will store their data in a DBMS. To have any chance of meeting SEQUOIA 2000 client needs, a DBMS must support spatial data structures such as points, lines, polygons, and large multidimensional arrays (e.g. satellite images). Currently these data are not supported by popular general-purpose relational and object-oriented DBMSs [STON91, DOZI92]. The best fit to SEQUOIA 2000 client needs would be either a special-purpose Geographic Information System (GIS) or a next-generation prototype DBMS. Since we have one such next-generation system within the project, we have elected to focus our DBMS work on this system, POSTGRES [STON90, STON91b].

To make POSTGRES suitable for SEQUOIA 2000 use, we require a **schema** for all SEQUOIA 2000 data. This database design process is evolving as a cooperative exercise between various database experts at Berkeley, SDSC, CERL, and SAIC. As we develop the schema, we are loading it with several terabytes of client data; we expect this load process to continue for the duration of the project. As the schema evolves, some of the already-loaded data will need to be reformatted. How to reformat a multi-terabyte database in finite time is an open question that is troubling us.

Suppose a client wants to move data from one machine to another, say to run them through a program that resides on a supercomputer. There must be a way to transfer the metadata along with the data, so that complete information is available at the remote site. This function requires an **on the wire** protocol, and we are working on the definition of this protocol.

In addition to schema development, we are tuning POSTGRES to meet the needs of our clients. The interface to POSTGRES arrays is being improved, and a novel **chunking** strategy [SARA93] is being prototyped. The R-tree access method in POSTGRES is being extended to support the full range of SEQUOIA 2000 spatial objects. Moreover, our clients typically use pattern classification functions in POST-QUEL queries that are very expensive to compute. For example, Query 3 in the SEQUOIA 2000 benchmark selects AVHRR data for a given time and geographic rectangle and then calculate an arithmetic function of the five wavelength band values for each cell in the study rectangle, i.e:

retrieve (raster-avg {clip (RASTER.data), RECTANGLE})
where RASTER.time = TIME

Here, raster-avg is a user-defined function that computes a weighted average of the individual cell, and is CPU intensive. We have been working on the POSTGRES optimizer to deal intelligently with such queries [HELL93].

A second approach to distribution in SEQUOIA 2000 is a distributed database effort called **Mariposa**. Unlike a distributed file system that moves data on demand from one or more remote sites to the user's program as needed, a distributed database system has the option of moving the user's query to the data or moving the data to the query, whichever is thought to be more efficient.

Unlike previous distributed DBMSs, which have assumed that data are statically partitioned among the sites in a computer network, Mariposa will assume that data will freely migrate among sites, and that data placement is a dynamic optimization issue. Lastly, Mariposa will attempt to make placement decisions by constructing a rule engine that will interpret a rule base. In this way, it is easy for a user to freely change the behavior of the system by changing a few rules. Mariposa is at its initial design stage.

Our last thrust is a facility to interface the UCLA General Circulation Model (GCM) to POSTGRES. This interface is a "data pump" because it pumps data out the simulation model and into POSTGRES. As such, it has been named the **big lift** after the DWR pumping station that raises Northern California water over the Tehachapi Mountains into Southern California.

The UCLA GCM produces a vector of simulation output variables for each time step of a lengthy run, for each cell in a three-dimensional grid of atmosphere and ocean. Depending on the scale of the model, its resolution, and the capability of the serial or parallel machine on which the model is running, the UCLA GCM can produce anywhere from 0.1 to 10 Mbytes/sec of output. The purpose of the big lift is to install these data into a POSTGRES database in real time. It is likely that the big lift will have to exploit parallelism in the data manager if it has to keep up with the execution of the model on a massively parallel architecture.

3.4. The Network Project

It is possible for the implementation of each layer in the SEQUOIA 2000 architecture to exist on a different machine. Specifically, the application can be remote from the DBMS , which can be remote from the file system, which can be remote from the storage device. Each layer assumes a local UNIX socket connection or a LAN or WAN connection using TCP. Actual connections among SEQUOIA 2000 sites use either the Internet or a dedicated T1 (1.54 Mbit/sec) network, contributed to SEQUOIA 2000 by the University of California.

The SEQUOIA 2000 T1 network uses DECstation 5000's (soon to become Alphas) as routers, instead of "custom iron." The project will soon upgrade to T3 (45 Mbit/sec) lines, and the computer science researchers in charge of the network are confident that workstation-based routers will continue to be fast enough. Furthermore, the SEQUOIA 2000 network is installing a **guaranteed delivery** service, through which a client program can **contract** with the network to guarantee a specific bandwidth and latency if the client agrees not to try to send faster than the contract. This service requires a "set-up" phase for a connection that will allocate bandwidth on all the lines and in all the switches [FERR90].

The network researchers are concerned that Ultrix copies every byte four times between retrieving it from storage and sending it out over a network connection. Even Alphas may not be fast enough to overcome this bottleneck. We are modifying Ultrix to "fast-path" network connections through the operating system, bypassing the redundant copyings.

3.5. The Visualization Project

SEQUOIA 2000 has standardized on IDL and AVS as our "official" off-the-shelf visualization software packages. AVS is liked for its easy-to-use "boxes and arrows" user interface, while IDL has a more conventional procedural programming notation. On the other hand, IDL is liked for its more flexible 2D graphics features. Both IDL and AVS allow a user to read and write file data.

To connect to the DBMS, we have written an AVS-POSTGRES bridge. This program allows one to construct an ad-hoc POSTGRES query and pipe the result into an AVS boxes-and-arrows network. Our clients can thus use AVS for further processing of any data retrieved from the DBMS . IDL is being interfaced to AVS by the vendor, so data retrieved from the database will be moved into IDL using AVS as an intermediary.

AVS has a collection of severe disadvantages as a visualization tool for our clients:

1) A type system that is different from the POSTGRES type system, without direct knowledge of the common SEQUOIA 2000 schema.

2) A severe appetite for main memory. AVS depends on virtual memory to pass results between various boxes. It maintains the output of each box in virtual memory for the duration of an execution session, so if a user changes a run-time parameter somewhere in the network, AVS will recompute only the "downstream" boxes, by taking advantage of the previous output. As a result, SEQUOIA 2000 clients, who produce large intermediate results, consume large amounts of both virtual and real memory: they report that 64 megabytes of real memory on a workstation is often not enough to enable serious AVS use.

3) No support for "zooming" into data of interest to obtain higher resolution.

4) No history of how any given data element was constructed, the so-called **data lineage** of an item.

4) A "video player" model for animation, which is too primitive for many SEQUOIA 2000 clients.

To correct these deficiencies, we have designed **Tioga,** a new boxes-and-arrows programming environment that is "DBMS-centric," i.e. the environment's type system is the same as the DBMS type system. The user interface presents a "flight simulator" paradigm for browsing the output of a boxes-and-arrows network, allowing the user to "navigate" around his data and then zoom in to obtain additional data on items of particular interest. Tioga [STON92] is a joint project between Berkeley and SDSC, and a prototype "early Tioga" [CHEN91] is currently running.

3.6. The Electronic Repository

Our final project considers the entire 10 Tbyte Bigfoot repository as a large electronic library. Although it has some textual information, including all of the UC Berkeley Computer Science Technical reports, Bigfoot contains primarily raw satellite data, "cooked" data, typically processed into polygons of constant classification, images, simulation output, and computer programs. Our clients want to retrieve objects from the library, usually by content. For example, DWR is digitizing their 500,000 slide media library and wants to retrieve it by content. For example, they might want to find all the images of ducks in the Sacramento River delta with blue sky in the background.

The purpose of the repository project is to support such information retrieval from Bigfoot. So far, we have focused on the textual portion of Bigfoot, and have designed **Lassen,** a browsing capability for textual information. Lassen has two components. The first is **Cheshire** [LARS91], a facility for constructing weighted keyword indices for the words in a document, stored as an instance of some particular POSTGRES type. Cheshire builds on the pioneering work of the Cornell Smart system. and operates as the action part of a POSTGRES rule that is triggered on each document insertion, update, or removal. The second piece of Lassen is a front-end query tool with natural language understanding, allowing a user to ask for all documents that satisfy a collection of keywords, by inquiring in a subset of Natural English.

Lassen is now operational, and retrievals can be requested against the currently loaded collection of SEQUOIA 2000 documents. This document collection includes some (soon to be all) Berkeley Computer Science technical reports, a collection of DWR publications, the Berkeley Cognitive Science technical reports, and the technical reports from the UC Santa Barbara Center for Remote Sensing and Environmental Optics.

Over the next year, we expect to:

1) Install phrase recognition software in Cheshire that will extend its indexing capabilities from single words to noun phases. Other research has shown this to be a good way to increase the precision of the answer to a query [EVAN91].

2) Move Lassen to a Z39.50 protocol [LYNC91] The client portion of Lassen would emit Z39.50 and we would write a Z39.50 to POSTGRES translator on the server side. This would allow the Lassen client code to access non-SEQUOIA 2000 information, and the SEQUOIA 2000 server to be accessed by text retrieval front ends other than Cheshire.

3) Extend Lassen coverage to include non-document materials such as business cards, marketing reports, etc.

4. COMMON CONCERNS

Four concerns of SEQUOIA clients cannot be isolated to a project area;
        guaranteed delivery;
        abstracts;
        compression;
        integration with other software.

4.1. Guaranteed Delivery

Guaranteed delivery must be an **end-to-end contract.** Suppose a SEQUOIA 2000 client wishes to visualize a specific computation, for example, observing Hurricane Andrew as it moves from the Bahamas to Florida to Louisiana. Specifically, the client wishes to visualize appropriate satellite imagery at 500x500 resolution, in 8-bit color, at 10 frames per second. This requires 2.5 Mbytes/sec of bandwidth to the client's screen. The following scenario might be the resulting computation steps:

The DBMS runs a query to fetch the satellite imagery. It might require returning a 16-bit data value for each pixel that will ultimately go to the screen, so the DBMS agrees to execute the query in such a way that it returns 5.0 Mbytes/sec.

The storage system at the server fetches some number of I/O blocks from secondary and/or tertiary storage. DBMs query optimizers can accurately guess how many blocks they need to read to satisfy a query. It is an easy extension for the DBMS to generate a guaranteed delivery contract that the storage manager must satisfy that will in turn allow the DBMS to satisfy its contract.

The network agrees to deliver 5.0 Mbytes/sec over the link connecting the client to the server. The SEQUOIA 2000 network software is designed to accommodate exactly this sort of contract request.

The visualization package agrees to translate the 16-bit pixels into 8-bit colors, and to render the result onto the screen at 2.5 Mbytes/sec.

In short, guaranteed delivery is a collection of contracts that must be adhered to by the storage system, the DBMS, the visualization system, and the network. One approach to implementing the required contracts is discussed in [STON92].

4.2. Abstracts

The SEQUOIA 2000 visualization process needs abstracts. Consider again the Hurricane Andrew example. The client might initially want to browse the hurricane at 100x100 resolution. Then, if he found something of interest, he would like to zoom in and increase the resolution, usually to the maximum available in the original data. This ability to change the amount of resolution in an image dynamically has been termed **abstracts** [FINE92].

Abstracts are a much more powerful construct than merely providing resolution adjustment. Obtaining more detail may entail moving from one representation to another. For example, one could have an icon for a document, zoom in to see the (textual) abstract, and then zoom in further to see the entire document. This use of abstracts was popularized in the DBMS community by SDMS [HERO80].

SEQUOIA 2000 clients wish to have abstracts. However, they could be managed by any combination of the visualization tool, the network, the DBMS, or the file system. In the visualization tool case, abstracts are defined for boxes-and-arrows networks [STON92]. In the DBMS case, abstracts would be defined for individual data elements or for data classes. If the network manages abstracts, then it will use them to automatically lower resolution to eliminate congestion. Much research on the optimization of network abstracts (called hierarchical encoding of data in that community) has been presented [DIXI91]. Lastly, in the file system case, abstracts would be defined for files. There are SEQUOIA 2000 researchers pursuing all four possibilities.

4.3. Compression

The SEQUOIA 2000 clients are open to any compression scheme as long as it is lossless. For many satellites, the characteristics of the sensor and the quantization and transmission of the data were designed around processing algorithms for interpretation of geophysical phenomena. Hence every bit is significant, and a lossy compression algorithm would probably introduce large errors into the interpretation of the data.

"Old" data also must be preserved. Twenty years ago, the equatorial Pacific Ocean was less interesting than in the last decade, when the El Nino has been discovered to affect weather patterns in the Western United States. Old data about El Nino are now central to many scientific research agendas. Such unpredictability of the future importance of data can be expected to continue indefinitely and leads to the decision to keep everything at its finest available resolution.

Some SEQUOIA 2000 data are not economically compressible, and should be stored in clear (uncompressed) form. For such data, the use of abstracts offers a mechanism to lower the bandwidth required between the storage device and the visualization program. However, little saving of tertiary storage space via compression is available for such data.

On the other hand, some SEQUOIA 2000 data are compressible and should be stored in compressed form. When should compression and decompression occur? The only concept that makes any sense is the principle of **just in time** decompression. For example, if the storage manager compresses data as they are written and then decompresses them on a read, then the network manager may then recompress the data for transmission over a WAN to a remote site where they will be decompressed again. Obviously, data should be moved in compressed form and only decompressed when necessary. In general, this will mean in the visualization system on the client machine. If the data are searched by some criteria, then the DBMS may have to decompress the data to search through them. Lastly, it is possible that an application resides on the same machine as the storage manager. If so, the file system must be in charge of decompressing the data. All software modules in the SEQUOIA 2000 architecture must co-operate to decompress just-in-time and compress as-early-as-possible. Like guaranteed delivery, compression is a task where every element must cooperate.

4.4. Integration with Other Software

SEQUOIA 2000 researchers will always need access to other commercial and public-domain software packages. It would be a serious mistake for the project to develop every tool the researcher needs, or to add a needed function to our architecture when it can be provided by integration with another package. SEQUOIA 2000 thus needs "grease and glue," so that interface modules to other packages, e.g. S, are easily written.

5. LESSONS RELEVANT TO GIS SYSTEMS

In this section we share some of the lessons we have learned about large spatial database applications from our SEQUOIA 2000 experience.

First, it is essential to find out what the real problem is. SEQUOIA 2000 users are beset with a hugh number of inadequacies with current technology in many areas. However, they are quick to point out which ones are major showstoppers and which ones are a minor annoyance. For example, our users report that storing raster data is a serious problem, while storing vector data is only a minor nuisance. Basically, raster data comes in terabytes, while vector data comes in megabytes. This huge difference in scale makes it the important "gorilla" to deal with. Also, our users are inundated with a myriad of formats for data that they have to "crack". Hence, any data integration project is measured in months, and essentially all of the delay occurs in writing the program to convert from one format to another. Our users are desperate for standards, that would cut down on the number of formats, and for general purpose conversion tools to deal with format conversion. Furthermore, our users invariably want to correlate disparate kinds of data, i.e. raster data to vector data and raster data to simulation output. They need a general purpose DBMS that will allow such correlations between disparate objects to take place, and are frustrated with the inability of current commercial GIS products to do this. Lastly, they occasionally mention the storage and indexing of vector data, but seem unconcerned with performance. Also, the exact nature of the spatial access method that is used to retrieve their data does not concern them.

Second, it is essential to realize that large spatial applications are **end-to-end** problems, i.e. they require the storage manager, the DBMS, the network and the visualization tool to cooperate. The failure of any piece dooms the application to the performance of the failed piece. Also, many functions (e.g. compression, abstracting) can be done by several different subsystems. It is essential that each function be done only by the subsystem(s) best able to perform it. Hence, one must adopt a **total** systems view of the problem.

Next, building a schema for geographic data has been a very hard problem for us. Raster data is very complex, since it entails recording data in units specific to the satellite, for a tile spacing also unique to the satellite. Moreover, information should be retained about the calibration of the on-board instruments and about the cartographic projection system that is used for processed data. Data recorded for GCMs includes all of the above information, plus parameters used for the model run and an additional vector of output variables.

We assembled a committee of experts to design a schema, and they immediately became lost in the potential complexity of the task they had undertaken. Moreover, there were "religious" wars over whether meta data should be encapsulated with the object that it represents, or put in a separate schema where it could be queried easily.

The only way we have made progress is to drastically curtail the scope of the activity to describing a few data sets. In this way, we are doing a schema for a simple subset of SEQUOIA 2000 objects and will then expand it over time. Hence, we are learning to "walk" before trying to "run", and it has been a humbling experience.

Furthermore, in the process of loading Bigfoot with data, we have found that virtually every data set that we receive is in a customized format. Hence, a large amount of effort has been spent "cracking" each code. As such, data load, not data retrieval, has been the biggest problem so far.

Lastly, SEQUOIA 2000 is a multi-disciplinary project in which the participants are geographically dispersed. It has taken a lot of time for the computer scientists and the Earth scientists to understand each other. For example the work "benchmark" means very different things to the two communities. Also, electronic mail and airplane tickets are an inadequate means of maintaining a sense of project coherency. We have purchased video teleconferencing equipment for each site, and make very heavy use of it. Even with this technology, staying in touch is a major challenge.

6. CONCLUSIONS

The SEQUOIA 2000 project plans an initial software distribution consisting of Highlight, Inversion, POSTGRES, the AVS-POSTGRES bridge, the big lift, Lassen, and perhaps an early version of Tioga during 1993. Sequoia Global Change investigators plan to use the prototype tools for analysis of Earth science data and models, in innovative ways that would have been difficult without the SEQUOIA 2000 environment.

REFERENCES

[CHEN91]   Chen, J. et. al., "The SEQUOIA 2000 Object Browser," University of California, Berkeley, SEQUOIA 2000 Technical Report 91/4 December, 1991.

[DIXI91]   Dixit, S. and Feng, Y., "Hierarchical Address Vector Quantization for Image Coding," CVGIP--Graphical Models and Image Processing, January, 1991.

[DOZI92]   Dozier, J., "How SEQUOIA 2000 Addresses Issues in Data and Information Systems for Global Change, University of California, Berkeley, SEQUOIA 2000 Technical Report 92/14, August, 1992.

[EVAN91]   Evans, D. et. al., "A Summary of the CLARIT Project," Laboratory for Computational Linguistics Report CMU-LCL-91-2, Carnegie Mellon University, November, 1991.

[FERR90]   Ferrari, D., "Client Requirements for Real-time Communication Services," IEEE Communications Magazine, November 1990.

[FINE92]   Fine, J., "Abstracts: A Latency-Hiding Technique for High-Capacity Mass-Storage Systems," University of California, Berkeley, SEQUOIA 2000 Technical Report 92/11, June, 1992.

[HELL93]   Hellerstein, J. and Stonebraker, M., "Predicate Migration: Optimizing Queries with Expensive Predicates," Proc. 1993 ACM-SIGMOD International Conference on Management of Data, Philadelphia, Pa., May 1993.

[HERO80]   Herot, C., "SDMS: A Spatial Data Base System," ACM TODS, June 1980.

[KATZ91]   Katz, R., "High Performance Network and Channel-Based Storage," University of California, Berkeley, SEQUOIA 2000 Technical Report 91/2, October, 1991.

[KOHL93]   Kohl, J. et. al., "Highlight: Using a Log-structured File System for Tertiary Storage Management," USENIX Association Winter 1993 Conference Proceedings, San Diego, January, 1993.

[LARS91]   Larson, R., "Classification, Clustering, Probabilistic Infor-
                mation Retrieval and the Online Catalog," Library Quarterly,
                April, 1991.

[LYNC91]   Lynch, C., "SIG LAN and ASIS Standards Committee -- The
                NISO Z39.50 Information Retrieval Protocol: Applications
                and Implementation," Proceedings of the ASIS Annual
                Meeting, 1991.

[MILL92]   Miller, E. and Katz, R., "Input/Output Behavior of Super-
                computing Applications," Proceedings of Supercomputing
                '91, November, 1991.

[NRC92]   National Research Council, Computer Science and Telecom-
                munications Board, "Computing the Future: A Broader
                Agenda for Computer Science and Engineering," National
                Academy Press, Washington, D.C., 1992.

[OLSO93]   Olson, M., "The Design and Implementation of the Inversion
                File System," USENIX Association Winter 1993 Conference
                Proceedings, San Diego, CA., January 1993.

[PATT88]   Patterson, D. et. al., "RAID: Redundant Arrays of Inexpen-
                sive Disks," Proc. 1988 ACM-SIGMOD International
                Conference on Management of Data," Chicago, Ill, June
                1988.

[ROSE92]   Rosenblum, M. and Ousterhout, J., "The Design and Imple-
                mentation of a Log-structured File System," ACM Transac-
                tions on Computer Systems, February 1992.

[SARA93]   Sarawagi, S., "Improving Array Access Through Chunking,
                Reordering, and Replication," (in preparation).

[SELT93]   Seltzer, M. et. al., "An Implementation of a Log-structured
                File System for UNIX," USENIX Association Winter 1993
                Conference Proceedings, San Diego, January, 1993.

[STON90]   Stonebraker, M. et. al., "The Implementation of
                POSTGRES," IEEE Transactions on Knowledge and Data
                Engineering, March, 1990.

[STON91]   Stonebraker, M. and Dozier, J., "SEQUOIA 2000: Large
                Capacity Object Servers to Support Global Change
                Research, University of California, Berkeley, SEQUOIA
                2000 Technical Report 91/1, July, 1991.

[STON91b]   Stonebraker, M., and Kemnitz, G., "The POSTGRES Next
                Generation Database Management System," CACM,
                October 1991.

[STON92]   Stonebraker, M., "Tioga: Providing Data Management Sup-
                port for Scientific Visualization Applications," University of
                California, Berkeley, SEQUOIA 2000 Technical Report
                92/20, December, 1992.

412

[STON93]   Stonebraker, M. and Olson, M., "Large Object Support in POSTGRES," Proceedings of the 1993 International Conference on Data Engineering, Vienna, Austria, April, 1993.

[STON93b]   Stonebraker, M. et. al., "The Sequoia 2000 Storage Benchmark," Proc. 1993 ACM-SIGMOD International Conference on Management of Data, Philadelphia, Pa., May 1993.

Neighborhood query and analysis with GeoSAL, a spatial database language

Zhexue Huang
Environmental and Natural Resources Information Systems
Royal Institute of Technology
S - 100 44 Stockholm, Sweden

Per Svensson
Division of Applied Mathematics and Data Processing
National Defence Research Establishment
S - 172 90 Sundbyberg, Sweden

Abstract

Although some database query languages provide basic functions useful for statistical data analysis and others contain spatial query capabilities, there is as yet no database language implementation which satisfies even basic requirements of spatial analysis.

GeoSAL is a database language being designed to address the solution of descriptive data analysis tasks in general, and spatial analysis problems in particular. The objective of the development of GeoSAL is to free analyst users from procedural programming while retaining a systematic and parsimonious language structure embedding fundamental as well as domain-specific concepts.

A number of spatial queries and analyses are characterized by the application of neighborhood conditions to spatial objects. Thus, the specification and evaluation of neighborhood conditions within a spatial database language is an important issue in spatial database research.

In this paper, several kinds of neighboring relationships are formulated in GeoSAL and the use of the resulting expressions is shown in examples. The capacity of GeoSAL to perform spatial operations involving non-trivial neighborhood conditions is thus demonstrated.

1. Introduction

In recent years substantial efforts have been made to extend conventional query languages [Egen89, Lori91, Aref91] or to design new ones [Guti88, Main90, Goh89] to suit spatial applications.

Although some query languages provide basic functions for statistical calculations, like average, standard deviation, minimum, maximum, etc., and others contain capabilities for spatial querying, there is as yet no query language implementation which satisfies even basic requirements of spatial analysis tasks. Such tasks usually have to be solved with the aid of application-specific modules of a geographical information system (GIS).

GISs as tools for spatial analysis have been widely used in different applications. Some GIS products have reached an impressive level of functionality. Thus, in many cases the major obstacle to the use of GIS in spatial analysis applications is not lack of functionality but the large number of concepts and commands that have to be mastered [Good90a].

In two previous papers [Sven91, Huan92a], we have discussed classes of operations required for spatial analysis and proposed a database language, GeoSAL, which has been designed to provide the required functionality. We have also given examples of the use of GeoSAL in spatial analysis applications. This paper continues our discussion by showing how GeoSAL can be used to express the solution of several problems in neighborhood analysis.

Neighborhood is a fundamental concept in spatial analysis [Unwi81, Davi86, Berr87, Toml90]. Typical examples of spatial analysis using the neighborhood concept include surface interpolation [Gold89], slope and gradient analysis [Unwi81], and nearest-neighbor analysis [Davi86].

An elegant presentation of neighborhood operations was given in [Toml90]. Based on the classical raster model [Fran91] (which we will henceforth call the square regular tessellation model), Tomlin defines a neighborhood as any set of one or more locations (a location is identical to a raster element or a pixel) that bear a specified distance and/or directional relationship to a particular location, the neighborhood focus. Then, the concepts focal location, adjacency, distance and direction are used to specify a neighborhood so that the locations within a neighborhood can be identified. Also, a number of operations were proposed to analyze locations within a neighborhood.

The neighborhood concept has been introduced in spatial database languages by including functions and operators such as distance, neighbor, meets, nearest, furthest, voronoi [Egen89, Rous88, Guti88, Sven91]. Even some very vague concepts, such as near, close to, left, right, etc., have been proposed. Only a few operators (e.g., adjacency) were illustrated by concrete query examples [Egen89, Guti88, Huan92a, 92b].

In this paper, we summarize in Section 2 the basic concepts of our spatial database language GeoSAL. In Section 3, we review several previously introduced definitions of neighborhood and, in Section 4, we show how they can be expressed in GeoSAL. Operations valid under specific neighborhood conditions on regular tessellation data types are discussed. Then, certain operations are extended to the irregular tessellation data type. The presentation is supported, in Section 5, by query and analysis examples expressed as GeoSAL statements.

Gold has pointed out [Gold91] that the Voronoi diagram [Aure91] can be used to transform the distance-based neighborhood concept to the topological concept of adjacency. We review the Voronoi neighborhood concept in Section 3.2. In Sections 4.2 and 5, we show how the Voronoi neighborhood concept can be expressed in GeoSAL and used in neighborhood analyses.

In Section 3.3.3, we review the distance transformation concept [Borg86, 88]. Given a set of initial raster elements, a distance transformation converts a binary raster, representing accessible and non-accessible regions, to a distance raster, where all raster elements in the accessible regions have been replaced or extended with an approximate value of the distance to the nearest initial raster element. Using this technique, one can efficiently compute good approximate values of the distance from a set of initial raster elements to all other elements in the raster, a frequently occurring task in spatial analysis applications. In Section 4, we show how such a computation can be compactly expressed in GeoSAL, using a recursive query expression. Given efficient optimization techniques for queries of this kind, the example provides evidence of the expressive power of the database language approach to spatial analysis.

This work is part of the GeoSAL project [Sven91, Huan92a]. GeoSAL is a spatial query language based on an extended relational data model which integrates the object and layer models commonly found in GISs. It is designed for a prototype spatial analysis and decision support system which is being developed as an extension of the relational data analysis system Cantor, designed and built by the National Defence Research Establishment (FOA) in Stockholm [Kara83, 85].

The objective of the development of GeoSAL is to free analyst users from procedural programming while retaining a systematic, parsimonious, and extensible language structure embedding fundamental as well as domain-specific concepts.

In view of these overall objectives, the present paper aims at demonstrating the feasibility of designing a declarative (non-procedural) database language which bridges the gap between database access and analytic problem solving facilities, here in particular for the solution of neighborhood problems.

In the now completed first phase of the GeoSAL project, our main concerns have been expressive power and semantic correctness of the language. A formal EBNF syntax has been developed, which can be fed into an object-oriented parser and syntax-tree generator [Grap92] to produce a tool which accepts queries in the language.

2. A review of GeoSAL concepts

GeoSAL is a development of the non-procedural query language SAL [Arnb80], which strictly follows set-algebraic semantic conventions and syntactically resembles a mathematician's set algebra notation.

The GeoSAL type system includes system types, the possibility for the user to define new types, type inheritance (both for system and user defined types), generic types and structured types. It is designed to be expressive and easily extendible. It provides a range of system defined types, as well as mechanisms for defining new types.

Operators are defined on these data types. Some of them are polymorphic, i.e., change their algorithmic behaviour automatically as required by the current representation of their operands.

In spatial modeling two views, object and layer, are commonly used [Good90b]. In GeoSAL these two views are integrated in the sense that spatial objects can be organized into layers based on their spatial types and non-spatial category attributes. GeoSAL provides the generic type (see below) Tessellation for layers of polygons in vector representation. For the representation of raster layers, the generic type Raster is provided, which is a specialization of Tessellation.

The semantic properties of the GeoSAL data model can be summarized as follows:

(1) Every database object has a well-defined, named type. Type names may be used in other type and object definitions.

(2) Attributes and tuples may be structured. Conceptually, an attribute type is a pair (<name>, <value type>), where <value type> can be any GeoSAL type expression.

Syntactically, attribute types are specified as <attribute name> <value delimiter> <value type>, where <value delimiter> is either "::", denoting key attributes (see (6) below), or ":".

(3) The instances of a given tuple type are individual database objects, i.e., they have a name, unique within their contextual scope, may have a defining view and may possess a value. Tuple operations can be used to identify, aggregate, and disaggregate tuples.

(4) Set types are ordered sets of scalars of the same type ("scalar sets") or sets of tuples of the same type ("relations"). Set operations may be applied to expressions of any set type, relation operations only to expressions of relation type.

(5) Although a tuple instance is an individual object, it may contain attributes whose values are relations.

(6) The notion of key applies to both tuple and relation types. A key is a subtuple whose value must be unique for each tuple instance in a relation. A relation key induces an ordering relationship on the tuples of the relation. The key propagation semantics is well-defined for each tuple, set, and relation operator.

2.1 Predefined non-spatial types

GeoSAL types are divided into three categories: scalar valued, tuple valued and set valued. Predefined scalar valued types are Integer, Float, Logical, and Literal. Predefined tuple types are all spatial (see Table 1). Predefined types will also be called system types.

A set valued type MySet is defined by:

TYPE MySet := SET_OF T;

where T can be either scalar valued, thus forming a scalar set object, or tuple valued, forming a tuple set object (a relation). Sets of sets are not allowed.

The simplest form of a tuple type is a:T, where a is the attribute name and T its type value. Tuples of more than one attribute are formed by the tuple concatenation operator .(,,,) that takes any number of arguments separated by commas.

Tuple valued types can be defined in two ways:

(1) By construction, that is, specification of the tuple structure.

(2) By restriction of an existing tuple valued type, for example:

TYPE MyPoint := Point with [xc = 0];

Generic types are not types that can be instantiated but rather type patterns from which a number of types can be derived by substituting actual type parameters. The effect is one of text substitution, as in a macro expansion. Syntactically, a generic type is denoted by a bracketed list of formal generic parameter specifications. A generic parameter can be constrained to a specific inheritance hierarchy, for example:

TYPE XY_raster [T -> Tuple] := Raster [XY_square, T];

Here, the formal generic type parameter T can only be assigned an actual type which is a descendant of the predefined type Tuple.

2.2 Predefined spatial types

In addition to the scalar valued system types already mentioned there are a number of predefined spatial types in GeoSAL.

In Table 1, below, we give their definitions as if they were user defined, starting with tuple valued non-generic types:

```
TYPE Point := .(id::Integer, xc:Float, yc:Float);
TYPE Line := .(id::Integer, vertices:SET_OF Point);
TYPE Closed_Line := .(id::Integer, vertices:SET_OF Point);
TYPE Polygon := .(id::Integer, vertices:SET_OF Point);
TYPE Reg_polygon := .(id::Integer, geometry:.(nsides:Integer,
                                    origin:Point, rot:Float, side:Float));
TYPE Square := Reg_polygon WITH [geometry.nsides = 4];
TYPE XY_Square := Square WITH [geometry.rot = 0];
TYPE Reg_hexagon := Reg_polygon WITH [geometry.nsides = 6];
TYPE Topup_hexagon := Reg_hexagon WITH [geometry.rot = 0];
TYPE Sideup_hexagon := Reg_hexagon WITH [geometry.rot = pi_div6];
```

Tuple valued generic types:

```
TYPE Pixel [T -> Tuple] := .(index:.(i::Integer, j::Integer), attr:T);
TYPE Polygon_ext [T -> Tuple] := .(pg::Polygon, attr:T);
TYPE Tessellation [T -> Tuple] := .(id::Integer, SET_OF Polygon_ext [T]);
TYPE Raster [R -> Reg_polygon, T -> Tuple] := .(id::Integer,
                                    shape:.(ll:R, m:Integer, n:Integer),
                                    image:SET_OF Pixel [T]);
TYPE Square_raster [T -> Tuple] := Raster [Square, T];
TYPE XY_raster [T -> Tuple] := Raster [XY_square, T];
TYPE Hex_raster [T -> Tuple] := Raster [Reg_hexagon, T];
TYPE Topup_raster [T -> Tuple] := Raster [Topup_hexagon, T];
TYPE Sideup_raster [T -> Tuple] := Raster [Sideup_hexagon, T];
```

Table 1. Predefined spatial data types in GeoSAL.

We expect most of the concepts presented in Table 1 to be self-explanatory. Note that Reg_Polygon represents a regular polygon and that Topup_hexagon and Sideup_hexagon represent regular hexagons, oriented with one corner respectively one side in the "north" direction.

It is not possible to create named types from either Reg_polygon or Raster. They are only conceptual types introduced to clarify the type hierarchy. Tuple is conceptual (has no structure and cannot be instantiated), but can still be used in generic type definitions to restrict the actual parameters.

In GeoSAL, a spatial data type, such as Point, Line, or Polygon, defines an abstract data structure as a specialization of a tuple or relation type, and is used to model spatial objects in vector representation.

The GeoSAL type system is visualized in Fig. 1.

418

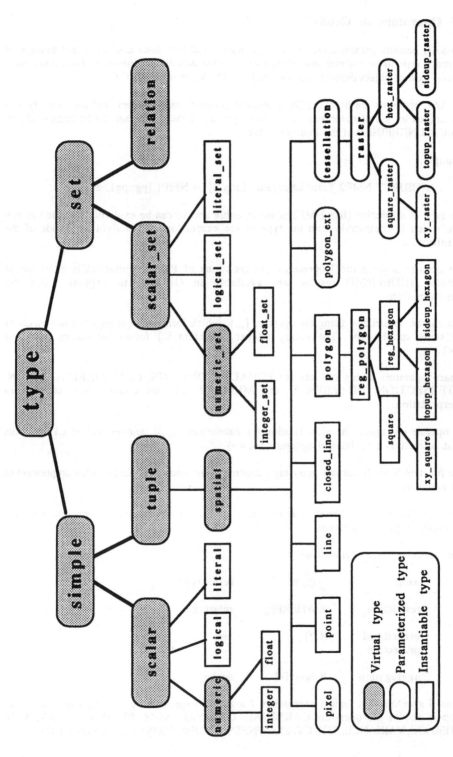

Fig. 1 Inheritance structure for the predefined types of GeoSAL

2.3 Operators in GeoSAL

GeoSAL permits parameterized or non-parameterized functions and other expressions of arbitrary type to be defined and referenced in other definitions. Function definitions are a special case of object definitions, designated by the keyword OBJECT.

GeoSAL operators are functions from operand values to result values, and the result type is determined by the operator and the operand type(s). If the result can not be computed, the result is UNDEFINED of the appropriate type.

Example:

OBJECT NMP2:Tessellation[attr1:Literal] := NMP1 [pg::pg1, attr1];

The type of a function (like NMP2 in the example above) can be explicitly specified as any type which is compatible with the type of the expression on the right hand side of the definition.

The built-in mathematical operators and functions of Pascal, semantically extended to include UNDEFINED results, are available in GeoSAL to express arithmetic transformations.

Sets can be constructed using the operator {,,,}, which forms a set from a list of objects of the same simple type. The binary integer operation i..j forms the enumeration set $i, i+1, ..., j$.

Binary operators acting on sets are EQUALS, CONTAINS, CONTAINEDIN, UNION, INTERSECTION, DIFFERENCE, and MEMBER with the conventional set algebra interpretation.

To operate on tuples, the identification (:), catenation (.(,,,)), and extraction (.) operators exist, as well as the relational operators (=, <>).

The function VALUE takes a unary tuple argument and returns the scalar value component of the argument.

There are two kinds of operators acting on relations, namely functional form operators and the cartesian product operator.

The functional form operators are:

name	syntax	result type
restriction	R WHERE[l]	relation
generalized projection	R [f]	set
aggregation	R agop [e]	scalar

where l symbolizes a logical expression, f a simple expression, e a scalar expression, and agop is one of the operators CARDINAL, ORDINAL, SUM, PRODUCT, MAX, MIN, AVERAGE, VARIANCE, STD, CV, SKEWNESS, EXCESS, EXISTS, ALL, and COUNT.

The function ELEMENT takes a set argument. If the cardinality of the set is 1, it returns the unique set element, otherwise it returns UNDEFINED.

A generalized projection expression may involve aggregation over the set of tuples of the argument relation, or over specified partitions. Assume, for example, that the relation R has attributes age, sex, and salary. Then, the expression

R [agegroup:: age DIV 5, sex:: sex, n: CARDINAL, ss: SUM(salary)]

is a generalized projection which produces a partitioning of R with respect to agegroup and sex, containing the number of cases and total salary for each value of the key .(agegroup, sex). All attributes of a partitioned aggregation whose value expressions do not involve aggregation operators must belong to the partitioning key.

The cartesian product operator *(,,,) takes one or more relations (factors) as argument and produces a result relation, whose attributes are the union of the sets of attributes of the factors.

The following classes of spatial operators are defined:

(1) Unary geometrical operators which compute scalar geometrical data from one object.

AREA	Area of polygon.
LENGTH	Length of line or segment.

(2) Binary geometrical operators which compute scalar geometrical relationships between two or more objects.

DIRDISTANCE	Distance in/along a given direction.
DIRECTION	Direction of segment.
DISTANCE	Shortest Euclidean distance.

(3) Unary object transformation operators that transform one spatial object into another.

BOUNDARY	Boundary curve of polygon.
CENTER_POINT	Center point of a raster element.
CLOSELINE	Closes a line, i.e. connects its start- and endpoint.
EP	End point of line.
EXTEND	Grows or shrinks a point, line or polygon.
NODE	m:th node point of a line.
NODES	Ordered set of points from a line.
POLYGON	Creates a polygon from a simply closed line.
RASTER_ELEMENT	(i,j):th polygon of a raster.
ROTATE	Rotate segment, line, or polygon.
SCALE	Changes size of an object.
SEGMENT	m:th segment of a line.
SEGMENTS	Ordered set of segments from a line.
SP	Start point of line.
TRANSLATE	Translates an object by a given vector.

(4) Binary topological operators which test topological relationships of two objects.

ADJOINS	Decides whether the boundary of two objects have common points while their interiors are disjoint.
CONTAINS	Decides whether one object contains another.

EQUALS	Decides whether two objects are equal.
INTERSECTS	Decides whether two objects intersect.
OVERLAPS	Decides whether two objects overlap.

(5) Object construction operators which construct new objects from several existing objects.

CUT	Cuts a line or a polygon into two or more parts, defined by an intersecting line.
DIFFUSE	Computes arrival times for a diffusion process over a raster.
VISIBLE	Creates a visibility raster for a given point.
VORONOI	Computes a voronoi tessellation for a given set of disjoint spatial objects.

In addition, the set operators UNION, INTERSECTION, and DIFFERENCE can be applied to spatial objects of the same type. The operators AUNION and AINTERSECTION [Huan92a] are "spatial aggregation" operators acting on sets of polygons, in particular tessellations and rasters.

3. Neighborhood and neighboring relationships

Three kinds of topological relationship between two spatial objects are immediately distinguishable:

(1) Disjoint, i.e., two objects are separated by other objects or empty space.
(2) Adjacent, i.e., two objects touch each other.
(3) Overlapping, i.e., two objects occupy some common space.

In the irregular tessellation model (the layer model), a set of objects with relationships of the first two kinds can be represented in a single layer, whereas objects satisfying the third kind of relationships have to be represented using several layers. If objects in different layers are involved in a problem, they can be transformed into a single layer by using overlay and reclassification operations [Huan92a].

A neighborhood is characterized by the following properties:

(1) It has a unique focal object.
(2) Objects within it relate to the focal object by well-defined neighboring relationship(s).
(3) Objects within it do not overlap each other.
(4) It can be represented by the set of all objects which satisfy properties 2 and 3.

A neighborhood is used to specify which objects are participating in a localized spatial query or analysis.

In the following subsections, we discuss several kinds of neighboring relationships and show how these relationships are used together with different object types.

3.1 Adjacency

The simplest neighboring relationship is adjacency. This relationship is the basis for local computations in digital image processing. Many operations like edge detection, smoothing, thinning, median filtering, sharpening, thresholding, counting, skeletonizing, matching, border following, etc., are based on the adjacency relationship [Levi83]. A number of operations in raster-based GISs are also based on this relationship [Toml90]. In GeoSAL, the adjacency relationship is represented by the operator ADJOINS (called MEETS in [Sven91, Huan92a]).

In the square regular tessellation model [Fran91, Sven91], space is partitioned into square objects (pixels) of the same size and orientation. Every square is surrounded by eight adjacent squares (see Fig.2a). If r is a focal object, then the other eight objects are adjacent neighbors of r.

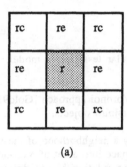
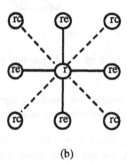

(a)   (b)

Fig. 2. A focal object and its 8-neighborhood in the square regular tessellation model.

Objects within this neighborhood are related to the focal object by two kinds of adjacency relationships: objects connected by a common boundary (r and re in Fig. 2a) and objects connected by a common corner point (rc and r in Fig. 2a). In digital image processing it is important to distinguish these two adjacency relationships, since obviously the same operations on the neighborhoods defined by them may produce very different results.

The neighborhood defined by combining the two kinds of adjacency relationships is called 8-neighborhood. This neighborhood can be represented as a graph in which objects are represented as nodes and the adjacency relation as arcs (Fig. 2b). We denote the first kind of adjacency by solid lines and the second kind by broken lines.

The adjacency relationships can also be applied to objects in the irregular tessellation model. Assume that we want to specify a neighborhood of the object c in Fig. 3a using an adjacency relationship. As before, two distinct adjacency relationships exist (see connections of objects 2 and 6 to c).

Based on the adjacency relationships, the map in Fig. 3a can also be represented as the graph of Fig. 3b. The neighborhood of object c defined by two adjacency relations is represented as the subnetwork of Fig. 3c.

3.2 The Voronoi neighboring relationship

The neighboring relationship of adjacency can only be applied to objects which share one or more boundary points. There is no unique way to define a neighboring relationship between discrete objects irregularly scattered in space. Distance functions are widely used to describe the neighboring relationship between such objects, as will be discussed in the next section.

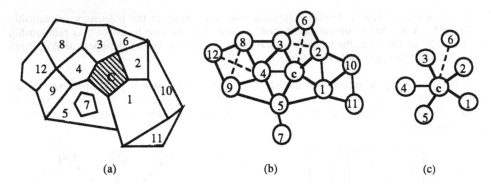

Fig. 3. Adjacency relationships in the irregular tessellation model.

In this section we discuss a topological approach - the Voronoi approach [Gold91, 92] - to define the neighboring relationship between spatially disjoint objects.

Given a set of point objects (Fig. 4a), we want to specify a neighborhood of the focal point c. First, we use the Voronoi diagram to subdivide the space into a set of Voronoi regions, each containing a point object. Then, the neighboring relationship is defined by the adjacency of Voronoi regions, i.e., if two Voronoi regions have a common boundary segment, then the points inside them are neighbors. For points on such a boundary segment, the two neighboring objects are the closest among all the objects in the given set.

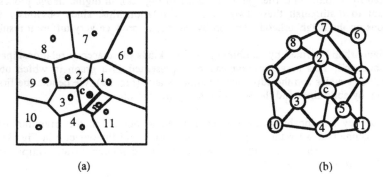

Fig. 4. The Voronoi neighboring relationship.

Obviously, the neighborhood of point c in Fig. 4, defined by the Voronoi neighboring relationship, consists of points 1, 2, 3, 4, and 5. The graph representation of the Voronoi neighboring relationship is shown in Fig. 4b.

In principle, the Voronoi neighboring relationship can be applied to any combination of spatial object types. Since the Voronoi diagram is unique for each set of discrete objects, the Voronoi neighboring relationship between two objects is also uniquely defined.

A basic algorithm for constructing the Voronoi diagram for a point set can be found in [Prep85]. A comprehensive survey of algorithms and applications of Voronoi diagrams is given in [Aure91].

3.3 Distances

The neighborhood concept is frequently defined by reference to a distance measure: all the objects whose distances from a focal object are smaller than a given threshold form the neighborhood of the focal object.

Distances can be defined and computed in a number of ways, useful in different GIS applications [Toml90, Sven91]. The basic concept is the Euclidean distance between two points.

In GeoSAL, the distance between two composite objects is by definition the shortest straight-line Euclidean distance between pairs of boundary elements, one from each object.

In applications, the relevant distance measure usually has to take interspersed non-accessible regions, or linear paths in an otherwise non-accessible region, into account. Such global shortest distance, or more generally, shortest travel time problems may require complicated algorithms (see, e.g., [Mitch88]). Problems get even more difficult when the extension and kinematics of moving objects must be taken into account (motion planning [Hwan92]).

In Section 3.3.3, we discuss a computational technique which can be used to provide good approximations for global shortest distances in regular tessellation models, and is simple enough to be expressed directly in GeoSAL.

3.3.1 Distance in the square regular tessellation model

The square regular tessellation model partitions space into a set of small squares (called raster elements or pixels) of the same size and orientation. Each element is a basic unit for registering spatial information and can be identified by a pair of row and column indices (i,j). Fig. 5 shows the relationship between row and column indices and spatial coordinates for the four corner points and the center of a pixel at (i,j).

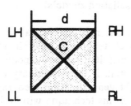

coordinates	LL	LH	C	RL	RH
x	d*(i-1)	d*(i-1)	d*(i-1/2)	d*i	d*i
y	d*(j-1)	d*j	d*(j-1/2)	d*(j-1)	d*j

Fig. 5. Parameters of a raster element

In GeoSAL, raster data are viewed in an object-based manner [Huan92a]. Four composite objects in raster representation are shown in Fig. 6. A, B, D and E are the category attribute values of the composite objects. The double arrows indicate the distances between pairs of composite objects.

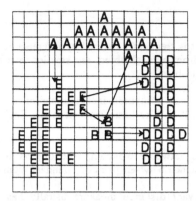

Fig. 6. Distance between composite objects in the square regular tessellation model.

3.3.2. Distance in the irregular tessellation model

Objects represented in the irregular tessellation model are represented by their closed-line boundaries. The distance between two points is their Euclidean distance. The distance between a point and an extended object (line, polygon, set of lines etc) is defined as the minimum distance between the point and the set of points belonging to the extended object. The distance between two extended, disjoint objects is analogously defined as the shortest distance between two arbitrary points, one from each object. Obstacles are not taken into account. The distance between objects which share interior points is undefined.

3.3.3 Computing global shortest distances using distance transformations

A frequently occurring task in spatial analysis applications is the computation of global shortest distances in regular tessellation models.

To solve problems of this kind, one may use so-called distance transformations [Borg86, 88], an iterative computational technique which allows efficient computation of approximate distance from a set of initial raster elements to all other elements in the raster. Obstacles can be taken into account, if their boundary features are large in comparison to the raster elements. With a slight generalization, geographically varying speed limitations can also be considered. The use of this technique will be illustrated in Example 4.7, below.

Given a set of initial raster elements, a distance transformation converts a binary raster, representing accessible and non-accessible regions, to a numeric distance raster, whose raster elements represent the distance to the nearest initial raster element.

Distance transformation algorithms which produce correct Euclidean distance rasters are known for regular square rasters, but they are computationally demanding and require an intermediate storage twice as large as the original image. Approximate Euclidean distance rasters can be obtained by iterative application of a local raster operator which takes as input previously computed distance values in a small neighborhood around each accessible raster element.

Initially, all points outside the initial region are assigned infinite distance values. In each iteration, the previous iteration's distance value at the raster element is compared with the shortest total distance for paths via neighborhood elements and is replaced by the smaller of the two. The distance via a neighborhood element is computed as the sum of the neighborhood element's global distance value and the operator's approximation of the distance between the neighborhood element and the given raster element.

Fast approximate Euclidean distance transformations have been developed and analyzed for square and hexagonal rasters. Using these approximations, it is possible to compute a distance transformation with an error of only a few percent. The integer Euclidean distance transformation operator using a 3x3 neighborhood shown in Fig. 7a has an approximation error of less than 8%, and the best 5x5 integer operator (Fig. 7b) has an error less than 2%.

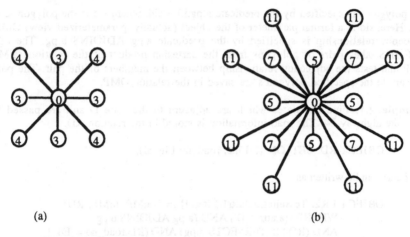

(a)   (b)

Fig. 7. Optimal 3x3 (a) and 5x5 (b) integer distance transformation operators (see [Borg86]).

By generalizing the concept of distance transformation operators, the local metric may be taken into account. Thus, distance transformation algorithms can be used to compute lowest cost paths in spatial raster models.

4. Neighborhood queries in GeoSAL

4.1 Queries based on the adjacency relationship

The operator ADJOINS is defined in GeoSAL as a fundamental topological operator to detect the adjacency relationship between two objects. ADJOINS does not apply to point objects. Neither is there much to be gained by defining an adjacency relationship between two lines [Huan92b]. On the other hand, the adjacency relationship between two polygons is a useful and well-defined concept [Egen90, 91].

ADJOINS can be applied to both raster and vector objects. Different types of objects require different algorithms. The type system of GeoSAL enables the query evaluator to select the appropriate algorithm in each situation.

Suppose we have a layer defined by:

```
TYPE Layer[T] := Tessellation[T];
OBJECT MP : Layer[attr1:Literal,  attr2:Integer];
```

Query type 1: Find polygonal objects in MP adjacent to the specified polygon s. s may be specified by its identifier or by its spatial or non-spatial properties.

GeoSAL expression:

> OBJECT OMP(sid:Integer): Tessellation[attr1:Literal] :=
> *(a:MP, b:MP)
> WHERE [(a.pg.id = sid) AND (a.pg ADJOINS b.pg)]
> [pg::b.pg, attr1:b.attr1];

The polygon s is specified by the predicate a.pg.id = sid, where sid is the polygon identifier of s. Here, sid is a formal parameter of the object (actually, parameterized view) OMP. The adjacency relationship is specified by the predicate a.pg ADJOINS b.pg. The operator ADJOINS takes pairs of polygons from the cartesian product of the relations a:MP and b:MP and tests the adjacency relationship between the members of the pair. The polygons adjacent to the specified polygon s are saved in the relation OMP.

Example 4.1: Find the states which are adjacent to the state D and are passed by the interstate highway E4. The road information is stored in the relation RD:

> OBJECT RD: SET_OF .(l::Line, road_no:Literal);

The query can be written as:

> OBJECT LR2: Tessellation[attr1:Literal] := *(a:MP, b:MP, RD)
> WHERE [(a.attr1='D') AND (a.pg ADJOINS b.pg)
> AND (RD.l INTERSECTS b.pg) AND (RD.road_no = 'E4')]
> [pg::b.pg, attr1:b.attr1];

The polygonal and linear objects are combined in the same query and are specified by the adjacency and intersection relationships.

Query type 2: Find objects with specified adjacent objects.

Example 4.2: Find objects that have adjacent objects with an attribute value B.

GeoSAL expression:

> OBJECT NMP: Tessellation[attr1:Literal] := *(a:MP, b:MP)
> WHERE [(b.attr1 = 'B') AND (a.pg ADJOINS b.pg)]
> [pg::a.pg, attr1:a.attr1];

NMP contains objects which are adjacent to objects with the attribute value B. This query differs from queries of type 1 in that the neighboring relationships and the properties of the neighboring objects are specified, whereas the focal objects having the specified neighbors are selected.

If information about the adjacent objects is needed, the query can be modified as:

> OBJECT NMP1: SRelation := *(a:MP, b:MP)
> WHERE [(b.attr1='B') AND (a.pg ADJOINS b.pg)]
> [pg1::a.pg, pg2::b.pg, attr1:a.attr1, attr2:b.attr1];

where SRelation is defined as:

    TYPE SRelation := SET_OF
    .(pg1::Polygon, pg2::Polygon, attr1:Literal,attr2:Literal);

Note that precise result type specification is not mandatory, but allows the system to type-check the result of the expression.

pg1 and attr1 represent the focal objects, and pg2 and attr2 the neighboring objects. SRelation is no longer a tessellation but combines two sets of polygons.

The focal objects can be found by projection of the first part from relation NMP1:

    OBJECT NMP2: Tessellation[attr1:Literal] :=
        NMP1 [pg::pg1, attr1];

and the neighboring objects by projection:

    OBJECT NMP3: Tessellation[attr1:Literal] :=
        NMP1 [pg::pg2, attr2];

The repeated objects in the second part of NMP1 are removed after the projection.

Example 4.3: Find a set of objects which have adjacent objects with attribute values A, B, C. Suppose MP represents the map in Fig.8.

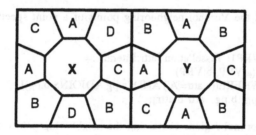

Fig. 8. A set of objects in an irregular tessellation.

GeoSAL expression:

    OBJECT NMP4:Tessellation[attr1:Literal] :=
        *(x:MP, a: MP, b:MP, c:MP)
        WHERE [(a.attr1='A') AND (x.pg ADJOINS a.pg)
        AND (b.attr1='B') AND (x.pg ADJOINS b.pg)
        AND (c.attr1='C') AND (x.pg ADJOINS c.pg)
        [pg::x.pg, attr1:x.attr1];

The result relation NMP4 will contain the two objects X and Y.

If we also include the objects with attribute value D, then the result relation will contain only the object X.

4.2 Queries based on neighboring relationships between disjoint objects

The operator VORONOI is defined to construct a set of Voronoi regions from a set of disjoint objects. Each Voronoi region is identified by the identifier of the object contained in it. Then, ADJOINS is used to detect the Voronoi neighboring relationship between objects (see Fig. 4).

Suppose a set of points is defined as:

> OBJECT PS: PointSet;

where type PointSet is defined by

> TYPE PointSet := SET_OF .(pt::Point, attr:Literal);

Query type 3: Create a tessellation of Voronoi regions from the point set PS:

> OBJECT VRP:Tessellation[attr:Literal] :=
> *(v:VORONOI(PS [pt]), p:PS)
> WHERE [v.pg CONTAINS p.pt]
> [pg::v.pg, attr:p.attr];

Neighborhood queries about point sets are transformed into queries about polygon sets. All the techniques shown above can be applied.

Example 4.4: Find the Voronoi neighboring points of a point specified with an attribute value.

> OBJECT VRP1: Tessellation [attr:Literal] :=
> *(a:VRP, b:VRP)
> WHERE[(a.attr='A') AND (a.pg ADJOINS b.pg)]
> [pg::b.pg, attr:b.attr];

VRP1 is a set of Voronoi regions containing the neighboring points of the specified point. We can get the neighboring points by the expression:

> OBJECT NPS: SET_OF .(p::Point, attr:Literal) :=
> *(a:VRP1, b:PS) WHERE[a.pg CONTAINS b.p]
> [p::b.p, attr:b.attr];

Similarly, we can apply the VORONOI operator to a line or a polygon set.

4.3 Queries based on distance

Suppose the set of attributed points PS is defined as:

> OBJECT PS: SET_OF .(p::Point, attr:Literal);

Example 4.5: Find pairs of points in PS whose mutual distance is less than a given number d. Also extract the attributes of these points and their distance.

```
TYPE PRelation := SET_OF
.(p1::Point, p2::Point, attr1:Literal, attr2:Literal, d:Float);

OBJECT PS1(d: Float): PRelation := *(a:PS, b:PS)
        WHERE [ dis:DISTANCE(a.p, b.p) < d ]
        [p1::a.p, p2::b.p, attr1:a.attr, attr2:b.attr, d:dis];
```

Example 4.6: Find the nearest neighbor(s) of each point in PS:

```
OBJECT PS2: Relation :=
        *(a:PS, b:PS)
        [p::a.p, d:MIN(DISTANCE(a.p, b.p))];

OBJECT PS3: Relation :=
        *(a:PS2, b:PS)
        WHERE [ a.p = b.p ]
        [p::a.p, attr:b.attr, d:a.d];

OBJECT PS4: PRelation :=
        *(a:PS3, b:PS)
        WHERE [ DISTANCE(a.p, b.p) = a.d ]
        [p1::a.p, p2::b.p, attr1:a.attr, attr2:b.attr,
        d:a.d];
```

Since this is a fairly complicated sequence of expressions, one would probably find it useful to define a parameterized view which solves the problem for any point set with a single attribute.

Example 4.7: Compute the distance from a given set of pixels to all other pixels in a raster by recursive application of a distance transformation operator. Assume that Draster.image takes the value zero at the initially occupied set of pixels and "infinity" at all other pixels.

```
OBJECT DRaster: XY_raster[dv:Integer];        -- initial data
```

-- define the raster index type Tindex as an (i, j)-tuple:

```
TYPE Tindex := .(i::Integer, j::Integer);
```

-- We also define some auxiliary functions:

-- the function dvalue returns the value of DRaster.image
-- (cf. Table 1) at a given focus:

```
OBJECT dvalue(focus: Tindex):Integer :=
        ELEMENT(DRaster.image
        WHERE[index=focus] [VALUE(attr.dv)]);
```

-- the function offset returns the index difference between
-- two given raster points:

```
OBJECT offset(i1: Tindex, i2:Tindex):Tindex :=
        .(i:i1.i-i2.i, j:i1.j-i2.j);
```

-- the 3x3 distance transformation operator (Fig. 7a)

```
-- is expressed as a function table, using the offset
-- from the focus as argument:

OBJECT distmask: Relation :=
        (off: *(i:-1..1, j:-1..1)  WHERE [off <> .(i:0, j:0)])
        [off, v: IF i=j THEN 3 ELSE 4];


-- the function maskvalue returns the value of the
-- operator distmask for a given offset from the focus:

OBJECT maskvalue(offset:Tindex): Integer :=
        ELEMENT (distmask WHERE [offset=off] [v]);


-- We are now able to formulate a pair of recursive
-- functions whose fixpoint is the required distance
-- image. The recursion converges to the correct value
-- because Dist is, by definition, initially an empty set:

OBJECT Dist1: SET_OF Pixel [dv:Integer] :=
        Dist UNION (DRaster.image WHERE [attr.dv = 0]);


OBJECT Dist:  SET_OF Pixel [dv:Integer] :=
        *(Dist1, d:Dist1)
        WHERE [(offset(index, d.index) MEMBER distmask)
            AND (attr.dv > 0)]
            [index, attr: dv: MIN(
                                maskvalue(offset(index,d.index))
                                + dvalue(d.index))];
```

5. Neighborhood operation examples

A neighborhood operation is a process that extracts information about objects within a neighborhood. The objects are represented as a relation in GeoSAL. If several neighborhoods are involved, the relation is partitioned with respect to focal objects. Therefore, a neighborhood operation can be defined as an aggregation function which is applied to each subset of the partition, i.e., to the objects within each neighborhood.

Example 5.1: Compute elevations of a set of grid points from a set of irregularly located elevation points. Assume that GridPoints and IrrPoints are the two point sets.

Step 1: For each grid point extract its neighboring points from the irregular point set. The distances between the neighboring points and the grid point are less than 100:

```
OBJECT  GridPoints: SET_OF p::Point;
OBJECT IrrPoints: SET_OF .(p::Point, elev:Float);

OBJECT NSet: SET_OF .(p1::Point, p2::Point, elev:Float) :=
        *(a:GridPoints, b:IrrPoints)
        WHERE [DISTANCE(a.p, b.p) <= 100]
        [p1::a.p,  p2::b.p,  elev:b.elev];
```

Step 2: Compute the elevation for each grid point by interpolating the elevations of its neighboring points:

```
OBJECT GridDEM: SET_OF .(p::Point, elev:Float) :=
    NSet [p::p1, elev:INTERPOLATION(elev)];
```

INTERPOLATION is an aggregation function which calculates elevations at the grid points from their neighboring irregular elevation points according to some interpolation method. The simplest method is to compute the average or the weighted average by distance, of elevations at the neighboring points. The former can be expressed by using the GeoSAL operator AVERAGE, and the latter by defining an interpolation function as a composite GeoSAL expression. More complex interpolation methods can be written in a programming language and then added to GeoSAL as a language extension.

In Example 5.1, we specified the neighborhood by using the distance function. The distance threshold specifies the maximum distance to neighboring objects. An alternative is to specify the neighborhood by the Voronoi relationship, in which case the neighborhoods are determined by the local distribution of the irregular points:

Example 5.2: Compute slopes and aspects from an elevation model. Assume that ElePoints is a set of elevation points.

Step 1: Extract the neighboring points of each elevation point using the Voronoi neighboring relationship.

```
OBJECT ElePoints: SET_OF .(pt::Point, elev: Float);

OBJECT VPolygons: Tessellation[pt:Point, elev:Float] :=
    *(v:VORONOI(ElePoints [pt]), p:ElePoints)
    WHERE [v.pg CONTAINS p.pt]
    [pg::v.pg, pt:p.pt, elev:p.elev];

OBJECT NSet1 : SET_OF .(p1::Point, p2::Point,
                        elev1:Float,elev2:Float) :=
    *(a:VPolygons, b:VPolygons)
    WHERE[(a.pg ADJOINS b.pg)]
    [p1::a.pt, p2::b.pt, elev1:a.elev, elev2:b.elev];
```

Step 2: Compute slope and aspect at each point using given functions Slope and Aspect:

```
OBJECT Slope :SET_OF .(p::Point, slope:Float) :=
    NSet1 [p::p1, slope:Slope(p1,elev1,p2,elev2)];

OBJECT Aspect :SET_OF .(p::Point, aspect:Float) :=
    NSet1 [p::p1, aspect:Aspect(p1,elev1,p2,elev2)];
```

Slope and Aspect are two functions which we can specify in GeoSAL. For example, Slope can be implemented as ARCTAN(ABS(elev2 - elev1)/DISTANCE(p1,p2)). The following example shows how a slope function based on a regular digital elevation model can be expressed in GeoSAL.

Example 5.3: An implementation of a slope function, which computes slope along the coordinate directions. A scalar slope value can be computed as SQRT(Eslope ** 2 + Nslope ** 2).

```
-- Eslope and Nslope represent the slope value in the
-- east and north direction, respectively:
```

```
      TYPE TSlope :=     .(Eslope:Float, Nslope:Float);
-     TYPE Tpos :=        .(i:Integer, j:Integer);
      TYPE Tpz :=         .(p::Tpos, z:Float);
      TYPE TpSlope :=    .(p::Tpos, slope:TSlope);
```

-- HTab is the initial elevation data set:

OBJECT HTab: SET_OF Tpz;

-- the function ISlope computes the eastward and northward
-- slopes from values of HTab at points in a 3x3 neigh-
-- borhood of p:

```
OBJECT ISlope(p:Tpos): TSlope :=
          .(Eslope:(hz(.(i:p.i+1,j:p.j)) - hz(.(i:p.i-1,j:p.j)))/(2*k),
            Nslope:(hz(.(i:p.i,j:p.j+1)) - hz(.(i:p.i,j:p.j-1)))/(2*k));
```

OBJECT SlopeTab: SET_OF TpSlope := HTab [p, slope:ISlope(p)];

where:

-- hz extracts the value of htab at the position pp:

OBJECT hz(pp:Tpos):Float := (ELEMENT (HTab WHERE [p=pp])).z;

-- k is the side length of each cell in the elevation
-- data set:

OBJECT k:Float := 0.0625;

Example 5.4: Statistical computations over neighborhoods.

We have seen in the examples above how the focal objects and their neighboring objects can be represented in the same relation, say R(A1,A2,..,B1,B2,..), where A1,A2,.. are attributes of focal objects and B1,B2,.. of their neighboring objects. The relation represents a partitioning of the set of neighboring objects by the focal objects. Therefore, statistical computations can be implemented as aggregation functions operating on the set of neighboring objects.

A simple example is calculation of the average of an attribute of the neighboring objects. Assume GM is a tessellation:

```
      OBJECT FN: SET_OF .(pg1::Polygon, pg2::Polygon, area:Float) :=
              *(a:GM, b:GM) WHERE[a.pg ADJOINS b.pg]
              [pg1::a.pg, pg2::b.pg, area:AREA(b.pg)];

      OBJECT AverArea: Tessellation[average:Float] :=
              FN [pg::pg1, average:AVERAGE(area)];
```

The relation AverArea contains a set of polygons which have an attribute containing the average of areas of the surrounding polygons.

In [Toml90] Tomlin proposes a number of operations like Combination, Variety, Majority, Minority, Percentage, Percentile, Ranking, etc. which can be easily implemented with GeoSAL in a similar way.

6. Conclusions and future work

We have shown in this paper that a number of basic spatial analysis problems involving several neighborhood concepts can be expressed in the declarative extended relational algebra GeoSAL. Although the formulation of query expressions is not always obvious, we claim that the expressive power of GeoSAL is sufficient to make procedural programming superfluous in a large number of spatial analysis tasks. Neither is it necessary to memorize hundreds of unstandardized concepts and special-purpose functions to successfully express the solutions of spatial analysis problems. On the contrary, most of the concepts required in the treated problems could be developed within the language itself, by reference to more fundamental previously developed concepts and finally, relatively few predefined operators.

However, it would be ridiculous to spread the impression that any conceivable kind of spatial analysis problem could be solved within a declarative language like GeoSAL. For example, problems that require complex mathematical modelling, like hydrological dynamics problems, obviously have to be programmed using some kind of procedural programming language. A query language based analysis system which wants to serve such purposes must therefore provide a well-defined interfacing mechanism, by which a user can extend the "query" language with new high-level operators. The precise specification of this interface mechanism remains to be worked out.

Several example queries given in this paper will require carefully designed optimization techniques if they are to be efficiently supported by a spatial analysis system based on the GeoSAL language. Such a set of optimization rules and a corresponding rule manager remains to be specified and implemented.

Fuzzy neighborhood concepts were not treated in this paper, although simple cases of fuzzy neighborhood relationships can be easily expressed in the GeoSAL language. To keep the complexity of the language within bounds, we have chosen not to include any built-in fuzzy operations in the language, although we strongly believe that operations on uncertain data will be a required feature in the spatial analysis systems of the future.

Acknowledgments

The authors acknowledge the contributions to the definition of the syntax and semantics of GeoSAL by several members of the GeoSAL project group. Of particular significance to the issues discussed in this paper are the many important improvements made by Per Grape and Kim Walden to the GeoSAL grammar and type system, and the analysis of the semantics of spatial operators done by Karsten Jöred. Of great importance to the development of a new language is the testing of its concepts in a large number of applications. Such testing is under way, with contributions from Mats Åkerlund, Göran Neider and Johan Schubert. Comments from Prof. Friedrich Quiel are also acknowledged.

References

[Aref91] Aref, W. G. & Samet, H., Extending a DBMS with spatial operations. In: O. Gunther & H.-J. Schek (eds.), Advances in Spatial Databases. Lecture Notes in Computer Science 525, Springer-Verlag 1991.

[Arnb80] Arnborg, S., A Simple Query Language Based on Set Algebra, BIT 20 (1980), 266-278.

[Aure91] Aurenhammer, F., Voronoi Diagrams - A Survey of a Fundamental Geometric Data Structure. ACM Computing Surveys, Vol. 23 (1991), No. 3, 345-405.

[Berr87] Berry, J. K., Fundamental Operations in Computer-Assisted Map Analysis. Int. J. of Geographical Information Systems, Vol. 1 (1987), No. 2, 119-136.

[Borg86] Borgefors, G., Distance Transformations in Digital Images. Computer Vision, Graphics, and Image Processing, Vol. 34 (1986), 344-371.

[Borg88] Borgefors, G., Distance Transformations in Hexagonally Digitized Images. Report C 30497-3.3, National Defence Research Establishment, Linkvping, Sweden, June 1988.

[Davi86] Davis, J. C., Statistics and Data Analysis in Geology. John Wiley & Sons, New York 1986.

[Egen89] Egenhofer, M. J., A Spatial Query Language, Report 103, Dept. of Surveying Engineering, Univ. of Maine, 1989.

[Egen90] Egenhofer, M. & Herring, J.R., A Mathematical Framework for the Definition of Topological Relationships. Proc. 4th Int. Symp. on Spatial Data Handling, Zurich 1990, 803-813.

[Egen91] Egenhofer, M. & Franzosa, R., Point-set topological spatial relations. International Journal of Geographical Information Systems, Vol. 5(1991), No. 2, pp. 161-174.

[Fran91] Frank, A. & Mark, D., Language Issues for GIS. In: Maguire, Goodchild, Rhind (eds), Geographical Information Systems: Principles and Applications, Longman 1991.

[Goh89] Goh, P.-C., A Graphic Query Language for Cartographic and Land Information Systems. Int. J. of Geographical Information Systems, Vol. 3 (1989), No. 3, 245-255.

[Gold89] Gold, C.M., Surface Interpolation, Spatial Adjacency and GIS. In: J. Raper (ed.), Three Dimensional Applications in Geographic Information Systems, Taylor and Francis, London 1989, 21-35.

[Gold91] Gold, C.M., Problems with Handling Spatial Data - the Voronoi Approach. CISM Journal, Vol. 45 (1991), No. 1, pp. 65-80.

[Gold92] Gold, C.M., The Meaning of "Neighbour". In: GIS, from Space to Territory. Theories and Methods of Spatio-Temporal Reasoning. Lecture Notes in Computer Science, Springer-Verlag 1992.

[Good90a] Goodchild, M. F., Spatial Information Science. In: Proceedings of the 4th International Symposium on Spatial Data Handling, Zurich 1990.

[Good90b] Goodchild, M. F., Tutorial on Spatial Data Analysis at 4th Int. Symp. on Spatial Data Handling (lecture notes), Zurich, 1990.

[Grap92] Grape, P. & Walden, K., Automating the Design of Syntax Tree Generators for an Evolving Language. Proceedings of the Tools USA 92 Conference, 1992.

[Guti88] Gueting, R.H., Geo-Relational Algebra: A Model and Query Language for Geometric Database Systems. In: Schmidt, J.W., Ceri, S., & Missikoff, M. (eds), Proc. of the Int. Conf. on Extending Database Technology, Venice 1988, 506-527.

[Huan92a] Huang, Z., Svensson, P. & Hauska, H., Solving Spatial Analysis Problems with Geo-SAL, a Spatial Query Language. Proc. of Sixth Int. Working Conf. on Scientific and Statistical Database Management, Ascona 1992.Dept. Informatik, ETH Zurich 1992.

[Huan92b] Huang, Z., Topological spatial relations and operators. In: Proc. of the 17th ISPRS Congress, Washington D.C. 1992.

[Hwan92] Hwang, Y.K. & Ahuja, N., Gross-Motion Planning, ACM Computing Surveys, Vol. 24 (1992), No. 3, 219-291.

[Kara83] Karasalo, I. & Svensson, P., An Overview of Cantor - a New System for Data Analysis. In: Proc. of the Second Int. Workshop on Statistical Data Base Management, Los Altos 1983. Dept. of Computer Science and Applied Mathematics, Lawrence Berkeley Laboratory 1983.

[Kara85] Karasalo, I. & Svensson, P., Solving Data Analysis Problems with CANTOR, a Relational SDBMS. In: P.S. Glaeser (ed.), The Role of Data in Scientific Progress, Elsevier Science Publishers B.V. 1985.

[Levi83] Levialdi, R., Neighborhood Operators: An Outlook. In: R. M. Haralick (ed), Pictorial Data Analysis, Springer-Verlag 1983.

[Lori91] Lorie, R. A., The Use of a Complex Object Language in Geographic Data Management. In: O. Gunther & H.-J. Schek (eds.), Advances in Spatial Databases. Lecture Notes in Computer Science 525, Springer-Verlag 1991.

[Main90] Mainguenaud, M. & P., Marie-Aude, CIGALES: A Graphical Query Language for Geographical Information Systems. In: Proceedings of the 4th Int. Symposium on Spatial Data Handling, Zurich 1990.

[Mitc88] Mitchell, J.S.B., An Algorithmic Approach to Terrain Navigation. Artificial Intelligence, Vol. 37 (1988), No. 1-3, 171-201.

[Prep85] Preparata, F. P., & Shamos, M.I., Computational Geometry, An Introduction. Springer Verlag, New York 1985.

[Sven91] Svensson, P. & Huang, Z., Geo-SAL: A Query Language for Spatial Data Analysis. In: O. Gunther & H.-J. Schek (eds.), Advances in Spatial Databases. Lecture Notes in Computer Science 525, Springer-Verlag 1991.

[Toml90] Tomlin, C. D., Geographic Information Systems and Cartographic modeling. Prentice-Hall 1990.

[Unwi81] Unwin, D., Introductory Spatial Analysis. Methuen, New York 1981.

Application of a Reciprocal Confluence Tree Unit to Similar-Picture Retrieval

Daniel J. Buehrer and C. C. Chang

Institute of Information Engineering and Computer Science
National Chung Cheng University
MinHsiung, Chiayi, Taiwan
dan@cs.ccu.edu.tw

Abstract. S. K. Chang et al. [1] defined three types of pattern matching to retrieve "similar" symbolic pictures from a symbolic picture database. Symbolic pictures are composed of icons. Each pair of icons have 9 possible spatial relationships, depending on whether their x an y coordinates are <, =, or >. In this paper we propose the use of a reciprocal confluence tree unit [2] to compute and represent each symbolic picture as a large integer. An algorithm is then given for determining whether or not a pattern picture matches a subject picture. This algorithm runs in $O(n^2 \log(m) + m^2)$ time, where n is the number of icons in the pattern and m is the number of icons in the subject.

1 Introduction

In the past few years, researchers have designed hardware units which are capable of performing high-speed arithmetic on very large integers [3]. These devices are based on the famous residue numbering system (RNS) which was invented by the ancient Chinese mathematician Sun Tze. These devices use relatively prime numbers to compute integers in a way such that no carry operations need to be performed when doing addition. This form of carry-free arithmetic makes it possible to do parallel addition, subtraction, and multiplication.

One hardware unit which is based on such residue numbering systems is the reciprocal confluence tree unit [2]. This device is able to quickly calculate an integer C which encodes n small integers. In this paper we use this device to encode the spatial relationships between the icons of a symbolic picture. Each symbolic picture can then be represented as a list of icons along with a single integer which represents the spatial relationships between those icons. An algorithm is then presented for using this representation to check whether or not a pattern picture is contained within a subject picture.

The definition for symbolic picture matching is given in Section 2. A more detailed mathematical description of the reciprocal confluence tree unit is presented in Section 3, as well as the description of how it is used to store symbolic pictures. Then our pattern matching algorithm is presented in Section 4, along with its runtime analysis. Section 5 presents a summary and conclusions.

2. A Review of Symbolic Picture Matching

Recently, the problem of querying image databases has become a focus of considerable interest [3-6]. Since pattern matching of real images is very slow, the images are very often stored in two forms; the original image and a symbolic image. Pattern matching is performed using the symbolic form of the pictures. After a pattern match succeeds, the corresponding original image is retrieved and displayed. One such system [3], called IIDS (Intelligent Image Database System), is based on the use of a data structure called a 2D string. The 2D string efficiently stores the spatial relationships between the icons of a picture. Unfortunately, the pattern matching algorithm becomes equivalent to a two-dimensional version of the longest-common subsequence algorithm, which has nonpolynomial run-time.

In this paper we propose using the reciprocal confluence tree unit to transform the spatical relationships between icons to a single integer. The pattern matching can be performed by an algorithm which is given in Section 4.

The pattern matching which we will be using permits rows and columns of the subject picture to be deleted, and also permits deletion of icons from the subject. If there exists a set of such deletions which permits the subject to become the same as the pattern picture, then the pictures are said to type-1 match. As defined by S.K. Chang, type-0 matching also would permit merging of subject rows and columns, whereas type-2 matching does not permit either deletion or merging of rows and columns. For example, see Fig. 1, where only patterns 2 and 3 type-1 match the subject picture.

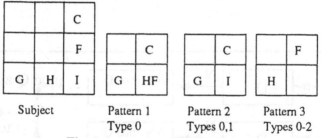

Fig. 1: 3 Types of Pattern Matching

Our method is based on the 9-directional lower triangular (9-DLT) matrix representation of C.C. Chang [5]. In this representation, the n icons of the picture are sorted by their type names and are used as the row and column indices of a lower-triangular nXn matrix. Each matrix element [r,c] at row r and column c (numbered from the upper left corner) has an integer from 0 to 8 indicating one of the 9 possible directions between the icon in row r and the icon in column c. The directions are assigned numbers as follows: 0=same position, 1=north, 2=northwest, 3=west, ..., 7=east, 8=northeast. For example, the lower triangular matrix for Pattern 1 is given in Fig. 2.

		Column			
		1 C	2 F	3 G	4 H
1	C				
2	F	5			
Row 3	G	4	3		
4	H	5	0	7	

Fig. 2: 9-DLT Representation of Pattern 1 of Fig. 1

3. A Reciprocal Confluence Tree

The Recprocal Confluence Tree (RCT) unit is based on an extension to a theorem by Jaeschke [4]. Let $q_1, q_2, \ldots, q_n$ be n coprime integers, and let $x_1, x_2, \ldots, x_n$ be n other integers such that $\max\{|x_i|\} < n < \min\{q_i\}$. The J-conditions (named after Jaeschke) involve finding an integer C in the residue class $n \prod_{i=1}^{n} q_i$ such that $x_i = \lfloor C/q_i \rfloor \bmod n$ for all $1 \le i \le n$. Here, a=b mod c means that a is the least positive residue of b modulo c, and $\lfloor \ \rfloor$ is the floor operator. In [2], the number $C = \sum_{i=1}^{n} nQ_iP_i$ is shown to satisfy the J-conditions, where $Q_i = \prod_{j \ne i} q_j$, $P_i = N_i b_i \bmod q_i$, each b_i satisfies $Q_i b_i = 1 \bmod q_i$, and $N_i = \lceil x_i q_i / n \rceil$. The RCT unit is then designed to calculate this number C in $O(\log_2 n)$ time.

In [2], Chang and Lin implemented the RCT unit, a hardware computation unit, as in Fig. 3.

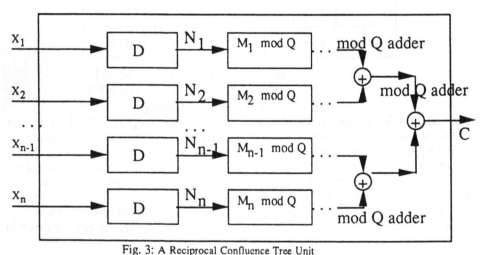

Fig. 3: A Reciprocal Confluence Tree Unit

Example 3.1:

Let $q_{1\ldots9} = [11, 13, 17, 19, 23, 29, 31, 37, 39]$ and let $x_1=3$, $x_2=5$, $x_3=6$, $x_4=2$, $x_5=8$, $x_6=0$, $x_7=0$, $x_8=0$, $x_9=0$. Here, n=9, and $x_i<9<q_j$, as is necessary for the J-conditions to be satisfied. Then the RCT unit would calculate the numbers $b_{1\ldots9}=[6, 8, 15, 14, 16, 24, 1, 30, 35]$ and the numbers $p_{1\ldots9}=[12, 10, 13, 14, 0, 0, 0, 0, 0]$ as well as the number C=38,935,817,811,729 . It can be checked that $\lfloor C/q_i \rfloor \bmod 9 =$

x_i for all values of i from 1 to 9. For example, $\lfloor C/q_2 \rfloor$ mod 9 = $\lfloor 38935817811729 / 13 \rfloor$ mod 9 = 5.

The RCT unit is used to store the spatial relationships between the icons of a picture as follows. First, the icons are sorted according to their types. The sorted lists of icons can then be compared to make sure that the sorted pattern icons form a subsequence of the sorted subject icons. Each possible correspondence can be located in $O(n \cdot \log m)$ time, where n is the number of icons in the pattern and m is the number of icons in the subject. Each possible correspondence is then checked to see whether or not all spatial relationships in the pattern also hold in the subject. This is checked by using the algorithm given in the next section, using the C values for the subject and pattern images.

4 Our Scheme

Let the directions between the icons in a picture be stored in the 9-DLT matrix representation above. That is, the matrix entry m(r,c) represents the direction from object O_r to object O_c, where r and c are unique icons with types type(r) and type(c), respectively. Assume that the objects in the rows and columns of the matrix have been sorted by their types, according to some fixed ordering of icon types (e.g. alphabetizing the type names). Let this ordering be called the "type-sorted list" of icons of the picture.

Definition 4.1: Matching subsequence

A type-sorted list $N_P=[P_1,...,P_m]$ for a pattern picture P type-1 matches a type-sorted list $N_S=[S_1,...,S_n]$ for a subject picture S if type(P_i)=type(S_{j_i}) for all $1 \leq i \leq m$ and some sequence $j_1<j_2<...<j_m$ and if $m_P(P_i,P_k)=m_S(S_{j_i},S_{j_k})$ for all $1 \leq i<k \leq m$ (i.e. the directions between all matching pattern icons are the same as the directions between the corresponding icons in the subject). Efficient algorithms which can find such common subsequences in $O(m \cdot \log(n))$ time or better are well-known.

ENCODE THE PICTURES:

First, process each pattern picture and the subject picture:

Sort the icons in each picture by their types to get a type-sorted list of icons N.
Calculate the 9-DLT spatial relationships m_{ij} between every two objects O_i and O_j of N

where $1 \leq j < i \leq |N|$

$m_{ij}=$ 0 if r(i)=r(j) and c(i)=c(j)
          1 if r(i)=r(j) and c(i)>c(j)
          ...
          8 if r(i)<r(j) and c(i)=c(j).

Transform the 9-DLT matrix into a list L by using the transformation
$L_{f(i,j)} = m_{ij}$. for $[i,j]=\{[2,1],[3,1],[3,2],[4,1],[4,2],...,[|N|, |N|-1]\}$
         where f(i,j)= (i-2)(i-1)/2+j.
Feed the list L into the RCT unit to get an integer C.

         (Since the encoding of integers from 0-9 requires that we have at least 9 elements, it is necessary to add 0's on to the end of the list L until getting 9 elements.)

The picture is represented as <N,C>.

MATCH THE PICTURES S and P:
Find the next subsequence of N_S which matches N_p using the above definition of a matching subsequence, where $|N_p|=m(m-1)/2$ and $|N_S|=n(n-1)/2$:

> For each r from 2 to m
>> For each c from 1 to i-1
>>> If $\lfloor C_P / q_{f(r,c)} \rfloor \bmod 9 = \lfloor C_S / q_{f(r,c)} \rfloor \bmod 9$ then continue
>>> Else return failure.
> Print out the above match.

Notice that the division in the above matching algorithm can be performed very efficiently in the special-purpose hardware for the residue numbering system. It is evident that the nested loops in the matching algorithm run in $O(m^2)$ time, whereas finding the common subsequences in the first step of the matching algorithm takes $O(m \log(n))$ time for each match. If icon types are all unique for one of the pictures, there will be only one match.

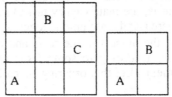

Fig. 4: Subject and Pattern for Example 4.1

Example 4.1: For a simple example, consider the pictures given above in Fig. 4. After the subject has been put into the sorted list [A,B,C] the list form of the 9-DLT matrix is calculated to be $L_S=[8, 6, 4]$. Since the list has fewer than 9 elements, it is padded with 0's. When this is fed through the RCT unit with $q_1...9= [11, 13, 17, 19, 23, 29, 31, 37, 39]$ as in Example 3.1, the result is $C_S=13715130584223$. Similarly, the sorted list for the pattern is [A,B], and the list form of the 9-DLT matrix is $L_P=[8]$. This is again padded with 0's to get [8,0,0,0,0,0,0,0,0] and fed throught the RCT unit with the above q_i's to get $C_P=5926953185595$.

The matching algorithm then compares the lists [A,B,C] and [A,B] to find the matching object pair(s), which in this case is {[A,B]}. The subscript for the pair [A,B] is 1 for both lists. The matching algorithm then checks that $\lfloor C_P /11 \rfloor \bmod 9 = 8 = \lfloor C_S /11 \rfloor \bmod 9$, so the pictures match.

5   Conclusions

The residue numbering systems can be used to efficiently store symbolic pictures so that similar symbolic pictures can be retrieved in time $O(m \log(n) + m^2)$ where m is the number of icons in the pattern picture and n is the number of icons in the subject picture. This compares favorably with other methods that have been presented for this problem.

References

1. S.K. Chang, Q.Y. Shi, and C.W. Yan: Iconic Indexing by 2-D Strings. *IEEE Transactions on Pattern Analysis and Machine Intelligence*, Vol. PAMI-9, No. 3, 413-428 (1987).

2. C.C. Chang, C.H. Lin: A Reciprocal Confluence Tree Unit and Its Applications. *BIT*, Vol. 30, 27-33, 1990.

3. F.J. Taylor: Residue Arithmetic: A Tutorial with Examples. *Computer*, Vol. 17, No. 5, .540-546 (1984).

4. G. Jaeschke: Reciprocal Hashing: A Method for Generating Minimal Perfect Hashing Functions. *Communications of the ACM*, Vol. 24, No. 12, .829-833 (1981).

5. C.C. Chang: A Fast Algorithm to Retrieve Symbolic Pictures. *International Journal of Computer Mathematics*, Vol. 43, No. 1&2 (1992).

6. S.K. Chang: *Principles of Pictorial Information Systems Design*, Prentice-Hall International, Englewood Cliffs, New Jersey, 1989.

Deduction and Deductive Databases for Geographic Data Handling

A. I. Abdelmoty, M. H. Williams and N. W. Paton

Department of Computing and Electrical Engineering, Heriot-Watt University, Riccarton, Edinburgh EH14 4AS, United Kingdom

Abstract. The representation of complex spatial domains in conventional databases suffers from fragmented representation of object structure, lack of instance-level spatial relationships, and the generation of large combinatoric search spaces in query analysis. The deductive capabilities provided by a deductive database offer some assistance in solving these problems, in particular by enabling spatial reasoning to be performed by a Geographic Information System (GIS). Deduction in the database is used to support the natural representation of complex spatial object structures in single and multi-layered Geographic DataBases (GDB), inference of implicit spatial relationships, and the manipulation of multiple resolution spatial representations. In addition, deductive capabilities are shown to be essential for automatic data input and update in a GDB. Coupled with appropriate structural representation, spatial reasoning is an important tool for the realization of an effective GDB.

1 Introduction

Complex real-world decision making tasks typically required in a GIS depend on a human's natural spatial, temporal and hierarchical reasoning ability. The automation or partial automation of such tasks depends heavily on search efficiency which in turn depends heavily on data modelling and representation. Modelling geographic data combines the complexity of modelling large spatial domains with the complexity incurred from the type of applications which have to be handled. This paper presents an investigation into the application of deduction in the context of databases to the representation and manipulation of geographic data with the aim of optimizing data storage and showing intelligent behaviour, which reflects itself in more efficient GISs.

Manipulating geographic data involves evaluation of spatial properties and relationships which necessitates the existence of a spatial model for data representation. This is usually achieved by viewing the geographic space as a collection of spatial entities such as points, lines, polygons or point sets, and representing objects and spatial relationships accordingly [27]. On the other hand, a different type of model is required to represent the aspatial aspects of geographic data. The hierarchical nature of the spatial data and the complex relationships to be represented have limited the use of the relational approach [7] and led towards modelling using an object-oriented representation [35, 9, 20]. However, using a single data model for representing both the spatial and aspatial aspects of geographic data meant forcing the spatial aspects of the data into the underlying data model whether relational [15] or object-oriented [33]. A model which is used to represent geographic data should ideally,

- Provide a rich set of semantic modelling capabilities to represent geographic entities as a coherent combination of spatial and aspatial aspects.
- Enable one to reason over the data in the same way as a pure spatial model would, viz. representation of complex spatial structures, multiple representation of geographic entities, and representation and inference of spatial relationships.

To this end we are currently investigating the application of the deductive object-oriented approach to databases to the realization of GDBs as a specialization of large spatial databases, taking into account the types of analysis and manipulation required in a GIS. Deduction in the database is a powerful mechanism for expressing queries, deriving data, and expressing integrity constraints, while object-orientation is appropriate for representing complex object structures and semantic relationships using concepts of data abstraction, encapsulation of structure and behaviour, and inheritance.

In this paper a comprehensive overview of the application of deduction in large GDBs is reported, covering different areas and levels in a GIS. It focuses on the representation of the spatial structure of a geographic object, spatial reasoning and spatial relationship inference, the definition of object classes over more than one data layer, and the choice of an appropriate spatial representation for a geographic object during query analysis.

A hypothetical geographic application based on resource management and allocation has been designed to test some of the issues discussed in this paper and will be used as test example for a prototype deductive object-oriented database system [12]. The application of a rule-based approach to feature extraction from digital maps has already been implemented using Prolog applied to data from Ordnance Survey large scale maps. Implementation issues are outside the scope of this paper and will be covered in future work.

The paper is organized as follows. Section 2 presents our view of a GDB as an object-oriented database with deductive capabilities. In section 3 the analysis of a GDB as a multidimensional framework for data is presented, pointing out areas where deduction in a database is applicable and useful. Expressing geographic database queries using a logic language is presented in section 4, while section 5 gives a general account of the application of deduction in automating the process of object recognition from input data sources in the form of maps and images.

2 Overview of a Deductive Object-Oriented Geographical Database

In this work a geographical database is regarded as consisting of two disjoint sets of database relationships, as shown in figure 1: one is the set of base or extensional database relationships (*EDB* relationships) and the other is the set of derived or intensional database relationships (*IDB* relationships). The *EDB* in turn contains two different levels of data representation, viz.

1. *Primitive level*, which is a spatial representation of geographic objects using an appropriate geometric data model [14], either in vector form (points, lines, and polygons) or tesselated (raster) form. Data from multiple sources is initially transformed and represented at this level. Spatial indexing structures are used to implement the geometric data model to improve performance, especially in search operations. Computational geometry algorithms necessary for spatial operations are also defined on the geographic data at this level.

2. *Object level*, where real world phenomena are represented as classes of objects which encapsulate their structure and behaviour. A rich set of semantic relationships including aggregation, specialization, association, etc. are used to represent complex abstract geographic phenomena. A mapping exists between the object level and the primitive one, i.e. there exists a function or a sequence of functions for every geographic object which leads to its spatial representation.

The *IDB* is the set of rules over objects in the *EDB*, which are used for spatial reasoning over the geographic space (as will be discussed later) and for feature extraction, whereby object level entities are inferred from the corresponding primitive primitive level objects. This is seen to be a necessary part of a GDB system for initial data loading and updating.

3 Deduction for Managing Geographic Database Dimensions

While knowledge of its shape and location in space might be enough to define a spatial entity, this is not sufficient for defining objects in a geographic space. This is due to the wide range of different applications that can be associated with the same area in space. There are as many different applications of geographic databases as there are kinds of maps or combinations of different kinds of maps.

A GIS user is interested not only in the extension of a particular object in space, but also in the different phenomena collected over a particular location in space, the ways in which these change over time, and the different representations of objects under different manipulation operations. By classifying the different kinds of maps used, a general view of the "dimensions" through which a geographic database has to extend can be obtained. Four different dimensions have been identified, namely, space, theme, resolution and time, as illustrated in figure 2. In this section a detailed definition of the first three dimensions is presented along with the effect of these dimensions on the representation of data in a GDB. This study is essential for pointing out particular areas in geographic data modelling which cannot be readily handled using a conventional DBMS and to show how the deductive capabilities of a database system can be used to handle some of these representational problems.

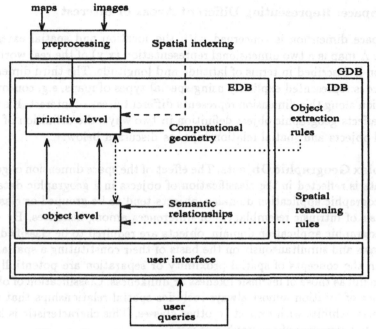

Fig. 1. Components of a deductive object-oriented GDB

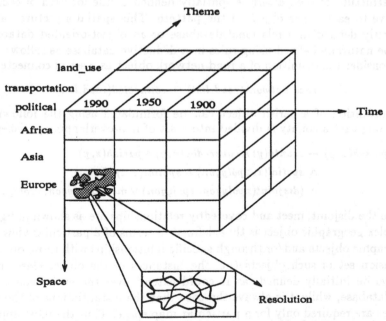

Fig. 2. Different dimensions of geographic data

3.1 Space: Representing Different Areas of Interest

The space dimension is concerned with the location and spatial extent of an object. A map is a two dimensional representation (x,y) of the real world, where location is described in terms of latitude and longitude. The third dimension (z) in space is represented explicitly using special types of maps, e.g. contour maps. Variation along this dimension represents different areas of interest. Existence in space affects geographic object definition in two ways: the definition of complex spatial objects and spatial relationships, as discussed below.

Complex Geographic Objects. The effect of the space dimension of geographical data is reflected in the classification of objects in a geographic database. In non-geographic application domains, objects tend to be grouped or classified on the basis of intrinsic resemblances or differences among instances. By contrast, in a geographic application domain, objects are required to be classified both on that basis and simultaneously on the basis of their constituting a spatial totality wherein the concepts of spatial proximity or separation are potentially just as meaningful as those of intrinsic likeness or unlikeness. Classification of objects on the basis of location almost always includes spatial relationships that the class of objects exhibits with respect to other classes. This characteristic is known as the *spatial structure* of geographic objects.

Thus the definition of an object could comprise a complex pattern of properties and spatial relationships, rather than a simple grouping of the related objects. The structure of the pattern is spatially defined as the location of each object relative to each other object in the pattern. This spatial structure cannot be explicitly defined in a relational database or an object-oriented database, but can be naturally defined using rules in a deductive database as follows.

Consider the definition of a road network object as a set of connected roads,

$$road\_network(road\_list) \leftarrow connected(road\_list).$$

The definition of a parish object can be formulated using the following rule, assuming that a county is divided into a set of non-overlapping parishes.

$$parish(x, y) \leftarrow county(y) \land coveredby(x, y) \land parish(z, y)$$
$$\land \; spatial(x, xpolygon) \land spatial(z, zpolygon)$$
$$\land \; (disjoint(xpolygon, zpolygon) \lor meet(xpolygon, zpolygon)).$$

where the disjoint, meet and coveredby relationships are as shown in figure 3. A complex geographic object is thus defined in terms of a particular view of other geographic objects and/or through specific relationships with those objects. The extension set of such objects (i.e. the instances of the object class) need not always be initially defined, as it could extend over the entire space limit of the database, while it is always the case that the instantiations of those object classes are required only for a particular map space. Thus the most appropriate way of defining these classes is through general rules in the *IDB*. To conduct any analysis procedure over a geographic database, the user has to specify the spatial limits of the data involved in the process (i.e. specify the area of interest to which analysis has to be limited and the rules to be applied).

Rules defining a particular class of objects could change from one location to another for several reasons. In particular,

1. The shapes and properties of man-made objects can be different in different areas. For example, grain silos in the US are round, while those in Canada are square; buildings with associated area might be interpreted as garages in some parts of a city (too small for a dwelling) whereas in other parts of the city they may be taken as modern housing.

$$grainsilo(x) \leftarrow building(x) \wedge round(x) \wedge \ldots$$
$$garage(x) \leftarrow building(x) \wedge area(x, y) \wedge lessthan(y, a) \wedge \ldots$$

2. A particular law may apply in one location and not in another. For example, laws governing the construction of houses, roads, etc. may differ from one area to another; parking laws may be different for different road and street types and so on.

$$parking\_law(x, metred\_parking) \leftarrow road(x) \wedge road\_type(x, major)$$
$$\wedge \neg day(saturday) \wedge \neg day(sunday)$$
$$\wedge timeofday('9-18').$$

Consequently some rules may be constrained over particular space limits in the database, with different versions of the rule defined for different spatial areas.

Spatial Relationships. In other application domains, relationships between objects are defined at the object class level. For example, *lecturer teaches course* and *student takes course*. In a geographic domain an object exhibits spatial relationships with all other objects in the database. Some spatial relationships are general (depending on the application, and on the spatial context) and apply to all objects within a class, whereas others are specific relationships between instances of geographic objects. In the latter case, a geographic object is considered to be in association or correlation with some other object or group of objects in space, which implies the relative description of its location. For example, objects are frequently used as landmarks to define locations of other objects, (the second house beside the church, the first street on the right after the national theater, and so on), or just expressing an ad hoc relationship between objects such as, city A is near lake B, or country C is in Western Europe.

This kind of object instance relationship is common in GIS queries. The representation and efficient retrieval of such relationships are essential functions of a GIS. It is not feasible to store all such relationships explicitly. Consequently, the dynamic evaluation of spatial relationships is necessary. On the other hand, it is not practical to specify explicitly the computations involved in the relationship every time a query is invoked. One way of supporting efficient computation involving spatial relationships is through special indexing structures, such as quad-trees, kd-trees, etc. [31, 25], over the primitive representation level of the geographic space to support different types of space analysis. Evaluation of relationships using this method requires the transition between the two different levels of representation, which can result in large computational overheads.

Alternatively, spatial reasoning can be applied over entities on the object level[1]. The identification, classification, and formal definition of spatial relationships is necessary for any spatial reasoning to be applied. Two specific frameworks for the representation of spatial relationships on spatial regions have been presented in Egenhofer[8] and Randell[30]. In what follows, both are reviewed and we show how such representation frameworks can be effectively implemented within a database using deductive rules.

Relationships Involving Regions.

(A) Egenhofer's Mathematical Model: A formal model for the combination of topological knowledge and the derivation of compositions of binary topological relationships is proposed by Egenhofer [8], based on a model for spatial data and relationship representation [29, 6, 11, 10, 8] which is based on concepts of point-set topology with open and closed sets [23]. Topological relationships between two point sets are defined through intersection relations of their boundary, interior and complement.

Reasoning over spatial relationships is then the composition of two binary relations over a common object i.e. $R_3(a,c)$ can be derived from $R_1(a,b)$ and $R_2(b,c)$. An exhaustive set of 64 such compositions based on 8 relationships (disjoint, meet, equal, inside, coveredby, contains, covers, overlap) between two point-sets have been defined in [8]. Figure 3 shows the representation of these relations.

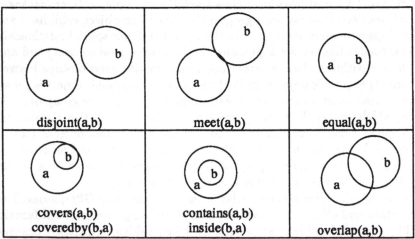

Fig. 3. Relationships between two regions in 2-dimensional space adapted from [8]

Such a representation framework can be implemented in a deductive database. The composition of spatial relationships can be rewritten as database clauses where the conjunction of two binary relationships $R_1(a,b)$ and $R_2(b,c)$ can be

---

[1] *Spatial reasoning* is the method by which spatial information which has not been explicitly recorded can be deduced.

mapped to a disjunctive set of base relations, for example,

$$inside(a, c) \leftarrow inside(a, b) \land inside(b, c). \tag{1}$$

$$disjoint(a, c) \lor meet(a, c) \lor equal(a, c) \lor$$
$$coveredby(a, c) \lor cover(a, c) \lor overlap(a, c) \leftarrow meet(a, b) \land meet(b, c). \tag{2}$$

$$coveredby(a, c) \lor inside(a, c) \lor overlaps(a, c) \leftarrow meet(a, b) \land inside(b, c). \tag{3}$$

$$contains(a, c) \lor cover(a, c) \lor overlap(a, c) \leftarrow contains(a, b) \land coveredby(b, c). \tag{4}$$

$$inside(a, c) \lor coveredby(a, c) \leftarrow coveredby(a, b) \land coveredby(b, c) \tag{5}$$

$$contains(a, c) \lor covers(a, c) \leftarrow covers(a, b) \land covers(b, c). \tag{6}$$

From the examples above it is clear that the composition of two topological relationships can result in indefinite database clauses, i.e. a clause whose consequent (or conclusion) is the disjunction of more than one atom.

Our study is concerned only with definite deductive databases, and as such a valid clause is a clause with only one conclusion. Compositions of the above mentioned topological relationships can be transformed to the required form by noting the following observations, and applying the required transformations.

- The composition results in only one topological relationship. This case is directly transformed to a normal clause, and no transformation is needed. Clause 1 is an example of such a relation.
- The composition results in a subset of probable relationships, in which case one can deduce the negation of the improbable one(s), i.e. the impossibility of existence of the rest of the relationships set. For example, clause 2 can be rewritten as follows,

$$\neg inside(a, c) \land \neg contains(a, c) \leftarrow meet(a, b) \land meet(b, c).$$

- The topological relationships *cover, coveredby, contains, inside and overlap* can be regarded as specializations of a relationship goverlap (general overlap), which indicates an intersection between the interior of the two point sets. Compositions resulting in the disjunction from this category viz., *cover* $\lor$ *contains* $\lor$ *overlap* and *coveredby* $\lor$ *inside* $\lor$ *overlap* can be generalized to a single relation goverlap. For example, clause 3 can be rewritten as follows,

$$goverlap(a, c) \leftarrow meet(a, b) \land inside(b, c).$$

- Similarly the relationships *coveredby* and *inside* can be regarded as specializations of a relationship ginside (general inside), which indicates that the interior of one set is a proper subset of the other. Compositions resulting in disjunctions of the form coveredby $\lor$ inside can be generalized to a single relationship ginside.
For example, clause 5 can be rewritten as follows,

$$ginside(a, c) \leftarrow coveredby(a, b) \land coveredby(b, c).$$

The converse relationships *covers* and *contains* can be generalized to the same relationship *ginside* with the arguments interchanged, for example, clause 6 can be rewritten as follows,

$$ginside(c, a) \leftarrow covers(a, b) \land covers(b, c).$$

– For the conjunction $< R_1(a, b) and R_2(b, c) >$ where no base relation is excluded, no definite database clause can be defined, for example,

$$disjoint(a, c) \lor meet(a, c) \lor equal(a, c) \lor$$
$$inside(a, c) \lor coveredby(a, c) \lor contains(a, c) \lor$$
$$covers(a, c) \lor overlap(a, c) \leftarrow disjoint(a, b) \land disjoint(b, c).$$

Using the above observations, a transformation of the results in [8] is presented in the transitivity table shown in figure 4, which shows an $n \times n$ relationship composition matrix M. For example, $M_{3,2}$ (disjoint(a,c)) is the result of the composition of $M_{3,0}$ (inside(a,b)) and $M_{0,2}$ (meet(b,c)) and so on.

Deduction of negative relations cannot be expressed readily as *Horn clauses*. Deduction of unique positive atoms is probably the most useful in a GDB, and is the subject of our current research.

Consider an example database where *landuse, vegetation, rainfall,* and *slope* data layers are considered. If region #1 in a landuse data layer contains regions #55, covers region #25, and overlaps region #33 from the vegetation layer, then this can be expressed by the following set of clauses.

$\vdots$

$contains(landuse(\#1, urban), vegetation(\#55, grass)).$
$covers(landuse(\#1, urban), vegetation(\#25, none)).$
$overlap(landuse(\#1, urban), vegetation(\#33, wheat)).$

$\vdots$

$coveredby(vegetation(\#33, wheat), rainfall(\#101, 35)).$
$contains(vegetation(\#25, none), slope(\#1001, 5)).$
$meet(vegetation(\#55, grass), vegetation(\#57, grass)).$

$\vdots$

$goverlap(a, c) \leftarrow contains(a, b) \land meet(b, c).$
$contain(a, c) \leftarrow covers(a, b) \land contains(b, c).$
$goverlap(a, c) \leftarrow overlap(a, b) \land coveredby(b, c).$

One can deduce the following relations between the landuse layer and the rainfall, slope and vegetation layers,

$goverlap(landuse(\#1, urban), rainfall(\#101, 35)).$
$contains(landuse(\#1, urban), slope(\#1001, 5)).$
$goverlap(landuse(\#1, urban), vegetation(\#57, grass)).$

Thus deduction of useful spatial relationships can be done automatically without the need for the application of computational geometry algorithms.

(B) Randell's Logic Theory: Alternative approaches for spatial relationship representation can be used. For example, in [30] Randell et al introduce a theory based on a first order formalism for reasoning over space, time and processes. It

	d(b,c)	m(b,c)	i(b,c)	cb(b,c)	ct(b,c)	cv(b,c)	o(b,c)
d(a,b)	noinfo	¬ ct(a,c) ∧ ¬ cv(a,c)	¬ ct(a,c) ∧ ¬ cv(a,c)	¬ ct(a,c) ∧ ¬ cv(a,c)	d(a,c)	d(a,c)	¬ ct(a,c) ∧ ¬ cv(a,c)
m(a,b)	¬i(a,c) ∧ ¬cb(a,c)	¬i(a,c) ∧ ¬ct(a,c)	go(a,c)	¬ct(a,c) ∧ ¬cv(a,c)	d(a,c)	¬go(a,c)	¬ct(a,c) ∧ ¬cv(a,c)
i(a,b)	d(a,c)	d(a,c)	i(a,c)	i(a,c)	noinfo	¬ct(a,c) ∧ ¬cv(a,c)	¬ct(a,c) ∧ ¬cv(a,c)
cb(a,b)	d(a,c)	¬go(a,c)	i(a,c)	gi(a,c)	¬i(a,c) ∧ ¬cb(a,c)	¬i(a,c) ∧ ¬ct(a,c)	¬ct(a,c) ∧ ¬cv(a,c)
ct(a,b)	¬i(a,c) ∧ ¬cb(a,c)	go(a,c)	¬d(a,c)	go(a,c)	ct(a,c)	ct(a,c)	¬ct(a,c) ∧ ¬cv(a,c)
cv(a,b)	¬i(a,c) ∧ ¬cb(a,c)	¬ct(a,c) ∧ ¬cv(a,c)	go(a,c)	go(a,c)	ct(a,c)	gi(a,c)	go(a,c)
o(a,b)	¬i(a,c) ∧ ¬cb(a,c)	¬i(a,c) ∧ ¬cb(a,c)	go(a,c)	go(a,c)	¬i(a,c) ∧ ¬cb(a,c)	¬i(a,c) ∧ ¬cb(a,c)	noinfo

Fig. 4 Transitivity table for the set of base relations in figure 3,
showing the transformation of composition results to one
relationship or the conjunction of more than one relationship.

is the spatial part of this theory which is of relevance here. Ontological primitives include regions where every region coincides with a set of incident points, and is contained in a distinguished region called the universe. Unlike Egenhofer [8], the basic part of the formalism assumes one primitive dyadic relation $C(x,y)$ read as 'x connects with y' which includes relationships between objects from external contact to identity in terms of mutually shared parts (this includes all the relationships in figure 3 except for the disjoint case) from which a basic set of dyadic relations are defined.

Some examples of this set expressed in IDB clauses would be,

$$DisConnected(x,y) \leftarrow \neg Connected(x,y).$$
$$ProperPart(x,y) \leftarrow Part(x,y) \wedge \neg Part(y,x).$$
$$Identical(x,y) \leftarrow Part(x,y) \wedge Part(y,x).$$
$$Overlap(x,y) \leftarrow Part(z,x) \wedge Part(z,y).$$
$$ExternallyConnected(x,y) \leftarrow Connected(x,y) \wedge \neg Overlap(x,y).$$

In terms of points incident in regions, $C(x,y)$ holds when two regions connect; of the incident points contained in both regions, at least one incident point is shared. Compositions of topological relationships using the above definitions can be axiomatized in a similar manner.

In the representation formalism of [8], topological relationships between two point-sets, A and B, was described by nine possible set intersections (3 x 3 matrix) of A's boundary, interior, and complement with the boundary, interior, and complement of B. In order to establish a fact based on such relations using Egenhofer's model, a function is needed for describing the boundary, interior and the complement of an object in the geographic space. However, the problem is more complex in a GDB, where objects can be defined as specializations of point-sets (regions with holes) or as sets of other objects. In this case proving the composition of two topological relationships would be difficult, and consequently the composition matrices are more difficult to formulate. Note, however, that in a geographic space the 9-intersection matrix of [8] can be reduced to a 4-case intersection matrix by eliminating the complement intersections of the point-sets. Removing the complements in this case would neither affect the definition of the relationships nor their compositions, and thus greatly reduces the computation needed.

The power of Randell's formalism [30] can readily be recognized. If the connectivity relationship can be computed for the whole space, then a systematic derivation of the whole set of specialized relationships can be achieved without the need for the application of computational geometry algorithms, based solely on the satisfaction of the axioms defined. One can envisage a GDB where indexing structures can be used for the computation of the connectivity relationships for the space required, rules derive topological relationships between objects, and finally rules derive compositions of topological relationships as required.

Non-areal Spatial Relationships. Whatever formalism is used for defining spatial relationships, the main point to emphasize is that deduction mechanisms in a database can prove to be of major importance in the realization of large spatial databases in general and GDBs in particular. Although spatial relationships in the research work surveyed cover a basic representation primitive (a region), in a geographic context however, the line and point primitives possess the same functional and representational importance. Based on either formalism, a detailed study of topological relationships that these objects exhibit with themselves and the interrelationships between all the primitives is still needed.

For example, a line primitive has as a boundary its two end points and as interior the connection curve between its boundaries. Relationships may be defined on the basis of the boundary (represented by the two end points, ∂_1 and ∂_2) and the interior, denoted by $\circ$ [2]. The intersection matrix in this case is,

$$I_n(A, B) = \begin{bmatrix} \partial_1 A \bigcap \partial_1 B & \partial_1 A \bigcap \partial_2 B & \partial_1 A \bigcap B^\circ \\ \partial_2 A \bigcap \partial_1 B & \partial_2 A \bigcap \partial_2 B & \partial_2 A \bigcap B^\circ \\ A^\circ \bigcap \partial_1 B & A^\circ \bigcap \partial_2 B & A^\circ \bigcap B^\circ \end{bmatrix}$$

Figure 5 shows some of the possible relationships. All the possible base relationships between 2 line primitives can be derived, and consequently transitivity tables formed. The same methodology can be applied to deriving relationships between different primitives, i.e. line and region, point and line and point and region. Of these the useful relationships in a geographic context can be extracted and represented by rules in the *IDB*.

Subjective Spatial Relationships. In a deductive database, the inexactness of the spatial relationships described in [28] resulting from the variety of

---

[2] notations as used in Egenhofer [11]

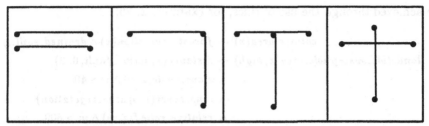

Fig. 5. Examples of relationships between two line primitives in 2-dimensional space

shape representations of spatial objects, (for example, in calculating the distance between two polygonal features, the problem is how to determine the points on the shape with which to apply the computation; is it the minimum, the maximum or the centroid distance that is required), can be resolved by defining rules in the database which correspond to different user views of the relationship. For example, in computing the distance between two cities, the definition of the relationships will differ if an areal representation is considered as opposed to a point representation. Also in the case of an areal representation, besides having to choose the point on each city object on which to carry out the computation, the definition would differ if the required distance is the shortest distance between the two points or the distance of the roads joining the cities, and so on.

Furthermore, subjective relationships which vary according to the class of objects considered can be expressed using rules.

$$near(building1, building2) \leftarrow buffer\_zone(building1, 20, x)$$
$$\wedge \ inside(building2, x)$$
$$near(city1, city2) \leftarrow centroid\_distance(city1, city2, 100).$$

Note that in a deductive object-oriented database, such relationships would be defined as methods on the appropriate object classes where inheritance of structure and behaviour is used.

3.2 Theme: Representing Different Themes of Interest

Information collected about geographic objects may be of different types. This is reflected in the different kinds of maps produced and used. Data sets representing the different types of information are referred to as *data layers*, and maps representing those data sets as *map layers*. Each data set might be analyzed and/or mapped individually. Alternatively, data sets may be combined to produce more meaningful information. For example, crop boundaries and types of soils can be used to determine the most productive soil for a particular crop. However, combining data sets can lead to an inordinate number of possible combinations.

Thus it is not practical to derive and represent instances of the results of such combinations of data sets apriori, as they could extend over the whole database space extension and might only be needed occasionally, if at all. Representation of object classes defined through the combination of more than one data set can be achieved through the use of rules, for example [2, 26],

$$cottage\_area(x) \leftarrow forest\_vegetation(x) \wedge drained\_soil(x).$$
$$landslide\_susceptible\_area(x, high) \leftarrow distance(x, active\_fault, 0..2)$$
$$\wedge slope\_angle(x, v) \wedge v > 40$$
$$\wedge land\_cover(x, sparse\_vegetation)$$
$$\wedge relative\_relief(x, w) \wedge w > 800$$
$$\wedge distance(x, ridge\_top, 0..900).$$

Thus in non-geographic applications, object class definition is usually achieved through a pre-conceived template of properties and relationships where instances of the object class are explicitly created and attached to a class. For example, *X is an instance of person, and Y is an instance of a car.* In the geographical domain, however, instances of a geographic object class would have to be inferred according to the rules, rather than simply stated. Overlay operations and rules for deriving relationships are used to find instances of such object classes. The resulting objects are generally physically colocated with part-of or all-of other objects in the database, i.e. they have arbitrary spatial shapes depending on their definition and constraints. The deductive definition of thematic concepts eases experimentation with alternative criteria, which increases the number of ways in which the underlying data can be used.

3.3 Resolution: Representing Different Details (or Scales) of Interest

For practical reasons, most maps are scaled representations. It is impossible to represent all geographic information on a one-to-one basis, so a scale is devised to retain the data required and to present it as a map of a particular size. The amount of detail required in the representation determines the choice of a particular representation scale. Too many irrelevant details can hinder the conveyance of the information in the map. For example, a map representation which shows the unemployment distribution, which is usually collected for large areas, need not show the name of every street in the area.

The process of scaling the map can involve screening out some details from a spatial scene as well as using different spatial representations of objects, for example, merging shapes or transforming an area to a line or a point, etc. The resolution dimension can be seen from two points of view,

- Cartographic: scaled representation of database objects used solely for cartographic purposes.
- Analytic: where a different spatial representation of the geographic object is needed to model the application under analysis, for example, studying a problem of path finding using a graph to represent the road network, and planning maintenance schedules using an area representation of the road network.

Although small scale representations of geographic objects can be derived from high resolution representations using generalization rules [22], the storage of multiple representations of geographic objects is sometimes necessary where situations involving large degrees of generalization can cause delays in computation which could not be tolerated in an interactive GIS. Representing multiple representations of objects in a GDB is a problem which is not readily handled using existing data models and is part of our research goals in this project, where extensions are sought to the object data model presented in [13].

In the context where an object can have more than one spatial representation several problems arise, which include maintaining correct links between related multi-represented objects, maintaining database integrity during update, and choosing the appropriate representation during manipulation. Integrity constraint-type rules can be formulated to handle the first two cases, while specific database rules are used for the third. For example,

$$spatial(X, Scale, Rep) \leftarrow equal(Scale, 1 : 50,000)$$
$$\land\ point(X, Rep).$$
$$spatial(X, Scale, Rep) \leftarrow equal(Scale, 1 : 1250)$$
$$\land\ region(X, Rep).$$
$$route(X, Y, S) \leftarrow scale(S)$$
$$\land\ spatial(X, S, P) \land spatial(Y, S, R)$$
$$\land\ path(P, R).$$

where different object representations and different levels of detail are associated to each representation scale.

3.4 Time: Representing the Change in the Data Over Time

Maps are also used to reflect the change in features over time whether as a record of past events (historical maps) or as prediction of future events (modeling and planning maps). Modeling the change of the data over time is a general requirement in any database system. A study of the implication of this dimension in a geographic database is not considered in the scope of our research.

4 Deduction in GDB Queries

Although conventional query languages such as SQL have been successfully used as query languages for many applications which can be easily expressed in terms of tables, its use is very limited when dealing with new applications such as image databases and GISs which need more complex underlying structures than tables. Extensions to such query languages have been proposed to cope with properties of spatial data [16, 5]. Such extensions are considered unnatural and at best short term solutions, as the real problem lies in forcing spatial concepts into a framework designed for data modelled as tables. Using a suitable geographic data model such as an object-oriented model coupled with deductive capabilities, as proposed here, provides an effective framework for the expression of queries against geographic data.

Three major advantages can be observed from the use of a logic query language for expressing geographic queries:

Firstly, declarative expression of geographic queries is offered using a first order language. An example of a typical GDB query is to find the objects satisfying particular spatial and aspatial conditions. For example, to select potential areas for waste disposal sites the following query can be used:

$$\leftarrow \quad close(x, waste\_source) \wedge close(x, railway\_station)$$
$$\wedge \, close(x, main\_road) \wedge inside(x, low\_quality\_agricultural\_buffer)$$
$$\wedge \, distance(x, residential\_dwellings, y) \wedge y >= 500$$
$$\wedge \, \neg site\_special\_scientific\_interest(x).$$

As shown in the above query, the evaluation of a spatial relationship can be invoked directly (distance/3) or from within other clauses (close/2). In both cases the spatial relationship is implemented using computational geometry. Such expressions are possible in our database system [12] where two languages based on the same data model coexist, viz. a logic language used for logical expression of queries and an imperative database programming language for implementing methods (including spatial) over geographic objects. The logic language can invoke methods defined in the imperative language and logic language expressions can be embedded in the imperative language.

Secondly, recursive queries which cannot be expressed using conventional query languages are directly expressible using the logic language. This type of query is essential for expressing network-oriented queries which are a subset of GIS queries which can be modeled using *Horn clauses*. For example, a query such as "What are the common parts of the paths between London and Edinburgh using British Rail *(BR)*" can be evaluated by finding all *BR* paths (recursive definition) between London and Edinburgh and then recursively selecting all the common path segments from the resulting path list.

Finally, expressing derived data in the *IDB* using the same language as that which is used for querying provides two major advantages, viz.

– Queries against geographic data can directly call rules in the *IDB*, which results in easier query formulation.
– Queries formulated during geographic analysis can be stored as derived data in the *IDB*, and can thus be reused for future analysis and manipulation.

Both features are unique to a deductive database and are useful in a GDB where complex spatial queries and results of queries can be used to enrich the database.

5 From the Primitive to the Object level: A Deductive Approach

As noted in section 2, data input to a GDB may come from different sources, whether as *"paper maps"* or *"images"*. In either form, the data has to pass through a process of digitization to produce a result in computer-readable form. The result of this digitization process is a geographic data set at the primitive level. An interpretation process is needed to transform the geographic data from this level to the object level needed for a GDB, as shown in figure 6. This task can be aided by automatic object recognition, which is important for the following reasons:

1. Currently the capturing and updating of data for a GDB is based on multiple primitive data sources. The data is initially stored at the primitive level, and later during an update process, changes to the primitive level must be propagated manually to the corresponding object level objects.
2. The huge amount of data stored and the frequency of its update makes a manual interpretation process costly and limited in its application.
3. The existence of data at the object level is essential in a GIS environment where one of the requirements is to have a user interface and a query language which are insensitive to the underlying geometrical representation of objects (i.e. the primitive level of representation).

The above facts support the inclusion of an object recognition module as a component of a GDB system. This module is essentially deductive in nature, where the hypotheses used by the map reader are mapped naturally into rules for automatic recognition. Rules in this object recognition module require access to computational geometry algorithms defined on the objects (primitive level) in the *EDB* during compilation.

Using deductive rules for object extraction from the primitive data representation means:

1. Detaching the recognition criteria from low-level algorithms.
2. Expressing the extraction criteria more concisely.
3. Easier modification of extraction criteria.

A rule-based approach for automatically extracting road networks from Ordnance Survey 'OS' large scale (1:1250) maps has been implemented in [1] and is used as the preprocessing stage for data input to the GDB.

Approaches to object (feature) recognition from multiple data sources, both *paper maps* and *images*, that have been investigated in the literature can be classified according to the properties utilized, into: *attribute-based map interpretation* and *structure-based map interpretation*. Both are discussed below.

5.1 Attribute-Based Object Recognition

This approach is suitable for object classes which can be described by a set of features or measurable attributes in isolation from other object classes. The power of this approach depends upon:

1. The availability of attributes for the object type that are invariant. For example, for any type of road, approximate parallelism of its sides is always a valid property.

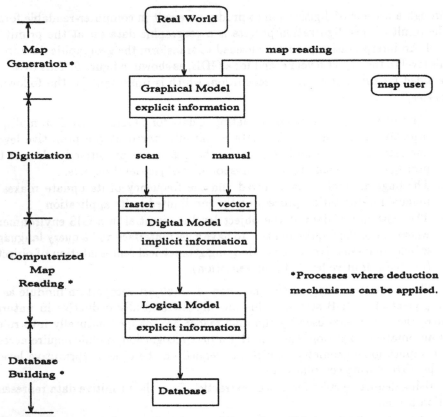

Fig. 6. The process of converting a map of the real world into a database representation

2. The amount of discriminatory information contained in the properties. The basic recognition process usually results in noise objects which are incorrectly identified as instances of the original object class. This is due to the fact that not all the characteristics of an object class are utilized in the interpretation process, as this may result in redundancy and inefficiency. More attributes can then be used to eliminate the noise objects.

The first step in this approach is to have a suitable classification and careful choice of the object attributes needed for the recognition process. If a complete set of discriminatory attributes for each object class can be determined from the data, then the recognition and classification of objects may be reduced to a matching process which is essentially a "table look-up" scheme. Since each pattern of object classes is considered in isolation from other patterns, there is no use for a specific search strategy as the order of extraction does not affect the interpretation process, and the matching is done for every shape of interest. An obvious disadvantage of this method is that it is a single step method where extracted information is not utilized for other object interpretation.

One classification of spatial attributes of an object is between *qualitative*
and *quantitative*. Qualitative or descriptive properties, such as parallelism or
curvature, smoothness, and homogeneity are obvious to a human interpreter,
but can be computationally time consuming to determine from a digital model
as they involve evaluation of the property on the micro level for the whole object.
On the other hand, the quantitative or objective properties, such as the area of
a polygon, length of a line, etc., are computationally easier to evaluate, although
they are probably not as obvious to a human interpreter as qualitative properties.
In most cases it is the qualitative properties which most surely distinguish an
object type, which means that high computation overheads will be a particular
characteristic of this approach.

Examples of extraction criteria utilizing only the attributes of geographic
phenomena can be found in the [3, 24, 17, 21, 34]. An example of criteria used
in [4] can be expressed as rules as follows,

A shape is a railway if
> It has a uniform width equal to the standard gauge of railways, and
> Sides have certain degree of straightness, and
> Sides are parallel, and
> It has no more than 4 sharp turns .

A shape is a pavement if
> Sides are parallel, and
> Each side is almost straight, and
> Has a narrow width within a certain limit.

A shape is a house if
> Its width is of the same order of magnitude as its length, and
> Its area is within a certain range, and
> The ratio of the area to the perimeter is within a certain range.

The disadvantages of relying solely on an attribute-based approach can be
summarized as follows,

1. It fails to extract complex map objects, as they are usually characterized by
   complex spatial structure. The recognition of such objects necessitates the
   extraction of spatial relationships between objects.
2. It can be ineffective if object classes with no strong discriminative attributes
   are extracted. For example, objects that can have similar shapes (a garage,
   or a garden as big as a house).
3. It can become inefficient when attributes are expensive to compute, as it
   involves repeating the same evaluation process for every existing shape.

5.2 Structure-Based Object Recognition

As described earlier, spatial structure is the pattern of existence of objects in
specific spatial relationships with respect to each other. This can be attributed

to the fact that some real world objects are functionally related (for example, houses having access to roads, and bridges connect roads), while others are naturally structured (such as drainage patterns). The structure-based approach to map interpretation involves the utilization of both spatial attributes of objects and spatial relationships between objects. This ensures recursive use of properties for extracting new objects on a map. This approach normally involves the application of a search strategy, where a search strategy can be defined as the process of selecting objects and defining the order in which the interpretation process is carried out.

Two different strategies can be recognized,

1. Identify an object class and then use spatial relationships between objects to extract instances of related object classes and so on, which is the approach followed by [17, 32, 19].
2. Identify a distinctive complex structure and then divide it up into its subparts using knowledge of their properties, which is the approach followed by [18].

The choice of a particular search strategy in structure-based interpretation is crucial to the efficiency and sometimes the success of the interpretation process.

The second strategy has been implemented [1] to extract the road network from large scale maps where the network is extracted as a complete object using spatial relationships between land parcels and the road boundaries. Then the first strategy is used to divide the network into its individual roads for the assignment of postal addresses. To achieve this, houses are grouped in chains to indicate that they should have the same road name in the address. Chains are classified according to their shapes, for example, closed chains indicate houses in a cul-de-sac. Thus,

$$enclosed(RoadSeg, Chain) \leftarrow closed\_loop\_chain(Chain) \land$$
$$junction(J, RoadSeg) \land$$
$$point\_in\_polygon(J, Chain).$$

The geometrical relationships between road segments are used to extend road names when the above method fails using the following rules,

$$extend\_name(S_1, S_2) \leftarrow dead\_end\_extension(S_1, S_2).$$
$$extend\_name(S_1, S_2) \leftarrow same\_alignment(S_1, S_2).$$

6 Conclusion

In this paper, the application of deduction to a GDB has been presented. This was based on a comprehensive analysis of the requirements for a GDB in terms of representation and data input. Four dimensions which need to be catered for within a GDB have been identified, namely, space, theme, resolution and time. Deduction in a GDB was found to be useful for:

1. Defining a complex geographic phenomenon through its spatial structure, i.e. the spatial relationships between its component objects.
2. Reasoning over the geographic space for the inference of implicit spatial relationships which otherwise are not generally defined over object classes and would require the application of computational geometry algorithms.
3. Defining geographic object classes which extend over more than one data layer, thus obviating the need to explicitly create instances of such numerous object combinations.
4. Defining generalization rules for extracting one spatial object representation from another for cartographic and analytical purposes.
5. Declarative and recursive formulation of GDB queries, for storing frequently asked queries as rules in the database.
6. Automatic extraction of object level concepts from primitive level representations, which is a necessary operation in a GDB either for initial data loading or subsequent map updating.

In the DOOD project, the integration of deductive and object-oriented approaches in the design of spatial databases is proposed. Our intention is to demonstrate the usefulness of deduction for spatial databases (in particular GDBs) focusing on issues 1,2,3,5 and 6 above. Towards this aim, a prototype rule-based object extraction module for road network extraction and naming has been implemented. In addition a hypothetical resource management and allocation geographic application has been designed and is currently being implemented to test the GDB.

Acknowledgments The work that resulted in this paper has been funded by the Science and Engineering Research Council through the IEATP programme, and their support is duly acknowledged. Many improvements were suggested by our colleagues A.A.A. Fernandes and M.L. Barja, for which we are sincerely thankful. We would also like to thank Mr Neil Smith of Ordnance Survey and Dr. J.M.P. Quinn representing ICL, as the industrial partners in the project, for their assistance and support and useful discussions on the subject of this paper. Finally, thanks are due to Dr. Keith G. Jeffery of Rutherford Appleton Laboratory for his support and advice on the subject.

References

1. A.I. Abdelmoty, M.H. Williams, and J.M.P Quinn. A Rule-Based Approach To Computerized Map Reading. to be published in Information and Software Technology, 1993.
2. S. Arnoff. *Geographic Information Systems: A Management Perspective.* WDL Publications, Ottawa, Canada, 1989.
3. M. David and Jr. McKeown. Towards Automatic Cartographic Feature Extraction. In L.F. Pau, editor, *Mapping and Spatial Modelling for Navigation*, pages 150–180. Springer-Verlag, 1990.
4. M. De Simone. *Data Structures and Feature Recognition: From the Graphic Map to a Digital Database.* PhD thesis, North East London Polytechnic, 1985.

5. M.J. Egenhofer. An Extended SQL Syntax to Treat Spatial Objects. In *Second International Seminar on Trends and Concerns of Spatial Sciences*, pages 83–95, 1987.

6. M.J. Egenhofer. A Formal Definition of Binary Topological Relationships. In *Proc. 3rd International Conference on Foundations of Data Organization and Algorithms, FODO 89*, Paris, June 1989.

7. M.J. Egenhofer. Deficiencies of SQL as a GIS Query Language. In D.M. Mark and A.U. Frank, editors, *Cognitive and Linguistic Aspects of Geographic Space*, pages 477–491. NATO ASI Series, 1990.

8. M.J. Egenhofer. Reasoning About Binary Topological Relations. In O. Gunther and H.J. Scheck, editors, *Advances in Spatial Databases, 2nd Symposium, SSD'91*, Lecture Notes in Computer Science, 525, pages 143–161, Zurich, Switzerland., 1991. Springer-Verlag.

9. M.J. Egenhofer and A. Frank. Object-Oriented Databases: Database Requirements for GIS. In *Proc. Int. GIS Symposium: The Research Agenda*, volume 2, pages 189–211, 1987.

10. M.J. Egenhofer and R.D. Franzosa. PointSet Topological Spatial Relations. *Int. J. Geographic Information Systems*, 5(2):161–174, 1991.

11. M.J. Egenhofer and J.R. Herring. A Mathematical Framework for the Definition of Topological Relationships. In *Proceedings of the 4th international Symposium on Spatial Data Handling*, volume 2, pages 803–13, 1990.

12. Alvaro A.A. Fernandes, Maria L. Barja, Norman W. Paton, and M. Howard Williams. An Object-Oriented Database for Large-Scale Application Development, 1993. To appear in *Proceedings of the Eleventh British National Conference on Databases (BNCOD 11)* .

13. Alvaro A.A. Fernandes, M. Howard Williams, and Norman W. Paton. A Formal Abstract Definition of Objects as a Data Modelling Primitive. Technical Report TR92003, Department of Computing and Electrical Engineering, Heriot-Watt University, Riccarton, Edinburgh EH14 4AS, Scotland, April 1992. Revised June 1992.

14. A.U. Frank. Spatial Concepts, Geometric Data Models and Data Structures. Technical Report 90-11, National Center Geographic Information and Analysis, 1990. Two Perspectives on Geographical Data Modelling.

15. R.H. Guting. Gral: An Extensible Relational Database System for Geometric Applications. In *Proceedings of the Fifteenth International Conference on Very Large Data Bases*, pages 33–44, 1989.

16. J. Herring, R. Larsen, and J. Shivakumar. Extensions to the SQL Language to Support Spatial Analysis in a Topological Database. In *GIS/LIS'89*, pages 741–750, 1989.

17. L.M. Jensen. Knowledge-Based Classification of an Urban Area Using Texture and Context Information in Landsat-TM Imagery. *Photogrammetric Engineering and Remote Sensing*, 56(6):899–904, 1990.

18. D.M. Mckeown, W.A. Harvey, and J. Mckdermot. Rule-Based Interpretation of Aerial Imagery. *IEEE Transactions on Pattern Analysis and Machine Intelligence*, PAMI-7:570–585, 1985.

19. G. Mehldau and R. Schowengredt. A C-Extension for Rule-Based Image Classification Systems. *Photgrammetric Engineering and Remote Sensing*, 56(6):887–892, 1990.

20. L. Mohan. An Object Oriented Knowledge Representation for Spatial Information. *IEEE Transactions on Software Engineering*, 14:675–80, 1988.

21. O.A. Morean and R. Kasturi. Symbol Identification in Geographical Maps. In *Seventh International Conference on Pattern Recognition*, volume 2, pages 966–7, USA, 1984. SILVER SPRING.

22. J.C. Muller. Rule Based Generalization: Potentials and Impediments. In *Proceedings of the Fourth International Symposium on Spatial Data Handling*, volume 1, pages 317–334. IGU, 1990.

23. J. Munkers. *Elementary Differential Topology*. Princeton University Press, Princeton, NJ, 1966.

24. T. Nagao, T. Agui, and M. Nakajima. Automatic Extraction of Roads Denoted by Parallel Lines from 1/25,000-Scaled Maps Utilizing Skip-Scan Method. *SYST. COMPUT. JPN. (USA)*, 21(11):96–105, 1990.

25. B.C. Ooi. Efficient Query Processing in Geographic Informatiᵤn Systems. In G. Goos and J. Hartmanis, editors, *Lecture Notes in Computer Science, 471*. Springer Verlag, 1990.

26. A.K. Pachauri and P. Manoj. Landslide Hazard Mapping based on Geological Attributes. *Engineering Geology*, 32:81–100, 1992.

27. D.J. Peuquet. A Conceptual Framework and Comparison of Spatial Data Models. *Cartographica*, 21(4):66–113, 1984.

28. D.J. Peuquet. The Use of Spatial Relationships to Aid Spatial Database Retrieval. In *Proc. 2nd Int. Symp. on Spatial Data Handling*, pages 459–71, 1986.

29. D.V. Pullar and M.J. Egenhofer. Towards Formal Definition of Topological Relations Among Spatial Objects. In *Proc. 3RD International Symposium on Spatial Data Handling*, pages 225–241, Sydney, Australia, 1988.

30. D. A. Randell, Z. Cui, and Cohn G. A Spatial Logic Based on Regions and Connection. In *Proccedings of the third International Conference on Principles of Knowledge Representation and Reasoning KR'92*. 1992. Yet to appear.

31. H. Samet. Heirarchial Data Structures For Spatial Reasoning. In *Mapping and Spatial Modeling for Navigation*, pages 41–58. Springer-Verlag, 1990.

32. T. Schenk and O. Zierstein. Experiments with a Rule-Based System for Interpreting Linear Map Features. *Photogrammetric Engineering and Remote Sensing*, 56(6):911–917, June 1990.

33. T.R. Smith, R. Ramakrishnan, and A. Voisard. Object-Based Data Model and Deductive Language for Spatio-Temporal Database Applications. In G. Gambosi, M. Scholl, and H.W. Six, editors, *Database Management Systems for Geographical Applications*, 1991.

34. S. Suzuli and T. Yamada. MARIS: Map Recognition Input System. In L.F. Pau, editor, *Mapping and Spatial Modelling for Navigation*, pages 95–116. Springer Verlag, 1990.

35. M.F. Worboys, H.M. Hearnshaw, and D.J. Maguire. Object-Oriented Data and Query Modeling for Geographical Information Systems. In *Proceedings of the Fourth International Symposium on Spatial Data Handling*, pages 679–688, Zurich, 1990.

Representing Expectations
in
Spatial Information Systems
A Case Study

Graham J. Williams[1] and Steven G. Woods[2]

[1] Centre for Spatial Information Systems,
CSIRO Division of Information Technology,
GPO Box 664 Canberra 2601 Australia
Graham.Williams@csis.dit.csiro.au
[2] now with Command and Control Division
Defence Research Establishment Valcartier
2459 Pie XI Blvd., North,
Courcelette, Quebec, Canada G0A 1R0
Woods@drev.dnd.ca

Abstract. Expectations are important in reasoning, providing a framework within which decisions can be made. This paper describes a spatial information system which couples a large object-oriented spatial database with a graphical user interface, and incorporates ideas from artificial intelligence research, allowing the representation and use of expectations. In particular, the decision support role of spatial information systems is enhanced by the incorporation of reasoning with justifications and truth maintenance. The resulting system facilitates the assimilation, handling, and access to large amounts of dynamic and static spatial data for decision support. Inferential information of an application can be recorded, monitored, and updated.

1 Introduction

Spatial Information Systems (SIS) deal with the storage, manipulation, and display of spatially indexed data. Geographic Information Systems (GIS) are those SIS which particularly pertain to geographic applications. They are used by decision makers to access large amounts of stored data, to view the spatial relationships between the data, and to provide basic analyses of the data.

SIS have tended to be static tools for viewing data. The user of the system specifies data to be retrieved and displayed, specifies operations to be performed using that data, and then commits new or modified data to a persistent store. The systems are generally not actively involved in the decision making process other than to provide the data on which decisions might be made.

In this paper, we describe an interactive SIS designed to allow the input, display, manipulation, and storage of extensive spatial data in an object-oriented database. We view the database as an on-line system, continually being updated as new information arrives. The system described here implements a pro-active extension on top of the

SIS/database which introduces the concept of Expectations. Expectations provide a decision support mechanism by which the SIS can actively monitor its own operation in order to recognise the occurrence of significant events, such as the entry into the database of important information. These expected events can either be described by the user of the SIS or automatically generated by the SIS itself. In the latter case, the concept of templates, which represent typical patterns of both spatial relationships and temporal progressions, are introduced.

A military application is used here to illustrate the functionality of Expectations. The example is one of a class of generic problems which can be characterised by their requirement that they dynamically handle real-world entities whose identities are often uncertain and whose locations typically change over time.

Section 2 describes the example. Sections 3 and 4 identify both the generic and domain-specific components of the basic SIS which has been developed. Section 5 introduces the concept of Expectations, and describes how they are supported in the SIS. Section 6 introduces the idea of automatically identifying expectations.

2 An Overview of the Problem Domain

TMIPS (Tactical Military Intelligence Processing System) is a decision support system for military intelligence assessment. It has been developed jointly by the Australian Government's Commonwealth Scientific and Industrial Research Organisation (CSIRO) and the Defence Science and Technology Organisation (DSTO).

The identification and location of opposing military units is of prime concern for an intelligence officer during military conflicts. Information is received by the intelligence officer in the form of messages from field observers. These messages contain information about the location and constitution of opposing forces, and often have some amount of uncertainty and error. A particular message records information about the identity and purpose of units sighted at a *single* location.

A map forms the key tool used by an intelligence officer. The field observations are marked on a map as they arrive. The terrain, the location of roads, cities, etc., as recorded on the map, play a vital role in understanding the position of the sighted units, and in predicting their possible courses of action.

The intelligence officer's vast knowledge and experience is used to explain and predict the behaviour of the opposing forces. Detailed knowledge of the hierarchical structure of the opposing forces is used in attempting to identify the units sighted in the field. This information is specific to an opposing force and contains details about the equipment, size, and structure of units, and their relationships with other units. The intelligence officer also uses domain knowledge in the form of military doctrine which describes the behaviour of a particular opposing force. Both the hierarchical unit knowledge and doctrinal domain knowledge are non-monotonic, being subject to continual refinement as more is revealed of the opposing forces.

Mechanisation of the intelligence recording and structuring process is quite complex and presents some difficult problems in knowledge representation as well as in information retrieval and display. While there is often a great deal of information available, it may be incomplete, and sometimes inaccurate. For example, from the description of equipment contained in a message from a field observer, an intelligence officer might identify several possible units which contain such equipment and could potentially be situated at the reported location.

In interpreting a single sighting the global picture plays a very significant role. The volume of information (messages, domain knowledge, maps, satellite images, etc.) which is available when interpreting a message can be overwhelming, even for an experienced officer. This information overload can easily lead to important information being overlooked, and is a significant problem for any domain involving large amounts of data.

The SIS must assist the user in dealing with competing information, particularly as it pertains to the existence and identity of sighted units. The SIS must simplify the task of collating and organising the information as it arrives rather than adding unwanted complexity to an already difficult problem. In addition, the SIS must not allow important information to become lost in the mass of data in the database or the confusion of symbols on the map.

TMIPS is a SIS which assists the intelligence officer in the task of accumulating, visualising, and interpreting large amounts of spatially oriented data. This example military domain provides a fertile environment in which the effective representation and visualisation of data, and developments in spatial reasoning, can be explored.

3 Representation and Visualisation

An important goal of any spatial information system must be to capture the domain nomenclature and symbology and to use them in the human-computer interface. The military domain has a rich set of terms and symbols which are used to capture and communicate concepts and ideas. Whilst the SIS must support these, the underlying framework must be generic, allowing different domains to be easily accommodated.

An object-oriented approach for modelling is adopted here The data required for TMIPS includes the predominantly static information about terrain, and the location of key facilities like roads, rivers, and populated areas, and the predominantly dynamic information about the location of the military units. Each of these are modelled as objects, and are persistent in an ONTOS (Ontos 1991) object-oriented database.

This section reviews both the generic (object-oriented) toolkits which make up the SIS and the domain specific structures (also object-oriented) layered above the toolkit.

3.1 Underlying Toolkits

Two toolkits for the display and manipulation of objects for map-based applications have been developed by the Centre for Spatial Information Systems. Xs (Milton and Campbell 1992) is a graphic object mapping system based on the X11 windowing system. The Spatial Object Library, or SOL (Milne, Milton and Smith in print), is a toolkit for representing spatially located objects. SOL provides a persistent representation of map objects (roads, units, etc.) through an ONTOS database, and Xs is used for the display of these objects. Intermediate between SOL and Xs is the Spatial Object Display Library, which essentially provides the interfaces for the persistent SOL objects implemented using Xs. Textual interfaces have also been developed, allowing objects to be viewed both textually and graphically.

Objects that are to be represented by symbols on a map must have attribute information describing their location. Some objects, such as those representing topology, will have static, and specific locations, but the objects of primary interest to an application will typically have locations which are dynamically updated. The location of these latter objects is often not particularly precise (referring, for example, to field observations of moving entities).

Objects can be displayed graphically (on a map) or textually (text window) as in Figure 1. Each display representation of an object is identical from the point of view of the persistent object it represents. Notionally, the only difference between a text-based window interface to the data object and a graphic display of this object is implementational. Changes to the real object in the persistent database are reflected in all display objects—any display changes required for a persistent object are handled locally by the interface and are thus detached from the object itself.

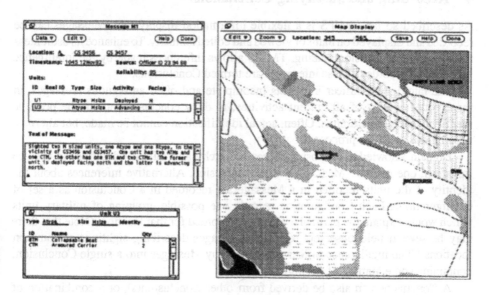

Fig. 1. Textual and graphical display of Object data. The rectangular icon near the centre of the map identifies the location referred to in the message. The boxed unit (U3) in the Message window identifies a selected Unit, which is displayed in a separate window.

The predominantly static type of data usually forms the base of the graphical (map) display. The dynamic data is typically displayed as a layer above the base map display. With the large amount of data available, retrieval and display of the data must be detailed enough to capture the information required by the user, and yet sparse enough to be easily comprehensible. This goal is accomplished using focus of attention, and smart map displays.

3.2 TMIPS and Messages

These toolkits provide much of the functionality often found in GISs with significant extensions based upon the object-oriented approach. TMIPS is built upon these tools. Static data consists of map-based objects such as topology and domain specific dynamic data consists of objects such as messages from field observers. Messages form the basis upon which the user (the intelligence officer) builds a model of the unfolding proceedings and makes predictions about future events.

Messages are reported in to the intelligence command post from field observers, and are entered into TMIPS by a clerk. Each message contains a time stamp, the identity of the sender of the message, an indication of the reliability and accuracy of the message, and details of the sighting itself, including the location, the type of activity observed, and descriptions of each unit at this location. Each Message may describe several sighted units, and each unit may be identified to be of a particular size and type, and having some set of equipment associated with it. Figure 1 illustrated both a textual and a map representation of a message.

4 Recording and Justifying Conclusions

As described so far, TMIPS is a flexible information display tool. Messages can be recorded and displayed on maps or viewed and edited textually. To enhance its usefulness in its support of decision making, TMIPS allows inferences made by the intelligence officer to be recorded. These inferences are termed Conclusions.

The intelligence officer interprets incomplete and often ambiguous messages, in the broader context of all current activities, to draw conclusions about the possible identity of the reported units. Often, actual identification cannot be made, but alternate possibilities might be proposed.

Domain knowledge (opposing forces hierarchy and military doctrine) is used to transform one or more Messages into a Conclusion. Alternative inferences about the identity of the units reported in a Message are recorded in a Conclusion as a set of Configurations. Each Configuration records one possible grouping of military units which would explain the particular sightings recorded for that location. (Note that there may be several field observers reporting messages describing sightings at common locations.) The intelligence officer can fuse many Messages into a single Conclusion, containing some number of Configurations.

A Conclusion can also be derived from other Conclusion(s), or a combination of Conclusions and Messages. Such derivations reflect the intelligence officer's evolving understanding about the configuration of the opposing forces. Figure 2 is an example of the formulation of a Conclusion. Ambiguity can be represented in the Conclusion and resolved later in other Conclusions as the intelligence officer learns more about the situation.

Relationships are maintained between Conclusions and Messages. This link records the Messages and Conclusions which were considered significant in arriving at a particular Conclusion. Such linkages define a Justification Network from which explanations of the reasoning leading to the assertion of a particular Conclusion can be composed.

The Justification Network can be used to monitor the validity of Conclusions. At any time, a Conclusion can be refuted on the basis, for example, of new information or insights by the user. The refuted Conclusion will have a new link to the Message(s) and/or Conclusion(s) which lead to its refutation. When a Conclusion is refuted, any other Conclusions justified by this one, either directly or indirectly, must also be reconsidered. Such dependencies between objects can easily be followed using a graphical Justification Browser. This can lead to Conclusions being withdrawn or otherwise justified.

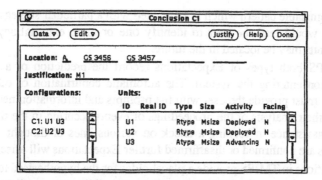

Fig. 2. The textual display of a Conclusion object. Within the area delineated by grid squares GS3456 and GS3457 a sighting was made, and that sighting can be explained by one of two Configurations. Configuration 1 consists of Unit 1 and Unit 3, and Configuration 2 consists of Unit 2 and Unit 3.

Conclusions, then, facilitate the intelligence officer's difficult task of assimilating and integrating the incoming reported sightings. Distinct messages, having locations in close proximity, can be quickly identified on the map, and drawn together into a Conclusion about the activities at that location, removing unnecessary redundancy and clutter. The dependencies between objects are visualised with a Justification Browser, providing easy access to related Conclusions, ensuring that the impact of new information can easily be propagated through the system.

5 Expectations

Often, in analysing a situation, and in particular when the situation is one that is dynamically changing, the user will identify the likely location and identity of further, as yet unreported, units. In addition, with the user's experience and knowledge, likely scenarios will be developed which will predict future movements of already reported units. In either of these situations, the user would be significantly assisted if they were able to record such predictions or expectations in the information system. The system could then automatically monitor new messages as they arrive, to determine whether the expectations have been met, or indeed, whether certain expectations cannot be met. The Expectations Model described here provides a facility for recording such speculation, enhancing the general functionality of spatial information systems.

5.1 Overview

Two types of Expectations are observed: expectations about the location of yet to be reported units, and expectations about the movement of currently reported units.

The first type of Expectation arises when a pattern in the layout of the reported units is recognised, leading to the hypothesised existence of other related units. For example, the reported sighting or conclusion of two units which typically form a larger unit when a third unit is also included, would lead the user to the expectation that the third unit will be located somewhere nearby.

The second type of Expectation hypothesises the future location of units already reported. For example, the observed relative location of a number of reported units may form a recognisable pattern which is associated with a particular strategy. Recognising this pattern would lead the user to identify one or more expectations about where particular units may be located in the future.

In TMIPS both types of Expectations record the prediction of a new Message or Conclusion entering the system. The automatic confirmation or otherwise of an Expectation must provide the user with the prompts and information needed to amend and extend their analysis of the proceedings of events occuring in the field. They will also be of assistance in keeping a check on various lines of thought. As the user's expectations are confirmed or disaffirmed further Expectations will arise.

Expectations in TMIPS provide a placeholder for the hypothesised locations of opposing forces and assist the intelligence officer in building an overall battle picture. In a hypothetical based reasoning system it is conceivable that multiple competing arguments or justifications for the location of opposing units exist. Individual Expectations are placed within the Justification Network, with links to supporting Conclusions and Messages, and to other Expectations.

Expectations are active objects—Expectations monitor the arrival of Messages and Conclusions for any that *match*. If a match occurs, the user is immediately notified with an Alert. The user will examine the Alert to determine whether a valid match occurred. If so, the evolving picture of the situation can be updated, with appropriate modifications to the Justification Network.

Within TMIPS, an Expectation is represented as an object having a form similar to that of a Conclusion (and in fact inherits from the same base class object). Thus, an Expectation has associated with it a location and a description of the units expected to be found at that location. In making predictions though, time is also a factor, and so an Expectation also possesses a time range for which it is valid.

5.2 Recording an Expectation

An Expectation is entered into the system using an interface similar to that used for entering Conclusions. An example of an Expectation Edit Window is illustrated in Figure 3. In practice, an Expectation will usually be derived from one or more Conclusions, with the relevant Conclusion data providing the initial and default values for the Expectation.

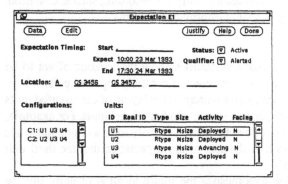
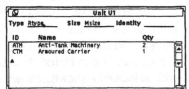

Fig. 3. Expectation Edit Window and Unit Edit Window.

As with Messages and Conclusions, the Expectation refers to a particular location. In common with Conclusions, the Expectation has associated with it a description of the units. Alternative configurations are permitted, identifying some degree of uncertainty of the identity of the units involved.

An Expectation, however, need not have any configurations associated with it. In such a case the Expectation anticipates some unit to be sighted at the specified location, without specifying the actual unit composition. This allows the user to identify a location which is to give rise to an alert immediately when some activity occurs at that location.

Similarly, an Expectation need not have a location specified, having only configurations and units. This Expectation anticipates some activity associated with particular units, without actually specifying where the activity is to occur. Thus, any relevant activity reported to the system as Messages or Conclusions will be brought to the attention of the user. This allows the user to monitor sightings of important units.

Additional information that an Expectation carries includes a Status and Status Qualifier recording the state of the Expectation, and a time-range within which the Expectation is predicted to occur.

An Expectation is either Active or InActive as indicated by the Status. The Qualifier identifies further information about the status. Expectations are recorded as Active if they correspond to a current valid prediction. Active Expectations monitor new or changed Messages and Conclusions, alerting the user of any matches. The Qualifier of an Active Expectation is automatically changed to "Alerted" when such a match occurs. When the user determines that the Expectation is of no further use, it will be flagged as InActive. For archival and explanatory purposes all Expectations are persistent, even if they are inactive. An InActive Expectation can be qualified as Satisfied if it has been entirely satisfied by one or more Messages or Conclusions. It can also automatically time out, in which case the user is alerted and must determine whether or not the Expectation is of any further significance. Possible actions at this stage include leaving the Status as InActive, or editing the Expectation's period of validity, and thereby re-activating the Expectation. Alternatively, an Expectation can be recorded as having been replaced by another Expectation or as no longer required, for whatever reason.

The time specified on an Expectation has three components. The Start Time refers to the earliest time at which a sighting is anticipated. When this time arrives, the Expectation is changed to Active and it will then attempt to match any subsequent Conclusions or Messages. The Expect Time is the most likely time for this particular sighting to occur. Matching could take into account the difference between this Expect Time and the sighting time of a Message by considering that certain activities have a regular nature and sightings near certain times have some explanations that are more likely than others. The Expectation End Time indicates the latest time a sighting is expected. Once this time elapses, an Expectation alerts the user to the expiry of its validity and the user can decide whether to re-Activate the Expectation or not.

Each Expectation will be a node in the Justification Network. Links identify the supports for an Expectation, which may be Messages, Conclusions and other Expectations. Links can be of different types, indicating the different relationships between these objects. For example, the user might identify two Messages as evidence of the existence of another unit at this location. The first two Messages could be linked (via the Conclusions) to an Expectation for this as yet unsighted unit by a *doctrinal* link which may also contain a description or pointer to the appropriate military doctrine that suggests the existence of the third unit. The user can obtain an "explanation" of an Expectation (or Conclusion) by viewing the links in the Justification Network, using the browser as in Figure 4.

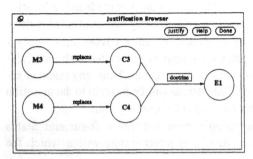
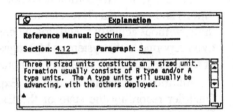

Fig. 4. The Justification Network browser. The explanation for a selected dependency (the doctrinal inference link) is shown.

5.3 Monitoring Events

An active daemon associated with the Expectations has the task of monitoring new Messages as they arrive and Conclusions as they are entered or modified, looking out for evidence supporting or invalidating the Expectation. The user is alerted to such changes as soon as they occur. The user then has the option of modifying the status and qualifier of the Expectation, possibly creating new Expectations and Conclusions. An Expectation that has been confirmed, for example, will usually be transformed into a Conclusion.

An Alert will be raised whenever it is deemed that the user should be informed of any significant events related to the Expectations. Events which merit attention include: a possible match of a new or modified Conclusion or Message with an Active Expectation; the timeout of an Active Expectation; or a change to the Conclusions or Messages which support an Active Expectation, as recorded by the Justification Network.

When an Alert occurs, the associated Expectation is added to a list of active alerts. A window is displayed informing the user of the new Alert. The user can choose to resolve the Alert immediately or to postpone this until convenient. The Alert (but not necessarily the window) will remain until it has been resolved. To resolve an Alert an appropriate course of action must be decided upon by the user.

If an Expectation matches a Message or Conclusion the Expectation status can be changed from Alerted to either Satisfied (by identifying one of the matching Messages or Conclusions as satisfying the Expectation, and replacing the Expectation and the "satisfier" Message or Conclusion with a new Conclusion based upon the "satisfier" Message or Conclusion), or InActive (simply causing the Expectation to be ignored by the system at present—no matching is performed on InActive Expectations). If an Expectation times out, the status of the Expectation can be changed from TimedOut to either: Active, (by modifying the Expectation to extend its time range), or InActive. If any of the Messages or Conclusions which support the Expectation in the Justification

Network change, the Expectation status can be changed to either: Active, (indicating that the support changes do not affect the Expectation in question), or InActive, (indicating that the support changes invalidate the Expectation as it exists). New Expectations can be constructed at any time by the user.

Of central importance to the monitoring of Expectations is the idea of matching Expectations with Messages and Conclusions. Matching is the automatic process of identifying a Message or Conclusion which has some similarity to an Active Expectation. The process of bringing the match to the attention of the user, as described above, is an Alert. There are two scenarios under which matching is initiated. If a Message or Conclusion is created or modified, all Active Expectations will be searched to determine if this new or modified object is *expected*. If an Expectation is created or modified, all Messages and Conclusions will be searched to determine if the expected situation has already been identified.

In TMIPS, matching is based upon location and identity. Location matching involves determining if the two regions intersect. Identity matching involves determining whether the configurations, and in turn the units of the two objects, match. In determining this the type, size and identity fields can be used.

In comparing locations and identities, imprecise matches may arise. Two types are distinguished: *possible* matches, and *necessary* (or exact) matches. A possible match describes the case where, for example, two locations overlap but do not coincide. An exact match occurs when the two values of an attribute in different objects are identical. A number can also be associated with the match, as an alternative means of specifying the degree of match.

6 Automatic Generation of Expectations

Conclusions, then, provide the user with the ability to capture inferences about how a particular situation is evolving as Messages arrive over time. This capability of revisiting earlier Conclusions and replacing them with new ones based upon new information is enhanced by the ability to explain current beliefs about the situation via the Justification Network. Expectations support the user with the additional ability to identify situations expected to arise in the future. Since the user creates these expectations based upon experience and domain knowledge, further support can be provided by identifying expected events automatically. This automatic generation of Expectations is driven by an understanding of the motivations and strategies of the opposing forces. A limited form of plan recognition is required.

Plan recognition is the process of determining how a set of perceived events in some domain are related, with the underlying desire of predicting what future events are likely to occur. Events can take the form of the sighting of new domain objects, or possibly of the movement over time of a single domain object, or perhaps even the non-movement or non-sighting of some object or objects. The definition of an event is domain dependent.

Traditional plan recognition involves fitting currently perceived events to a library of known domain plans. The process of identifying which plan is currently occuring consists of constructing a mapping from the "perceived" situation to one of the known plans. Of considerable interest as well is the explanation of the hypothesised mapping(s).

One way in which to address plan recognition from the standpoint of spatial information systems is to attempt to express the known (or common) domain plans in very general terms, typically as a pattern. An actual partial plan will be an instantiated pattern which may match some part of any one or more of the stored common plans (un-instantiated patterns). Matching a partial plan with a common plan will result in the identification of expectations of future events. Matching multiple common plans will result in multiple (or alternative) expectations. A general model of expectations, borrowing ideas from Truth Maintenance Systems (Winston 1984) and Possible Worlds (Charniak and McDermott 1985), is devised.

This general approach is being developed in TMIPS. Currently, all objects are archived so that partial plans which describe military unit movements are available. These partial plans can be matched against patterns (or templates) derived from military doctrine relating to general strategies of the opposing forces. When matching occurs, TMIPS Expectations can be automatically generated, using the Expectations Model already developed. Also, new strategies adopted by the opposing forces can be "learnt" by the system from its observations, employing common machine learning approaches (Kodratoff and Michalski 1990).

Spatial and temporal templates, derived from doctrine, can be used to guide the intelligence officer's assessment. Spatial templates describe the relative spatial positions of the opposing forces. Temporal templates provide indicators of the progress of the opposing forces over time. Key to the concept of spatial and temporal templates is the concept of expectations. Spatial templates give rise to expected locations of units yet to be sighted given sightings of other related units. Temporal templates give rise to expectations associated with troop movement.

Uncertainty needs to be represented in templates. The distance between the expected units described in a spatial template, for example, must contain some flexibility. A rubber sheeting type of approach is envisaged whereby the units of the template can be visualised as having stretchable and shrinkable rubber bands between them. The amount of stretch and shrinkage permitted is specified as part of the template. If the current layout of actually sighted units falls within these bounds, then the template is applicable. Direction and time can similarly be rubber banded.

Introducing the idea of plan recognition into the spatial information systems arena through the conception of templates is an important step in the incorporation of more powerful spatial reasoning capabilities. Such enhanced systems can play an even more supportive role in the decision making process.

7   Summary and Conclusions

The problem of formulating a decision support system based upon manipulation and display of spatially oriented, complex and dynamic information provides many different challenges, both technical and conceptual. Data representation, technical mapping approaches, multiple simultaneous views of complex and uncertain objects, and the complications at all levels of interleaving hypothetical information with factual information are only a few of the difficulties that provide ample opportunity for investigation in this domain. While each of these problems have been addressed in the course of the TMIPS project, the focus of this paper has been upon the representation, explanation, and future evolution of predictions of change for data that has a spatial orientation.

Expectations are a hypothetical representation of spatial data that may or may not exist, and may or may not be confirmed or dismissed at some future time. Evidential relationships exist and need to be recognised explicitly in the process of developing individual Expectations and in fact, in meeting those Expectations.

The support role of a decision support system can be enhanced by allowing the user to record their expectations, and have these expectations automatically monitored as the system evolves. Further, patterns can be identified and brought in to play a further supportative role in the identification of possible future events.

While the problem domain presented in this paper has been that of an interactive military intelligence system, many other domains with spatially oriented aspects offer different applications of these same ideas. Where there is a need to form a general picture of an evolving situation based upon intermittent and sparse observations, the ideas introduced here are relevant. One example is the task of tracking sightings of rare animal species. Here an Expectation could serve to help resolve many sporadic sightings into a general prediction of future sightings or perhaps even help understand other patterns such as migration. Domain knowledge about animal likes, dislikes, and habits could drive a plan recognition system that effectively combined spatial information such as vegetation, topography, water availability, etc., with sighting information over time.

In general, many environmental and infrastructure type applications could benefit from the use of an Expectations Model. Other potential applications in spatial information systems include weather observation and prediction, water quality measurements and inferences, and traffic flow measurements and consequent diagnosis of congestion over a network.

Acknowledgements

The seeds for the ideas which emerged as Expectations were planted by our colleague and mentor John Smith of the CSIRO Division of Information Technology. Early discussion with John helped to nurture the seedling. Discussion with our DSTO colleagues (particularly Ronnie Gori and Peter Calder) provided many insights into the application of the ideas to the military domain.

The original design and implementation of TMIPS was lead by Peter Milne, with Scott Milton and David Campbell contributing.

References

Charniak, E. and McDermott, D.: 1985, *Introduction to Artificial Intelligence*, Addison-Wesley, Reading, Massachusetts.

Kodratoff, Y. and Michalski, R. (eds): 1990, *Machine Learning: An artificial intelligence approach*, Vol. 3, Morgan Kaufmann Publishers, Inc., Palo Alto, California.

Milne, P., Milton, S. and Smith, J. L.: in print, Geographic object-oriented databases, a case study, *International Journal of Geographic Information Systems*. Accepted for publication 1993.

Milton, S. and Campbell, D.: 1992, A graphic object mapping system for Xwindows, *Tools Pacific '92*, Sydney, Australia.

Ontos: 1991, *ONTOS Developers Guide*, Ontos Inc., Three Burlington Woods, Burlington Massachussetts, USA 01803.

Winston, P. H.: 1984, *Artificial Intelligence*, 2nd edn, Addison-Wesley, Reading, Massachusetts.

Volumes From Overlaying 3-D Triangulations in Parallel

Wm. Randolph Franklin

Electrical, Computer & Systems engineering Department
Rensselær Polytechnic Institute
Troy, NY, 12180 USA

Internet: wrf@ecse.rpi.edu

Mohan S. Kankanhalli

Institute of Systems Science
National University of Singapore
Kent Ridge, Singapore 0511

Internet: mohan@iss.nus.sg

Abstract. Consider a polyhedron that is triangulated into tetrahedra in two different ways. This paper presents an algorithm, and hints for implementation, for finding the volumes of the intersections of all overlapping pairs of tetrahedra. The algorithm should parallelize easily, based on our experience with similar algorithms. One application for this is, when given data in terms of one triangulation, to approximate it in terms of the other triangulation. One part of this algorithm is useful by itself. That is to locate a large number of points in a triangulation, by finding which tetrahedron contains each point.

Keywords: tetrahedron, triangulation, overlay, uniform grid, finite element model, mass property, uniform grid, parallel, point location

1 Introduction

A given polyhedron may be partitioned, or triangulated, into tetrahedra in more than one way. No one triangulation is best since it may be easier to gather data for one set of tetrahedra, while another set might be more compatible with finite element analysis. However, then we must transfer some approximation of the data from the first triangulation to the second. If the data are smoothly varying one reasonable method might be as follows.

Let the input be two different triangulations, $\mathcal{A}$ and $\mathcal{B}$, of the same 3-D object. Assume that we can calculate a set of the pairs of tetrahedra which intersect each other, and the volumes of the intersections. Assume, e.g., that we wish to approximate the mass of each tetrahedra of $\mathcal{B}$ from the mass of each tetrahedron of $\mathcal{A}$, where the density is not constant, so the mass is not simply the volume.

Let m_i be the mass of the i-th tetrahedron of $\mathcal{A}$.

Let u_i be the volume of the i-th tetrahedron of $\mathcal{A}$.

Let v_j be the volume of the j-th tetrahedron of the $\mathcal{B}$.

Let w_{ij} be the volume of the intersection of the i-th tetrahedron of $\mathcal{A}$ with the j-th tetrahedron of $\mathcal{B}$. Note that $u_i = \sum_j w_{ij}$ and $v_j = \sum_i w_{ij}$.

Then the approximate mass of the j-th tetrahedron of $\mathcal{B}$ is

$$\sum_i \frac{w_{ij}}{u_i} m_i$$

If the tetrahedra are generalized, another application is to transfer data between input k-cells and the octree obels when building an octree.

We will see how to do this in several stages: the mathematical foundation, finding the volume of the intersection of two tetrahedra, intersecting two complete triangulations, efficient point location, how to implement on a parallel computer, actual implementations of related algorithms, and handling degenerate input.

The ideas of this paper were first developed in 2D in the context of cartographic map overlay in Geographic Information Systems[Fra90, FS90, Sun89, Siv90]. For some algebraic topological considerations in 2-D overlaying, see [Saa91]. Topological consistency and topology in 3-D are discussed in [ES92, Pig92]. For the latest on plane-sweep overlaying, see [vR91].

This paper is focussed on a specific problem; it takes the triangulations as given, and does not concern itself with their initial generation or later application, although that is clearly necessary. For an treatment of some 2-D triangulation algorithms, see [Ilel90]. For another application of tetrahedra in GIS, see [KV92].

2   Mathematical Foundation

Volume, and other mass properties, of a polyhedron can be determined using only the location and local neighborhood of each vertex. The polyhedron can contain multiple nested disjoint components and holes. It may be non-manifold. The only requirements are that it be finite, that there be a boundary that separates the inside from the outside, and the given data correctly represent it.

The data structure is a set of quadruples of vectors: (P, T, N, B), with one tuple for each case of a face, edge, and vertex all adjacent. (E.g., consider the cube in Figure 1, which has 48 tuples.) The components have the following meanings.

P Cartesian coordinates of the vertex.

T Unit tangent vector along the adjacent edge of this vertex-edge-face adjacency.

N Unit vector perpendicular to T, in the plane of the face.

B Unit vector perpendicular to both T and N, pointing into the interior of the polyhedron. B adds only one extra bit of information, but this is a convenient form for it.

Now, the mass properties, L, A, and V, can be calculated as follows. L is the total edge length, counted once per each face adjacent to each edge, A is the total face area, and V is the total volume.

$$L = -\sum P \cdot T$$

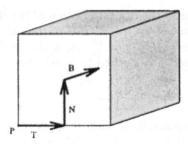

Fig. 1. The Local Data Topological Data Structure for a Polyhedron

$$A = \frac{1}{2} \sum P \cdot T \, P \cdot N$$

$$V = -\frac{1}{6} \sum P \cdot T \, P \cdot N \, P \cdot B \tag{1}$$

The difficult step is finding the volumes of the intersection polyhedra. Note that we do not need the intersection polyhedra themselves, but only their volumes, which is simpler. We assume that our input data structure includes all the vertices, edges, faces, tetrahedra, and adjacency information.

3 The Volume of the Intersection of Two Tetrahedra

To apply equation 1 to finding the volume of particular intersection polyhedron, we need its vertices, and their local neighborhoods. Such an *output vertex* is one of two types:

1. an input vertex, from one of the intersecting tetrahedra, or
2. the intersection of an edge of a tetrahedron of $\mathcal{A}$ with a face from $\mathcal{B}$ (or vice-versa).

If p is a type-1 vertex, then its adjacent edges and faces are the same as in the original tetrahedron. If p is type-2, the situation is more complicated, as shown in Figure 2. T and F are the input edge and face from $\mathcal{A}$ and $\mathcal{B}$, respectively. $G1$ and $G2$ are the two faces of the $\mathcal{A}$ tetrahedron that are adjacent to T. Now, what is the neighborhood of the new vertex, P?

P has three adjacent edge rays and face planes. Call them $T1$, $T2$, $T3$, $F1$, $F2$, and $F3$, respectively. $T1$ is just the input edge T, properly oriented. $T2$ and $T3$ are the intersection lines $F \times G1$ and $F \times G2$, respectively. $F1$ and $F2$ are $G1$ and $G2$, resp. Finally, $F3 = F$. This gives us the tangents and normals for the neighborhood; all we need now are the binormals.

Since we are intersecting the two polyhedra, the interior of the output polyhedron is interior to both input polyhedra. Therefore the binormals of the output faces are

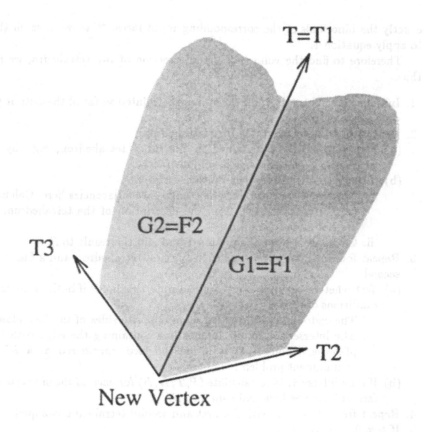

Fig. 2. New Type-2 Vertex

exactly the binormals of the corresponding input faces. Now we have all the data to apply equation 1.

Therefore to find the volume of the intersection of two tetrahedra, we proceed thus:

1. Initialize the subtotal, S, for the volume calculated so far of the output polyhedron, to zero.
2. Repeat for each vertex of the first tetrahedron:
   (a) Test whether it is contained in the other tetrahedron, e.g., by testing whether it is on the inside of all four faces.
   (b) If the vertex is inside, then do this:
       i. Note that there are six vertex–edge–face adjacencies here. Calculate the (P, T, N, B) for each, from the description of the tetrahedron, if they are not already known.
       ii. Calculate a term of equation 1 and add the result to S.
3. Repeat for each pair of an edge from the first tetrahedron and a face from the second.
   (a) Test whether they intersect. For example, this holds if both of the following conditions are true.
       i. The endpoints of the edge are on opposite sides of the face plane.
       ii. The intersection of the infinite line containing the edge with the face plane is a point that is inside the face, considered as a 2-D point-containment problem.
   (b) If they intersect, then calculate (P, T, N, B) for each of the six vertex–edge–face adjacencies here and sum into S.
4. Repeat from step 2 for with the first and second tetrahedra swapped.
5. If $S \neq 0$, then record it.

4 Using Triangulations, not Single Tetrahedra

The above section described how to process two single tetrahedra, but we have two whole triangulations of tetrahedra, A and B. Although we could apply the above to all pairs of tetrahedra with one from each triangulation, that would be expensive since it would take quadratic time.

Using some culling operation to select pairs of tetrahedra likely to intersect would be better, but still quite suboptimal. It ignores optimizations resulting from the sharing of vertices, edges, and faces by adjacent tetrahedra. A much better solution is as follows.

1. Initialize a hash table to store the partial volumes of all the output polyhedra, as they are calculated. The key is to be (a, b) for the volume of the intersection of tetrahedron a with tetrahedron b. We choose a hash table since we don't know in advance which intersection polyhedra will be nonzero, and our abstract operations are to test the existence of a key, read the associated record (partial volume) if the key exists, and write a replacement record for that key.

2. Repeat for each vertex, p, of $\mathcal{A}$.
   (a) Determine which tetrahedron, b, of $\mathcal{B}$ contains p. Store this information with p.
   (b) Find all the adjacent tetrahedra, a_i, in $\mathcal{A}$, to p.
   (c) Since p is a vertex of a_i that is inside b, calculate the resulting partial volume for each (a_i, b) and add into the hash table.
3. Repeat for each edge e of $\mathcal{A}$.
   (a) Get the tetrahedra of $\mathcal{B}$ containing each end of e.
   (b) If they are the same, then go on to the next edge. Otherwise:
   (c) Get the tetrahedra a, of $\mathcal{A}$ adjacent to e.
   (d) Trace through $\mathcal{B}$ to determine which faces of $\mathcal{B}$, e intersects.
   (e) Repeat for each face such face, f :
       i. Find the intersection of e and f.
       ii. Apply the equation.
       iii. Add the resulting partial volumes into the hash table.
4. Repeat the above steps 2 through 3 with $\mathcal{A}$ and $\mathcal{B}$ swapped.

The resulting volumes in the hash table should all be nonnegative. A negative quantity indicates a error, either in the implementation or in the input data.

5 Point Location

Given a vertex p and a triangulation of tetrahedra, $\mathcal{A}$, how do we determine which tetrahedron contains p? We recommend an extension of the uniform grid[FKN89, FNK+89]. For an analysis of the uniform grid on a transputer, see [HH90]. For a comparison of the grid to other methods, and related issues, see [Pul90, HHW92].

Build the data structure as follows.

1. Choose a grid-cell length, λ, proportional to the average edge length. The optimal value is a subject of future research; however in 2-D, being off the optimal by a factor of three either way has never increased the time more than 50%.
2. Construct a 2-D grid on the XY plane.
3. Project the vertices onto the grid to determine which cells they fall in. Use this to determine which PROJECT DATA which cells each edge and face intersect. The accurate method uses Bresenham's algorithm.
   Another method is to find the smallest enclosing box around the edge or face and then write the edge or face into all the cells that the box intersects. This will put the edge or face into too many cells, which will make the later point location slower. However this step will be faster, so the question is which part of the algorithm dominates the total time. Note that with this method, the result is still correct, since the grid is used later merely to cull objects.
4. Repeat for each cell, c: test each face intersecting c to see whether the projected face completely covers c. Such *blocking faces* partition the objects in the cell into those above and those below the blocking face. The resulting data structure for each cell will be an ordered list of blocking faces, with an unordered set of edges and other faces between each pair of adjacent blocking faces.

Since the number of objects in any cell will vary widely, a good data structure is an *expandable array*:

1. Initially, each cell, c, is a null pointer.
2. When we find the first object in c, allocate a block sufficient to hold a counter, and, say, five objects, perhaps with the C language **malloc** routine.
3. If more space is needed, then allocate a larger block and copy the old data, say with **realloc**.

The advantages of this method are as follows.

1. Variable numbers of objects per call can be accommodated without artificial limits.
2. Less space is wasted for pointers than with a linked list.
3. The objects in a cell can be accessed randomly with array indexing. If the cell is an array of pointers to integers, i.e., **int ***grid**, then the k-th object of **grid[i][j]** is simply **grid[i][j][k]**.
4. Again unlike with linked lists, the information for one cell is stored contiguously, which makes virtual memory managers perform better. (However, since real memory is becoming so inexpensive, about US$40 per megabyte as this is written, this factor will become less important in the future.)

The creation cost of expandable arrays depends on how much the array is grown each time it overflows. Suppose, for example, we double the array each time, and add one million elements to it, one-by-one. How expensive is this? The average element will be copied only once, there will be 20 reallocations, and a total of 2 000 000 words of memory will be allocated and 1 000 000 words freed. This is quite good performance.

With this data structure, locating a point, p, goes as follows.

1. Project p onto the XY plane, and determine which cell, c, contains it.
2. If c contains blocking faces, then locate p between an adjacent pair of them. Recommended procedures for this include a binary search or an interpolation search[PIA78]. The latter uses an expected $(\log \log N)$ queries if the statistical distribution of the elements is known. $(\log \log N)$ is effectively a small constant. Only the faces in the cell between these two blocking faces, and the upper blocking face, are relevant to what follows. See Figure 3.
3. Run a vertical semi-infinite ray up from p and intersect it with all the relevant faces.
4. Find the lowest such intersection point. The tetrahedron on the bottom side of this face contains p.
5. If there is no intersection, then p is not in any tetrahedron.

How does this perform? The only serious uncertainty has to do with the number of faces between adjacent blocking faces in each cell. For efficient performance, the input data must not be distributed "too" unevenly, which means no more than, say, a factor of ten variation in density throughout the space. The exact characterization of acceptable data is a research topic. However, in 2-D, we have never seen bad data.

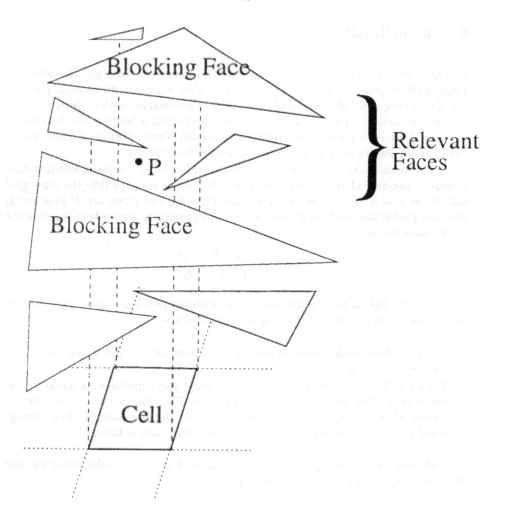

Fig. 3. Blocking Face Concept

If the data are reasonably random, and if the cell size is proportional to the average face size, then the probability that a particular face blocks a cell, given that it is in the cell, is constant. Therefore the expected number of faces between each pair of adjacent faces is constant, independent of the total number of faces in the cell.

Therefore, the expected time to locate a point is effectively constant.

6   Parallelizability

The algorithm presented here is clearly parallelizable for a data-parallel machine. Related algorithms on a uniform grid, such as finding all intersections among a large set of small edges, an object-space hidden-surface removal algorithm, determination of mass properties of polygonal CSG objects, and finding a boolean combination of polygons have been parallelized successfully[Kan90, Nar91, NF92a, NF92b, FK90, FNK+89]. Consider the point-location algorithm for example.

When we insert an object into the uniform grid to build the point-location data structure, the only clash might occur if two objects are inserted into the same grid cell. If the grid is $G \times G$, so that there are G^2 cells, and there are P processors, then the probability that, in parallel write, two processors somewhere try to write to the same cell is

$$1 - \left(1 - \frac{1}{G^2}\right)^P \approx \frac{P}{G^2}$$

if $P << G^2$. This is simply the coincident birthday problem. There are different solutions for this problem, depending on the hardware.

- On a machine with hardware semaphores, such as a Sequent, we lock a cell before appending to it.
- On a CM-2 Connection Machine, if we attempt two simultaneous writes to the same word, then one succeeds and one loses. Therefore we must read back a datum after writing, and rewrite it if the write did not succeed. The average number of necessary repetitions can be calculated, and is tolerable.

Performing the actual point location in parallel is even simpler since we only read the data structure, but don't write it.

7   Observed 2-D Performance for Map Overlay Areas

Some indication of the possible performance might be gained from seeing the efficient 2-D performance of the map overlay area program. The largest input data had these statistics.

Database	Vertices	Edges	Faces
US counties	55068	46116	2985
Hydrography	76215	69835	2075

When executed on a Sun IPC (25 MHz, 10 MIPS, ≈1990), we observed the following performance.

Operation	CPU Time
Read map	99.32
Scale vertices	1.03
Extract edges from chains	2.38
Calculate input polygon areas	3.65
Make grid	1.28
Add map to grid	8.60
Intersect edges	6.50
Locate map 0 points in map 1	5.83
Locate map 1 points in map 0	8.17
Accumulate output areas	14.35
Print areas	17.23
TOTAL TIME	168.35

After building the data structure, locating a point took 100μseconds on the average. Simply reading the input data from an ASCII file took more time than everything else combined.

8 Observed 2-D Performance for Parallel Object Mass Property Determination

We might obtain some idea of this algorithm's performance on a parallel machine by considering a the performance of a related problem. This is to determine the 2-D mass properties edge length and area of the union of many rectangles. We implemented this on a CM-2 Connection Machine, with 32786 processors. The highlights of the implementation are as follows.

1. Each processor serves first as an edge processor, then as a cell processor.
2. We distribute the edges to the processors.
3. Each (edge) processor finds the cells its edges pass thru, and sends messages to the cell processors.
4. Because of collisions, it reads back to check success, and retransmits if necessary. We can analyze expected number of retries. Experimentally, the maximum was 1–11, and the average number 1–4.
5. Each (cell) processor then intersects its edges to find some possible output vertices.
6. We do a point inclusion to select which are the actual output vertices.
7. Finally, we apply the formula.

The test data were part or all of a VLSI chip containing isothetic edges in rectangles. Notable observations included these.

1. The time to distribute the two million edges to processors is 216 secs.
2. If data size < P, then the time is rather constant, else it grows linearly.
3. Some actual times for various sizes of input are as follows.

# Edges	Grid size	# Procs	# Virt. procs	Time CM-2	Time 4/280
1000	90	8k	8k	1.42	
10000	90	8k	8k	1.41	3.3
100000	512	32k	32k	1.59	34
200000	512	32k	64k	3.42	73
400000	512	32k	128k	7.48	213
1819064	512	32k	512k	36.21	1066

The Sun 4/280 execution times are given for comparison since that is a much less expensive machine.

This suggests that overlaying tetrahedra in 3-D should also be quite parallelizable.

9 Degenerate Data

Degeneracies, such as a vertex falling exactly on a face of another tetrahedron, can be handled by Simulation of Simplicity[EM90]. This requires that calculations be exact. One solution is to scale the data so that edge and face equations are exact, and that tests against them can be performed without roundoff. Assume that the input coordinates are scaled to the range $[-M, M]$. Then in a face equation, $Ax + By + Cz + D = 0$, we have $-2M \leq A, B, C \leq 2M$ and $-6M^2 \leq D \leq 6M^2$. Testing a point against this can generate temporary numbers up to $12M^2$. With single-precision integers on a 32-bit machine, $M \approx 14000$. This may appear imprecise but might well be adequate for volume calculations.

For greater precision, we can use double-precision floats, considered as integers, to get seven digits of precision. However, many, though not all, workstations calculate with floating point much more slowly than with integers.

10 Summary

Transferring data between two triangulations of the same polyhedron is possible by finding the intersection volumes of the tetrahedra. We do not need to find the intersection polyhedra themselves. This algorithm is parallelizable, and, based on past experience, should parallelize well.

11 Acknowledgements

Parts of this work were supported by NSF grant CCR-9102553, by the Directorate for Computer and Information Science and Engineering, NSF Grant CDA-8805910, and by the Gruppo Nazionale Informatica Matematica of the Italian National Research Council.

References

[BCC92] P. Bresnahan, E. Corwin, and D. Cowen, editors. *Proceedings of the Fifth International Symposium on Spatial Data Handling*. International Geographical Union, Commission on GIS, 3-7 August 1992. ISBN 0-9633532-2-5.

[BK90] Kurt Brassel and H. Kishimoto, editors. *4th International Symposium on Spatial Data Handling*, Zürich, 23-27 July 1990.

[EM90] H. Edelsbrunner and E. P. Mücke. Simulation of simplicity: A technique to cope with degenerate cases in geometric algorithms. *ACM Trans. Graphics*, 9(1):66-104, January 1990.

[ES92] Max Egenhofer and J. Sharma. Topological consistency. In Bresnahan et al. [BCC92], pages 335-343. ISBN 0-9633532-2-5.

[FK90] Wm Randolph Franklin and Mohan Kankanhalli. Parallel object-space hidden surface removal. In *Proceedings of SIGGRAPH'90 (Dallas, Texas) in Computer Graphics*, volume 24, August 1990.

[FKN89] Wm Randolph Franklin, Mohan Kankanhalli, and Chandrasekhar Narayanaswami. Geometric computing and the uniform grid data technique. *Computer Aided Design*, 21(7):410-420, 1989.

[FNK+89] Wm Randolph Franklin, Chandrasekhar Narayanaswami, Mohan Kankanhalli, David Sun, Meng-Chu Zhou, and Peter YF Wu. Uniform grids: A technique for intersection detection on serial and parallel machines. In *Proceedings of Auto Carto 9: Ninth International Symposium on Computer-Assisted Cartography*, pages 100-109, Baltimore, Maryland, 2-7 April 1989.

[Fra90] Wm Randolph Franklin. Calculating map overlay polygon' areas without explicitly calculating the polygons — implementation. In *4th International Symposium on Spatial Data Handling*, pages 151-160, Zürich, 23-27 July 1990.

[FS90] Wm Randolph Franklin and Venkatesh Sivaswami. OVERPROP — calculating areas of map overlay polygons without calculating the overlay. In *Second National Conference on Geographic Information Systems*, pages 1646-1654, Ottawa, 5-8 March 1990.

[Hel90] Martin Heller. Triangulation algorithms for adaptive terrain modeling. In Brassel and Kishimoto [BK90], pages 163-174.

[HH90] Sara Hopkins and Richard G. Healey. A parallel implementation of Franklin's uniform grid technique for line intersection detection on a large transputer array. In Brassel and Kishimoto [BK90], pages 95-104.

[HHW92] Sara Hopkins, R.G. Healy, and T.C. Waugh. Algorithm scalability for line intersection detection in parallel polygon overlay. In Bresnahan et al. [BCC92], pages 210-218. ISBN 0-9633532-2-5.

[Kan90] Mohan Kankanhalli. *Techniques for Parallel Geometric Computations*. PhD thesis, Electrical, Computer, and Systems Engineering Dept., Rensselaer Polytechnic Institute, October 1990.

[KV92] Menno-Jab Kraak and E. Verbree. Tetrahedrons and animated maps in 2d and 3d space. In Bresnahan et al. [BCC92], pages 63-71. ISBN 0-9633532-2-5.

[Nar91] Chandrasekhar Narayanaswami. *Parallel Processing for Geometric Applications*. PhD thesis, Electrical, Computer, and Systems Engineering Dept., Rensselaer Polytechnic Institute, 1991. UMI no. 92-02201.

[NF92a] C. Narayanaswami and W. R. Franklin. Boolean Combinations of Polygons in Parallel. In *Proceedings of the 1992 International Conference on Parallel Processing*, volume tbd, page tbd, August 1992.

[NF92b] Chandrasekhar Narayanaswami and Wm Randolph Franklin. Determination of mass properties of polygonal CSG objects in parallel. *International Journal on Computational Geometry and Applications*, 1(4), 1992.

[PIA78] Y. Perl, A. Itai, and H. Avni. Interpolation search – a log log n search. *Comm. ACM*, 21(7):550–553, July 1978.

[Pig92] Simon Pigot. A topological model for a 3-d spatial information system. In Bresnahan et al. [BCC92], pages 344–360. ISBN 0-9633532-2-5.

[Pul90] David Pullar. Comparative study of algorithms for reporting geometrical intersections. In Brassel and Kishimoto [BK90], pages 66–76.

[Saa91] Alan Saalfeld. An application of algebraic topology to an overlay problem of analytical cartography. *Cartography and Geographic Information Systems (formerly The American Cartographer)*, 18(1):23–36, 1991.

[Siv90] Venkateshkumar Sivaswami. Point inclusion testing in polygons and point location in planar graphs using the uniform grid technique. Master's thesis, Rensselaer Polytechnic Institute, Electrical, Computer, and Systems Engineering Dept., May 1990.

[Sun89] David Sun. Implementation of a fast map overlay system in c. Master's thesis, Rensselaer Polytechnic Institute, Electrical, Computer, and Systems Engineering Dept., May 1989.

[vR91] Jan W. van Roessel. A new approach to plane-sweep overlay: Topological structuring and line-segment classification. *Cartography and Geographic Information Systems (formerly The American Cartographer)*, 18(1):49–67, 1991.

A Declarative, Object-Oriented Interface to a Solid Modeler

Michael L. Heytens
Hewlett-Packard Laboratories
1501 Page Mill Road
Palo Alto, CA 94304, USA
heytens@hpl.hp.com

Cristiano Sacchi
CNR - IMU CAD Group
Via Ampere, 56
Milano, Italy
cris@cad.imu.mi.cnr.it

Abstract. We describe an integration of Iris, an object-oriented database system, and ACIS, a solid modeler, into a single, unified environment for the management of both geometric and non-geometric data. Objects and operators of the modeler are accessible through OSQL, the database query language, in a completely transparent manner. This provides access to functionality of the modeler through a declarative, object-oriented language, and allows both geometric and non-geometric data to be manipulated easily and uniformly. To test the integration of the two systems, we developed an application program that managed three-dimensional part assemblies. Our experience in developing and using the application is: (1) the uniform and declarative OSQL interface greatly simplified application development; and (2) the ad hoc query capability of Iris proved to be very useful, as it allowed sophisticated users to interrogate the object base in ways unanticipated by the application developer, and to effectively extend the set of operators beyond those hard-wired in the application.

1 Introduction

Many application systems, such as those for assembly modeling and plant design, must manage both geometric and non-geometric data. Providing efficient persistent storage and manipulation of such a diverse set of data is a challenging problem. General-purpose database management systems (DBMS) effectively support many forms of non-geometric data, but do not include built-in facilities for efficient representation and manipulation of geometric objects. Special-purpose systems such as solid modeling packages do provide such facilities, but lack the generality of DBMSs.

As a number of researchers have observed (e.g., [2, 8]), it is desirable to integrate database systems and special-purpose packages into a single, unified environment, providing a powerful platform on which applications may be developed. The resulting environment includes: the declarative, optimizable query language of the DBMS; highly-tuned functionality of the special-purpose systems; and traditional DBMS features such as persistence, concurrent access control, transactions, and failure recovery.

In this paper, we describe the integration of Iris, a state-of-the-art, object-oriented database system developed at Hewlett-Packard Laboratories [4], and

ACIS, a solid modeling package from Spatial Technology Inc. [21] The main idea behind our approach is to make objects and operators supported by the modeler accessible from OSQL, the Iris query language, in a completely transparent manner. This provides access to functionality of the modeler through a declarative, object-oriented language, and allows both geometric and non-geometric data to be manipulated easily and uniformly. We refer to the integration of ACIS and Iris, and the OSQL types and operators that define the interface to ACIS, as GEO-DB.

The purpose of this work was (1) to test and validate the idea of integrating a DBMS and a solid modeler by constructing a simple but working prototype, and (2) to investigate the use of facilities provided by Iris for integration of external systems (the modeler, in this case). Our focus in this paper is on evaluating the suitability of OSQL for modeling the objects and operators provided by ACIS, and understanding the ramifications of using a declarative, object-oriented database language for development of applications that manipulate geometric data. To aid in our study, we constructed a simple application program that managed part assemblies.

In the next section, we give a brief overview of ACIS and Iris, and then describe the interface to, and implementation of, GEO-DB. Section 3 describes the assembly manager application, and includes many example queries which access both geometric and non-geometric data. Section 4 contrasts the Iris query language and facilities for integration with those of other extensible and object-oriented DBMSs. Section 5 summarizes the work and presents conclusions.

2 GEO-DB

GEO-DB consists of an interface containing geometric types and functions, specified in OSQL, and an underlying implementation on Iris and ACIS (see Figure 1). The modeler is accessed through a facility of Iris called external functions (to be described in Section 2.2). The geometric types and functions represent a seamless embedding of ACIS functionality in OSQL. As we shall see shortly, the entire OSQL language, including declarative queries and user-defined functions, is available for manipulating geometric objects. In the remainder of this section, we describe ACIS and Iris, and then the GEO-DB interface and implementation.

2.1 ACIS

ACIS is a three-dimensional, boundary-representation geometric modeler from Spatial Technology Inc. [21] It consists of two main components: (1) the *Kernel Modeler*, which is a basic solid modeler; and (2) the *Geometric Modeler*, which extends the kernel to accommodate sculptured surfaces.

We used only the Kernel Modeler in our work. The kernel supports explicit representations of solids such as blocks, spheres, and torii, and basic manipulations such as boolean operations union, difference, and intersection. The kernel

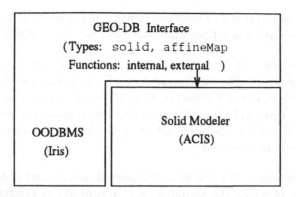

Fig. 1. GEO-DB architecture.

is intended to be embedded in application systems for design, analysis, or manufacture. Services provided by the kernel are accessible through an application procedural interface (API), which consists of a collection of routines. For example, procedure `api_make_torus` constructs a torus object, and `api_intersect` returns the intersection of two objects.

2.2 Iris

Iris is an object-oriented database system developed at Hewlett-Packard Laboratories [4]. It serves as a vehicle for research in many areas of database systems, and is the basis of a product now available from HP, called OpenODB [9]. In the remainder of this section we give a brief introduction to the Iris data model; for a more thorough treatment of this material, the interested reader is referred to [1, 4, 14, 26].

The Iris data model has three primary constructs: *objects*, *functions*, and *types*. Objects model real and conceptual entities from an application domain. For example, in an automotive design application, objects would model entire automobiles as well as components such as rims, tires, and engines.

Functions model all attributes, relationships, and behavior of objects. For example, the width of a tire object is obtained by applying the `width` function to it, and the weight of an engine object is computed (say, by summing the weights of component parts) by applying the `weight` function to it. This is in contrast to "classical" object-oriented models such as SmallTalk [6], where objects encapsulate all behavior and state information, and object interrogation is performed solely via message passing. In Iris, behavior and state information are *not* stored in objects, but rather in the functions which may be applied to them. In other words, the state and behavior of an object is not encapsulated within it, but distributed amongst the various functions which may be applied to it. This organization means that object behavior is easily extended by creation of new functions that implement new behavior. Data independence is maintained in the sense that pre-existing functions and code need not be modified or recompiled.

The *declaration* of a function specifies its name and the types of its argument(s) and result(s). The *implementation* of a function specifies its behavior; functions may have either *internal* or *external* implementations. Internal implementations are compiled into efficient executable representations and placed in the database. When an internal function is invoked at run-time, this representation is fetched and executed.

Two kinds of internal functions are supported: *stored*, and *computed*. A stored function is one in which the mapping from arguments to results is enumerated explicitly by the user through update statements, and stored in a table in the database. The width function, for example, would most likely be implemented as a stored function. When a stored function is applied to an argument, the mapping table for the function is consulted, and the result value is returned. If the user has not defined a mapping for a particular argument, then the result is null.

A computed function does not store its mapping of arguments to results in a table, but rather computes the result each time the function is invoked. The implementation of a computed function is defined in terms of other OSQL statements, i.e., the code that computes the result. The weight function, which traverses the hierarchy of component parts and sums their weights, is an example of a computed function. As we shall see in later sections of this paper through a number of examples, OSQL supports declarative queries, recursive functions, conditionals, and data structures such as bags, sets and tuples, so the database programmer has available a rich and complete programming language for defining computed functions.

External functions, unlike internal functions, have implementations defined outside of Iris in, for example, traditional programming languages such as C. External functions provide transparent access to information and functionality outside of Iris.

Types in Iris classify objects into named collections. Types also constrain functions, by defining the set of objects to which a function may be applied. For example, tire may be the type over which the width function is defined. Thus, the width function may be applied only to tire objects. A type may be declared to be a *subtype* of other types. This allows a type to inherit the structure and behavior of (i.e., the functions defined on) other types.

For the prototyping work described in this paper, we used WorkStation-Iris, a single-user, easy-to-use version of Iris that cached all database objects in main memory for high performance [20]. This was done solely for ease of development; a port of GEO-DB and the assembly manager to multi-user Iris or OpenODB would be straightforward, as all support the same basic language, OSQL.

2.3   GEO-DB Interface

The GEO-DB interface contains two types, **solid** and **affineMap**, and approximately twenty functions defined on them.[1] Let us first look at type **solid**, and then type **affineMap**.

Type solid. Type **solid** represents a geometric model (or object), which may be viewed as a subset of three dimensional Euclidean space [19]. The functions defined on type **solid** are shown in Figure 2. Constructor functions support creation of five pre-defined solids: block, sphere, cylinder, cone, and torus. For example, the OSQL statement

```
:s1 := cone('cone1', 1.2, 2.3);
```

applies constructor function **cone** to arguments representing the name, radius and height of the new cone, and binds the result to variable **s1**. By convention, all cones returned by **cone** are located at the origin.

Additional constructor functions allow creation of more complex solids from simpler ones via set operations union, intersection, and difference. The following statement, for example, creates and binds to **s3** a new solid named "cone-block", which is the union of solids bound to **s1** (a cone) and **s2** (say, a block).

```
:s3 := unite('cone-block', :s1, :s2);
```

Such set operations provide a simple but powerful mechanism for creating complex solids. For example, four copies of a wheel object built from approximately ten set operations are shown in Figure 3.

Each solid has name and volume attributes, accessible via functions **name** and **volume**, respectively. The following OSQL query utilizes these functions to return the names and volumes of all solids in the database.

```
SELECT    name(s), volume(s)
FOR EACH solid s;
```

The query returns a bag (like a set, but duplicates are allowed) of two-tuples containing the name and volume of each solid. The **SELECT** construct is similar to its counterpart in SQL, the standard language for relational databases, and is the central construct of the OSQL query language.

The GEO-DB interface includes predicate function **staticInterference**, which checks whether two solids "interfere" with each other, i.e., intersect in space. Here is an example query that utilizes the predicate.

```
SELECT    name(t)
FOR EACH solid s, solid t
WHERE     name(s) = 'cone-block' and staticInterference(s,t);
```

---

[1] Our intent in defining the GEO-DB interface was not to identify a complete set of objects and operators appropriate for all applications that manipulate geometric objects, but rather to identify an interesting subset capable of meeting the requirements of the part-assembly application we developed. The interface may be easily modified as necessary to reflect the changing needs of applications and/or new functionality provided by the solid modeler.

```
Type
        solid
Functions
    Constructors
        block(char(64) name, float x, float y, float z) -> solid;
        sphere(char(64) name, float radius) -> solid;
        cylinder(char(64) name, float radius, float height) -> solid;
        cone(char(64) name, float radius, float height) -> solid;
        torus(char(64) name, float radius, float height) -> solid;
        unite(char(64) name, solid s1, solid s2) -> solid;
        subtract(char(64) name, solid s1, solid s2) -> solid;
        intersect(char(64) name, solid s1, solid s2) -> solid;
        duplicate(char(64) name, solid s) -> solid;

    Destructors
        delete(solid s) -> boolean;

    Accessors
        name(solid s) -> char(64);
        volume(solid s) -> float;

    Mutators
        transform(solid s, affinemap am) -> solid;

    Predicates
        staticInterference(solid s1, solid s2) -> boolean;

    Miscellaneous functions
        export(solid s, char(256) fileName) -> boolean;
        import(char(256) fileName) -> solid;
```

Fig. 2. Type solid and associated functions.

The query returns the name of each solid t, where t intersects solid s, and the name of s is "cone-block".

The use of OSQL for describing and manipulating geometric objects enables easy and uniform access to both geometric and non-geometric data. Say, for example, we wanted to record, for each solid, the engineer that designed it. This can be implemented by a function with the following signature.

```
designer(solid s) -> engineer;
```

Let us assume that **engineer** is a type in the database, with functions such as **name**, **manager**, etc. defined on it. Function **designer** maps a solid to the engineer that designed it. This function may be utilized in queries such as the following, that access both solids and engineers.

```
SELECT   name(t), name(designer(t))
FOR EACH solid s, solid t
```

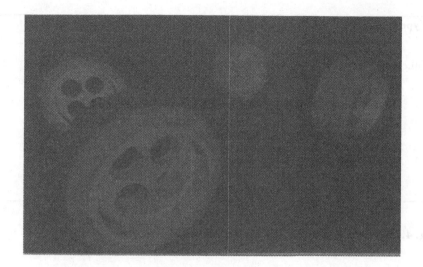

Fig. 3. Wheel objects.

WHERE name(s) = 'cone-block' and staticInterference(s,t);

The query returns, for each solid that interferes with "cone-block", the name of the solid and the name of its designer.

Type affineMap. The second type in the interface, affineMap, models transformations of geometric objects.[2] The functions defined on type affineMap are shown in Figure 4. The three transformations supported are: translation, rotation, and scaling. Here is an example that translates the cone bound to s1.

```
:t1 := translate(1, 1, 1);
:s1 := transform(:s1, :t1);
```

Function translate creates an affine map object, which transform then applies to s1, translating it by one unit in each dimension.

Note that it is not strictly necessary to make transformations first-class objects in the language, as we have done. We could have, for example, created three separate transform functions, one each for translation, rotation and scaling. The transformation in the previous example, then, could have been expressed as follows.

```
:s1 := translateSolid(:s1, 1, 1, 1);
```

In this case the translateSolid function updates s1 based on the translation factors, and does not create a separate object describing the transformation as before. While this might provide a small improvement in performance (and may be worth adding to the interface), we chose to model transformations as first class objects because it allows manipulation of them independent of the

---

[2] The name affineMap was chosen because geometric transformations are called affine maps in mathematics.

```
Type
        affineMap

Functions

    Constructors
        rotate(float x, float y, float z) -> affineMap;
        translate(float x, float y, float z) -> affineMap;
        scale(float f) -> affineMap;
        concatenate(affineMap am1, affineMap am2) -> affineMap;

    Mutators
        reset(affineMap am) -> affineMap;
```

Fig. 4. Type affineMap and associated functions.

objects to which they may be applied. For example, we may wish to create a
new transformation based on t1 as follows.

```
    :t2 := concatenate(:t1, rotate(90, 0, 0));
```

Function **concatenate** creates a new affine map which is the concatenation of
t1 and the affine map created by **rotate**. In other words, the new affine map
includes both the translation and rotation. Affine map t2 may then be passed
to functions, applied to individual or collections of solids, etc. For example, the
following code creates a cylinder, and applies t2 to it.

```
    :c1 := cylinder('cylinder1', 1, 10);
    :c1 := transform(:c1, :t2);
```

The first statement creates a cylinder, located at the origin (see Figure 5). The
second statement applies the affine map bound to t2 to the cylinder, translating
and rotating it (again, see Figure 5).

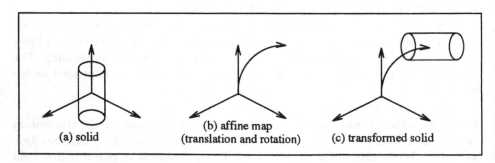

Fig. 5. Translation and rotation of cylinder object.

2.4   GEO-DB Implementation

Types and functions in the GEO-DB interface are implemented in both Iris and ACIS; connectivity between the two systems is achieved through the use of OSQL external functions (described previously in Section 2.2).

Type solid. Let us first examine the implementation of type solid and one of the functions defined on it. The persistent state of a solid consists of the name, which is stored in Iris, and the geometric representation of the solid (called a *body*), which is stored in ACIS. The persistent state of a solid is initialized by its constructor function. For example, here is the actual OSQL definition of constructor torus.

```
create function torus(char(64) tname, float radius,
                      float height) -> solid
  as osql
  begin
      declare solid s;                          /* 1 */
      create solid s;                           /* 2 */
      name(s) := tname;                         /* 3 */
      makeTorusBody(tname, radius, height);     /* 4 */
      return s;                                 /* 5 */
  end;
```

Keywords **as osql** in the definition indicate that **torus** is a computed function. The first line of the function body declares s to be a local variable of type solid. The second creates an instance of type solid and binds it to s. The third statement sets the name of s to be the value bound to formal parameter tname. As we shall see in a moment, the call to function makeTorusBody in the fourth statement constructs the ACIS body describing the torus. The final statement returns the newly-constructed solid bound to s.

Function makeTorusBody implements the link to ACIS; it is an external function, declared as follows.

```
create function makeTorusBody(char(64) tname, float radius,
                      float height) -> void
  as external simpleExtFun('CmakeTorusBody');
```

The keyword **simpleExtFun** indicates that makeTorusBody is a "simple" external function in the sense that its result type is not a bag or set. CmakeTorusBody is the name of the C routine that implements makeTorusBody. Thus, when makeTorusBody is invoked at run-time from function torus, control is transferred to CmakeTorusBody for execution of the call. Function CmakeTorusBody is implemented as follows.[3]

```
void CmakeTorusBody(char* tname, float radius, float height)
{
```

---

[3] In OpenODB, CmakeTorusBody would take only a single argument (a database structure) from which code in the body would extract the tname, radius, and height argument values. Here, for clarity, we show the three arguments as separate parameters.

```
        SOLID *s = api_make_torus(...);   /* 1 */
        api_save_body(tname, s);          /* 2 */
        addHashTableMapping(tname, s);    /* 3 */
}
```

The first statement of the function body constructs the solid body describing the torus by calling ACIS routine api_make_torus. The value returned by api_make_torus is a pointer to an ACIS-format, in-memory data structure. The second statement instructs ACIS to make the solid persistent by storing it in file tname.[4] The final statement adds an entry to an in-memory hash table that maps names of solids to their ACIS representations. As we shall see later, functions in the GEO-DB implementation need to map Iris solids to ACIS bodies. The name of a solid serves as a key in this mapping process, which first probes the in-memory hash table and, if not found, reads and constructs the body from the appropriate ACIS file.

Other functions defined on type solid are implemented in a similar manner.

Type affineMap. Now let us examine the implementation of type affineMap. The persistent state of an affine map consists of a 4x4 matrix that describes the transformation [5]. The matrix resides in Iris, and is implemented by the following stored function:

```
    create function amMatrix(affineMap am, integer row,
                            integer col) -> float as stored;
```

which maps an affineMap object and row and column indexes to the value of the desired matrix entry. Constructor functions rotate, translate, and scale create a new affineMap object, and define its matrix appropriately. For example, the following code utilizes scale to construct an affine map object, and then apply it to the solid bound to s1.

```
    :t1 := scale(1.4);
    :s1 := transform(:s1, :t1);
```

The first statement is executed entirely within Iris. It first creates an instance of type affineMap, and then defines its matrix to represent scaling by a factor of 1.4. The second statement transforms the solid bound to s1 by (1) accessing the transformation matrix associated with t1, (2) using the name of s1 to get a reference to its ACIS body, and (3) calling the ACIS API routine to transform the body.

Limitations of Current Implementation. An important issue related to the implementation of GEO-DB that we have not addressed is transaction management (i.e., concurrency control and recovery) that spans both ACIS and Iris.

---

[4] As described at the end of this section, a limitation of our current prototype is the lack of transaction management across both ACIS and Iris. For now, we simply make ACIS bodies persistent immediately after they are created, instead of at the end of a transaction.

Currently concurrency control and recovery are performed only on computations and data in Iris, since the modules in Iris that implement transaction management do not interact with external systems such as ACIS.

One approach to implementing transaction management across a DBMS such as Iris, and a special-purpose data manager such as ACIS, is to utilize the Encina Toolkit from Transarc [24]. The Toolkit may be used to make the special-purpose data manager transactional, and to coordinate transactions across the two systems. Some of the issues and tradeoffs in using the Toolkit in this context are investigated in [18].

There is also a need for comprehensive optimization of external functions. Some of the functions implemented in ACIS, such as predicate `staticInterference`, are computationally intensive. Since the implementation is external to Iris, the query optimizer has no way of knowing its cost. Thus, it is important for characteristics such as the cost of invocation to be described and made available to the Iris optimizer so that it may perform most effectively. Some issues related to optimization of external functions are identified and discussed in [10].

3   Assembly Manager

To test the GEO-DB interface, we developed on top of it a simple application that managed assemblies of mechanical parts. The application consisted of OSQL types and functions that modeled structured assemblies, and an interactive interface for visualization of objects and menu-based access to a number of common tasks (see Figure 6). The interface between the interactive layer and the underlying GEO-DB and assembly manager was OSQL.

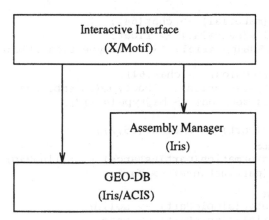

Fig. 6. Assembly manager architecture.

In the remainder of this section, we present the types and functions that model part assemblies; describe the interactive interface; and discuss ramifications of using OSQL for application development.

3.1 Types and Functions

The types and functions used in the assembly manager are shown in Figure 7. Types **solid** and **affineMap** were described previously in Section 2. Type **assemblyEntity** is a supertype of **part** and **partInstance**. Type **part** and its subtypes **simplePart** and **complexPart** record the description of a kind of part, while **partInstance** models actual instances. The motivation for distinguishing between information associated with a kind of part (type **part**) and that associated with a particular instance (type **partInstance**) is to avoid storing redundant information in the database.

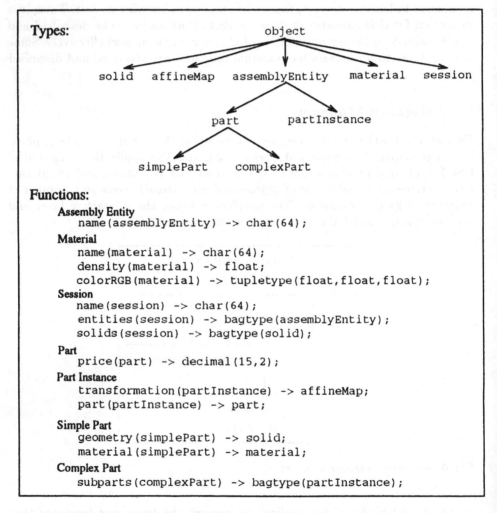

```
Types:                            object

      solid   affineMap   assemblyEntity   material   session


                    part        partInstance


             simplePart    complexPart
```

Functions:

Assembly Entity
```
    name(assemblyEntity) -> char(64);
```
Material
```
    name(material) -> char(64);
    density(material) -> float;
    colorRGB(material) -> tupletype(float,float,float);
```
Session
```
    name(session) -> char(64);
    entities(session) -> bagtype(assemblyEntity);
    solids(session) -> bagtype(solid);
```
Part
```
    price(part) -> decimal(15,2);
```
Part Instance
```
    transformation(partInstance) -> affineMap;
    part(partInstance) -> part;
```
Simple Part
```
    geometry(simplePart) -> solid;
    material(simplePart) -> material;
```
Complex Part
```
    subparts(complexPart) -> bagtype(partInstance);
```

Fig. 7. Assembly manager type hierarchy and functions.

For instance, consider a common screw used in the construction of an automobile. A single **simplePart** object would be created to record the name, geometry (i.e., shape), price, and material of the screw, while a **partInstance** object would be created for each of the many instances used in the car. For example, the following code creates two instances of a particular type of screw.

```
create partInstance :s1;                        /* 1 */
name(:s1) := 'screwA';                          /* 2 */
part(:s1) := :screw278;                         /* 3 */
transformation(:s1) := translate(1,2,4);  /* 4 */

create partInstance :s2;
name(:s2) := 'screwB';
part(:s2) := :screw278;
transformation(:s2) := concatenate(translate(2,2,2),
                                   rotate(90,30,30)));
```

Let us assume that variable **screw278** is bound to a part object that describes a kind of screw. The first statement creates an instance of the screw, and binds it to **s1**. The second statement sets the name of the screw to "screwA". The third defines the part-type of the screw to be the object bound to **screw278**, and the fourth sets its position in space to be a translation about the principal axes. The remaining statements create another instance in a similar manner.

As this example illustrates, each **partInstance** object references and thus shares information common to a class of parts, and also records, via function **transformation**, an instance-specific affine map describing the position of the object in space. This organization not only saves space, but allows shared information, such as price (a function defined on type **part**), to be updated quickly and easily.

Type **part** is capable of modeling not only simple part types such as screws, but also complex parts such as entire automobiles. Type **simplePart** models atomic part-types, i.e., those describable by a single solid. Type **complexPart** models the assembly of parts, either simple or complex.

For example, let us consider construction of the part-type shown in Figure 8, which consists of a center piece, ball-bearings around it, and an outer covering. The part-type is modeled via an object of type **complexPart**, created as follows.

```
create complexPart :roller;
name(:roller) := 'roller';
```

The first statement creates an object of type **complexPart** and binds it to variable **roller**. The second sets its name to "roller".

Next we need to describe the type and location in space of each component part. This is done by creating part instances that describe all components, and adding them to the bag of parts associated with **roller**. For example, the following code adds to roller a description of the center piece.

```
create partInstance :cp;                        /* 1 */
name(:cp) := 'roller-center';               /* 2 */
```

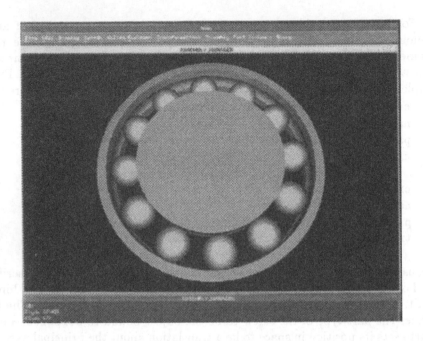

Fig. 8. Complex part "roller".

```
part(:cp) := :centerpiece;                /* 3 */
transformation(:cp) := translate(1,1,1);  /* 4 */
subparts(:roller) += bag(:cp);            /* 5 */
```

The first statement creates a **partInstance** object and binds it to **cp**. The second sets its name to "roller-center", and the third defines its part-type to be the object bound to **:centerpiece** (let us assume that an appropriate **part** object is bound to **centerpiece**). The fourth statement defines the position of the center piece in the roller. The fifth statement adds the center piece to the bag of subparts that define the complex part. Part instances describing the ball-bearings and outer covering may be created and added to the roller in a similar manner.

As this example illustrates, complex part-types can be constructed easily in a hierarchical manner; the richness of OSQL allows the structure of such objects to be modeled directly in the database. Also, the expressive power of the query language allows complex objects to be manipulated easily and naturally. For example, consider the **price** function, which maps a **part** to its price. The function is defined as follows.

```
create function price(part) -> decimal(9,2) as stored;

create function price(complexPart p) -> decimal(9,2)
as osql
    SELECT   single atomic sum(i)
    FOR EACH decimal i, partInstance pi
```

```
WHERE    i = price(part(pi)) and pi occurs in subparts(p);
```

The first statement defines **price** to be a stored function from **part** to **decimal(9,2)** (a fixed-point decimal number with 9 digits to the left of the decimal point, and 2 to the right). The definition is inherited by both **simplePart** and **complexPart**, the subtypes of **part**. This implementation of **price** is appropriate for **simplePart**, but not for **complexPart**, where the price must be computed from component parts. The second implementation given above defines the **price** of a complex part **p**, to be the sum of all prices **i**, where **i** is the price of a part instance **pi**, and **pi** is in the bag of parts of which **p** is comprised. By default the **SELECT** statement returns a bag of tuples, so keywords **single** and **atomic** are necessary in this case to return just the sum.

As described previously in Section 2, GEO-DB enables easy integration and querying of both geometric and non-geometric data. For example, the assembly manager includes a type **material**, which records the name, density, and color (RGB values) of a part. The following query accesses both parts and materials to find the names of all components of part "mercedes" that are made of asbestos.

```
SELECT   name(sp)
FOR EACH part p, simplePart sp, material m
WHERE    sp occurs in partExplode(p) and name(p) = 'mercedes'
         and material(sp) = m and name(m) = 'asbestos';
```

The query returns the names of all **sp**, where **sp** occurs in the bag returned by **partExplode(p)**, the name of **p** is "mercedes", the material of **sp** is **m**, and the name of **m** is "asbestos". Function **partExplode** returns all of the simple parts of which a part is comprised; it is defined as follows.

```
create function partExplode(part p) -> bagtype(simplePart)
as osql
begin
    return bag(p);
end;

create function partExplode(complexPart p)
       -> bagtype(simplePart)
as osql
    SELECT   sp
    FOR EACH simplePart sp, partInstance pi
    WHERE    pi occurs in subparts(p) and
             sp occurs in partExplode(part(pi));
```

The first definition simply returns, for a part **p**, a one-element bag containing **p**. When **p** is a **simplePart**, this definition applies. When **p** is a **complexPart**, however, the second definition applies. The second definition returns, for a part **p**, all simple parts **sp**, where **sp** occurs in the part explosion of a subpart of **p**.

Finally, the assembly manager includes one remaining type, **session**, which provides a mechanism for grouping objects in a database. This may be used, for example, to record all objects used in a design session.

3.2   Interactive Interface

To simplify use of the assembly manager, we constructed a simple interactive interface to it. The interface is written in C++, and utilizes X windows, Motif, and the HP Starbase graphics library. It consists of a menu-bar at the top of the screen, a large area for visualization of objects in the middle, and a small area at the bottom for issuing OSQL queries (see Figure 8).

The pull-down menus accessible through the menu-bar provide easy access to a number of common operations such as creating and transforming solids, assembling parts, and computing the price of an assembly. C++ code that implements the various menus executes an operation selected by the user by calling the appropriate database function. The database is accessed through the application call interface (ACI), which allows OSQL to be executed from a host programming language. All operations supported by the interactive interface can also be executed by the user by issuing the appropriate OSQL statements directly to Iris.

An external OSQL function, `displayObject`, was created for visualization of database objects. Internally, it accesses the ACIS representation of an object, and utilizes the Starbase graphics library to display it. This provides a powerful tool, as it enables the results of database queries to be displayed graphically. For example, the following query displays all part-types that cost more than 10,000 dollars.

```
SELECT   displayObject(p)
FOR EACH part p
WHERE    price(p) > 10000;
```

3.3   Discussion

In the development of GEO-DB and the assembly manager, we were able to exploit three important aspects of OSQL: (1) its rich, object-oriented modeling capability; (2) its high-level, declarative query language; and (3) its dynamic nature. We now discuss each of these, in turn.

Modeling Capability. As described earlier in this section, the object-orientation and inheritance of the Iris data model allowed complex, nested objects to be modeled directly in the database. Because the structure of such objects is visible in the database (and not encoded in binary strings, for example), it can be accessed and manipulated via the query language. A number of examples were given, such as the `price` function, illustrating how complex objects may be queried in a straightforward manner.

Declarative Query Language. Application development was greatly simplified by the declarative nature of the database language. The assembly manager, excluding the interactive interface, was developed in one person-month and consisted of only a few hundred lines of OSQL. While we have not constructed an equivalent assembly manager using a more imperative language, such as C, we believe that it would take approximately an order of magnitude more effort. This is consistent with observations made by Newell, based on experience in implementing a GIS using a high-level, object-oriented language [15].

Dynamic Nature of OSQL. OSQL is a dynamic language in the sense that arbitrary, ad hoc queries may be posed at any time, and new types and functions can be defined on-the-fly, without requiring recompilation or relinking of the application. The key to this flexibility is the OSQL interpreter embedded in Iris. This capability not only simplifies application development, but also allows users of the assembly manager to interrogate the database in ways unanticipated by the application developer.

It also enables sophisticated users to define their own functions, thus customizing the system and extending the set of operators beyond those predefined by the application. This is similar to the manner in which Lisp and the Lisp interpreter embedded in GNU Emacs may be used to customize and extend Emacs functionality [22].

4 Related Work

In this section, we contrast facilities of Iris that support extensibility and integration of external systems with those of other DBMSs. Our main focus is on data model and query language.

Most early work in this area was done in the context of relational systems, and involved extending the DBMS with user-defined abstract data types (ADT) [12]. An ADT may be used as a data type for columns of a relation, or to provide the implementation of an entire relation. In either case, the ADT implementor must provide routines that implement ADT operators, perform conversion to an external (i.e., printable) representation, etc.

Examples of systems that were extended with ADTs are Ingres [16] and RAD [17]. While ADTs did provide a form of extensibility in these systems, they were still limited in their ability to handle complex data and operators. For example, lacking were objects, type inheritance, and expressive power in the query language. Such features are present in the Iris data and computational models, and are common in many other modern DBMSs.

Extended relational systems, such as Postgres [23], Starburst [13], and Gral [7] also support a similar notion of extensibility through ADTs. While the data models of these systems are quite different from that of Iris, due to their relational origins, they provide the necessary flexibility and modeling power to successfully integrate a solid modeler. A thorough discussion of how Starburst could be extended to handle spatial data is given in [8], and a description of how a GIS system was developed on top of Postgres is given in [25].

Object-oriented database systems are easily extensible, as creation of new types and operators is a common and fundamental activity. However, there are important differences amongst object-oriented DBMSs that have significant ramifications on application development. One popular approach to building an OODBMS (e.g., [11]) is to add persistence and transactions to C++. Since ACIS is implemented in C++, one could put such an OODBMS underneath it, thus making ACIS data structures persistent. While this provides transparent persistence of geometric objects, transactions, and easy integration with non-geometric data, as in GEO-DB, it differs in the following ways.

1. No high-level, declarative query language such as OSQL is available for accessing the database. All access to the database is through C++, possibly embellished slightly to allow things like simple associative lookups.
2. C++ implementations are not dynamic, in the sense that ad hoc queries (or code) cannot be executed, and new classes and functions cannot be defined on-the-fly, as in Iris. To extend or modify an application system, the new or modified code must be compiled, and the system relinked.
3. Application development in languages other than C++ is difficult. When the application language happens to be C++, integration with the database is obviously very tight, thus completely eliminating the so-called impedance mismatch [3]. When the application language is not C++, access to the database is extremely difficult. In contrast, OSQL is not tightly bound to a single language, which increases the impedance mismatch slightly, but makes access to the database from multiple languages (e.g., Ada and Fortran) much easier.

5   Summary and Conclusions

Iris, an object-oriented database system developed at Hewlett-Packard, and ACIS, a solid modeling package from Spatial Technology Inc., were integrated to provide a single, unified environment for the management of geometric and non-geometric data. The resulting environment, called GEO-DB, provided transparent access to the geometric objects and operators of the solid modeler through OSQL, the database query language.

To test the integration, a simple assembly-manager application was developed on top of GEO-DB. The application consisted of OSQL types and functions that modeled structured assemblies, and an interactive interface for visualization of objects and menu-based access to common operations. The powerful modeling constructs and declarative nature of OSQL, and the unified interface to both geometric and non-geometric data, greatly simplified application development. We were able to implement the assembly manager in about one person-month of effort and with only a few hundred lines of OSQL code. We estimate that a similar implementation using a more imperative language, such as C, would have taken an order of magnitude more effort.

The OSQL interpreter embedded in Iris enabled users of the assembly manager to pose ad hoc queries and to extend the system dynamically with new operators. This capability proved to be very useful, as it allowed users to interrogate the object base in ways unanticipated by the application developer,

508

and to effectively extend the set of operators beyond those hard-wired in the application.

Acknowledgements

We thank Dan Fishman, Curt Kolovson and Marie-Anne Neimat for their comments on an early version of this paper, and for insightful discussions of this work. We also thank Spyros Potamianos for his help in producing some of the figures included in the paper.

References

1. J. Annevelink. Database Programming Languages: A Functional Approach. In *Proceedings of the 1991 ACM SIGMOD Conference*, Denver, CO, May 1991. ACM.
2. T. Connors, W. Hasan, C. Kolovson, M.-A. Neimat, D. Schneider, and K. Wilkinson. The Papyrus Integrated Data Server. In *Proceedings of First International Conference on Parallel and Distributed Information Systems*, December 1991.
3. G. Copeland and D. Maier. Making Smalltalk a Database System. In *Proceedings of the 1984 ACM SIGMOD Conference*, New York, June 1984. ACM.
4. D. Fishman, J. Annevelink, E. Chow, T. Connors, J. Davis, W. Hasan, C. Hoch, W. Kent, S. Leichner, P. Lyngbaek, B. Mahbod, M.-A. Neimat, T. Risch, M. Shan, and W. Wilkinson. Overview of the Iris DBMS. In W. Kim and E. Lochovsky, editors, *Object-Oriented Concepts/Applications and Databases*. Addison-Wesley, 1989.
5. J. Foley, A. van Dam, S. Feiner, and J. Hughes. *Computer Graphics Principles and Practice*. Addison-Wesley, Reading, Massachusetts, 1990.
6. A. Goldberg and D. Robson. *Smalltalk-80: The Language and Its Implementation*. Addison-Wesley, Reading, Mass., 1983.
7. R. H. Guting. Gral: An Extensible Relational Database System for Geometric Applications. In *Proceedings of the 15th International Conference on Very Large Data Bases*, Amsterdam, August 1989.
8. L. Haas and W. Cody. Exploiting Extensible DBMS in Integrated Geographic Information Systems. In *Second Symposium on Large Spatial Databases, Lecture Notes in Computer Science, vol. 525*, Zurich, Switzerland, August 1991. Springer-Verlag.
9. Hewlett-Packard Company. OpenODB Reference Document, HP Part No. B2470A-90001, 1992.
10. C. P. Kolovson, M.-A. Neimat, and S. Potamianos. Interoperability of Spatial and Attribute Data Managers: A Case Study. 3rd International Symposium on Large Spatial Databases, June 1993.
11. C. Lamb, G. Landis, J. Orenstein, and D. Weinreb. The ObjectStore Database System. *Communications of the ACM*, 34(10):50–63, October 1990.
12. B. Liskov and S. Zilles. Programming with Abstract Data Types. *ACM SIGPLAN Notices*, April 1974.
13. G. M. Lohman, B. Lindsay, H. Pirahesh, and K. B. Schiefer. Extensions to STAR-BURST: Objects, Types, Functions, and Rules. *Communications of the ACM*, 34(10):94–109, October 1990.

14. P. Lyngbaek and OODB Team in CSY. OSQL: A Language for Object Databases. Technical Report HPL-DTD-91-4, Hewlett-Packard Laboratories, Palo Alto, CA, January 1991.

15. R. G. Newell. Practical Experiences of Using Object-Orientation to Implement a GIS. In *Proceedings 1992 GIS/LIS Conference and Exposition*, San Jose, CA, November 1992.

16. J. Ong, D. Fogg, and M. Stonebraker. Implementation of Data Abstraction in the Relational Database System INGRES. *ACM SIGMOD Record*, 14(1), March 1984.

17. S. Osborne and T. Heaven. The Design of a Relational Database System with Abstract Data Types for Domains. *ACM Transactions on Database Systems*, 11(3), September 1986.

18. R. Rastogi and M.-A. Neimat. On Using the Encina Toolkit to Provide Recovery and Support for Data Managers. Technical Report HPL-DTD-92-21, Hewlett-Packard Laboratories, November 1992.

19. A. Requicha. Representations for Rigid Solids: Theory, Methods, and Systems. *ACM Computing Surveys*, 12(4), December 1980.

20. T. Risch. WS-IRIS, A Main Memory Object-Oriented DBMS. Technical Report HPL-DTD-92-5, Database Technology Department, Hewlett-Packard Laboratories, 1501 Page Mill Road, Palo Alto, CA 94304, April 29 1992.

21. Spatial Technology Inc. ACIS Interface Guide, March 1992.

22. R. Stallman. GNU Emacs Manual, 1987.

23. M. Stonebraker and G. Kemnitz. The POSTGRES Next-Generation Database Management System. *Communications of the ACM*, 34(10):78–93, October 1990.

24. Transarc Corporation. Encina Toolkit Server Core: Programmer's Reference.

25. T. Vijlbrief and P. van Oosterom. The GEO++ System: An Extensible GIS. In *Proceedings 5th International Symposium on Spatial Data Handling*, Charleston, SC, August 1992.

26. W. K. Wilkinson, P. Lyngbaek, and W. Hasan. The Iris Architecture and Implementation. *IEEE Trans. on Knowledge and Data Engineering*, 2(1):63–75, March 1990.

Indexing on Spherical Surfaces Using Semi-Quadcodes

Ekow J. Otoo and Hongwen Zhu

School of Computer Science
Carleton University
Ottawa, Ontario, Canada, K1S 5B6

Abstract. The conventional method of referencing a point on a spherical surface of known radius is by specifying the angular position of ϕ and λ with respect to an origin at the centre. This is akin to the $\langle x, y \rangle$ coordinates system in R^2 cartesian plane. To specify a region in the cartesian plane, two points corresponding to the diagonal points $\langle x_1, y_1 \rangle$ and $\langle x_2, y_2 \rangle$ are sufficient to characterize the region. Given any bounded region, of $2^h \times 2^h$ an alternate form of referencing a square subregion is by the linear quadtree address [10] or quadcode [13]. Corresponding encoding scheme for spherical surfaces is lacking. Recently a method similar to the quadtree recursive decomposition method has been proposed independently by Dutton and Fekete. Namely, the *quaternary triangular mesh (QTM)* [4] and the *spherical quadtree (SQT)* [8]. The addressing method of the triangular regions suggested are very similar. We present a new labeling method for the triangular patches on the sphere that allows for a better and more efficient operation and indexing on spherical surfaces.

1 Introduction

Advances in computer graphics technology now provide capability to model 3-dimensional objects with added manipulative functions such as real-time rotations, etc. In certain disciplines such as in the earth and space science, it is becoming increasing desirable to model spherical surfaces. In geography, the idea of map projections, is effectively a form of modeling the spatial features on spherical surfaces as a flat or planar surfaces, e.g., paper maps, to the extent that actual measurement on the map can be translated, by scaling to the actual physical distances on the ground. The concept of paper maps is an abstract model of the physical world. Given the current state of computer and graphics technology one should be able to visualize information depicted in a map as an actual 3-dimensional model of the physical world. To achieve this, we need a convenient way of representing, storing, retrieving and accessing information relating to spherical regions of the globe.

Techniques of visualizing data of planar regions have benefited considerably from the use of hierarchical data structuring methods such as the quadtrees [20, 19]. To put the problem in perspective, consider a square planar region (A, B, C, D) of figure 1.1. A location in this region may be defined, to some degree of precision, by the Cartesian coordinate system with respect to an origin, say in the lower left hand corner. To specify a region in this system, for example, region (a, b, c, d) of figure 1.1, the coordinates of two diagonal points $a = \langle x_1, y_1 \rangle$ and $c = \langle x_2, y_2 \rangle$, are specified. Alternatively, using a quadtree decomposition, of the space, the subregion (a, b, c, d) can be defined by a linear quadtree code [10] or quadcode [13]. In general, an arbitrary subregion will be defined by a list of quadcodes.

The quadtree like decomposition of planar regions into rectangular cells, and also volumetric space into voxels or cuboids, have had extensive applications in graphics, spatial searching and solid modelling. The address of a cell may be specified by the string of quaternary digits from the root to the terminal node representing the subregion. Such an address embeds the spatial coordinates as well. It is natural then to explore the extension of quadtree-like decomposition method to spherical surfaces. In this respect, we note some properties of the region quadtree decomposition.

- It preserves the rectilinear shapes of the cells at any level.
- The cells, at any level, have equal parametric measures: equal area, perimeter, volume, etc.

The natural extension of the concept of quadtrees to decomposing spherical surfaces so that regions can be appropriately indexed, has been addressed in [2, 21, 15, 16]. Unfortunately this has been found to be inappropriate. Its inappropriateness is exacerbated by the fact that the two desired properties, mentioned above, are not preserved. The shapes of the cells are rectilinear for regions around the equator but triangular near the poles, see figure 1.2. The cells at the same level of decomposition neither have equal shapes or equal areas. The question then is whether there is some other hierarchical decomposition method for spherical surfaces that lends itself to the operations much like the quadtree is to planar surfaces. Such a decomposition and representation can be used for the construction of 3-D model of the globe and for the rendering of both volume and spherical surface data so that distribution over the surfaces can be displayed in vector form or in discrete element of forms as rendered triangles [12].

The answer to this question is in the affirmative and it has been addressed by a number of researchers. Variants of the same idea have been proposed and associated with different names. Dutton [4, 6, 5] proposed a triangular decomposition method which he refers to as *the Quaternary Triangular Mesh (QTM)*. He proposed this as an alternative method for geographically referencing locations on planetary surfaces. He showed that the method has considerable advantages over other conventional methods such as the geographic coordinate system, of longitude and latitude. We briefly elaborate on his approach in the next section. The method has since been studied by Goodchild and Shiren [12] and they conclude that the method serves as a better alternative to the quadtree for global indexing in Geographic Information Systems. A similar approach has been proposed by Fekete [9, 8]. He referred to his approach as *Spherical Quadtree (SQT)* and calls the triangular cells *trixels*.

In either of the two methods, the spherical surface is approximated by a set of triangular patches. Each triangular patch is recursively tessellated by bisecting the edges to form a median point. These median points are then projected to the surface. By joining the new median points, four new triangular patches are generated. One interesting characteristic of the scheme is that the higher the degree of tessellation, the better the triangular patches approximate the shape of the sphere. The two schemes, however, differ with respect to: i) the initial number of triangular patches of the base platonic solid and ii) the labeling schemes used for addressing the triangular cells; Dutton uses labels 0 - 3 while Fekete uses labels 1 - 4. Otherwise, they are the same.

We observe that the QTM method is to region encoding of spherical surfaces as the linear quadtree [10] is to region encoding of planar surfaces. In proposing the use of QTM, Dutton recommends its use for point location. This requires an arbitrary long string of QTM digits when the depth of tessellation is high. A number of open questions were raised. In particular he raised the question of how best to implement the variable resolution aspects of QTM codes on a hardware that is designed to process fixed-precision data. We believe the significance of the QTM encoding is diminished when stretched in this manner for point location instead of it being used simply to address regions on spherical surfaces. Given the success and dominant use of the region quadtree and related quadtree-like structures [10, 11, 20, 19] in image processing and spatial indexing, the QTM encoding holds great promise in its use for indexing on spherical surfaces.

In proposing a similar idea called the Spherical Quad-trees (SQT), Fekete [8] presents arguments for its importance in a number of applications. Namely:

- generalization in cartographic visualization;
- efficient access to spherically distributed data;
- development of graphical browser to select metadata of regions. The *metadata* is a database that describes the available databases on specific regions of the globe.

In this paper, we address some of the problems related to the use of the QTM and SQT codes for spatial indexing and we show how it may be used effectively for indexing regions on spherical surfaces We propose an alternate labeling scheme which we refer to as the *semi-quadcode (SQC)*. Our SQC (not to be confused with the abbreviation (SQT)) is actually a variant of the QTM scheme of Dutton. We would like to emphasize that all three schemes are similar except for the initial base structures inscribed in the sphere. They differ also in the manner in which they generate the address labels and ultimately the algorithms for basic operations such as neighbour finding, adjacency detection, connected component labeling, etc.

We utilize the scheme more for addressing triangular regions only up to the level of precision tolerable by the integer representation of the hardware. The highlights and major contribution of this paper are:

1. the development of a new labeling scheme termed semi-quadcodes (SQC) in place of QTM methods;

2. the design of simpler algorithms for operations on spherical surfaces: neighbour finding, union, intersection, difference, rotation, etc.;

3. development of new transformation algorithm from angular coordinates to semi-quadcode addresses;

4. derivation algorithm of the angular coordinates of the three points that define the triangular cell of a given SQC address;

5. application of the scheme to indexing regions on spherical surfaces;

We discus the background to the development of the SQC scheme in the next section and show how it relates to the earlier QTM and SQT methods. In section three, we present some properties of the method and its related arithmetic operations. We compare the scheme with the earlier proposed schemes in section four and suggest other applications of it. We conclude in section five, giving an outline of future direction of its use in modeling the globe in Geographic Information Systems.

2 Background

The basic idea of the Quaternary Triangular Mesh (QTM), Spherical Quadtree and Semi-Quadcode is to recursively approximate the surface of a sphere by a set of triangular patches. The method is similar to the digitization of a curve whereby the curve is approximated by a set of line segments. Consider the arc segment, ABC, of figure 2.1a. This may be approximated by the chord AC. Suppose we recursively perform the following procedure: At each level of the recursive process, the midpoint B, of each line segment, say (AC) of the preceding level, is projected radially to intersect the arc at B'. The new approximation to the arc is now $(AB'C)$. Continuing the process to a sufficiently high level of segmentation, the circular arc AC can be approximated by a series of equal line segments as shown in figure 2.1b. This basic idea is carried over to the spherical surface except that a group of three points, forming a triangular patch, is used.

The development of the Quaternary Triangular Mesh (or QTM code) begins by conceiving one of the platonic solids, i.e., the octahedron, as inscribed in a sphere such that the vertices touch the surface. The octahedron is chosen because of the property that it can be orientated so that the geographic coordinates (ϕ, λ), of a point on the surface of the earth, consistently and unambiguously, map to a triangular region of a QTM code Q, where $Q = \mathcal{F}(\phi, \lambda)$ and $\mathcal{F}$ is the mapping function. Figures 2.2a and 2.2b show the first two levels of tessellations in such a scheme. We will call the platonic solid inscribed in the sphere (in our case the octahedron), the *base solid* of the QTM scheme and refer to one of the eight triangles of the base solid as *a base triangular facet*. The eight base triangular facets are addressed as 0, 1, ..., 7. In the subsequent sections, we will focus on addressing on the spherical surface defined by the representative facet 0.

Like the quadtree, one can construct a hierarchical tessellation of the triangular facet into smaller and smaller regular cells starting from the base triangular fact as shown in figure 2.3a. The QTM region labelling scheme proposed by Dutton is carried out is as follows. Given a triangular facet that is tessellated regularly into four sub-triangular regions, the middle triangle is labelled 0, the one to the left is labelled 1, the one to the right is labelled 2 and the upper triangular cell is labelled 3. Although Dutton proposed the method for point location, we believe the method is most appropriate for addressing regions on spherical surfaces. Consequently, the hierarchical decomposition process terminates when a "small enough" cell is generated. A triangular cell becomes small enough when either the error introduced by approximating it simply as a flat surface is negligible or the longest code string occupies the full integer word of the hardware.

Goodchild and Shiren [12] simplify Dutton's cell labelling approach to facilitate transformation from latitude and longitude to the quaternary code of the cell that a point lies in and vice versa. In the use of the quaternary codes as a global tessellation method, Goodchild and Shiren consider the projection of a sphere onto the eight distinct planer surfaces of the octahedron. These planer surfaces are then recursively tessellated and labelled. In their subsequent decomposition process, the midpoints of the edges of the triangular cells are not projected to intersect the spherical surfaces for the next level tessellation. One major drawback of this approach is that the error introduced as a result of the first level projection onto one of the eight base planes, remain the same irrespective of the subsequent levels of tessellations.

The Spherical Quadtree of Fekete [8] begins with an inscribed platonic solid of an icosahedron in the sphere. The sphere is therefore approximated initially by the 20 base planar facets of the icosahedron. The approximation is improved by successively subdividing the planar surfaces into four triangular cells. The new triangular cells for the next level are formed by bisecting the edges of the current triangular cells and projecting the new vertices out onto the surface of the sphere. This process is repeated until any desired resolution is attained. Like the QTM code, the approximation to the spherical surface is represented as a forest of 20 spherical quadtrees, one for each base planar region of the icosahedron. Each cell within each forest can be labeled by a unique code defined by the path from the root to the leaf cell.

Unlike the method of Goodchild and Shiren which is asymmetric, the cell labelling is similar to that proposed by Dutton and is symmetric. The SQT, uses the symbols $\{1, 2, 3, 4\}$ for labelling in place of $\{0, 1, 2, 3\}$. Let (A, B, C) be the vertex label of a triangle and let (A', B', C') be the set of midpoints of the sides opposite the vertices A, B and C respectively. The new generated triangular cells are labeled as illustrated in the figure 2.3b.

The two methods described briefly, share a number of common properties. We distinguish between the two methods of labelling by referring to them simply as QTM-code and SQT-code. In the sequel, we will refer simply to the QTM-codes with the understanding that in some cases the discussion applies to both methods. A number of useful operations and functions are necessary for the use of QTM in spatial indexing on spherical surfaces. These include the following:

- given the angular measure of ϕ and λ, compute the QTM code, $Q = \mathcal{F}(\phi, \lambda)$, that contains the point;
- given a QTM address of a triangular cell, compute the address of an edge or a node adjacent cell in a given direction.
- given the resolution and QTM-code of a cell, compute the angular coordinates of the vertices of the triangular cell.
- given an arbitrary figure on the surface of a sphere of known radius, the level h, of the tessellation, and the set of QTM codes of a connected region, compute the approximate area or perimeter of the defined region.
- *Connected Component Labeling:* assign a unique label to each maximal connected region of cells that share a common property.
- given two lists S_1 and S_2, of QTM codes compute the union $S = S_1 \cup S_2$.
- given two lists S_1 and S_2, of QTM codes compute the intersection $S = S_1 \cap S_2$.
- given a set of QTM codes representing a region at level h, enhance the resolution of the image by generating the representation at level h+1.

Earlier papers have addressed some but not all of the above operations. We propose a new method, *the semi-quadcode*, as an alternative to the QTM codes that gives a different perspective of the QTM scheme. Due to space limitations this paper focuses on the data structure, the representation of semi-quadcodes and some relevant operations. We present a detailed algorithms for the use of the semi-quadcode in [18]. Some concerns were raised about the size of the index generated when the level of tessellation becomes high. Specifically, one may ask whether an initial index, after h levels of tessellation, could be allocated on secondary storage and then subsequently extended to h+1 levels of tessellation without reorganizing the previous assignments made.

This is similar to the resolution enhancement problem mentioned above and is easily realized by organizing the QTM-codes into a B-tree structure [1, 3]. We utilize a similar idea in constructing the index for spherical surfaces except that semi-quadcodes are used.

The use of the semi-quadcodes greatly facilitates the operations mentioned above. We also address the problem of the use of semi-quadcodes for *Global Spatial Indexing*. In using SQC for global spatial indexing, the triangular cells are conceived as corresponding to data pages or buckets that hold detailed description of vector or raster data of the spatial objects that fall within the cells. The SQC's are used as keys to construct an order m B^+-tree index whose leaves hold pointers to the locations where detailed information relating to the cells (e.g., the vector map data of the cells) are kept.

The technique achieves $O(log_m N)$ page accesses to retrieve information the features of the spherical surface contained in any one of the N triangular cells. This access complexity is independent of the resolution k, $1 \leq k \leq h$, where h is the maximum resolution of the quadcodes. In this manner both horizontal and vertical navigation through the data is achieved with the same access cost irrespective of the size of the region. This paper highlights the significance of the SQC as a variation of the QTM encoding scheme. We point out its relevance to other applications such as visualization of data on the surface of the globe, rendering of maps as an aid in browsing the metadata of global databases in the geosciences.

3   Geometry of Semi-Quadcode

The semi-quadcode (SQC) is a labeling method for spherical regions of arbitrary resolution based on the subdivision of a base octahedron inscribed in the sphere. The structure formed approximates the sphere by subdividing the 8 triangular planar faces as shown in the figure 2.2b. It is perceived as a hierarchical structure with the planar regions of the inscribed base octahedron forming level 0 of the hierarchy. The hierarchical approximation is formed by recursively tessellating the surface at level h-1 to form the new structure at level h. Each of the edges of the triangular facets at level h-1 are bisected and the midpoints pushed radially to the surface. The new triangular facet formed by joining the midpoints at level h effectively partitions the facet at level h-1 into four new ones. As in [6], the 8 base octants are labelled by $\{0, 1, 2, ..., 7\}$. In what follows we concentrate on the subdivision of facet 0 since the discussion easily carries over to the other base facets by translation, inversion or both.

3.1   Coordinate System of SQC

The semi-quadcode adopts the main concepts of *Quadcodes* [13, 14] to address QTM cells. Quadcode is a linear quadtree encoding scheme with no *Don't Care* digits. To contrast the SQC with QTM, consider first the QTM labelling of the 0 triangular facet that has been tessellated up to level 2 as shown in figure 2.3a. Some triangular cells are upright while others are inverted. Given a QTM code of a cell computing the adjacency of a cell in a specific direction, requires setting up state transition tables [9, 12]. The algorithm for adjacent cell detection and similar others can be simplified considerably by the use of the semi-quadcode labelling.

The QTM encoding scheme has a number of interesting properties described by Dutton. He observed that:-

- As the level of the tessellation increases, facets grow smaller, the QTM codes grow longer and they tend to be more unique thus allowing for unique address assignment to locations.
- A QTM address at level 16 provide the same order of resolution as LAND-SAT pixels. At level 24, a QTM addresses a region the size of an average door mat.
- By interpreting the QTM location codes as integers, and mapping them into linear storage, they exhibit the property that numerically similar codes tend to lie in close spatial proximity to one another.
- Facets at the same level having QTM codes terminated by the digits 1, 2 or 3 form hexagonal groups of six triangles, such that codes terminating 1 gravitate towards a vertex labelled 1. Those terminating in 2 gravitate

towards a vertex labelled 2 and those terminated by 3 gravitate towards a vertex labelled 3. These nodal points are termed *attractors*. Attractors serve to tie adjacent sub-trees together. They unite cousins, rather than siblings.

- Suppose an edge (x, y) at level h is bisected to generate a midpoint z where x, y and z are 1-digit basis numbers {0, 1, 2 or 3}. The value of z is given by the expression $z = 6 - (x + y)$. A nodes basis number labels all tiles incident to it at level h+1.

Suppose we perceive the QTM of one base plane as a graph G = (V, E) where V is the set of nodes and G is the set of edges. Then we may also add to the above the following property.

Proposition 1. *The mesh of a base planar surface constructed by the recursive partitioning in of the quaternary triangular mesh decomposition to any level h, is a graph that always has an Eulerian tour.*

This follows from the fact that the base triangular cell has three nodes each of even degree 2. Subsequent tessellations, to any level, introduce new nodes that are always of even degree.

Consider a 2-dimensional square space oriented so that the bottom and left edges are parallel to the X- and Y-axes. Let the bottom triangle be the half-space formed by the diagonal joining the top-left corner to the bottom-right corner of square space. Let this half-space be recursively partitioned by the lines that constitute the quadtree partitioning of the full square region except that each square region so formed is split into two triangular regions by a line joining the top-left corner to the bottom right corner of each quad cell. This half-space partitioning will be termed the *semi-quadtree*. Figure 3.1a illustrates the tessellation of half-space up to level 2. Let $G' = (V', E')$, denote the graph formed by the set of nodes V' and edges E' of the mesh shown in figure 3.1b.

The key observation of the property of the QTM method that led to the development of the Semi-Quadcode (SQC) is given in the next proposition.

Proposition 2. *The graph G, formed by the Quaternary Triangular Mesh tessellation of the base plane upto level h, is isomorphic to the graph G' generated by the quadtree-like tessellation of corresponding square grid of the base plane restricted only to the half-space, complete with the diagonal lines as shown in figure 3.1b.*

The isomorphism established between the QTM graph G and the semi-quadtree graph G' suggests that a number of the quadtree properties should hold naturally for the semi-quadtree and consequently for the QTM.

3.2 SQC Addressing

To demonstrate the significance of the SQC scheme, we show how the linear quadtree labeling [10, 11] is adopted. First, observe that the semi-quadtree tessellation is exactly the quadtree tessellation of the square region restricted only to one triangular half of it. At each level of recursion, a full quad cell either lies entirely in the subspace below the diagonal line or lies along the diagonal line, i.e., it is a diagonal cell. If it lies entirely below the diagonal line it contains two triangular cells corresponding to the upright and inverted QTM cells respectively. Otherwise it contains only one triangular cell corresponding to an upright QTM cell. We will refer to a *"triangular cell"* as a *tricell*.

Each normal rectangular quad cell contains two triangular cells of the QTM scheme. These are designated as the *u-tricell* for the "upright" triangular cell, and the *i-tricell* for the "inverted" triangular cell. We can now apply the addressing scheme of the linear quadtree to the quad cells and then distinguish between the *u-tricells* and *i-tricells* within the same quad cell by appending the digit 1 and 2 respectively to the corresponding linear quadtree code. The above discussion effectively describes a semi-linear quadtree scheme or what we call *semi-quadcode*.

Let the spherical surface defined by one of the base triangular planes of the inscribed octahedron be mapped onto the lower left half space of a square region with the bottom and left edges defined by the X- and Y-axis. A quadtree-like tessellation to level h will partition the space into $2^h \times 2^h$ quad cells. Each quad cell can be addressed by the pair of indices $x \in X$ and $y \in Y$, i.e., $\langle x, y \rangle$ or by an address formed from the linear quadtree addressing scheme. From now on we will refer to the quadcode addresses instead of linear quadtree labelling. For example in figure 3.1b, where h = 2, the space is tessellated into a 4×4 quad cells. The subspace equivalent to the QTM scheme of figure 2.3a, is that triangular region 0AB. The quad cell (S,T,U,V) has the indices $\langle 1, 1, \rangle$. The corresponding quadcode address is $(03)_4$. The *u-tricell* and *i-tricell* of the quad cell $(03)_4$ are $(031)_4$ and $(032)_4$ respectively.

Recall that the quadcode label of a node in a quadtree is a string of quaternary digits that defines the path, from the root to the node. More importantly, the coordinate indices $\langle x, y \rangle$ and the quadcode address are related by the Proposition 3 stated below.

Proposition 3. *Given the X- Y- coordinates $\langle x, y \rangle$ of a quad cell in a quadtree tessellated square region to level h, denote by $(\beta_{h-1}^x \beta_{h-2}^x \ldots, \beta_0^x)$ and $(\beta_{h-1}^y \beta_{h-2}^y \ldots, \beta_0^y)$ the h binary digit representation of x and y respectively. Then the string of quaternary digits formed by taking pairs of bits of the interlaced binary digits of the form $(\beta_{h-1}^x \beta_{h-1}^y \beta_{h-2}^x \beta_{h-2}^y \ldots \beta_0^x \beta_0^y)$ constitutes the quadcode address of the quad cell.*

Denote the mapping of the $\langle x, y \rangle$ coordinate address to the quadcode Q, by a function $\mathcal{F}$ and conversely denote the inverse mapping by $\mathcal{F}^{-1}$. We have then that $Q = \mathcal{F}(\langle x, y \rangle)$, and $\langle x, y \rangle = \mathcal{F}^{-1}(Q)$. Both the function $\mathcal{F}$ and its inverse $\mathcal{F}^{-1}$ are computed by h bit shifts where h is the length of the quadcode or the highest resolution $(2^h \times 2^h)$ of the tessellated space.

For a black and white image representation, the quadcode encodes only the black regions of the space. The quadcode representation is a sorted sequence of the quadcode labels. If four connected square block of the form { $q_{h-1} q_{h-2} \ldots q_1 0$,

$q_{h-1}q_{h-2} \ldots q_1 1$, $q_{h-1}q_{h-2} \ldots q_1 2$ and $q_{h-1}q_{h-2} \ldots q_1 3$ } appear in the sequence, these four are replaced by the singly code $q_{h-1}q_{h-2} \ldots q_1$. With the knowledge of the resolution of the space in which the image is embedded, each string of quaternary digits can be interpreted correctly.

The quadcode representation of the tessellated space is what we adopt in the semi-quadcode labelling of the triangular patches of spherical surfaces. The triangular regions are tessellated exactly as in the quaternary triangular mesh but we always count two tricells as being contained within one quad cell except for the diagonal quad cells which contain only one tricell. The semi-quadcode addresses of the two QTM cell in a quad cell are formed by appending to the quadcode the digit 1 or 2, according to whether the tricell is upright or inverted.

3.3 Further Properties of SQC

Further properties of the SQC method are worth noting:

- Within any base triangular facet tessellated to level h, each of the X, and Y indices range over the set $\{0, 1, \ldots, 2^h - 1\}$ and the valid coordinate $\langle x, y \rangle$ of quad cells are those for which $(x + y) \leq 2^h - 1$.
- Starting from a perfect sphere and an inscribed octahedron, all cells resulting from tessellating a base triangular plane in the manner described have triangular shapes. However, the triangular patches deviate from equilateral to right isosceles triangles and subsequently to cells of unequal edge length and unequal areas. The range of variation in area has a limit of $\pi/2$ [12].

4 Operations on Semi-Quadcodes

One of the main virtues of the SQC addressing scheme is that it considerably simplifies computations of neighbours of a cell. Other related operations, such as detecting the boundary of SQC cells and connected component labelling, are easily computed. Used as a global indexing scheme, the SQC facilitates conversion of latitude and longitude values to the SQC address containing the point. Conversely given and SQC code, one can compute the latitude and longitude values of three vertices of the tricell or its centroid.

4.1 Neighbour Finding

In discussing neighbours of a SQC cell, we need to define a sense of direction in which the neighbour is required. We discuss edge-adjacent neighbours only in this paper. The same strategy can be extended to compute the addresses of the 5 vertex adjacent neighbours as well, if desired. Relative direction of a cell can be defined in two ways: either i) by the direction of the line joining a vertex to the midpoint of the opposite edge or ii) by referring to the direction in the sense of West, East and North or South. A tricell may have either a northern or southern neighbour depending on whether the cell in question is a u-tricell or an i-tricell. Direction in this paper is defined in the sense of the latter.

The suffixes of the SQC address, indicating the triangular cell type either upright or inverted, are two binary bits even though one bit suffices. Within each quad cell, a u-tricell is always an upright triangular cell, has the suffix code 1 and forms the lower off-diagonal triangle of a quad cell. An i-tricell is always inverted, has suffix digit 2 and forms the upper triangular cell of a quad cell. The edge adjacent cells of a u-tricell are all i-tricells and conversely the edge-adjacent cells of an i-tricell are all u-tricells.

Since the length of the quadcode implicitly defines the level for which the code applies, we will use the suffixes 0 to signify the end of a string representing a quad cell if the level is less than h. The terminal digit 3 in a quadcode of (k+1)-digits implies the presence of both the u-tricell and the i-tricell of the quad cell given by the k-digits. This means that semi-quadcodes at level k, $0 < k < h$, has k+1 quaternary digits. These terminal digits allows us to develop a very simple algorithm for determining the semi-quadcode of an edge adjacent neighbour to a given cell.

Algorithm for determining the edge adjacent neighbours
SemiQcode **EdgeAdjacent** (SemiQcode Q, Direction Dir)
{

        l ← lengthOf(Q) ; //length of SQC string
        tcode ← SuffixCode(Q); //extract the terminal digit.
        Q ← ClearRight(Q, 2); // delete the terminal digit
        $\langle x, y \rangle \leftarrow \mathcal{F}^{-1}(Q)$;
        switch (Dir) {
West: if $(- - x < 0)$ return (NullSQC) ;
        break ;
East: x++;
        if $(x + y > 2^h - 1)$ return (NullSQC);
        break;
North: if (tcode $= 1 \vee (+ + y > 2^h - 1)$) return (NullSQC)
        break
South if (tcode $= 2 \vee (- - y < 0)$) return (NullSQC)
        }   AdjToQ ← $\mathcal{F}(\langle x, y \rangle)$;
        if (tcode $= 1$)
        AdjToQ ← AppendToQ(AdjToQ, 2);
    else
        AdjToQ ← AppendToQ(AdjToQ, 1);
        return (AdjToQ);

}

The value NullSQC is defined as '0' and indicates a possible error condition or an attempt to cross the boundary of the current base facet. The function SuffixCode() returns the suffix digit of the semi-quadcode, ClearRight(Q, n) drops the n suffix bits of the semi-quadcode Q, and the function AppendToQ(Q, d) appends the quadcode "d" as the terminal digit of Q. In a similar discussion of adjacent neighbour finding, detecting when the boundary of a base facet is crossed was not handled. Boundary detection is simple in the SQC scheme. Whenever any of the coordinate values of the pair $\langle x, y \rangle$, become negative or $(x + y) \geq 2^h - 1$ we know a boundary of the base facet is being crossed. In that case we translate our origin to the new origin of the adjacent base planar facet.

4.2 Detecting Sons and Parents of Cells

Related to the problem of neighbour finding is the question of determining the semi-quadcode address of either the sons or the parent of a tricell. For the QTM addressing scheme, the sons of a tricell addressed by $(q_{h-1}q_{h-2} \ldots q_0)$ are determined by appending the digits 0, 1, 2 or 3, to obtain $(q_{h-1}q_{h-2} \ldots q_0 0)$, $(q_{h-1}q_{h-2} \ldots q_0 1)$, $(q_{h-1}q_{h-2} \ldots q_0 2)$ and $(q_{h-1}q_{h-2} \ldots q_0 3)$. The address of the parent of a QTM tricell is obtained by simply discarding the trailing quaternary digit.

In the SQC scheme, computing the address of the children or the parent is not that straight forward. It depends on the suffix digit q_0. If $q_0 = 1$ we have a u-tricell if $q_0 = 2$ we have an i-tricell. If $q_0 = 0$ or $q_0 = 3$ we have the occurrence of both an u- and i-tricells with a common parent. Let $(q_k q_{k-1} \ldots q_1 q_0)$ be the address of a semi-quadcode. If $q_0 = 1$, the children are $(q_k q_{k-1} \ldots q_1 01)$, $(q_k q_{k-1} \ldots q_1 02)$, $(q_k q_{k-1} \ldots q_1 11)$ and $(q_k q_{k-1} \ldots q_1 21)$. These are formed by replacing q_0 by the pairs of quaternary digits {01, 02, 11, 21}. Similarly if $q_0 = 2$ the children are derived by replacing q_0 with the pairs of digits { 12, 21, 31, 32 }.

The algorithm for the parent node of $(q_k q_{k-1} \ldots q_1 q_0)$ is the reverse operation for computing children and the pair of trailing digits "$q_1 q_0$" are replaced by either the digit 1 or 2. If $q_0 = 1$ then if also $q_1 < 3$ the parent address is $(q_k q_{k-1} \ldots 1)$ otherwise the parent address is $(q_k q_{k-1} \ldots 2)$. If $q_0 = 2$ then if also $q_1 > 0$ the parent address is $(q_k q_{k-1} \ldots 2)$ otherwise the parent address is $(q_k q_{k-1} \ldots 1)$.

4.3 Conversions from Latitude/Longitude to SQC Addresses

The angular measures of the location of a point on a sphere with respect to the origin in the center correspond to the geographic coordinates of latitude (ϕ) and longitude (λ). In anticipation of the application domain for which the SQC was developed, we will refer to the geographic coordinates (ϕ, λ) of a point on the globe. Although in reality the globe is an ellipsoid, we will continue to assume that we are dealing with spherical surfaces. This difference will impact our transformation algorithms but it is not essential for now. We will also limit our conversion algorithm to the 0 base plane since this is easily carried over to other base facet planes by changing the origin or the orientation of the X-Y- axes. The base facet 0 is assumed to be the quarter northern hemisphere lying above the equator ($\phi = 0$) and between longitudes $\lambda = 0$ and $\lambda = \pi/2$. Figure 3.1b illustrates the subdivision of the base 0 plane to level 2.

Let h be the highest level of subdivision of the base plane 0. We shall assume that the sense of orientation of triangles is as illustrated in figure 4.1. The vertices of a u-tricell are assumed to be numbered 0, 1 and 2 and those of an i-tricell as being numbered 1, 2 and 3. The X and Y axes in the corresponding $\langle x, y \rangle$ coordinate system are subdivided into 2^h intervals. The coordinate conversion algorithms is performed simply by first converting (ϕ, λ) values into $\langle x, y \rangle$ and then converting from $\langle x, y \rangle$ coordinates to the SQC address. First we state the following propositions. Their proofs are straight forward and are left out.

Proposition 4. *Let (ϕ, λ) be the angular coordinate of a point on the surface of a spherical region defined by the lines of longitude $\phi = 0$, $\phi = \pi/2$ and the latitude $\lambda = 0$. Let the degree of tessellation of the region into quaternary triangular mesh be h. Then in the SQC encoding of the space, the corresponding $\langle x, y \rangle$ coordinate of the quad cell that the point lies is defined by*

$$y = \lfloor \frac{2^{h+1} * \phi}{\pi} \rfloor \tag{1}$$

and

$$x = \lfloor \frac{2\lambda(2^h - y)}{\pi} \rfloor. \tag{2}$$

Proposition 5. *Let (ϕ, λ) be the angular coordinates of a point in the quarter hemisphere that is defined by the lines of longitudes $\lambda = 0$ and $\lambda = \pi/2$ and let this point lie in the quad cell given by the $\langle x, y \rangle$ in the SQC tessellation method. If the three vertices of the u-tricell in the corresponding quad cell are denoted by (ϕ_0, λ_0), (ϕ_1, λ_1) and (ϕ_2, λ_2), then these angular coordinates are defined by the expressions:*

$$\phi_0 = y * \tfrac{\pi}{2^{h+1}}; \quad \lambda_0 = x * \frac{\pi}{2(2^h - y)} \tag{3}$$

$$\phi_1 = (y+1) * \tfrac{\pi}{2^{h+1}}; \quad \lambda_1 = x * \frac{\pi}{2(2^h - y - 1)} \tag{4}$$

$$\phi_2 = y * \tfrac{\pi}{2^{h+1}}; \quad \lambda_2 = (x+1) * \frac{\pi}{2(2^h - y)} \tag{5}$$

The propositions (4) and (5) form the bases for the conversion algorithm from angular coordinates to SQC address and vice versa. We assume that within a given cell ϕ varies linear with λ. The algorithm to derive the SQC address given the angular coordinate (ϕ, λ) is stated below.

Semi-Qcode **Address**(integer h, double ϕ, double λ)

```
{
        integer x, y ;
        Semi-Qcode Q;
        y ← ⌊ (2^{h+1}*φ)/π ⌋;
        x ← ⌊ (2λ(2^h−y))/π ⌋;
        φ₁ ← (y + 1) * π/2^{h+1};
        λ₁ ← x * π/(2(2^h−y−1));
        φ₂ ← y * π/2^{h+1};
```

$$\lambda_2 \leftarrow (x + 1) * \frac{\pi}{2(2^k - y)};$$
$$Q \leftarrow \mathcal{F}(\langle x, y \rangle) ;$$
if $(\phi \geq (\frac{\phi_1 - \phi_2}{\lambda_1 - \lambda_2}) * (\lambda - \lambda_1) + \phi_2)$
$\qquad Q \leftarrow \text{AppendToQ}(Q, 2) ;$
else
$\qquad Q \leftarrow \text{AppendToQ}(Q, 1);$
return (Q);
}

The above algorithm for computing the SQC address of a point given its location in angular measure is $O(1)$. Note also that it implicitly computes the angular coordinates of two diagonal vertices of the corresponding quad cell. This is easily extended to compute all three vertices of a given SQC address.

4.4 Other Operations

In general an image on the sphere will be given as a set of semi-quadcodes. Other desired operations on the codes are intersection, union and difference of two sets of semi-quadcodes. Although the triangular facets at any given resolution are not all of the same shape, for any given radius and a given resolution, the area and edge lengths of the triangles, depending on the level and address are predefined. For this reason, it is easy to compute the area of a figure inscribed on a spherical surface, to a sufficiently good approximation, given the set of SQC addresses that represent it. Another important operation often desired is the connected component labeling of images on the sphere. All of these operations are easily computed by representing the image as a set of SQC addresses.

5 Applications of SQC

The semi-quadcode was the result of developing data structures for building a model of the globe as an interface to a spatial browser for a global databases. Since its development, it has found a number of applications. The SQC scheme, we believe, is an alternative scheme for applications currently supported by the QTM and SQT schemes. We illustrate this with an application of the SQC to global indexing.

5.1 Global Indexing

One major application of the SQC is for organizing spatial indices into geoscience database. Consider the alternative in which the globe is subdivided along the boundaries of parallels and meridians, at say intervals of 6 degrees. Let each of the quadrangles by further subdivided into regions using the quadtree tessellation method. Traditionally, these subregions correspond to map sheets of increasing map scales. If we now consider that the information related to one of these defined regions are clustered, then we need a consistent method of indexing the locations where each cluster of information is stored.

The problem of global indexing has been previously addressed [2, 21, 15, 17, 16]. One idea suggested is a decomposition of space along lines of meridians and parallel so that regions are assigned their equivalent linear quadtree labels. The quadtree labels serve as the keys to locations where the clusters of information related to the regions are stored. These linear quadtree codes are then organized into B^+-tree index. The main objection to the scheme is the fact the spherical surface subdivided along lines of meridian and parallel, do not maintain the same shape. They are triangular at the poles and rectangular along the 0-parallel.

Since the SQC method maintains the triangular shapes for any level of decomposition, it serves as a better alternative for global indexing. First we note that, given one of the initial 8 base planar facets, the semi-quadcode addresses of regions up to level 13 can be compacted into a 32-bit integer words. The first 4 bits gives the length of the semi-quadcode, the right most 2-bits give the tricell type, i.e., "01" for a u-tricell, "10" for an i-tricell and "11" for the occurrence of two triangular cell of the same parent in quad cell. This representation assumes that the whole spherical surface is represented as a forest of 8 distinct semi-quadtrees.

To represent semi-quadcodes up to 19 levels for the whole spherical surface (equivalent to a resolution of about $6 \times 6 \ m^2$ for the globe), requires at least 48-bit (or a 6-byte) words. Within the first byte, the first 3-bits represent the facet number, the next 5-bits represent the length of the semi-quadcode. Of the remaining 40-bits, the last 2-bits designate the cell type. This leaves 38 bits to maintain at most 19 levels (or 19 digits) of the semi-quadcode. This may be extended to a 64-bit representation for a point level precision as was originally proposed by Dutton.

To use the semi-quadcode as a global index, we simply tessellate the surface of the sphere in the manner consistent with the semi-quadcode scheme. For each region that has information to be stored, we associate with it the corresponding semi-quadcode address as its key. Let this location be perceived as a location pointer. The pairs of values (key and pointer) are then organized as the content of the leaf nodes of a B^+-tree.

Irrespective of the level or resolution of the region for which information is maintained, this indexing method gives the same access complexity of $O(\log N)$ for an index of N cells. The main drawback of the scheme is that information must be grouped in units consistent with the triangular subdivision of space. This historically has not been the case.

5.2   Seamless Horizontal and Vertical Navigation

Our treatment of the SQC scheme has concentrated on the representation of one of the base triangular facet. We have also illustrated how to detect when facet boundaries are crossed. All our algorithms are easily extended to cover the entire sphere, simply by detecting when a boundary cell is crossed and then making the appropriate change of origin and orientation of the axes, with exception loops for crossing the 6 prime vertices.

One immediate requirement in the application of the SQC method to global indexing scheme is the realization of a seamless traversal of cells that are at the same level of tessellation or traversal of the cells at different levels. We refer to the former as a *"horizontal navigation"* of space and to the latter as *"vertical navigation"*. To access information related to an adjacent tricell of some given one we apply the neighbour finding algorithm to locate the address of the neighbour tricell. This address is then used as the search key in the B^+-tree index to locate the location of the data related to the new tricell. In the same manner, we can access information related to one of the children of a given cell by first applying the algorithm for determining the children of a node. The SQC address computed is then used as the search key of the index tree to locate the information related to the higher level cell.

6 Conclusion

We have illustrated how the SQC scheme is used for addressing tricells resulting from the triangular decomposition of the surface of a sphere. By this means we are able to treat region addressing on spherical surface much like quadcode addressing of quadtree subdivision of planer regions.

The SQC scheme is an alternative to the QTM and SQT representation of spherical surfaces. The main virtues of our scheme is that it gives simplified and efficient algorithms for nearly all the operations required to represent an image on a spherical surface. Like the QTM and SQT methods, it has applications for:

- global spatial indexing;
- developing a model of the globe in 3D instead of reliance on projections onto planes;
- improving the speed of rendering maps on the globe;
- rendering information on spherical surfaces;
- developing a spatial browser interface for rapid data selection and analysis;
- developing a new dynamic projection of the globe that varies with change of origins of the planes. This is essentially the orthographic (or Gnomic) projection. A similar idea uses the QTM concept in a Zenithial Orthotriangular Projection [7].

Using 32-bit integer words, with each base planar facet represented independently, we can achieve up to 13 SQC digits, or 13 levels of tessellations. With 48-bit words we can achieve up to 19 SQC digits and still address location on the sphere to sufficient high degree of precision. Note that the errors resulting from projections, diminish by projecting onto triangular facets at high levels of subdivision. Presently, our use of SQC is in modeling the globe. This is the first level of interaction for a spatial browser used to explore the metadata of the Canadian Geomatic databases. Other scheduled works include its use in terrain model building on surfaces of the globe. QTM and SQT form some of the early works in global geographic information systems. The SQC scheme provides an enhanced but simplified scheme that is used to achieve the same objectives.

Acknowledgement

This work is supported in part by a joint grant from the Geographic Information Systems Division, Surveys Mapping and Remote Sensing Sector, Energy Mines Resources, Canada and the Natural Sciences and Engineering Research Council of Canada. We appreciate the careful reading and suggestions of G. Dutton in improving the quality of this paper.

References

1. R. Bayer and E. McCreight. Organization and maintenance of large ordered indexes. *Acta Informatica*, 1:173 – 189, 1972.
2. Z. T. Chen. Quad tree spatial spectra — its generation and applications. In *Proc. International Symposium on Special Data Handling*, pages 218 – 237, 1984.
3. D. Comer. The ubiquitous b-tree. *ACM Comput. Surveys*, 11(2):121 – 137, Jun. 1979.
4. G. H. Dutton. Geodesic modelling of planetary relief. *Cartographica*, 21(2&3):188 – 207, 1984.
5. G. H. Dutton. Locational properties of quaternary triangular meshes. In *Proc. 4th Int'l Symp. on Spatial Data Handling*, pages 901 – 910, Zurich, Switzerland, 1990.
6. G. H. Dutton. Planetary modelling via hierarchical tessellation. In *Proc. Auto-Carto 9, ACSM-ASP*, pages 462 – 471, Baltimore, U.S.A., 1989.
7. G. H. Dutton. Zenithial orthotriangular projection.
8. G. Fekete. Rendering and managing spherical data with sphere quadtrees. In *Proc. Visualization '90*, pages 176 – 186, San Francisco, 1990.
9. G. Fekete and L. S. Davis. Property spheres: a new representation for 3-d object recognition. In *Proceedings of the workshop on Computer Vision: Representation and Control*, pages 192 – 201, Annapolis, MD, April 1984. (also University of Maryland Computer Science Tech Report-1355).
10. I. Gargantini. An effective way to represent quad-trees. *Comm. ACM*, 25(12):905 – 910, Dec. 1982.
11. I. Gargantini. Linear octtrees for fast processing of three dimensional objects. *Comput. Gr. Image Process.*, 20(4):365 – 374, Dec. 1982. File = D4B, *.
12. M. F. Goodchild and Y. Shiren. A hierarchical data structure for global geographical information systems. *Graphical Models and Image Processing*, 54(1):31 – 44, Jan. 1992.
13. S. X. Li and M. H. Loew. Adjacency detection using quadcodes. *Comm. ACM.*, 30(7):627 – 631, Jul. 1987.
14. S. X. Li and M. H. Loew. The quadcode and its arithmetic. *Comm. ACM.*, 30(7):621 – 626, Jul. 1987.
15. F. D. Libera and F. Gosen. Using b-trees to solve geographic range queries. *Comput, Journal*, 29(2):176 – 181, 1986.

16. D. M. Mark and J. P. Lauzon. Approaches for quadtree-based geographic information systems at a continental or global scales. In *Proc. AutoCarto 7, Digital Representation of Spatial Knowledge*, Amer. Soc. of Photogamm., Falls Church, Virginia, Mar. 1985.

17. D. M. Mark and J. P. Lazon. Linear quadtrees for geographic information systems. In *Proc. Int'l. Symp. on Spatial Data hasndling*, pages 412 – 430, Zurich, Switzerland, Aug. 1984.

18. E. J. Otoo. *Semi-Quadcode and Its Operations on Spherical Surfaces*. Technical Report, School of Computer Science, Carleton Univ., Ottawa, Canada, 1992.

19. H. Samet. *Applications of Spatial Data Structures*. Addison-Wesley, Reading, Mass., 1990.

20. H. Samet. *The Design and Analysis of Spatial Data Structures*. Addison-Wesley, Reading, Mass., 1990.

21. W. Tobler and Z-T. Chen. A quadtree for global information storage. *Geographical Analysis*, 18(4):360 – 371, Oct. 1986.

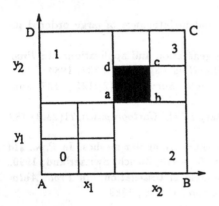

Figure 1.1: A quadtree tessellation

Figure 1.2: Tessellation of a Spherical surface along lines of meridians and parallel

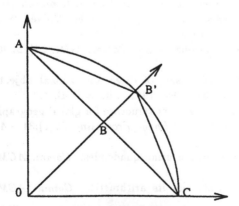

Figure 2.1a: First level approx. of the arc AB'C by the arc AB' and B'C

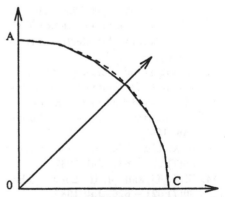

Figure 2.1b: Approx. of the arc AC by a sequence of line segments.

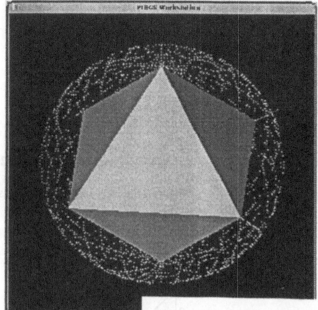

Figure 2.2a: The base octahedron inscribed
in a sphere

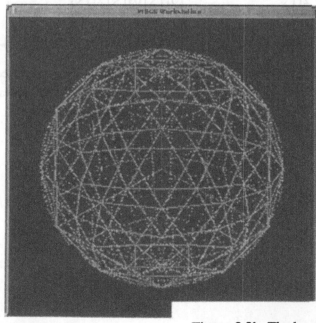

Figure 2.2b: The level 3 tessellation of the
base planes of the octahedron.

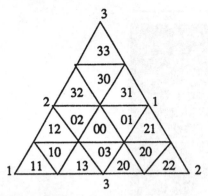

Figure 2.3a: QTM labelling

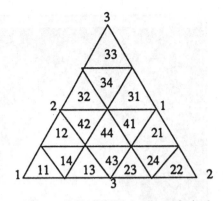

Figure 2.3b: SQT labelling of trixels

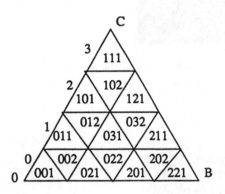

Figure 3.1a SQC Labelling of tricells

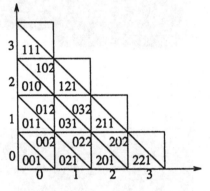

Figure 3.1b: Graph of triangular facets orientated to show correspondance with quadtree tessellation.

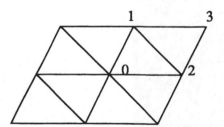

Figure 4.1: Illustration of transformation from angular measure to SQC labels

Springer-Verlag
and the Environment

We at Springer-Verlag firmly believe that an international science publisher has a special obligation to the environment, and our corporate policies consistently reflect this conviction.

We also expect our business partners – paper mills, printers, packaging manufacturers, etc. – to commit themselves to using environmentally friendly materials and production processes.

The paper in this book is made from low- or no-chlorine pulp and is acid free, in conformance with international standards for paper permanency.

Springer-Verlag
and the Environment

We at Springer-Verlag firmly believe that an international science publisher has a special obligation to the environment, and our corporate policies consistently reflect this conviction.

We also expect our business partners – paper mills, printers, packaging manufacturers, etc. – to commit themselves to using environmentally friendly materials and production processes.

The paper in this book is made from low- or no-chlorine pulp and is acid free, in conformance with international standards for paper permanency.

Lecture Notes in Computer Science

For information about Vols. 1–610
please contact your bookseller or Springer-Verlag

Vol. 650: T. Ibaraki, Y. Inagaki, K. Iwama, T. Nishizeki, M. Yamashita (Eds.), Algorithms and Computation. Proceedings, 1992. XI, 510 pages. 1992.

Vol. 651: R. Koymans, Specifying Message Passing and Time-Critical Systems with Temporal Logic. IX, 164 pages. 1992.

Vol. 652: R. Shyamasundar (Ed.), Foundations of Software Technology and Theoretical Computer Science. Proceedings, 1992. XIII, 405 pages. 1992.

Vol. 653: A. Bensoussan, J.-P. Verjus (Eds.), Future Tendencies in Computer Science, Control and Applied Mathematics. Proceedings, 1992. XV, 371 pages. 1992.

Vol. 654: A. Nakamura, M. Nivat, A. Saoudi, P. S. P. Wang, K. Inoue (Eds.), Prallel Image Analysis. Proceedings, 1992. VIII, 312 pages. 1992.

Vol. 655: M. Bidoit, C. Choppy (Eds.), Recent Trends in Data Type Specification. X, 344 pages. 1993.

Vol. 656: M. Rusinowitch, J. L. Rémy (Eds.), Conditional Term Rewriting Systems. Proceedings, 1992. XI, 501 pages. 1993.

Vol. 657: E. W. Mayr (Ed.), Graph-Theoretic Concepts in Computer Science. Proceedings, 1992. VIII, 350 pages. 1993.

Vol. 658: R. A. Rueppel (Ed.), Advances in Cryptology – EUROCRYPT '92. Proceedings, 1992. X, 493 pages. 1993.

Vol. 659: G. Brewka, K. P. Jantke, P. H. Schmitt (Eds.), Nonmonotonic and Inductive Logic. Proceedings, 1991. VIII, 332 pages. 1993. (Subseries LNAI).

Vol. 660: E. Lamma, P. Mello (Eds.), Extensions of Logic Programming. Proceedings, 1992. VIII, 417 pages. 1993. (Subseries LNAI).

Vol. 661: S. J. Hanson, W. Remmele, R. L. Rivest (Eds.), Machine Learning: From Theory to Applications. VIII, 271 pages. 1993.

Vol. 662: M. Nitzberg, D. Mumford, T. Shiota, Filtering, Segmentation and Depth. VIII, 143 pages. 1993.

Vol. 663: G. v. Bochmann, D. K. Probst (Eds.), Computer Aided Verification. Proceedings, 1992. IX, 422 pages. 1993.

Vol. 664: M. Bezem, J. F. Groote (Eds.), Typed Lambda Calculi and Applications. Proceedings, 1993. VIII, 433 pages. 1993.

Vol. 665: P. Enjalbert, A. Finkel, K. W. Wagner (Eds.), STACS 93. Proceedings, 1993. XIV, 724 pages. 1993.

Vol. 666: J. W. de Bakker, W.-P. de Roever, G. Rozenberg (Eds.), Semantics: Foundations and Applications. Proceedings, 1992. VIII, 659 pages. 1993.

Vol. 667: P. B. Brazdil (Ed.), Machine Learning: ECML – 93. Proceedings, 1993. XII, 471 pages. 1993. (Subseries LNAI).

Vol. 668: M.-C. Gaudel, J.-P. Jouannaud (Eds.), TAPSOFT '93: Theory and Practice of Software Development. Proceedings, 1993. XII, 762 pages. 1993.

Vol. 669: R. S. Bird, C. C. Morgan, J. C. P. Woodcock (Eds.), Mathematics of Program Construction. Proceedings, 1992. VIII, 378 pages. 1993.

Vol. 670: J. C. P. Woodcock, P. G. Larsen (Eds.), FME '93: Industrial-Strength Formal Methods. Proceedings, 1993. XI, 689 pages. 1993.

Vol. 671: H. J. Ohlbach (Ed.), GWAI-92: Advances in Artificial Intelligence. Proceedings, 1992. XI, 397 pages. 1993. (Subseries LNAI).

Vol. 672: A. Barak, S. Guday, R. G. Wheeler, The MOSIX Distributed Operating System. X, 221 pages. 1993.

Vol. 673: G. Cohen, T. Mora, O. Moreno (Eds.), Applied Algebra, Algebraic Algorithms and Error-Correcting Codes. Proceedings, 1993. X, 355 pages 1993.

Vol. 674: G. Rozenberg (Ed.), Advances in Petri Nets 1993. VII, 457 pages. 1993.

Vol. 675: A. Mulkers, Live Data Structures in Logic Programs. VIII, 220 pages. 1993.

Vol. 676: Th. H. Reiss, Recognizing Planar Objects Using Invariant Image Features. X, 180 pages. 1993.

Vol. 677: H. Abdulrab, J.-P. Pécuchet (Eds.), Word Equations and Related Topics. Proceedings, 1991. VII, 214 pages. 1993.

Vol. 678: F. Meyer auf der Heide, B. Monien, A. L. Rosenberg (Eds.), Parallel Architectures and Their Efficient Use. Proceedings, 1992. XII, 227 pages. 1993.

Vol. 683: G.J. Milne, L. Pierre (Eds.), Correct Hardware Design and Verification Methods. Proceedings, 1993. VIII, 270 Pages. 1993.

Vol. 684: A. Apostolico, M. Crochemore, Z. Galil, U. Manber (Eds.), Combinatorial Pattern Matching. Proceedings, 1993. VIII, 265 pages. 1993.

Vol. 685: C. Rolland, F. Bodart, C. Cauvet (Eds.), Advanced Information Systems Engineering. Proceedings, 1993. XI, 650 pages. 1993.

Vol. 686: J. Mira, J. Cabestany, A. Prieto (Eds.), New Trends in Neural Computation. Procdings, 1993. XVII, 746 pages. 1993.

Vol. 687: H. H. Barrett, A. F. Gmitro (Eds.), Information Processing in Medical Imaging. Proceedings, 1993. XVI, 567 pages. 1993.

Vol. 688: M. Gauthier (Ed.), Ada - Europe '93. Proceedings, 1993. VIII, 353 pages. 1993.

Vol. 689: J. Komorowski, Z. W. Ras (Eds.), Methodologies for Intelligent Systems. Proceedings, 1993. XI, 653 pages. 1993. (Subseries LNAI).

Vol. 690: C. Kirchner (Ed.), Rewriting Techniques and Applications. Proceedings, 1993. XI, 488 pages. 1993.

Vol. 691: M. Ajmone Marsan (Ed.), Application and Theory of Petri Nets 1993. Proceedings, 1993. IX, 591 pages. 1993.

Vol. 692: D. Abel, B.C. Ooi (Eds.), Advances in Spatial Databases. Proceedings, 1993. XIII, 529 pages. 1993.

Vol. 694: A. Bode, M. Reeve, G. Wolf (Eds.), PARLE '93. Parallel Architectures and Languages Europe. Proceedings, 1993. XVII, 770 pages. 1993.